Fodor's

PROVENCE AND THE FRENCH RIVIERA

Welcome to Provence and the French Riviera

Provence's azure skies, brilliant sunlight, and windswept landscapes have inspired artists like Cézanne and Van Gogh, as well as countless travelers. Medieval villages perch on hilltops between rolling vineyards, fragrant lavender fields, and craggy mountains. Port towns and glamorous resorts are scattered amid the French Riviera's sparkling beaches. Savor the region's civilized pleasures, too: Aix's elegant boulevards, Arles's and Avignon's archaeological treasures, and Marseille's lively restaurants and architectural gems. As you plan your trip, confirm that places are still open and let us know when we need to make updates by emailing editors@fodors.com.

TOP REASONS TO GO

★ **Natural beauty:** The dazzling Mediterranean and the untamed Camargue beckon.

★ **Food and wine:** France's regional cuisines pair perfectly with great local vintages.

★ **Lofty views:** Built to ward off pirates and pillagers, hilltop villages are stunning.

★ **Market day:** Farmers display the local bounty at markets in every town and village.

★ **Seaside splendor:** Sunny beaches and glitzy nightlife define the alluring Côte d'Azur.

★ **Modern art:** Marvelous museums display masterpieces by residents Picasso and Matisse.

Contents

Fodor's Features

MAPS

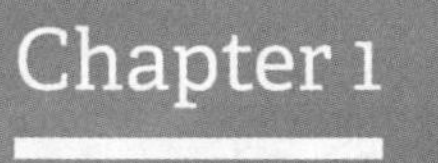

Chapter 1

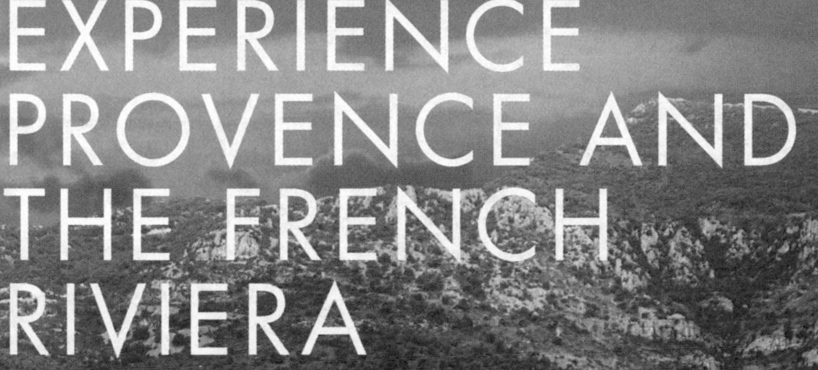

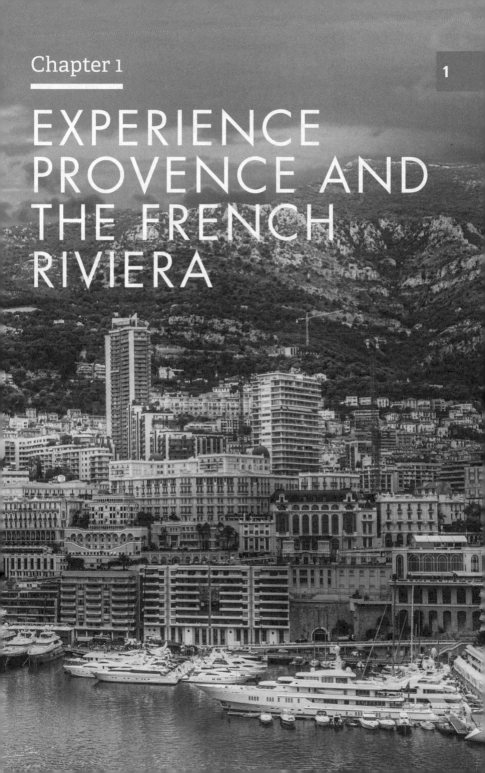

EXPERIENCE PROVENCE AND THE FRENCH RIVIERA

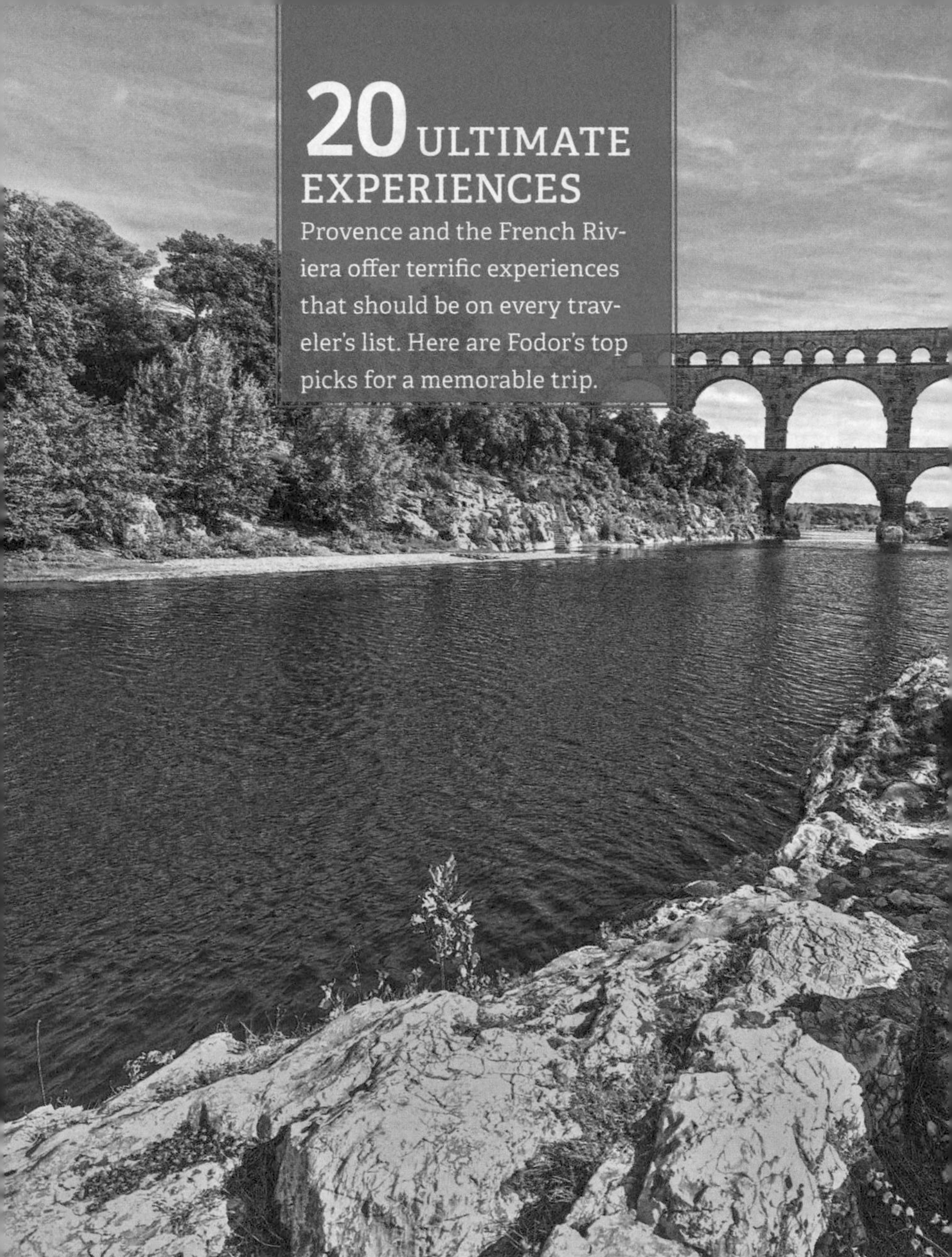

20 ULTIMATE EXPERIENCES

Provence and the French Riviera offer terrific experiences that should be on every traveler's list. Here are Fodor's top picks for a memorable trip.

1 Pont du Gard

Rising 160 dramatic feet above the Gardon River, the triple-tiered Pont du Gard is France's highest and most beautifully preserved Roman bridge. *(Ch. 3)*

2 Carnaval in Nice

Started in 1924, Carnaval de Nice is now the third largest carnival celebration in the world, with the Flower Battle parade its biggest event. *(Ch. 7)*

3 Aix-en-Provence

Spend an afternoon at a café on one of Aix-en-Provence's tree-shaded avenues and elegant streets lined with graceful old *hôtel particulières* (family mansions). *(Ch. 5)*

4 The Lavender Route

Join the lavender-happy crowds from June to mid-July and travel the Route de la Lavande amid the 560-mile blue-purple swath that produces a third of the world's lavender. *(Ch. 4)*

5 Corniche d'Estérel

Bordered by rocky cliffs and impossibly turquoise waters, the Corniche d'Estérel is one of the most scenic drives along the Riviera. *(Ch. 6)*

6 Èze

The expression "bird's-eye view" takes on new meaning in Èze, a tiny medieval jewel soaring 1,400 feet above the Riviera. *(Ch. 7)*

7 Arles

Immortalized by Vincent van Gogh, who was enchanted with its clear light, ancient Arles has lots of art museums, galleries, and festivals. *(Ch. 3)*

8 Art Museums

Provence's numerous excellent art museums are filled with works by artists who fell in love with the region, including Matisse, Renoir, Picasso, Van Gogh, and more. *(Ch. 3–7)*

9 Cannes

Home to the world's most famous film festival, Cannes is an epicenter of French Riviera glamour and bling. *(Ch. 7)*

10 Grasse

The cradle of modern perfumery, Grasse is home to names like Fragonard, Galimard, and Molinard, where you can take workshops to learn the industry's secrets and create your very own perfume. *(Ch. 7)*

11 The Camargue

At the southern reaches of Provence is the Camargue, where you'll feel you've come to the ends of the earth. The nature park is filled with French cowboys, bulls, and birds, including 50,000 flamingos. *(Ch. 3)*

12 Perched Villages

Provence's gravity-defying medieval perched villages, from Gordes to Lacoste, are little glimpses into another time. *(Ch. 3–7)*

13 Avignon

Once the Holy Roman Empire's papal seat, today ancient Avignon holds some of the region's most important arts festivals, like the Avignon Festival and Le Festival OFF. *(Ch. 4)*

14 Wine-Tasting on the Côtes du Rhône

The celebrated appellations of the Côtes du Rhône are named for its villages and regions: Gigondas, Beaumes-de-Venise, Châteauneuf-du-Pape, Côtes du Luberon, and more. *(Ch. 4)*

15 Beaches in St-Tropez

When Brigitte Bardot kicked up some sand on the Plage de Pampelonne, St-Tropez became an emblem of beachside glam and still beckons with its white sand beaches (a rarity on the Riviera). *(Ch. 6)*

16 Cap d'Antibes

The Riviera's most exclusive corner is filled with luxury hotels and Michelin-starred restaurants inviting you to live lavishly like Zelda and F. Scott Fitzgerald did, even for just one afternoon. *(Ch. 7)*

17 Gambling in Monte Carlo

This gilded playground in Monaco has captivated European royalty and the international elite since the Belle Époque years of the late 19th century. *(Ch. 8)*

18 Gorges du Verdon

The Gorges du Verdon's vertiginous limestone cliffs have earned the natural wonder the nickname of the Grand Canyon of Europe. *(Ch. 6)*

19 Antique Shopping in L'Isle-sur-la-Sorgue

Famed for its Sunday markets, L'Isle-sur-la-Sorgue is literally wall-to-wall with antique stores of every shape, size, and caliber. *(Ch. 4)*

20 Marseille

Marseille has always been France's quintessential melting pot. Nowadays, its cultural richness is reflected in everything from its museums to its cuisine. *(Ch. 5)*

WHAT'S WHERE

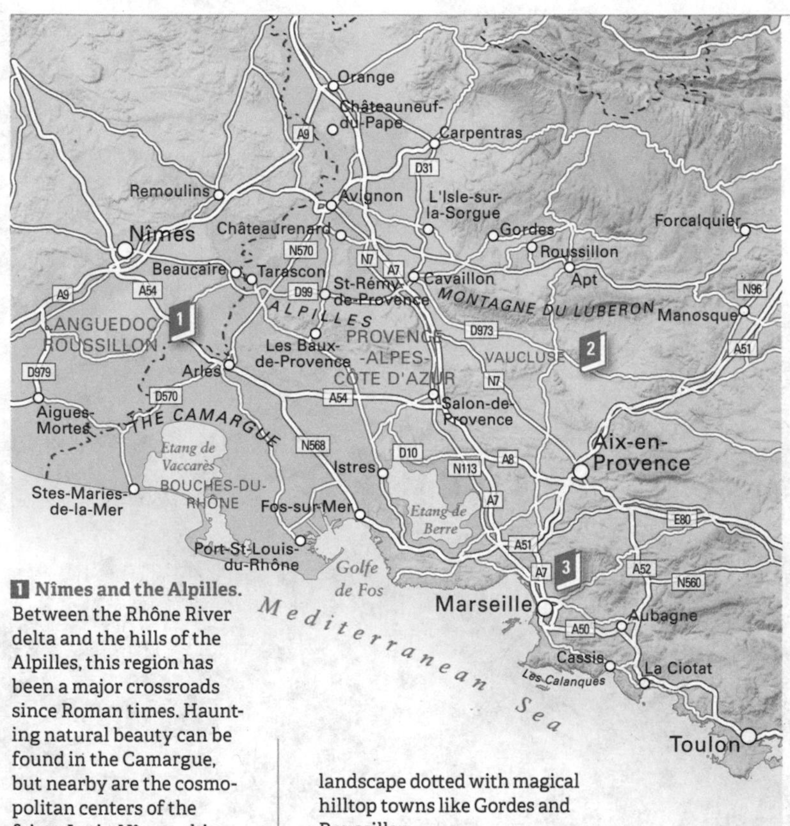

1 Nîmes and the Alpilles. Between the Rhône River delta and the hills of the Alpilles, this region has been a major crossroads since Roman times. Haunting natural beauty can be found in the Camargue, but nearby are the cosmopolitan centers of the feisty Latin Nîmes, chic St-Rémy, and Van Gogh's golden Arles.

2 Avignon and the Vaucluse. Anchored by the medieval city stronghold of Avignon, the Vaucluse spreads luxuriantly north into the Rhône vineyards of Châteauneuf-du-Pape and east along the Lavender Route. Visit the Roman theater in Orange, then head to the Luberon—the quintessential Provençal landscape dotted with magical hilltop towns like Gordes and Roussillon.

3 Aix, Marseille, and the Central Coast. Famous for its boulevards, Aix-en-Provence has a bevy of posh cafés where you can enjoy people-watching, just as Cézanne used to do. South lies Marseille, France's second-largest city and a Mediterranean melting pot. Studded with rocky calanques (inlets), the nearby coast has pockets of tremendous natural beauty.

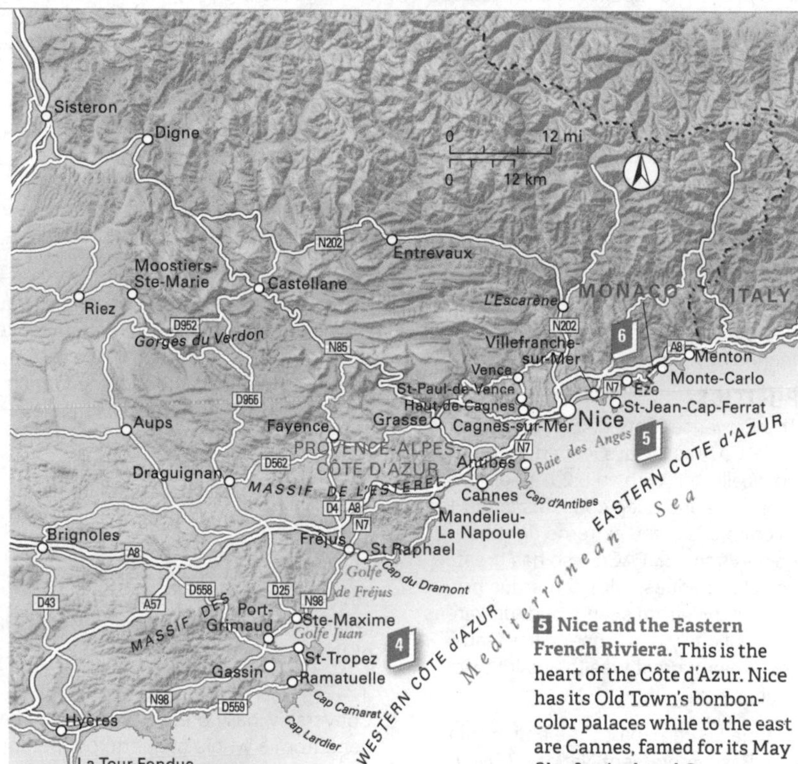

4 The Western French Riviera. The legend begins here: palm trees, parasol pines, and improbably blue sea against the backdrop of the red-rock Massif de l'Estérel. There's St-Tropez, with its white-sand beaches and celeb-filled port bars, and there are *sportif* resorts like St-Raphaël. Inland, the woolly Haute-Provence backcountry is home to the Gorges du Verdon.

5 Nice and the Eastern French Riviera. This is the heart of the Côte d'Azur. Nice has its Old Town's bonbon-color palaces while to the east are Cannes, famed for its May film festival, and Cap d'Antibes with its zillion-dollar hotels. The sky may kiss the perched village of Èze, but the rainbow ends in places beloved by artists: Renoir's Haut-de-Cagnes, Picasso's Antibes, and Matisse's Nice and St-Paul de Vence.

6 Monaco. Take the high-rises of Hong Kong, add the amusement-park feel of Disneyland, and mix in an aristocratic touch, and there you have all 473 acres of Monaco, the playground of royalty, wealthy playboys, and glamorous film stars.

Provence Today

If you've experienced the hustle and bustle of Paris, the Mediterranean mindset in Provence and the French Riviera may come as a welcome surprise. Daily life here revolves around the weather, people stroll without purpose, businesses still close for a leisurely lunch (or for the entire winter), and a "big city" like Nice has a population just shy of a million.

The region is moving forward into the 21st century, but don't be surprised if you can't get a strong Wi-Fi signal from your perched medieval village. Sixteenth-century buildings just weren't designed with technology in mind.

POLITICS

The Provence–Cote-d'Azur region, known as PACA, has always leaned to the right politically, but with an 8.2% unemployment rate and deep concerns about the migrant crisis, the extreme-right has gained traction. PACA also has great social disparities, with numerous pockets of poverty—from abandoned rural areas to notoriously gritty inner cities—amid the region's great wealth and influx of tourist euros.

Marine Le Pen's party, the anti-immigration Rassemblement National (RN or National Rally)—formerly the National Front but renamed in an effort to soften a racist image dating back to its founder, Jean-Marie Le Pen, Marine's father—has a foothold in the south. Despite Emmanuel Macron's wins over Marine Le Pen in the 2017 and 2022 presidential elections, she still garnered 42% of the 2022 votes, and half of the PACA MPs chosen in the 2022 legislative elections were RN candidates.

The south also harbors resentment over Paris's central role in French politics, and it shares in the widespread dissatisfaction with Macron's policies that led to pre-Covid Gilet Jaunes (Yellow Vests) demonstrations and subsequent countrywide strikes and protests. Indeed, many in the laid-back south found Macron's initiative to raise the retirement age from 62 to 64 particularly loathsome. Although there are places where the RN has been less successful (in Marseilles, Jean-Luc Mélenchon's far left party, La France Insoumise, made a robust showing), many pundits believe Macron's missteps will give Le Pen leverage in 2027.

FOOD

Many locals posit that American trends arrive in Provence and the rest of France about five years later than in the rest of the world. Take fast food: the French are second only to Americans in the consumption of Big Macs, and sales at fast-food chains now outpace those in the country's traditional restaurants. In addition, the French spend, on average, less than 30 minutes eating a meal (down from 1 hour and 20 minutes in 1975), and national obesity rates have reached unprecedented heights, at 17% of the population (compared to 39% stateside).

Conversely, daily bread consumption has gone from a whole baguette per person 30 years ago to less than half of one today—despite the baguette's inclusion on UNESCO's Intangible Cultural Heritage list in 2022—and France's sales of gluten-free bread has tripled in recent years. Following this trend, Provence is seeing the rise of non-gluten haute cuisine, with trendy vegan cafés and organic shops popping up along the coast.

One thing you still won't see in the south of France, though, is people eating on the go (unless it's a picnic). Civility still rules when it comes to sitting down for a meal, however quick.

LANGUAGE

Although some waiters and shopkeepers will grunt a few reassuring words in English, if you want to buy a train ticket from a station machine here, the only language option is French. Also, referring to the south's coastal region in English instead of *en français* distinguishes American visitors from those of other nationalities, so consider forgoing "French Riviera" in favor of "Côte d'Azur," a term coined by Stéphen Liégeard in 1887.

Pronunciation is also key. For example, when Americans say the name of the city famous for its international film festival, it comes out as "cans." In French, however, the "s" at the end of a word is silent. Ditto for Antibes, Picasso's adopted town east of *Can-ne*.

That said, Monaco's Riviera Radio 106.5 broadcasts news, weather, and traffic in English, and you can download the free *Riviera Reporter* magazine to your iPad or buy a copy at one of the few English-language bookstores in Antibes, Cannes, or Valbonne. If all else fails, Google Translate or a free language app is just one tablet or smartphone touch away.

CAFÉS

Café culture is very much alive in the south of France. You won't see the French sipping from an insulated mug in their car or on the bus. Although the craft-coffee craze has arrived, with barista cafés springing up everywhere, most people still stop by their favorite local haunt for an unhurried *café* (espresso), and they sip every last caffeinated drop while sitting at a table or standing at the bar.

So what to order? Well, if you request a *petit café* or *un express,* you'll get a tiny shot of espresso; if you want to cut its bitterness, order a *noisette,* which will have a dab of steamed milk. A *café américain* (also known as a *café allongé*) is espresso diluted with more water and put in a bigger cup. Sugar will always be served on your saucer, but you'll need to ask for milk.

Dairy options are still limited, but some cafés have low-fat milk, and an increasing number in cities like Nice offer soy milk. One last piece of advice: it's only tourists who order their evening coffee at the same time as dessert—everyone else orders it afterward.

THE WEALTHY

If you want to be part of the Riviera in-crowd, you have to be prepared to spend money like the richest 1%. They don't bat an eyelash at dropping €50 for a breakfast that consists of a croissant and coffee or €14 for a beer in a hotel. And €500 for a bottle of Champagne to spray poolside at Nikki Beach in St-Tropez? Well, they'll probably order two!

Even though you might find such prices vexing, there are times when it pays to be a bit more extravagant. It's absolutely worth spending extra for that upgraded sea-view suite or for that meal at a Michelin-starred restaurant overlooking the water. The impeccable service and superstar treatment will truly make for a once-in-a-lifetime vacation experience.

One caveat: although the jet-setter at the next table might be wearing a Philippe Patek watch and your watch might be a Timex, in the eyes of would-be thieves, any English-speaking tourist or expat here is considered rich.

What to Eat and Drink in Provence and the French Riviera

BOUILLABAISSE
Originating from the fishing port of Marseille, this iconic dish consists of a broth of small fish, tomatoes, onion, garlic, fennel, olive oil, and saffron, served with a garlicky bread crumb sauce called rouille. Next, four to six larger fish are added to the soup and served as a second course.

PROVENÇAL ROSÉ WINE
Provence is the world's largest rosé producer, using Grenache, Cinsault, Mourvedre, and Syrah grapes, which help create that pale orange-tinted pink color. You'll find plenty of options to sample here, and you can even visit a few vineyards specializing in rosé production.

FOUGASSE
The Provençal answer to Italian focaccia, this soft flatbread is distinguished by holes that give it the appearance of a lacy leaf. It can be made savory—flavored with olives, anchovy, bacon, cheese, or anything else the baker has on hand—or sweet, enriched with olive oil and dusted with icing sugar.

SALADE NIÇOISE
Forget politics, nothing divides the residents of Nice more than the question of what goes in their beloved salade Niçoise. Cooked vegetables are banned from the salad, that's the one rule. And, contrary to popular belief, no green beans either. It's a simple recipe of tomatoes, cucumber, peppers, onions, and cooked eggs, with a few leaves of lettuce and tuna if you want to get fancy.

DAUBE DE BOEUF
To distinguish their prized beef stew from *boeuf bourguignon*, Provençal chefs make a point of not marinating the meat, instead cooking it very slowly in tannic red wine that is often flavored with orange zest. In the Camargue, *daube* is made with local *taureau* (bull's meat) and is considered a specialty of the region, while the Avignon variation uses lamb.

SOUPE AU PISTOU
The Provençal version of pesto, *pistou* consists of the simplest ingredients—garlic, olive oil, fresh basil, and Parmesan—ideally pounded together by hand in a stone mortar with an olive wood pestle. Most traditionally it delivers a potent kick to *soupe au pistou*, a kind of French minestrone made with green beans, white beans, potatoes, and zucchini.

PASTIS
What could be more Provençal than sipping—before or after dinner—pastis, the chalky-light

Daube de Boeuf

amber, anise-flavored spirit that's served on ice with a side carafe of cold water? But not all pastis are equal. Ricard (now Ricard Pernod) was the first to produce the silky beverage, after the ban of the hallucinogenic absinthe in 1915, and newcomer Pastis des Creissauds takes 18 months to make each bottle.

CITRON PRESSÉ
Order a satisfying *citron pressé* in a café, and you'll be served a tall glass filled with ice, the juice of a just-squeezed lemon, a little pitcher of water, and a dish of sugar cubes to sweeten your ultra-fresh and ultra-refreshing lemonade as you wish.

NIÇOIS SOCCA
Nice is known for *socca*, a sort of chickpea flour pancake that Chez Pipo has been making and serving since 1923. It takes a bit of time to get perfectly cooked, so order some of the delicious *tartinades*, or local dips, while you wait.

L'ORANGERIE LIQUEUR
What else can you do with Monaco's 600 organic bitter orange trees but make a refreshing liqueur? Food trader Philip Culazzo first bottled the premium bitter orange liqueur (30% alcohol) in 2017. Try the Monaco Spritz, L'Orangerie topped up with Prosecco and orange zest, or pick up a three-miniature gift-pack as a souvenir.

TAPENADE
When you order an *apéritif* in Provence-Côte d'Azur you'll often receive a bowl of tapenade, an inky black dip that contains olives, capers, garlic, and olive oil and is served with bread, toast, or breadsticks. There are several variations, including those featuring green olives, anchovies (anchoïade), mostly garlic, or sun-dried tomatoes.

What to Buy in Provence and the French Riviera

HERBS DE PROVENCE
This rock star of spice blends consists of the usual suspects of thyme, rosemary, and bay leaf, with other herbs like oregano, basil, tarragon, marjoram, savory, sage, fennel, and dill thrown in—with everything grown in the southeast of France.

CALISSON
There are sweets, and then there's the *calisson* d'Aix, a regal candy first served in 1473 at the second wedding of King René and made from a paste of candied fruit and almonds topped with icing sugar. In the 16th century, as almond trees started to grow around Aix-en-Provence, production of the diamond-shape morsels took off, and today the strict method of making them is protected in France. You can find the region's favorite treat in stores throughout Provence, but Le Roy René in Aix has a museum that showcases their origins (with samples!).

PERFUME
North of Cannes, follow your nose to the microclimatic town of Grasse, the perfume capital of the world, thanks to Jean de Galimard, who developed gloves fragranced with perfume that masked the unpleasant smell of substances used to tan leather hides. Eventually, Grasse went from a tanning town to a perfume town, and, 250 years later, fragrances comprise a $49.4 billion global industry. But why choose from the more than 8,000 perfumes on the market when you can create your own scent? Galimard, Fragonard, and Molinard all offer make-your-own workshops.

PROVENÇAL FABRIC
Known as *les indiennes*, Provence's colorful cottons date from the 16th century, when they were first imported from India to Marseille. The material was so popular with the high bourgeoisie that, in 1686, French textile manufacturers in Lyon—worried about competition—ordered an import ban. This led to Armenian craftsmen coming to France to create similar patterns, which are still seen today in everything from tablecloths and napkins to clothing.

LAVENDER PRODUCTS
Driving through the lavender fields of Provence should be on everyone's bucket list. During the summer bloom, you'll see endless rows of vibrant purple lavandin, a French lavender hybrid created in 1920 for the country's perfume industry. The less fragrant lavandin produces almost five times more essential oil than true lavender, with 1 ton generating 25 to 40 liters. That's plenty to scent the pretty soaps and candles for sale, along with the creams and aromatic sprays that can act as disinfectants or help with sunburned lips, dry skin, insect bites, and nausea. But remember: only the label "PDO (AOC or AOP) Lavender Essential Oil" tells you that a product is made with authentic, Haute-Provence ingredients.

Olive oil

CERAMICS
Thanks to its clay-rich soil, Provence has a long history of pottery making. In 1946, however, after Picasso met Suzanne and Georges Ramié at their ceramics factory in the town of Vallauris, the industry was transformed. Picasso created 633 original pieces over 23 years, and the Madoura workshop still attracts art enthusiasts eager to see his clay masterpieces. Many villages continue to produce earthenware items, including the iconic sunshine-yellow-colored water jugs and two-part olive bowls. Detailed clay *santons* (little saints), particularly Christmas crèche figures, also beckon from shop windows (especially in the town of Aubagne), and it's easy to get hooked on building a collection to lovingly display every holiday season.

OLIVE OIL
Although olive-oil production in France doesn't quite match that of Italy, Spain, and Greece, the French choose to emphasize quality over quantity. Historically, the town of Roussillon has been the country's leading producer, creating aromatic and organic olive oils, but French olive oil is sold in stores and street markets throughout the country.

SOCCA CHIPS
Though shaped like nacho chips, the crunchy, 100% natural, gluten-free Socca Chips, created by Niçois chef Luc Salsedo in 2016, are made from chickpea flour, olive oil, salt, pepper, and sunflower oil—the same ingredients used to make the socca, Nice's version of a pancake. There are lots of knockoffs, but Salsedo's chips are the originals, and they pair well with a rosé or any *apèro*. He also offers SoccApero, an organic liquid batter in a bottle: just add water to make your own socca at home.

SAVON DE MARSEILLE
Only four soap makers in France still produce *le vrai* savon de Marseille in the traditional way: cooked in giant vats, with at least 72% pure olive oil and without fragrances (or with only natural essential oils added later), and air-dried and aged on wooden slats. Look for *savonneries* Marius Fabre, Fer à Cheval, du Midi, and Le Sérail—age-old companies that are fighting for a label to distinguish the real from the faux. If you're in Marseille, Maison Empereur, the 190-year-old housewares emporium, is a great place to find them.

Best Villages in Provence

GORDES

Often listed as one of the most beautiful villages in France, Gordes is a charming mix of sleepy French hillside community and posh resort town. Although the village is favored by celebrities as a quiet summer retreat, its atmosphere is unpretentious.

MÉNERBES

This charming village, whose sand-color buildings seem to disappear into the leafy landscape, is dominated by the Protestant-built citadel, a remnant from Ménerbes's time as an important Protestant stronghold during the French Wars of Religion.

SAINT-RÉMY-DE-PROVENCE

If the rolling wheat fields and gnarled olive groves surrounding Saint-Rémy-de-Provence look familiar, don't be surprised. Van Gogh spent a year in a psychiatric hospital here, and it was during this productive period that he created *Starry Night*.

CASSIS

No longer a true hidden gem, Cassis still offers a pleasant respite from Provence's more popular port cities with its dramatic seaside setting, framed by the imposing russet cliffs and the calanques (narrow inlets) tucked among them. Wine making is now the primary activity in the region, but Cassis has maintained its idyllic fishing-village vibe.

PORQUEROLLES

The largest of the Îles d'Hyères, Porquerolles has some of the best beaches in all of Provence. Built in the 19th century, its small village is new compared with most of Provence, and it has an atmosphere more akin to that of an Italian port town than of a hillside Roman village.

L'ISLE-SUR-LA-SORGUE
On the banks of the Sorgue River, this town is a shopper's paradise, only instead of malls and boutiques, it has fabulous antiques stores and bustling markets. Wake up early to stroll along the stalls at the famous Sunday market.

ROUSSILLON
At sunset, Roussillon practically glows, its fiery red and orange buildings brightening the surrounding landscape. Its unique color palette—most Provençal towns are a study in sandy beiges and creamy whites—is due to the area's large ocher clay deposits.

LACOSTE
Old houses made from ocher limestone are just the first pages of this storybook village. As you walk deeper through the streets, history unfolds to reveal medieval architecture, including an 11th-century château that was home to the Marquis de Sade.

LE BARROUX
Few places in Provence feel farther off the well-trod tourist path than Le Barroux. Alleyways in the tiny village are impossibly narrow, and rugged stone structures are adorned with flower-filled window boxes and mint-green or robin's-egg-blue shutters.

VAISON-LA-ROMAINE
It wasn't the Romans but the Celts who first settled on this picturesque hill in the Vaucluse department. Today, Vaison-la-Romaine is a charming mix of old and new, with steep medieval-era streets leading up to the Colline de Château on the south side of Ouvèze River.

Best Beaches in the French Riviera

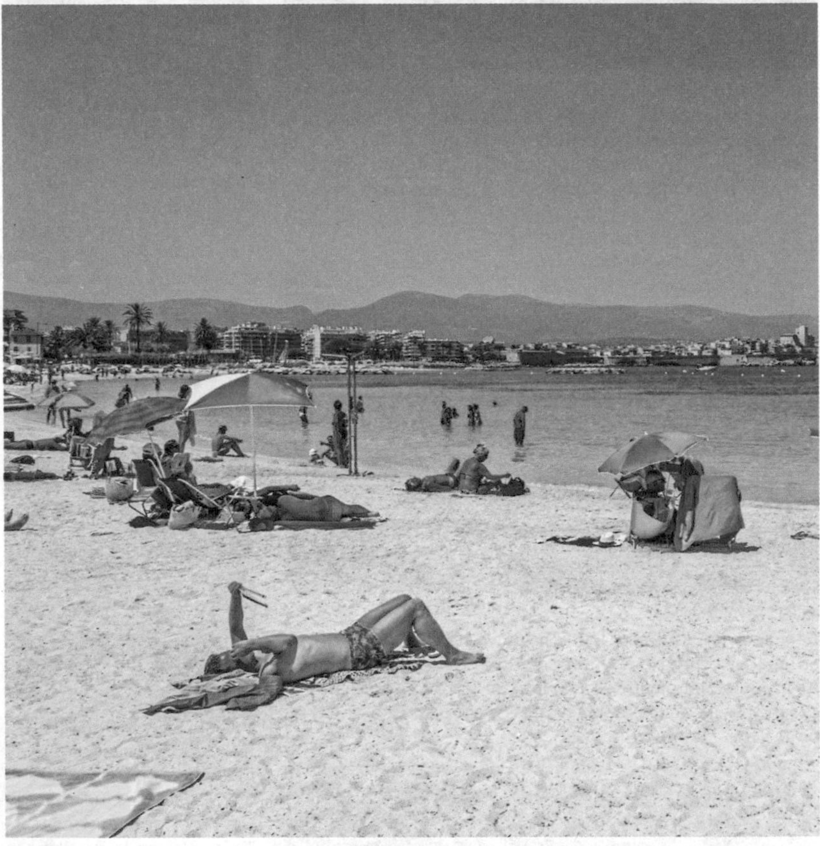

Plage de la Salis, Antibes

PLAGE DE LA SALIS, ANTIBES
One of the coastline's more glamorous addresses, Antibes is lined with beaches both public and private. The Plage de la Salis has golden sands (don't dig too deep as there are pebbles underneath) and stunning views of the Old Town, mountains, and the Garoupe lighthouse.

PLAGE DE LA GAROUPE, CAP D'ANTIBES
A long, sandy beach on a sparkling bay favored by sailboats, Plage de la Garoupe is one of the loveliest in Cap d'Antibes. While several sections of the beach are private (it's the only beach in Cap d'Antibes with any private sands), there are designated public areas.

PORT DE CROUTON PLAGE, JUAN-LES-PINS
On the west side of Cap d'Antibes lies the charming village of Juan-les-Pins, well known as the 1920s home of writer F. Scott Fitzgerald, his wife, Zelda, and their daughter, Scottie (their actual house is now the five-star Belles Rives Hotel). Port de Crouton is smaller than Juan-les-Pins's other main beaches and sheltered by stone jetties on either side.

The Calanques, Cassis

THE CALANQUES, CASSIS
Like tiny pockets of paradise, more than a dozen azure blue *calanques* (inlets) can be found tucked away in the rocky cliffs between Marseille and Cassis, a charming fishing village that's now a favorite of European tourists.

PLAGE DES MARINIÈRES, VILLEFRANCHE-SUR-MER
Just east of Villefranche-sur-Mer city center, the Plage des Marinières curves around the bay for nearly a mile past the Old Town. Between steep cliffs and the glimmering sea, with excellent views of Villefranche, this narrow, coarse white sand beach is a stunner.

PLAGE DE PALOMA, ST-JEAN-CAP-FERRAT
Jutting into the sea between Nice and Monaco, St-Jean-Cap-Ferrat is a coveted address that's a haven of calm. Plage de Paloma, one of the peninsula's five beaches, is the top contender for St-Jean-Cap-Ferrat's most Instagrammable beach.

TAHITI BEACH, ST-TROPEZ
The famous Tahiti Beach is at the northernmost edge of Pampelonne Beach's 3-mile stretch of white sand—half in St-Tropez and half in Ramatuelle—that can be reached from Pampelonne. Head for the stand of pine trees and be prepared for bathers in various stages of undress, as this is the Riviera's legendary "clothing-optional" beach.

PLAGE DE LA RÉPUBLIQUE, FRÉJUS
A long, sprawling beach fronting the pleasant town of Fréjus, in the Var region of Provence, Plage de la République is the most central of Fréjus's four beaches. Its large expanse of fine-grained sand and calm waters attract serious swimmers, while its proximity to the Fréjus Nautical Club makes it an ideal beach for water sports.

PLAGE BEAU-RIVAGE, ST-RAPHAEL
Set between the Veillat Beach and the Santa Lucia port, Plage Beau-Rivage is lined by a pretty promenade and a leafy park. The beach itself is a mix of sand and pebbles, with tranquil waters and wonderful views of the bay of St-Raphael and Lion de Mer Island.

Best Art Towns in Provence and the French Riviera

ARLES
The light, the landscapes, and the characters here inspired Van Gogh's greatest masterpieces. The Fondation Vincent van Gogh commemorates the artist, and the cultural center Luma Arles adds to the city's artistic allure.

HAUT-DE-CAGNES
Cagnes-sur-Mer may seem like nothing to write home about, but its hilltop Old Town, one of Provence's loveliest perched villages, was adored by Auguste Renoir. The town is home to Musée Renoir, the building where the artist spent his last 12 years.

ST-PAUL-DE-VENCE
At the town's famed La Colombe d'Or, artists once paid for their stays with artwork, and today the inn proudly displays works by Picasso, Matisse, and Miro. St-Paul-de-Vence is also home to one of Europe's largest modern art collections at the Fondation Maeght.

NICE
Henri Matisse's love affair with Nice lasted 37 years until the artist's death in 1954; he had a total of four dwelling places in the city, and the fourth and final is now the Musée Matisse. The city also has the Musée National Marc Chagall and the Musée des Arts Asiatiques.

ANTIBES
Several famous artists have fallen in love with the ancient city of Antibes, including Monet, Cross, Boudin, and Harpignies, but Picasso left the biggest mark. On a cobbled street in the charming Old Town, the Musée Picasso is housed in the 17th-century Château Grimaldi, where Picasso worked in an attic studio for six happy months.

MARSEILLE
The robust cultural scene in Marseille includes such famed institutions as the Musée des Civilisations de l'Europe et de la Méditerranée (aka the MuCEM); the Musée Regards de Provence; and the Unité d'Habitation Cité Radieuse, Le Corbusier's experiment in collective living.

Nice's Musée des Arts Asiatiques

AVIGNON
Avignon is an epicenter for the arts in Provence, starting with the Avignon Festival, and its offshoot, the edgier Le Festival OFF, Europe's biggest contemporary performing arts festival and France's oldest. Art museums also flourish here, with the Musée du Petit Palais; Musée Calvet; Musée Angladon; and the Collection Lambert, one of France's great bodies of modern and contemporary works.

VALLAURIS
Picasso's giant Riviera footprint extends 6 km (4 miles) from Antibes and Juan-les-Pins to Vallauris, an old pottery town where he lived from 1948 until 1955, where he married François Gilot in top secret at the town hall, and where he began his pivotal and fertile foray into ceramics and sculpture.

VENCE
Among the many attractions in Vence are a charming Old Town, a top-notch morning market, and Henri Matisse's exquisite Chapelle du Rosaire, aka the Matisse Chapel. The immaculate white structure, a gift to the nuns who nursed him through an illness, is all the more moving for its purity and simplicity.

AIX-EN-PROVENCE
Famed Postimpressionist painter Paul Cezanne was born, raised, and died in Aix-en-Provence, and the city's gorgeous light and stunning colors are said to have inspired much of his work. Today, its famed art museums include Musée Granet, the Fondation Victor Vasarely, and Atelier Cézanne.

What to Read and Watch

A YEAR IN PROVENCE BY PETER MAYLE

For years, the south of France was a mecca for British expats, many of whom were inspired by Peter Mayle's book—half cautionary tale and half amusing memoir—about trying to live the good life in an exceptional corner of the world.

JAMES BALDWIN: ESCAPE FROM AMERICA, EXILE IN PROVENCE BY JULES B. FARBER

Driven from America by pervasive racism and homophobia, the great writer James Baldwin eventually settled in St-Paul-de-Vence, where his small house became a mecca for French and American artists, writers, and musicians. Author Jules B. Farber explores these 17 years through interviews with town residents, as well as Toni Morrison, Maya Angelou, Quincy Jones, and others.

BONJOUR TRISTESSE BY FRANÇOISE SAGAN

Although today's teenagers aspire to go viral, back in the day, writers like Françoise Sagan dreamt of literary accolades. Her first novel, published in 1954 when she was just 18, became an overnight sensation. The plot revolves around a bored young girl and her equally bored philandering father who both find themselves bereft of meaning and love while summering on the French Riviera. Spoiler alert: there is no happy ending.

TWO TOWNS IN PROVENCE BY M.F.K. FISHER

In this tale of two rival cities, Marseille and Aix-en-Provence, Fisher—a friend of Julia Child, Richard Olney, and others who put Provençal cooking on the map—reveals a Provence still reeling from World War II, often through insightful descriptions of those she meets, from proud yet penniless aristocrats to her café waiter, during a stay in Aix from 1954 to 1955.

TENDER IS THE NIGHT BY F. SCOTT FITZGERALD

In the 1920s, F. Scott Fitzgerald and his wife, Zelda, spent time in the French Riviera, and their lifestyle there inspired his fourth and final novel, which he considered his best work.

MARSEILLE

The south of France is famous for sea views and abundant rosé, but it can also have a darker side. This Netflix series, which explores the politics and culture of France's second-largest city, stars Gerard Depardieu as the mayor of 20 years, who enters a war of succession with his political rival.

TRANSATLANTIC

Based on the novel *The Flight Portfolio* (2019) by Julie Orrigner, this Netflix series tells the true story of the Emergency Rescue Committee, created in 1940 by American and German academics to rescue artistic luminaries and others who had fled from Paris to the Riviera to escape the Nazis and the Vichy collaborationist government.

PROVENCE 1970: M.F.K. FISHER, JULIA CHILD, JAMES BEARD, AND THE REINVENTION OF AMERICAN TASTE

These three great American chefs, along with the American writer and cook Richard Olney, Simone Bec—one of Julia Child's coauthors on *Mastering the Art of French Cooking*—and their editor, Judith Jones, revolutionized food in the United States. Taken from chronicles by the brilliant Fisher, the book captures these tastemakers gossiping, arguing, eating, drinking, and, of course, cooking.

Chapter 2

TRAVEL SMART

Updated by
Nancy Heslin

POPULATION:
5 million

LANGUAGE:
French

$ CURRENCY:
Euro

COUNTRY CODE:
33; 337 Monaco

EMERGENCIES:
112

DRIVING:
On the right

ELECTRICITY:
220v/50 cycles; electrical plugs have two round prongs

TIME:
Six hours ahead of New York

WEB RESOURCES:
cotedazurfrance.fr
provence-alpes-cotedazur.com
www.visitmonaco.com

Know Before You Go

Provence is a large region, with several distinct cultures and landscapes, but no matter where you're going, here are a few tips that will help your trip go as smoothly as possible.

SUMMER IS A TOUGH TIME TO VISIT.

July and August can be stifling here, not only because of the intense heat but also because of the crowds (almost all of France goes on vacation the second half of July and all of August). Don't travel on or around July 14 (Bastille Day) or August 1, 15, and 31, when every French family is either driving to or from home. Free of midsummer crowds, June comes with balmy weather and long daylight hours.

May is riddled with church holidays—one per week—and the museum and store closings they entail, as well as reduced public transportation. After November 1, the whole region begins to shut down for winter, and main resort hotels don't open until Easter.

The shoulder seasons of March–April and September–October have their charms: prices are lower, many days are warm enough to soak up the sun, the pétanque pitches are just for the townsfolk, and the most touristy hill towns are virtually abandoned. What's more, although April and October have traditionally been the wettest months, with climate change this isn't a given.

Note, however, that in winter (and sometimes into spring), *le mistral*, a bone-chilling north wind phenomenon, brings 60-mph (100-kph) gusts, making the area less hospitable.

FRANCE HAS A LOT OF HOLIDAY CLOSURES.

With 11 national *jours feriés* (holidays) and five weeks of paid vacation, the French have their share of downtime. Tourist sites are nearly all closed on January 1 (New Year's), May 1 (Labor Day), and December 25 (Christmas). Check social media feeds or directly with museums, restaurants, and hotels in advance to ensure they will be open on these key dates as well: early to mid-April, Easter and Easter Monday; May 8, VE Day; mid- to late May, Ascension; late May–early June, Pentecost Monday; July 14, Bastille Day; August 15, Assumption; November 1, All Saints; and November 11, Armistice.

THE BEACHES MIGHT NOT BE WHAT YOU EXPECT.

Although renowned as being the world's most glamorous coastline, much of the Côte d'Azur is lined with rock and pebble, and the beaches are narrow swaths backed by city streets or roaring highways—all of which comes as a shock to first-timers. Some beaches are reviled for their *galets*, or round white stones the size of a fist, heaped along the shoreline, just where the sand should be.

There are some natural-sand beaches on the southern French coast—especially between St-Tropez and Cannes—and beaches like La Garoupe on Cap d'Antibes enjoy legendary status. Provence's coastline—between the Camargue and St-Tropez—alternates sandy pockets with inlets called *criques* and *calanques*, where you can perch on black rocks and ease yourself into turquoise waters.

To use the restaurant/hotel beaches in many of the resort towns you are charged a fee that usually includes a sun-lounger and a parasol (you can often use many hotel beaches for free if you order drinks or food). There are stretches of public beach where you'll need to bring your own parasol, sun chair, and towel. Be sure to arrive early in the summer, as all *plages* are popular with locals.

A sign of the times: there are now more than 20 smoke-free beaches (*plage sans tabac*) along the Côte d'Azur and half a dozen beaches now, including those in Monaco, have jellyfish (*méduse*) nets. Both public and private beaches usually post warnings daily if there are jellies. And, if you're on the fence about ditching that bikini top, according to a survey by the French Institute for Public Opinion published a few years back, the number of French women who sunbathe topless dipped to 19% from 43% in 1984.

BE ON THE LOOKOUT FOR A PÉTANQUE GAME.

In every village from the Rhône Valley to the Italian border, under every deep-shaded plane tree, the theater of Provençal life plays itself out slowly, serenely, and sociably. The café is a way of life in Provence, a cool outdoor living room where friends gather like family and share the ritual of the long, slow drink, the discussion of the weather (hot), and an amble over to the *pétanque* (lawn-bowling) court. The players stand, somber and intense, hands folded behind backs, and watch the intricate play of heavy metal balls rolling and clicking. A knot of onlookers gathers, disperses, is reinforced. In this region of the animated debate, the waving gesture, the forefinger punching the chest, it is a surprisingly quiet pastime.

RENTING A CAR MIGHT BE THE WAY TO GO.

When not on strike, the SNCF train service is a scenic and time-efficient option to travel along the coast, but if you want to reach all those perched villages, driving is the only option. When it comes to car rentals, forget the SUV and go for a small car that's easy to maneuver along tiny village cobblestone streets or to parallel park. Check that the vehicle has GPS (and in English!) and be sure to enter the full name of your destination: for instance, use "St-Paul-de-Vence" and not just St-Paul. The downside of driving is that France's toll highways can add up quickly; Paris to Nice is nearly €77.10 one-way, so if you have the time, stick to the National (RN) or District (RD) roads.

PRICES ARE HIGH (LIKE, REALLY HIGH) IN SOME PLACES, BUT YOU CAN STILL VISIT WITHOUT BREAKING THE BANK.

Yes, this region is widely considered a playground for the rich and famous. Yes, it's true that you could easily spend a lifetime's fortune in just a weekend. It's also true, however, that mere mortals can (and do) visit this area without going bankrupt. Many French tourism websites have a section that lists free stuff (concerts, Wi-Fi, exhibits, food, etc.), local "greeters" offer free tours (tip recommended), and national museums are free the first Sunday of each month.

Buy tickets online when you can; most cultural centers, museums, and tour companies offer reduced prices on tickets purchased in advance, and the tradeoff for possibly having to pay a small service fee is that you'll save time by not having to wait in line. City tourism cards, like the French Riviera Pass, can also help you save money (and bypass lines) at sights. They also usually feature public transport discounts.

Remember, too, that this is France, where nearly every town has a food market, so you can pack reasonably priced picnics. Also, look into the Too Good to Go "end food waste" app, which gets you end-of-the-day bargains at participating eateries. You can stay hydrated on the cheap by carrying a water bottle to fill up for free at one of the numerous *eau pótable* fountains. Later in the day, look for reduced-price happy hour drinks in bars and cafés.

There are free public restrooms in department stores, and many parks and cultural sites have toilets. And even if you end up spending €27 for a glass of water at Jimmy'z in Monaco or €150 on a piece of langouste you unknowingly ordered that is priced per 100/grams, remind yourself you're lucky to be experiencing a part of the world many others can only dream of—and think of the colorful story you'll be able to tell post-trip.

Getting Here and Around

The "Getting Here and Around" sections listed under towns in the regional chapters of this book provide detailed information about bus and train routes. In many cases, prices, transport companies, and schedules to and from the towns are listed.

It's possible to see the entire region just by taking the train, as there are comprehensive connections all the way from Montpellier to Avignon to Marseille and on to the full length of the Italian coast. There are also good regional bus networks that connect out of train stations. Although trains and buses may not be the best thing for quick village-hopping and multistop sightseeing (their schedules rarely intersect with yours), they can prove highly useful. When in doubt, check out tourist office websites or ask your hotel concierge for more information.

Air

Flying time to Paris is 80 minutes from London, 7½ hours from New York, 8 hours 10 minutes from Chicago, and just under 11 hours from Los Angeles. A direct flight from New York to Nice is eight hours. Scheduled flying time between Paris to either Marseille or Nice is approximately 1½ hours. Given the possibility of strikes in France, it's a good idea to confirm your flight online the day before.

AIRPORTS

The major gateways to France are Paris's Orly and Charles de Gaulle airports. Nice, Marseille, and Montpellier's airports are also served by frequent flights from Paris and London, and daily connections from Paris arrive at the smaller airports in Avignon and Nîmes.

FLIGHTS

Most major airlines fly to Paris and have connecting flights to the south of France on domestic airlines. The one exception is Delta, which flies nonstop to Nice from New York. From the United Kingdom, easyJet offers inexpensive nonstop service to Nice and Marseille; British Airways has direct flights to Nice and Marseille; low-cost Ryanair flies to Nîmes and Marseille.

Within France, Air France flies frequently from Paris to Marseille, Nice, Montpellier, and Toulon. EasyJet has flights from both Paris airports to Nice.

Bus

Long-distance buses are rare; regional buses are found mainly where train service is spotty. The weakest rail links in the south lie in the Luberon region of the Vaucluse, in the Alpilles, and in the back-country of the Haut Var, Haute-Provence, and the pre-Alpes behind Nice. To explore these regions, you must work closely with a bus schedule (available at most train stations and online through tourist offices), but don't plan on too much multistop sightseeing if you're limited to bus connections, as they rarely dovetail with your plans. To visit the popular hill towns just behind the Côte d'Azur—Grasse, St-Paul, Vence, and Biot—you can catch a regional bus or watch for commercial bus excursions advertised in the bigger coastal resorts. Tourist offices and their websites provide information on accompanied excursions.

Buses from the United Kingdom generally depart from London, traveling via hovercraft or ferry from London to Paris. If you're planning to travel extensively throughout Europe, you may wish to purchase a Eurolines Europass, valid for unlimited bus travel between 50 European cities (London, Paris, and Marseille included) for up to 30 days.

 Car

Car travel is the best way to see Provence, especially because buses go to the famous hilltop villages only once a day. However, a car may not be the fastest or most economical way to actually get to Provence: consider flying into Paris, connecting via a smaller airline to Nice or Marseille, and then renting a car in the south. Or purchase a rail-drive pass (TER + *voiture*), available from the SNCF (French national rail company), which gives discounts on car rentals or even car-share options. This will allow a few days' train travel—say, from Paris to Nice—and a block of car-rental time. By using the train to cover the long distances, then exploring the region in depth by car, you can make the most of both modes of transit.

France's roads are classified into three types and prefixed *A, N,* or *D.* For the fastest roads between two points, look for roads marked *A* for *autoroutes.* A *péage* (toll) must be paid on most expressways: rates vary but can be steep, for example it's €86.30 from Paris to Nice and €20.20 from Nice to Aix-en-Provence. Retrieve a ticket at your first toll stop and pay at the next toll. You may pay by credit card; Visa and American Express are accepted at most toll booths. The main toll roads through Provence are the A6 and A7, which connect Paris to Marseille via Lyon, Avignon, and Aix, and the east–west A8, which traverses the region from the Italian border to Aix via Nice.

The *N* (Route Nationale) roads, which are sometimes divided highways, are the route of choice for heavy freight trucks and are often lined with industry and large chain stores. More scenic, though less trafficked than the Ns, are the *D* (Route Départementale) roads, often also wide and fast. Although routes are numbered, the French generally guide themselves from city to city and town to town by destination name.

Negotiating the back roads requires a careful mix of GPS navigation and sign reading, often at high speeds around suburban *giratoires* (rotaries, also known as roundabouts). But once you head out into the hills, give yourself over to road signs and pure faith. Directions are indicated by village name only, with route numbers given as a small-print afterthought. Of course, this means you have to recognize the names of minor villages en route.

To leave Paris by car, figure out which of the *portes* (gates) corresponds to the direction you are going. Major highways connect to Paris at these points, and directions are indicated by major cities. For instance, heading south out of the city, look for Porte d'Orléans (direction Lyons and Bordeaux); after Lyons, follow Avignon, and after Avignon follow Nice and/or Marseille. It's best to steer clear of rush hours (6:30–9:30 am and 4:30–7:30 pm), although this is only a real concern between Aix and Marseille and around Nice.

GASOLINE

Between supply shortages and refinery strikes, gas prices in France are nearly 6% higher than in 2022. When possible, buy gas (*essence*) before you get on expressways or into rural areas, and keep an eye on pump prices as you go. These are roughly €1.91 per liter, or about $7.20 per gallon. The cheapest gas can be found at *hypermarchés* (very large supermarkets), but be ready for long lines. It

Getting Here and Around

is possible to go for many miles in the country without passing a gas station—don't let your tank get too low in rural areas. Diesel cars used to be a more economic option but, at €1.84 per liter, the difference is marginal. Diesel fuel at gas pumps can be labeled as *diesel, gasoil,* or *gazole;* unleaded gas will be labeled as *sans plomb* (SP95 for regular unleaded and SP98 for super unleaded). A handy site to source all pump prices is 🌐 *www.prix-carburants.gouv.fr.*

PARKING

In large towns, especially in a metropolis like Nice or Marseille, your best option is to duck into the parking garage nearest the neighborhood you want to visit. Carry the ticket with you, and pay at the vending machine–style ticket dispenser before returning to your car. On the street, ticket machines (pay and display) are common, and you'll need to put the receipt, which must be clearly visible to the meter patrol, on the dashboard on the inside of the front window on the passenger side. Be sure to check the signs before you park, as rules vary. You can pay with coins, credit card, or download the PayByPhone app, which can be used in most French cities.

Be careful when parking your car overnight, especially in towns and village squares; if your car is still there in the early morning on a market day, it will be towed. In smaller towns, parking may be permitted on one side of the street only—alternating every two weeks—so pay attention to signs.

The coastal area of Provence—especially the Camargue and the Calanques—as well as overlooks along the Riviera are extremely vulnerable to car break-ins. Never leave valuables visible in the car, and think twice about leaving them in the trunk. Any theft should be reported formally to the police.

RENTAL CARS

You must be at least 21 to rent a car. When you reserve, request car seats and extras such as GPS, and ask about cancellation penalties, taxes, drop-off charges (for picking up the car in one city and leaving it in another), and surcharges (for being under or over a certain age, for additional drivers, or for driving across regional or country borders or beyond a specific distance from your point of rental). All these things can add substantially to your costs.

Rates are sometimes better if you book in advance or reserve through a rental agency's website. There are other reasons to book ahead, though: for popular destinations, during busy times of the year, or to ensure that you get certain types of cars (vans, SUVs, exotic sports cars). **■ TIP→ Make sure that a confirmed reservation guarantees you a car. Agencies sometimes overbook, particularly for busy weekends and holiday periods.**

Though renting a car in France is expensive—up to twice as much as in the United States—and the cost of gas is very high as well, it may pay off if you are traveling with two or more people and want to move around at your own pace. Rates begin at about €100 per day and €350–€400 per week for an economy car with a manual transmission (an automatic transmission will cost more). Be sure to check whether the price includes the 20% V.A.T. tax or, if you pick up from the airport, the airport tax.

Also, check rates offered by local car-rental companies. Although their service and maintenance may not be as good as those of major rental agencies, their prices might be lower. ADA, a French-owned rental company, has offices in towns, train stations, and airports throughout Provence. The Renault Eurodrive program lets non-EU citizens visiting between

21 days and 6 months lease new cars short-term. Offices are at Paris CDG and in Marseille, Montpellier, and Nice. ■ **TIP→ Do yourself a favor, and opt for all-inclusive insurance.** This is France, and almost every time you park on the street, you'll be bumped by another parking car.

ROAD CONDITIONS

Road conditions in Provence are above average and potholes are rare, especially on highways. Check with the highway information website (🌐 *www.vinci-autoroutes.com/fr/autoroutes-temps-reel*) or listen to FM107.7 (the traffic station in French) or Riviera Radio in English FM106.5 and online to find out whether there's anything you should know before setting off.

RULES OF THE ROAD

In France your own driver's license is acceptable, provided you have an official translation. Most visitors don't actually have one, but in the event of a fender-bender that's not your fault, it will save hassle. You don't need an International Driver's Permit unless you are planning on a long-term stay; you can get one from the American or Canadian automobile associations, and, in the United Kingdom, from the Automobile Association or Royal Automobile Club. You must also be able to prove you have third-party insurance, which most car rental companies provide.

Drive on the right and yield to drivers coming from streets to the right. However, this rule does not necessarily apply at roundabouts, where you are obligated to yield to those already within (to your left)—but you should watch out for just about everyone. You must wear your seat belt, and children under 10 may not travel in the front seat.

French speed limits vary depending on weather conditions and are lower in rural areas. The limits in dry weather are 130 kph (80 mph) on freeways, 110 kph (70 mph) on divided highways, 90 kph (55 mph) on other roads, 50 kph (30 mph) in towns, and 30 kph (15 mph) in school zones. French drivers break these limits often, but France has 4,447 radar devices, and police hand out hefty on-the-spot fines. The cops are also fast to fine when it comes to using a mobile phone while driving: €135 and 3 points—which applies also to foreign licenses.

 Train

The SNCF is one of Europe's best national rail services: it's fast, punctual (when not on strike), comfortable, and comprehensive. You can get to Provence and the coast from all points west, north, and east, though lines out of Paris are by far the most direct. There are various options: local trains, overnight trains with sleeping accommodations, and the high-speed TGV (Trains à Grande Vitesse, or high-speed trains).

France is rightly proud of its TGV lines, which zoom along at 300 kph (186 mph). The LGV Méditerranée connects Paris to Avignon and Aix-en-Provence. With the hassles of airport check-in and transfer, you may find train travel the most efficient way to get from Paris to Provence.

All TGV trains to Provence leave from Paris's Gare de Lyon, and Ouigo trains—the low-cost service operated also by SNCF—leave from stations across the country. Travel time from Paris is 2 hours, 40 minutes to Avignon; between 3 to 3½ hours to Nîmes, Marseille, and Aix-en-Provence; 3¼ hours to Montpellier; 4 hours to Toulon; and 5½ hours to Nice.

Getting Here and Around

Certain models of the TGV, called *train duplex,* offer luxurious comfort, with double-decker seating and panoramic views. When one of these passes along the coast—especially from Nice to Menton—it makes for a dramatic sightseeing excursion, though it pokes along at a local-train snail's pace. When you're connecting from one coastal city to another (Marseille–Toulon–Fréjus–Cannes–Nice–Menton), you're also likely to board a regional TER double-decker train.

Traveling first-class can cost about 50% more than second class, but, with the exception of wider seats, you won't get many more amenities, and, unless you're traveling internationally, you'll still need to buy your own food at the onboard café-bar. All TGVs now offer Wi-Fi.

BOARDING THE TRAIN

Before boarding, you must validate your ticket (but not Eurail Pass or e-ticket) in one of the yellow machines at the entrance to the platforms, or else you risk a €50 minimum fine plus a processing fee, which has to be paid on the spot. If you board your train on the run and don't have time to punch it, look for a conductor (*contrôleur*) as soon as possible and get him to sign it. In main cities, like Nice, you have to scan your ticket's QR code to open the electronic entry gate. In theory, the same process applies to exit the station, though the gates often open automatically; still, it's best to have your ticket handy.

RAIL PASSES

France is one of 33 countries where you can use Eurail Passes, which provide unlimited first- and second-class rail travel, in all of the participating European countries, for the duration of the pass. Select between a one-country pass with up to eight days of travel within one month, or a Global Pass with four, five, or seven days travel within one month; 10 or 15 days within two months; or unlimited travel over 15 or 22 consecutive days, or one, two, or three months.

You must book seats ahead even if you are using a rail pass. You also have to make a seat reservation for the TGV—easily done on the app, online, or from an automatic machine. Seat reservations are reassuring but seldom necessary on other main-line French trains, except at busy holiday times (as in summer), particularly on popular routes. You will also need a reservation for sleeping accommodations.

SNCF offers a number of discount rail passes, which are available only for purchase in France. You can get a reduced fare if you are 60 or older with the SNCF's Carte Senior, which costs €49 and entitles the bearer to deep discounts on rail and TGV travel for a year. There are also passes for young people (12 to 27), weekend passes (for ages 27 to 59), and passes for those traveling with at least three children.

Essentials

Dining

When dining out, it's best to relax and go with the French flow. If you keep one eye on your watch and the other on the waiter, you'll miss the point and spoil the meal. Allowing 90 minutes for lunch, savoring three courses and talking over the wine, is reasonable; allow even more time for dinner.

Diners in France don't generally request special preparations, so expect a blank stare if you order off menu. Always request your coffee or tea after dessert, not at the same time, and when you're ready for the check, ask for it: no professional waiter would dare put a bill on your table while you're still enjoying the last sip of coffee. And the once frowned-upon doggy bag is now à la mode since a law introduced in July 2021 says restaurateurs must offer customers reusable "doggy bag" containers.

Rather than soda or coffee, the French usually drink wine or mineral water with their food. In regard to water, it's not that what comes out of the tap is unsafe (indeed, you can order *une carafe d'eau* if you prefer)—rather, it's just not as tasty as Evian or slightly fizzy Badoit. To order flat mineral water, ask for *eau naturelle*; fizzy is *eau gazeuse*.

Coastal restaurants are generally more expensive than those inland. Basic prix-fixe menus average €22–€32, though the high end of this range represents the usual cost of seafood so often featured on menus. In high summer, reserve ahead at popular restaurants, especially if you want a coveted outdoor table.

MEALS AND MEALTIMES

Breakfast is usually served 7–10; if you want it earlier, arrange a time the night before with your hotel. Morning meals are light, usually consisting of croissants and baguettes, jam and butter, and coffee. Many hotels also serve yogurt, fruit juice, cereal, cheese, and eggs on request.

Here, more than anywhere in France, the local lunch hour begins after 1; some places don't even open before that. If you're antsy to get to the next museum, or if you plan to spend the evening dining in grand style, consider lunch in a brasserie, where quick, one-plate lunches and full salads are available.

Cafés often serve *casse croûtes* (snacks), including sandwiches, which are simply baguettes lightly filled with ham or cheese, or *croques monsieurs,* grilled ham and cheese open-face sandwiches with a rich layer of béchamel. Bakeries and *traiteurs* (delis) tend to sell savory items like quiches, tiny pizzas, or pastries filled with pâté. On the Riviera, there's a wealth of street food, from the chickpea-based crêpes called *socca* to *pissaladière* (onion-olive pizza) to *pan bagnat* (a tuna-and-egg-stuffed pita-style bun).

Dinner is usually eaten at 8, and most restaurants do not open for the evening meal before 7:30. Unless otherwise noted, the restaurants listed in this guide are open daily for lunch and dinner.

Lodging

In Provence, you can go native in a country *gîte* (rental house), be pampered in a luxury penthouse overlooking the Mediterranean, or get to know the locals in a converted *mas* (farmhouse). Regardless of the type of accommodation, it's essential to book well in advance for stays in July and August and a good idea to do so for visits in late spring or early fall.

Essentials

APARTMENT AND HOUSE RENTALS

Although Paris mayor Anne Hidalgo is still considering banning Airbnb from certain arrondissements, the service is popular in France. Alternatively, check with town tourist offices, which usually publish lists of independent rentals, many of them inspected and classified by the tourist office itself.

There is also Gîtes de France, a nationwide organization that rents vacation homes by the week, in the countryside, by the sea, or in the mountains. Properties are rated according to comfort on a scale of one to five and are strictly supervised, with an on-site welcome from either a representative or the owners. Some gîtes are quaint, restored farmhouses or village row houses. Others are quite posh, with a swimming pool and other amenities.

In addition, Gîtes de France can, for extra fees, arrange *table d'hôte* dinners—meals often made with farm produce and cooked by and eaten with the owners—as well as activities such as hiking and biking tours, canyoning excursions with certified instructors, or wine experiences with an enologist.

The region west of Nîmes, including some parts of the Camargue, lies in the *département* of Hérault. Gîtes de France offices for this department are based in Montpellier. Nîmes itself and environs are processed by the Gard office. For Arles and the Alpilles, contact the Bouches-du-Rhône office.

BED-AND-BREAKFASTS

France's bed-and-breakfasts are known as *chambres d'hôtes*. To find listings—from rustic options to luxurious châteaux—check local tourist office websites or Chambres-Hotes.fr, an organization that list thousands of B&Bs all over the country. Gîtes de France also has a list of regional B&Bs. **■TIP→ Although there are a good number of British-run B&Bs in Provence and the Riviera, it is more likely that the owners will speak only French.**

HOTELS

Hotels are classified by the French government from one- to five-star up to Palace. Rates must, by law, be posted at the hotel entrance and should include taxes and service; you are always charged per room, not per person. Remember that in France the first floor is one floor up (what Americans call the second floor), and the higher up you go, the quieter the room will be. Note, too, that the quality of accommodations, particularly in older properties, can vary greatly from room to room, as hotels are often renovated floor by floor; if you don't like the room you're given, ask to see another.

Unless otherwise noted, lodging listings in this book include a private bathroom with a shower or tub. Because replumbing drains is often very expensive, if not impossible, old hotels may have added bathrooms—often with *douches* (showers), not *baignoires* (tubs)—to the guest rooms, but not toilets, although this is becoming a rarity.

If you want a queen- or king-size bed, ask for a *grand lit* when making your reservation. Also check in advance that your hotel room is *climatisé* (air-conditioned), which isn't a given, even at hotels in inland Provence, far from sea breezes. Note, too, that window screens (*moustiquaires*) are rare, except, perhaps, at some properties in the Camargue marshlands, where mosquitoes are an issue.

Breakfast is rarely included in the price, but you're sometimes expected to have it and are occasionally charged for it regardless, so be sure to inform the hotel if you are not going to be eating the *pétit-déj* there. In smaller rural hotels, you may be expected to have your evening meal at the hotel, too.

Safety

Car break-ins have become common in the south, especially in the isolated parking lots where hikers set off to explore for the day. Be especially careful around the marshes of the Camargue, the departure point for the Îles d'Hyères ferries, the rocky Esterel between Fréjus and Cannes, and the coastal path around St-Tropez. Take valuables with you, and, if possible, leave luggage at your hotel.

Also beware of petty theft—purse and phone snatching and pickpocketing. Avoid pulling out a lot of money in public, and keep wallets up front or otherwise safely tucked away. Consider wearing a money belt or a handbag with a zippered compartment for your money and passport and with long straps so that you can sling it across your body, bandolier-style. At airports and train stations, never leave luggage unattended even for a minute.

Although cities in Provence are relatively safe during the day, be cautious at night, especially in Avignon, Marseille, Nice, and Toulon. Marseille is particularly known for its drug-related crime, although tourists generally aren't targeted.

Taxes

In France, all taxes must be included in posted prices, even if the abbreviation TTC (*toutes taxes comprises*—taxes included) doesn't appear on price lists.

Restaurant and hotel prices must also include taxes, including any daily habitation taxes, which can run €0.20–€4.10 a day (depending on room size).

Stores participating in the Tax-Free Shopping "PABLO" program (you'll see a sticker in the shop window) offer V.A.T. refunds to foreign shoppers. To qualify, you must be a national of a non-EU country, at least 16 years old at the time of purchase, and visiting France for less than six months. Also, the total amount of your purchases from one store, tax included, must be more than than €100. If you qualify, you're entitled to an export discount of up to 20%. Some items are exempt, like cigarettes.

Tipping

The French have a clear idea of when they should be tipped. Bills in bars and restaurants include a 15% service fee, but it is customary to round out the total of your tab slightly. The amount varies: anywhere from €0.10 if you've merely bought a beer to €2–€5 for a meal.

At hotels, leave about €2 per day for the housekeeper and tip bellhops about €1.50 per item. For concierges and other staffers, tips depend on how much you've used (and the quality of) their services.

Train and airport porters get €1–€1.50 per bag. Tip taxi drivers and hairdressers about 5%. Coat check attendants expect nothing if there's a sign saying "*pourboire interdit*" (tips forbidden); otherwise give them €1. The same goes for washroom attendants, unless another sum is posted.

On the Calendar

Spring

Antibes Art Fair. At this antique and modern art fair, held for two weeks in April, some 20,000 people from all over the world come to view the treasures and pick up a little something for back home. ✉ *Old Port, Antibes* ☎ *04–93–34–65–65* 🌐 *www.antibesartfair.com.*

Cannes International Film Festival. The Riviera's cultural calendar is splashy and star-studded, and never more so than during May's Cannes International Film Festival. Screenings aren't open to the public, so unless you have a pass, your stargazing will be on the streets or in restaurants (though if you hang around the backstreet exits of the big hotels around 7 pm, you may bump into a few celebs on their way to the red carpet). Cinéma de la Plage shows Cannes classics and out-of-competition films free at Macé beach at 9:30 pm. In addition, Cannes Cinéphiles (🌐 *www.cannes-cinema.com*) gives 4,000 film buffs a chance to view Official Selections; you can apply online starting in February. ✉ *Cannes* 🌐 *www.festival-cannes.com.*

Summer

Festival d'Aix-en-Provence. Every July, you can see world-class productions in the courtyard of the Palais de l'Archevêché during one of Europe's most important opera festivals. The repertoire is varied and often offbeat, featuring works like Britten's *Curlew River* and Bartók's *Bluebeard's Castle* as well as the usual Mozart, Puccini, and Verdi. Most of the singers are not celebrities but rather elite students who spend the summer with the Académie Européenne de Musique, training and performing under the tutelage of stars like Robert Tear and Yo-Yo Ma. Buy tickets online beginning in January. ✉ *Palais de l'Ancien Archevêché, 28 pl. des Martyrs de la Résistance, Aix-en-Provence* ☎ *08–20–67–00–57 €0.12/min.* 🌐 *festival-aix.com/fr.*

Festival d'Avignon. Held annually over three weeks in July, the Festival d'Avignon has brought the best of world theater to this ancient city since 1947. Avignon's version of fringe, the OFF Festival (🌐 *www.festivaloffavignon.com*) is staged at the same time. The two combined host more than 1,600 performances, with the main venue being the Palais des Papes. Tickets go on sale around mid-June and sell out quickly. ✉ *Avignon* ☎ *04–90–27–66–50 tickets and information* 🌐 *festival-avignon.com.*

Festival International Jazz à Juan. Launched in 1960 and held in July, this world-renowned jazz festival hosts a stellar lineup in a romantic venue under ancient pines. In the early years, stars such as Miles Davis and Ray Charles made their European debuts here. More recently, the festival has spawned the fringier Jazz OFF, with 200 musicians and free street concerts, as well as the Jazz Club at Les Ambassadeurs beach, where you can enjoy a drink with live music (headliners have been known to pop in for impromptu concerts here). Book online or buy tickets directly from the tourist office in Antibes or Juan-les-Pins. ✉ *Juan-les-Pins* ☎ *04–22–10–60–01 ticket information* 🌐 *jazzajuan.com.*

Grande Féria. This highly anticipated, mid-August festival brings the Camargue to St-Rémy-de-Provence. Bullfights (don't worry, they're not killed) and bull runs, *peñas flamencas* (flamenco "clubs"), DJs, parades, kids' races, and plenty of food are all on offer during its four days. 🌐 *www.saint-remy-de-provence.com/feria-de-st-remy-de-provence.*

International Cannes Fireworks Festival. On various nights in July and August, six countries compete in an amazing 25-minute musical fireworks display that lights up both the water and the sky. The fireworks are set off from barges 400 meters offshore from the Baie of Cannes. You can watch beachside for free among the masses of locals who come early. ✉ *Cannes* 🌐 *www.festival-pyrotechnique-cannes.com.*

Les Rencontres d'Arles. In July, movers and shakers in international photography gather at the Théâtre Antique for five days of specialized colloquiums and other events. Ordinary folks can take in 35 exhibitions of mostly unpublished work that are held in various heritage sites throughout town from July to September. Tickets, which range from €5.50 for a single entry to €37 for a pass, can be purchased online or from various locations in Arles, including the festival office. The app is super helpful. ✉ *Office, 34 rue du Docteur Fanton, Arles* ☎ *04–90–96–76–06* 🌐 *www.rencontres-arles.com.*

Monte-Carlo Sporting Summer Festival. Since its creation in 1974, the Monte-Carlo Sporting Summer Festival has brought the biggest names in music to the open-air Salle des Étoiles in July and August. John Legend, Lady Gaga, Tom Jones, Elvis Costello, and Duran Duran are a few recent performers at these intimate dinner shows. For a chance to see Sting in 2023, tickets started at €225 per person, but hey, at least it included valet parking. ✉ *Monaco* ☎ *98–06–41–59* 🌐 *www.montecarlosbm.com/fr/spectacles-monaco.*

Nice Jazz Festival. For five days in July, the Nice Jazz Festival and Jazz OFF draw performers from around the world to Place Masséna and Théâtre de Verdure. Normal tickets cost €45 per show and can be purchased online or at Place Masséna. ✉ *Pl. Masséna and Théâtre de Verdure, Nice* 🌐 *www.nicejazzfestival.fr.*

Voiles d'Antibes. In the first week of June, the Match Race regatta sets sail across 23 km (14 miles) of coastline. The event marks the official opening of the classic yachting season, with other regattas in Cannes and St-Tropez in September, and features beautiful old teak and brass sailing vessels, metric classes, and maxi-cruisers more than 20 meters long. ✉ *Old Port, Antibes* ☎ *04–93–34–42–47 for info* 🌐 *www.voilesdantibes.com.*

Winter

Menton Lemon Festival. Running 15 days in February through the first week of March, this full-blown lemon love-in features 140 tons of the citrus fruit on floats during daily parades and in gardens, which are lit up at night as part of the Les Jardins de Lumières (tickets are needed for both). Think of this as France's answer to the Rose Bowl Parade. ✉ *Menton* ☎ *04–92–41–76–95* 🌐 *www.fete-du-citron.com.*

Nice Carnaval. During the two weeks leading up to Mardi Gras and Lent, the Niçois let loose in disguise during this carnival, which attracts roughly 250,000 visitors. The parades in Place Masséna include €30,000 floats made up of some 80,000 flowers, dancers of varying levels of expertise and enthusiasm, more than 1,600 musicians, and face-painting stands for kids. For the best view, it's worth investing in tickets (book seats online, up to €32, standing-room from €10). The main event also incorporates Lou Queernaval, the first Gay Carnival Parade in France (free). ✉ *Nice* 🌐 *www.nicecarnaval.com.*

Helpful French Phrases

BASICS

Yes/no	wee/nohn	Oui/non
Please	seel voo play	S'il vous plaît
Thank you	mair- **see**	Merci
You're welcome	deh ree- **ehn**	De rien
Excuse me, sorry	pahr- **don**	Pardon
Good morning/ afternoon	bohn- **zhoor**	Bonjour
Good evening	bohn- **swahr**	Bonsoir
Good-bye	o ruh- **vwahr**	Au revoir
Mr. (Sir)	muh- **syuh**	Monsieur
Mrs. (Ma'am)	ma- **dam**	Madame
Miss	mad-mwa- **zel**	Mademoiselle
Pleased to meet you	ohn-shahn- **tay**	Enchanté(e)
How are you?	kuh-mahn-tahl-ay **voo**	Comment allez-vous?
Very well, thanks	tray bee-ehn, mair- **see**	Très bien, merci
And you?	ay voo?	Et vous?

NUMBERS

one	uhn	un
two	deuh	deux
three	twah	trois
four	**kaht**-ruh	quatre
five	sank	cinq
six	seess	six
seven	set	sept
eight	wheat	huit
nine	nuf	neuf
ten	deess	dix
eleven	ohnz	onze
twelve	dooz	douze
thirteen	trehz	treize
fourteen	kah- **torz**	quatorze
fifteen	kanz	quinze
sixteen	sez	seize
seventeen	deez- **set**	dix-sept
eighteen	deez- **wheat**	dix-huit
nineteen	deez- **nuf**	dix-neuf
twenty	vehn	vingt
twenty-one	vehnt-ay- **uhn**	vingt-et-un
thirty	trahnt	trente
forty	ka- **rahnt**	quarante
fifty	sang- **kahnt**	cinquante
sixty	swa- **sahnt**	soixante
seventy	swa-sahnt- **deess**	soixante-dix
eighty	kaht-ruh- **vehn**	quatre-vingts
ninety	kaht-ruh-vehn-**deess**	quatre-vingt-dix
one hundred	sahn	cent
one thousand	meel	mille

COLORS

black	nwahr	noir
blue	bleuh	bleu
brown	bruhn/mar- **rohn**	brun/marron
green	vair	vert
orange	o- **rahnj**	orange
pink	rose	rose
red	rouge	rouge
violet	vee-o- **let**	violette
white	blahnk	blanc
yellow	zhone	jaune

DAYS OF THE WEEK

Sunday	dee- **mahnsh**	dimanche
Monday	luhn- **dee**	lundi
Tuesday	mahr- **dee**	mardi
Wednesday	mair-kruh- **dee**	mercredi
Thursday	zhuh- **dee**	jeudi
Friday	vawn-druh- **dee**	vendredi
Saturday	sahm- **dee**	samedi

MONTHS

January	zhahn-vee- **ay**	janvier
February	feh-vree- **ay**	février
March	marce	mars
April	a- **vreel**	avril
May	meh	mai
June	zhwehn	juin
July	zhwee- **ay**	juillet
August	ah- **oo**	août
September	sep- **tahm**-bruh	septembre
October	awk- **to**-bruh	octobre
November	no- **vahm**-bruh	novembre
December	day- **sahm**-bruh	décembre

USEFUL PHRASES

Do you speak English?	par-lay **voo** ahn- **glay**	Parlez-vous anglais?
I don't speak …	zhuh nuh parl pah …	Je ne parle pas …
French	frahn- **say**	français
I don't understand	zhuh nuh kohm-**prahn** pah	Je ne comprends pas
I understand	zhuh kohm- **prahn**	Je comprends
I don't know	zhuh nuh say **pah**	Je ne sais pas
I'm American/ British	zhuh sweez a-may-ree- **kehn** / ahn- **glay**	Je suis américain/ anglais
What's your name?	ko-mahn vooz a-pell-ay- **voo**	Comment vous appelez-vous?
My name is …	zhuh ma- **pell** …	Je m'appelle …
What time is it?	kel air eh- **teel**	Quelle heure est-il?
How?	ko- **mahn**	Comment?
When?	kahn	Quand?
Yesterday	yair	Hier
Today	o-zhoor- **dwee**	Aujourd'hui

Tomorrow	duh- **mehn**	Demain
Tonight	suh **swahr**	Ce soir
What?	kwah	Quoi?
What is it?	kess-kuh- **say**	Qu'est-ce que c'est?
Why?	poor- **kwa**	Pourquoi?
Who?	kee	Qui?
Where is …	oo ay	Où est …
the train station?	la gar	la gare?
the subway station?	la sta- **syon** duh may- **tro**	la station de métro?
the bus stop?	la-ray duh booss	l'arrêt de bus?
the post office?	la post	la poste?
the bank?	la bahnk	la banque?
the … hotel?	lo- **tel**	l'hôtel …?
the store?	luh ma-ga- **zehn**	le magasin?
the cashier?	la **kess**	la caisse?
the … museum?	luh mew- **zay**	le musée …?
the hospital?	lo-pee- **tahl**	l'hôpital?
the elevator?	la-sahn- **seuhr**	l'ascenseur?
the telephone?	luh tay-lay- **phone**	le téléphone?
Where are the …	oo sohn lay	Où sont les …
restrooms?	twah- **let**	toilettes?
(men/women)	(**oh**-mm/ **fah**-mm)	(hommes/femmes)
Here/there	ee- **see** /la	Ici/là
Left/right	a goash/a draht	A gauche/à droite
Straight ahead	too drwah	Tout droit
Is it near/far?	say pray/lwehn	C'est près/loin?
I'd like …	zhuh voo- **dray**	Je voudrais …
a room	ewn **shahm**-bruh	une chambre
the key	la clay	la clé
a newspaper	uhn zhoor- **nahl**	un journal
a stamp	uhn **tam**-bruh	un timbre
I'd like to buy …	zhuh voo- **dray ahsh**-tay	Je voudrais acheter …
cigarettes	day see-ga- **ret**	des cigarettes
matches	days a-loo- **met**	des allumettes
soap	dew sah- **vohn**	du savon
city map	uhn plahn de **veel**	un plan de ville
road map	ewn cart roo-tee- **air**	une carte routière
magazine	ewn reh- **vu**	une revue
envelopes	dayz ahn-veh- **lope**	des enveloppes
writing paper	dew pa-pee- **ay** a **let**-ruh	du papier à lettres
postcard	ewn cart pos- **tal**	une carte postale
How much is it?	say comb-bee- **ehn**	C'est combien?
A little/a lot	uhn peuh/bo- **koo**	Un peu/beaucoup
More/less	plu/mwehn	Plus/moins
Enough/too (much)	a-say/tro	Assez/trop
I am ill/sick	zhuh swee ma- **lahd**	Je suis malade
Call a …	a-play uhn	Appelez un …
doctor	dohk- **tehr**	docteur
Help!	o suh- **koor**	Au secours!
Stop!	a-reh- **tay**	Arrêtez!
Fire!	o fuh	Au feu!
Caution!/Look out!	a-tahn-see- **ohn**	Attention!

DINING OUT

A bottle of …	ewn boo- **tay** duh	une bouteille de …
A cup of …	ewn tass duh	une tasse de …
A glass of …	uhn vair duh	un verre de …
Bill/check	la-dee-see- **ohn**	l'addition
Bread	dew panh	du pain
Breakfast	luh puh- **tee** day-zhuh- **nay**	le petit-déjeuner
Butter	dew burr	du beurre
Cheers!	ah **vo**-truh sahn- **tay**	A votre santé!
Cocktail/aperitif	uhn ah-pay-ree- **teef**	un apéritif
Dinner	luh dee- **nay**	le dîner
Dish of the day	luh plah dew **zhoor**	le plat du jour
Enjoy!	bohn a-pay- **tee**	Bon appétit!
Fixed-price menu	luh may- **new**	le menu
Fork	ewn four- **shet**	une fourchette
I am diabetic	zhuh swee dee-ah-bay- **teek**	Je suis diabétique
I am vegetarian	zhuh swee vay-zhay-ta-ree- **en**	Je suis végétarien(ne)
I cannot eat …	zhuh nuh puh pah mahn- **jay** deh	Je ne peux pas manger de …
I'd like to order	zhuh voo- **dray** ko-mahn- **day**	Je voudrais commander
Is service/the tip included?	ess kuh luh sair- **veess** ay comb- **pree**	Est-ce que le service est compris?
It's good/bad	say bohn/mo- **vay**	C'est bon/mauvais
It's hot/cold	say sho/frwah	C'est chaud/froid
Knife	uhn koo- **toe**	un couteau
Lunch	luh day-zhuh- **nay**	le déjeuner
Menu	la cart	la carte
Napkin	ewn sair-vee- **et**	une serviette
Pepper	dew **pwah**-vruh	du poivre
Plate	ewn a-see- **et**	une assiette
Please give me …	doe-nay- **mwah**	Donnez-moi …
Salt	dew sell	du sel
Spoon	ewn kwee- **air**	une cuillère
Sugar	dew **sook**-ruh	du sucre
Waiter!/Waitress!	muh- **syuh** / mad-mwa- **zel**	Monsieur!/ Mademoiselle!
Wine list	la cart day vehn	la carte des vins

Great Itineraries

Best of Provence

To focus only on the best of Provence—its history, its architecture, its markets, and its cafés—devote your time to the "three As": Avignon, Arles, and Aix, as well as the area between them that anchors the heart of the region.

DAYS 1–2: AVIGNON

The population of Avignon swells most during the extensive midsummer Drama Festival that sees the gateway city to Provence at its liveliest. Yet this historic town, with its protective medieval ring of muscular towers, is seldom dull at any time of year.

In the 14th century, this was the center of Christendom, when French-born Pope Clement V shifted the papacy from Rome to Avignon's magnificent Palais des Papes (Papal Palace). Spend your first day viewing the palace, the Pont St-Bénezet, and the Rocher des Doms Park, then escape into the cobblestone alleys to see the Avignonnais living their daily lives. Pop into the Musée Angladon to view Van Gogh's *Wagons de Chemin de Fer*, and then see modern and contemporary works at the Collection Lambert.

The next morning, head to a food or flea market or to the gorgeous indoor Marché des Halles with its 40 local vendors (⏲ *Closed Mon.*). Pick up a snack for an afternoon road trip 25 km (15 miles) west of Avignon to the three-tier stone spectacle that is the Pont du Gard, built by the Romans in 19 BC as an aqueduct and known today as one of the wonders of the classical world.

DAY 3: ST-RÉMY

Escape to "the Hamptons of Provence," the picturesque town of St-Rémy-de-Provence, where mellow 18th-century mansions line the streets, some of which lead to St-Paul-de-Mausolée, the ancient monastery where Vincent van Gogh spent some of his most productive months. From here, take the 90-minute guided tour, "In the Footsteps of Vincent van Gogh," or download a free map from the tourist office and make your own tour.

Stop for lunch at the Café de Place before heading to the 6th-century archaeological site Glanum. You then might want to squeeze in Les Baux-de-Provence, one of the country's most spectacular perched villages.

DAYS 4–5: ARLES

Head 33 km (21 miles) southwest to Arles, which competes with Nîmes for the title "Rome of France" thanks to its famous Roman theater, *arènes* (amphitheater), Alyscamps, and Cryptoporticus. All the main sights are in the small *vieille ville* (Old Town), speckled with pockets where time seems to have stood still since 1888, the year Vincent van Gogh immortalized the town in his paintings. Study reproductions of the best canvases, which have come to define Provence as much as its herbs and traditional costumes, at Arles's Fondation Vincent van Gogh and see the places he painted along the town's Promenade Vincent van Gogh.

Just off the Rond-Point des Arrènes, have your camera ready for a stroll up Rue Ernest Renan, the idyllic Provençal street. Over at the 15th-century priory, the Musée Réattu (the first fine art museum in the country to have a photography section) has more Van Gogh, as well as a collection of Picasso drawings. Underneath Forum Square, wildly famous for Van Gogh's *Starry Night*, you'll discover the Cryptoporticus du Forum, with foundations dating from 1 BC.

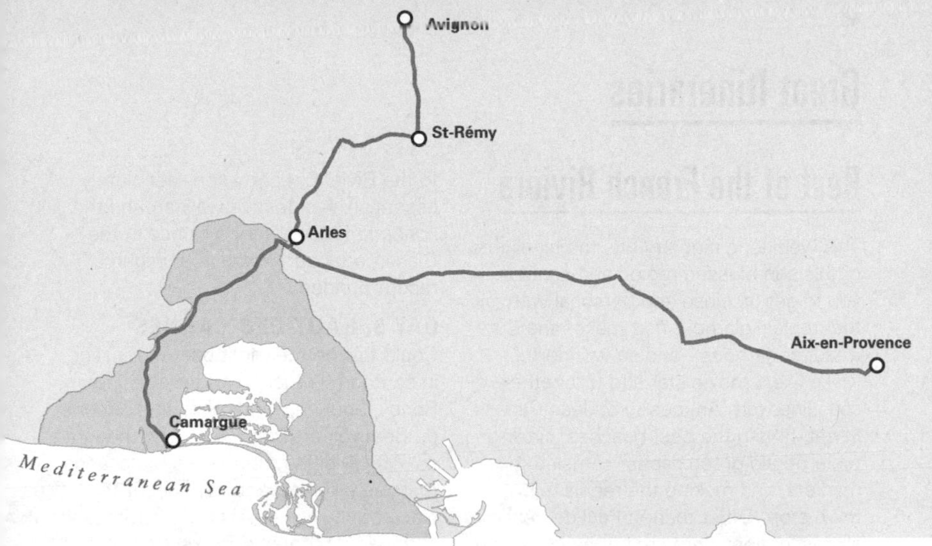

DAY 5: CAMARGUE

You need at least a day to take in the Parque Natural Régional de Camargue, a nature preserve that protects both coastal and wetland areas and is famed for its pink flamingos, black bulls, white horses, and gardens. Base yourself in Ste-Maries-sur-Mer, which is entirely within the park and is where Roma from around the world pilgrimage to honor their patron saint, Sarah.

Inquire at the tourist office about bus, bike, or walking tours of the park, and set aside some time to roam the town's cobblestone streets and climb the tower of its 9th-century church. If you happen to be here during one of the processions, horse fairs, or bullfights, you're in for a real treat.

DAYS 6–7: AIX-EN-PROVENCE

The museums and churches in Aix are overshadowed by the town itself, an enchanting beauty with elegant *hôtels particuliers* (mansions), luxurious fountains, and an architectural layout that attests to Aix's prominent past as the 17th-century cultural and political capital of Provence. Walking is not only the easiest way to get around but also the best, as the center is a maze of narrow streets and lovely squares where people and café tables take up every available inch.

The tree-lined Cours Mirabeau divides old Aix in half, with the Quartier Ancien's medieval streets to the north and the 18th-century mansions of the Quartier Mazarin to the south. Connecting most of the dots—including such sightseeing musts as the Musée Granet, the Cathédrale St-Sauveur, and the gorgeous Pavillon de Vendôme—is the Paul Cézanne Trail, which allows you to follow in the footsteps of Aix's most famous native son, including at his Jas de Bouffan home. Alas, his favorite hangout, the Café-Brasserie Les Deux Garçons, was ravaged by fire in 2019 and is still under construction.

Great Itineraries

Best of the French Riviera

This weeklong itinerary hits the highlights of this sun-blessed region and enables you to get up close and personal with the tropical glamour that makes the Côte d'Azur so famous—and so wonderful. Make like a movie star and follow the coastline from Antibes to St-Jean-Cap-Ferrat, hitting the best beaches, circling the emerald-green capes, perusing the markets, and making the requisite hill-town stop. Other than St-Paul-de-Vence, all destinations here are on the coast and linked by the wonderful coastal railway.

DAY 1: ANTIBES

Although bustling, Antibes is a little slice of heaven on the western side of the Baie des Anges (Bay of Angels). The town's waterfront is so picturesque that you'll be tempted to set up an easel like Picasso, whose works are on view in the Château Grimaldi. The surrounding alleys are a maze of enchantment with the Cours Masséna overflowing with charm and Le Safranier, an independent historic quarter of tiny cobblestone streets and flower box–filled windowsills.

Enjoy a day of tropical hedonism on the Cap d'Antibes, a rocky promontory (which juts out into the Bay of Millionaires) adorned with Gilded Age mansions, one of which, the Villa Eilenroc, is open to the public. Catch the sunset at Plage des Ondes, a sandy public beach frequented by locals.

DAY 2: ST-PAUL-DE-VENCE

Drive up to the pretty perched medieval village of St-Paul to take a selfie with a panoramic backdrop and to explore a seemingly endless array of galleries. Have lunch at the Picasso-blessed Colombe d'Or—a high point of any trip to the Riviera (reservations absolutely essential). A digestive walk around the Fondation Maeght for a glance at the Giacometti courtyard comes highly recommended.

DAY 3: HAUT-DES-CAGNES

Could this be the most beautiful village in southern France? Part-time residents Renoir, Soutine, Modigliani, and Simone de Beauvoir are just a few who thought so. After visiting, there's a good chance that you will forever dream about this place of tiny medieval streets, 15th- and 17th-century houses, corkscrew alleys, and vaulted arches draped with bougainvillea. It is truly a lovely dip into the Middle Ages.

Many of the pretty residences are like dollhouses (especially those on Rue Passebon), but looming over all is the medieval town castle, with a grand Renaissance courtyard and three quirky collections. After a morning of exploring, head to Cagnes-sur-Mer for an afternoon beverage at one of the many beach cafés and a refreshing dip in the Mediterranean.

DAYS 4–5: NICE

Just 15 minutes from Haut-des-Cagnes by train, Nice is the big-city leg of your trip, so immerse yourself in culture, perhaps at the Matisse and Chagall museums, set in the Cimiez suburb high over the city, or at the cutting-edge modern art museum. Start the day, though, at the magnificent Cours Saleya Market, which shuts down by 1 pm—if you're up early enough, you can watch the chefs squabble over the best produce.

Then wander through the labyrinthine Old Town. A few steps away lies the shoreline, where you can spend an hour or two strolling the famed Promenade

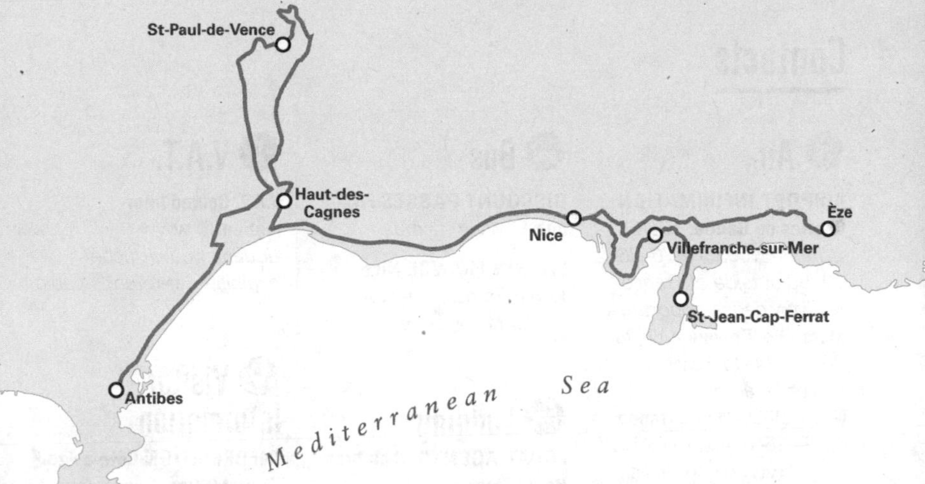

des Anglais bordering Nice's vast crescent of beach. Amble toward the port, and you'll find La promenade des Amateurs d'Art et d'Antiquités, which runs up to Place Garibaldi. You could easily spend a whole day on the shore here: rent a lounger, order a seaside lunch, and relax amid sea breezes and sunshine.

DAY 6: VILLEFRANCHE-SUR-MER AND ST-JEAN-CAP-FERRAT

Either of these pretty ports towns will take you back to the days before the Riviera became the land of pink it is today. First, marvel at Villefranche's deep-blue bay, study its hillside estates, and visit its Chapelle St-Pierre, decorated by Jean Cocteau. Then, take the bus or walk over to Cap Ferrat, a favorite getaway of the sunglasses-and-sapphires set.

Be sure to tour the art-charged rooms and expansive gardens of the Villa Ephrussi de Rothschild. Or set out on a half-hour hike along the Promenade Maurice Rouvier (lots of movie stars do their power-walking here) to nearby Beaulieu-sur-Mer, home to the fabulous re-creation of ancient Greece that is the Villa Kerylos.

DAY 7: ÈZE

Your final destination is the sky-high village of Èze, an eagle's-nest wonder threaded by stone alleys that lead to the most spectacular vistas of the coast. One step higher and you will indeed be in paradise.

Both Fragonard and Galimard perfumeries have boutiques here and offer free tours, but you can also take a perfume workshop guided by a professional nose. Alternatively, if you prefer the smell of burning rubber to lavender, you can test-drive a Lamborghini from outside Fragonard's factory with Liven Up. Take the free electric shuttle (in summer) back down to the coast and then hop a train back to Nice.

Contacts

Air

AIRPORT INFORMATION Charles de Gaulle. (*CDG*). ✉ *Paris* ☎ *0033/1–70–36–39–50 outside of France* 🌐 *www.parisaeroport.fr.* **Marseille–Provence.** ☎ *08–20–81–14–14* 🌐 *www.marseille.aeroport.fr.* **Montpellier–Meditérranée.** ☎ *08–25–83–00–03 €0.12/min* 🌐 *www.montpellier.aeroport.fr.* **Nice–Côte d'Azur.** ☎ *08–20–42–33–33 €0.12/min* 🌐 *www.nice.aeroport.fr.* **Nîmes–Arles–Camargue.** ☎ *04–66–70–49–49* 🌐 *www.nimes.aeroport.fr.* **Orly.** ✉ *Paris* ☎ *33/1–70–36–39–50 from outside France* 🌐 *www.parisaeroport.fr.* **Toulon Hyères.** ☎ *08–25–01–83–87* 🌐 *www.toulon-hyeres.aeroport.fr.* **Avignon–Provence Airport.** ✉ *100 rue Marise Bastié, Montfavet* ☎ *04–90–81–51–42* 🌐 *avignon.aero.*

Bus

DISCOUNT PASSES Flixbus. 🌐 *www.flixbus.fr.*

WITHIN FRANCE Nice AirportXpress. 🌐 *www.niceairportxpress.com/en.*

Lodging

LOCAL AGENTS Chambres Hôtes France. 🌐 *www.chambres-hotes.fr.* **Gîtes Vacation Rentals.** 🌐 *www.gites-de-france.com/fr.*

Train

INFORMATION Eurail. 🌐 *www.eurail.com.* **Eurostar.** 🌐 *www.eurostar.com.* **Rail Europe.** 🌐 *www.raileurope.com.* **SNCF.** ☎ *3635* 🌐 *www.sncf-connect.com.*

V.A.T.

V.A.T. Refund Information. 🌐 *www.douane.gouv.fr/fiche/eligibility-vat-refunds-pablo.*

Visitor Information

INFORMATION Côte d'Azur Tourist Office. 🌐 *cotedazur-france.fr.* **France Tourism.** 🌐 *www.france.fr/en.* **Monaco Tourist Office.** ✉ *2a bd. des Moulins, Monte Carlo* ☎ *377/92–16–61–66* 🌐 *www.visitmonaco.com.* **Provence-Alpes-Côte d'Azur Tourisme.** (*CRT PACA*). ✉ *Marseille* 🌐 *provence-alpes-cote-dazur.com.*

Chapter 3

NÎMES AND THE ALPILLES

Updated by
Jennifer Ladonne

Sights
★★★☆☆

Restaurants
★★★☆☆

Hotels

Shopping

Nightlife

WELCOME TO NÎMES AND THE ALPILLES

TOP REASONS TO GO

★ **Vincent van Gogh's Arles:** Ever since the fiery Dutchman immortalized Arles in all its chromatic drama, this town has had a starring role in museums around the world.

★ **Medieval history:** Channel the Middle Ages at the ghostly ruins of the Château des Baux atop Les Baux-de-Provence and then wander the charming village.

★ **Camargue Nature Park:** The windswept lagoons of the Camargue will swamp you with their charms as soon as you catch sight of their white horses, pink flamingos, and black bulls.

★ **St-Rémy-de-Provence:** Find inspired gourmet cooking, meditate quietly on Greco-Roman antiquity, or browse bustling markets, basket in hand, at this fashionable village enclave.

★ **The Pont du Gard:** This aqueduct of the ancient Roman era is also a spectacular work of art.

1 Nîmes. A classic Roman town turned lively modern city.

2 Uzès. A medieval and Renaissance jewel in a marvelous setting.

3 Pont du Gard. A famed Roman bridge.

4 Aigues-Mortes. A walled fortress-town.

5 Parc Naturel Régional de Camargue. One of France's most remarkable terrains.

6 Stes-Maries-de-la-Mer. A pilgrimage town located within the Camargue.

7 Arles. Splendid Roman ruins and contemporary art in the footsteps of Van Gogh.

8 Abbaye de Montmajour. Once Provence's spiritual center.

9 Tarascon. Home to a folk hero who slayed the mythical Tarasque monster.

10 Fontvieille. Hometown to writer Alphonse Daudet.

11 Les Baux-de-Provence. A lively tangle of medieval streets and views for miles.

12 St-Rémy-de-Provence. Van Gogh's famous refuge, now a ritzy retreat.

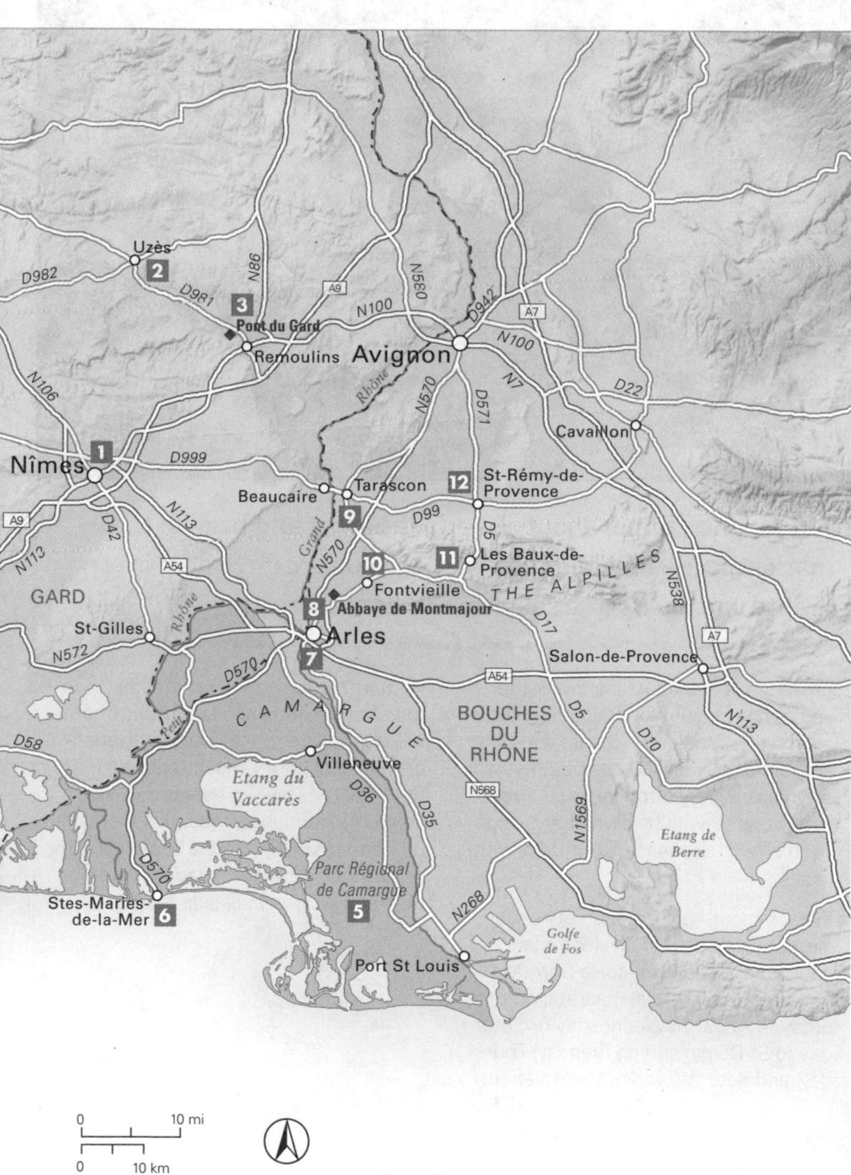

Uzès
D982
D981
N86
A9
Pont du Gard
Remoulins
Avignon
N100
N580
D942
A7
N106
Rhône
N570
D571
N7
D22
Cavaillon
Nîmes
D999
Beaucaire
Tarascon
St-Rémy-de-Provence
A9
D42
N113
D99
D5
Les Baux-de-Provence
THE ALPILLES
N538
N113
A54
Grand
Fontvieille
Abbaye de Montmajour
GARD
Rhône
St-Gilles
Arles
D17
A7
N572
D570
Salon-de-Provence
A54
CAMARGUE
BOUCHES DU RHÔNE
D5
N113
D58
Petit
Villeneuve
D10
Etang du Vaccarès
D36
N568
D35
N1569
Etang de Berre
D570
Parc Régional de Camargue
Stes-Maries-de-la-Mer
N268
Golfe de Fos
Port St Louis
0
10 mi
0
10 km

PROVENCE'S VILLAGE MARKETS

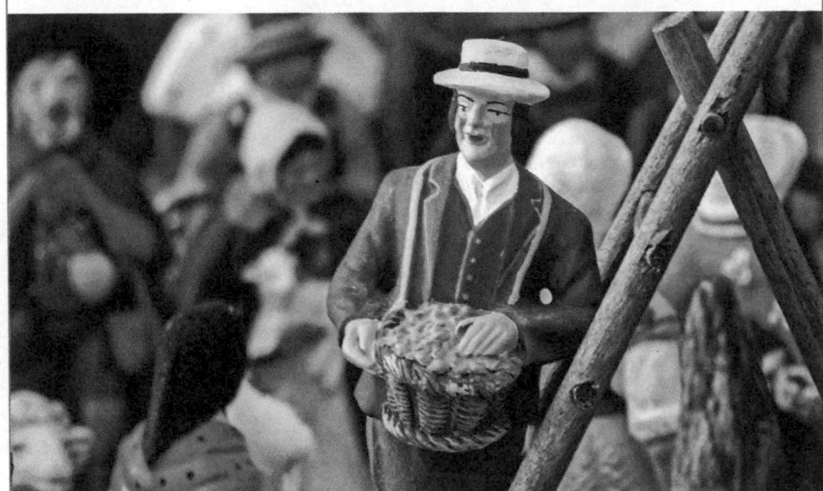

In Provence, forget about the supermarket and head to the marketplace—an integral part of the culture anywhere in France, but even more so in this bountiful region.

Provence is market heaven, whether you're on the hunt for antiques and collectibles or foodstuffs, crafts, and other authentic souvenirs. Just about every town has a (very often famous) street market, each with its own energy and each offering a chance to interact with locals.

What's more, regional markets occur almost daily. On Sunday, for instance, you can head to L'Isle-sur-la-Sorgue's antiques and farmers' markets; on Saturday to Arles; on Wednesday or Saturday to St-Rémy; and on Tuesday, Thursday, and Saturday to Aix-en-Provence.

Remember to separate the wheat from the chaff. Friends and family back home will appreciate those lavender sachets or that local honey much more than they will the Day-Glo versions of Van Gogh masterpieces. Plus, there's really no harm in yielding to the temptation of buying that tablecloth made with sky-blue-and-yellow Souleiado fabric.

AIX-EN-PROVENCE

The markets in Aix are more focused on food. You can find rare delicacies side by side with cured sausages flavored with Provençal spices; vats of olives, tapenade, and oils from the Pays d'Aix region; or neat boxes of ellipse-shaped *calissons* (almond-paste confections made with candied fruit like orange or melon). The main food markets take place on Tuesday, Thursday, and Saturday in the Cours Mirabeau and every day in Place Richelme. There's also a daily flower market in the beautiful Place de l'Hôtel de Ville opposite Aix's majestic town hall.

ARLES AND THE CAMARGUE

Every Saturday morning, a more than 2-km (1-mile) stretch of Boulevard des Lices hosts one of the area's richest and most varied markets. Stands overflow with all the generous bounty of Provence—olives of every kind, fresh-pressed oils, herbs, cheeses, tapenade, lavender, handcrafted soaps. You can also find the famous *boutis* (cotton throws), as well as textured fabrics and an endless array of tablecloths, children's clothes, and Arlesian costumes. On the first Wednesday of every month, Boulevard Emile Combes becomes an antiques and collectibles market.

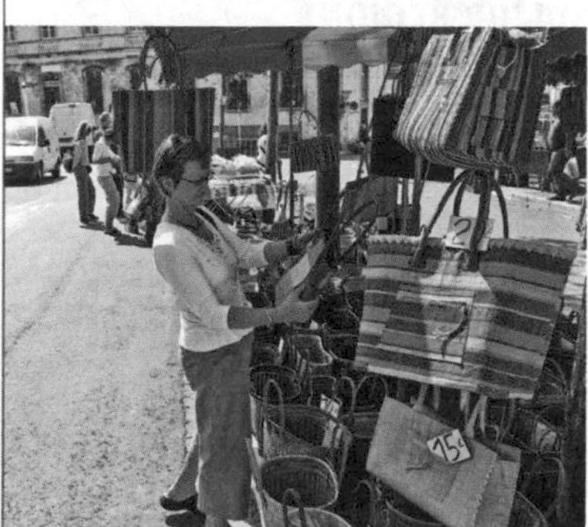

MARSEILLE

The main shopping drag lies between La Canebière and the Préfecture—and there are scores of new stores and boutiques around the Old Port—but Marseille also has an assortment of street markets, from the daily Marché de Noailles, the liveliest and most bustling food market, and the daily morning fish market in the Old Port to the stamp market every Sunday morning in Cours Julien, which is also home to the Wednesday organic market. Probably the most famous item you'll find around town is Savon de Marseille (Marseille soap).

THE SORGUE VALLEY

The best place to go trolling for time-burnished treasure is the famed antiques market held in the lovely town of Isle-sur-la-Sorgue every weekend. Twice a year, around Easter and on All Saints Day (November 1), the town's 300 art and antiques dealers are joined by some 200 antiques and vintage collectibles merchants, who set up shop around town during the four-day Upcycling Festival.

Scoured by the mistral and leveled to flat prairie lands by eons of earth deposits carried south by the Rhône, this region is Provence in its rawest form. At first glance, its endless space seems broken only by the occasional wildflower-lined gully, yet, after a few moments, a mysterious, romantic, and very beautiful landscape—colored with lavenders, wheat-yellows, vibrant greens, and burnt reds—comes into focus.

Only the giant, rocky outcrops of the Alpilles interrupt this colorful horizon. Along the southern coast, the windswept, wide-open marshlands of the Camargue conceal exotic wildlife—richly plumed egrets, rare black storks, clownish flamingos—as well as domestic oddities like dappled white horses and lyre-horned *taureaux*, bulls descended from ancient indigenous species. In May and October, the Roma from all over Europe arrive, as they have since the Middle Ages, for a procession to the sea that honors their patron saint, Sarah.

The scenery is surpassed only by the genuine warmth of the people and the feisty energy of their cities. In addition to having a plethora of Roman architectural marvels, in-your-face Nîmes has a raffish urban lifestyle that's most evident in its picturesque Old Town. Graceful, artsy Arles, harmonious in Van Gogh hues, mixes serious culture with a healthy dose of late-night café life. This town, too, has a Colosseum-like Roman arena. Outside St-Rémy—a chic village that appeals to a cosmopolitan crowd—are the ruins of Glanum, first settled in the 6th century BC.

Add to this mix the miniature fortified towns of Aigues Mortes and Les Baux-de-Provence, Romanesque châteaux and abbeys, and seaside fortresses that launched crusades—all set amid the sun-sharpened landscapes beloved and painted by Van Gogh and Gauguin—and you have a region not only worth exploring, but also savoring.

MAJOR REGIONS

Nîmes and around. The westernmost edge of Provence is highlighted by Nîmes, which competes with Arles and Orange for the title of "the Rome of France" and is home to the Arènes, among the most complete Roman amphitheaters in the world, and the Maison Carrée, the best preserved ancient temple in France. (Thomas Jefferson admired it so much he used it as a model for the Virginia state capitol.) To the north is the Pont du Gard,

Provence and the Languedoc

Nîmes and its famous aqueduct are in the Gard *département*, an administrative area that is part of the Languedoc region, rather than Provence, but is considered a kindred southern spirit because of its location and its similar climate, terrain, and architecture. Linguistics also ties this area to its Provençal neighbors.

The *langue d'oc* (language of "oc") refers to the ancient southern language, Occitane, which evolved from Latin. Northern parts of France developed their own *langue d'oïl*. The two terms are derived from the word "yes," which was *oc* in the south and *oïl* in the north. Per a 16th-century edict from Paris, the *oïls* had it, and *oui* and its northern dialect became standard French. That said, Languedocien and Provençal merely went underground, popping up from time to time then and even now—perhaps during chatter (or a gesture-filled dispute) at a farmers' market.

most awe-inspiring in the early-morning light or lit up at nightfall.

The Camargue. A bus ride away from Arles and bracketed by the towns of Aigues Mortes and Stes-Maries-de-la-Mer, the vast Camargue nature park is a desolate land of haunting natural beauty—a forgotten area of France until a few decades ago. Today, thousands of visitors come to experience its singular ecosystem. Ride horseback across its mysterious marshlands or discover its exceptional bird-watching, then enjoy home-style cooking at one of the exclusive *mas* (converted farmhouse) hotels.

Arles and around. Reigning over the austere but evocative landscape of the Camargue marshlands, the small city of Arles is fiercely Provençal, nurturing its heritage and parading its culture at every colorful turn. Although little is left of the town Van Gogh once painted, there are spots where you can still channel his spirit. With its atmosphere, animation, and culture, it is a patch of golden color in a sepia landscape—and an excellent home base for sorties into the raw natural beauty and eccentric villages of the Rhône delta.

The Alpilles. Whether you approach from the damp lowlands of Arles and the Camargue or the pebbled vineyards around Avignon, the countryside changes dramatically as you climb into the arid heights of the low mountain range called the Alpilles (pronounced "ahl-*pee*-yuh"). A rough-hewn, rocky landscape rises into nearly barren limestone hills, the fields silvered with ranks of twisted olive trees and alleys of gnarled *amandiers* (almond trees). These spiky mountains guard treasures like Les Baux-de-Provence—be bewitched by both its *ville morte* (dead town) and its luxurious L'Oustau de la Baumanière inn, the first restaurant in the region to gain a Michelin star in 1947 (today it has three). Nearby is ritzy St-Rémy-de-Provence, Van Gogh's famous retreat.

Planning

When to Go

July and August are the high season, especially along the coast, and are best avoided, both because of the crushing crowds and the grilling heat. Fall's golden vineyards and still-warm days make September till mid-November delightful. In winter (January and February, even into March), some hotels and restaurants are closed, and the café culture is driven indoors by cool temperatures and wind. Around Easter, the cherry and almond trees blossom, the plane trees bud, and the outdoor tables emerge—it's the beginning of an enchanting time to visit that lasts right up until the summer crowds return.

Planning Your Time

The best place to start your trip is in Arles or Nîmes, because they both have direct train links to most major cities in France. In either city you can also begin to slow down—Provence, after all, is about leisurely mornings and lazy afternoons—before heading into the countryside by bus or by car.

You can move from site to site or choose a central base and explore without traveling more than an hour to any one attraction. For instance, Nîmes and the lovely Uzès belong in spirit to the Languedoc but are also close to the Camargue, Arles, and the Pont du Gard. The Alpilles are a world apart but are easily accessible from Arles and environs.

A couple of days in the region will enable you to see world-class antiquities; five days allows time to wander the Camargue; a week lets you see the principal sites, enjoy a nature tour, and take a break by the sea. And don't forget that the ravishing old city of Avignon is an hour's easy run up from Arles.

Getting Here and Around

Public transportation is well organized in the Alpilles, Arles, and the Camargue, with most towns accessible by train or bus. It's best to plan on combining the two: smaller Provençal towns often won't have their own train station, but a local bus connects to the train station at the nearest town. For instance, take a train to Nîmes or Arles and then a bus to Les Baux or St-Rémy.

Driving is perhaps the best option, since you can travel national or district roads or brave the speeding highways to go quickly from point to point. But be sure to get a good map—road signs can be confusing—and slow down to enjoy all the scenery.

AIR

Marseille (an hour's drive from Arles) is served by frequent flights from Paris and London and a direct flight from San Francisco. Daily flights from Paris arrive at the smaller airport in Nîmes. Air France flies direct from New York to Nice, 200 km (124 miles) from Arles.

BUS

A moderately good network of private bus services links places not served, or badly served, by trains. Arles is one of the largest hubs, serviced out of the *gare routière* (bus station) on Avenue Paulin-Talabot, opposite the train station. Within the city, bus stations are mainly on Boulevard G. Clémenceau.

You can travel from Arles on the bus or the TER regional train to such stops as Nîmes (liO Ligne 130, €1.50, 50 minutes, 11 daily) and Avignon (Zou! Ligne 18, €7.10, 1 hour, 10 daily). Ten buses daily also head out to Aix-en-Provence (only two run on Sunday).

Popular destinations include the Camargue's Stes-Maries-de-la-Mer (Envia A50, €1, 1 hour, seven daily), Mas du Pont de Rousty, and Pont de Gau.

Stops in the Alpilles area include Les Baux-des-Provence and St-Rémy-de-Provence (neither have train stations). You can also reach the latter's bus station at Place de la République aboard one of the frequent buses from Avignon.

From Nîmes's bus station on Rue Ste-Félicité, you can connect to Avignon and Arles, while Edgard runs you into the deep country. As for Pont du Gard, this is a 40-minute ride from Nîmes; you are dropped off at Auberge Blanche, 1 km (½ mile) from the bridge.

BUS INFORMATION Edgard. ☎ *08–10–33–42–73* 🌐 *www.edgard-transport.fr.* **Envia.** ☎ *04–90–54–86–16* 🌐 *www.tout-envia.com.* **LER.** ☎ *08–09–40–04–15* 🌐 *www.info-ler.fr.* **LiO.** 🌐 *www.lio-occitanie.fr.* **Zou!** 🌐 *zou.maregionsud.fr.*

CAR

The A6/A7 toll expressway (*péage*) channels all traffic from Paris toward the south. It's called the Autoroute du Soleil (Highway of the Sun) and leads directly to Provence. From Orange, A9 (La Languedocienne) heads southwest to Nîmes. Arles is a quick jaunt from Nîmes via A54.

With its swift autoroute network, it's a breeze traveling from city to city by car in this region. But some of the best of Provence is experienced on back roads and byways, including the isolated Camargue and the Alpilles.

Navigating the flatlands of the Camargue can feel unearthly, with roads sailing over terrain uninterrupted by hills or forests. Despite this, routes don't always travel as the crow flies and can wander wide of a clean trajectory, so don't expect to make good time.

Rocky outcrops and switchbacks keep you a captive audience to the arid scenery in the Alpilles. Even if you could hurry along the roads here, it would be a waste.

HORSE

A novel way to tour a slice of the Camargue park is on horseback, although the wild glamour of the ancient breed of Camargue horses becomes downright pedestrian when the now-domesticated beauties are saddled en masse. Rent-a-horse stands proliferate along the highways, especially near the major towns. Much of this marshy land is limited to walkers and riders, so a trip on horseback lets you experience this landscape without getting your feet wet—literally.

TRAIN

Two Arles-bound TGV (Trains à Grands Vitesses) trains arrive direct from Paris daily; from the Gare Centrale station (*Av. Paulin Talabot*) you can connect to Nîmes (€11.30, 30 minutes), Marseille (€16.30, 1 hour), Avignon Center (€9.20, 20 minutes), and Aix-en-Provence (€29.70, 1 hour 30 minutes with connection).

The Gare Avignon TGV station is a few miles southwest of the city in the district of Courtine (a navette shuttle bus connects with the train station in town); other trains (and a few TGV) use the Gare Avignon Center station at 42 boulevard St-Roch, where you can find trains to destinations like Orange (€5.20, 20 minutes) and Arles (€7.90, 20 minutes).

To Nîmes, there are more than a dozen TGV trains daily on the three-hour trip from Paris; frequent trains connect with Avignon Center (€9.60, 30 minutes) and Arles (€9.90, 22 minutes). To reach the *vieille ville* (Old Town) from the station, walk north on Avenue Feuchères.

CONTACTS SNCF. ☎ *3635* 🌐 *www.sncf-connect.com.*

Hotels

Although Arles, Les Baux, and St-Rémy have stylish hotels—with all the requisite creature comforts and such Provençal touches as wrought-iron decorative elements and *folklorique* cottons—Nîmes is a latecomer to the party. A few marvelous properties aside, its hotels tend to be more prosaic.

Throughout the region you'll find lovely converted mas (farmhouses). Although they blend into the landscape as if they'd been there a thousand years, they also offer modern pleasures like swimming pools and sophisticated restaurants.

Restaurants

In this corner of Provence, you need only spend 30 minutes in a picturesque town market to get a sense of the region's myriad culinary pleasures—from piquant tapenades produced using the area's green or black olives to *crème d'ail* (roasted garlic cream) to salty *anchoïade* made with Camargue anchovies. And all of this bounty is enhanced by deliciously sun-kissed local wines. The region also abounds with top-notch restaurants, both modest and exalted—including some that have earned Michelin stars.

⇨ *Hotel and restaurant reviews have been shortened. For full information, visit Fodors.com. Hotel prices are the lowest cost of a standard double room in high season. Restaurant prices are the average cost of a main course at dinner or, if dinner is not served, at lunch.*

What It Costs in Euros

$	$$	$$$	$$$$
RESTAURANTS			
under €18	€18–€24	€25–€32	over €32
HOTELS			
under €125	€125–€225	€226–€350	over €350

Tours

Arles Guided Visits

GUIDED TOURS | Throughout the year, the Arles tourist office offers a wide variety of guided English-language tours, including those of the antiquities and monuments, notable houses, museums, and the Camargue. Tour descriptions and prices are readily available on the website and listed according to date. You can also hire a private English-speaking guide to escort you through the major sites or tailor a tour according to your interests. ✉ *Bd. des Lices, Arles* ☎ *04–90–18–41–20* 🌐 *www.arlestourisme.com* 🎫 *From €75.*

Visitor Information

Most of the region's towns are handled by the Comité Regional du Tourisme de Provence-Alpes-Côte d'Azur. The Comité Régional du Tourisme Occitanie, however, provides information on towns west of the Rhône, including Nîmes, Uzès, and Pont du Gard.

CONTACTS Comité Regional du Tourisme de Provence-Alpes-Côte d'Azur. ✉ *62–64 La Canebière, Marseille* ☎ *04–91–56–47–00* 🌐 *provence-alpes-cotedazur.com* Ⓜ *Noailles.* **Comité Régional du Tourisme Occitanie.** ✉ *64 rue Alcyoné, Montpellier* ☎ *04–30–63–84–20* 🌐 *www.tourisme-occitanie.com.*

Nîmes

714 km (444 miles) south of Paris; 44 km (27 miles) southwest of Avignon; 33 km (21 miles) northwest of Arles.

If you've traveled south seeking well-preserved Roman treasures, you need look no farther than Nîmes (pronounced *neem*). Here, the Arènes (a 24,000-seat coliseum), Maison Carrée (patterned after Rome's Temple of Apollo), and public waterworks fed by the Pont du Gard attest to its classical prosperity, which began in the 1st century BC. In addition, the city's compact medieval Old Town has all the grace of Arles or St-Rémy but little of the tourist congestion or the snobbishness.

Nîmes has also invested in progressive architecture. Indeed, the ancient and the modern are perfectly juxtaposed in this proud, lively city. The pillars of the Maison

Carrée are reflected in the glass of Sir Norman Foster's neighboring modern-art museum and municipal library—dubbed the Carrée d'Art (Art Square) because of its four-square form. The Musée de la Romanité—whose rippling, white facade evokes the fabric of a well-draped toga—sits across from the Arènes and offers wonderful views of the ancient amphitheater and the clay-tiled rooftops beyond from its rooftop and restaurant.

■ TIP➔ To see as much as possible in Nîmes, invest in a Citypass: it costs €29, is valid for two days (€37 for four days, €39 for seven days), and can be purchased at most local monuments and sites.

GETTING HERE AND AROUND

On the Paris–Avignon–Montpellier train line, Nîmes has a direct link to and from Paris (about a three-hour ride). The Nîmes gare routière (bus station) is just behind the train station. Several buses run to and from Arles (11 daily Monday–Saturday, two on Sunday); there are also buses (Monday–Saturday) between Avignon and Nîmes and Uzès and Nîmes. Some Uzès buses stop at Remoulins for the Pont du Gard and a few continue on to St-Quentin-la-Poterie.

Although Tango buses (€1.60) loop from the bus station, passing many of the city's principal sites, Nîmes is an ideal city for walking. For a lovely tour on foot, start at the Jardin de la Fontaine, which is worth at least an hour's exploration, and then follow the canal down to the graceful Quai de la Fontaine, an elegant neighborhood that recalls Aix-en-Provence. The Maison Carré, Carré d'Art, Arènes, and Musée de la Romanité are all just a few minutes' walk farther along. The mazelike Old Town, a stone's throw away, is a joy to wander for its many cafés and épiceries selling all the specialties of Nîmes.

VISITOR INFORMATION

CONTACTS Nîmes Tourist Office. ✉ *6 bd. des Arènes, Nîmes* ☎ *04–66–58–38–00* 🌐 *www.nimes-tourisme.com.*

Sights

★ Arènes

RUINS | The best-preserved Roman amphitheater in the world is a miniature of the Colosseum in Rome (note the small carvings of Romulus and Remus, the wrestling gladiators, on the exterior, and the intricate bulls' heads etched into the stone over the entrance on the north side). More than 435 feet long and 330 feet wide, it had a seating capacity of 24,000 in its day. Bloody gladiator battles, criminals being thrown to animals, and theatrical wild-boar chases drew crowds to its bleachers. Nowadays it hosts bullfights, which transform the arena (and all of Nîmes) into a sangria-flushed homage to Spain, and summer concerts. Self-guided audio tours are available. ✉ *Bd. des Arènes, Nîmes* ☎ *04–66–21–82–56, 04–66–02–80–80 for féria box office* 🌐 *www.arenes-nimes.com* 🎫 *€10.*

Carrée d'Art

ART MUSEUM | Directly opposite the Maison Carrée and looking a bit like an airport terminal, the glass-fronted Carrée d'Art was designed by British architect Sir Norman Foster. It literally reflects the Maison Carrée's creamy symmetry and figuratively answers it with a featherlight deconstructed colonnade. In addition to a library and archives, the sleek, modern structure houses the Musée d'Art Contemporain (Contemporary Art Museum), with a permanent collection of works that date from 1960 and onward and fall into three categories: French painting and sculpture; English, American, and German works; and Mediterranean styles. There are often temporary exhibits of new work, too. Atop the museum, enjoy spectacular city views over lunch at the Ciel de Nîmes. The restaurant, which

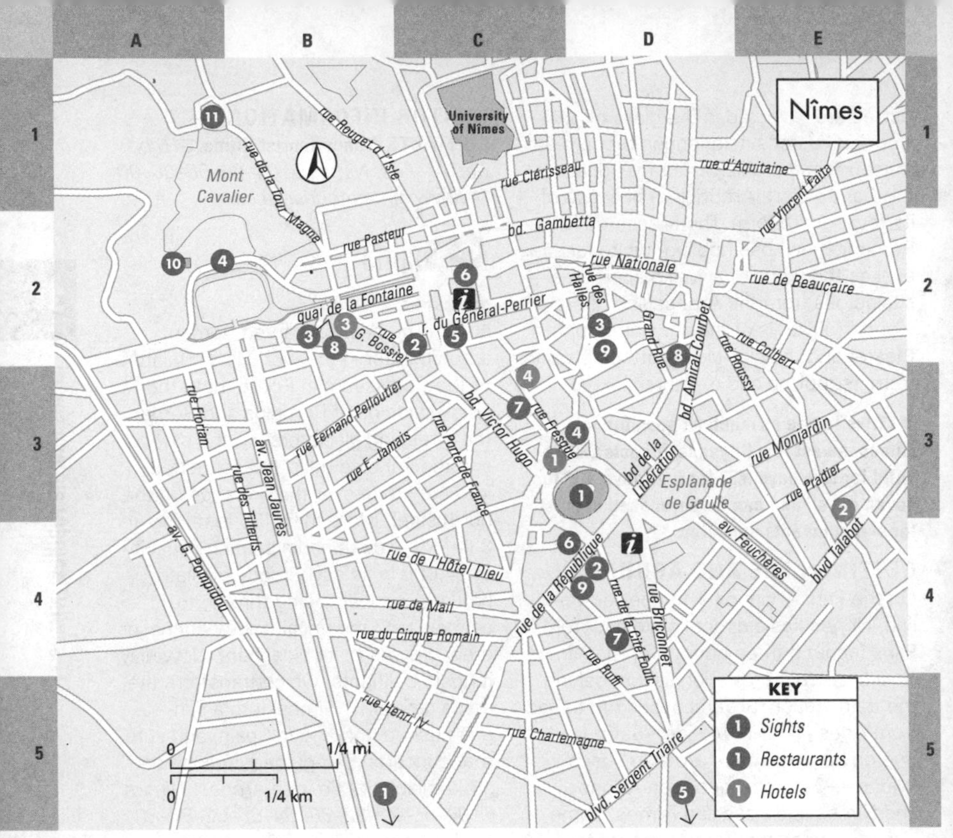

Sights	
1 Arènes	D3
2 Carrée d'Art	C2
3 Cathédrale Notre-Dame et St-Castor	D2
4 Jardins de la Fontaine	A2
5 Maison Carrée	C2
6 Musée de la Romanité	D4
7 Musée des Beaux-Arts	D4
8 Musée d'Histoire Naturelle	D2
9 Musée du Vieux Nîmes	D2
10 Temple de Diane	A2
11 Tour Magne	A1

Restaurants	
1 Alexandre	B5
2 Bistrot Le République	D4
3 Duende	B2
4 Gard Ô Vin	D3
5 Jérôme Nutile	D5
6 La Marmite	C2
7 Le Chabinais	C3
8 L'Impé Brasserie	B2
9 Skab	D4

Hotels	
1 Hôtel de l'Amphithéâtre	C3
2 La Maison de Sophie	E3
3 L'Imperator	B2
4 Margaret Hôtel Chouleur	C3

closes at 6 pm, is also an excellent spot for afternoon tea or a drink. ✉ *Pl. de la Maison Carrée, Nîmes* ☎ *04–66–76–35–70* 🌐 *www.carreartmusee.com* 🎫 *€8.*

Cathédrale Notre-Dame et St-Castor (*Nîmes Cathedral*)
CHURCH | Nîmes Cathedral was damaged by Protestants during the 16th-century Wars of Religion but still shows traces of its original construction in 1096. A remarkably preserved Romanesque frieze portrays Adam and Eve cowering in shame, the gory slaughter of Abel, and a flood-wearied Noah. Inside, look for the 4th-century sarcophagus (third chapel on the right) and a magnificent 17th-century chapel in the apse. ✉ *Pl. aux Herbes, Nîmes* ☎ *04–66–67–27–72* 🎫 *Free.*

Jardins de la Fontaine (*Fountain Garden*)
GARDEN | FAMILY | A testimony to the taste of the Age of Reason, this elaborate formal garden was created on the site of the Roman spring in the 18th century, when the Source de Nemausus, a once-sacred spring, was channeled into pools and a canal. The shady haven of mature trees and graceful stonework makes for a lovely approach to the Temple de Diane and the Tour Magne. ✉ *Corner of Quai de la Fontaine and Av. Jean-Jaurès, Nîmes* ☎ *04–66–58–38–00* 🎫 *Free.*

Maison Carrée (*Square House*)
RUINS | FAMILY | Lovely and forlorn in the middle of a busy downtown square, this exquisitely preserved temple strikes a timeless balance between symmetry and whimsy, purity of line and richness of decoration. Modeled on the Temple to Apollo in Rome, adorned with magnificent limestone columns and elegant pediments, the Maison Carrée remains one of the most noble surviving structures of ancient Roman civilization anywhere.

Built around 5 BC and dedicated to Caius Caesar and his brother, Lucius, the temple has survived subsequent use as a medieval meeting hall, an Augustinian church, a storehouse for Revolutionary archives, and a horse shed. In addition to hosting temporary art and photo exhibitions, it contains a permanent display of photos and drawings of ongoing archaeological work. Don't miss the splendid Roman fresco of Cassandra (being dragged by her hair by a hunter) that was discovered in 1992 and carefully restored. There's also a fun 3-D projection of the heroes of Nîmes. ✉ *Pl. de la Maison Carrée, Nîmes* ☎ *04–66–21–82–56* 🌐 *www.arenes-nimes.com/maison-carree* 🎫 *From €6.*

★ **Musée de la Romanité**
HISTORY MUSEUM | FAMILY | The newest museum in Nîmes is impossible to miss: first for its location, just opposite the Arènes, and second for its exterior featuring a gleaming, translucent facade meant to evoke a Roman toga. Exhibits inside this luminous edifice showcase the city's Roman past with more than 5,000 artifacts, as well as touch screens, interactive displays, and other state-of-the art features that will delight both adults and kids. Highlights include intact mosaics discovered during recent excavations, a model of a *domus* (Roman house), and a green roof with panoramic views of the amphitheater and all the city's major sites. The sidewalk café is great for a quick lunch or afternoon drink, and the upstairs La Table du 2—which also has impressive views—is a Michelin-starred brasserie that serves lunch and dinner. ✉ *16 bd. des Arènes, Nîmes* ☎ *04–48–21–02–10* 🌐 *museedelaromanite.fr* 🎫 *€9* 🕒 *Closed Mon.*

★ **Musée des Beaux-Arts** (*Fine Arts Museum*)
ART MUSEUM | The centerpiece of this early-20th-century building, stunningly refurbished by architect Jean-Michel Wilmotte, is a vast ancient mosaic depicting a marriage ceremony that provides intriguing insights into the lifestyle of Roman aristocrats. Also in the varied collection are seven paintings devoted

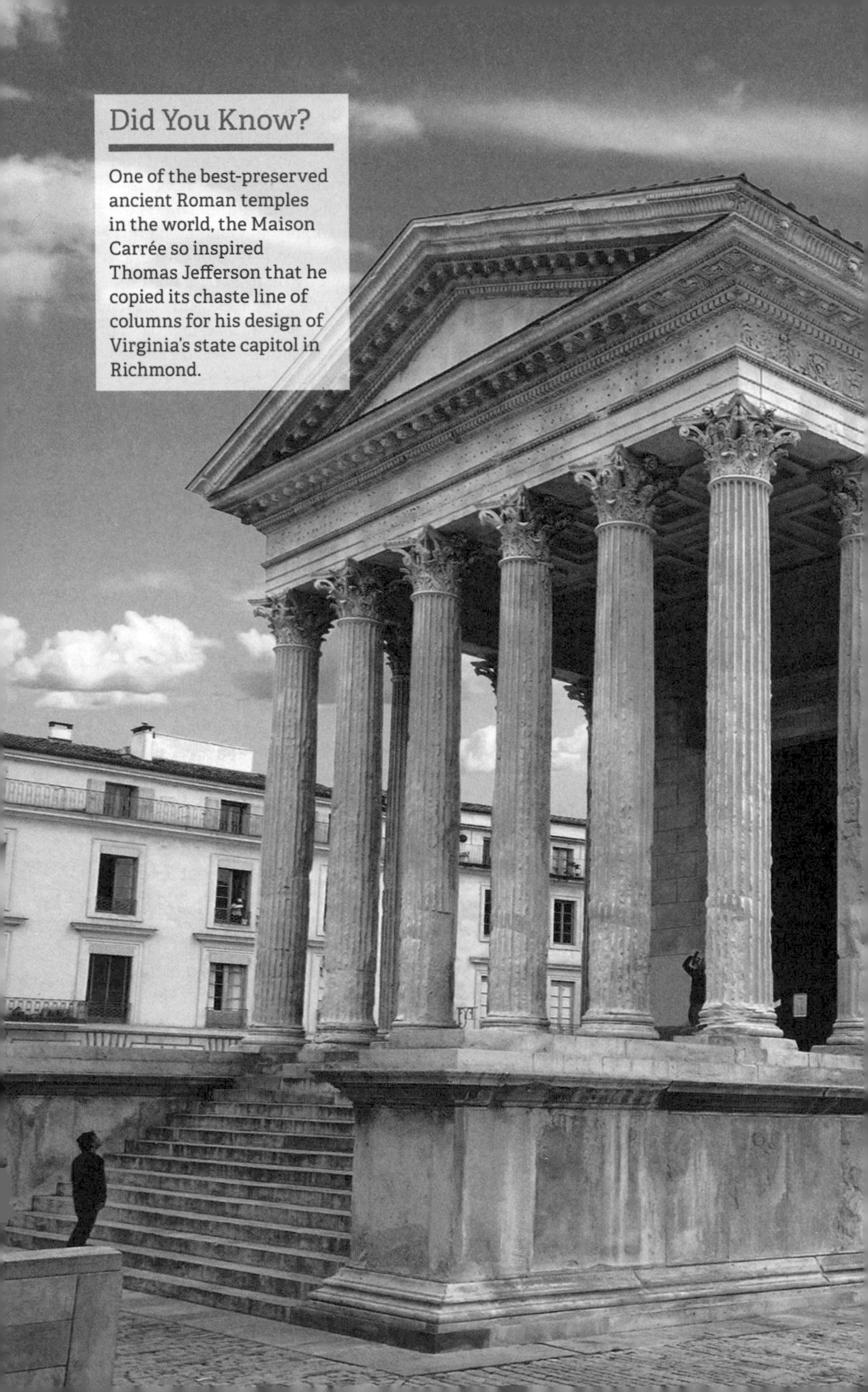

Did You Know?

One of the best-preserved ancient Roman temples in the world, the Maison Carrée so inspired Thomas Jefferson that he copied its chaste line of columns for his design of Virginia's state capitol in Richmond.

to Cleopatra by 18th-century Nîmes-born painter Natoire Italian, plus some fine Flemish, Dutch, and French works (notably Rubens's *Portrait of a Monk* and Giambono's *The Mystic Marriage of St. Catherine*). ✉ *23 rue de la Cite Foulc, Nîmes* ☎ *04–66–76–71–82* 🌐 *www.nimes.fr/musees* 🎫 *€5* 🕓 *Closed Mon.*

Musée d'Histoire Naturelle

HISTORY MUSEUM | FAMILY | Nîmes's oldest museum, inaugurated in 1895 in a listed 17th-century chapel, contemplates the natural and human sciences via a vast collection of stuffed beasts, menhirs, and other wonders. The setting has barely changed since 1930s, when France was a still a vast colonial power. There's a planetarium, too. ✉ *13 bd. Amiral Courbet, Nîmes* ☎ *04–66–76–73–45* 🌐 *www.nimes.fr/musees* 🎫 *€9* 🕓 *Closed Mon.*

Musée du Vieux Nîmes (*Museum of Old Nîmes*)

HISTORY MUSEUM | FAMILY | Housed in the 17th-century bishop's palace opposite the cathedral, this museum shows off garments embroidered in the exotic and vibrant style for which Nîmes was once famous. Look for the 18th-century jacket made of blue *serge de Nîmes,* the renowned fabric—now simply called denim—from which Levi Strauss first fashioned blue jeans. ✉ *Pl. aux Herbes, Nîmes* ☎ *04–66–76–73–70* 🌐 *www.nimes.fr/musees* 🎫 *€5* 🕓 *Closed Mon.*

Temple de Diane (*Temple of Diana*)

RUINS | FAMILY | This shattered Roman ruin dates from the end of the 1st century BC. The temple's function is unknown, though it's thought to have been part of a larger complex that is still unexcavated. In the Middle Ages, Benedictine nuns occupied the building before it was converted into a church. Destruction came during the Wars of Religion. ✉ *Jardins de la Fontaine, Nîmes.*

Tour Magne (*Magne Tower*)

RUINS | FAMILY | At the far end of the Jardins de la Fontaine are the remains of a tower the emperor Augustus had built on Gallic foundations; it was probably used as a lookout post. Despite losing 30 feet in height over the course of time, the tower still provides fine views of Nîmes for anyone energetic enough to climb the 140 steps. ✉ *Jardins de la Fontaine, Pl. Guillaume-Apollinaire, Nîmes* ☎ *04–66–21–82–56* 🌐 *www.arenes-nimes.com* 🎫 *From €3.50.*

Restaurants

★ Alexandre

$$$$ | MODERN FRENCH | Double Michelin–starred chef Michel Kayser adds a personal touch both to the elegant modern dining room and library sitting room where you can enjoy a drink before tucking into local specialties and seasonal menus transformed into delicious works of art. Scallops from the Camargue coast served with a luscious ravioli stuffed with celery cream and black garlic; plump white asparagus from the sands of Aigues Mortes with a sabayon and elderberry vinegar; and thyme-infused Aveyron lamb with carrots, turnip, and kumquat may not leave room for tender local strawberries from the Gard infused with kaffir lime served with sage sorbet. **Known for:** top-notch tasting menus; lovely garden terrace; seasonal, regional products. $ *Average main: €70* ✉ *2 rue Xavier Tronc, Rte. de l'Aeroport, Nîmes* ☎ *04–66–70–08–99* 🌐 *www.michelkayser.com* 🕓 *Closed Mon. and Tues. No dinner Sun. and Wed.*

★ Bistrot Le République

$$ | FRENCH | This quintessential locals' hangout is packed for lunch pretty much year-round thanks to dishes that are deeply French and deeply satisfying. The traditional bistro decor—long bar, leatherette banquettes, large mirrors, and brass railings—has something to do with the appeal of this marvelous restaurant that's casual in every sense except when it comes to food and wine. **Known for:** exceptional service;

unpretentious atmosphere; bistro lunch classics. *Average main: €19 3 rue de la République, Nîmes 04-66-64-26-17 www.facebook.com/bistrotlerepublique Closed weekends. No dinner.*

★ Duende

$$$$ | MODERN FRENCH | Duende, that irresistible magnetic force radiated by a performer to transport an audience, is precisely what two Michelin-star chef Nicolas Fontaine (channeling Pierre Gagnaire who designed the menus) conjures in the dining room of the Art Deco–era Hotel L'Imperator. A sophisticated spot to be sure, but it's also expressive of Nîmes's earthy, independent spirit in dishes that pair the exotic with the local: Mediterranean jumbo shrimp à l'Amontillado with local Camargue rice and mango in a passion fruit emulsion or a butter-poached catch of the day with camus artichokes, green olives, and a parsley-anchovy sauce. **Known for:** 1,000-plus wines to choose from; historical dining room; impeccable service. *Average main: €70 15 rue Gaston Boissier, Nîmes 04-66-21-94-34 www.maison-albar-hotels-l-imperator.com No dinner Mon.–Thurs.*

★ Gard Ô Vin

$ | WINE BAR | This convivial wine bar, tucked in a corner near a pretty square in the Old Town, is the best place for tasting local wines. The selection of excellent-value wines by the glass allows you to take in (literally) the vast wealth of the Côtes du Rhône, deliciously accompanied by local cheeses, charcuterie, or salad plates. **Known for:** friendly and fun atmosphere; top-quality food; wine-lover's paradise. *Average main: €13 3 pl. du Marché, Nîmes 09-52-15-79-74 www.facebook.com/gardovin.nimes Closed Sun. and Mon. No lunch Tues. and Wed.*

★ Jérôme Nutile

$$$$ | MODERN FRENCH | The vaulted dining room provides an excellent backdrop for camera-ready "haute couture" dishes that taste as good as they look and have garnered the chef a Michelin star. For an atmosphere that's a little less formal, the colorful Bistr'AU offers a fine prix-fixe menu; both restaurants are part of the Jérôme Nutile empire—which also includes a hotel and a boutique—that's set on a pretty old farm just outside the city. **Known for:** warmest welcome; quality service; beautiful bucolic setting. *Average main: €60 351 chemin Bas du Mas de Boudan, Nîmes 04-66-40-65-65 www.jerome-nutile.com Closed Tues. and Wed.*

Local Tastes

While in Western Provence, consider trying *tellines*, salty, thumbnail-size clams from the Camargue coast, or *gardianne*, a sinewy stew of beef from regional prairies ladled over chewy red Camargue rice. *Brandade*, a creamy spread made of salt cod pestled with olive oil and milk, has an interesting backstory: in the Middle Ages, Breton fishermen traded dried salt cod for south-coast salt and, thus, a delectable Nîmois staple was born.

La Marmite

$ | MODERN FRENCH | On nice days, the lively scene in the dining room spills out onto a spacious terrace, though both are lovely places to enjoy something from the short menu of home-style dishes that's made even more irresistible by the fact that nothing on it costs more than €17 (three-course lunch menu, €16). Look for such comfort foods as spelt risotto with veal and cèpes or pork *caillettes* (meatballs) with chard and pickles; for dessert, consider the melting chocolate mousse cake that's just like the one grandmère makes. **Known for:** fresh, home-cooked dishes; great value; central location. *Average main: €15 13 rue*

In Nîmes, the pleasure of relaxing in a square is greatly enhanced with a pitcher of local rosé, a bowl of olives, and a plat du jour.

de l'Agau, Nîmes ☎ *04–66–29 98–23* 🌐 *lamarmite.business.site* ⏲ *Closed Sun. and Mon. No dinner Tues. and Wed.*

Le Chabanais

$ | **MODERN FRENCH** | This under-the-radar *cave à manger,* for people who want to eat and drink well without the fuss of a fancier place, specializes in small plates with big flavors. Try the morteau sausage with lentils and pickled onions, the briny oysters in an herb-infused broth, or the tender pork cheeks with sweet corn cream—all accompanied by a feisty natural wine. **Known for:** big selection of wines for any budget; sidewalk dining; gently priced. [$] *Average main: €14* ✉ *13 rue de l'Étoile, Nîmes* ☎ *06–64–85–77–03* 🌐 *restaurantlechabanaisnimes.fr* ⏲ *No lunch. Closed Sun. and Mon. Sept.–June and weekends July–Aug.*

L'Impé Brasserie

$$$$ | **MODERN FRENCH** | The chic little sister brasserie to the Hôtel L'Imperator's gastronomic Duende restaurant is your best bet in the city for a memorable meal that won't break the bank. What's more, Duende's Michelin-starred chef presides over the kitchen, putting out perfectly executed comfort food made with ingredients sourced from the Occitane. **Known for:** Nicolas Fontaine's second restaurant (menu by Pierre Gagnaire); beautiful terrace; top-quality products. [$] *Average main: €54* ✉ *15 rue Gaston Boissier, Nîmes* ☎ *04–66–21–03–74* 🌐 *www.maison-albar-hotels-l-imperator.com.*

★ Skab

$$$$ | **FRENCH** | Don't be put off by the name—a blend of the initials of owners Sébastien Kieffer and Alban Barbette—because this restaurant has an enchanting shaded garden terrace and a seasonal menu by chef Damien Sanchez that will not disappoint. Crispy Provençal lamb with fresh vegetables makes for a great main dish, and for dessert there's poached apple on a crispy pastry with apple jelly, nougat, heavy cream, and gingerbread ice cream. **Known for:** outstanding wine list; pretty outdoor courtyard; gluten-free and vegetarian options. [$] *Average main: €50* ✉ *7 rue de*

la République, Nîmes ☎ *04–66–21–94–30* 🌐 *www.restaurant-skab.fr* ⊙ *Closed Sun., Mon., and last 2 wks in Apr.*

Hotels

Hôtel de l'Amphithéâtre
$ | **HOTEL** | This old private home has, fortunately, fallen into the hands of a loving and very hospitable owner, who has refinished 18th-century double doors and fitted rooms with restored-wood details, white-tiled bathrooms, and antique bedroom sets. **Pros:** ideally located; good value; friendly hosts. **Cons:** underground parking is a few blocks away; amenities are limited; no elevator. $ *Rooms from: €90* ✉ *4 rue des Arènes, Nîmes* ☎ *04–66–67–28–51* 🌐 *www.hoteldelamphitheatre.com* *14 rooms* *No Meals.*

La Maison de Sophie
$$$ | **B&B/INN** | Outside the hustle of town and yet just five minutes from the Arènes, this luxurious Art Deco *hôtel particulier* has lots of charm—especially in its large, airy, individually decorated guest rooms. **Pros:** big-city elegance mixes nicely with quiet nights; warm welcome; easy walk from city center and train station. **Cons:** often fully booked far in advance; pool is quite small; breakfast, though very good, is expensive. $ *Rooms from: €249* ✉ *31 av. Carnot, Nîmes* ☎ *04–66–70–96–10* 🌐 *www.hotel-nimes-gard.com* *7 rooms* *Free Breakfast.*

★ L'Imperator
$$$$ | **HOTEL** | **FAMILY** | This local grande dame—in a lovely neighborhood near the canal and just across from the Jardins de la Fontaine—has been transformed into a gorgeous contemporary hotel, complete with indoor and outdoor pools, a bistro, and a gastronomic restaurant overseen by superstar chef Pierre Gagnaire. **Pros:** richly atmospheric; excellent location; wonderful restaurant and bar. **Cons:** pricey; some rooms have better views than others; books up quickly in June around féria time. $ *Rooms from: €350* ✉ *15 rue Gaston Boissier, off Quai de la Fontaine, Nîmes* ☎ *04–66–21–90–30* 🌐 *www.maison-albar-hotels-l-imperator.com* *61 units* *No Meals.*

★ Margaret Hôtel Chouleur
$$$$ | **HOTEL** | Just five minutes from the Arènes and the Maison Carrée, this stunning hotel, which opened in 2022, fills three floors of a graceful private mansion—a classified historical monument—and offers amenities-filled guest rooms with contemporary chic furnishings and state-of-the-art lighting and fixtures. **Pros:** Diptyque bath products; butler service on demand; beautiful setting and dining. **Cons:** restaurant closed Sunday and Monday; small pool; dark color schemes in some rooms can be off-putting. $ *Rooms from: €420* ✉ *6 rue Fresque, Nîmes* ☎ *04–48–27–08–00* 🌐 *www.margaret-hotelchouleur.com* *10 rooms* *No Meals.*

Shopping

Antiques and collectibles are found in tiny shops throughout the city's backstreets, but there is a concentration of them in the Old Town, which also has, amid the chain stores, fabulous interior-design boutiques and fabric shops selling the Provençal cottons (Les Indiennes de Nîmes, Les Olivades, Souleiado) that were once produced here en masse.

★ Ateliers de Nîmes
MIXED CLOTHING | Where else should you buy blue jeans but in the birthplace of denim? Guillaume Sagot's hand-cut options for men and women are not only of supremely elegant cut and fit, but they're also sustainably produced, a rarity for denim. Made using 17th-century weaving techniques, the fabric is soft yet durable, so this chic boutique-atelier draws fashionistas from near and far. ✉ *2 rue Auguste Pellet, Nîmes* ☎ *09–53–40–15–89* 🌐 *www.ateliersdenimes.com.*

★ Les Halles de Nîmes
MARKET | FAMILY | With more than 100 stalls, Nîmes's central covered market is an excellent spot to grab a quick bite while stocking up on all the area's gastronomic specialties: crisp PDO (Protected Designation of Origin) picholine olives and olive oil, anchoïade (a heady mix of anchovies crushed with garlic and olive oil), Pélardons goat cheeses from nearby Cévennes, and Costières de Nîmes wines. **■ TIP→ For deeply satisfying regional cuisine—think brandade de morue (salt cod gratin) or taureau (bull's meat) with Camargue rice—and the convivial company of locals, head to Halles Auberge, which is open daily for lunch.** ✉ *5 rue des Halles, Nîmes* ☎ *04–66–21–52–49* 🌐 *leshallesdenimes.fr.*

Les Indiennes de Nîmes
MIXED CLOTHING | FAMILY | This deeply Provençal boutique, known for its beautiful cotton textiles and smart tailoring, has been dressing elegant men and women, kids, and cowboys, since 1938. The colorful prints are original 18th- and 19th-century designs from the manufacturer's archives. You'll also find a range of quality accessories, home goods, and fabrics sold by the meter. ✉ *2 bd. des Arènes, Nîmes* ☎ *04–66–21–69–57* 🌐 *indiennesdenimes.fr.*

Maison Villaret
FOOD | FAMILY | The longtime local favorite boulangerie–patisserie is the best place to buy yet another of Nîmes's many specialties: the jaw-breaking *croquant,* a confection made with roasted almonds and caramelized sugar. ✉ *13 rue de la Madeleine, Nîmes* ☎ *04–66–67–41–79* 🌐 *maison-villaret.com.*

Souleiado
MIXED CLOTHING | All those famous, gorgeous Provençal fabrics can be found at Souleiado, made into scarves and tailored shirts, dresses, and skirts. There's also a selection of bags, shoes, and other accessories. ✉ *Av. du Général Perrier, Rue Guizot, Nîmes* ☎ *04–66–23–76–97* 🌐 *www.souleiado.com/fr/boutiques.*

The Birthplace of Denim 

The word "denim" is derived from a cloth known as *serge de Nîmes.* Originally used by farmers in this region to make wagon covers and work clothes, this fabric made its way to San Francisco, where Bavarian merchant Levi Strauss used it for the durable trousers that became popular with gold miners. And the word "jeans"? Well, it comes from "Gênes," French for the Italian port of Genova, from which the fabric was initially shipped.

Activities

The *corrida* (bullfight) is a quintessential Nîmes experience, taking place as it does in the ancient Roman arena. There are usually two bullfighting seasons a year, always during the carnival-like citywide férias: at Pentecost (end of May) and during the wine harvest (end of September). The férias feature not only gentle Camargue-style bullfights (where competitors pluck a ring from the bull's horns) but also parades and a running of the bulls.

For many, however, the focal point is the Spanish-style bullfight, held twice daily and complete with *l'estocade* (the final killing) and the traditional cutting of the ear. Although this practice is frequently criticized, it is, nevertheless, a longstanding regional tradition. If you're squeamish or value animal rights you should avoid such events during the férias.

Pont du Gard

24 km (15 miles) northeast of Nîmes.

No other ancient Roman sight in the region rivals the Pont du Gard, a mighty, three-tiered aqueduct midway between Nîmes and Avignon—the highest bridge the Romans ever built. Erected some 2,000 years ago as part of a 48-km (30-mile) canal supplying water to Nîmes, it is astonishingly well preserved. You can't walk across it anymore, but you can get close enough to see the amazing gigantic square blocks of stone (some weighing up to 6 tons) by traversing the 18th-century bridge built alongside it.

GETTING HERE AND AROUND

The best way to get to Pont du Gard is via Nîmes, which is on the direct TGV line from Paris and takes about three hours. The Nîmes bus station is right behind the train station, and several buses daily except Sunday between Nîmes and Pont du Gard (about one hour, €1.50 one-way). If you are coming by car, take the A9 to Nîmes, Exit 50; then take the D979 in the direction of Uzès. Pont du Gard is 14 km (9 miles) southeast of Uzès on the D981.

Sights

★ Pont du Gard

RUINS | FAMILY | The ancient Roman aqueduct is shockingly noble in its symmetry, and its strong arches are a testimony to engineering concepts that were relatively new in the 1st century AD, when the structure was built under Emperor Claudius. Today, the surrounding nature is unsullied, with the Gardon River flowing through a rocky gorge unperturbed by the work of master engineering that straddles it. In fact, one of the preferred ways of viewing the bridge is via canoe or kayak, which are for rent upstream.

You can approach the aqueduct from either side of the Gardon River. If you choose the south side (Rive Droite), the walk to the *pont* (bridge) is shorter and the views arguably better. Although the spectacular walkway along the top of the aqueduct is now off-limits, the sight of the bridge is still breathtaking. The nearby Espaces Culturels details the rich history of the bridge—and Roman France at the time—and includes an interactive area for kids. ✉ *400 rte. du Pont du Gard, Vers-Pont-du-Gard* ☎ *04–66–37–50–99* 🌐 *www.pontdugard.fr* 🎫 *Guided tour €15.*

Hotels

La Bégude Saint Pierre

$$ | HOTEL | A mere 2 km (1 mile) from Pont du Gard, a 17th-century coach house on 30 acres of greenery has been lovingly converted into this boutique hotel and gourmet restaurant. **Pros:** practical location; friendly staff; lovely pool. **Cons:** street-facing rooms can be noisy; can be difficult to find; rustic atmosphere not for everyone. 💲 *Rooms from: €165* ✉ *295 chemin des Bégudes, Vers-Pont-du-Gard* ☎ *04–66–02–63–60* 🌐 *www.hotel-pontdugard.com* 🛏 *26 rooms* 🍽 *No Meals.*

★ Le Vieux Castillon

$$ | HOTEL | A five-minute drive from Pont du Gard, in a charming village setting with panoramas of vineyards and olive groves, this one-time residence of the Bishop of Uzès is an excellent choice for rest and relaxation. **Pros:** exquisite mix of modern and medieval; lovely location near Uzès; excellent price-to-quality ratio. **Cons:** not open year-round; pool on the small side; some rooms lack views. 💲 *Rooms from: €134* ✉ *10 rue Turion Sabatier, Castillon-du-Gard* ☎ *04–66–37–61–61* 🌐 *www.vieuxcastillon.com* 🕒 *Closed Nov.–Mar.* 🛏 *34 rooms* 🍽 *No Meals.*

Uzès

14 km (8½ miles) northwest of Pont du Gard; 24 km (15 miles) north of Nîmes.

The village of Uzès (pronounced "ou-zes") is a tiny Renaissance gem polished to a mellow shine. In the 1950s, the village was falling to ruin, and then saved, as were many villages in France, by André Malraux, the French minister of culture from 1959 to 1969, who designated funds to safeguard France's heritage. As one of the prettiest villages in the region, Uzès caught the eye of wealthy investors from all over Europe and the United States, who sped its recovery by investing in second homes here. Now Uzès is a handsome upscale destination, full of stately Renaissance architecture, lovely boutiques, and a leafy market square (Place du Marché aux Herbes) whose pretty arcades are in full charm during the Saturday and Wednesday morning markets.

GETTING HERE AND AROUND

The nearest TGV station is in Avignon, and four buses a day make the trip from Avignon Station to Uzès. The direct trip takes about 48 minutes and costs €4 each way. By car, follow the N100 to D981, which takes about 41 minutes.

VISITOR INFORMATION

CONTACTS Uzès Tourist Office. ✉ *Chapelle des Capucins, Pl. Albert 1er, Uzès* ☎ *04–66–22–68–88* 🌐 *www.uzes-pont-dugard.uk/.*

Sights

Cathédrale Saint-Théodont

CHURCH | The onetime home of the Bishops of Uzès, the original Saint-Théodont was built in 1090 on the site of a Roman temple, but it was demolished during the ensuing religious wars. Though the impressive Fenestrelle Tower—a ringer for the Tower of Pisa minus the tilt—remains, it is too delicate to actually visit. The 19th-century neo-Romanesque facade shelters a pared-down interior and one of the oldest pipe organs in France. The views from the grounds are lovely. ✉ *Rue du Portalet, Uzès* ☎ *04–66–22–68–88* 🌐 *www.cathedrale-uzes.fr.*

Ducal Palace

CASTLE/PALACE | The Middle Ages, the Renaissance, and the 17th century are on display at the 1,000-year-old-and-counting residence of the Dukes of Uzès (when the blue flag is flying you know the duke is at home). Tours (in French) from the cellars to the Bermonde tower narrate the history of the castle (which is also basically the history of France), including one of its most colorful residents, Anne de Mortemart, wife of the 12th duke. She was the first woman in France to earn a driver's license and also the first to get a speeding ticket. ✉ *Pl. du Duché, Uzès* ☎ *04–66–22–18–96* 🌐 *www.uzes.com/en/chateau/histoire.php* 🎫 *€14, €22 with guided tour.*

Jardin Médiéval

GARDEN | **FAMILY** | This lovely compact garden on a 12th-century site re-creates a typical botanical garden with plants commonly used in medieval medicines. It's well worth the steep 100-step climb up the King's tower for the eye-popping views of the town. Afterward, you'll be served a refreshing *tisane* made from garden herbs. There's also a fascinating 19th-century jail and several art galleries showing works by local artists. ✉ *BP Hôtel de Ville, Rue Port Royal, Uzès* ☎ *04–66–22–38–21* 🌐 *jardinmedievaluzes.com* 🎫 *€7.*

Restaurants

La Table d'Uzès

$$$$ | **FRENCH** | Uzès's only Michelin-starred restaurant has a stately but cozy dining room that sets the stage for a memorable meal from start to finish. Give yourself time to fully appreciate the dishes of chef Christophe Ducros, whose magic lies in the seasonal pairings of the freshest ingredients from both the countryside (like lamb served three ways) and coast (coquilles Saint-Jacques with butternut squash, yuzu, and trompette mushrooms) with complementary local wines. **Known for:** set in the town's most elegant hotel; Michelin-star dining; good price-to-quality ratio. *Average main: €45 18 rue du Dr Blanchard, Uzès 04–66–20–07–00 www.lamaisonduzes.fr/en/gastronomy Closed Mon. and Tues. year-round. Closed Wed. mid-Oct.–Apr.*

Racines

$$ | MODERN FRENCH | Locals appreciate this cozy, contemporary dining room, set in an old stone house a 10-minute walk from the town center, so a table here is one of Uzès's most coveted. After training in top Parisian kitchens, chef Axel Grousset-Bachelard traveled the world tasting as he went, so expect a touch of the exotic in his seasonal dishes made with market-fresh produce (if you're here in winter, order any of the dishes featuring the local black truffles) and meat and fish sourced from the finest Occitane and Provence purveyors. **Known for:** true culinary genius; fancy without the fuss; good-value prix-fixe menus. *Average main: €21 1 rue Masbourguet, Uzès 04–66–63–30–59 racines.restaurant Closed Sun. and Mon. No lunch Tues.*

Ten

$ | MODERN FRENCH | FAMILY | This favorite spot in the center of town draws crowds, especially after the morning market, for its excellent French comfort food with a twist. It's a great place to relax—inside the cheerful dining room or outdoors in the garden or under the 16th-century building's beautiful stone vaulting—and feast on rotisserie chicken with crispy frites, fresh oysters on the half shell, jumbo shrimp with mango and avocado, or a charcuterie plate. **Known for:** always lively and fun; super welcoming; delicious small plates. *Average main: €16 10 pl. Dampmartin, Uzès 04–66–22–10–93 www.tenuzes.com.*

Hotels

Boutique Hôtel Entraigues

$ | HOTEL | This appealing boutique hotel on a charming cobbled street in the Old Town has 15th-century bones (it was once a private mansion) and a thoroughly contemporary spirit. **Pros:** small enough that it never feels crowded; beverages and wine available for around the pool or on the terrace; warm welcome. **Cons:** rooms lack character; some rooms have low ceilings; small staff sometimes elsewhere. *Rooms from: €120 4 pl. de l'Évêché, Uzès 04–66–72–05–25 www.hotel-entraigues.com/en/hotel 19 rooms No Meals.*

★ La Maison d'Uzès

$$$ | HOTEL | Each of the spacious rooms in this exquisite hotel—created by merging three buildings of a 17th-century mansion—is unique, but they all have beautiful decor, high ceilings (many beamed) and other elegant architectural details, enormous baths, modern amenities, and typical Uzès charm. **Pros:** on-site L'Occitane spa; easy walk to all of the town's major sights; Michelin-starred restaurant. **Cons:** only one of the three buildings has an elevator; books up quickly in summer; not ideal for kids. *Rooms from: €290 18 rue du Dr Blanchard, Uzès 04–66–20–07–00 www.lamaisonduzes.fr/en 9 rooms Free Breakfast.*

Aigues-Mortes

39 km (24 miles) south of Nîmes; 45 km (28 miles) southwest of Arles.

Like a tiny illumination in a medieval manuscript, Aigues-Mortes (pronounced "ay-guh-*mort*-uh") is a precise and perfect miniature fortress-town, with perfectly symmetrical castellated walls and streets laid out in grids. Now amid

Aigues-Mortes is a precise and perfect medieval fortress town, whose grid of streets is contained within castellated walls.

flatlands of sand, salt, and marsh, it once was a major port town from whence no less than St-Louis himself (Louis IX) set sail to conquer Jerusalem in the 13th century. In 1248, some 35,000 zealous men launched 1,500 ships for Cyprus, engaging the enemy on his own turf and suffering swift defeat; Louis himself was briefly taken prisoner. A second launching in 1270 led to more crushing losses, after which Louis succumbed to typhus in Tunis.

GETTING HERE AND AROUND

Several trains a day run to Aigues-Mortes from Nîmes. The trip takes 45 minutes to an hour and costs €8.30. Buses, which cost €1.50 each way, make the hourlong trip between the two towns every two hours. By car, take the A9 to exit Gallargues (direction Aimargues–St-Laurent-d'Aigouze) and take the D979 directly to Aigues-Mortes.

VISITOR INFORMATION

CONTACTS Aigues-Mortes Tourist Office. ✉ *Pl. St-Louis, Aigues-Mortes* ☎ *04–66–53–73–00* 🌐 *ot-aiguesmortes.com.*

Sights

Place St-Louis

PLAZA/SQUARE | FAMILY | A 19th-century statue of the father of the fleur-de-lis reigns under shady pollards on this square with a mellow village feel, a welcome retreat from the clutter of souvenir shops on surrounding lanes. The pretty, bare-bones Église Notre-Dame des Sablons, on one corner of the square, has a timeless air (the church dates from the 13th century, but the stained glass is modern), and the spectacular Chapelle des Pénitents Blancs and Chapelle des Pénitents Gris are Baroque-era marvels. ✉ *Aigues-Mortes.*

Tour et Remparts d'Aigues Mortes

MILITARY SIGHT | FAMILY | The stout walls and ramparts of this Gothic fortress, once a state-of-the-art marvel, are astonishingly well preserved. The tower is particularly impressive, as are the vistas of the surrounding Camargue. Temporary exhibitions are held along the ramparts in summer; there's also a permanent exhibit on the history of Protestantism in the region. ✉ *Pl. Anatole France, Porte de la Gardette, Aigues-Mortes* ☎ *04-66-53-61-55* 🌐 *www.aigues-mortes-monument.fr* 🎫 *€8.*

 Restaurants

L'Atelier de Nicolas

$$$ | BISTRO | An open kitchen, a chalkboard menu, a bright terrace, and friendly service combine to create a laid-back atmosphere here, but, when it comes to the food, chef Nicolas Epiard is on his toes, serving up traditional local cuisine with flair and exuberance. Try dishes like the meltingly tender, slow-cooked bull with wild morels and a puree of root vegetables or the sea bass with savory herb *pistou* (Provence's answer to pesto) and crisp vegetables. **Known for:** sophisticated dining in a casual, amiable atmosphere; wine list with lots of local options; excellent taureau (slow-cooked bull), a local specialty. 💲 *Average main: €29* ✉ *28 rue A. Lorraine, Aigues-Mortes* ☎ *04-34-28-04-84* 🌐 *restaurant-latelierdenicolas.fr* ⏲ *Closed Sun., Wed., and Thurs.*

Ni Vu Ni Connu

$ | SEAFOOD | Finding a decent place for a sit-down meal amid the village's head-spinning number of tourist cafés is challenging, but you can't go wrong with this welcoming eatery at the historic port. Watch the boats pass by while dining on heaping platters of shellfish or the catch of the day. **Known for:** great prices; outdoor seating with sea views; freshest seafood in town. 💲 *Average main: €16* ✉ *Rue du Port, Aigues-Mortes* ☎ *07-71-94-30-29* ⏲ *Closed Tues.*

 Hotels

Les Templiers

$$ | HOTEL | A 17th-century residence within the ramparts is the setting of this delightful hotel featuring stone, stucco, and terra-cotta details as well as classically simple and antique furnishings. **Pros:** wonderfully warm welcome; charmingly intimate space; delightful restaurant with home cooking. **Cons:** some rooms are small; amenities are lacking (no minibars); simple decor. 💲 *Rooms from: €180* ✉ *23 rue de la République, Aigues-Mortes* ☎ *04-66-53-66-56* 🌐 *www.hotellestempliers.fr* *14 rooms* 🍽 *No Meals.*

Villa Mazarin

$$ | HOTEL | Spacious, romantic rooms and Provençal styling are among the things that make this surprisingly peaceful, town center hotel so popular that guests often rebook immediately for next year's trip. **Pros:** indoor heated swimming pool; lots of amenities; Clarins products in bathroom. **Cons:** restaurant on the pricey side; books up quickly; inconsistent service. 💲 *Rooms from: €180* ✉ *35 bd. Gambetta, Aigues-Mortes* ☎ *04-66-73-90-48* 🌐 *www.villamazarin.com* *23 rooms* 🍽 *No Meals.*

Parc Naturel Régional de Camargue

10 km (6 miles) southeast of Aigues-Mortes; 25 km (16 miles) southeast of Nîmes; 6 km (4 miles) southwest of Arles.

Between the endless flow of sediment from the Rhône and the erosive force of the sea, the shape of the 1,500-square-km (580-square-mile) alluvial delta known as the Camargue is constantly changing. This austere, flat marshland is scoured by the mistral and swarmed over by mosquitoes. Yet its harsh landscape harbors wildlife unique in all of Europe. Birds, in particular, find the Camargue irresistible. Indeed, it lures some 400 species, including little egrets, gray herons, spoonbills, bitterns, cormorants, redshanks, and grebes—as well as those famous flamingos.

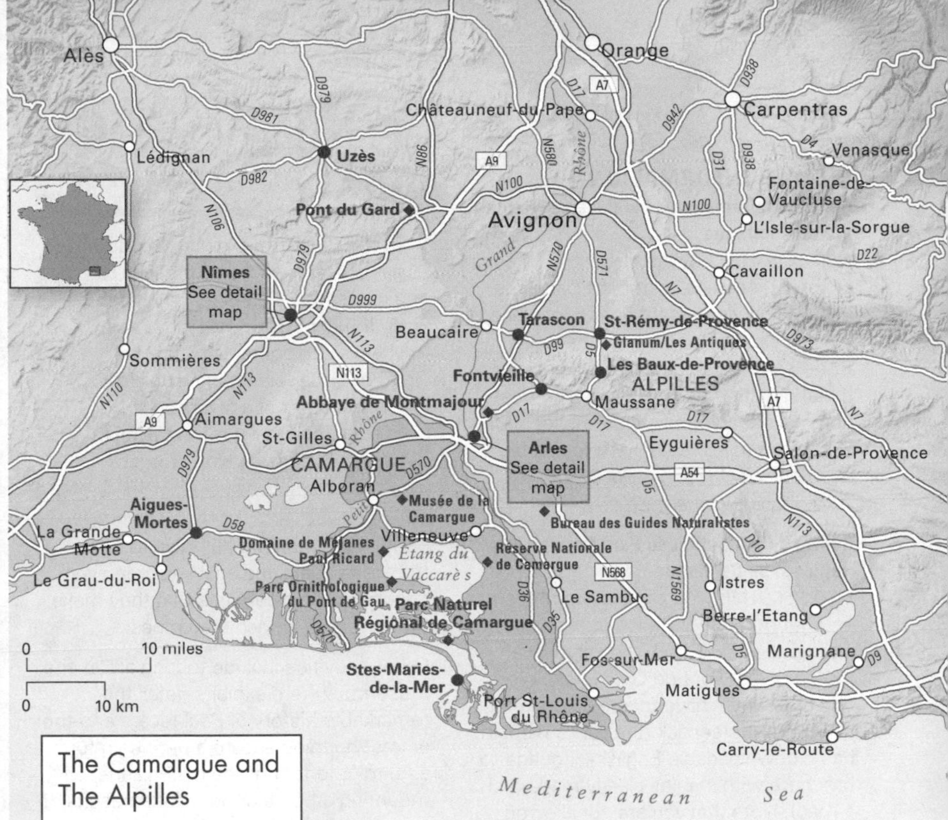

This isolated, natural world surrounds a few far-flung villages. All are rich in the region's quirky culture and intriguing history, and all make good points of departure for forays by car, or in the wildest reaches, on foot or on horseback.

GETTING HERE AND AROUND

The best way to explore the park is by car. Roads around and throughout it have parking areas from which you can set out on foot. You can also explore by bicycle, boat, on horseback, or guided tour. Detailed information on trails and rentals can be found at the tourist offices in both Aigues-Mortes and Stes-Maries-de-la-Mer—the park's major points of entry—and through the main Centre d'Information Parc Naturel Camargue at La Capelière.

TOURS

★ Bureau des Guides Naturalistes

ECOTOURISM | FAMILY | Covering nearly 1,000 square miles, the triangle between the Camargue, Crau, and the Alpilles (known by naturalists as the *triangle d'or de la biodiversité*) is France's—and one of the world's—most biodiverse regions, home to myriad plant and wildlife species, many rare or endangered. Frédéric Bouvet, an ornithologist who studied extensively in England, organizes small, personalized outings focusing on birdlife and conducted year-round. Tours are customized to your interests, last either a half day or a full day (or up to several days if desired), and can start anywhere in or near the area. A natural raconteur, Bouvet's passion, enthusiasm, and exceptional knowledge ensure an unforgettable experience. ✉ *Arles*

☎ *06–20–70–09–61* 🌐 *www.guide-nature.fr* 💳 *€230 half day, €350 full day.*

VISITOR INFORMATION

Centre d'Information de la Réserve Nationale de Camargue

VISITOR CENTER | At the easternmost point of the Etang du Vaccarès, La Capeliére has a good visitor center with maps as well as exhibits on wildlife. There are three *sentiers de découverte* (discovery trails) radiating from its pond-side position, each leading to a small observatory. ✉ *5 km (3 miles) south of Villeneuve/Romieu, off D37* ☎ *04–90–97–00–97* 🌐 *www.parc-camargue.fr.*

Centre d'Information du Parc Naturel Régional de Camargue

VISITOR CENTER | You can pick up maps and get other information at this center, just up the D570 from the Parc Ornithologique at Pont de Gau. To explore this area, you'll have to strike out on foot, bicycle, or horseback (the park's website has a downloadable English-language brochure with stables clearly marked on a map). Note that you are not allowed to diverge from marked trails. ✉ *D570, Stes-Maries-de-la-Mer* ☎ *04–90–97–10–40* 🌐 *www.parc-camargue.fr.*

Sights

★ Domaine de Méjanes Paul Ricard

NATURE PRESERVE | **FAMILY** | Near the northern shore of the Etang de Vaccarès, 4 km (2½ miles) north of Albaron on the D37, this unique cultural center, funded by the Ricard family of pastis fame and set on one of the larger estates in the Camargue, is a place to meet *gardians* (French cowboys) and learn about the *toro,* or bull—virtually a totemic creature in these parts. You'll also gain a better understanding of the regional spectacle known as the *course camarguaise,* in which *raseteurs* (runners) try to pluck off a red cockade and two white tassels mounted on the bull's horns. There is no *mise à mort* (as in Spanish-style *corridas,* or bullfights), so the bulls live to enter the arena again and again—some even become such celebrities that they make the covers of French magazines.

Other activities include touring an on-site museum, where exhibits detail the remarkable history of Paul Ricard and the estate; hopping aboard a *petit* train for a 20-minute tour of the marshlands; or mounting a horse or pony for a beachside trot. At Chez Hélène et Néné restaurant, you can feast on Camargue seafood while gazing at the beach and the ocean. If you want to stay the night, the estate has several charming accommodation options—from guest rooms to cottages to colorful wooden, Roma-style caravans. ✉ *D37, on edge of Etage de Vacarrès* ☎ *04–90–97–10–10* 🌐 *mejanes-camargue.fr.*

Musée de la Camargue

HISTORY MUSEUM | **FAMILY** | North of the village of Albaron, between Arles and Stes-Maries-de-la-Mer, this former sheep ranch is now a museum devoted to the region's history, produce, and people, including the gardians. It's also a good place to pick up information about nature trails. ✉ *Mas de Pont de Rousty, D570, Albaron* ☎ *04–90–97–10–82* 🌐 *www.museedelacamargue.com* 💳 *€7.*

Flamingos in the Camargue

In the Camargue, ivory-pink flamingos are as common as pigeons on a city square. Their gangly height, dodolike bill, and stilty legs give them a cartoonish air, and their flight style seems comic up close. But the sight of a few thousand of these creatures taking wing in unison is one you won't forget.

Gardians are a type of open-range cowboy you might see herding horses in the Camargue.

Parc Naturel Régional de Camargue

NATIONAL PARK | FAMILY | As you drive the few roads that crisscross the Camargue, you'll usually be within the boundaries of the Parc Naturel Régional de Camargue. Unlike most state and national parks in the United States, this area is supervised by the state but privately owned, primarily by the *manadiers,* small-scale ranchers who graze their wide-horned bulls and broad-bellied, white-dappled horses here and are helped by the gardians—French cowboys who ride through the marshlands wearing leather pants and wide-rimmed black hats and wielding long cattle prods.

Some posit that the Camargue's curved-horned *taureaux* (bulls) were imported by Attila the Hun; others, that they are descended from ancient, indigenous wild animals. Regardless, they bear the noble marks of their ancestors. The strong, heavy-tailed Camargue horse has been traced to the Paleolithic period (though some claim the Moors imported an Arab strain) and is prized for its endurance and tough hooves.

The gardians are as fascinating as the animals they herd. Their homes—tiny, whitewashed, cane-thatched huts with the north end raked and curved apselike as protection from the vicious mistral—dot the countryside. The signature wrought-iron crosses at the gable invoke holy protection and serve as lightning rods. ☎ *04–90–97–10–82* 🌐 *www.parc-camargue.fr.*

Parc Ornithologique du Pont de Gau (*Pont du Gau Ornithological Park*)

NATURE PRESERVE | FAMILY | The easiest place to view birdlife is the Parc Ornithologique du Pont de Gau. On some 150 acres of marsh and salt lands, birds are protected, and injured birds are treated and kept in large pens, to be released if and when they're deemed able to survive. A series of boardwalks (including a short, child-friendly inner loop) snakes over the wetlands, the longest leading to an observation blind, where a half hour of silence, binoculars in hand, can reveal unsuspected satisfactions. ✉ *D570, 5 km (3 miles) north of Stes-Maries-de-la-Mer, Stes-Maries-de-la-Mer* ☎ *04–90–97–82–62* 🌐 *www.parcornithologique.com* 🎟 *€8.*

Réserve Nationale de Camargue
NATURE PRESERVE | FAMILY | If you're an even more committed nature lover, venture into this inner sanctum of the Camargue, an intensely protected area that contains the central pond called Le Vaccarès and is mostly used for approved scientific research. The wildlife (birds, nutria, fish) is virtually undisturbed here, and you won't come across the cabins and herds of bulls and horses found elsewhere in the Camargue. ☎ *04–90–97–00–97* 🌐 *www.snpn.com/reservedecamargue.*

Hotels

★ Le Mas de Peint
$$$ | HOTEL | Sitting on roughly 1,250 acres of Camargue ranch land, this 17th-century farmstead is a study in country elegance, with several buildings containing rooms done in soft Provençal colors and featuring wooden beams, polished stone floors, brass beds, dreamy linen fabrics, and bathrooms with claw-foot tubs. **Pros:** isolated setting makes for a romantic getaway; on-site pool and lots of activities offered; no detail is missed in service or style. **Cons:** not all rooms have showers; a bit rustic, including lots of mosquitoes; not much to do once sun goes down, which some appreciate. $ *Rooms from: €350* ✉ *D36, 20 km (12 miles) south of Arles, Le Sambuc* ☎ *04–90–97–20–62* 🌐 *www.masdepeint.com* ⏲ *Closed mid-Nov.–Mar.* *15 rooms* *No Meals.*

Stes-Maries-de-la-Mer

31 km (19 miles) southeast of Aigues-Mortes; 40 km (25 miles) southwest of Arles.

The principal town within the confines of the Parc Naturel Régional de Camargue, Stes-Maries has a fascinating history. Provençal legend has it that, around AD 45, a band of the first Christians was rounded up and set adrift at sea in a boat without a sail and without provisions. Their stellar ranks included Mary Magdalene, Martha, and Mary Salome, mother of apostles James and John; Mary Jacoby, sister of the Virgin; and Lazarus, risen from the dead (or another Lazarus, depending on who you ask). Joining them in their fate: a dark-skinned servant girl named Sarah.

Miraculously, their boat washed ashore in this area, and the Marys built a chapel in thanks. Martha moved on to Tarascon to tackle dragons, and Lazarus founded the church in Marseille. But Mary Jacoby and Mary Salome remained, and Sarah stayed with them, begging in the streets to support them in their ministry. The three women died around the same time and were buried together at the site of their chapel.

A cult grew up around this legendary spot, and a church was built around it. In the 15th century, a stone memorial and two female bodies were found under the original chapel, and the Romanesque church was expanded to receive an influx of pilgrims. But not all of them were lighting candles to the two St. Marys: the servant girl Sarah has been adopted as an honorary saint by the Roma of the world.

Two extraordinary annual festivals honor these women, one held May 24–25 and the other on the Sunday nearest to October 22. On May 24, Roma pilgrims gather from across Europe and carry the wooden statue of Sarah from her crypt, through the streets of the village, and down to the sea to be washed. The next day, they carry a wooden statue of the two Saint Marys, kneeling in their wooden boat, to the sea for its own holy bath—a ritual that is repeated by non-Roma pilgrims in October.

As you enter this town's mammoth Église des Stes-Maries, a sign on the door wrenches you back to this century from the Middle Ages: the sign notes that visitors are forbidden to enter *torse nu* (topless). It's a reminder that, in addition to being a a pilgrimage center, Stes-Maries is a beach resort. Unless you've come to make a pilgrimage to the sun and sand, you probably won't spend much time in the town center. And if you've chosen Stes-Maries as a base for viewing the Camargue, consider staying in one of the discreet country inns outside the city limits.

GETTING HERE AND AROUND

The nearest train station with bus connections to Stes-Maries-de-la-Mer is in Arles. Several buses a day run from Arles to Stes-Maries-de-la-Mer. The trip takes about one hour and costs €1 each way. By car, your best bet by far is to take the A54 and at Exit 4 take the D570 directly to Stes-Maries-de-la-Mer.

VISITOR INFORMATION

CONTACTS Stes-Maries-de-la-Mer Tourist Office. ✉ *5 av. Van Gogh, Stes-Maries-de-la-Mer* ☎ *04–90–97–82–55* 🌐 *www.saintesmaries.com.*

Sights

Église des Stes-Maries

CHURCH | This mammoth, Romanesque fortress-church, built in the 9th century, is almost devoid of windows, and its tall, barren nave is cluttered with florid and sentimental ex-votos (tokens of blessings, prayers, and thanks) and primitive artworks depicting the famous trio of Marys. For €3, you can climb up to the terrace for a panoramic view of the Camargue (hours vary depending on the season). ✉ *2 pl. de l'Église, Stes-Maries-de-la-Mer* ☎ *04–90–97–80–25* 🌐 *www.sanctuaire-des-saintesmaries.fr.*

Hotels

★ Cacharel Hôtel

$$ | **B&B/INN** | **FAMILY** | Nestled in the middle of 170 acres of private marshland, this quiet, laid-back retreat has simple whitewashed buildings with equally simple guest rooms that feature terra-cotta tiles, jute rugs, white cotton throws, and large picture windows with hauntingly beautiful views of of rose-color reeds. **Pros:** can view flamingos from your window; scintillating taste of the real Camargue in a beautiful wild setting; fabulous pool. **Cons:** rooms are very sparse, almost monastic; not much to do; a drive into town. *$ Rooms from: €220* ✉ *Rte. de Cacharel, 4 km (2½ miles) north of town on D85, Stes-Maries-de-la-Mer* ☎ *04–90–97–95–44* 🌐 *www.hotel-cacharel.com* *16 rooms* *No Meals.*

Mas de la Fouque

$$$ | **HOTEL** | With stylish rooms and luxurious balconies that overlook a beautiful lagoon, this upscale converted farmhouse, just 2 km (1 mile) from deserted beaches, is a perfect escape from the rigors of horseback riding and bird-watching. **Pros:** excellent spa; in the heart of nature, with all the wildlife to prove it; eco-friendly ethos. **Cons:** no nightlife for those who need to be entertained; expensive (but worth it); breakfast not included in rate. *$ Rooms from: €320* ✉ *Rte. du Petit Rhone, Stes-Maries-de-la-Mer* ☎ *04–90–97–81–02* 🌐 *www.masdelafouque.com* *Closed Jan.* *26 rooms* *No Meals.*

Shopping

★ **La Botte Gardiane**

SHOES | This family enterprise (since 1957) earned the coveted status of Entreprise du Patrimoine Vivant (Living Heritage Company) as the last shoemaker offering authentic boots for the famous Camargue cowboys, les gardians. Aside from some chic cowboy-esque models, there are stylish and durable full-length fashion boots and booties, suede and leather chukka boots, supersoft espadrilles, and strappy sandals—all made from supple, vegetable-tanned calfskin provided by the same tanner that supplies Hermès. ✉ *38 rue Victor Hugo, Stes-Maries-de-la-Mer* ☎ *09–81–07–22–51* 🌐 *labottegardiane.com.*

Arles

31 km (19 miles) southeast of Nîmes; 40 km (25 miles) northwest of Stes-Maries.

Although it has an abundance of well-preserved ancient and Romanesque structures, Arles is more charming than it is austere. Here, shuttered town houses shade graceful Old Town streets and squares that are often the sites of pageantry, festivals, and cutting-edge arts events. The many atmospheric restaurants and picturesque small hotels also make Arles an ideal base for forays into the Alpilles and the Camargue.

Seated in the shade of plane trees on Place du Forum, sunning at the foot of the obelisk on Place de la République, meditating in the cloister of St-Trophime, or strolling the rampart walkway along the sparkling Rhône, you can see what enchanted Gauguin and drove Van Gogh mad with inspiration: multihued Arles—with its red-and-gold ocher, cool gray stone, and blue-black shade—is bathed in an intense, vivid, crystalline light. It's no wonder that UNESCO has listed the entire old city as historical monument.

It wasn't always such a low-key place. A Greek colony since the 6th century BC, little Arles took a giant step forward when Julius Caesar defeated Marseille in the 1st century BC, transforming it into a formidable civilization—by some accounts, the Rome of the north. Fed by aqueducts, canals, and solid roads, it profited from all the Romans' modern conveniences: straight paved streets and sidewalks, sewers and latrines, thermal baths, a forum, a hippodrome, a theater, and an arena. It became an international crossroads by sea and land and a market to the world. The emperor Constantine himself moved to Arles and brought with him Christianity.

■ **TIP→ If you plan to visit many of the monuments and museums in Arles, purchase a visite générale ticket for €16, which covers admission to all of them.**

GETTING HERE AND AROUND

Arles is roughly 20 km (12 miles) from the Nîmes-Arles-Camargue airport, and a taxi into town costs about €35. Buses run between Nîmes and Arles 11 times daily on weekdays and four times on Saturday (not at all on Sunday). Four buses run weekdays between Arles and Stes-Maries-de-la-Mer, and there are three buses Monday–Saturday connecting Avignon and Arles. Arles is along the main coastal train route, and you can take the TGV to Avignon from Paris, and jump on the local connection to Arles. You can also reach Arles directly by train from Marseille.

VISITOR INFORMATION

CONTACTS Arles Tourist Office. ✉ *9 bd. des Lices, Arles* ☎ *04–90–18–41–20* 🌐 *www.arlestourisme.com.*

Sights

★ **Arènes** (*Arena*)

RUINS | Rivaled only by the even better-preserved version in Nîmes, the arena dominating old Arles was built in the 1st century AD to seat 21,000 people, with

Van Gogh immortalized the courtyard of this former hospital—now the Espace Van Gogh, a center devoted to his works—in several masterpieces.

large tunnels through which wild beasts were forced to run into the center. Before being plundered in the Middle Ages, the structure had three stories of 60 arcades each; the four medieval towers are testimony to a transformation from classical sports arena to feudal fortification. Complete restoration of the arena began in 1825. Today it's primarily a venue for the traditional spectacle of the corridas, which take place annually during the *féria pascale,* or Easter festival. The less bloodthirsty local variant *course carmarguaise* (in which the bull is not killed) also takes place here. Festival season starts with the Fête des Gardians on May 1, when the Queen of Arles is crowned, and culminates in early July with the award of the Cocarde d'Or (Golden Rosette) to the most successful *raseteur.* It's best to book event tickets in advance. ✉ *24 bis, Rond Point des Arènes, Arles* ☎ *04–90–18–41–20 for arena info, 08–91–70–03–70 for courses carmarguaise info* 🌐 *www.arenes-arles.com* 🎫 *€9, includes admission to Théâtre Antique.*

Cloître St-Trophime (*St. Trophime Cloister*)
RELIGIOUS BUILDING | This peaceful haven, one of the loveliest cloisters in Provence, is tucked discreetly behind St-Trophime, the notable Romanesque treasure. A sturdy walkway above the Gothic arches offers good views of the town. ✉ *Off Pl. de la République, Arles* ☎ *04–90–18–41–20* 🎫 *€6.*

Cryptoportiques
RUINS | Entering through the elegant 17th-century City Hall, you can gain access to these ancient underground passages dating from 30–20 BC. The horseshoe of vaults and pillars buttressed the ancient forum from belowground. Used as a bomb shelter in World War II, the galleries still have a rather ominous atmosphere. Yet openings let in natural daylight and artworks of considerable merit have been unearthed here, adding to the mystery of the site's original function. ✉ *Pl. de la République, Arles* ☎ *04–90–18–41–20* 🎫 *€5.*

Église St-Trophime

CHURCH | Classed as a world treasure by UNESCO, this extraordinary Romanesque church alone would justify a visit to Arles. The side aisles date from the 11th century and the nave from the 12th. The church's austere symmetry and ancient artworks (including a stunning early Christian sarcophagus) are fascinating. But it's the church's superbly preserved Romanesque sculpture on its 12th-century portal, the renovated entry facade, that earns it international respect. Particularly remarkable is the frieze of the Last Judgment, with souls being dragged off to Hell in chains or, on the contrary, being lovingly delivered into the hands of the saints. Christ is flanked by his chroniclers, the evangelists: the eagle (John), the bull (Luke), the angel (Matthew), and the lion (Mark). ✉ *Pl. de la République, Arles* 🌐 *paroisse-catholique-arles.fr/eglises* 🎟 *Free.*

★ Espace Van Gogh

GARDEN | The hospital to which the tortured Van Gogh repaired after cutting off his earlobe is a strikingly resonant site. Its courtyard has been impeccably restored and landscaped to match one of Van Gogh's paintings. The cloistered grounds have become something of a shrine for visitors, and there is a photo plaque comparing the renovation to some of the master's paintings, including *Le Jardin de la Maison de Santé*. The exhibition hall is open for temporary shows; the garden is always on view. ✉ *Pl. Dr. Félix Rey, Arles* ☎ *04–90–18–41–20* 🎟 *Free.*

Fondation Vincent Van Gogh

ART MUSEUM | Located in the beautifully restored 15th-century Hôtel Léautaud de Donines, the Fondation Vincent van Gogh houses a superb collection of contemporary art and hosts temporary art exhibitions, concerts, and other cultural events. Originally conceived in the mid-1980s in response to the 100th anniversary of the artist's arrival in Arles, the Fondation pays homage to Van Gogh's legacy and monumental influence via an impressive range of artworks contributed by 90 contemporary artists. Van Gogh's 15-month stay in Arles represented a climax in the artist's career. Enchanted with Arles's limpid light, vibrant landscape, and scenic monuments, Van Gogh experienced here what was to be his greatest blossoming as a painter in a decade. ✉ *35 rue du Docteur Fanton, Arles* ☎ *04–90–93–08–08* 🌐 *www.fondation-vincentvangogh-arles.org* 🎟 *From €10.*

Les Alyscamps

CEMETERY | Although the romantically melancholic Roman cemetery lies 1 km (½ mile) southeast of the Old Town, it's worth the hike—certainly Van Gogh thought so, as several of his famous canvases prove. This long necropolis amassed the remains of the dead from antiquity to the Middle Ages. Greek, Roman, and Christian tombs line the shady road that was once the main entry to Arles, the Aurelian Way. The finest stone coffins have been plundered over the centuries, thus no single work of surpassing beauty remains here (they're in the Musée Départmental Arles Antiques). Next to the ruins rise the Romanesque tower and ruined church of St-Honorat, where (legend has it) St-Trophime fell to his knees when God spoke to him. ✉ *Allée des Sarcophages, Arles* 🎟 *€5.*

★ Luma Arles

ARTS CENTER | This arts center focuses on the pioneers of contemporary art and culture, bringing together sculpture, painting, dance, philosophy, literature, gastronomy, sustainability, and design. It has several spaces used for cutting-edge exhibitions and workshops geared toward art lovers and the curious of all ages, and its Frank Gehry building, a twisting silo sheathed in glittering silver scales, is spectacular. ✉ *45 ch. des Minimes, Arles* ☎ *04–88–65–83–09* 🌐 *www.luma.org* 🕓 *Closed Tues.*

Musée Départemental Arles Antiques (*Museum of Ancient Arles*)
HISTORY MUSEUM | FAMILY | Although it's a hike from the center, this state-of-the-art museum is a good place to start your exploration of Arles. You can learn all about the city in its Roman heyday, from the development of its monuments to details of daily life. The bold, modern triangular structure (designed by Henri Ciriani) lies on the site of an enormous Roman *cirque* (chariot-racing stadium).

The permanent collection includes jewelry, mosaics, town plans, and carved 4th-century sarcophagi. One wing of the museum features a rare intact barge dating from AD 50, as well as a fascinating display illustrating how the boat was meticulously dredged from the nearby Rhône. Seven superb floor mosaics can be viewed from an elevated platform, and you exit via a hall packed with magnificently detailed paleo-Christian sarcophagi. As you leave you will see the belt of St-Césaire, the last bishop of Arles, who died in AD 542 when the countryside was overwhelmed by the Franks and the Roman era met its end. Ask for an English-language guidebook. ✉ *Av. de la 1ère Division Française Libre, Presqu'île du Cirque Romain, Arles* ☎ *04–13–31–51–03* 🌐 *www.arlesantique.fr* 🎫 *€8; free 1st Sun. of month* ⏲ *Closed Tues.*

Musée Réattu
ART MUSEUM | Three rooms of this museum, housed in a Knights of Malta priory dating from the 15th century, are dedicated to local painter Jacques Réattu. But the standouts are works by Dufy, Gauguin, and 57 drawings (and two paintings) done by Picasso in 1971—including one delightfully tongue-in-cheek depiction of noted muse and writer Lee Miller in full Arles dress. They were donated to Arles by Picasso himself, to thank the town for amusing him with bullfights. ✉ *10 rue Grand Prieuré, Arles* ☎ *04–90–49–37–58* 🌐 *www.museereattu.arles.fr* 🎫 *€6; free 1st Sun. of month* ⏲ *Closed Mon.*

Place de la République
PLAZA/SQUARE | FAMILY | On this broad square, the slender, expressive saints of St-Trophime overlook wide steps that attract sun worshippers and foot-weary travelers. The square is also home to the 17th-century Hôtel de Ville, a noble Italianate landmark by the great Parisian architect François Mansart (as in mansard roofs); a passageway allows you to cut through its graceful vestibule from Rue Balze. The obelisk of Turkish marble once stood in the Gallo-Roman cirque but was hauled to the square in the 18th century. ✉ *Arles.*

Place Lamartine
PLAZA/SQUARE | FAMILY | Stand on the site of Van Gogh's residence in Arles—the famous Maison Jaune (Yellow House), which was destroyed by bombs in 1944. The artist may have set up his easel on the Quais du Rhône, just off Place Lamartine, to capture the view that he transformed into his legendary *Starry Night.* Eight other sites—each featured in one Van Gogh canvas or another—are highlighted on the city's (🌐 *www.arles-tourisme.com*) "Arles and Vincent van Gogh" tour, including Place du Forum, the Trinquetaille bridge, Rue Mireille, the Summer Garden on Boulevard des Lices, and the road along the Arles à Bouc canal. ✉ *Arles.*

Pont Van Gogh (*Langlois Bridge*)
BRIDGE | He immortalized many everyday objects and captured views still seen today, but Van Gogh's famous painting of the Langlois Bridge over the Canal d'Arles à Bouc—on the southern outskirts of Arles, about 3 km (2 miles) from the Old Town—seems to strike a particular chord among locals. Bombed in World War II, the bridge has been restored to its former glory. ✉ *Rte. de Port St-Louis, Arles.*

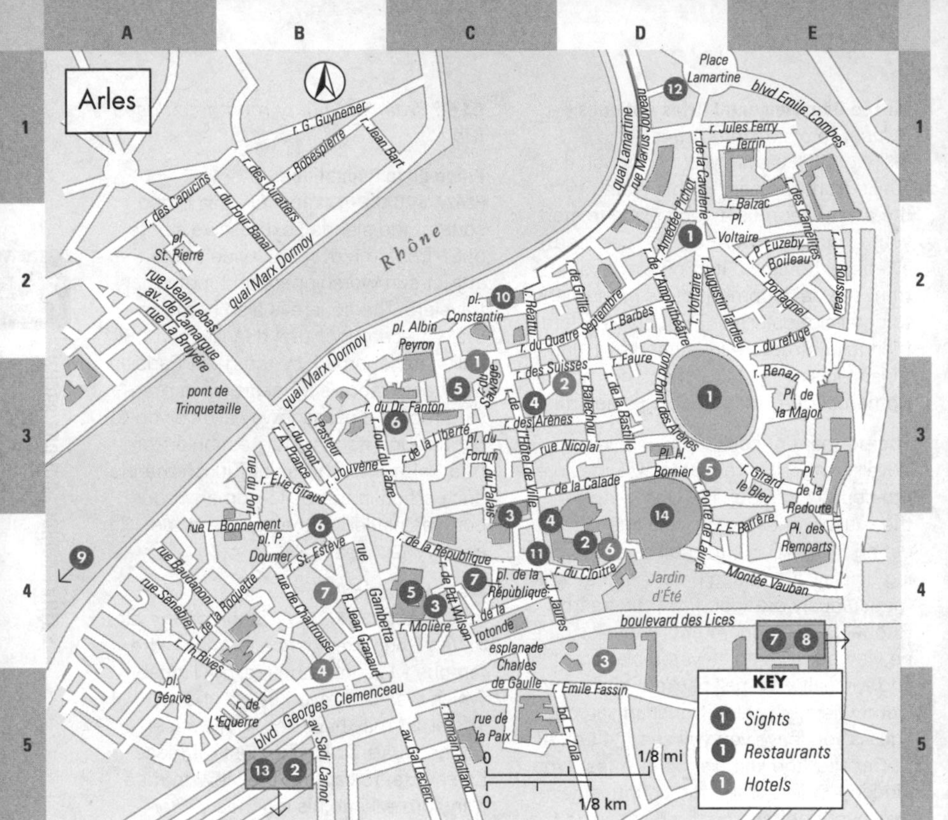

Sights

1 Arènes D3
2 Cloître St-Trophime..... D4
3 Cryptoportiques.......... C3
4 Église St-Trophime...... D4
5 Espace Van Gogh........ C4
6 Fondation Vincent Van Gogh........ C3
7 Les Alyscamps........... E4
8 Luma Arles E4
9 Musée Départemental Arles Antiques A4
10 Musée Réattu C2
11 Place de la République C4
12 Place Lamartine D1
13 Pont Van Gogh B5
14 Théâtre Antique......... D3

Restaurants

1 Inari D2
2 La Chassagnette......... B5
3 L'Affenage C4
4 La Gueule du Loup...... C3
5 Le Galoubet.............. C3
6 Le Gibolin B4
7 Le Greenstonome....... C4

Hotels

1 Hôtel d'Arlatan........... C2
2 Hôtel de La Muette..... D3
3 Hôtel Jules César....... D4
4 La Maison Molière B4
5 Le Calendal.............. D3
6 Le Cloître................. D4
7 L'Hôtel Particulier....... B4

Van Gogh in Arles and St-Rémy

It was the light that drew Vincent van Gogh to Arles. For a man raised under the iron-gray skies of the Netherlands and the city lights of Paris, Provence's clean, clear sun was a revelation. In his last years, he turned his frenzied efforts to capture the town's magic.

Arles, however, was not drawn to Van Gogh. Although it has since worked hard to make up for its misjudgment, Arles treated the artist badly during the time he passed here near the end of his life—a time when his creativity, productivity, and mental illness all reached a climax. It was 1888 when he settled in to work in Arles with an intensity and tempestuousness that first drew, then drove away, his companion Paul Gauguin, with whom he had dreamed of founding an artists' colony.

Frenziedly productive—he applied a pigment-loaded palette knife to some 200 canvases in 1888 alone—he nonetheless lived in intense isolation, counting his *sous*, and writing his visions in lengthy letters to his long-suffering, infinitely patient brother, Theo. Often drinking heavily, Vincent alienated his neighbors, goading them to action. In 1889, a petition circulated to have him evicted, a shock that left him less and less able to cope with life and led to his eventual self-commitment to an asylum in nearby St-Rémy. The houses he lived in are no longer standing, though many of his subjects remain as he saw them. The paintings he daubed and splashed with such passion have been auctioned off elsewhere.

Thus you have to go to Amsterdam or Paris to view Van Gogh's work. But with a little imagination, you can glean something of Van Gogh's Arles from a tour of the modern town. In fact, the city has provided helpful markers and a numbered itinerary to guide you between landmarks. You can stand on Place Lamartine, where his famous Maison Jaune stood until it was destroyed by World War II bombs. *Starry Night* may have been painted from the Quai du Rhône just off Place Lamartine, though another was completed at St-Rémy.

The Café La Nuit on Place Forum is an exact match for the terrace platform, scattered with tables and bathed in gaslight under the stars, from the painting *Terrasse de Café le Soir*; Gauguin and Van Gogh used to drink here. Both the Arènes and Les Alyscamps were featured in paintings, and the hospital where he went after he broke down and cut off his earlobe is now a kind of shrine, its garden reconstructed exactly as it figured in *Le Jardin de l'Hôtel-Dieu*.

About 25 km (15½ miles) away is St-Rémy-de-Provence, where Van Gogh retreated to the asylum St-Paul-de-Mausolée. Here he spent hours in silence, painting the cloisters. On his ventures into town, he painted the dappled lime trees at the intersection of Boulevard Mirabeau and Boulevard Gambetta. Between Arles and St-Rémy-de-Provence are the orchards whose spring blooms ignited his joyous explosions of yellow, green, and pink.

Théâtre Antique (*Ancient Theater*)
RUINS | **FAMILY** | Directly up Rue de la Calade from Place de la République, are these ruins of a theater built by the Romans under Augustus in the 1st century BC. It's here that the noted Venus of Arles statue, now in the Louvre, was dug up and identified. The theater was once an entertainment venue that held 10,000 people, and is now a pleasant, parklike retreat that's used as a site for the Festival d'Arles, in July and August, and for Les Recontres d'Arles (Photography Festival) from early July to mid-September. Only two columns of the amphitheater's stage walls, one row of arches, and vestiges of the original stone benches remain, as much of the theater's fine local stone was repurposed in early Christian churches. ✉ *Rue de la Calade, Arles* 🎫 *€10, includes admission to Arènes.*

Restaurants

Inari
$$ | **MODERN FRENCH** | Franco-Vietnamese chef Céline Pham, a talented veteran of top restaurants in Paris, headlines at this chic bistro set in a 13th-century chapel. This is a food lover's destination, not only for the seasonal dishes with subtle and surprising combinations but also for the excellent-value menus (three courses at lunch, €41; dinner, €55 or €85 with wine pairings). **Known for:** watch the chef work in the open kitchen; chic dining room; spacious terrace. 💲 *Average main: €20* ✉ *16 pl. Voltaire, Arles* ☎ *09–82–27–28–33* 🌐 *www.inari-arles.com/en* 🕒 *Closed Mon. and Tues. No lunch Wed.*

★ La Chassagnette
$$$$ | **FRENCH** | Sophisticated yet comfortable, this organic restaurant, 12 km (7½ miles) south of Arles at the entrance of the Camargue, has a fetching dining room that extends to an outdoor area with large, family-style picnic tables under a canopy and overlooking extensive gardens. The mix of modern and French-country dishes on master chef Armand Arnal's prix-fixe menus are made using ingredients grown right on the property. **Known for:** bucolic setting; outdoor dining; local, seasonal products. 💲 *Average main: €38* ✉ *Rte. du Sambuc, D36, Arles* ☎ *04–90–97–26–96* 🌐 *www.chassagnette.fr* 🕒 *Closed Tues., Wed., and Dec.–mid-Mar. No dinner Thurs., Sun., and Mon.*

L'Affenage
$$ | **FRENCH** | Locals come to this restaurant in a former fire-horse shed for Provençal hors d'oeuvres like fried eggplant, green tapenade, chickpeas in cumin, and a slab of ham carved off the bone, perhaps followed by roasted potatoes with lamb chops grilled in the great stone fireplace. Call at least a week in advance to reserve table in summer, when you can opt for just the first-course buffet—and go back for seconds or even thirds. **Known for:** generous portions of local fare; terrace dining; reservations needed in summer. 💲 *Average main: €19* ✉ *4 rue Molière, Arles* ☎ *04–90–96–07–67* 🕒 *Closed Sun.*

La Gueule du Loup
$$ | **FRENCH** | You reach your table through the kitchen, bustling with chopping, sizzling, and wafting scents, which is a nice introduction to what awaits. The cooking is serious, featuring Provençal specialties such as *rouget* (red mullet) with pureed potatoes or *caillette d'agneau* (lamb baked in herbs). **Known for:** rustic, stone-and-beam interior; best-ever crème brûlée; convivial atmosphere. 💲 *Average main: €22* ✉ *39 rue des Arènes, Arles* ☎ *04–90–96–96–69* 🌐 *www.restaurant-lagueuleduloup.fr* 🕒 *Closed Wed. and Thurs.*

★ Le Galoubet
$$ | **MODERN FRENCH** | Tucked away under a canopy of green, this cozy local favorite serves contemporary French fare far above the usual offerings. Relax in a vintage armchair while enjoying appetizers like creamy burrata cheese with perfectly

ripe heirloom tomatoes or grilled sardines with arugula and olives and entrées such as succulent guinea fowl or steak smothered in fresh morels with a side of golden frites. **Known for:** excellent seafood dishes; terrific natural wines; bistro vibe. *Average main: €21 18 rue du Dr. Fanton, Arles 04-90-93-18-11 Closed Sun. and Mon.*

Le Gibolin

$ | **MODERN FRENCH** | This classic wine bar is ever popular for its great location and reliably good French food. The menu features modern riffs on the classics—pigs' feet (and ears if you're lucky), ricotta-spinach dumplings with mushrooms spiked with pecorino cheese, or asparagus eggs Benedict—and the owners also have a tender spot for vegetarians. **Known for:** cozy atmosphere; sidewalk terrace; easy walk to sights (five-minute walk from the Fondation Vincent Van Gogh). *Average main: €16 13 rue des Porcelets, Arles 04-88-65-43-14 www.facebook.com/LeGibolinArles Closed Sun. and Mon. No lunch Tues.*

Le Greenstronome

$$$$ | **MODERN FRENCH** | Visionary Jean-Luc Rabanel is the culinary success story of the region—he was one of the first organic chefs in France to merit two Michelin stars and is renowned for the fresh, garden-inspired cuisine that he features in this stylish restaurant and cooking school. Menus are prix-fixe only, and the seven-dish tapas-style lunch (€65) and six-course "Emotion" dinner (€145) are unforgettable. **Known for:** dedication to local and organic cuisine; veggie-centric menu; sophisticated presentation and pairings. *Average main: €132 7 rue des Carmes, Arles 04-90-91-07-69 www.rabanel.com/le-greenstronome-restaurant.html Closed Mon. and Tues.*

Hotels

Hôtel de la Muette

$ | **HOTEL** | This prosaic Old Town option has 12th-century exposed stone walls, a 15th-century spiral staircase, weathered wood everywhere, and homey touches like cream-colored linens. **Pros:** good value; convenient to all landmarks; generous buffet breakfast included in price. **Cons:** some rooms can be noisy, especially in summer; Wi-Fi can be spotty; no elevator. *Rooms from: €100 15 rue des Suisses, Arles 04-90-96-15-39 www.hotel-muette.com Closed Jan. 18 rooms Free Breakfast.*

Hotel Jules César

$$$ | **HOTEL** | A 17th-century Carmelite convent provides an intriguing backdrop for fashion designer Christian Lacroix's *fantaisie* interiors, which feature ultra-modern color schemes, large (sometimes jarring) motifs, and furnishings in a jumble of periods and styles. **Pros:** central location; lovely spa and pool; beautiful gardens. **Cons:** indifferent staff; parking not included in price; mod-Baroque decor can be distracting. *Rooms from: €240 Bd. des Lices, Arles 04-90-52-52-52 www.hotel-julescesar.fr 52 rooms No Meals.*

★ **Hôtel L'Arlatan**

$$$ | **HOTEL** | Not only is this gem of a hotel ideally situated near the Fondation Vincent Van Gogh, but it's also set in a 15th-century stone house—once home to the counts of Arlatan—on the site of a 4th-century basilica whose excavated vestiges are visible through a glass floor in the lobby. **Pros:** whimsical decor with a cool history; lively atmosphere in the bar and restaurant; exceptional value. **Cons:** heated pool is small; rooms range dramatically in price; mad color schemes may prove distracting to some. *Rooms from: €240 26 rue du Sauvage, Arles 04-90-93-56-66 www.arlatan.com 45 rooms No Meals.*

La Maison Molière

$$$ | **B&B/INN** | Resident *chineur* (that's fancy for "antiques hunter") Michel Montagne decorated his 18th-century home in the heart of Arles with furniture and paintings from the 19th and 20th centuries, creating a setting so flawless that it feels like a stage and enabling you to relax in an arcaded courtyard, lounge in a library, or retire to a spacious and luxurious guest room. **Pros:** quiet and central; a little-known gem; breakfast and Wi-Fi included. **Cons:** on the expensive side; limited parking; can be hard to book in summer. *Rooms from: €230* *37 rue Molière, Arles* *06–87–73–39–59* *lamaisonmoliere.fr* *5 rooms* *Free Breakfast.*

Le Calendal

$$ | **HOTEL** | This hotel, in a prime Old Town location just steps from the Théâtre Antique, lacks nothing in the way of charm or service—indeed, it would be hard to find a more welcoming staff. **Pros:** extremely central location; some rooms have stunning views of the arena; discounted parking for guests. **Cons:** rooms are basic and can be dark; breakfasts plentiful but standard-issue (and an extra fee); strict no-food policy in rooms. *Rooms from: €175* *5 rue Porte de Laure, Arles* *04–90–96–11–89* *www.lecalendal.com* *38 rooms* *No Meals.*

Le Cloître

$$ | **HOTEL** | Tucked away on a pretty Old Town side street, this intimate, vine-clad hotel received a stylish makeover by Parisian interiors star India Mahdavi, who preserved the elegant bones of the grand medieval building—once the home for the provost of the Cloisters—but added chic touches, like vividly colored fabrics and rattan or burnished-wood furniture, that contrast with the limestone walls and other original details (some rooms have arches or a fireplace). **Pros:** lovely architecture enhanced by clever use of color; top-notch service; excellent location. **Cons:** no elevator or air-conditioning; dinner only on weekends; no cars permitted in this part of town. *Rooms from: €199* *18 rue du Cloître, Arles* *04–90–96–29–50* *www.lecloitre.com* *19 rooms* *No Meals.*

★ **L'Hôtel Particulier**

$$$$ | **HOTEL** | Once owned by the Baron de Chartrouse, this extraordinary 18th-century *hôtel particulier* is delightfully intimate and elegant, decorated with gold-framed mirrors, white-brocade chairs, marble writing desks, artfully hung curtains, and hand-painted wallpaper. **Pros:** combines historical style with high-tech conveniences; quiet and secluded; only a five-minute walk to town center. **Cons:** nonrefundable deposit required when booking; small swimming pool; expensive breakfast (€26). *Rooms from: €415* *4 rue de la Monnaie, Arles* *04–90–52–51–40* *www.hotel-particulier.com* *Closed Jan.–mid-Mar.* *18 rooms* *No Meals.*

Nightlife

Patio de Camargue

BARS | Although Arles seems like one big sidewalk café in warm weather, the best place to drink is at the hip bar-restaurant Patio de Camargue, with its great location on the banks of the Rhône. It serves terrific tapas, and you can hear guitar music and watch traditional dance from Chico and Los Gypsies, led by a founding member of the Gypsy Kings. Reservations are a good idea in high season. *49 ch. de Barriol, Arles* *04–90–49–51–76* *patiodecamargue.com.*

Performing Arts

Association du Méjan

ARTS CENTERS | Housed in the beautiful Chapelle St-Martin du Méjan, this arts organization hosts a year-round program of classical and sacred music; a revolving series of exhibitions featuring painting, sculpture, and photography; and the

One of the centers of Provençal folklore, Arles is host to a bevy of parades featuring locals dressed in regional costume.

superb Arles Jazz Festival, held every year in May. ✉ *Pl. Nina Berberova, Arles* ☎ *04–90–49–56–78* 🌐 *www.lemejan.com.*

Cinémas Actes Sud

FILM | Run by a large publishing house, this arts complex has a first-rate movie theater. ✉ *Pl. Nina Berberova, Arles* ☎ *04–90–99–53–52* 🌐 *www.cinemas-actes-sud.fr.*

Shopping

Despite being chic and popular, Arles doesn't have the rows of designer shops found in Aix-en-Provence and St-Rémy. Its stores remain small and eccentric and contain an overwhelming variety of Provençal goods. The city's colorful market, with produce, regional products, clothes, fabrics, wallets, frying pans, and other miscellaneous items, takes place every Saturday morning along Boulevard des Lices, which flows into Boulevard Clemenceau.

Christian Lacroix

JEWELRY & WATCHES | This shop has picks for women—bold jewelry, exuberant scarves, and colorful sunglasses (Jackie O herself once bought a pair here)—as well as a selection of scented candles, stationery, and glassware in a range of gorgeous jewel tones. There are also some vintage items. ✉ *52 rue de la République, Arles* ☎ *04–90–96–11–16* 🌐 *www.christian-lacroix.com.*

★ La Parfumerie Arlésienne

PERFUME | Maire Duchêne, an independent perfumer trained in Grasse, the world capital of perfumes, dreamed of creating fragrances that would capture the essence of Arles and its beautiful surroundings. Her dream has been realized in this jewel of a boutique where her five sensuous perfumes evoke the spirit of Arles in a mix of citrus and pink peppercorn, the Camargue in notes of vetiver and amber, and Les Baux in lemon and white flowers. Her sublime smelling soaps and candles make for heady mementos of Provence. ✉ *5 rue du*

Palais, Arles ☎ 04–90–97–02–07 🌐 www.la-parfumerie-arlesienne.com.

Le Château du Bois
COSMETICS | This boutique specializes in a huge range of pure, plant-based cosmetics from Le Château du Bois, one of Provence's oldest and most venerable producers of fine lavender oil. The range includes face creams, hand and body lotions, toning gels, massage oil, bath milk, hydrosols, and much more. ✉ *42 rue de la République, Arles ☎ 04–90–52–01–35 🌐 www.lavandeandco.fr.*

L'Occitane
COSMETICS | The products of this world-renowned fragrance and skin care company are still made in nearby Manosque using regional ingredients. Make sure to sniff Jasmine Immortelle Neroli, the newest women's fragrance, and Arlésienne, a floral tribute to the women of the South of France. ✉ *58 rue de la République, Arles ☎ 04–90–96–93–62 🌐 www.loccitane.com.*

Savonnerie Marius Fabre
COSMETICS | The soaps, cosmetics, and products for the home sold here are of exceptional artisanal quality. Marius Fabre is one of only six soap makers in France that still produce "le vrai" savon de Marseille the traditional way: cooked in giant vats with at least 72% pure olive oil, no fragrances (or only natural essential oils added later), and air-aged on wooden slats. ✉ *11 rue du Palais, Arles ☎ 04–12–04–62–75 🌐 www.marius-fabre.com.*

Souleiado
MIXED CLOTHING | This well-stocked boutique has a good selection of clothing for men and women, as well as table linens and fabrics. ✉ *10 bd. des Lices, Arles ☎ 04–90–18–25–91 🌐 www.souleiado.com/en/boutiques.*

Abbaye de Montmajour

6 km (4 miles) north of Arles.

Once the spiritual center of the region and a major 12th-century pilgrimage site (it contained a small relic of the true cross), the haunting ruins of the Abbaye de Montmajour still dominate this romantic windswept landscape.

GETTING HERE AND AROUND

From Arles by car, take the D17 in the direction of Fontvieille, and follow the signs to the Abbaye. Buses from Arles run 10 times per day on weekdays and twice per day on weekends (€2).

Sights

★ Abbaye de Montmajour
RELIGIOUS BUILDING | This magnificent Romanesque abbey looming over the marshlands north of Arles stands in partial ruin. Founded in the 10th century by a handful of Benedictine monks, the abbey grew according to an ambitious plan of church, crypt, and cloister and, under the management of worldly lay monks in the 17th century, became more sumptuous. When the Catholic church ejected those monks, they sacked the place, and what remained was eventually sold off as scrap. A 19th-century medieval revival spurred a partial restoration, but portions are still in ruins; what remains is a spare and beautiful piece of Romanesque architecture.

The cloister rivals that of St-Trophime in Arles for its balance, elegance, and air of mystical peace. Van Gogh, drawn to isolation, came often to the abbey to reflect, but the strong mistral winds kept him from painting here. The interior, renovated by architect Rudy Ricciotti, is used for world-class contemporary art exhibitions. ✉ *Rte. de Fontvieille, Arles ☎ 04–90–54–64–17 🌐 www.abbaye-montmajour.fr 🎫 €6 🕓 Closed Mon. Oct.–Mar.*

Tarascon

18 km (11 miles) north of Arles; 16 km (10 miles) west of St-Rémy.

Tarascon's claim to fame is the mythical Tarasque, a monster said to emerge from the Rhône to gobble up children and cattle. Luckily, St. Martha (Ste-Marthe), who washed up at Stes-Maries-de-la-Mer, tamed the beast with a sprinkle of holy water, after which the natives slashed it to pieces.

This dramatic event is celebrated on the last weekend in June with a parade and was immortalized by Alphonse Daudet, who lived in nearby Fontvieille, in his tales of a folk hero known to all French schoolchildren as *Tartarin de Tarascon.* Unfortunately, a saint has not yet been born who can vanquish the fumes that emanate from Tarascon's enormous paper mill.

GETTING HERE AND AROUND

By car, take the D999 (which turns into the D99) from Nîmes or the N570 from Arles. Local trains also stop at Tarascon on the Avignon–Centre–Arles line. Several buses run between Arles and Tarascon (three buses Monday–Saturday, €2.80, 30 minutes). There are also buses from Nîmes (€1.50), although this is a longer journey (1¼ hours).

VISITOR INFORMATION

CONTACTS Tarascon Tourist Office. ✉ *62 rue des Halles, Tarascon* ☎ *04–90–91–03–52* 🌐 *www.tarascon.org.*

Sights

Château

CASTLE/PALACE | **FAMILY** | Despite Tarascon's modern-day drawbacks, with the walls of its formidable château plunging straight into the roaring Rhône, this ancient city on the river presents a daunting challenge to Beaucaire, its traditional enemy across the water. Begun in the 15th century by the noble Anjou family on the site of a Roman *castellum,* the castle grew through the generations into a splendid structure, crowned with both round and square towers and elegantly furnished. René the Good (1409–80) held court here, entertaining luminaries of the age.

The castle owes its superb preservation to its use, through the ensuing centuries, as a prison. It first served as such in the 17th century, and it released its last prisoner in 1926. Complete with a moat, a drawbridge, and a lovely faceted spiral staircase, it retains its beautiful decorative Renaissance stonework and original cross-mullioned windows. ✉ *Bd. du Roi René, Tarascon* ☎ *04–90–91–01–93* 🌐 *chateau.tarascon.fr* 🎫 *€8* 🕒 *Closed Mon. Oct.–Mar.*

Hotels

★ Mas de Prêcheurs

$$$ | **HOUSE** | This grand, 17th-century farmstead in the shadow of the Alpilles was once populated by Dominican monks (hence the name "farmhouse of the preachers") and is now a serene and beautiful country-house hotel, where you're encouraged to treat the place as your own—perhaps wandering the lovely grounds, walking along the miles of trails, taking a dip in the pool, or lounging in chairs amid the olive groves. **Pros:** huge rooms; amazing breakfasts; close to major sights. **Cons:** a bit bobo; 17th-century stairs are precarious; rusticity isn't for everyone (though we love it). $ *Rooms from: €228* ✉ *1136 chemin de la Chapelle Saint Victor, Tarascon* ☎ *09–78–07–00–05* 🌐 *www.masdesprecheurs.com* 🕒 *Closed Dec.–Mar.* *5 rooms* *Free Breakfast.*

Fontvieille

19 km (12 miles) northeast of Arles; 20 km (12½ miles) southeast of Tarascon.

The village of Fontvieille (pronounced "fohn-*vyay*-uh"), set among the limestone hills, is best known as the home of 19th-century writer Alphonse Daudet.

GETTING HERE AND AROUND

The nearest train station is in Arles, and from there several buses run daily to Fontvieille. The direct trip takes about 30 minutes and costs €1.50 each way. By car, take the A54 to RN113, then the RN568 in the direction of Fontvieille.

 Sights

Château de Montauban

CASTLE/PALACE | FAMILY | Summering in the Château de Montauban brought French journalist and author Alphonse Daudet a peace he missed in literary Paris. Daudet frequently climbed the windswept, pine-studded hilltop to the rustic old windmill that ground the local grain from 1814 to 1915—the inspiration for his famous folkloric short stories *Lettres de Mon Moulin.* The windmill is now closed to the public, but the graceful château houses a museum devoted to Daudet's writings, and you can freely stroll the grounds to enjoy the peace and sweeping views of the Rhône valley and the Alpilles that so inspired him. ✉ *Ch. Montauban, Fontvieille* ☎ *04–90–54–75–12* 🌐 *www.alpillesenprovence.com/fiches/chateau-de-montauban* 🎫 *€5* ⏲ *Closed Oct.–Mar.*

Les Baux-de-Provence

9 km (5½ miles) east of Fontvieille; 19 km (12 miles) northeast of Arles.

When you first search the craggy hilltops for signs of Les Baux-de-Provence (pronounced "*boh*"), you might find it hard to distinguish between bedrock and building, so naturally does the ragged skyline of towers blend into the sawtooth jags of stone. It was from here that the lords of Baux ruled throughout the 11th and 12th centuries over some 80 towns and villages—one of the largest fiefdoms in the south. Their virtually unchallenged power led to the flourishing of a rich medieval culture: courtly love, troubadour songs, and knightly gallantry. By the 13th century, however, the lords of Baux had fallen from power, and their stronghold was destroyed.

Today Les Baux offers two faces to the world: the ghostly ruins of its fortress, once referred to as the *ville morte* (dead town), and its beautifully preserved Renaissance village. As dramatic in its perched isolation as Mont-St-Michel in Brittany and St-Paul-de-Vence, this tiny château-village is one of the most visited sites in France, yet it has escaped most of the usual tourist trappings.

Lovely 16th-century stone houses (even their window frames still intact) shelter the elegant shops, cafés, and galleries that line its car-free main street, which is redolent of the smell of lavender-scented souvenirs. But don't deprive yourself for fear of crowds: stay late in the day, after the tour buses leave, or spend the night in one of the two splendid domaine hotels. You could also experience the spectacular blend of medieval color and natural beauty on a more peaceful, off-season visit.

GETTING HERE AND AROUND

The easiest way to get to Les Baux is by car. Take the A7 until you reach Exit 25, then the D99 between Tarascon and Cavaillon. Les Baux is 8 km (5 miles) south of St-Rémy by the D5 and the D27. Otherwise, a bus runs between Arles and Les Baux (summer only, €2.30). Local trains stop at Tarascon; from here, in summer, you can take a bus both to St-Rémy and Les Baux (20 minutes, €1).

Rising up from a calcareous rock valley, the Château des Baux is the most extraordinary landmark of the "dead city" of Les-Baux-de-Provence.

VISITOR INFORMATION

CONTACTS Les Baux-de-Provence Tourist Office. ✉ *Maison du Roy, Rue Porte Mage, Les Baux-de-Provence* ☎ *04–90–54–34–39* 🌐 *www.lesbauxdeprovence.com.*

Sights

★ Carrières des Lumières

ARTS CENTER | FAMILY | This vast old limestone quarry has 66-foot-high stone walls that make a dramatic setting for a multimedia show in which thousands of images are projected onto the walls. Exhibitions change yearly, but recent showings have showcased the life and work of Van Gogh, Picasso, Dali, and Cézanne. ✉ *Rtes. des Carrières, Les Baux-de-Provence* ☎ *04–90–49–20–02* 🌐 *www.carrieres-lumieres.com* 🎫 *From €14.*

Château des Baux

RUINS | FAMILY | A 17-acre cliff-top sprawl of ruins is contained beneath the Château des Baux. At the entrance, the Tour du Brau has a small collection of relics and models, as well as a music-and-slideshow called *Van Gogh, Gauguin, Cézanne au Pays de l'Olivier,* which features artwork depicting olive orchards in their infinite variety. From April through September there are fascinating medieval events: people dressed up in authentic costumes and displays of medieval crafts. The exit gives access to the wide and varied grounds, where the tiny Chapelle St-Blaise and towers mingle with skeletal ruins. ✉ *Rue du Trencat, Les Baux-de-Provence* ☎ *04–90–49–20–02* 🌐 *www.chateau-baux-provence.com* 🎫 *From €8.*

Hôtel de Manville

GOVERNMENT BUILDING | Vestiges of the Renaissance remain in Les Baux, including the pretty Hôtel de Manville, built at the end of the 16th century by a wealthy Protestant family. Step into its inner court to admire the mullioned windows, stained glass, and vaulted arcades. Today it serves as the *mairie* (town hall). Up and across the street, the striking remains of the 16th-century Protestant temple still bear a quote from Jean Calvin: "*post tenebras lux*" ("after the shadows, light"). ✉ *Grand rue Frédéric Mistral, Les Baux-de-Provence* ☎ *04–90–54–34–03.*

Musée Yves Brayer (*Yves Brayer Museum*)

ART MUSEUM | The Hôtel de Porcelet, which dates from the 16th century, contains this museum with works by the local 20th-century artist Yves Brayer. Figurative and accessible to the point of näiveté, his paintings highlight Italy, Spain, and even Asia, but demonstrate, most of all, his love of Provence. His grave is in the château cemetery. The house at No. 4 on Place de l'Église is also decorated with frescoes by the artist. ✉ *Pl. François Hérain, Les Baux-de-Provence* ☎ *04–90–54–34–39* 🌐 *www.yvesbrayer.com* 🎫 *€8* 🕒 *Closed Jan. and Feb. and Tues. Oct.–Apr.*

Restaurants

★ Le Bistrot du Paradou

$$$ | **FRENCH** | **FAMILY** | This spot has seen its share of famous diners, from French movie stars to politicians, but you'd never know it from the friendly, laid-back atmosphere cultivated by the longtime chef and his loyal staff who loudly greet their friends—meaning everyone. From the apéritif until the bill comes (which could be a while, as you'll want to take your time here), you're drawn into the rhythm of Provençal bistro dining, with a bottle of the house red wine ready at your table and a stellar cheese platter all to yourself. **Known for:** exceptional atmosphere; high-quality ingredients; set menus with choice between two starters, two mains, and six desserts. [$] *Average main: €28* ✉ *57 av. de la Vallée des Baux, Les Baux-de-Provence* ☎ *04–90–54–32–70* 🕒 *Closed Sun. and Mon.*

★ Les Baux Jus

$$ | **VEGETARIAN** | Who would have thought that you could find a 100% organic, raw, gluten-free, and vegan restaurant of this caliber in the heart of meat-centric Provence? It's foodie heaven to those with restricted diets, offering a tantalizing range of cold-pressed juices, salads, pastries, and smoothies so good that even carnivores will appreciate them. **Known for:** vegan and gluten-free dishes; 100% organic ingredients; friendly atmosphere. [$] *Average main: €20* ✉ *Rue de la Calade, Les Baux-de-Provence* ☎ *09–86–39–84–96* 🌐 *www.facebook.com/lesbauxjus* 🕒 *Closed Tues.*

★ L'Oustau de Baumanière

$$$$ | **FRENCH** | Year after year, diners return to this temple to haute cuisine for updated versions of dishes they might have first tried three decades ago. This was the first establishment outside of the Riviera to earn three Michelin stars, and, under legendary chef Raymond Thuillier, it rose from being the dining room of a small country inn to a restaurant whose guest list has included leading artists, movie stars, and heads of state (Picasso, Queen Elizabeth, Churchill, and Harry Truman all dined here). **Known for:** gorgeous setting in a five-star country hotel; refined Provençal cuisine made with ingredients from the hotel garden; Provence's most respected wine list with options from the hotel domaine. [$] *Average main: €85* ✉ *Mas de Baumanière, Les Baux-de-Provence* ☎ *04–90–54–33–07* 🌐 *www.baumaniere.com/en* 🕒 *Closed Thurs.*

Hotels

★ Baumanière Les Baux-de-Provence

$$$$ | **HOTEL** | Just outside the village, amid terraces and formal gardens sheltered by rocky cliffs, the five buildings of this fabled hotel contain guest rooms that are breezy, private, and chic. **Pros:** two of the great restaurants of Provence; full-service spa; three pools. **Cons:** a bit of a snobby atmosphere; service can be hit-or-miss; expensive. [$] *Rooms from: €380* ✉ *Val d'Enfer, Les Baux-de-Provence*

☎ *04–90–54–33–07* 🌐 *www.baumaniere.com/en* ⏲ *Closed Mon. and Tues. early Jan.–early Mar.* 🛏 *54 rooms* 🍽 *No Meals.*

★ Domaine de Manville

$$$$ | **HOTEL** | **FAMILY** | With sumptuous decor, an idyllic setting amid olive groves and gardens, impeccable service, a spa, an 18-hole golf course, a pool, and a choice of rooms and suites or villas, the Domaine de Manville is as ideal for a romantic getaway as it is for a family retreat. **Pros:** full-service spa; superb gastronomic restaurant; well-equipped golf center and boutique. **Cons:** expensive; not lacking in snob appeal; some rooms need touching up. 💲 *Rooms from: €360* ✉ *Les Baux-de-Provence* ☎ *04–90–54–40–20* 🌐 *www.domainedemanville.fr* 🛏 *38 units* 🍽 *No Meals.*

La Benvengudo

$$$ | **HOTEL** | **FAMILY** | Featuring interior details like heavy old beams, a stone fireplace, and terra-cotta tiles, this graceful, shuttered, family-owned mas, set on manicured grounds dotted with tall pines, feels centuries old, but it was built to look that way some 30 years ago. **Pros:** quiet and secluded; lovely pool; excellent on-site restaurant. **Cons:** set on a main road; strict dining hours observed; need to reserve meals in advance in high season to be sure to get a table. 💲 *Rooms from: €270* ✉ *1800 rte. d'Arles, Les Baux-de-Provence* ☎ *04–90–54–32–54* 🌐 *www.benvengudo.com* ⏲ *Closed Nov.–Mar.* 🛏 *28 units* 🍽 *No Meals.*

Shopping

★ Mas de la Dame

WINE/SPIRITS | This fourth-generation winemaker's organic reds, whites, and rosés are served in gastronomic restaurants countrywide, so what better place to taste and buy these award-winning wines than at the source? How is it that they're allowed to reproduce a Van Gogh painting on their labels? Well, because the family mas is featured in the work! ✉ *Chemin Départemental 5, Les Baux-de-Provence* ☎ *04–90–54–32–24* 🌐 *masdeladame.com.*

★ Moulin Castelas

FOOD | Here you can purchase top-quality, AOC (controlled origin) olive oils and learn how they're made, from picking and pressing to blending and bottling. Free tours and tastings (in English) demonstrate why these regional oils—most made from green olives and some made from fermented black olives—end up on tables in some of the best restaurants in France. ✉ *Mas de l'Olivier, Les Baux-de-Provence* ☎ *04–90–54–50–86* 🌐 *www.castelas.com.*

St-Rémy-de-Provence

11 km (7 miles) northeast of Les Baux; 25 km (15½ miles) northeast of Arles; 24 km (15 miles) south of Avignon.

There are other towns as pretty as St-Rémy-de-Provence, and many also have dramatic or picturesque settings, ancient ruins, and/or authentic village life. So what makes this market town in the heart of the Alpilles a standout? It's the steady infusion of style, art, and imagination—all brought by people with a respect for and love of traditional Provençal ways.

Here, more than anywhere, you can meditate quietly on antiquity; browse aromatic markets with a basket in hand; peer down the very row of plane trees you remember from a Van Gogh painting; and enjoy urbane galleries, cosmopolitan boutiques, and specialty food shops. There are lots of chic restaurants, mas, and even châteaux, and almond and olive groves conceal dozens of stone-and-terra-cotta *gîtes,* many with pools.

The village of Glanum was established by an indigenous Celtic-Ligurian people who worshipped the god Glan. In the 2nd and 3rd centuries BC, it was adopted by the Greeks of Marseille, who brought in sophisticated building techniques. Rome moved in to help ward off Hannibal, and, by the 1st century BC, Caesar had taken full control. The Romans eventually fell, but the community of St-Rémy that was developed beside their ruins became an important market town. Wealthy families built fine *hôtels* (mansions) in its center—among them the de Sades, whose distant black-sheep relation held forth in the Lubéron at Lacoste.

Another famous native son was the eccentric doctor, scholar, and astrologer Michel Nostradamus (1503–66), who is credited by some with having predicted many events of the modern age. Perhaps the best known of St-Rémy's residents, though, was the ill-fated Vincent van Gogh. Shipped unceremoniously out of Arles at the height of his madness (and creativity), he had himself committed to the asylum St-Paul-de-Mausolé and wandered through the ruins of Glanum during the last year of his life.

GETTING HERE AND AROUND

Like Les Baux-de-Provence, the easiest way to get to St-Rémy is by car. Take the A7 until you reach Exit 25. Follow the D99 between Tarascon and Cavaillon and then take the D5 in the direction of St-Rémy. In summer, though, there is an Arles–St-Rémy–Les Baux bus service (€2.30, Monday–Saturday). Local trains stop at nearby Tarascon, and from there you can take a bus to St-Rémy (€1, 20 minutes).

VISITOR INFORMATION

CONTACTS St-Rémy Tourist Office. ✉ *Pl. Jean-Jaurès, St-Rémy-de-Provence* ☎ *04–90–92–05–22* 🌐 *www.alpillesen-provence.com.*

Sights

Collégiale St-Martin

CHURCH | St-Rémy is wrapped by a lively commercial boulevard, lined with shops and cafés and anchored by its 19th-century church Collégiale St-Martin. Step inside—if the main door is locked, the side door is always open—to see the magnificent 5,000-pipe modern organ, one of the loveliest in Europe. Rebuilt to 18th-century specifications in the early 1980s, it has the flexibility to interpret new and old music with pure French panache; you can listen for free on weekends mid-April–September. ✉ *Pl. de la République, St-Rémy-de-Provence* 🎫 *Free.*

Glanum

RUINS | **FAMILY** | A slick visitor center prepares you for entry into the ancient village of Glanum, with scale models of the site in its various heydays. A good map and an English brochure guide you stone by stone through the maze of foundations, walls, towers, and columns that spread across a broad field; helpfully, Greek sites are denoted by numbers, Roman ones by letters. Note that Glanum is across the street from Les Antiques and set back from the D5, and the only parking is in a dusty roadside lot on the D5 south of town (in the direction of Les Baux). In addition, hours vary, so check ahead. ✉ *Rte. des Baux de Provence, off D5, direction Les Baux, St-Rémy-de-Provence* ☎ *04–90–92–23–79* 🌐 *www.site-glanum.fr* 🎫 *€8* ⏲ *Closed Mon. Oct.–Mar.*

Hôtel de Sade

HISTORIC HOME | Make your way to the Hôtel de Sade, a 15th- and 16th-century private manor now housing the treasures unearthed from the ruins of Glanum. The de Sade family built the house around remains of 4th-century baths and a 5th-century baptistery, now nestled in its courtyard. ✉ *Rue du*

Did You Know?

Although St-Rémy-de-Provence has been gentrified through and through, it has also stayed true to its Provençal roots.

Parage, St-Rémy-de-Provence ☎ *04–90–92–64–04* 🌐 *www.hotel-de-sade.fr* 🎫 *€4* ⏲ *Closed mid-Sept.–May.*

Les Antiques

RUINS | **FAMILY** | Two of the most miraculously preserved classical monuments in France are simply called Les Antiques. Dating from 30 BC, the Mausolée (Mausoleum), a wedding-cake stack of arches and columns, lacks nothing but a finial on top and is dedicated to a Julian, probably Caesar Augustus. A few yards away stands the Arc Triomphal, dating from AD 20. A lovely spot for a stroll and within easy walking distance from the city center, the site is open during the day and at night—when it's handsomely illuminated. ✉ *Av. Vincent Van Gogh, St-Rémy-de-Provence* 🎫 *Free.*

Musée Estrine Présence Van Gogh

ART MUSEUM | The 18th-century Hôtel Estrine now houses this museum, which contains many reproductions of Van Gogh's work (along with letters to his brother, Theo) and hosts exhibitions of contemporary art, much of it inspired by Vincent. It also has a permanent collection dedicated to the father of Cubism, Albert Gleizes, who lived in St-Rémy for the last 15 years of his life. ✉ *Hôtel Estrine, 8 rue Lucien Estrine, St-Rémy-de-Provence* ☎ *04–90–92–34–72* 🌐 *musee-estrine.fr* 🎫 *€7* ⏲ *Closed Mon.*

St-Paul-de-Mausolé

HOSPITAL | This is the isolated asylum where Van Gogh spent the last year of his life (1889–90). Enter quietly: the hospital shelters psychiatric patients to this day, all of them women. You're free to walk up the beautifully manicured garden path to the church and its jewel-box Romanesque cloister, where the artist found womblike peace. ✉ *Chemin St-Paul, St-Rémy-de-Provence* ☎ *04–90–92–77–00* 🌐 *www.saintpauldemausole.fr* 🎫 *€7* ⏲ *Closed Jan.*

Vieille Ville

NEIGHBORHOOD | **FAMILY** | Within St-Rémy's fast-moving traffic loop, a labyrinth of narrow streets leads you away from the action and into the slow-moving inner sanctum of the Vieille Ville. Here trendy, high-end shops mingle pleasantly with local life, and the buildings, if gentrified, blend in unobtrusively. ✉ *St-Rémy-de-Provence.*

Restaurants

★ Chez Tata Simone

$$ | **FRENCH** | **FAMILY** | Set in an 18th-century Provençal mas once owned by the *grand-mère* of one of the owners, this countrified restaurant is a short drive outside the city but well worth the effort. Sit inside at wooden tables or out under towering plane trees to enjoy delicious dishes made with locally sourced ingredients that mix classic recipes (yes, from Tata Simone) with modern touches. **Known for:** country atmosphere; welcoming service; hearty home-cooked dishes. 💲 *Average main: €18* ✉ *Chemin du Mas de Jacquet* ☎ *04–90–99–65–12* 🌐 *chez-tata-simone.business.site* ⏲ *Closed Mon. and Tues. No lunch Wed.–Sat. No dinner Sun.*

L'Aile ou la Cuisse

$$$ | **BISTRO** | A popular place for lunch or dinner, this modern bistro and terrace in the heart of the Vieille Ville draws a lively mix of locals, expats, and tourists looking for authentic market-driven meals. A small but satisfying menu is generously laced with local delicacies—savory ragoût of wild boar, cod with puréed local vegetables and tapenade-laden croutons, and poached-egg cocotte with foie gras cream and turmeric-balsamic toast. **Known for:** long wine list with local options; classic French bistro cuisine; fantastic desserts. 💲 *Average main: €28* ✉ *34 bd. Mirabeau, St-Rémy-de-Provence* ☎ *04–32–62–00–25* 🌐 *www.laile-ou-la-cuisse-restaurant-saint-remy-de-provence.com* ⏲ *Closed Sun. and Mon.*

Olga by le Bistrot Découverte

$$$ | **BISTRO** | Claude and Dana Douard collaborated with some of the greatest chefs of our time before getting away from the big city lights to open this bistro–wine bar hot spot in the center of St-Rémy. The wine selection is magnificent, and so is the simple food—try the grilled sea bass with chorizo, mashed potatoes, and seasonal vegetables or the grilled Mont Ventoux spiced pork. **Known for:** emphasis on top-notch local ingredients; vegetarian-friendly options; terrace dining. *Average main: €25 ✉ 19 bd. Victor Hugo, St-Rémy-de-Provence ☎ 04–90–92–34–49 🌐 www.bistrotdecouverte.fr.*

★ Restaurant Fanny Rey et Jonathan Wahid

$$$$ | **FRENCH** | Named for its illustrious chef and pastry chef, the restaurant of the L'Auberge de Saint-Remy hotel draws foodies from near and far. Inventive, earthy, and refined, Rey's cuisine doesn't so much redefine Provençal cooking as expand it. **Known for:** refined and healthy cuisine; famous chef and pastry chef; glassed-in kitchen so you can watch the culinary team at work. *Average main: €55 ✉ 12 bd. Mirabeau, St-Rémy-de-Provence ☎ 04–90–92–15–33 🌐 www.aubergesaintremy.com ⏲ Closed Mon. No dinner Sun.*

 Hotels

Château de Roussan

$$$ | **B&B/INN** | Philippe Roussel, a descendant of the 17th-century owners, has filled his château with lovingly polished antique family furniture, buffed the red clay floors to their original shine, and ensured that guest rooms are light and airy and bathrooms are equipped with all the modern trinkets. **Pros:** eager-to-please, house-proud staff are happy to recount the hotel's history; rooms are very quiet; great restaurant. **Cons:** some rooms are small; elevator doesn't provide access to all rooms; on the pricier side. *Rooms from: €300 ✉ Rte. de Tarascon, D99, St-Rémy-de-Provence ☎ 04–90–90–79–00 🌐 chateauderoussan.com 20 rooms Free Breakfast.*

★ Château des Alpilles

$$$$ | **HOTEL** | Reached via a lane lined with majestic plane trees and set on 8 acres of luxuriant parkland, this gracious five-star manor (it's not exactly a château) dates from the Middle Ages and is one of St-Rémy's dreamiest spots—and that's saying a lot in this château-saturated territory. **Pros:** service that anticipates your every need; top-notch—and reasonably priced—on-site dining; spectacular country grounds only a five-minute drive from St-Rémy. **Cons:** expensive; not a lot to do after dark; if you prefer contemporary design, it isn't for you. *Rooms from: €389 ✉ Rte. de Rougadou, St-Rémy-de-Provence ☎ 04–90–92–03–33 🌐 www.chateaudesalpilles.com ⏲ Closed Jan.–mid-Mar. 21 rooms No Meals.*

★ Hotel de Tourrel

$$$ | **HOTEL** | This hotel, set in three 17th-century buildings and featuring a fabulous rooftop pool and lounge, is a model of contemporary refinement, with bright, spacious suites that have soaring ceilings, tasteful artwork, ample marble baths, and gorgeous color palettes that offset the building's creamy stone. **Pros:** St-Rémy's most beautiful hotel; Michelin-star dining and delicious breakfasts; in the center of town. **Cons:** not cheap; breakfast not included in price; books up quickly. *Rooms from: €350 ✉ 5 rue Carnot, St-Rémy-de-Provence ☎ 04–84–35–07–20 🌐 www.detourrel.com 9 rooms No Meals.*

Shopping

Every Wednesday morning, St-Rémy hosts one of the most popular and picturesque markets in Provence, during which Place de la République and narrow Vieille Ville streets overflow with herbs and spices, olive oil by the vat, and tapenade by the scoop, as well as fabrics and *brocante* (collectibles). There's a smaller version on Saturday morning.

Calanquet

FOOD | For five generations, this family-run outfit has produced some of the country's finest olive oils. You can buy several varieties at the centrally located boutique—which also has a tantalizing array of tapenades, sauces, condiments, and jams—or visit the mill a mile out of town to see firsthand how the oil is made. ✉ *8 rue de la Commune, St-Rémy-de-Provence* ☎ *04–32–26–20–90* 🌐 *www.moulinducalanquet.fr.*

Christallerie Alban Gaillard

GLASSWARE | Colorful, whimsical, elegant—the sculptural handblown glass creations sold here range from exquisite perfume flacons and decorative paperweights to everything you need to impress at the dining table. ✉ *1405 rte. de Maillane, St-Rémy-de-Provence* ☎ *04–32–60–10–28* 🌐 *www.cristallerie-dart.com.*

★ Florame

COSMETICS | Here you can stock up on fine soap, shampoo, body lotion, and other beauty products—all made using top-quality organic essential oils distilled in Provence. ✉ *6 av. de la Résistance* ☎ *04–32–60–05–18* 🌐 *fr.florame.com.*

Joël Durand Chocolatier

CHOCOLATE | FAMILY | Although he's known for his creamy ganaches, Joël Durand also offers a range of gourmet chocolates, nut creams, and toffees, as well as marmalades made in Provence from tree-ripened fruit. ✉ *3 bd. Victor Hugo, St-Rémy-de-Provence* ☎ *04–90–92–38–25* 🌐 *www.joeldurand-chocolatier.fr.*

★ Lilamand Confiseur

FOOD | FAMILY | This *confiseur* dates from 1866 and is in its fifth generation of family ownership on the same St-Rémy premises. It makes the famous Provençal *calisson,* an almond-shape marzipan confection, as well as a gorgeous array of candied fruits—from cherries and strawberries to kiwis and even whole pumpkins—using a recipe credited to Nostradamus (a native son of St-Rémy). There are also fruit syrups, jams, chocolates, and regional honey. A tour of the factory and a stop in the beautiful boutique are pleasurable ways to spend and hour or two. ✉ *5 av. Albert Schweitzer, St-Rémy-de-Provence* ☎ *04–90–92–11–08* 🌐 *confiserie-lilamand.com.*

Chapter 4

AVIGNON AND THE VAUCLUSE

Updated by
Jennifer Ladonne

Sights	Restaurants	Hotels	Shopping	Nightlife
★★★☆☆	★★★☆☆	★★★☆☆	★★★☆☆	★☆☆☆☆

WELCOME TO AVIGNON AND THE VAUCLUSE

TOP REASONS TO GO

★ **Avignon:** While most exciting during the theater festival at the Palais des Papes (Pope's Palace) in July, Avignon is surprisingly youthful and vibrant year-round.

★ **Châteauneuf-du-Pape:** Probably the most evocative Rhône appellation, this village is just one of many in the area where you can sample exceptional wines.

★ **The Lavender Route:** Get hip-deep in purple by touring the Lavender Route between the Abbaye de Sénanque and the historic towns of Sault and Gordes.

★ **Perched villages:** Experience the region's many *villages perchés,* including Gordes and Bonnieux, in a patchwork landscape right out of a medieval Book of Hours.

★ **Roussillon:** With its ocher cliffs that change tones—copper, pink, rust—depending on the time of day, this town is a gigantic ruby embedded in the Vaucluse bedrock.

1 **Avignon.**

2 **Villeneuve-lès-Avignon.**

3 **Châteauneuf-du-Pape.**

4 **Orange.**

5 **Beaumes-de-Venise.**

6 **Gigondas.**

7 **Séguret.**

8 **Vaison-la-Romaine.**

9 **Crestet.**

10 **Le Barroux.**

11 **Crillon-le-Brave.**

12 **Mont Ventoux.**

13 **Sault.**

14 **Forcalquier.**

15 **L'Isle-sur-la-Sorgue.**

16 **Fontaine-de-Vaucluse.**

17 **Gordes.**

18 **Roussillon.**

19 **Ménerbes.**

20 **Lacoste.**

21 **Bonnieux.**

22 **Buoux.**

23 **Saignon.**

24 **Apt.**

25 **Lourmarin.**

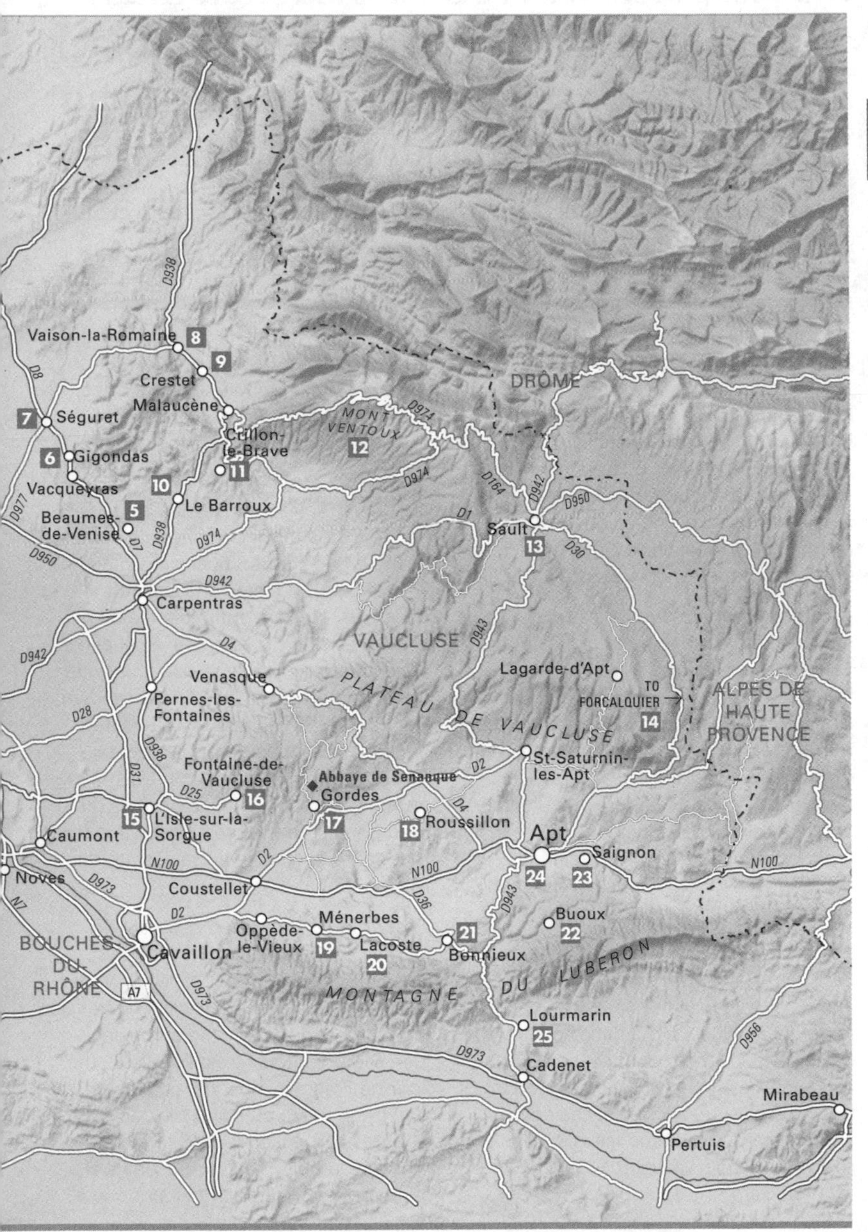

Vaison-la-Romaine
8
9
Crestet
Malaucène
7
Séguret
Crillon-le-Brave
MONT VENTOUX
12
6
Gigondas
11
Vacqueyras
10
Le Barroux
5
Beaumes-de-Venise
DRÔME
Sault
13
Carpentras
VAUCLUSE
PLATEAU DE VAUCLUSE
Lagarde-d'Apt
TO FORCALQUIER
14
ALPES DE HAUTE PROVENCE
Venasque
Pernes-les-Fontaines
Fontaine-de-Vaucluse
16
Abbaye de Senanque
Gordes
17
St-Saturnin-les-Apt
15
L'Isle-sur-la-Sorgue
Caumont
18
Roussillon
Apt
Saignon
24
23
Noves
Coustellet
Ménerbes
Oppède-le-Vieux
19
Lacoste
20
21
Bonnieux
Buoux
22
BOUCHES-DU-RHÔNE
Cavaillon
MONTAGNE DU LUBERON
Lourmarin
25
Cadenet
Mirabeau
Pertuis

For many, the Vaucluse is the only true Provence. It's like one vast Cézanne masterpiece, where sun-bleached hills and fields are laced with green-and-black grapevines or silver-gray olive trees, and rolling rows of lavender harmonize with purple mountains—all of it beneath an indigo sky.

It is here, in his beloved Luberon, that British author Peter Mayle discovered and described the simple pleasures of breakfasting on melons still warm from the sun, buying fresh-dug truffles from furtive farmers in smoke-filled bars, and life without socks. The world shared his epiphany, and vacationers now flock here in search of the same sensual way of life.

Anchored by the magnificent papal stronghold of Avignon, the glories of the Vaucluse spread luxuriantly eastward from the Rhône. The region's famous vineyards seduce connoisseurs, and its Roman ruins in Orange and Vaison-la-Romaine draw scholars, arts lovers, and history buffs. Plains dotted with orchards of olives, almonds, and cherries give way, around formidable Mont Ventoux, to a rich and wild mountainous terrain, then flow into the primeval Luberon.

The antiques market in L'Isle-sur-la-Sorgue makes for a terrific Sunday excursion, as does the nearby Fontaine-de-Vaucluse, a dramatic spring cascade (outside drought season). But the Luberon and its villages perched high up in the hills are a world of their own and worth allowing time for—perhaps even your whole vacation. Note that the Pont du Gard, the superbly preserved Gallo-Roman aqueduct, is a 30-minute drive west of Avignon, and that Arles, Nîmes, and the windswept Camargue are a stone's throw to the south and west.

Just north lies a wine-lover's paradise, as the Côtes du Rhône produce some of the world's most muscular vintages: Châteauneuf-du-Pape and Beaumes-de-Venise are two of the best-known villages, though the names Vacqueyras, Gigondas, and Cairanne also give wine buffs goosebumps. Despite its renown, though, this area feels off the beaten track even in midsummer, when it's favored by the French rather than foreign tourists. A brisk wind cools things off in summer, as do the broad-leaf plane trees that shade the sidewalk tables at village restaurants and cafés.

East of here, the countryside grows increasingly dramatic, first with the jagged Dentelles de Montmirail, whose landscape is softened by olive groves and orchards, and then by the surprisingly lush Mont Ventoux, best known as the Tour de France's most difficult stage. Along the way, you'll find villages such as Séguret and Vaison-la-Romaine, where you can sample the slow-paced local lifestyle over a game of pétanque or a lingering *apéro*. And all this lies a stone's throw from thriving Avignon, its feudal fortifications sheltering a lively arts scene and a culture determinedly young.

MAJOR REGIONS

Avignon. Avignon's most famous bridge—the subject of a French children's song—now stretches only halfway across the river, so don't make the mistake of trying to drive across it. Take the next bridge to L'Île de la Barthelasse, an amazingly rural setting minutes from the city where you can ride a bike through orchards and overnight in lovely auberges.

Lorded over by the Palais des Papes, home of the medieval French popes, this fortified city is still encircled by beautifully preserved ramparts. During the world-famous Avignon Festival in July, theater lovers can choose from more than 1,500 performances a day.

Haut Vaucluse. To the north and northeast of Avignon, this land of rolling orchards and vineyards spreads lazily at the foot of Mont Ventoux (Provence's highest peak), redolent of truffles, lavender, and fine wine. Perhaps that's why the Romans so firmly established themselves here, erecting grand arenas and luxurious villas that still in part remain.

From Avignon head north into the vineyards, making a brief tour of Châteauneuf-du-Pape, even if you don't stop to drink and buy wine. Orange is just up the highway; although the town isn't the most picturesque, its Roman theater is a must-see. Between Orange and Mont Ventoux are wine centers (Beaumes-de-Venise, Gigondas, Vacqueyras) and picturesque villages such as Crestet, Séguret, and Le Barroux, which the first French pope preferred to Avignon. Visit Vaison-la-Romaine for a strong concentration of Roman ruins.

The Sorgue Valley. This gentle, rolling valley east of Avignon follows the course of the River Sorgue, which wells up from caverns below the arid hills of the Vaucluse plateau, gushes to the surface at Fontaine-de-Vaucluse, and rolls down to turn the mossy waterwheels in picturesque L'Isle-sur-la-Sorgue. If you're fond of antiques, plan to join the festive hordes trawling for treasure at the famous Sunday flea market there. After exploring the fancier *antiquaires* (antiques stores) in town, enjoy an idyllic lunch by one of the town watermills, then track down the "source" of the River Sorgue in the famous spring of Fontaine-de-Vaucluse—the fifth largest in the world. It is a region of transition between the urban outskirts of Avignon and the wilds of the Luberon to the east.

The Luberon. The broad mountain called the Luberon is protected by the Parc Naturel Régional du Luberon, but that doesn't mean you should expect rangers, campsites, and his-and-her outhouses. It has always been and remains private land, though building and forestry are allowed in moderation, and hiking trails have been cleared. The D10, anchored to the west by the market town of Cavaillon and to the east by bustling Apt, parallels the long, looming north face of the Luberon, and from it you can explore the hill towns and valley villages on either side.

To its north, the red-ocher terrain around Roussillon, the Romanesque symmetry of the Abbaye de Sénanque, and the fashionable charms of Gordes punctuate a rugged countryside peppered with ancient stone *bories* (drystone huts). To its south lie Ménerbes, Lacoste, and pretty perched Bonnieux. From Bonnieux you can drive over the rugged crest through Lourmarin and explore the less gentrified south flank of the mountain. If you're a nature lover, you may want to venture into the wilder Grand Luberon, especially to the summit called Mourre Nègre.

Planning

When to Go

High heat and high season hit in July and August with a wallop: this lovely region is anything but undiscovered. Not only the French, but tourists from the four corners of Europe and beyond flock to the area for its legendary *savoir-vivre*. You'll miss the lavender if you visit in the spring (April, May, and early June) or in September or October, but the vines are golden, the crowds are bearable, and the weather is mild. Crowds or no crowds, it's still an unparalleled corner of the world.

Low season falls between mid-November and mid-March, when many restaurants and hotels take two or three months off. That leaves spring and fall: if you arrive after Easter, the flowers are in full bloom, the air cool, and the sun warm, and you'll still be able to book a table on the terrace. The same goes for October and early November, when the hills of the Luberon turn rust and gold, and game and wild mushrooms figure in every menu.

Planning Your Time

The Vaucluse is more refined than its flashy counterpart, the Côte d'Azur, so take advantage of its gastronomic blessings and sign up for a wine tasting or a cooking course. Hôtel de la Mirande in Avignon offers a superb roster for 6–12 people, in English, including courses around truffles, pastry, cheese, and wine. At La Maison sur la Sorgue, the owners will arrange visits (and be the designated drivers) to several local vineyards for a dose of viticulture and tasting. While you're in L'Isle-sur-la-Sorgue, arrange to stay over on a Saturday and wake up to the chatter and clatter of the Sunday antiques vendors.

Avignon is almost a never-ending festival: Les Hivernales dance festival (February); Jazz Festival (July and August); Theater Festival (July); Le Off Festival (also July); and the Gastronomy Festival (September). On another musical note for July: Lacoste has a successful arts festival; Orange takes on opera; and noted dance troops take part in Vaison-la-Romaine's Dance Festival, held at the town's Roman theater. But if you want to tiptoe through the best lavender, you'll want to drive through the Luberon between late June and early August to take in endless rows of glorious lavender before it's too late.

Getting Here and Around

If arriving in Avignon by TGV train (Paris–Avignon, 2 hours 40 minutes, Nice–Avignon, 3 hours 15 minutes), arrange for a rental car prior to arrival. Driving is the best choice, allowing you to control your schedule and not fall slave to a public system that isn't on par with that of the Alpes–Maritimes.

Even anxious drivers can find roads linking one village to the next rather easy (pleasant even!) to handle—the only downside is that the driver won't be able to take in all those breathtaking views, like the descent from Le Barroux into the Luberon. Note that country roads, especially over the mountain ranges, can be quite twisty and narrow—and French drivers are unnervingly speedy— but just take it slow, and you'll be fine.

Traveling by train in the region can be done from Avignon to L'Isle-sur-la-Sorgue, Cavaillon, Saint-Rémy, Aix, Arles, Orange, and Carpentras. Vaucluse regional buses are few and far between with infrequent schedules, though service has improved from the main towns; consult 🌐 *www.tcra.fror* for up-to-the-minute listings and fares for Avignon, Orange, Vaison, Saint-Rémy, Aix, Manosque, Castellane, and other bus routes.

AIR

Marseille's Marseille Provence, or MP, airport—commonly known as Marignane (which appears on all local signage)—is served by frequent flights from British cities in season; it's about an hour's drive from Avignon.

CONTACTS Avignon–Provence Airport. ✉ *100 rue Marise Bastié, Montfavet* ☎ *04–90–81–51–51* 🌐 *avignon.aero.* **Marseille Provence Airport.** (*Marignane*) ✉ *Marseille* ☎ *08–20–81–14–14* 🌐 *www.marseille.aeroport.fr.*

BUS

Major bus companies transport travelers from surrounding cities into towns not accessible by rail; bus and rail services usually dovetail. Avignon's *gare routière* (bus station) has the heaviest interregional traffic.

A reasonable network of private bus services (called, confusingly enough, *cars*) links places not served or poorly served by trains. Ask for bus schedules at train stations and tourist offices. Avignon has a sizable station, with posted schedules.

Bus companies serving the Vaucluse have essentially been consolidated under the Zou! Bus banner to provide more routes, easier schedules, and cheaper fares. The main destinations serviced to/from the Avignon bus station (10–20 buses daily) are Orange (€3, 45–60 minutes) and Carpentras (€2, 45 minutes). Five or fewer buses daily connect with: Aix-en-Provence (€7.60, 1½ hours), Apt (€5, 1½ hours), Arles (€6.60, 1½ hours), Cavaillon (€2, 1 hour), Nîmes (€1.50, 1½ hours), and Pont du Gard (€1.50, 1 hour).

You can access the Luberon villages, Cavaillon, L'Isle-sur-la-Sorge, Aix-en-Provence, and some of the hard-to-reach hilltop villages like Bonnieux from the main Avignon bus station on Avenue Monclar. Some destinations need a transfer.

CONTACTS Gare Routière. ✉ *5 av. Monclar at Bd. St-Roch, Avignon* ☎ *04–90–82–07–35.* **Zou!** ☎ *0809/400–415* 🌐 *zou.maregionsud.fr.*

CAR

The A6/A7 toll expressway channels all traffic from Paris to the south. Orange A7 splits to the southeast and leads directly to Avignon and D10 (in the direction of Apt), which dives straight east into the Luberon. To reach Vaison and the Mont Ventoux region from Avignon, head northeast toward Carpentras on D942. D36 jags south from D10 and leads you on a gorgeous chase over the backbone of the Luberon, via Bonnieux and Lourmarin; from there it's a straight shot to Aix and Marseille or to the Côte d'Azur. Or you can head back west up D973 to Cavaillon and Avignon.

With spokes branching out in every direction from Avignon and A7, you'll have no problem accessing the Vaucluse. The main *routes nationales* (national routes, or secondary highways) offer fairly direct links via D942 toward Orange and Mont Ventoux and via D10 into the Luberon. Negotiating the roads to L'Isle-sur-la-Sorgue and Fontaine-de-Vaucluse requires a careful mix of map and sign reading (or better yet just follow your GPS), often at high speeds around suburban *giratoires* (roundabouts). But when you strike out into the hills and the tiny roads—one of the best parts of the Vaucluse—give yourself over to GPS, road signs, and pure faith. As is the case throughout France, directions are indicated by village name only, with route numbers given as a small-print afterthought. Of course, this means you have to recognize the minor villages en route.

If you have access to the Internet while traveling, Vinci Autoroutes is a good website to consult. It not only gives directions for highways and village roads in southern France, but it also indicates weather conditions and traffic problems; although it's in French, it's not difficult to follow. Keep in mind that *péages* are toll booths and *aires* are gas and rest stops.

CONTACTS Vinci Autoroutes. 🌐 *www.vinci-autoroutes.com.*

TRAIN

Trains arrive in Marseille from many main cities, including Paris, Strasbourg, Nantes, and Bordeaux. Those from Paris and Strasbourg pass through Orange and Avignon. The quickest train connection remains the TGV *Méditerranée* line that arrives in Avignon after a 2-hour 40-minute trip from Paris. These TGV trains then connect with Nîmes (from €9.90, 18 minutes), Marseille (from €22.10, 35 minutes), and Nice (from €53, 3 hours).

From Avignon's central station, the Gare Avignon Centre, connections include Orange (€6.60, 15 minutes), Arles (€8, 20 minutes), and L'Isle-sur-la-Sorgue. Another big rail nexus is the city of Orange, but note that the city center is a 10-minute walk from the train station. Ticket prices range according to time of day and season, so look online before speaking with an agent.

CONTACTS SNCF. ☎ *3635 within France, 33–184–94–36–35 outside France* 🌐 *www.sncf.com.* **TGV.** ☎ *3635* 🌐 *www.sncf-connect.com.*

Hotels

One of the most popular vacation regions in France (after the seaside), the Vaucluse has a plethora of sleek and fashionable converted *mas* (farmhouses), landscaped in lavender, cypress, and oil jars full of vivid flowers, as well as luxurious inns that cater to people fleeing Avignon's summer crowds. There are budget accommodations, too, in the form of cheerful *chambres d'hôtes* and modest but well-run hotels, which often have good restaurants.

Given the crushing heat in high summer and the distance from the sea, most properties have swimming pools and, these days, air-conditioning, although it's wise to check ahead if you're counting on it. One alternative is to stay higher up in the mountains, where there is a refreshing breeze. Only a few lodgings provide *moustiquaires,* mosquito netting put over the bed or window screens to keep out troublesome flies. Reservations are essential most of the year, and many hotels close down altogether in winter.

⇨ *Hotel reviews have been shortened. For full information, visit Fodors.com. Prices are the lowest cost of a standard double room in high season.*

What It Costs in Euros

$	$$	$$$	$$$$
HOTELS			
under €125	€125–€225	€226–€350	over €350

Restaurants

As the cultural capital of the Vaucluse, Avignon might logically be considered the culinary capital, too. Visit during the July theater festival, however, and you'll have the opposite impression. Sunny sidewalk tables spill out temptingly onto the streets, but nearly all serve the kind of food designed for people on tight schedules: salads, pizzas, and charcuterie plates, often of indifferent quality.

For more generous and imaginative Provençal food, you will have to seek out Avignon's culinary gems or scour the countryside, where delightful meals can be had in roadside restaurants, renovated farmhouses, and restaurants with chefs whose talents are as stunning as the hilltop settings where they operate. It pays to do research—too many restaurants, especially in summer, are cashing in on the thriving tourist trade, and prices are generally high.

Be sure to indulge in the sun-drenched local wines from the Luberon, the Ventoux, and the Côtes du Rhône (especially its lesser-known appellations), and if a full bottle seems too much for two people, order one of the 50 cl bottles (the equivalent of two-thirds of a regular bottle).

⇨ *Restaurant reviews have been shortened. For full information, visit Fodors.com. Prices are the average cost of a main course at dinner or, if dinner is not served, at lunch.*

What It Costs in Euros

	$	$$	$$$	$$$$
RESTAURANTS	under €18	€18–€24	€25–€32	over €32

Visitor Information

The VPA Vaucluse Tourisme is a good source of information for the region. For the complete scoop on the hundreds of sights to see in Haute-Provence and other lavender-intensive areas, contact Les Routes de la Lavande.

CONTACTS Les Routes de la Lavande. ✉ *2 av. de Venterol, Nyons* ☎ *04–75–26–65–91* 🌐 *routes-lavande.com.* **VPA Vaucluse Tourisme.** ✉ *12 rue Collège de la Croix, Avignon* ☎ *04–90–80–47–00* 🌐 *www.provenceguide.com.*

Avignon

44 km (28 miles) northeast of Nîmes; 70 km (43 miles) northwest of Aix-en-Provence.

Of all the monuments in France—cathedrals, châteaux, fortresses—the ancient city of Avignon (pronounced "ah-veen-*yonh*") is one of the most dramatic. Wrapped in a crenellated wall punctuated by towers and Gothic slit windows, its historic center stands distinct from modern extensions, crowned by the Palais des Papes, a 14th-century fortress-castle that's nothing short of spectacular.

Standing on the Place du Palais under the gaze of the gigantic Virgin that reigns from the cathedral tower, with the palace sprawling to one side, the bishops' Petit Palais to the other, and the long, low bridge of childhood-song fame stretching over the river ("Sur le pont d'Avignon / On y danse tous en rond ..."), you can beam yourself briefly into the 14th century, so complete is the context, so evocative the setting.

Yet you'll soon be brought back to the present with a jolt by the skateboarders leaping over the smooth-paved square. Avignon is anything but a museum: it surges with modern ideas and energy, and it thrives within its ramparts as it did in the heyday of the popes—like those radical church lords, sensual, cultivated, and cosmopolitan, with a taste for lay pleasures.

For the French, Avignon is synonymous with its July theater festival. Thousands fill the city's hotels to bursting for the official festival and Le Festival OFF, the fringe festival with an incredible 1,500 performances each day. If your French isn't up to a radical take on Molière, look for English-language productions, or focus on the circus and the mimes. There are plenty of shows for children, and street performers abound.

GETTING HERE AND AROUND

Avignon is a major rail crossroads and springboard for the Vaucluse. Although the Gare Avignon TGV is a few miles southwest of the city, a shuttle bus runs between it and town every 15 minutes from early morning to late at night. There are also plenty of car-rental agencies at the station (it's best to reserve your vehicle in advance, though).

The quickest train link is the high-speed TGV (Trains à Grande Vitesse)

Méditerranée line that connects Paris and Avignon (2 hours 40 minutes); Nice to Avignon on the TGV (3 hours) costs €58. Other trains, such as the Avignon–Orange line (€6.60, 35 minutes) use the Gare Avignon Centre station; other lines go to Arles, Nîmes, Orange, Toulon, and Carcassonne.

Buses run to and from Avignon, Arles (€7.10, 1 hour), Carpentras (€2, 45 minutes), Cavaillon (€2, 1 hour), Nîmes (€1.50, 1½ hours), and farther afield to Orange, L'Isle-sur-la-Sorgue, Marseille, Nice, and Cannes. The Avignon–Orange bus runs several times during the day and takes less than an hour (€2 one-way). In addition, city buses and trams traverse Avignon itself.

BUS CONTACTS Avignon Bus Terminal. *5 av. Monclar, Avignon 04–90–82–07–35.* **Orizo.** *www.orizo.fr.*

TRAIN CONTACTS Gare Avignon Centre. *42 bd. St.-Roch, Avignon 3665 www.garesetconnexions.sncf.* **Gare Avignon TGV.** *Ch. du Confluent – La Courtine, Avignon 3665 www.garesetconnexions.sncf.*

TOURS

Le Petit Train d'Avignon

TRAIN TOURS | FAMILY | Resembling a children's party ride, this tourist train—a type of tram—travels the city streets for a 40-minute ride through the Rocher des Doms gardens, the historic city center, and by major monuments. It departs from the Popes' Palace Square daily 10–7, mid-March–October 30 (until 8 in July and August). *Pl. du Palais, Avignon From €9.*

Les Compagnie des Grands Bateaux de Provence

BOAT TOURS | FAMILY | Tired feet after too many rocky cobblestone paths? Take a cruise along the Rhône aboard *Le Saône,* a sightseeing vessel, or *Le Mireiro,* a larger boat with a restaurant. Excursions are offered year-round and range from a 45-minute "promenade" to wine discoveries and dinner and dancing cruises. Offerings and schedules vary according to season; check the website for a full listing. *Allées de L'Oulle, Avignon 04–90–85–62–25 bateauxdeprovence.fr From €13.*

VISITOR INFORMATION

CONTACTS Avignon Tourist Office. *41 cours Jean-Jaurès, Avignon 04–32–74–32–74 avignon-tourisme.com.*

Sights

Avignon has one of the most fabled and time-stained histories in France. It was transformed into the "Vatican of the north" when political infighting in the Eternal City drove Pope Clement V to accept Philippe the Good's invitation to start afresh. In 1309, his entourage arrived, with many of them staying in priories and châteaux near the city. In 1316, Clement was replaced by Pope John XXII, who moved into the bishop's palace (today the Petit Palais). It was his successor, Pope Benedict XII, however, who undertook construction of the magnificent palace that would house a series of popes.

During this, the so-called Avignon Papacy, the city became a sophisticated capital, drawing thousands of faithful pilgrims from across Europe. The University of Avignon, which was founded in 1303, also burgeoned, and the city attracted thinkers and artists, as well as stylish hangers-on.

As the popes' wealth and influence expanded, so, too, did their formidable palace. Indeed, its sumptuous architecture was legendary, inspiring disdain from the poet Petrarch, who wrote of "towers both useless and absurd that our pride may mount skyward, whence it is sure to fall in ruins." The Italians dubbed Avignon a "second Babylon."

In 1376, after a dispute with the king, Pope Gregory XI packed up for Rome,

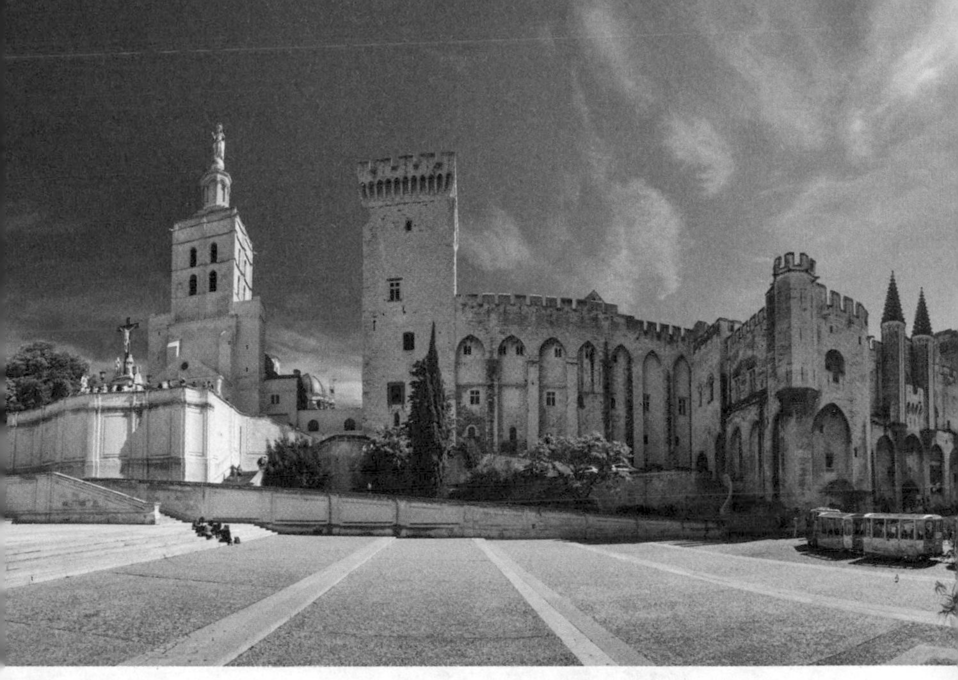

Side-by-side with Avignon's fortresslike Palais des Papes is the Byzantine-style Cathédrale Notre-Dame-des-Doms.

but Avignon held its ground. In 1378, while Gregory was on his deathbed, the French elected their own pope, Clement VII. This led to the Western Schism, which divided the Christian world. Popes and antipopes abused, insulted, and excommunicated each other in a conflict that seemed less about beliefs and faith and more about the power of the papacy. In 1417, Avignon lost out to Rome, and the extravagant court dispersed.

Although it is merely the capital of the Vaucluse these days, Avignon's lively street life, active university, and colorful markets present a year-round spectacle. At night, many of the landmark buildings and churches are beautifully lit, adding to the city's allure.

Cathédrale Notre-Dame-des-Doms

CHURCH | Built in a pure Provençal Romanesque style in the 12th century, this cathedral was soon dwarfed by the extravagant palace that rose beside it. The 14th century saw the addition of a cupola, which promptly collapsed. As rebuilt in 1425, the cathedral is a marvel of stacked arches with a strong Byzantine flavor and is topped with a gargantuan Virgin Mary lantern—a 19th-century afterthought—whose glow can be seen for miles around. ✉ *Pl. du Palais, Avignon* ☎ *04–90–80–12–21* 🌐 *www.metropole.diocese-avignon.fr.*

★ Collection Lambert

ART MUSEUM | Housed in two elegant 17th-century mansions, this impressive assembly of contemporary artworks came out of the private collection of Paris art dealer Yvon Lambert, who founded the museum in 2000 in honor of Avignon's designation as European Capital of Culture. The museum is known both for the breadth of its collection—more than 1,200 pieces dating from the 1960s to the present—and the scope of its three to four major exhibitions per year, as well as its cultural events, lectures, and arts eduction programs, done independently or in conjunction with other arts institutions worldwide. The foundation closes three months out of the year between exhibitions, so be sure to check before

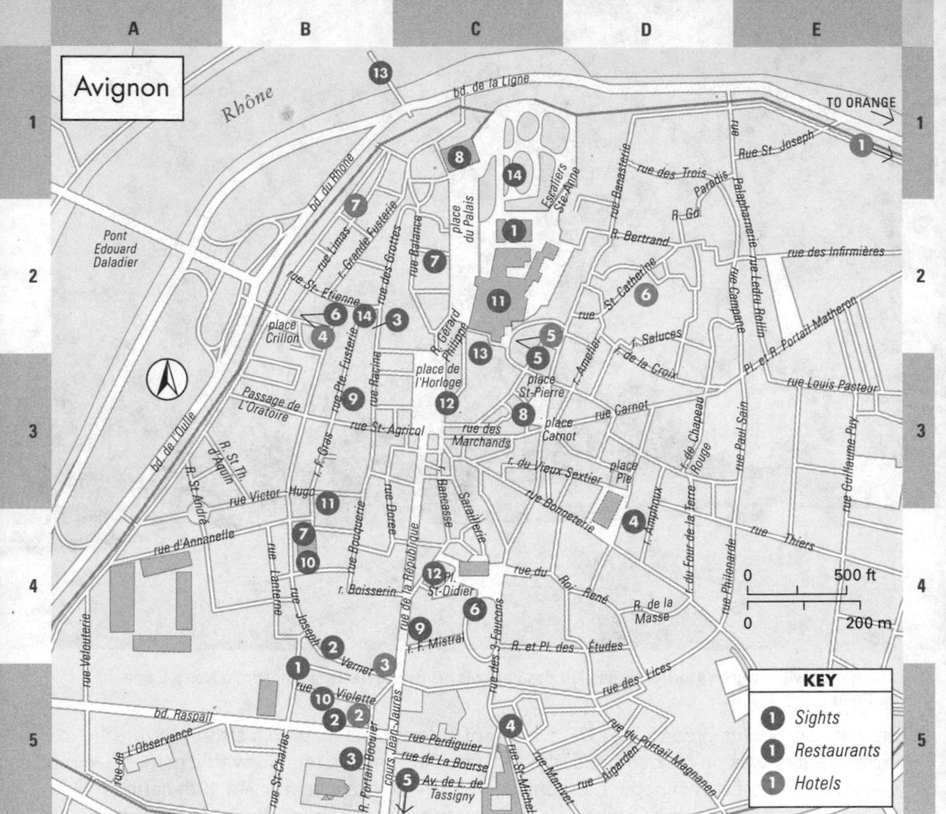

Sights

1 Cathédrale Notre-Dame-des-Doms........ C2
2 Collection Lambert B5
3 Espace St-Louis......... B5
4 Les Halles.............. D4
5 Les Remparts............ C5
6 Musée Angladon C4
7 Musée Calvet B4
8 Musée du Petit Palais... C1
9 Musée Lapidaire......... C4
10 Musée Requien......... B4
11 Palais des Papes C2
12 Place de l'Horloge....... C3
13 Pont St-Bénézet B1
14 Rocher des Doms........ C1

Restaurants

1 Bèou Bistrot............ B4
2 Bibendum............... B4
3 La Fourchette B2
4 L'Agape C5
5 La Mirande C2
6 La Vieille Fontaine B2
7 Le 46.................... C2
8 L'Epicerie C3
9 L'Essentiel B3
10 Le Violette B5
11 Pollen B3
12 Première Édition C4
13 Restaurant Sevin C3
14 Simple Simon............ B2

Hotels

1 Auberge de Cassagne................ E1
2 Hôtel Boquier B5
3 Hôtel de Cambis B5
4 Hôtel d'Europe B2
5 Hôtel de la Mirande C2
6 La Divine Comédie...... D2
7 Le Limas B2

going. The impressive bookshop carries dozens of original, limited-edition works by artists represented in the collection, including prints by Cy Twombly, Sol LeWitt, and Jenny Holzer, and the breezy courtyard café offers gourmet snacks, beverages, and light lunches under the shade of sleepy plane trees. ✉ *5 rue Violette, Avignon* ☎ *04–90–16–56–20* 🌐 *collectionlambert.com* 🎫 *€10* 🕓 *Closed Mon. Sept.–June.*

Espace St-Louis

NOTABLE BUILDING | This graceful, old 17th-century Jesuit cloister has been converted for office use by the well-known Avignon Festival—a performing arts event that lasts most of the month of July. The cloister's symmetrical arches (now partly enclosed as the sleek Hôtel Cloître St-Louis) are shaded by ancient plane trees. You can wander around the courtyard after you've picked up your festival information. Occasional exhibitions are held inside as well. ✉ *20 rue du Portail Boquier, Avignon* ☎ *04–90–27–66–50* 🌐 *festival-avignon.com.*

Les Halles

MARKET | **FAMILY** | By 6 am every day but Monday, merchants and artisans have stacked their herbed cheeses and arranged their vine-ripened tomatoes with surgical precision in arrangements that please the eye. This permanent covered market is as far from a farmers' market as you can get, each booth a designer boutique of *haute de gamme* (top-quality) goods, from jewel-like olives to silvery mackerel to racks of hanging hares worthy of a Flemish still life. Even if you don't have a kitchen to stock, consider enjoying a cup of coffee or a glass of (breakfast) wine while you take in the sights and smells. You can also tuck into a plate of freshly shucked oysters and a *pichet* of the crisp local white. ✉ *Pl. Pie, Avignon* ☎ *04–90–27–15–15* 🌐 *www.avignon-leshalles.com* 🕓 *Closed Mon.*

Avignon City Pass

The Avignon City Pass offers good value for the money. This prepaid card (24 hours, €21; 48 hours, €28) gives you access to the following museums in Avignon and Villeneuve Lez Avignon: Palais des Papes, Le Pont d'Avignon, Collection Lambert, Musée Angladon, Musée Louis Vouland, Tour Philippe Le Bel, La Chartreuse, Jardins de l'Abbaye St-André, Fort St-André, and Musée Pierre de Luxembourg.

Les Remparts (*The Ramparts*)

MILITARY SIGHT | More than 4 km (2½ miles) long, these crenellated walls and towers were built by the popes in the 14th century to keep out rampaging brigands and mercenary armies attracted by legends of papal wealth. They're extraordinarily well preserved, thanks in part to the efforts of architect Eugène-Emmanuel Viollet-le-Duc, who restored the southern portion in the 19th century. Modern-day Avignon roars around its impervious walls on a noisy ring road that replaced a former moat. ✉ *Pl. du Palais, Avignon.*

Musée Angladon

ART MUSEUM | This superb collection of major 18th- to 20th-century paintings and decorative arts was assembled by Parisian couturier Jacques Doucet (1853–1929), who befriended many of the major painters and writers of his day and, with an unerring eye, purchased—or funded—some of the great works of the 20th century (he was the original owner of Picasso's *Les Demoiselles d'Avignon*). He built this mansion toward the end of his life to house works by Degas, Van Gogh, Manet, Cézanne, Modigliani, and Picasso, along with important drawings, sculpture, photography, and furniture.

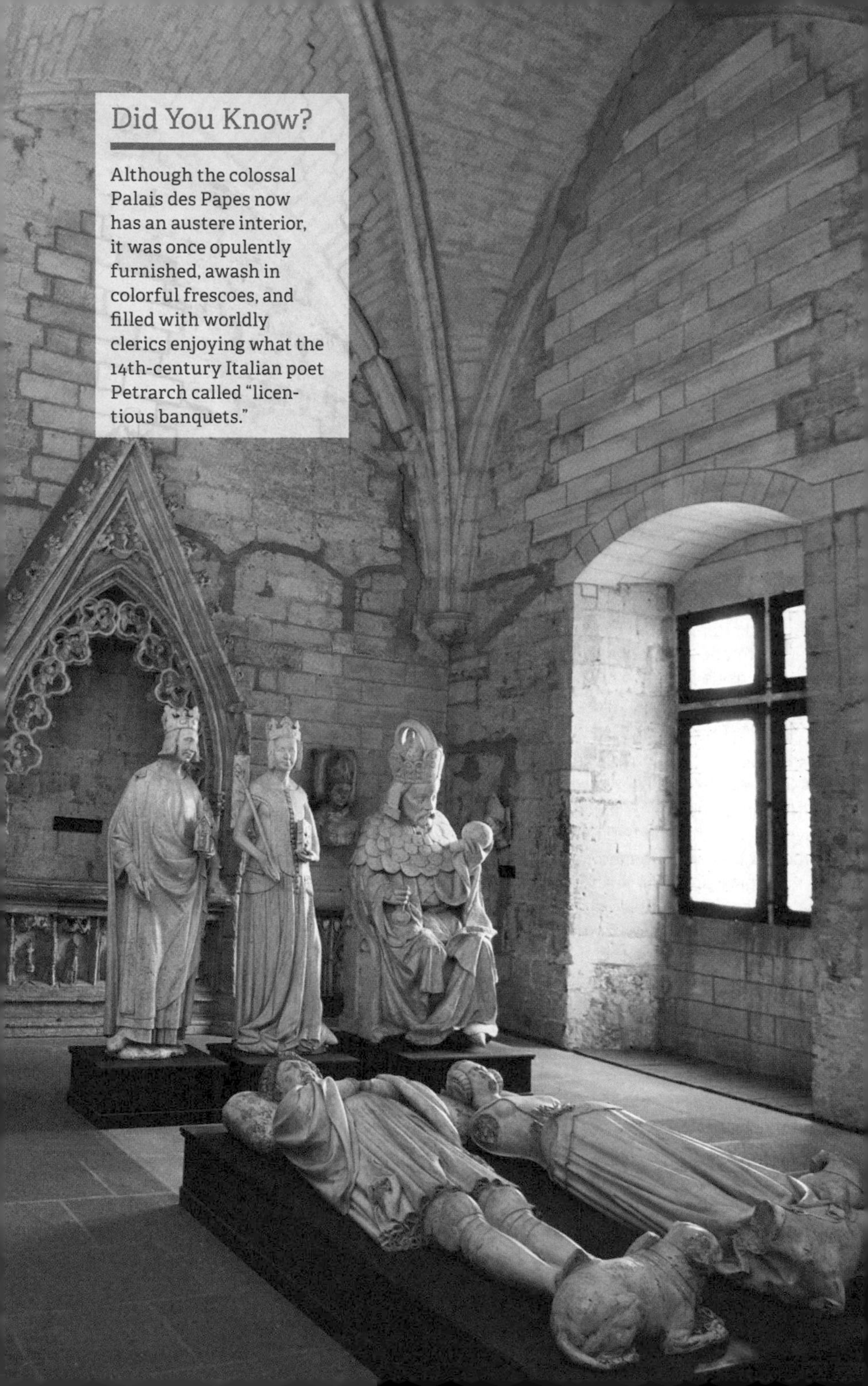

Did You Know?

Although the colossal Palais des Papes now has an austere interior, it was once opulently furnished, awash in colorful frescoes, and filled with worldly clerics enjoying what the 14th-century Italian poet Petrarch called "licentious banquets."

The museum also hosts temporary exhibitions. ✉ *5 rue Laboureur, Avignon* ☎ *04–90–82–29–03* 🌐 *angladon.com* 🎫 *€8* ⏲ *Closed late Dec.–Jan., Mon. year-round, and Sun. Nov.–Mar.*

Musée Calvet

ART MUSEUM | Worth a visit for the beauty and balance of its architecture alone, this fine old museum contains a rich collection of antiquities and classically inspired works. Acquisitions include neoclassical and Romantic pieces and are almost entirely French, including works by Manet, Daumier, and David. There's also a good modern section, with pieces by Bonnard, Duffy, and Camille Claudel (note Claudel's piece depicting her brother Paul, who incarcerated her in an insane asylum when her relationship with Rodin caused too much scandalous talk). The main building itself is a Palladian-style jewel in pale Gard stone dating to the 1740s; the garden is so lovely that it may distract you from the art. ✉ *65 rue Joseph-Vernet, Avignon* ☎ *04–90–86–33–84* 🌐 *www.musee-calvet.org* 🎫 *Permanent collections free* ⏲ *Closed Tues.*

Musée du Petit Palais

ART MUSEUM | This residence of bishops and cardinals before Pope Benedict XII built his majestic palace houses a large collection of old-master paintings, most of which are Italian works from the early Renaissance schools of Siena, Florence, and Venice—styles with which the Avignon popes would have been familiar. Later pieces here include Sandro Botticelli's *Virgin and Child* and Venetian paintings by Vittore Carpaccio and Giovanni Bellini. The museum café and tearoom, with a picturesque outdoor terrace in the mansion's ancient courtyard, is a favorite spot for lunch, coffee, or teatime (open 10–7). ✉ *Pl. du Palais, Avignon* ☎ *04–90–86–44–58* 🌐 *www.petit-palais.org* 🎫 *Permanent collections free* ⏲ *Closed Tues.*

Musée Lapidaire

ART MUSEUM | Housed in a pretty little Jesuit chapel on the main shopping street, this collection of sculpture and stonework is primarily from Gallo-Roman times but also includes Greek and Etruscan works. There are several interesting inscribed slabs, a selection of *shabtis* (small statues buried with the dead to help them get to the afterlife), and a notable depiction of *Tarasque of Noves,* the man-eating monster immortalized by Alphonse Daudet. Most items, unfortunately, are haphazardly labeled and insouciantly scattered throughout the chapel, itself slightly crumbling yet awash with light. ✉ *27 rue de la République, Avignon* ☎ *04–90–85–75–38* 🌐 *www.musee-lapidaire.org* 🎫 *Permanent collections free, special exhibits €3* ⏲ *Closed Mon.*

Musée Requien

HISTORY MUSEUM | **FAMILY** | Don't bother to rush to this eccentric little natural history museum, but since it's next door to the Calvet Museum (and free) you might want to stop in and check out the petrified palm trunks, the dinosaur skeleton, the handful of local beetles and mammals, and the careful and evocative texts (French only) that accompany them. The museum is named for a local naturalist and functions as an entrance to the massive library of natural history upstairs. ✉ *67 rue Joseph-Vernet, Avignon* ☎ *04–90–82–43–51* 🌐 *www.museum-requien.org* 🎫 *Free* ⏲ *Closed Sun. and Mon.*

★ Palais des Papes

CASTLE/PALACE | Although this disconcertingly fortresslike palace seems like just one colossal building, it actually consists of two different structures: the severe Palais Vieux (Old Palace), built between 1334 and 1342 by Pope Benedict XII, a member of the Cistercian order, which frowned on frivolity, and the more decorative Palais Nouveau (New Palace), built in the following decade by the artsy, lavish-living Pope Clement VI. The Great Court, entryway to the complex, links

Beautiful town squares form the hub of historic Avignon, as seen in this view from the roof of the famed Palais des Papes.

the two. The interiors are austere—many original furnishings were returned to Rome with the papacy, and others were lost during the French Revolution—so some imagination is required to picture the medieval splendor, awash with color and with worldly clerics enjoying what the 14th-century Italian poet Petrarch called "licentious banquets."

The main rooms of the Palais Vieux are the Consistory (Council Hall), decorated with some excellent 14th-century frescoes by Simone Martini; the Chapelle St-Jean, with original frescoes by Matteo Giovanetti; the Grand Tinel, or Salle des Festins (Feast Hall), with a majestic vaulted roof and a series of 18th-century Gobelin tapestries; the Chapelle St-Martial, with more Giovanetti frescoes; and the Chambre du Cerf, with a richly decorated ceiling, murals featuring a stag hunt, and a delightful view of Avignon. The principal attractions of the Palais Nouveau are the Grande Audience, a magnificent two-nave hall on the ground floor, and, upstairs, the Chapelle Clémentine, where the college of cardinals once gathered to elect new popes. ✉ *6 rue Pente Rapide, Avignon* ☎ *04–32–74–32–74* 🌐 *palais-des-papes.com* 🎫 *€12.*

Place de l'Horloge (*Clock Square*)
PLAZA/SQUARE | FAMILY | Shaded by plane trees, this square is the social nerve center of Avignon, with a concentration of bistros, brasseries, cafés, and restaurants that draw swarms of locals. ✉ *Avignon.*

Pont St-Bénézet (*St. Bénézet Bridge*)
BRIDGE | FAMILY | Unlike the London Bridge, this other subject of a childhood song (and a UNESCO World Heritage site) stretches only partway across the river. After generations of war and flooding, only half of the arched *pont* (bridge) remained by the 17th century. Its first stones were allegedly laid with the miraculous strength granted St-Bénezet in the 12th century, and it once reached all the way to Villeneuve. It's a bit narrow for dancing "*tous en rond*" (round and round), and the traditional place for dance

and play was under the arches. You can climb along its high platform for broad views of the Old Town ramparts. The ticket price includes an audio guide or tablet, and the latter (for which you'll need to show your passport or driver's license) illustrates how the bridge appeared in medieval times. ✉ *Port du Rhône, Avignon* ☎ *04–32–74–32–74* 🌐 *avignon-tourisme.com* 🎫 *€5.*

★ **Rocher des Doms** (*Rock of the Domes*)
GARDEN | FAMILY | Set on a bluff above town, this lush hilltop garden has grand Mediterranean pines, a man-made lake (complete with camera-ready swans), plus glorious views of the palace, the rooftops of Old Avignon, the Pont St-Bénézet, and formidable Villeneuve across the Rhône. On the horizon loom Mont Ventoux, the Luberon, and Les Alpilles. The garden has lots of history as well: often called the "cradle of Avignon," its rocky grottoes were among the first human habitations in the area. ✉ *Montée du Moulin, off Pl. du Palais, Avignon* ☎ *04–32–74–32–74* 🌐 *www.avignon-et-provence.com/sites-naturels/rocher-doms-avignon.*

Restaurants

Bèou Bistrot
$ | MODERN FRENCH | Set in a quiet, leafy courtyard a few steps from the Collection Lambert, this is a good place to enjoy fresh, unfussy, reasonably priced dishes paired with local wines and served by a friendly staff. The pretty dining room's bucolic frescoes set the tone for a cuisine based on whatever's fresh, and you can eat outside in nice weather. **Known for:** outdoor dining; specials on blackboard menu; good for vegetarians. $ *Average main: €14* ✉ *14 rue Violette, Avignon* ☎ *06–16–59–70–58* 🌐 *www.beou-bistrot-restaurant-avignon.com* ⏲ *Closed Sun. and Mon. No dinner Tues.*

Bibendum
$$$ | MODERN FRENCH | The more elegant sister to Mathieu Desmaret's locavore mecca, Pollen, this dining room set in a 14th-century cloister attracts a chic, upscale crowd that fits right in with the stunning decor. You'll find all the flair and precision that put this talented chef on the foodie map, but with an Asian touch in dishes like candied beets with miso yogurt and kumquat or roasted pollack with lemongrass, ginger, and lacquered leeks. **Known for:** outdoor dining; sophisticated decor; trendy. $ *Average main: €25* ✉ *83 rue Joseph Vernet, Avignon* ☎ *04–90–91–78–39* 🌐 *www.bibendumavignon.fr* ⏲ *Closed Sun. and Mon.*

La Fourchette
$$ | FRENCH | FAMILY | The service here is friendly, and the food is delicious and satisfying—as evidenced by the bevy of locals clamoring to get in. Dig in to heaping portions of escalope of salmon, chicken cilantro à l'orange, or what just might be the best Provençal daube (served with macaroni gratin) in France. **Known for:** cozy, elegant atmosphere; family-friendly vibes; reasonable prices, especially for fixed-price menus. $ *Average main: €21* ✉ *17 rue Racine, Avignon* ☎ *04–90–85–20–93* 🌐 *www.la-fourchette.net* ⏲ *Closed weekends and 1st 3 wks in Aug.*

★ **L'Agape**
$$$ | MODERN FRENCH | At this gastropub hot spot in the heart of the city, chef Julien Gleize applies light, playful, modern touches to dishes that are steeped in French tradition, made with local ingredients, and beautifully presented. Options might include rabbit farci perfumed with wild cèpes and served over a cloud of whipped potatoes and shallot confit or wild salmon caramelized in olive oil with watercress, black sesame seeds, and luscious cream of corn. **Known for:** devotion to the freshest ingredients; superb price-to-quality ratio; excellent wine list. $ *Average main: €30* ✉ *21 pl. des Corps-Saints, Avignon* ☎ *04–90–85–04–06*

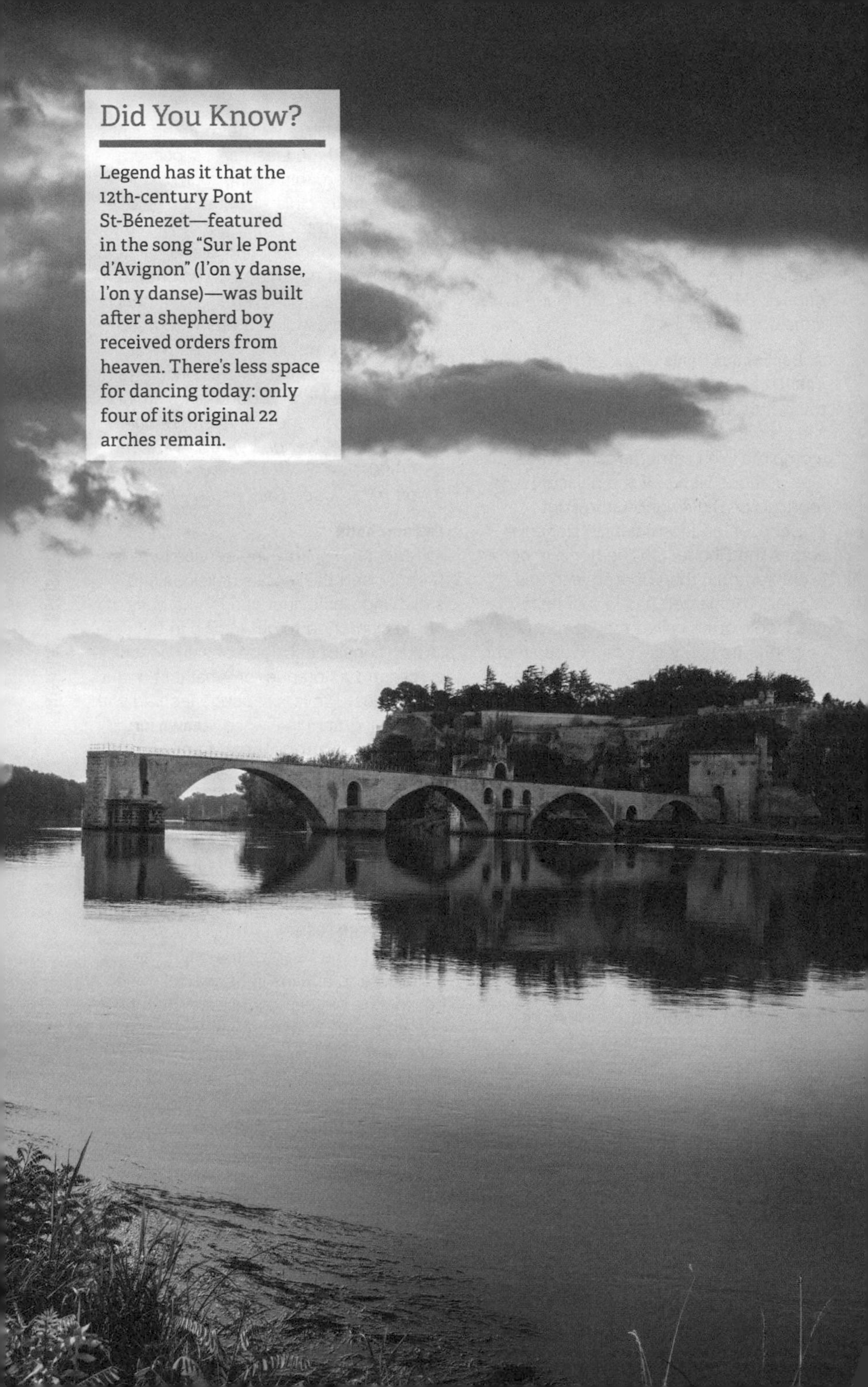

Did You Know?

Legend has it that the 12th-century Pont St-Bénezet—featured in the song "Sur le Pont d'Avignon" (l'on y danse, l'on y danse)—was built after a shepherd boy received orders from heaven. There's less space for dancing today: only four of its original 22 arches remain.

🌐 *www.restaurant-agape-avignon.com* ⏲ *Closed Sun. and Mon.*

★ La Mirande

$$$$ | FRENCH | Whether you dine under the 14th-century coffered ceilings, surrounded by exquisite paintings and Renaissance tapestries, or in the intimate garden under the walls of the Palais des Papes, the restaurant of the luxurious Hôtel de la Mirande transports you to another time. Chef Florent Pietravalle offers original haute-cuisine dishes with a focus on local products, perhaps wild cèpes with caviar and razor clams, line-caught dorade with roasted cucumber and a Granny Smith apple emulsion, or aged beef with Jerusalem artichokes and wild blackberries. **Known for:** Michelin-starred chef; unparalleled elegance; chef's table and wonderful food and wine workshops. *Average main: €45* ✉ *4 pl. de la Mirande, Avignon* ☎ *04–90–85–93–93* 🌐 *www.la-mirande.fr* ⏲ *Closed Tues., Wed., and 3 wks in Jan.*

La Vieille Fontaine

$$$$ | FRENCH | Summer evening meals around the old fountain and boxwood-filled oil jars in the courtyard of the Hôtel d'Europe would be wonderful with *filet de boeuf* alone, but combine this romantic backdrop with top-notch southern French cuisine and you have a special event. Give yourself over to one of the great restaurants of the Vaucluse, complete with fine regional wines and an army of urbane servers—and hope for moonlight. **Known for:** beautiful setting; outdoor courtyard dining; exquisite presentation. *Average main: €38* ✉ *12 pl. Crillon, Avignon* ☎ *04–90–14–76–76* 🌐 *www.heurope.com* ⏲ *Closed Sun. and Mon.*

Le 46

$$$ | MODERN FRENCH | A 200-plus wine list is a big highlight of this restaurant and *bar à vins,* yet the main focus is squarely on the food. Beautiful to behold and even better to eat, the Mediterranean-inspired dishes flaunt the bounty of Provence in options like beef carpaccio, sliced razor-thin and served with shaved Parmesan and crispy house frites; a tender zucchini tartlette with chèvre and herbes de Provence; or a salad of heirloom tomatoes, bufala mozzarella, Serrano ham, and basil sorbet. **Known for:** loved by the locals; accommodating to different diets and food allergies; lovely outdoor terrace. *Average main: €26* ✉ *46 rue de la Balance, Avignon* ☎ *04–90–85–24–83* 🌐 *www.le46avignon.com* ⏲ *Closed Wed. and Sun.*

L'Epicerie

$$ | FRENCH | This restaurant doesn't have great gastronomic pretensions, but the delicious food, hip waiters, and charming terrace in the quiet, cobblestone Place St-Pierre make it a local favorite. Order a steak with *vraies frites* (real chunky French fries), and soak up the atmosphere with the help of some well-chosen local wine. **Known for:** wonderful terrace on historic Square St-Pierre; charming interiors; reasonable prices. *Average main: €21* ✉ *10 pl. St-Pierre, Avignon* ☎ *04–90–82–74–22* 🌐 *www.facebook.com/lepicerieavignon84* ⏲ *Closed Tues., Wed., Jan., and Feb.*

L'Essentiel

$$$ | FRENCH | This chic hot spot, steps from the Palais des Papes, is part of the "bistronomy" movement, which focuses on creative cooking, a casual atmosphere, and reasonable prices. The quaint terrace on a side street will lure in passersby, and the romantic 17th-century interior courtyard will keep them coming back. **Known for:** quality ingredients highlighting seafood; beautiful dining room; good-value lunch menu. *Average main: €25* ✉ *2 rue Petite Fusterie, Avignon* ☎ *04–90–85–87–12* 🌐 *restaurantlessentiel.com* ⏲ *Closed Sun. and Mon.*

★ Le Violette

$ | FRENCH | You could hardly beat the location of this (mostly outdoor) bistro in the shady, elegant courtyard of the Collection Lambert. Hearty lunches and dinners include a fish and meat choice with plenty of fresh local vegetables and salads on the side—perhaps, salmon gravlax with an Asian-inflected cabbage salad or roasted lamb with bright steamed veggies. **Known for:** superfresh ingredients; unbeatable shaded terrace; organic wines by the glass. *Average main: €16* *5 rue Violette, Avignon* *04–90–85–36–42* *restaurant-le-violette-avignon.eatbu.com* *Closed Mon. No dinner Sun. and Tues.*

★ Pollen

$$$ | **FRENCH** | This luminous, casual dining room is an absolute must on any foodie circuit of Provence. Michelin-starred chef Mathieu Desmaret's thoughtful approach to seasonal Provençal products and wild ingredients and exquisite attention to unusual flavor pairings make for a revelatory experience far beyond the usual gourmet cuisine. **Known for:** on a charming street at the center of town; prix-fixe menus; casual setting for elegant dishes. *Average main: €29* *18 rue Joseph Vernet, Avignon* *04–86–34–93–74* *pollen-restaurant.fr* *Closed weekends.*

★ Première Édition

$$ | **FRENCH** | Tucked away on a pretty street in the center of Avignon, this cozy duplex restaurant with a Japanese vibe is the city's newest hot spot for delicious, locally sourced small plates that elevate the humble vegetable. Aurélie Tomassin's thoughtful cuisine follows the seasons in dishes like squash-blossom-and-cheese-stuffed fritters, anchovy toast with sweet onion and homemade aioli, tender shredded chicken sandwich with lemon and frisée, or spicy hummus with homemade pita. **Known for:** great for vegetarians; outdoor seating in warm weather; everything homemade with all local ingredients. *Average main: €18* *5 rue Prévôt, Avignon* *04–84–14–59–85* *premiereedition.fr* *Closed Sun.–Tues.*

★ Restaurant Sevin

$$$$ | **FRENCH** | The stellar period interior of this renovated 12th-century mansion makes for an impressive backdrop to innovative and delicious cuisine. Try the pan-roasted veal medallion with dried porcini blinis and thinly sliced mushrooms with chervil, or splurge for the whole lobster sautéed in olive oil, muscat grapes, and beurre blanc with verjuice. **Known for:** meticulous sourcing and presentation; romantic setting with views of Papal Palace; one of Avignon's top restaurants. *Average main: €36* *10 rue de Mons, Avignon* *04–57–70–00–29* *www.restaurantsevin.fr* *Closed Wed. and Thurs.*

Simple Simon

$ | **BRITISH** | Since the 1970s, this quaint (there is no other word for it) English tearoom—dark wooden beams, teapots on shelves, a table laden with cakes and pies—has catered to locals and homesick expats, all of whom are intrigued by the pieman's tempting wares and properly brewed teas served in silver pots. Owned from the beginning by a Frenchwoman whose mother was English, Simple Simon is a real ode to British tradition, with Cornish salad, bacon and eggs, and hot dishes like shepherd's pie, cheese-and-onion crumble tart, or turkey hot pot at lunch. **Known for:** traditional English tearoom experience; excellent desserts; delicious scones. *Average main: €16* *26 rue Petite Fusterie, Avignon* *04–90–86–62–70* *simplesimon.monboutigo.fr* *Closed Mon., Sun. May–Sept., and Aug. No dinner (except during festival).*

Hotels

★ Auberge de Cassagne

$$$ | **HOTEL** | Once you get beyond the residential surroundings, an oasis of splendid gardens, indoor and outdoor pools, a full-service spa and fitness room, an excellent gastronomic restaurant, and an old-world welcome await. **Pros:** some

rooms overlook gardens; exemplary service and fantastic restaurant; prices reasonable in most seasons. **Cons:** residential neighborhood doesn't appeal to everyone; 15-minute drive from Avignon; breakfast not included. *Rooms from: €296 450 allée de Cassagne, Avignon 09–75–18–85–28 www.aubergedecassagne.com 42 rooms No Meals.*

Hôtel Boquier

$ | HOTEL | FAMILY | You might not guess that this friendly, family-run, shabby-chic hotel, convenient to both the train station and the Palais des Papes, is a budget option. **Pros:** good continental breakfast; homey touches, like lavender on the pillows; air-conditioning. **Cons:** no elevator; some rooms dated; resident cat might bother allergic guests. *Rooms from: €120 6 rue du Portail-Boquier, Avignon 04–90–82–34–43 www.hotel-boquier.com 12 rooms No Meals.*

★ Hôtel de Cambis

$$ | HOTEL | FAMILY | Perfectly situated in a historic building that's a short walk from Avignon's principal attractions, this chic boutique hotel has quiet, colorful, beautifully designed rooms with every amenity, ample bathrooms, and plenty of closet space; some rooms also have a balcony or a fireplace. **Pros:** well priced; fun wine bar on premises; chic and lively hotel. **Cons:** no spa; rooms are on the small side; fills up quickly in summer. *Rooms from: €200 89 rue Joseph Vernet, Avignon 04–90–14–62–73 www.hoteldecambis.com 42 rooms No Meals.*

Hôtel d'Europe

$$$$ | HOTEL | This classic, vine-covered 16th-century home once hosted Emperor Maximilian (as well as Victor Hugo and Napoléon Bonaparte), and some of its guest rooms are emperor size. **Pros:** authentic historical setting; romantic hideaway; close to everything. **Cons:** least expensive rooms are small and slightly shabby; high season can mean noisy evenings, especially from nearby bars; service could be better. *Rooms from: €390 12 pl. Crillon, Avignon 04–90–14–76–76 heurope.com/fr 44 rooms No Meals.*

★ Hôtel de la Mirande

$$$$ | HOTEL | A romantic's dream of a hotel, this *petit palais* enables you to step into 18th-century Avignon—complete with painted coffered ceilings, precious antiques, extraordinary handmade wall coverings, and beautiful Asian rugs. **Pros:** a step back into a more gracious era; luxurious toiletries; beautiful courtyard garden. **Cons:** old-fashioned baths may not appeal to all; very pricey rooms and dining; breakfast not included. *Rooms from: €611 Pl. de la Mirande, Avignon 04–90–14–20–20 www.la-mirande.fr 27 rooms No Meals.*

★ La Divine Comédie

$$$$ | HOTEL | One of Avignon's loveliest hotels is in an 18th-century mansion not far from the Palais des Papes and set amid lush gardens with towering plane trees, flowers, and palms, as well as a koi pond, swimming pool, and spa pavilion. **Pros:** tranquil setting; stunning interiors; delightful hosts. **Cons:** no restaurant; not ideal for young kids (but they're welcome); quite pricey. *Rooms from: €550 16 impasse Jean Pierre Gras 06–77–06–85–40 www.la-divine-comedie.com 5 rooms No Meals.*

Le Limas

$$ | B&B/INN | Two minutes from the famous Avignon bridge, this contemporarily decorated B&B offers a rooftop terrace view of the palace but also tranquility away from the noisy palace streets. **Pros:** rooftop terrace fridge stocked with rosé; convenient location; air-conditioning. **Cons:** only one room can accommodate more than two people; limited parking; fills up quickly in high season. *Rooms from: €160 51 rue de Limas, Avignon 06–69–00–60–37 www.le-limas-avignon.com 4 rooms Free Breakfast.*

Within its fusty old medieval walls, Avignon teems with modern nightlife well into the wee hours.

★ **AJMI** (*Association Pour le Jazz et la Musique Improvisée*)
LIVE MUSIC | At AJMI, in La Manutention arts center, you can hear live jazz acts of some renown. ✉ *4 rue des Escaliers Sainte-Anne, Avignon* ☎ *04–90–86–08–61* 🌐 *www.ajmi.fr.*

Bistrot d'Utopia
BARS | Enjoy drinks in this dark, intimate space just outside the Utopia movie theater in La Manutention arts center. ✉ *4 rue des Escaliers Ste-Anne, Avignon* ☎ *04–90–82–65–36.*

Le Delirium
LIVE MUSIC | An übercool hangout for live music, performance, and entertainment during the Avignon Festival and on weekends, Le Delirium covers its walls with ongoing exhibits to create a truly artsy atmosphere. ✉ *23 rue de la République, Avignon* ☎ *04–90–85–44–56* 🌐 *www.ledelirium.net.*

Le Rouge Gorge
CABARET | This venue for cabaret-style dinner shows also hosts jazz, blues, and rock concerts and theater performances. ✉ *10 bis rue Peyrollerie, Avignon* ☎ *04–90–14–02–54* 🌐 *www.lerougegorge.fr.*

Performing Arts

Small though Avignon is, its inspiring art museums, strong university, and 60-some years of saturation in world-class theater have made the city a second center for the arts, after Paris.

Your best bets for year-round programs of theater, ballet, opera, and classical music are the Opéra-Théâtre d'Avignon or La Manutention arts center, which also screens art films plus first-run, mainstream movies in *v.o.* (*version originale*, meaning in the original language with French subtitles). The center also has a café, a restaurant, and a jazz club.

Cinéma Utopia–La Manutention
FILM | This theater shows hard-to-find international independent works. There's another location on Rue Figuière. ✉ *4 rue des Escaliers Ste-Anne, Avignon* ☎ *04–90–82–65–36* 🌐 *www.cinemas-utopia.org/avignon* 🎫 *€7.*

★ **Festival d'Avignon**
ARTS FESTIVALS | **FAMILY** | Founded in 1947, this is the oldest theater festival in France and one of the biggest in the world. It takes place over three weeks in July and features more than 1,500 performances held in venues throughout the city. The Off Festival (🌐 *www.festivaloffavignon.com*), which is held simultaneously, is less formal and highlights productions by smaller, more experimental companies. ✉ *Avignon* 🌐 *festival-avignon.com/en.*

FNAC
CONCERTS | For information on events and tickets, stop at this massive book-and-record chain. ✉ *19 rue de la République, Avignon* ☎ *08–25–52–00–20* 🌐 *www.fnac.com.*

★ **La Manutention**
ARTS CENTERS | This hip cultural complex, on a picturesque cobbled street just behind the Palais des Papes, includes the Utopia–La Manutention movie theater, a well-regarded restaurant, the AJMI jazz club, and a relaxed bar that's popular even with those not seeing a show. Its location in front of the Avignon School of the Arts and its eclectic style—a mix of antique and contemporary touches—make it a big draw for the town's artsy crowd. ✉ *4 rue des Escaliers Ste-Anne, Avignon* ☎ *04–90–86–08–61 for jazz club, 04–90–86–86–77 for restaurant.*

Opéra-Théâtre d'Avignon
ARTS CENTERS | This theater proves that culture and the arts are not limited to festival season, with a year-round schedule that ranges from classical concerts, ballet, and opera to Broadway musicals. ✉ *1*

rue Racine, Avignon ☎ *04–90–14–26–40* 🌐 *www.operagrandavignon.fr.*

 Shopping

Avignon has a cosmopolitan mix of French chains and youthful clothing shops (it's a college town), many of which are along a few plummy fashion streets. Rue des Marchands, off Place Carnot, and Rue de la République are two key stretches. The largest concentration of high-end clothing, jewelry, vintage, and fashion-forward stores, however, is along Rue Joseph Vernet.

★ CQFD
OTHER SPECIALTY STORE | Part charming café serving lunch, snacks, and coffee and part concept store, CQFD (Créations Éthiques Franco Décalées) is hands-down Avignon's chicest shopping destination. Its spacious rooms brim with a curated selection of whimsical clothing and jewelry, chic stationery, tableware, soaps, cosmetics, and handmade housewares (including eco-paints and hand-blocked wallpapers). Everything is eco-conscious—and made in France. ✉ *7 rue des Trois Faucons, Avignon* ☎ *04–90–01–70–64* 🌐 *cqfd-avignon.fr.*

Fusterie Quarter
NEIGHBORHOODS | If you're into Louis XVI, the Fusterie quarter caters to antiques hunters and interior decorators. ✉ *Rue Petit Fusterie, Avignon.*

Joseph Vernet Quarter
NEIGHBORHOODS | The more luxurious shops along Rue Joseph-Vernet and St-Agricol in the Joseph Vernet quarter merit some *lèche-vitrine* (window licking, as the French say). ✉ *Avignon.*

Les Délices du Luberon
FOOD | For those with a taste for all things Provençal, this gourmet épicerie sells many of the delicacies found in the region's best local markets, all neatly packaged and suitcase ready—if they make it that far. Shop for olive oils, tapenades, herbs, preserves, bottled soups, fruit jams, honey, pastries, lavender-based sweets or cosmetics, and so much more. ✉ *20 pl. du Change, Avignon* ☎ *04–90–84–03–58* 🌐 *www.delices-du-luberon.fr.*

Mouret Chapelier
OTHER ACCESSORIES | This shop has a cornucopia of old-fashioned, old-world, and marvelously eccentric hats in a jewel-box setting. ✉ *20 rue Marchands, Avignon* ☎ *04–90–85–39–38* 🌐 *www.facebook.com/chapelleriemouret84.*

Pure Lavande
COSMETICS | For all things lavender—and not just any lavender—this shop has the best AOC essential oil (it must be from flowers that grow above 2,600 feet) from the famous Château de Bois, plus a range of top-quality soaps, body lotions, and other fine cosmetics made with lavender essential oil. ✉ *61 rue Grand Fusterie, Avignon* ☎ *04–90–14–70–05* 🌐 *www.lavandeandco.fr.*

Souleïado
MIXED CLOTHING | All those famous, gorgeous Provençal fabrics can be found at Souleïado—sold by the meter or as elegantly tailored shirts, dresses, and skirts. There's also a fine selection of leather boots, bags, and other accessories. ✉ *19 rue Joseph-Vernet, Avignon* ☎ *04–90–86–32–05* 🌐 *www.souleiado.com.*

Villeneuve-lès-Avignon

3 km (2 miles) northwest of Avignon.

In the 14th century, when Avignon became home to the papacy, a flood of wealthy cardinals poured across the Rhône and into the hilltop town of Villeneuve-lès-Avignon (aka Villeneuve-lez-Avignon). No fewer than 15 of the status-seeking princes of the church built magnificent homes here—though, in truth, some simply requisitioned existing mansions, and these "freed" town palaces became known as *livrées cardinalices*. In addition, kings Philip the Fair and Louis VIII built formidable defenses on the site to keep an eye on papal territories. Nowadays, the town's abbey, fortress, and quiet streets offer a pleasant respite from Avignon's bustle.

GETTING HERE AND AROUND

The No. 5 from the Avignon "center" train station runs every 20 minutes and costs €1.40 for the five-minute ride. To drive, it's 3 km (2 miles) from Avignon; just follow the signs.

VISITOR INFORMATION

CONTACTS Villeneuve-lès-Avignon/Greater Avignon Tourism. ✉ *Pl. Charles David, Villeneuve-lès-Avignon* ☎ *04–90–03–70–60* 🌐 *avignon-tourisme.com.*

Sights

Abbaye St-André Gardens

GARDEN | FAMILY | Don't miss the formal Italianate gardens of Fort St-André, littered with remains of the abbey that preceded the fortifications. The gardens are now privately owned. ✉ *Rue Montée du Fort, Villeneuve-lès-Avignon* ☎ *04–90–25–55–95* 🌐 *www.grandavignon.fr* 🎫 *€9* ⏲ *Closed Mon. Mar.–Oct.*

Chartreuse du Val-de-Bénédiction

RELIGIOUS BUILDING | The bounty of the cardinals nourished this abbey, whose name translates, literally, to the Charterhouse of the Valley of Blessings. Inside it are spare cells with panels illuminating monastic life; the vast 14th-century *cloître du cimetière* (cemetery cloister); a smaller Romanesque cloister; and, within what remains of the abbey church, the Gothic tomb of Pope Innocent VI. Theatrical events are staged here during Avignon's annual theater festival. ✉ *58 rue de la République, Villeneuve-lès-Avignon* ☎ *04–90–15–24–24* 🌐 *www.chartreuse.org* 🎫 *€8.*

Fort St-André

MILITARY SIGHT | FAMILY | At the top of the village is the Fort St-André, which once ostensibly protected the town of St-André, now absorbed into Villeneuve. The fortress's true importance was as a show of power for the kingdom of France in the face of the all-too-close Avignon popes. You can explore the fortress grounds and the ruined walls of inner chambers. There's a good view from the Notre Dame de Belvézet church within the fort, and you can also climb into the twin towers for broad views over Avignon, the Luberon, and Mont Ventoux. ✉ *Rue Montée du Fort, Villeneuve-lès-Avignon* ☎ *04–90–25–45–35* 🌐 *www.fort-saint-andre.fr* 🎫 *Towers €6.*

Musée Pierre-de-Luxembourg

ART MUSEUM | Below the abbey, one of the luxurious, 14th-century cardinals' manors today contains a notable collection of art, including the spectacularly colorful and richly detailed *Couronnement de la Vierge* (*Coronation of the Virgin*), an altarpiece painted in 1453 by Enguerrand Quarton. One of the greatest paintings of the 15th century, it shows rows and rows of Avignonnais hieratically sitting around the figures of God the Father and God the Son. Depicted by Quarton—the leading painter of the Avignon School—as identical twins, they bless Mary and hover over a surreal landscape that places Montagne St-Victoire in between Heaven and Hell. ✉ *2 rue de la République, Villeneuve-lès-Avignon* ☎ *04–90–27–49–66* 🌐 *www.museepierredeluxembourg.gard.fr* 🎫 *€4* ⏲ *Closed Mon.*

Hotels

Le Prieuré

$$$ | HOTEL | Heavenly peace is the theme at this charming five-star hotel, set in a medieval convent amid enchanting gardens with a pool, shady terraces, and a highly regarded restaurant. **Pros:** very good restaurant; a good base for exploring Avignon and area villages;

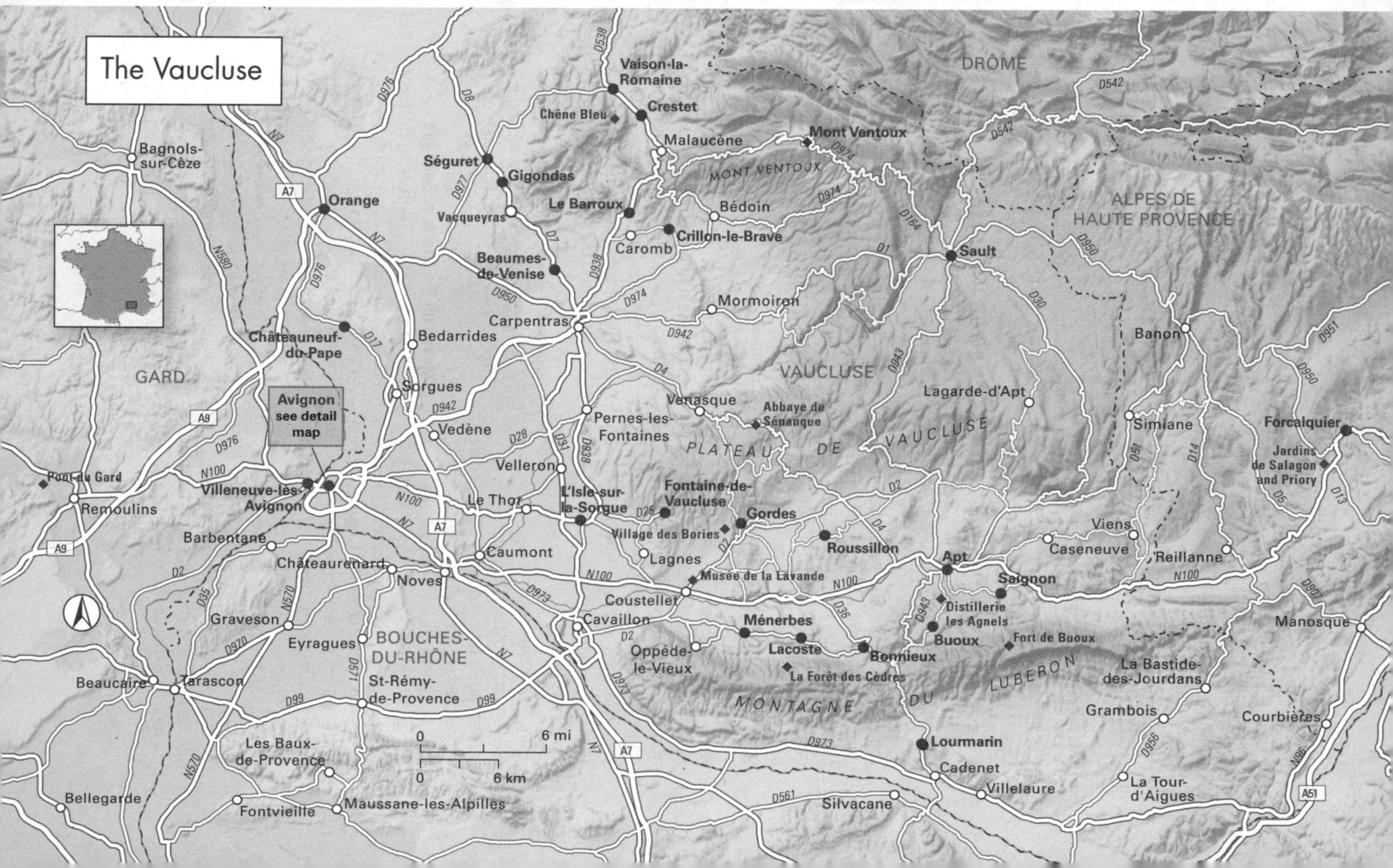
The Vaucluse
DRÔME
ALPES DE HAUTE PROVENCE
GARD
BOUCHES-DU-RHÔNE
VAUCLUSE
PLATEAU DE VAUCLUSE
MONT VENTOUX
MONTAGNE DU LUBERON
Vaison-la-Romaine
Crestet
Chêne Bleu
Malaucène
Mont Ventoux
Séguret
Gigondas
Le Barroux
Vacqueyras
Bédoin
Crillon-le-Brave
Caromb
Beaumes-de-Venise
Orange
Bagnols-sur-Cèze
Sault
Carpentras
Mormoiron
Châteauneuf-du-Pape
Bedarrides
Banon
Sorgues
Avignon see detail map
Venasque
Abbaye de Sénanque
Lagarde-d'Apt
Simiane
Forcalquier
Jardins de Salagon and Priory
Vedène
Pernes-les-Fontaines
Velleron
Pont du Gard
Villeneuve-lès-Avignon
Remoulins
Le Thor
L'Isle-sur-la-Sorgue
Fontaine-de-Vaucluse
Gordes
Village des Bories
Roussillon
Viens
Caseneuve
Reillanne
Barbentane
Caumont
Lagnes
Apt
Saignon
Châteaurenard
Noves
Musée de la Lavande
Coustellet
Distillerie les Agnels
Graveson
Cavaillon
Ménerbes
Buoux
Fort de Buoux
Manosque
Eyragues
Oppéde-le-Vieux
Lacoste
Bonnieux
La Forêt des Cèdres
La Bastide-des-Jourdans
Beaucaire
Tarascon
St-Rémy-de-Provence
Grambois
Courbières
Les Baux-de-Provence
Lourmarin
Cadenet
Villelaure
La Tour-d'Aigues
Bellegarde
Fontvieille
Maussane-les-Alpilles
Silvacane
0
6 mi
0
6 km
A7
A9
A51
N7
N100
N580
N570
N96
D538
D976
D8
D977
D7
D938
D950
D974
D164
D1
D542
D942
D17
D4
D943
D30
D951
D28
D31
D25
D2
D51
D14
D5
D13
D907
D973
D36
D943
D35
D970
D571
D99
D561
D956

private terraces with some rooms. **Cons:** some rooms on the dark side; expensive in high season; some buildings could use a spruce-up. *Rooms from: €290* ✉ *7 pl. du Chapitre, Villeneuve-lès-Avignon* ☎ *04–90–15–90–15* 🌐 *www.leprieure.com* *39 rooms* *No Meals.*

Châteauneuf-du-Pape

17 km (10 miles) north of Avignon.

A patchwork of rolling vineyards—green-and-black furrows striping the landscape in endless, retreating perspective—welcomes you to one of France's great wine regions. Once the source of the table wine of the Avignon popes, who kept a fortified summer house here (hence the name of the town, which means "new castle of the pope"), these vineyards were wiped out by phylloxera in the 19th century and subsequently re-grafted with resistant American root stock. The wine's revival as a muscular and resilient mix of up to 13 varieties with an almost portlike intensity (it can reach 15% alcohol content) moved it to the forefront of French reds. The whites, though less known, can also be sublime.

There are *caves de dégustation* (wine-tasting cellars) on nearly every street; get a free map from the tourist office. Also head to the discreet *vignobles* (vineyards) at the edge of town. Some of the best (and oldest) Châteauneufs come from Château la Nerthe, Château de Vaudieu, and Château Fortia, and they are priced accordingly. If you're not armed with the names of a few great houses, look for *medaille d'or* (gold medal) ratings from prestigious wine fairs; these are usually indicated by a gold sticker on the bottle. Better yet, for the best selection of wines in one place as well as expertise to match, go to Vinadea, the official *maison des vins* of Châteauneuf.

GETTING HERE AND AROUND

There's no direct bus from Avignon to Châteauneuf-du-Pape, but you can take a Zou! bus to Orange (€3) and connect with another bus for the 25-minute journey to Châteauneuf (€2.10). Several buses make these trips in both directions throughout the day. It's easier to drive, however: take the D225, the D907, and then the D17, direction Orange, and follow signs to Châteauneuf-du-Pape (about 30 minutes).

VISITOR INFORMATION

CONTACTS Châteauneuf-du-Pape Tourist Office. ✉ *3 rue de la République, Châteauneuf-du-Pape* ☎ *04–90–83–71–08* 🌐 *www.poptourisme.fr/contact-chateauneuf-du-pape-tourisme.*

Sights

Château

CASTLE/PALACE | If you're disinclined to spend your vacation sniffing and sipping, climb the hill to the ruins of the château. Though it was destroyed in the Wars of Religion (1562–98) between Catholics and Huguenots and its remaining donjon (keep) blasted by the Germans in World War II, it still commands a magnificent position. From this rise in the rolling vineyards, you can enjoy wraparound views of Avignon, the Luberon, and Mont Ventoux. ✉ *Châteauneuf-du-Pape.*

Musée du Vin Brotte et Boutique

HISTORY MUSEUM | There's no better way to learn about the local wine production than to spend an hour at the Musée du Vin Maison Brotte, a private collection of wine-making equipment displayed in the *caveau* (wine cellar) of the Brotte family. ✉ *Av. St-Pierre de Luxembourg, Châteauneuf-du-Pape* ☎ *04–90–83–59–44* 🌐 *www.museeduvinbrotte.com* *Free.*

★ Vinothèque

OTHER ATTRACTION | Put yourself in the hands of an expert under the arched ceilings of this new, state-of-the-art tasting room set in an ancient wine cave. This is

Châteauneuf-du-Pape, a beautiful hillside town just a half-hour bus ride from Avignon, lends its name to some of the world's most renowned wines.

a great opportunity to sample the region's majestic reds and dazzling whites side by side, or you can custom-design your own tasting from the 200 wines offered by the 120 estates represented here. All of the wines can be purchased at Vinadea, just above the Vinothèque. ✉ *9 rue de la République, Châteauneuf-du-Pape* ☎ *04–12–04–45–86* 🌐 *www.vinadea.com* ⏲ *Closed Mon. and Tues.*

Wine Appreciation Classes

OTHER ATTRACTION | Held in the wine cellar of her "wine B&B" in the heart of Châteauneuf-du-Pape, Danièle Raulet-Reynaud's informative classes (in English) cover everything you'll need to know about this world-class appellation: tasting, buying, storing, serving, and pairing. A master sommelier of France, gastronomic cook, vice president of the Women Vignerons of the Rhône, and a charming raconteur, Raulet-Reynaud has taught wine courses around the world for 40 years. Her popular Apéro Fun (€30) Friday workshops are a wonderful way to spend an hour or an afternoon learning about and tasting these magnificent wines. ✉ *20 av. Charles de Gaulle, Châteauneuf-du-Pape* ☎ *06–16–48–61–87* 🌐 *www.chateauneuf-wine-bb.com* 🎫 *Fees upon request.*

Restaurants

★ La Maisouneta

$$ | FRENCH | FAMILY | This cozy restaurant with cheerful planters and original art is run by a young husband-and-wife team and specializes in pasta dishes and regional French comfort food (from Savoie, Nice, and Provence). Dishes such as basil-and-cheese ravioli, stuffed peppers farci, and *crème anchoïade* (anchovy cream) are seasonal, beautifully prepared, and deeply satisfying. **Known for:** reliably excellent food; little-known Châteauneuf-du-Pape wines; lovely outdoor terrace. $ *Average main: €18* ✉ *Pl. Jean Moulin, Châteauneuf-du-Pape* ☎ *04–90–32–55–03* 🌐 *www.lamaisouneta.fr* ⏲ *Closed Jan. and Sun and Mon.*

★ La Mère Germaine

$$$$ | **MODERN FRENCH** | The dazzling new La Mère Germaine restaurant earned a Michelin star within seven months of reopening as part of the hotel of the same name, and now, with two-star Belgian chef Christophe Hardiquest at the helm, it has further refined its locavore offerings. Dishes on the seasonal, five-course menus (€98 at lunch, €118 at dinner) might include celery root and shredded truffle ravioli with fermented shiitake or melt-in-your-mouth quail *suprême* with almond hummus and artichoke hearts. **Known for:** beautiful decor; outdoor dining; impressive wine list. *Average main: €48 Hôtel La Mère Germaine, 3 rue Commandant Lemaître, Châteauneuf-du-Pape 04–90–22–78–34 www.lameregermaine.com/restaurant-gastronomique Closed Mon.–Wed.*

Le Comptoir de la Mère Germaine

$$ | **MODERN FRENCH** | This chic new bistro, a hit among locals, was designed with all the care and taste as the nearby Hôtel La Mère Germaine. On cool days, you can relax in its light-filled dining room and watch preparations in the open kitchen; in warm weather, you can sit on the terrace and take in the endless vineyard views. **Known for:** fresh daily dishes; great location in the village center; superb (bien sûr) wine list. *Average main: €18 4 rue des Consuls, Châteauneuf-du-Pape 04–28–69–00–60 www.lameregermaine-chateauneufdupape.fr/le-comptoir Closed Tues. and Wed.*

Le Verger des Papes

$$ | **FRENCH** | It's well worth the slog up the hill to the château simply to linger on the terrace of this long-established restaurant and savor the view over Mont Ventoux, Avignon, the Luberon, and the Rhône—and you can visit the restaurant's well-stocked wine cellar on your way to the top. The tarte *à la tomate confite* with goat cheese and iced white cheese is a specialty that reveals a love for the region's cuisine. **Known for:** family-run for generations; fabulous views; excellent wine list. *Average main: €24 Rue Montée du Château, Châteauneuf-du-Pape 04–90–83–50–40 vergerdespapes.com Closed Sun., Mon., and mid-Dec.–Feb.*

Hotels

★ Coucou Grands Cépages

$$$ | **RESORT** | **FAMILY** | Behind a locked gate at this sprawling property five minutes from Châteauneuf-du-Pape center, contemporary, wooden *eco-cabanes* sit beside, just over, or even on top of a secluded emerald-green lake. **Pros:** total peace and privacy; beautifully designed cabins; food delivery and spa treatments available. **Cons:** must have a car to get here; no hot meals unless you go out to a restaurant; less delightful in cold or windy weather. *Rooms from: €280 2061 chemin des Pompes, Châteauneuf-du-Pape 04–88–95–87–58 www.cabanesdesgrandscepages.com 15 cabins No Meals.*

★ Hôtel La Mère Germaine

$$ | **HOTEL** | **FAMILY** | This jewel of a hotel—complete with a spa and a Michelin-starred restaurant—is set in two 18th-century buildings and has sleek guest rooms that feature pale wood, ocher walls, colorful kilims, charming art, contemporary designer furnishings, and high-quality bedding. **Pros:** easy walking distance to town and vineyards; parking; great price-to-quality ratio. **Cons:** small breakfast room in winter; no pool; books quickly in high season. *Rooms from: €170 3 rue Commandant Lemaître, Châteauneuf-du-Pape 04–90–22–78–34 www.lameregermaine.com/hotel 8 rooms No Meals.*

L'Espace de L'Hers

$$ | **B&B/INN** | The charming hosts at this serene B&B set amid vineyards and forest make every effort—from organizing wine tastings and tours to offering cooking classes—to ensure that you

enjoy a true Provençal experience. **Pros:** gourmet meals are served by advance reservation; price includes breakfast; free Wi-Fi. **Cons:** fills up quickly; no nightlife for miles around; no elevator. *Rooms from: €150* ✉ *5 chemin de L'Hers, Châteauneuf-du-Pape* ☎ *06–22–65–41–18* 🌐 *www.espacedelhers.com* 💳 *No credit cards* *4 rooms* *Free Breakfast.*

Shopping

★ Vinadea

WINE/SPIRITS | The official *maison des vins* of Châteauneuf-du-Pape, Vinadea has the town's best selection of wines, along with wine expertise if you have questions. Tastings are offered daily, and wines can be shipped internationally. Keep in mind that shipping rates are offset by the fact that you're getting "cellar door" prices with no markup. ✉ *8 rue Maréchal Foch, Châteauneuf-du-Pape* ☎ *04–90–83–70–69* 🌐 *www.vinadea.com.*

Orange

12 km (7 miles) north of Châteauneuf-du-Pape; 31 km (19 miles) north of Avignon.

Cradled in northern Provence in the land of Côtes du Rhône vineyards, Orange really isn't very big, but when compared with the sleepy wine villages that surround it, it's a thriving metropolis. In many ways, the town captures the essence of the region: the Provençal accent here is quite thick, and savory food and wine can be had—for a price. Come to see its two ancient Roman monuments, the Théâtre Antique and the Arc de Triomphe, spectacular vestiges of history that seem transported from a different world.

GETTING HERE AND AROUND

The Paris TGV at 3 hours 20 minutes serves Orange twice daily, but from Nice to Orange by TGV is more complicated, involving a change of trains at Marseille; the fare is about €67, but with the stop-over it takes about 5½ hours. From Gare Avignon Centre to Orange, it costs €6.40 for the 20-minute train ride. Orange's center is a 10-minute walk from the train station (head from Avenue F. Mistral to Rue de la République, then follow signs).

By bus from Avignon's gare routière (bus station) there are 10–20 buses daily at €2.60 one-way (45 minutes), arriving at the train station in Orange.

VISITOR INFORMATION

CONTACTS Orange Tourist Office. ✉ *5 cours Aristide Briand, Orange* ☎ *04–90–34–70–88* 🌐 *www.poptourisme.fr/orange/orange.*

Sights

Arc de Triomphe

RUINS | North of the city center is the Arc de Triomphe, which once straddled the Via Agrippa between Lyon and Arles. Three arches support a heavy double attic (horizontal top) floridly decorated with battle scenes and marine symbols, references to Augustus's victories at Actium. The arch, which dates from about 20 BC, is superbly preserved—particularly its north side—but to view it on foot, you'll have to cross a roundabout seething with traffic. ✉ *Av. de l'Arc de Triomphe, Orange.*

Musée d'Orange

HISTORY MUSEUM | **FAMILY** | Across the street from the Théâtre Antique, this small museum displays artifacts unearthed around Orange, including fragments of three detailed marble *cadastres* (land survey maps) dating from the first century AD. Upstairs, a vivid series of 18th-century canvases shows local mills producing Provençal fabrics, each aspect illustrated in careful detail. There are also personal objects from local aristocrats and a collection of faience pharmacy jars. ✉ *Rue Madeleine Roch, Orange* ☎ *04–90–51–17–60* 🌐 *www.*

theatre-antique.com 🎫 *€11.50 combined ticket with Théâtre Antique.*

Théâtre Antique

RUINS | Orange's spectacular Théâtre Antique, a colossal Roman theater, was built in the time of Caesar Augustus. The vast stone stage wall, bouncing sound off the facing hillside, climbs four stories high—a massive sandstone screen that Louis XIV once referred to as the "finest wall in my kingdom." The niche at center stage contains the original statue of Augustus, just as it reigned over centuries of productions of classical plays. Today the theater provides a backdrop for world-class theater and opera. ✉ *Pl. des Frères-Mounet, Orange* ☎ *04–90–51–17–60* 🌐 *www.theatre-antique.com* 🎫 *€11.50 combined ticket with the Musée d'Orange.*

Vieil Orange

NEIGHBORHOOD | **FAMILY** | This Old Town neighborhood, which you must cross to hike from one Roman monument to the other, carries on peacefully when there's not a blockbuster spectacle in the theater. Lining its broad squares, under heavy-leaved plane trees, are a handful of shops and a few sidewalk cafés. ✉ *Orange.*

Restaurants

Au Petit Patio

$$ | **BISTRO** | This ultrapopular eatery on the edge of Old Town consistently serves fresh, locally sourced cuisine with a price-to-quality ratio that keeps the locals coming back. Imaginative dishes like *pot au feu de coquilles Saint-Jacques* (stewed scallops and vegetables) and mussels in saffron broth are ample and served with flair. **Known for:** cozy, romantic atmosphere; pretty garden terrace; top-notch service. 💲 *Average main: €22* ✉ *58 cours Aristide-Briand, Orange* ☎ *04–90–29–69–27* 🌐 *au-petit-patio-orange.eatbu.com* ⏲ *Closed Sun. No dinner Wed. and Thurs.*

Le Mas des Aigras

$$$ | **FRENCH** | Set amid vineyards just outside Orange, this stone farmhouse restaurant recently updated its traditional dining room and its dishes, while maintaining its charm and its high standards. The sophisticated menu is based on the French classics like salmon mousse, house-made foie gras, beef cheeks, and a fish of the day. **Known for:** pretty setting; attention to presentation; outdoor terrace. 💲 *Average main: €25* ✉ *Chemin des Aigras, Orange* ☎ *04–90–34–81–01* 🌐 *www.masdesaigras.com* ⏲ *Closed Oct.–Mar.*

Hotels

Château de Massillan

$$ | **HOTEL** | **FAMILY** | Ancient meets modern at this 50-acre wine estate and gardens 9 km (5½ miles) from Orange, where you can stay in an elegant beamed aerie in the crenellated 16th-century castle or a chic contemporary abode in the stylish addition. **Pros:** superb "bio" spa with a sensorial pool, sauna, whirlpool, and steam rooms; an all-organic credo, with an emphasis on gluten-free foods; large luxurious bedrooms with all the amenities. **Cons:** some guests can't get past the ancient–modern thing; dining room lacks character; spa can get crowded. 💲 *Rooms from: €195* ✉ *730 chemin de Massillan, Uchaux* ☎ *04–90–40–64–51* 🌐 *www.chateaudemassillan.fr* *26 rooms* *No Meals.*

Grand Hôtel d'Orange

$$ | **HOTEL** | **FAMILY** | Tucked away in an 18th-century town house on a quiet city center street, just minutes from the Théâtre Antique, this chic boutique hotel—part of Best Western's Signature Collection—has stylishly furnished rooms; a wellness area with a fitness room, sauna, and steam room; and a spacious rooftop pool. **Pros:** well priced; lots of amenities; pool is refreshing during Provence's hot summers. **Cons:** not all rooms have great views; elevators reach only some rooms; corporate service. $ *Rooms from: €130* ✉ *8 pl. Langes, Orange* ☎ *04–90–11–40–40* 🌐 *www.grandhotelorange.com* 🛏 *40 rooms* 🍽 *No Meals.*

Performing Arts

Les Chorégies d'Orange

MUSIC FESTIVALS | To witness the torches of *Nabucco* or *Aïda* flickering against the 2,000-year-old Roman wall of the Théâtre Antique and to hear the extraordinary sound play around its semicircle of ancient seats is one of the great summer festival experiences in Europe. Every July, Les Chorégies d'Orange echo tradition and amass operatic and classical music spectacles under the summer stars in Orange. Be sure to book tickets well in advance; they go on sale in October. ✉ *15 pl. Silvain, Orange* ☎ *04–90–34–24–24* 🌐 *www.choregies.fr.*

Beaumes-de-Venise

23 km (14 miles) east of Orange.

Just west of the great mass of Mont Ventoux, surrounded by farmland and vineyards, is Beaumes-de-Venise, where streets of shuttered bourgeois homes slope steeply into a market center. This is the renowned source of a delicately sweet muscat wine, but if you're tasting, don't overlook the local reds. In the town center you can also buy fruity, unfiltered olive oil produced in the area; it's made in such small quantities that you're unlikely to see it elsewhere.

Beaumes lies at the foot of the Dentelles de Montmirail, a small range of rocky chalk cliffs eroded to lacy pinnacles—hence the name *dentelles* (lace). From tiny D21, east of town, you'll find dramatic views north to the ragged peaks and south over lush orchards and vineyards interspersed with olive groves and stands of pine or yew trees. It's a splendid drive, and if you love nature it would be well worth staying in this area—many of the stone houses have been converted into bed-and-breakfasts.

GETTING HERE AND AROUND

There is no direct bus service to Beaumes-de-Venise. You can take Bus 5.1 from Avignon to Carpentras, about 10 km (6 miles) away (€2.10, 1 hour) and take a taxi the rest of the way for about €20. The best way to get here is by car.

VISITOR INFORMATION

CONTACTS Beaumes-de-Venise Tourist Office. ✉ *140 pl. du Marché, Beaumes-de-Venise* ☎ *04–90–62–94–39* 🌐 *www.ventouxprovence.fr.*

Sights

Domaine des Bernardins

WINERY | This vineyard has a tasting cave, where you can sample some of the wines, which include mostly whites but also reds from grapes such as grenache. ✉ *138 av. Gambetta, Beaumes-de-Venise* ☎ *04–90–62–94–13* 🌐 *www.domaine-des-bernardins.com.*

Vacqueyras

TOWN | **FAMILY** | Smaller and more picturesque than Beaumes, with stone houses scattered along its gentle slopes, Vacqueyras gives its name to a robust, tannic red wine worthy of its more famous neighbors Châteauneuf-du-Pape and Gigondas. Wine domaines beckon from the outskirts of town, and the center is dotted with plane trees, adorned with cascading wisteria, and punctuated by discreet tasting shops. Thanks to its consistently rising quality, Vacqueyras is one of the latest of the Côtes du Rhônes to earn its own appellation—that is, the right to put its village name on the bottle instead of the less prestigious, more generic Côtes du Rhône label. ✉ *Vacqueyras.*

 Hotels

★ Domaine de Coyeux

$$$$ | **B&B/INN** | Luxury and privacy reign at this majestic lodging perched above the rolling hills of a 300-acre wine estate and backed by the jagged peaks of the Dentelles de Montmirail and the azure Provençal sky. **Pros:** splendid setting; enormous suites; boundless luxury. **Cons:** no nightlife if that's what you're looking for; you'll never want to leave; luxury comes at a price. *Rooms from: €2,500 ✉ 167 chemin du Rocher, Beaumes-de-Venise ☎ 04–90–12–42–42 🌐 www.domainedecoyeux.com ⏲ Closed Dec.–Mar. 5 rooms 🍽 Free Breakfast.*

 Shopping

★ Rhonéa

WINE/SPIRITS | This elegant cooperative features the best of the legendary Beaumes-de-Venise wines, made exclusively from the muscat grape, as well as the appellation's lesser-known but equally worthy reds, whites, and rosés. There are also options from the neighboring Gigondas and Vacqueyras. All can be tasted in the degustation room, as can local olive oil, fruit juices, and more. Wines can be shipped worldwide. *✉ 228 rte. de Carpentras, Beaumes-de-Venise ☎ 04–90–12–41–00 🌐 rhonea.fr.*

Gigondas

9 km (6 miles) northwest of Beaumes-de-Venise.

Dating from the 10th through the 14th centuries, Gigondas is the prettiest of all the Mont Ventoux Côtes-du-Rhône wine villages, with a cluster of stone houses stacked gracefully up a hillside overlooking the broad sweep of the valley below. At the top, a false-front Baroque church anchors a ring of medieval ramparts; from here you can take in views as far as the Cévennes.

Its few residents share one vocation: the production of the vigorous grenache-based red that bears the village name. At the more than 60 *caveaux* scattered throughout the area, you're welcome to visit, taste, and buy without ceremony. Pick up a contact list from the tourist office at the village entrance beside the town hall. **■ TIP→ While in town, be sure to visit the Caveau du Gigondas, a convivial tasting room and wine boutique.**

GETTING HERE AND AROUND

There is no direct bus service to Gigondas. The only way to get here is by car. From Beaumes-de-Venise, take the D81 to the D7.

VISITOR INFORMATION

CONTACTS Gigondas Tourist Office. *✉ 5 rue du Portail, Gigondas ☎ 04–90–65–85–46 🌐 www.ventouxprovence.fr.*

 Restaurants

★ L'Oustalet

$$$$ | **FRENCH** | Chef Laurent Deconinck won his first Michelin star in 2018, proving to the culinary mainstream what Provence gourmands have known all along—that this is one of the region's most coveted tables. In the elegant dining room, you're assured of a stellar meal and superb wines (the sommelier is expert at pairing the local nectars, as the winemakers all flock here) in a convivial atmosphere. **Known for:** gourmet Provençal cuisine; beautiful setting in the heart of the village; excellent wines. *Average main: €35 ✉ 5 pl. Gabrielle Andéol, Gigondas ☎ 04–90–65–85–30 🌐 www.loustalet-gigondas.com ⏲ Closed Sun.–Tues.*

 Hotels

Les Florêts

$$ | **HOTEL** | **FAMILY** | A good choice for hikers, this family-run lodging—a scenic, mile-long walk from town and set amid woods and vineyards at the foot of the

Dentelles de Montmirail—provides a warm welcome and basic but spacious guest rooms. **Pros:** great restaurant; all water is from the spring; gently priced. **Cons:** rooms need an upgrade; few in-room amenities; more practical than chic. $ *Rooms from: €145* ✉ *1243 rte. des Florêts, Gigondas* ☎ *04–90–65–85–01* ⊕ *www.hotel-lesflorets.com* ⏲ *Closed Jan.–mid-Mar.* *15 rooms* *No Meals.*

Villa Sainte-Anne

$$ | **HOUSE** | **FAMILY** | You'll feel right at home amid the vineyards at this restored winemaker's villa on one of Gigondas's most prominent estates, a 10-minute walk from the village. **Pros:** winery tours and tastings are just steps away; friendly welcome; great for families. **Cons:** set close to the road; pool is small; not in the village center. $ *Rooms from: €180* ✉ *345 rte. de Sable, Gigondas* ☎ *04–65–89–00–20* ⊕ *www.oenotourisme.pierre-amadieu.com* *5 rooms* *No Meals.*

Shopping

★ Caveau du Gigondas

WINE/SPIRITS | This is *the* place to sample more than 100 Gigondas vintages—all for free—and learn everything you want to know about the terroir, wine making, organic wines, and the AOP Gigondas appellation from friendly, highly knowledgeable staffers who speak English. Afterward, you can stock up on the best of these stunning wines. ✉ *Pl. Gabrielle Andéol, Gigondas* ☎ *04–90–65–82–29* ⊕ *www.gigondas-vin.com/le-caveau-du-gigondas.*

Séguret

7 km (4 miles) northeast of Gigondas.

Nestled into the sharp rake of a rocky slope and crowned with the ruins of a medieval castle, Séguret is a picture-book hill village that is only moderately commercialized. Its 14th-century clock tower, Romanesque Église St-Denis, and bubbling Renaissance fountain sit amid steep little stone streets and lovely views of the Dentelles de Montmirail cliffs. Here, too, you can find peppery Côtes du Rhône for the tasting.

GETTING HERE AND AROUND

There is no direct bus service to Séguret. The only way to get here is by car via the D7 and the D23.

Restaurants

Côté Terrasse

$$ | **BISTRO** | Like many restaurants in Provence, this one has a pleasantly shaded terrace with a view, but it also offers truly warm and welcoming service and consistently good food. Alongside hearty dishes like cod with aïoli and grilled vegetables, Iberian pork with chestnuts and whipped potatoes, or classic roasted duck breast, the menu features plenty of fresh, inventive salads—not always easy to find—like wild salmon with shrimp, melon, and tomato confit. **Known for:** nicely priced fixed menus (especially at lunch); very popular so book in advance; classic French food. $ *Average main: €18* ✉ *219 rue des Poternes, Séguret* ☎ *04–90–28–03–48* ⏲ *Closed Nov.–Mar.*

Hotels

La Bastide Bleue

$ | **HOTEL** | Once an idyllic youth hostel, this old stone farmhouse with blue-shuttered windows is now an unpretentious but enchanting country inn set in a pine-shaded garden court. **Pros:** garden-lined pool; very good on-site restaurant with courtyard; recently updated rooms. **Cons:** proper and clean, but design nothing special; books up quickly; breakfast not included. $ *Rooms from: €75* ✉ *Rte. de Sablet, 1 km (½ mile) south of Séguret on D23, Séguret* ☎ *04–90–46–83–43* ⊕ *www.bastide-bleue.com* *7 rooms* *No Meals.*

Vaison-la-Romaine

10 km (6 miles) northeast of Séguret; 29 km (18 miles) northeast of Orange.

As the town's name implies, the ancient Roman presence in Vaison was significant. A well-established Celtic colony here joined forces with Rome in the 2nd century BC, and the town had considerable status in the empire's glory days. No gargantuan monuments were raised, yet it's surmised that the luxury of the villas in Vaison surpassed that of those in Pompeii. Today, you can see what remains at the largest archaeological site in France.

In the medieval area of town, the 13th- and 14th-century houses owe some of their beauty to stone pillaged from the Roman ruins below. But the charm here is all derived from the Middle Ages: a trickling stone fountain, a bell tower with a wrought-iron campanile, soft-color shutters, and blooming vines. Set in a river valley lush with orchards of almonds and apricots, Vaison is also a modern-day market center. The Provençal market on Tuesday and the smaller organic farmers' market on Saturday morning are major draws, as is the five-day food festival in early November.

GETTING HERE AND AROUND

Several routes travel from Séguret to Vaison-la-Romaine; regardless of which one you choose, the drive is about 15 minutes. Bus 4 (€3; 40 minutes) runs throughout the day from the Orange SNCF station to Vaison, and Bus 11 runs from Carpentras (€2.10; 45 minutes). A taxi from Orange is €43; from Avignon, count on at least €85 on weekdays (weekend fares are 50% more).

VISITOR INFORMATION

CONTACTS Vaison-la-Romaine Tourist Office. ✉ *Pl. Chanoine Sautel, Vaison-la-Romaine* ☎ *04–90–36–02–11* 🌐 *www.vaison-la-romaine.com/tourisme.*

Sights

★ At Home with Patricia Wells Cooking Classes

OTHER ATTRACTION | Although Vaison has centuries-old attractions, the most popular for Americans may well be the classes offered by Patricia Wells, the food critic who made a name for herself writing posh columns and *The Food Lover's Guide to France.* She now introduces people to the splendors of French cooking—in her lovely farmhouse and above her own Chanteduc vineyards outside Vaison. Weeklong culinary seminars are deluxe ($6,000 a student) and exclusive (maximum of 12 students), and the January truffle workshop usually sells out, so book early (online only). ✉ *Vaison-la-Romaine* 🌐 *www.patriciawells.com.*

Cathédrale Notre-Dame-de-Nazareth

CHURCH | Fragments from a Gallo-Roman basilica were used to build this solemn, Romanesque cathedral, whose cloister is surrounded by richly sculpted columns and arches. ✉ *Av. Jules-Ferry, Vaison-la-Romaine.*

★ Les Sites Antiques de Vaison-la-Romaine

RUINS | **FAMILY** | Like a miniature Roman Forum, the ancient **Quartier de Puymin,** part of the largest archaeological site in France, spreads over a field and hillside in the heart of Vaison, visible in passing from the town's streets. Access to a garden, an archaeological museum, and the skeletal ruins of Roman villas below Vaison's ancient theater is via an entry booth across from the tourist office. Although it requires considerable imagination to visualize the structures as they once were, there are some poignant details, such as thresholds that still show the hinge holds for and scrape marks left by swinging doors.

Closest to the entrance, the foundations of the Maison des Messii (Messii House) indicate that it had a sumptuous design complete with a vast gentleman's library; reception rooms; an atrium with a rain-fed pool; a large kitchen (note the enormous stone vats); and baths with hot, cold, and warm water. To see the accoutrements of everyday Roman life, wander beneath the cypress trees and amid the flowering shrubs of a formal garden to the **Musée Archéologique Théo-Desplans.** Here, items are displayed by theme: pottery, weapons, gods and goddesses, jewelry, and, of course, sculpture—including a complete figure of the emperor Claudius (1st century) and a strikingly noble nude Hadrian (2nd century).

Cross the park behind the museum to climb into the bleachers of the 1st-century **Théâtre Romain,** smaller than the one in Orange but also used today for concerts and plays. Across the parking lot is the **Quartier de la Villasse,** where remnants of a lively market town indicate main-street shops, public gardens, and grand private homes complete with floor mosaics. The most evocative image of all is in the *thermes* (baths): a neat row of marble-seat toilets lined up over a raked trough that instantly rinsed waste away.

The best way to understand the sites is with a self-guided audio tour (€2, available at the museum). Guided tours led by certified docents are also a possibility, though availability, duration, prices, and themes vary. Check ahead with the museum or the tourist board. ✉ *Rue Burrus, Vaison-la-Romaine* ☎ *04–90–46–51–14 archaeology museum* 🌐 *www.provenceromaine.com* 🎫 *€9 (all sites; valid for 24 hrs)* ⏲ *Closed Jan.–Feb. 5.*

Pont Romain (*Roman Bridge*)
BRIDGE | The remarkable single-arch Roman bridge, built in the 1st century, stands firm across the Ouvèze River. ✉ *Vaison-la-Romaine.*

Restaurants

La Belle Étoile
$$ | **FRENCH** | **FAMILY** | The relaxed, welcoming atmosphere and lovely country setting here are worth the short drive to the town of Roaix. The affable owner and cook presents an ever-changing menu with an emphasis on what's fresh, local, and organic—salmon-and-sweet-onion tartlette nestled among a crisp mesclun salad might be among the starters, perhaps followed by chicken stuffed with local wild mushrooms. **Known for:** relaxed garden dining; fresh ingredients; beautiful outdoor terrace. $ *Average main: €20* ✉ *1234 rte. des Princes d'Orange, Roaix* ☎ *04–90–37–31–45* ⏲ *Closed Thurs. and mid-Feb.–mid-Mar.*

Hotels

★ Bastide la Combe
$$ | **B&B/INN** | A warm welcome awaits you at this picture-perfect country inn, just five minutes from town and set amid vineyards with sweeping views of Mont Ventoux and the Dentelles mountains. **Pros:** abundant breakfast served in the garden; homemade gourmet meals available upon request; bright, airy, tasteful rooms. **Cons:** closed November through March; breakfast not included in price; fills up very quickly. $ *Rooms from: €165* ✉ *1885 ch. de Sainte Croix, Vaison-la-Romaine* ☎ *04–90–28–76–33* 🌐 *www.bastide-lacombe.fr* ⏲ *Closed Nov.–Mar.* *5 rooms* *Free Breakfast.*

Évêché
$ | **B&B/INN** | In the medieval part of town, this turreted 16th-century former bishop's palace has rooms with rustic charm—delicate fabrics, exposed beams, and wooden bedsteads. **Pros:** generous breakfast is excellent; hosts are available to give advice; charming decor. **Cons:** some rooms are a little small (so opt for a suite); house can be cold in winter; books up quickly. $ *Rooms from: €100* ✉ *14 rue de l'Évêché, Vaison-la-Romaine* ☎ *06–03–03–21–42* 🌐 *eveche.free.fr* *5 rooms* *Free Breakfast.*

Le Beffroi
$ | **HOTEL** | Perched on a cliff top in the Old Town, this gracious grouping of

16th-century mansions comes together as a fine hotel, where an extravagant period salon leads to curving stone stairs that go up to sizable rooms with beamed ceilings and antiques. **Pros:** beautiful views; lovely garden; saltwater pool. **Cons:** pool on the small side; very narrow street to reach the hotel; some rooms are dated. *Rooms from: €120* *Rue de l'Évêché, Vaison-la-Romaine* *04–90–36–04–71* *www.le-beffroi.com* *Closed mid-Jan.–mid-Mar.* *22 rooms* *No Meals.*

Crestet

7 km (4½ miles) south of Vaison-la Romaine.

Another irresistible, souvenir-free aerie perched on a hilltop at the feet of the Dentelles de Montmirail cliffs and of Mont Ventoux, Crestet has it all: tinkling fountains, shuttered 15th-century houses, an arcaded *place* at the village's center, and a 12th-century castle crowning the lot. Views from its château terrace take in the concentric rings of tiled rooftops below, then the forest greenery and cultivated valleys below that.

GETTING HERE AND AROUND

You can take the bus from nearby Vaison-la-Romaine, but the best way to get here is by car. The drive along the D938 takes about 10 minutes.

Sights

★ Chêne Bleu

WINERY | This extraordinary domaine benefits from an ideal setting in the Mont Ventoux UNESCO Biosphere Reserve, with sweeping views of the Rhône Valley, the Dentelles de Montmirail, Mont Ventoux itself, and the medieval village of Crestet. The overarching principle here is to respect the land while benefiting from its incline and altitude to make handcrafted, fully organic wines of the highest quality. Comprehensive tours of the wine-making facilities and the estate include a tasting and a visit to the boutique where you can buy locally made gift items as well as wine.

Between mid-April and the end of October the domaine also serves lunches featuring all-organic dishes created by the in-house chef using ingredients from the kitchen gardens, charcuterie and cheese plates from local artisans, and, *bien sûr,* a glass or two of estate wines. Customized tastings can be arranged upon request, and the estate also has a separate house where up to 14 people can stay for a week in total luxury, including a private chef, a valet, and every imaginable comfort. Prices are through the roof, but the experience is assuredly one-of-a-kind. *Domaine de la Verrière, Crestet* *04–90–10–06–30* *www.visit.chenebleu.com* *Free.*

Le Barroux

15 km (10 miles) south of Crestet.

Of all the marvelous hilltop villages stretching across the South of France, this tiny ziggurat of a town has a special charm. Le Barroux has more than a whiff of fairy tale in the air, lording over a patchwork landscape as finely drawn as a medieval illumination, as bright as an illustration in a children's book.

This aerie has just one small church, a post office, and one tiny old *épicerie* (small grocery store) selling canned goods, yellowed postcards, and today's *La Provence.* You are forced, therefore, to look around you and listen to the trickle of the ancient fountains at every labyrinthine turn. Houses, cereal-box slim, seem to grow out of the bedrock, closing in around your suddenly unwieldy car.

GETTING HERE AND AROUND

There is no direct bus service to Le Barroux. The drive along the D938 from Crestet takes 20 minutes.

Sights

★ Château du Barroux

CASTLE/PALACE | With grand vaulted rooms and a chapel dating from the 12th century, this enormous château is picturesque Le Barroux's main draw. Some of its halls serve as venues for contemporary art exhibits, and the chapel's breathtaking frescoes—undergoing restoration but still accessible to the public—painted between the 16th and 19th centuries are a must-see. Ever full of surprises, the castle also harbors a whiskey distillery that produces a golden nectar from the local einkorn grain, which you'll learn all about on a comprehensive tour that ends with a tasting. Or you can relax in the charming gourmet tearoom, perfect for a refreshing break and an excellent coffee with your homemade pastry or ice cream and panoramic views. ✉ *Le Barroux* ☎ *06–59–13–13–21* 🌐 *www.chateaudubarroux.fr* 🎫 *€8.50; distillery and castle €17.50* 🕑 *Closed Jan. 1–15.*

Crillon-le-Brave

11 km (7 miles) southeast of Le Barroux.

On a knoll in a valley shielded by Mont Ventoux, with the craggy Dentelles in one direction and the hills of the Luberon in another, this hamlet named for a 16th-century soldier-hero is a good base for exploring the region—if you can afford to stay in its hotel. Indeed, in a village that doesn't have even a *boulangerie* (bakery), let alone a souvenir shop, the Hotel Crillon Le Brave is the main draw.

GETTING HERE AND AROUND

There is no direct bus service to Crillon-le-Brave. The drive from Le Barroux takes 15 to 20 minutes, depending on which routes you follow.

Hotels

Hotel Crillon le Brave

$$$$ | **HOTEL** | Like the views from its interconnected hilltop houses, prices at this sumptuous property are elevated—but, in return, you get a rarefied stage-set of medieval luxury. **Pros:** spa and heated outdoor pool; large, beautiful, bright rooms; most rooms have views. **Cons:** lots of stairs; restaurant isn't what it used to be; very expensive. 💲 *Rooms from: €420* ✉ *Pl. de l'Église, Crillon-le-Brave* ☎ *04–90–65–61–61* 🌐 *www.crillonlebrave.com* 🕑 *Closed Dec.–Feb.* 🛏 *34 rooms* 🍽 *No Meals.*

Mont Ventoux

27 km (17 miles) northeast of Crillon-le-Brave; 34 km (21 miles) east of Le Barroux.

The tallest mountain in the region, Mont Ventoux dominates the sweeping vistas and landscapes of northwestern Provence. The mountain's limestone peaks—often mistaken for snow cover—reach nearly 6,000 feet and harbor a unique wind-buffeted ecosystem recognized by UNESCO and strictly protected by France. It's also known for its foreboding role in the Tour de France bike race: if you can summit the "Beast of Provence" you'll be amply rewarded with truly breathtaking views.

GETTING HERE AND AROUND

The mountain is a favorite spot for hikers and cyclists (bike rentals are plentiful in Bédoin and Sault), but unless you're in tip-top shape, you'll need a car to explore the mountain. The drive from Crillon-le-Brave (along the D974, as well as the

D19 and D19A) takes about 40 minutes. From Le Barroux, it will take you about 50 minutes along the D974.

Sights

Mont Ventoux

MOUNTAIN | FAMILY | In addition to all the beautiful views *of* Mont Ventoux, there are equally spectacular views *from* Mont Ventoux. From any of the surrounding hill towns you can take an inspiring circle drive along the base and over the crest of the mountain, following the D974. This road winds through the extraordinarily lush south-facing greenery that Mont Ventoux protects from vicious mistral winds. Abundant orchards and olive groves peppered with stone farmhouses make this one of Provence's loveliest landscapes. Stop for a drink in busy Bédoin, with its 18th-century Jesuit church at the top of the Old Town maze.

Mont Ventoux was the site of the first recorded attempt at *l'escalade* (mountain climbing), when Italian poet-philosopher Petrarch grunted his way up in 1336. Although people had climbed mountains before, this was the first "do it because it's there" feat. Reaching the summit itself (at 6,263 feet) requires a bit of legwork. From either Chalet Reynard or the tiny ski center Mont Serein, you can leave your car and hike up to the peak's tall observatory tower. The climb is not overly taxing, and when you reach the top you are rewarded with gorgeous panoramic views of the Alps. And to the south, barring the possibility of high-summer haze, you'll take in views of the Rhône Valley, the Luberon, and even Marseille.

Hiking maps are available at *maisons de la presse* (newsstands) and tourist offices. Town-to-town treks are also a great way to explore the area; one of the most beautiful trails is from Malaucène to Séguret. In the off-season, lonely Mont Ventoux is plagued with an ungodly reputation due to destructive winds; attempts at saving its soul are evident from the chapels lining its slopes. Whether it's possessed by the devil or not, don't attempt to climb it in inclement weather; from late fall to early spring, in fact, the summit is closed by snow.

Restaurants

Le Chalet Reynard

$ | FRENCH | FAMILY | This restaurant, opened in 1927, is *the* spot to stop for lunch and to bask in the sun on your way up the eastern slope of Mont Ventoux. The food is far beyond the merely acceptable, whether you opt for simple omelets (with truffles in season), traditional options like *tartiflette* (a baked dish of potatoes, cheese, and bacon from the Savoie region) or even heartier fare such as a spit-roasted pig (for groups of 15 or more). **Known for:** basic French comfort food; hiker-friendly atmosphere; reasonable prices. *Average main: €17 Rte. du Mont Ventoux, Crillon-le-Brave At easternmost elbow of D974 04–90–61–84–55 www.chalet-reynard.fr Closed Nov. No dinner.*

Sault

38 km (24 miles) southeast of Crillon-le-Brave; 45 km (28 miles) southeast of Le Barroux.

Though at the hub of no fewer than six main roads, Sault remains an utterly isolated market town floating on a stony hilltop in a valley of lavender. Accessed only by circuitous country roads, it remains virtually untouched by tourism. The landscape is traditional Provence at its best: oak-forested hills and long, deep valleys purpled with the curving arcs of lavender. In the town itself, old painted storefronts exude the scent of honey and lavender. The damp church, Église Notre Dame de la Tour, dates to the 12th century; the long, lovely barrel nave was doubled in size in 1450.

From Sault all routes are scenic. You may head eastward into Haute-Provence, visiting (via D950) tiny Banon, source of the famed goat cheese. Wind up D942 to see pretty hilltop Aurel or down D30 to reach perched Simiane-la-Rotonde. Or head back toward Carpentras through the spectacular Gorges de la Nesque, snaking along narrow cliff-side roads through dramatic canyons carpeted with wild boxwood and pine. If you're exploring the Lavender Route, head eastward some 48 km (30 miles) to reach the epicenter of Haute-Provence's fabled lavender in the fields around the sleepy, dusty town of Forcalquier.

GETTING HERE AND AROUND

There is no direct bus service to Sault. The only way to get here is by car. Depending on which scenic routes you choose, the drive from Crillon-le-Brave takes 35 to 50 minutes; that from Le Barroux requires 40 to 50 minutes.

FESTIVALS

Fête de la Lavande

CULTURAL FESTIVALS | **FAMILY** | This daylong festival, usually held around August 15, is dedicated entirely to lavender. Village folk dress in traditional Provençal garb and parade on bicycles; horses leap over barrels of fragrant bundles of hay; and local producers display their wares at the market. It all culminates in a countryside lunch. ✉ *Hippodrome le Defends, along D950, Sault* 🌐 *www.fetedelalavande.fr.*

VISITOR INFORMATION

CONTACTS Ventoux-Sud Sault Tourist Office. ✉ *Av. de la Promenade, Sault* ☎ *04–90–64–01–21* 🌐 *www.ventoux-sud.com.*

Forcalquier

53 km (33 miles) southeast of Sault.

As a center of lavender production, this small town has a lively Monday-morning market—and an organic market on Thursday—with many lavender-based products. It also has a bohemian side, though: many artists have fled urban centers to draw inspiration from the area's bucolic surroundings, and the town is dotted with ateliers.

In the 12th century, Forcalquier was the capital of Haute-Provence and was called the Cité des Quatre Reines (City of the Four Queens) since the four daughters—Eleanor of Aquitaine among them—of this region's ruler, Raimond Beranger V, all married royals. In the vieille ville, this glorious era is evident in the Cathdédrale Notre-Dame and the Couvent des Cordeliers.

For most visitors, however, the town is significant as a departure point for walks, bike rides, horse rides, or drives into the surrounding world of lavender. You can pick up a brochure and map of the lavender route at the tourist office.

GETTING HERE AND AROUND

There is no direct bus service to Forcalquier. The only way to get here is by car. From Sault, the drive along the D950 takes just under an hour.

VISITOR INFORMATION

CONTACTS Forcalquier Office du Tourisme. ✉ *13 pl. Bourguet, Forcalquier* ☎ *04–92–75–10–02* 🌐 *www.haute-provence-tourisme.com.*

Sights

★ Artemisia Museum

OTHER MUSEUM | **FAMILY** | At this unique museum in the 13th-century Couvent des Cordeliers, you'll learn how the aromatic plants and medicinal herbs of the Montagne de Lure, part of a UNESCO Biosphere Reserve, have traditionally been grown, gathered, and used in remedies, perfumes, and cosmetics. Explanatory panels, botanical illustrations, plant specimens, and fragrance galleries are used to create a multisensory educational experience in themed exhibits such as Lavender, Pickers & Peddlers, The Druggists, Distillation, Plants & Elixirs, and Plants & Beauty. In addition, activity booklets and special displays help children navigate and understand the exhibits. For total immersion, sign up for one of the two-hour perfume workshops, which are offered for both adults (€45) and kids (€25). ✉ *Couvent des Cordeliers, Forcalquier* ☎ *04–92–72–50–68* 🌐 *www.artemisia-museum.fr* 🎫 *€6* ⏲ *Closed Tues., Sat., and Sun.*

Jardins de l'Abbaye de Valsaintes

GARDEN | FAMILY | The grounds of a Cistercian abbey—constructed in the late 11th century and rebuilt in the 17th century—contain a dry garden, a vegetable garden, and a spectacular rose garden with more than 500 varieties. Guided nature tours are offered, as are history tours that take in the church and might feature Gregorian chant. Open year-round, the on-site restaurant serves lunch and dinner Tuesday through Saturday and lunch on Sunday. A boutique sells gardening books and tools, as well as locally made fragrance and food items. ✉ *Lieu dit, Forcalquier* ☎ *04–92–75–94–19* 🌐 *www.valsaintes.org/en* 🎫 *€7* ⏲ *Closed late Dec.–early Feb.*

★ Jardins de Salagon and Priory

GARDEN | FAMILY | On a site occupied since the Gallo-Roman period, this picturesque 11th- to 12th-century priory—a rich archaeological site classed as a Historic Monument by the French Ministry of Culture—presides over 10 acres of themed gardens. The restored priory, with well-preserved Gothic and Romanesque flourishes, now houses an ethnological museum, a testament to the various cultures and peoples in this part of Provence. The garden functions as both a visual delight and a preserve for 2,500 species of plants and flowers native to the region, from ancient times to the present, organized into five themes—like "simple gardens and village plants," which includes field and cultivated plants that were both consumed and used medicinally. There's also a medieval garden, a fragrant garden with benches under the roses and honeysuckle for maximum sensory effect, and a modern "exotic" garden that crosses five continents. ✉ *Prieuré de Salagon, Mane* ☎ *04–92–75–70–50* 🌐 *www.musee-de-salagon.com* 🎫 *€8* ⏲ *Closed Tues.*

L'Occitane

FACTORY | FAMILY | Although the town of Manosque, 9 km (15 miles) south of Forcalquier, is not itself a draw, the town's main employer is. This where you'll find the factory of L'Occitane, the renowned Provençal purveyor of botanical skin-care products. You can make reservations for a one-hour tour of the production facility or just visit the gardens and shop in the company shop. ✉ *Z.I. chemin St-Maurice, Manosque* ☎ *04–92–70–32–08* 🌐 *fr.loccitane.com/visite-usine-loccitane-manosque* 🎫 *Gardens and shop free; tours €6.*

Hotels

La Bastide Saint-Georges

$$ | HOTEL | FAMILY | You can unwind in total comfort at this retreat—in a semirural area near the village of Forcalquier and amid the Luberon Natural Park—where each contemporary villa is done in earth tones and has a private terrace. **Pros:** close to sights and Lavender Route; free parking; Forcalquier's only five-star hotel. **Cons:** some rooms are a bit dark; no dinner on Sunday; updates needed in some bathrooms. $ *Rooms from: €180* ✉ *Rte. de Banon, Forcalquier* ☎ *04–92–75–72–80* 🌐 *www.bastidesaintgeorges.com/en/hotel-provence-luberon* 🛏 *22 rooms* 🍽 *No Meals.*

Le Couvent des Minimes

$$$ | HOTEL | It makes sense that L'Occitane, the regionally based cosmetics and fragrance giant, would have a spa hotel in the heart of lavender country, but this property is also housed in a

17th-century convent amid a medieval perched village—offering Provence-style old-world seclusion alongside modern luxury. **Pros:** two gastronomic restaurants and a wine bar; one of the region's most famous spas; historical setting. **Cons:** spa treatments are expensive; rude staff and lackluster service have been issues for some guests; restaurant is pricey. *Rooms from: €275 ✉ Chemin des Jeux de Maï, Mane ☎ 04-92-74-77-77 🌐 www.couventdesminimes-hotelspa.com 46 rooms No Meals.*

Shopping

★ Biscuiterie de Forcalquier

FOOD | FAMILY | Within walking distance of the town center and tourist office, this traditional bakery for the boat-shaped *navette*, an emblematic cookie of Marseille and Provence, was revived by the founder of the Provence-based cosmetics giant, L'Occitane. Delicately perfumed with orange flower water, the oblong cookie is said to represent the boat that brought saints Mary Magdalene and Martha to the coast near Marseille. Other traditional biscuits, flavored with lemon, almond, anise, or orange flower (including *calissons d'Aix* and macarons made from local almonds) are baked here by hand in gourmet versions updated by Paris superstar pâtissier Pierre Hermé. Though you'll also find them in gastronomic shops, all of the biscuits made here—easily transportable in tins—are sold in the Biscuiterie store at a 10% discount. *✉ 28 av. St-Promasse, Forcalquier ☎ 09-67-22-66-36 🌐 www.territoire-provence.com/forcalquier.*

Distilleries et Domaines de Provence

WINE/SPIRITS | This distiller, founded in 1898, makes aperitifs and digestives using aromatic ingredients such as gentian root, anise, thyme, wormwood, and peaches. Indeed, more than 65 plants and spices go into its famous Pastis Henri Bardouin. *✉ 9 av. St-Promasse, Forcalquier ☎ 04-92-75-00-58 🌐 www.distilleries-provence.com.*

Activities

Cycles Bachelas

BIKING | FAMILY | Just steps from Place du Bourguet, the town's main square, this reliable, well-equipped outfitter rents bikes, including mountain and electric bikes (which come in handy in this countryside, part of the Tour de France circuit). *✉ 5 av. de la République, Forcalquier ☎ 04-92-75-12-47 🌐 www.bachelas-bikeshop.com.*

France Montgolfière

BALLOONING | The blue-and-purple patchwork of the Luberon's famous lavender fields have never been seen to better effect than while floating freely in a ballon at 1,500 feet in the air. You can take in the whole vista of mountains, perched villages, and sprawling lavender fields on an hour-long flight at either dawn or dusk, when air currents are calm. The company picks you up in the village, gives you breakfast (or a snack), takes you up for an hour flight, and brings you to home base. After the balloon is packed away, your courage will be honored with a *flûte de champagne* and the traditional "*toast des aéronautes.*" *✉ Pl. du Village, Forcalquier ☎ 03-80-97-38-61 🌐 www.franceballoons.com €165 per person.*

L'Isle-sur-la-Sorgue

75 km (47 miles) west of Forcalquier; 30 km (19 miles) east of Avignon.

Crisscrossed with lazy canals and still alive with waterwheels that once drove its silk, wool, and paper mills, this charming valley town retains its gentle appeal—except on Sunday. Then this easygoing old town transforms itself into a Marrakech of marketeers, "the most charming flea market in the world," its streets crammed with antiques and *brocantes,* its cafés swelling with crowds of chic bargain browsers making a day of it.

After London's Portobello district and the flea market at St-Ouen outside Paris, L'Isle-sur-la-Sorgue is reputedly Europe's third-largest antiques market. It ratchets up to high speed twice a year when the town hosts a big antiques show, usually four days around Easter and another in mid-August, nicknamed the Grand Déballage (Great Unpacking). Prices can be high, but remember that many dealers expect you to bargain.

On a nonmarket day, life returns to its mellow pace. Dealers and clients catch up on gossip at the Place Gambetta fountain and at the Café de France, opposite the church of Notre-Dame-des-Anges. Wander the maze inside the ring to admire a range of architectural styles, from Gothic to Renaissance.

GETTING HERE AND AROUND

It's a 40-minute bus ride (No. 6) from the Avignon center train station to Place Robert Vasse in Isle-sur-la-Sorgue. It's €2 one-way or €1 if returning on the same day. By car the distance is 5 km (3 miles). The TER train line links Avignon and L'Isle-Fontaine train station in L'Isle-sur-la-Sorgue.

VISITOR INFORMATION

CONTACTS L'Isle-sur-la-Sorgue Tourist Office. ✉ *13 pl. Ferdinand Buisson, L'Isle-sur-la-Sorgue* ☎ *04–90–38–04–78* 🌐 *islesurlasorguetourisme.com.*

Sights

Campredon Centre d'Art
ART GALLERY | One of the finest of L'Isle's mansions, the 18th-century Hôtel de Campredon has been restored and reinvented as a modern-art gallery, mounting three temporary exhibitions per year. ✉ *20 rue du Docteur Tallet, L'Isle-sur-la-Sorgue* ☎ *04–90–38–17–41* 🌐 *www.campredonartetimage.com* 🎫 *€7* ⏲ *Closed Mon.*

Collégiale Notre-Dame-des-Anges
CHURCH | L'Isle's 17th-century church is extravagantly decorated with gilt, faux marble, and sentimental frescoes. The double-colonnade facade commands the center of the *vieille ville* (Old Town). Visiting hours change frequently, so check with the tourist office. ✉ *Pl. de la Liberté, L'Isle-sur-la-Sorgue* 🎫 *Free.*

★ Fondation Villa Datris
ART GALLERY | Housed in a stately Belle Époque mansion set on the river, this vibrant contemporary sculpture center is one of the most respected establishments of its kind in Provence. Its talented, far-sighted curators scour the European arts scene for ingenious themed shows that mix established names with up-and-coming sculptors. While the shows change only once a year, they are always revelatory, with artwork cleverly installed in every room of the house, including the old shower stalls, the pretty garden, and even from trees hanging over the canal. ✉ *7 av. des Quartres Otages, L'Isle-sur-la-Sorgue* ☎ *04–90–95–23–70* 🌐 *fondationvilladatris.fr* 🎫 *Free.*

★ La Filaventure Brun de Vian-Tiran
OTHER MUSEUM | FAMILY | Through eight generations on the same premises, the Brun de Vian-Tiran family has created France's most beautiful and luxurious woolens from fibers sourced throughout the world, including baby camel, cashmere, merino wool, alpaca, and baby llama. Housed in one of the company's old warehouses, this state-of-the-art museum takes you through the manufacturing process, from fiber to fabric, with interactive exhibits that are fascinating for kids as well as adults. The on-site boutique carries the entire range of luxury bedding and blankets, scarves, slippers,

Continued on page 150

Van Gogh may have made the sunflower into the icon of Provence, but it is another flower—one that is unprepossessing, fragrant, and tiny—that draws thousands of travelers to the region each year. They come to journey the famous "Route de la Lavande" (Lavender Route), a wide blue-purple swath that connects over 2,000 producers across the south of France.

THE LAVENDER ROUTE

Once described as the "soul of Haute-Provence," lavender has colored Provence's plains since the days of the ancient Romans. Today it brings prosperity, as consumers are crazy about buying beauty products that use lavender essence. Nostrils flared, they travel this route every summer. To help sate this lavender lust, the following pages present a detail-rich tour of the Lavender Route.

TOURING THE LAVENDER ROUTE

❶ Have your camera ready for the beautifully preserved Cistercian simplicity of the **Abbaye Notre-Dame de Sénanque,** a perfect foil for the famous waving fields of purple around it.

❷ No shrinking violet, the hilltop village of **Gordes** is famous for its luxe hotels, restaurants, and lavender-stocked shops.

❸ Get a fascinating A to Z tour—from harvesting to distilling to production—at the **Musée de la Lavande** near Coustellet.

❹ **Apt** is a good hub for visits to several lavender fields. For more insight, though, head just south of town to the **Distillerie les Agnels**, where you can tour the facility, visit the farm, and browse in the gift shop.

❺ Even if you miss the biggest blowout of the year, the Fête de la Lavande (usually on August 15) in the hillside town of **Sault**, you can spend some time shopping in its charming *vieille ville* boutiques before or after a drive through the surrounding fields of purple.

❻ Sault is also a good jumping off point for a side trip northwest to the summit of **Mont Ventoux**, where unrivaled views of lavender-filled valleys await.

❼ The artsy town of **Forcalquier** has an intriguing museum—set in a medieval-era convent—with displays on aromatic and medicinal plants. In addition, the factory of world-renowned botanical skin-care company, **L'Occitane**, is just south of town.

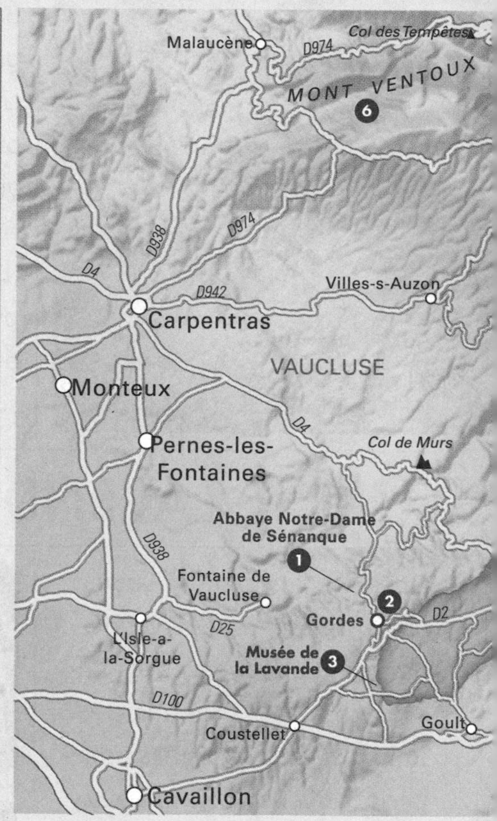

The wide-purple swath of the Lavender Route connects more than 2,000 producers and runs across the Drôme, the plateau du Vaucluse, and the Alpes-de-Haute-Provence, but our itinerary is lined with some of the prettiest sights—and smells—of the region. Whether you're shopping for artisanal bottles of the stuff (as with wine, the finest lavender carries its own Appellation d'Origine Contrôlée), spending time at a spa, or simply find yourself

Apt market

Purple haze

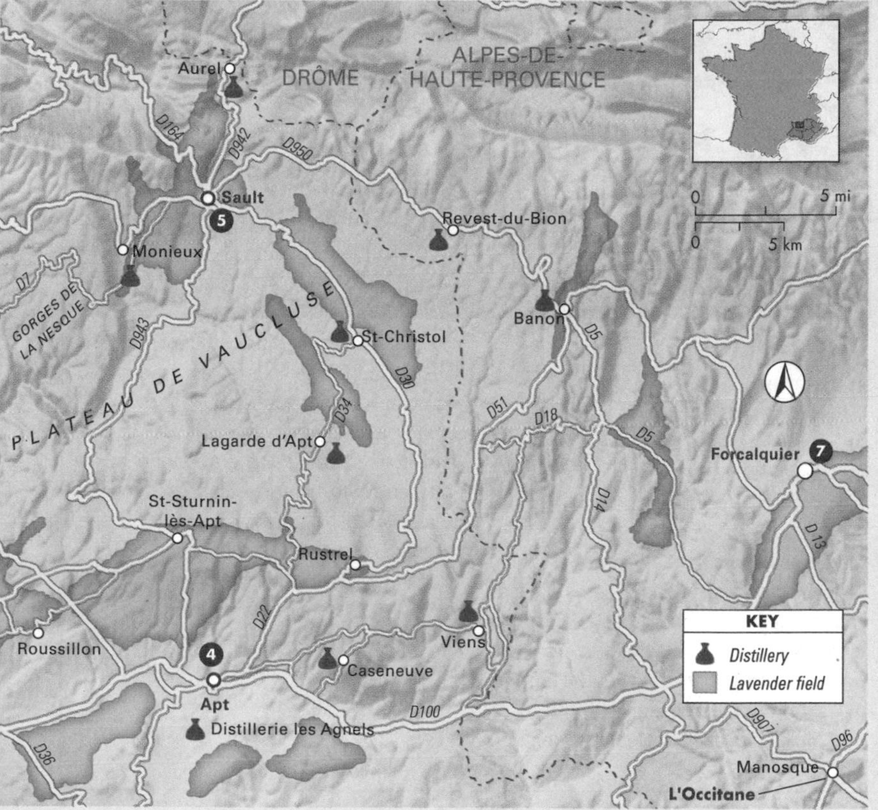

hip-deep in purple while walking the fields, the most essential aspect on this trip is savoring a magical world of lavender, one we usually only encounter on picture postcards.

To join the lavender-happy crowds, you have to go in season, which (if you're lucky) runs from June to early August. Like Holland's May tulips, the lavender of Haute-Provence is in its true glory only once a year: the last two weeks of July, when the harvesting begins—but fields bloom throughout the summer months for the most part. In this feature, we wind through the most generous patches of lavender, giving you good visiting (and shopping) time in a number of the villages that are *fou de la lavande* (crazy for lavender).

Abbaye Notre-Dame de Sénanque

DAY 1

SÉNANQUE

A Picture-Perfect Abbey

An invisible Master of Ceremonies for the Lavender Route would surely send you first to the greatest spot for lavender worship in the world: the 12th-century Cistercian **Abbaye Notre-Dame de Sénanque**, which in July and August seems to float above a sea of lavender, a setting immortalized in a thousand travel posters. Happily, you'll find it via the D177 only 4 km (2½ miles) north of Gordes, among the most beautiful of Provence's celebrated perched villages. An architecture student's dream of neat cubes, cylinders, and pyramids, its pure Romanesque form alone is worth contemplating in any context. But in this arid, rocky setting the gray stone building seems to have special resonance—ancient, organic, with a bit of the borie about it. Along with the abbeys of Le Thornet and Silvacane, this is one of the trio of "Three Sisters" built by the Cistercian order in this area. Sénanque's church is a model of symmetry and balance. Begun in 1150, it has no decoration but still touches the soul with its chaste beauty.

THE ESSENCE OF THE MATTER

Provence and lavender go hand in hand—but why? The flower is native to the Mediterranean, and grows so well because the pH balance in the soil is naturally perfect for it (pH 6–8). But lavender was really put on the map here when ancient Romans colonized Provence and used the flower to disinfect their baths and perfume their laundry (the word comes from Latin *lavare*, "to wash"). From a small grass-roots industry, lavender proliferated over the centuries until the first professional distillery opened in Provence in the 1880s to supply oils for southern French apothecaries. After World War I, production boomed to meet the demand of the perfumers of Grasse (the perfume center of the world). Once described as the "soul of Haute-Provence," lavender is now farmed in England, India, and the States, but the harvest in the South of France remains the world's largest.

The adjoining cloister, from the 12th century, is almost as pure, with barrel-vaulted galleries framing double rows of discreet, abstract pillars. Next door, the enormous vaulted dormitory and the refectory shelter a display on the history of Cistercian abbeys. The few remaining monks here now preside over a cultural center that presents concerts and exhibitions. The bookshop is one of the best in Provence, with a huge collection of Provençaliana (lots in English).

After spending the morning getting acquainted with the little purple flower at Sénanque, drive south along the D2 (or D177) back to **Gordes**, through a dry, rocky region mixed with deep valleys and far-reaching plains.

Wild lavender is already omnipresent, growing in large tracts as you reach the entrance of the small, unspoiled hilltop village, making for a patchwork landscape as finely drawn as a medieval illumination. A cluster of houses rises above the valley in painterly hues of honey gold, with cobbled streets winding up to the village's picturesque Renaissance château, making it one of the most beautiful towns in Provence.

ON THE CALENDAR

If you plan to be at the Musée de la Lavande between July 1 and August 25 you can watch animations of workers swathing lavender with copper scythes.

Gordes has a great selection of hotels, restaurants, and B&Bs to choose from. Spend the early afternoon among tasteful shops that sell lovely Provençal crafts and produce, much of it lavender-based, and then after lunch, head out to Coustellet.

COUSTELLET

A Great Lavender Museum

Set 2 miles south of Gordes, Coustellet is noted for its **Musée de la Lavande** (take the D2 southeast to the outskirts of Coustellet). Owned by one of the original lavender families, who have cultivated and distilled the flower here for over five generations, this museum sits at the edge of more than 815 acres of prime lavender-cultivated land.

Not only can you visit the well-organized and interesting museum (note the impressive collection of scythes and distilling apparatus), you can buy up a storm in the boutique, which offers a great selection of lavender-based products at very reasonable prices.

There are four main species. True lavender (*Lavandula angustifolia*) produces the most subtle essential oil and is often used by perfume makers and laboratories. Spike lavender (Lavandula latifolia) has wide leaves and long floral stems with several flower spikes. Hybrid lavender (*lavandin*) is obtained from pollination of true lavender and spike lavender, making a hybrid that forms a highly developed large round cluster. French lavender (*Lavendula stoechas*) is wild lavender that grows throughout the region and

is collected for the perfume industry. True lavender thrives in the chalky soils and hot, dry climate of higher altitudes of Provence. It was picked systematically until the end of the 19th century and used for most lavender-based products. But as the demand for this remarkable flower grew, so did the need for a larger production base. By the beginning of the 20th century, the demand for the flower was so great that producers planted fields of lavender at lower altitudes, creating the need for a tougher, more resistant plant: the hybrid *lavandin*.

In many towns, Provence's lavender harvest is celebrated with charming folkloric festivals.

DAY 2

APT

The Liveliest Market

On the second day of your lavender adventure, begin by enjoying the winding drive 25 km (15 miles) east of **Apt**. Although the town itself is unremarkable, it has a pretty setting, and it hosts the region's liveliest Saturday market—filled with fine Luberon and Haute-Provence products (arrive early for a parking spot). Apt also makes a good hub for visits to several area lavender fields.

For insight into lavender cultivation, harvesting, and distillation, drive 4 km (2½ miles) south of Apt to the **Distillerie les Agnels**, where you can tour the facility, visit the farm, and browse in the gift shop.

Althernatively, head east of Apt, where small, charming places to stop for a quick bite on a drive through rows upon rows of magnificent lavender include Caseneuve (10 km [6 miles] from Apt) and Viens (8 km [5 miles] from Casaneuve).

SAULT

The Biggest Festival

Beautifully perched on a rocky outcrop overlooking the valley that bears its name, the village of **Sault** is one of the key stops on the Lavender Route. Several highways head north to it from Apt, but if you make the 35-km (22-mile) drive along the D34, you can stop in Lagarde d'Apt, another lavender village, along the way.

If at all possible, however, time your visit to Sault for the **Fête de la Lavande**, a daylong festival—the best in the region—that's usually held around August 15. Village folk dress in traditional Provençal garb and parade on bicycles, horses leap over barrels of fragrant bundles of hay, and local producers display their wares at the market. The event culminates with a communal Provençal dinner.

For a peak lavender experience—literally—make the winding 40-minute drive (follow signs from Sault) northwest to the summit of **Mont Ventoux** for a spectacular view of the purple-hued valleys from on high.

DAY 3

FORCALQUIER

The Artsiest Town

On your third day, make the 55-km (34-mile) trip southeast from Sault to **Forcalquier**, an artists' town that hosts a Monday morning market featuring lavender-based products. From here, you can head out on walks, bike excursions, horseback rides, or drives into the surrounding purple fields.

Before leaving town, though, be sure to visit the family-friendly **Artemesia Museum**. In addition to engaging, multisensory exhibits (including a fragrance gallery) on aromatic plants and medicinal herbs, it offers fun perfume-making workshops for adults and children.

Set in the historical Couvent des Cordeliers, the museum also affords a glimpse into Forcalquier's medieval history. In the 11th century, when this was the capital of Haute-Provence, it was called the Cité des Quatre Reines (City of the Four Queens) because the region's ruler, Raimond Béranger V, had four daughters (Eleanor of Aquitaine among them) who all married royals.

For a more contemporary experience, consider heading to the town of Manosque, 9 km (15 miles) south of Forcalquier and home to **L'Occitane**, the world-renowned maker of botanical skin-care products. Book ahead for a factory tour, or just stop by to see the gardens and shop in the boutique.

MAKING SCENTS

BLOOMING

Lavender fields begin blooming in late June, depending on the area and the weather, and reach their peak from the end of July to early August. The first two weeks of July are considered the best time to catch the fields in all their glory.

HARVESTING

Lavender is harvested from July to September, when the hot summer sun brings the essence up into the flower. Harvesting is becoming more and more automated; make an effort to visit some of the older fields with narrow rows—these are still picked by hand. Lavender is then dried for two to three days before being transported to the distillery.

DISTILLING

Distillation is done in a steam alembic, with the dry lavender steamed in a double boiler. Essential oils are extracted from the lavender by water vapor, which is then passed through the cooling coils of a retort.

and other items, all of which are usually found only at high-end department stores in Paris. ✉ *2 cours Victor Hugo, L'Isle-sur-la-Sorgue* ☎ *04–90–38–73–31* 🌐 *www.lafilaventure.com* 🎫 *€7.50.*

Restaurants

Islo

$$ | MODERN FRENCH | This bright, elegant-modern dining room, tucked away behind the church in the vieille ville, is a real find for a market-fresh gourmet meal you won't soon forget. Beautifully presented dishes include a parfait of local wild mushrooms and poached egg to start, followed by perfectly poached dorade with roasted citrus-infused fennel or succulent guinea hen with oregano polenta. **Known for:** excellent cheese plates; local wines; good value prix-fixe dinner menu. $ *Average main: €22* ✉ *3 rue Molière, L'Isle-sur-la-Sorgue* ☎ *04–90–20–18–21* 🌐 *islo.fr* ⏲ *Closed Sun. and Mon. No lunch.*

Le Jardin du Quai

$$ | FRENCH | Local antiques dealers come here to eat, and the place feels so welcoming that it would be easy to linger for hours. Chef Daniel Hébet made his name at La Mirande in Avignon and Le Domaine des Andéols in St-Saturnin-lès-Apt before opening this bistro in his own image—young, jovial, and uncompromising when it comes to quality. **Known for:** choice of fine dining or bistro menu; charming setting and pretty terrace; well-priced wines. $ *Average main: €20* ✉ *91 av. Julien Guigue, L'Isle-sur-la-Sorgue* ☎ *04–90–20–14–98* 🌐 *www.jardinduquai.com* ⏲ *Closed Tues., Wed., and mid-Dec.–mid-Jan.*

★ Le 17 Place aux Vins

$ | WINE BAR | A *cave* (wine store) by day and a happening wine and tapas bar by night, this is a great place to sample the famous wines of the Côtes du Rhône—perhaps a local Beaume-de-Venise, which goes nicely with the house-made foie gras. Whether you sit inside or out on the terrace, charming, knowledgeable staffers will pour samples until you've found the perfect pairing for your charcuterie or artisanal cheese plate. **Known for:** local favorite; menu of local specialties; extensive list of wines by the glass. $ *Average main: €13* ✉ *17 pl. Rose Goudard, L'Isle-sur-la-Sorgue* ☎ *04–90–15–68–67* 🌐 *www.17placeauxvins.fr.*

★ Le Vivier

$$$ | FRENCH | Patrick Fischnaller returned to southern France from London and quickly won acclaim (and a Michelin star) with this dazzler just outside the town center. Start off by enjoying a glass of wine (from €8) while seated on the orange sofa in the Art Deco–style lounge before heading to a table for foie gras and smoked eel terrine, pigeon pie, or strawberry soup with basil and black olives from the €70 menu (or order à la carte). **Known for:** riverside views from the terrace; excellent roast beef with cherry marmalade; long, leisurely lunches. $ *Average main: €30* ✉ *800 cours Fernande Peyre, L'Isle-sur-la-Sorgue* ☎ *04–90–38–52–80* 🌐 *www.levivier-restaurant.com* ⏲ *Closed Mon., Tues., and late Feb.–mid-Mar. No lunch Sat. No dinner Sun.*

Coffee and Quick Bites

★ Pâtisserie Jouvaud

$ | BAKERY | FAMILY | You'll never feel more like a kid in a candy shop than when you feast your eyes on the scintillating pastries, candied fruits (a specialty of the Vaucluse since Roman times), chocolates, and other local sweets sold here. At the charming café next door you can enjoy your selection with tea or coffee; there's also a small menu of savory lunch dishes. **Known for:** the best of French pastries; everything made on the premises; friendly, English-speaking service. $ *Average main: €6* ✉ *5 av. des Quatre Otages, L'Isle-sur-la-Sorgue* ☎ *04–90–26–72–94* 🌐 *www.patisserie-jouvaud.com.*

Hotels

★ Grand Hôtel Henri

$$ | HOTEL | With bright, airy rooms and suites decorated with vintage and antique treasures, soothing contemporary color schemes, and chic carpets, the refurbished Grand Hôtel Henri has lots of panache that's matched by an utter lack of pretension, as evidenced by the friendly staff. **Pros:** nice restaurant; very reasonable prices; short walk from market and antiques shops. **Cons:** no in-room coffee; lower-category rooms could use more storage space; restaurant books up quickly. *Rooms from: €140* ✉ *1 cours René Char, L'Isle-sur-la-Sorgue* ☎ *04–90–38–10–52* 🌐 *www.grandhotelhenri.com* *17 rooms* *No Meals.*

★ La Maison sur la Sorgue

$$$$ | HOTEL | Obliging innkeepers Frédéric and Marie-Claude did their architectural homework before they transformed a 17th-century home into this elegant B&B, where four unique suites feature tasteful color schemes, original historical details, antique and vintage items, and modern fixtures. **Pros:** all-out treatment plus amenities (shampoos and soaps); courtyard breakfast goes beyond basic croissant-and-jam fare; true elegance. **Cons:** can be hard to find; some handheld showers; expensive (but worth it). *Rooms from: €370* ✉ *6 rue Rose Goudard, L'Isle-sur-la-Sorgue* ☎ *04–90–20–74–86* 🌐 *www.lamaisonsurlasorgue.com* *Closed 1st 2 wks of Nov. and 2 wks in Feb.* *4 suites* *Free Breakfast.*

★ La Prévôté

$$ | B&B/INN | With exquisitely styled, Provence-chic rooms, each done in soft colors, this property is an ideal respite after a long day of antiques shopping. **Pros:** price includes breakfast; wonderful dining room; antiques-bedecked interiors. **Cons:** a little tricky to find; parking may be difficult; decor in some rooms borders on kitschy. *Rooms from: €170* ✉ *4 bis rue Jean Jacques Rousseau, L'Isle-sur-la-Sorgue* ☎ *04–90–38–57–29* 🌐 *www.la-prevote.fr* *Closed Tues., Wed., 2 wks late Nov., and 2 wks late Feb.* *5 rooms* *Free Breakfast.*

Shopping

In the vieille ville, boutiques on pretty backstreets—especially between Place de l'Église and Avenue de la Libération—are filled with tempting goods that often spill out onto the sidewalk to lure you inside. Most shops focus on home design and Provençal wares.

Hôtel Dongier

ANTIQUES & COLLECTIBLES | A former inn built in the 17th century is the perfect setting for an emporium of roughly 30 antiques galleries selling art, furniture, and decorative *objets* from the 16th to the 20th centuries. ✉ *15 esplanade Robert Vasse, L'Isle-sur-la-Sorgue* ☎ *04–90–38–63–63.*

La Cour aux Saveurs

CHOCOLATE | FAMILY | You might just be lucky enough to arrive at this Old Town artisanal *chocolaterie* on a day when you can watch the confections being made by hand. Specialties include delicately perfumed ganache-filled chocolates, calissons, and chocolate bars laden with dried fruit and nuts. ✉ *4 rue Louis Lopez, L'Isle-sur-la-Sorgue* ☎ *04–90–21–53–91* 🌐 *www.lacourauxsaveurs.fr.*

L'Île aux Brocantes

ANTIQUES & COLLECTIBLES | Also known as Passage du Point, this is another of L'Isle's emporiums of vintage and antique wares. Here you'll find about 40 dealers under one roof. ✉ *7 av. des Quatre Otages, L'Isle-sur-la-Sorgue* ☎ *06–20–10–58–15* 🌐 *lile-aux-brocantes.business.site.*

Sous un Olivier

FOOD | FAMILY | This food boutique is stocked to the ceiling with bottles, jars, and tins of tapenade, mustard, vinegar, olive oil, honey, coffee, tea, and more. ✉ *16 rue de la République,*

L'Isle-sur-la-Sorgue ☎ *04–90–20–68–90* 🌐 *www.sousunolivier.com.*

Un Jour, La Suite
HOUSEWARES | For more than 200 years, Brun de Vian-Tiran has been making wool blankets, cozy quilts, throws, and other bedding accessories. You can find its signature items here amid housewares from other brands like Nina Ricci, Cire Trudon, Yves Delorme, and Le Jacquard Français. ✉ *1 rue Rose Goudard, L'Isle-sur-la-Sorgue* ☎ *04–90–26–34–37* 🌐 *www.facebook.com/unjourlasuite.*

Xavier Nicod
ANTIQUES & COLLECTIBLES | Higher-end antiques are in plentiful supply at Xavier Nicod, which "pays tribute to eclecticism" in art and architecture. ✉ *9 av. des Quatre Otages, L'Isle-sur-la-Sorgue* ☎ *06–07–85–54–59* 🌐 *xaviernicod.com.*

Fontaine-de-Vaucluse

7 km (4½ miles) east of L'Isle-sur-la-Sorgue; 30 km (19 miles) southeast of Avignon.

Like the spring and cascade for which it's named, this village has welled up and spilled over as a Niagara Falls–style tourist hub. The rustic, pretty, and slightly tacky riverside town is full of shops, cafés, and restaurants, all geared to serve the pilgrims who flock to its namesake. And neither the town nor its natural attraction should be missed if you're either a connoisseur of rushing water or a fan of foreign kitsch.

GETTING HERE AND AROUND

You can take Bus 6 (running eight times daily, twice on Sunday) from Avignon TGV station (€2; 1 hour). Otherwise arriving by car is your best option. It's about a 15-minute drive from L'Isle-sur-la-Sorgue; from Avignon, the drive is about 45 minutes.

VISITOR INFORMATION

CONTACTS Fontaine-de-Vaucluse Tourist Office. ✉ *4 rte. de Cavaillon, Fontaine-de-Vaucluse* ☎ *04–90–20–32–22* 🌐 *islesurlasorguetourisme.com.*

Sights

Château
CASTLE/PALACE | Fontaine has its own ruined château, perched romantically on a forested hilltop over the town and illuminated at night. First built around the year 1000 and embellished in the 14th century by the bishops of Cavaillon, the castle was destroyed in the 15th century and forms little more than a sawtooth silhouette against the sky. ✉ *Fontaine-de-Vaucluse.*

Fontaine-de-Vaucluse
WATERFALL | FAMILY | There's no exaggerating the magnificence of the Fontaine de Vaucluse, a mysterious spring that gushes from a deep underground source that has been explored to a depth of 1,010 feet—so far. Framed by towering cliffs, a broad, pure pool wells up and spews dramatically over massive rocks down a gorge to the village, where its roar soothes and its spray cools the visitors who crowd the riverfront cafés. You must pay to park, and then run a gauntlet of souvenir shops and tourist traps on your way up to the source of the water. ✉ *Rue des Bourgades, Fontaine-de-Vaucluse.*

Le Musée-Bibliothèque F. Pétrarque
OTHER MUSEUM | The great Renaissance poet Petrarch, driven mad with unrequited love for a beautiful married woman named Laura, retreated to this valley to nurse his heartache in a cabin with "one dog and only two servants." He had met the woman in the heady social scene at the papal court in Avignon, where she was to die years later of the plague. Sixteen years in this wild isolation didn't ease the pain, but the serene environment inspired him to poetry, and the lyrics of his *Canzoniere* were dedicated

to Laura's memory. The small museum, built on the site of his residence, displays prints and engravings of the virtuous lovers, both in Avignon and Fontaine de Vaucluse. ✉ *On left bank, direction Gordes, Fontaine-de-Vaucluse* ☎ *04–90–20–37–20 tourist office* 🎫 *€5* ⏲ *Closed Tues. and Wed.*

Moulin Vallis Clausa

FACTORY | FAMILY | Fontaine was once an industrial center, but its mills and factories were closed by strikes in 1968, and most never recovered. To learn more about this aspect of the town, consider visiting this working paper mill. Its reconstructed, 15th-century waterwheel drives timber crankshafts to mix rag pulp, and its artisans roll and dry thick paper *à l'ancienne* (in the old manner). The process is fascinating and free to watch, though it's almost impossible to resist buying the pretty note cards, posters, and even lamp shades in the on-site boutique. If you're feeling creative, you can make your own sheet during the paper-making experience (€15 per person). There are also 30-minute guided mill tours (€5, minimum of 10 people). Book either option online in advance. ✉ *Chemin de la Fontaine, Fontaine-de-Vaucluse* ☎ *04–90–20–34–14* 🌐 *www.moulin-vallisclausa.com* 🎫 *Free* ⏲ *Closed for 3 wks in Jan.*

Restaurants

Restaurant Philip

$$ | FRENCH | If you want a truly regional experience, take a seat on the shaded terrace of Restaurant Philip (circa 1926), enjoy the water views, and dig in to some *cuisses de grenouille* (frog's legs) or trout fished straight from the Sorgue River. Set apart from the other eateries, it's just before the trail to the spring. **Known for:** closest dining to the river; regional wine; good value fixed-price menus. 💲 *Average main: €19* ✉ *Chemin de la Fontaine, Fontaine-de-Vaucluse* ☎ *09–75–59–28–63 mobile phone, 04–90–20–31–81* ⏲ *Closed Oct.–Mar. No dinner Apr.–June and Sept.*

Hotels

Hôtel du Poète

$$$ | HOTEL | "A river runs through it" is no exaggeration at this amiable hotel in a former mill, where a romantic garden is laced with water channels and shaded by plane trees and where terraces and some of the pleasant, light-drenched guest rooms overlook the Sorgue River. **Pros:** a short walk from Fontaine de Vaucluse and restaurants; beautiful setting; great for families. **Cons:** some ground-floor rooms lack views; decor is a bit dated; sound of rushing water might bother some. 💲 *Rooms from: €240* ✉ *Le Village, Fontaine-de-Vaucluse* ☎ *04–90–20–34–05* 🌐 *www.hoteldupoete.com* 🛏 *24 rooms* 🍽 *No Meals.*

Gordes

10 km (6 miles) southeast of Fontaine-de-Vaucluse; 39 km (24 miles) southeast of Avignon.

The famous *village perché* (hilltop village) of Gordes is only a short distance from Fontaine-de-Vaucluse, but you must wend your way south, east, and then north on D100A, D100, D2, and D15 to skirt the impassable hillside. It's a lovely drive through dry, rocky country covered with wild lavender and scrub oak, and it may tempt you to have a picnic or take a walk.

How surprising, then, to leave such wildness behind and enter resort country. Once a summer retreat favored by modern artists such as André Lhôte, Marc Chagall, and Victor Vasarely, Gordes is now surrounded by luxury vacation homes, modern hotels, B&Bs, and restaurants—all often patronized by chic Parisians.

No matter: the ancient stone village still rises above the valley in painterly hues of honey gold, and its cobbled streets—lined with boutiques, galleries, and real-estate offices—still wind steep and narrow to its Renaissance château. Note, too, that Gordes's year-round farmers' market (Tuesday 8–1) is a grand event, with upscale offerings like truffle-infused olive oil, charcuterie, locally made foie gras, and pretty Provençal linens.

GETTING HERE AND AROUND

There's no bus service to Gordes, so you'll need a car. A taxi from Avignon will cost about €75; one from Fontaine-de-Vaucluse will be roughly €40.

VISITOR INFORMATION

CONTACTS Gordes Tourist Office. ✉ *Pl. Genty Pantaly, Gordes* ☎ *04–90–72–02–75* 🌐 *www.destinationluberon.com.*

Sights

★ Abbaye de Sénanque
RELIGIOUS BUILDING | If you've fantasized about Provence's famed lavender fields, head to the wild valley some 4 km (2½ miles) north of Gordes (via D177), where this photogenic, 12th-century, Romanesque abbey seemingly floats above a fragrant sea of purple blooms from late June through August. Begun in 1150 and completed at the dawn of the 13th century, the church and adjoining cloister are without decoration but still touch the soul with their chaste beauty. Along with the abbeys of Le Thornet and Silvacane, this is one of a trio of "Three Sisters" built by the Cistercian Order in this area.

Next door, the enormous vaulted dormitory contains an exhibition on Abbaye de Sénanque's construction, and the refectory shelters a display on the history of Cistercian abbeys. The few remaining monks here now preside over a cultural center presenting concerts and exhibitions. The bookshop has a huge collection of books about Provence (lots in English). ✉ *Gordes* ☎ *04–90–72–05–72* 🌐 *www.senanque.fr* 🎫 *€8.50.*

Belvédère
VIEWPOINT | FAMILY | From this spot you can overlook the area's fields and *mas* (farms), and the modern vacation homes are differentiated from the older properties only by their aqua-blue pools. Belvédère is just downhill from the château; look for the signs. ✉ *Gordes.*

Château de Gordes
CASTLE/PALACE | The only way you can get into this château is by paying to see a collection of photo paintings by Belgian pop artist Pol Mara, who lived in Gordes. It's worth the price of admission, though, just to look at the fabulously decorated stone fireplace, created in 1541. Unfortunately, hours change without warning (afternoon visits are your best bet). ✉ *Pl. Genty Pantaly, Gordes* ☎ *04–32–50–11–41* 🌐 *www.chateaudegordes.com* 🎫 *€4.*

Église St-Firmin
CHURCH | The interior of the village's Église St-Fermin is overblown Rococo—all pink and gold. ✉ *Rue du Belvédère, Gordes.*

Musée de la Lavande
OTHER MUSEUM | FAMILY | Owned by one of the original lavender families, who have cultivated and distilled the flower here for more than five generations, this chic museum sits at the edge of 80 or so acres of prime lavender fields about 3 km (2 miles) outside of Gordes (take the D2 southeast to the outskirts of Coustellet). Not only can you take in well-organized displays (note the impressive collection of scythes and distilling apparatus), see a fascinating movie, and play with interactive screens, but you can also participate in lavender workshops that are fun for adults and kids alike. The boutique sells a top-notch selection of sophisticated lavender-based cosmetics and essential oils. ✉ *276 rte. de Gordes, Coustellet* ☎ *04–90–76–91–23* 🌐 *www.museedelalavande.com* 🎫 *€8.*

Village des Bories

RUINS | FAMILY | Although the fascinating, hivelike structures called *bories* (shepherds' shelters built with tight-fitting, mortarless stone) are found throughout this region of Provence, this ancient community has about 20 of them. Their origins are provocatively vague—perhaps dating from the eras of the Celts or the Ligurians or even from the Iron Age—and they were inhabited or used for sheep through the 18th century. A photo exhibition shows structures similar to bories in countries around the world. Look for signs to the village just outside Gordes, on a lane heading north from D2. *Gordes* *04–90–72–03–48* *levillagedesbories.com* *€6.*

Restaurants

Restaurant l'Estellan

$$ | FRENCH | This restaurant is worth a trip just outside town for such delights as sea bream with cherry tomatoes and flax seed, a trilogy of goat and ewe cheeses with black-olive jam, or roasted pike perch with risotto. The bistro-Provençal interior and the terrace are the perfect settings for long, leisurely meals, and there are spectacular village views. **Known for:** generous portions; lovely garden dining in warm weather; meticulous presentation. *Average main: €20* *Mas de la Sénancole, Montée de Gordes, about 5 km (3 miles) southwest of Gordes via D15 and D2, Gordes* *04–90–72–04–90* *www.mas-de-la-senancole.com* *Closed Sun. and Mon.*

Hotels

★ Airelles Gordes La Bastide

$$$$ | HOTEL | FAMILY | Spectacularly perched on Gordes's hilltop, the 16th-century Bastide has both old-world charm and old-world elegance—it's also one of the few properties in Provence to have earned Palace status, meaning that it's among the best of the country's five-star hotels. **Pros:** views are unmatched in the area; impeccable service; excellent dining. **Cons:** €35 for breakfast; very expensive; street-side rooms disappointing considering views from other rooms. *Rooms from: €800* *Le Village, 61 rue de la Combe, Gordes* *04–90–72–12–12* *airelles.com/en/destination/gordes-hotel* *Closed Jan. and Feb.* *41 rooms* *No Meals.*

Domaine de l'Enclos

$$$ | B&B/INN | FAMILY | Though this cluster of private stone cottages has had a modernizing face-lift, the antique tiles and faux patinas keep things looking fashionably rustic, and the panoramic views are classics. **Pros:** ideal for families; stunning views from the terraces and some rooms; free parking. **Cons:** breakfasts could be bigger; narrow roads to the hotel; no full restaurant on-site. *Rooms from: €230* *Rte. de Sénanque, Gordes* *06–83–67–89–13* *www.domainedelenclos.com* *5 rooms* *Free Breakfast.*

★ Domaine Les Martins

$$$ | B&B/INN | A stay at this lovely restored farmhouse in the tiny hamlet of Les Martins—strategically set between the villages of Gordes, Ménerbes, and Lacoste—lets you enjoy all the wonders of the region without the crushing crowds. **Pros:** luxury touches; everything homemade; charming hosts. **Cons:** very few rooms; must have a car; need to book six months in advance. *Rooms from: €300* *Les Martins, Gordes* *04–90–72–09–56* *www.domainelesmartins.com/en* *5 rooms* *Free Breakfast.*

Le Phébus & Spa

$$$$ | HOTEL | This country hotel's beautiful setting, luxurious pool, full-service spa, Michelin-starred restaurant, and guest rooms with every modern convenience assure a high level of pampering. **Pros:** stupendous scenery; some rooms have terraces; glass of Champagne offered upon arrival. **Cons:** very expensive; some rooms lack character; out-of-the-way location. $ *Rooms from: €455* ✉ *220 rte. de Murs, Joucas* ✈ *Take D2 northeast of Gordes for about 7 km (4½ miles), then D102 into Joucas* ☎ *04–90–05–78–83* 🌐 *www.lephebus.com* *24 rooms* *No Meals.*

Shopping

Le Jardin

SOUVENIRS | If you're shopping for a gift or souvenirs, you'll find tasteful Provençal tableware at Le Jardin, which also has a charming tearoom in its leafy courtyard garden. ✉ *Rte. de Murs, Gordes* ☎ *04–90–72–12–34.*

Roussillon

14 km (9 miles) southeast of Gordes; 43 km (27 miles) southeast of Avignon.

A rich vein of ocher runs through the earth of Roussillon, occasionally breaking the surface in vivid displays of russet, rose, garnet, and orange. Roussillon is a mineral showcase, perched above red-rock canyonlands whose pigmentation is often echoed by the stone and stucco houses in town.

Indeed, the pleasure of a visit here lies in the panorama of these richly varied colors, which change with the light of day, contrasted with the countryside's deep-shadowed greenery, which sets off the red stone with Cézannesque severity. Here, too, you'll find pleasant *placettes* (tiny squares) in which to linger and a Renaissance fortress tower crowned with a 19th-century clock.

GETTING HERE AND AROUND

There is no direct bus service to Roussillon. The only way to get here is by car. The drive from Gordes, primarily along the D2 and D102, takes about 15 minutes. Though it depends on traffic and your routing, the drive from Avignon is just over an hour.

VISITOR INFORMATION

CONTACTS Tourist Office. ✉ *19 rue de la Poste, Roussillon* ☎ *04–90–05–60–25* 🌐 *otroussillon.pagesperso-orange.fr.*

Sights

Ôkhra, Écomusée de l'Ocre (*Roussillon's Mathieu Ocher Works*)

HISTORY MUSEUM | **FAMILY** | The area's famous vein of natural ocher, which runs for about 25 km (16 miles) along the foot of the Vaucluse Plateau, has been mined for centuries, beginning with the ancient Romans, who used ocher for their pottery. Visit this museum housed in a former factory to learn more about ocher's extraction and its modern uses. English-language guided tours (50 minutes) are available. If the landscapes of Provence that inspired so many great artists have also inspired you, head for the on-site gift shop to pick up some bottled pigments or a set of ocher and indigo watercolors to use in your own creative endeavors. ✉ *570 rte. d'Apt, Roussillon* ☎ *04–90–05–66–69* 🌐 *www.okhra.com* *From €9.50.*

Sentier des Ocres (*Ocher Trail*)

TRAIL | **FAMILY** | This popular trail starts out from the town cemetery and winds through a magical, multicolor palette *de pierres* (of rocks) replete with eroded red cliffs and chestnut groves. The circuit takes about 45 minutes. Its opening hours are complicated, so check ahead with the tourist office. ✉ *Roussillon* 🌐 *otroussillon.pagesperso-orange.fr* *From €3.50.*

Hotels

Hôtel les Sables d'Ocre

$$ | **HOTEL** | This small, picturesque hotel, set amid lovely gardens, is a 10-minute walk to town but far enough from its summer crowds to offer peace and quiet. **Pros:** exceptional service; lovely pool; air-conditioning. **Cons:** breakfast isn't included in price; reception closes

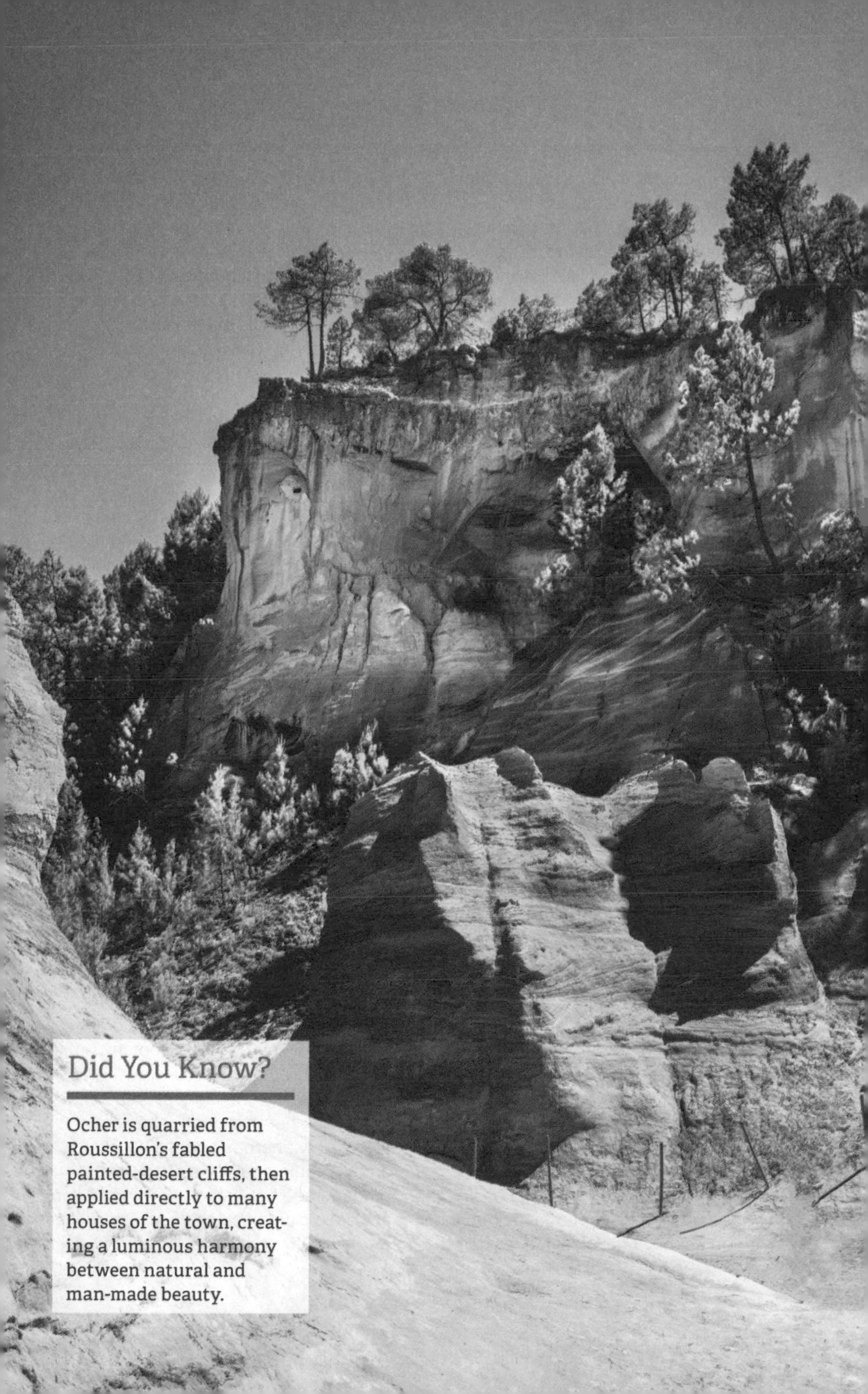

Did You Know?

Ocher is quarried from Roussillon's fabled painted-desert cliffs, then applied directly to many houses of the town, creating a luminous harmony between natural and man-made beauty.

The Earthly Source of a Heavenly Palette 

Since the first cave paintings, man has extracted ocher from the earth, using its extraordinary palette of colors to make the most of nature's play between earth and light. Grounded in these earth-based pigments, ancient frescoes seem to glow from within, and the houses of Provence seem to draw color from the land itself.

The source of all this luminosity is iron hydroxide, intimately allied with the purest of clays. Extracted from the ground in chunks and washed to separate it from its quartz-sand base, ocher is ground to fine powder and mixed with a binder of chalk and sand. This ancient blend is applied to the stone walls of Provençal houses, giving the region its heavenly repertoire of warm yellow, gold, brick, sienna, and umber.

at 8 pm sharp; decor quaint but dated. *Rooms from: €125 Quartier Les Sablières, Roussillon 04–90–05–55–55 www.sablesdocre.com 22 rooms No Meals.*

Le Clos de la Glycine

$$$ | **HOTEL** | Modern amenities like an elevator and air-conditioning combine with Provençal charm at this centrally located hotel, where some rooms have terraces with views of the ocher cliffs. **Pros:** perfect for sunrise views; easy walking distance to town; very good restaurant. **Cons:** often fully booked far in advance; not all rooms have showers; no tea or coffee in rooms. *Rooms from: €230 Pl. de la Poste, Roussillon 04–90–05–60–13 www.leclosdelaglycine.fr 9 rooms No Meals.*

Ménerbes

27 km (17 miles) southwest of Roussillon; 30 km (19 miles) southeast of Avignon.

This picturesque, fortified town isn't designated as one of the *"plus beaux villages du France"* for nothing. Perched high on a rocky precipice and anchored by a 15th-century castelet, beautiful Ménerbes is a place of charming narrow streets, winding passageways, and limitless views.

GETTING HERE AND AROUND

There is no direct bus service to Ménerbes. The only way to get here is by car. There are several routes from Roussillon, but regardless of which one you choose, the drive takes 15 minutes or so. From Avignon, it's about 75 minutes.

VISITOR INFORMATION

CONTACT Ménerbes Visitors' Bureau. *119 av. Marcellin Poncet, Ménerbes 04–90–72–21–80 www.menerbes.fr/en/visitors-bureau.*

Sights

★ Le Jardin Botanique de la Citadelle

GARDEN | **FAMILY** | The flowering of a 25-year project, this lovely botanical garden is planted on rediscovered 18th-century terraces at the highest point of La Citadelle vineyards, with magnificent views of Ménerbes and the Vaucluse and Ventoux mountains. Stroll its scenic paths to see hundreds of medicinal and aromatic plant species used in traditional medicines for millennia. Afterward, enjoy a tasting at the domaine and entrance to the Musée du Tire-Bouchon, the world's first museum dedicated to the corkscrew. ✉ *601 rte. de Cavaillon, Ménerbes* ☎ *04–90–72–41–58* 🌐 *www.jardindelacitadelle.com* 🎫 *€5* 🕒 *Closed Sun. Oct.–late Apr.*

★ **Musée du Tire-Bouchon** (*Corkscrew Museum*)
OTHER MUSEUM | **FAMILY** | Don't miss this quirky museum, which has some 1,200 corkscrews—the oldest dating from the 17th century—collected from all over the world, as well as interesting historical displays on various wine-related subjects. ✉ *Domaine de la Citadelle, Rte. de Cavaillon, Ménerbes* ☎ *04–90–72–41–58* 🌐 *www.museedutirebouchon.com* 🎫 *€5.*

Place de l'Horloge (*Clock Square*)
PLAZA/SQUARE | **FAMILY** | In pretty Place de l'Horloge, a campanile tops the Hôtel de Ville, and you can admire the delicate stonework on the arched portal and mullioned windows of a Renaissance house. Just past the tower on the right is an overlook taking in views toward Gordes, Roussillon, and Mont Ventoux. ✉ *Ménerbes.*

Hotels

★ **La Bastide de Marie**
$$$$ | **HOTEL** | A Provençal dream come true, this exclusive property—part of the Maisons et Hôtels Sibuet collection—is amid a 57-acre vineyard and has rustic-chic common areas and guest quarters in a restored stone farmstead. **Pros:** fantastic dining room and terrace; lovely full-service spa; perfectly located for touring Ménerbes and the Luberon. **Cons:** far from nightlife; some rooms on the smaller side; a car is essential. $ *Rooms from: €421* ✉ *64 chemin des Peirelles, Ménerbes* ☎ *04–90–72–30–20* 🌐 *labastidedemarie.com* 🛏 *16 rooms* 🍽 *No Meals.*

Lacoste

7 km (4 miles) east of Ménerbes; 37 km (23 miles) southeast of Avignon.

The gentrified hilltop town of Lacoste owes its fame to an infamous literary resident.

GETTING HERE AND AROUND

There is no direct bus service to Lacoste. The only way to get here is by car. It's a 10- to 15-minute drive from Ménerbes. The trip from Avignon takes 45 to 50 minutes.

VISITOR INFORMATION

CONTACT Lacoste Tourist Office. ✉ *Pl. de l'Eglise, Lacoste* ☎ *04–90–06–11–36* 🌐 *www.luberon-apt.fr.*

Sights

Château de Lacoste
CASTLE/PALACE | For many years, little but ruins remained of the once magnificent Château de Lacoste, where the Marquis de Sade (1740–1814) spent some 30 years of his life. Because his exploits, both literary and real, were judged obscene by various European courts, he was also imprisoned several times, including, in 1784, at the Bastille in Paris. It was there that he secretly wrote *Les 120 Journées de Sodome* (*The 120 Days of Sodom*), an unfinished novel that featured a Black Forest château very similar in description to de Sade's actual home. Though he had to leave his manuscript behind, de Sade escaped harm during the Storming of the Bastille on July 14, 1789. His Lacoste home, however, was not so lucky: it was destroyed with particular relish during the Revolution.

In 2001, wealthy Paris couturier Pierre Cardin bought the château and oversaw its restoration up until his death in 2020. His legacy lives on in the Festival Pierre Cardin (aka the Festival Lacoste), a two-week arts extravaganza held on the grounds in late July and early August. Events range from outdoor poetry recitals and open-air film screenings to ballet performances and colorful operettas. The castle is also open to the public between mid-June and late September. ✉ *Carrière du Château, Lacoste* ☎ *04–90–75–93–12* 🌐 *www.festivaldelacoste.com/chateaudumarquisdesade* 🎟 *Château €10, festival performances from €55* 🕒 *Closed Oct.–mid-June.*

★ La Forêt des Cèdres

FOREST | FAMILY | Created in part to fortify France's supply of cedar and cyprus wood, this magnificent forest, covering hundreds of acres, also provides a cool, quiet place for hiking and picnicking. Information on the forest is available at all of the local tourist offices, and the route to it is well marked from the village of Lacoste. The winding drive provides astounding views of the hilltop villages that dot the countryside. ✉ *Lacoste* ☎ *04–90–75–80–06* 🌐 *www.luberon-sud-tourisme.fr.*

Hotels

★ Domaine de Bonne Terre

$$ | B&B/INN | Though only a two-minute walk from Lacoste, a more captivating country setting would be hard to find, complete with extensive gardens and olive groves, a wooded park with picturesque stone walls, a pool, and breathtaking views everywhere—including from your room. **Pros:** freshly prepared breakfast included in price; short walk to Lacoste; very nice pool. **Cons:** closed in late fall and winter; rooms are lovely but basic; not for those seeking chic design. $ *Rooms from: €125* ✉ *Rte. de Sainte Veran, Lacoste* ☎ *04–90–75–85–53* 🌐 *www.luberon-lacoste.com* 💳 *No credit cards* 🕒 *Closed Nov.–Mar.* 🛏 *5 rooms* 🍽 *Free Breakfast.*

Bonnieux

5 km (3 miles) southeast of Lacoste; 42 km (26 miles) southeast of Avignon.

The most impressive of the Luberon's hilltop villages, Bonnieux (pronounced "bun-*yuh*") is a jumble of honey-color cubes, strewn along D36, wrapped in crumbling ramparts, and dug into bedrock and cliffs. Most of its steep streets take in wide-angle valley views, though you'll get the best vistas from the pine-shaded grounds of the 12th-century Église Vieille du Haut, reached by stone steps that wend past tiny niche houses. Shops, galleries, cafés, and fashionable restaurants abound here, but they don't dominate. It's possible to lose yourself in a *ruelle* (small street) most of the year.

If you have a car, you're in luck: lovely drives thread out from Bonnieux in every direction through Le Petit Luberon. Of the four routes, the best is the eastward course, along the D943 and D113, which leads to the Romanesque ruins of the Prieuré de St-Symphorien. You can also follow the road above Bonnieux toward Loumarin to the lofty Forêt des Cèdres. Perched on a mountaintop, the unparalleled 360-degree views and cool breezes make it a popular spot for a picnic or hike among majestic century-old cedars.

GETTING HERE AND AROUND

The Avignon–Apt bus line services Bonnieux. There are seven buses a day Monday–Saturday, three on Sunday, departing from Avignon's Gare Routière (€2, 1 hour 15 minutes). It's worth renting a car, though, to fully explore area ruins and other worthwhile sites.

VISITOR INFORMATION

CONTACTS Bonnieux Tourist Office. ✉ *7 pl. Carnot, Bonnieux* ☎ *04–90–75–91–90* 🌐 *www.luberon-apt.fr.*

Restaurants

★ La Table des Amis

$$$$ | MODERN FRENCH | Chef Christophe Bacquié spent a dozen years at the renowned Hotel & Spa de Castellet, where he earned three Michelin stars, before he and his wife, Alexandra, set off on their own in 2022. Now Alexandra presides over their welcoming restaurant and *chambres d'hôtes* (guest rooms), set amid vineyards and lavender fields, and the chef is just as likely to serve your amuse-bouche as he is to whisk away your plate—and then ask you what you thought. **Known for:** innovations in the kitchen; the kindest welcome; outstanding service. *Average main: €200* *Le Mas des Eydins, 2420 chemin du Four, Bonnieux* *06–33–63–81–24* *www.leseydins.com* *Closed Mon. and Tues. No lunch.*

★ Le Carillon

$$$ | FRENCH | If you're willing to travel 10 minutes to the tiny perched village of Goult, you'll be rewarded with a top-notch, thoroughly French meal at a restaurant that's elegant enough for a celebratory dinner, yet casual enough for a gourmet lunch on the go. Sea-crab soup with fricassee of cuttlefish and homemade aïoli makes a nice prelude to saddle of rabbit with local chanterelle mushrooms stewed with kale (a rarity in France). **Known for:** classic French dishes with a certain amount of elegance; homemade sorbet for dessert; outdoor terrace overlooking the town square. *Average main: €25* *Av. du Luberon, 8½ km (5 miles) from Bonnieux, Goult* *04–90–72–15–09* *www.restaurant-goult.com* *Closed Tues. and Wed.*

Le Fournil

$$$ | FRENCH | This restaurant's setting—in a former bakery that's tucked into a natural grotto and lighted by candles and arty torchères—is as memorable as the stylishly presented Provençal dishes on both the à la carte and prix-fixe menus. Try the thinly layered beetroot with feta cheese and walnut oil or the veal braised with anise and served with creamy polenta. **Known for:** beautiful terrace in the center of town; attentive service; focus on local wines. *Average main: €25* *5 pl. Carnot, Bonnieux* *04–90–75–83–62* *lefournil-bonnieux.fr* *Closed Mon. and Tues.*

Hotels

Le Clos du Buis

$$ | B&B/INN | At this Gîtes de France B&B, guest rooms have carefully chosen antiques and lovely tiled baths, and public spaces feel homey with scrubbed floorboards, a fireplace, and exposed stone. **Pros:** full access to kitchen to cook or keep supplies in fridge; plenty of restaurants nearby; guests can use washer and dryer, a rarity anywhere. **Cons:** parking is difficult; if "homey" isn't your thing, it might not be for you; not all rooms have separate showers. *Rooms from: €165* *Rue Victor Hugo, Bonnieux* *04–90–75–88–48* *leclosdubuis.fr* *Closed mid-Nov.–mid-Mar.* *8 rooms* *Free Breakfast.*

★ Le Mas des Eydins

$$$$ | HOTEL | Alexandra Bacquié and three-star Michelin chef Christophe Bacquié left the famed Hotel & Spa du Castellet in late 2022 to create this quintessentially Provençal idyll, where five farmhouse guest rooms, an apartment suite, and a separate cottage are set amid lavender fields and rolling vineyards and sheltered by olive and fig trees. **Pros:** warm but discreet service; picture-perfect setting in the heart of Provence; superlative breakfast included in the rates. **Cons:** best to have a car; prices are steep in high season; books quickly. *Rooms from: €420* *2420 chemin du Four, Bonnieux* *06–33–63–81–24* *www.leseydins.com* *7 rooms* *Free Breakfast.*

Buoux

8 km (5 miles) northeast of Bonnieux; 9 km (5½ miles) south of Apt.

To really get into backcountry Luberon, crawl along serpentine single-lane roads below Apt, past orchards and lavender fields. Deeply ensconced in the countryside, the tiny hamlet of Buoux (pronounced "bu-*ooks*") is sheltered by white brush-carpeted cliffs. If you squint, you can just make out the dozens of rock climbers dangling, spiderlike, from slender cables along the cliff face.

GETTING HERE AND AROUND

There is no direct bus service to Buoux. The only way to get here is by car. It's a 20-minute drive from Bonnieux via the D232.

Sights

Fort de Buoux

RUINS | This site contains the ruins of an ancient village and a fortification that defended the valley in both Ligurian and Roman times. Several houses and an entire staircase were chiseled directly into the stone; it's uncertain whether they're prehistoric or medieval. Louis XIV dismantled the ancient fortifications in the 17th century, leaving Turneresque ruins to become overgrown with wild box and ivy. It is a hike up, and it's not kid-friendly due to the drop-offs above the ravines. ✉ *D113, Buoux* ☎ *04–90–74–25–75* 🌐 *www.lefortdebuoux.e-monsite.com* 🎫 *€6.*

Saignon

15 km (9 miles) northeast of Buoux; 5 km (3 miles) southeast of Apt.

Set on the Plateau de Claparèdes and draped just below the crest of an arid hillside covered with olive groves, lavender, and stone farms, Saignon is an appealing hill town anchored by a heavyset Romanesque church. Neat cobbled streets wend between flower-festooned stone houses and surround a central *placette* (small square) with a burbling fountain. Yes, it's been gentrified, but the escapist feel hasn't been erased.

GETTING HERE AND AROUND

There is no direct bus service to Saignon. The only way to get here is by car, a 10-minute drive from Buoux along the D232.

Apt

40 km (25 miles) east of Avignon.

Actively ugly from a distance, with a rash of modern apartment blocks and industrial buildings, Apt doesn't attract the attention it deserves. It has a charming central vieille ville, with tight, narrow streets shaded by stone houses and strings of fluttering laundry. The best time to visit is Saturday, when the town buzzes with a vibrant Provençal market with crafts, clothing, carpets, jewelry, and—not incidentally—all the finest produce of the Luberon and Haute-Provence.

GETTING HERE AND AROUND

Multiple buses depart for Apt each day from Avignon's Gare Routière (€2, 1½ hours). If you prefer to drive, several routes travel here, and the drive from Avignon along any of them takes just over an hour.

Sights

Distillerie les Agnels

OTHER ATTRACTION | **FAMILY** | Since 1895, this important local distiller has been producing not only lavender, but also essential oils of lavendin and other aromatic plants. Tours of its facility, offered May through August, cover cultivating lavender and the distillation process. You can stock up on lavender, organic essential oils, floral waters, soaps, sachets, and plant-based cosmetics in the on-site shop. ✉ *Rte. de Buoux, Apt* ☎ *04–90–04–77–00* 🌐 *www.lesagnels.com* *€6* ⏲ *Closed Oct.–Mar. and Sun.*

Hotels

★ Domaine des Andéols

$$$$ | RESORT | In a complete departure from traditional Provençal chic, each of this contemporary property's individually decorated houses features the work of top designers and artists; all the units also have private terraces, and some have small private pools. **Pros:** lovely setting; superb dining choices, using the domaine's own olive oil, wine, and vegetables; total privacy and tranquility, even in high season. **Cons:** breakfast is expensive; rooms not available until 4 pm; must have a car to get here. *Rooms from: €460* ✉ *Rte. de Roussillon Les Andéols, St-Saturnin-lès-Apt* ☎ *04–90–75–50–63* 🌐 *www.andeols.com* *19 houses* *No Meals.*

★ La Coquillade

$$$$ | RESORT | Set amid gentle rolling hills, elegant gardens, and 90 sun-drenched acres of vineyards (from which the Aureto estate wine is produced), this upscale hideaway—with several historic country houses restored to designer perfection—is perfect whether you want a relaxing spa or wine-tasting getaway or a more active escape of hiking through vineyards or biking on one of the hotel's Swiss-made mountain bikes. **Pros:** total pampering; close to the Luberon's best sites; huge private terraces. **Cons:** some rooms have better views than others; expensive; some staff members could be friendlier. *Rooms from: €500* ✉ *Domaine de la Coquillade, Gargas* ☎ *04–90–74–71–71* 🌐 *www.coquillade.fr* *63 rooms* *No Meals.*

Shopping

★ La Maison du Fruit Confit

FOOD | FAMILY | Known for its lush orchards, Apt excels at a technique for preserving fresh fruit that dates back to Roman times and was prized by everyone from the French popes to Madame Sévigné. At this local cooperative, founded in 1962, the old techniques were updated to 20th-century standards, but the colorful local fruits preserved in all their sun-ripened glory are still a sight to behold, and you can taste things before buying. Bigarreau cherries from the Luberon are an absolute favorite, but you'll also find Cavaillon watermelons and melons, Provence apricots, figs, plums, pears, and Corsican clementines, as well as kiwi, pineapple, and, of course, candied ginger. ✉ *538 Quartier Salignan, Apt* ☎ *04–90–76–31–66* 🌐 *www.lesfleurons-apt.com.*

Lourmarin

21 km (13 miles) south of Apt; 54 km (33 miles) southeast of Avignon.

The highly gentrified, low-slung village of Lourmarin lies in the hollow of the Luberon's south face, a sprawl of manicured green. Albert Camus loved this place from the moment he discovered it in the 1930s. After he won his Nobel Prize in 1957, he bought a house here and lived in it until his death in 1960 (he is buried in the local cemetery). Today, the main draw is a restored, Renaissance-era château, though despite being a haven of French and European vacation homes, the lovely village is well worth a wander, too.

GETTING HERE AND AROUND

There is no direct bus service to Lourmarin. The only way to get here is by car. It's an hour-long drive along the A7 from Avignon. Along the D943 from Apt, the drive takes 30 minutes.

VISITOR INFORMATION

CONTACTS Lourmarin Tourist Office. ✉ *Pl. H. Barthélémy, Lourmarin* ☎ *04–90–68–10–77* 🌐 *www.luberoncoeurdeprovence.com.*

Sights

★ Château de Lourmarin

CASTLE/PALACE | **FAMILY** | The "new" wing (begun in 1526 and completed in 1540) of this château—which was restored to near perfection in the 1920s—is the prettiest, with a broad art collection, rare old furniture, and ornate stone fireplaces, including two with exotic *vases canopes* (ancient Aztec figure vases). The château also offers lots of fun activities for kids, and it hosts a series of highly regarded open-air concerts in summer and several contemporary art exhibitions throughout the year. ✉ *24 av. Laurent Vibert, Lourmarin* ☎ *04–90–68–15–23* 🌐 *chateaudelourmarin.com* *€7.50.*

Restaurants

★ Auberge La Fenière

$$$$ | **FRENCH** | Nadia Sammut, the third generation of female chefs in her family and the second to hold a Michelin star, crafts a cuisine of such sensuality, refinement, and soul that her dedicated fan base stretches well beyond France. Sammut's passion for fresh, local, and "living" foods is backed by the notion that each ingredient expresses itself differently, and she creates extraordinary flavor pairings in the dishes on her prix-fixe tasting menus. **Known for:** completely gluten- and dairy-free kitchen; personable chef who works closely with local producers for her ingredients; natural and biodynamic wines. [$] *Average main: €45* ✉ *Rte. de Lourmarin, Lourmarin* ☎ *04–90–68–11–79* 🌐 *www.aubergelafeniere.com.*

Hotels

★ Domaine de Fontenille

$$$ | **HOTEL** | Settling into this gracious retreat under the dappled shade of tall trees deep in the Provençal countryside is the easiest thing you'll ever do. **Pros:** gorgeous grounds; impossible not to relax; fine dining and wine tastings. **Cons:** breakfast expensive; rooms vary drastically in size; service can be spotty. [$] *Rooms from: €250* ✉ *Rte. de Roquefraiche, Lourmarin* ☎ *04–13–98–00–00* 🌐 *www.lesdomainesdefontenille.com* *19 rooms* *No Meals.*

★ Le Pavillon de Galon

$$$ | **B&B/INN** | Romantic doesn't begin to describe this beautiful eco-friendly B&B set in an 18th-century hunting lodge, where every detail is rendered with taste and refinement without an ounce of snobbery. **Pros:** magnificent setting close to the Luberon's best villages; breakfast included in price; intimate setting. **Cons:** only three rooms; minimum stay two nights, maximum four nights in high season; young children not allowed. [$] *Rooms from: €250* ✉ *Chemin de Galon, Cucuron* ☎ *06–13–39–17–31* 🌐 *www.pavillondegalon.com* *3 rooms* *Free Breakfast.*

Chapter 5

AIX, MARSEILLE, AND THE CENTRAL COAST

Updated by
Jennifer Ladonne

Sights ★★★★☆ | Restaurants ★★★★☆ | Hotels ★★★☆☆ | Shopping ★★★☆☆ | Nightlife ★★★☆☆

WELCOME TO AIX, MARSEILLE, AND THE CENTRAL COAST

TOP REASONS TO GO

★ **Cours Mirabeau in Aix:** The Champs-Elysées of posh Aix-en-Provence, this boulevard is lined with lovely cafés like Café Le Grillon, where the interior looks much as it did when it opened in 1896.

★ **Bouillabaisse in Marseille:** Order ahead at Chez Fonfon and indulge in classic bouillabaisse—this version will practically make your taste buds stand up and sing "La Marseillaise."

★ **The Calanques:** Near Cassis, these picturesque coves make you feel like you've stumbled onto a movie set.

★ **Paul Cézanne:** Tour Cézanne Country in the area around Montaigne Sainte-Victoire, outside the artist's hometown of Aix-en-Provence.

★ **Îles d'Hyères:** In season, the tourists arrive en masse, but the sense of pure escape can still be enjoyed on these forested islands.

Rough-hewn and fiercely beautiful, this is the sculpted land of Cézanne and Pagnol: from a coastline of lonely pine-studded cliffs and enchanting calanques to neat rows of touristy striped sun beds and seafood platters served with a saucy comment in the local patois. Sophisticated and posh Aix-en-Provence stands carefully aloof from Marseille, tough, vibrant, and larger-than-life. Yet the backcountry between them ambles along at a 19th-century pace with boules, pastis, and country markets.

1 Aix-en-Provence. The main hub of Provence and one of its cultural capitals.

2 Marseille. A vibrant port city that combines seediness with fashion and metropolitan feistiness with classical grace.

3 Aubagne. A low-key market town once home to filmmaker Marcel Pagnol.

4 Cassis. The prettiest coastal town in Provence.

5 Bandol. A seaside resort town that once rivaled the glitziness of the French Riviera.

6 Toulon. A bustling seaside city best known for its naval role in World War II.

7 Îles d'Hyères. A collection of verdant islands once known as a haven for pirates.

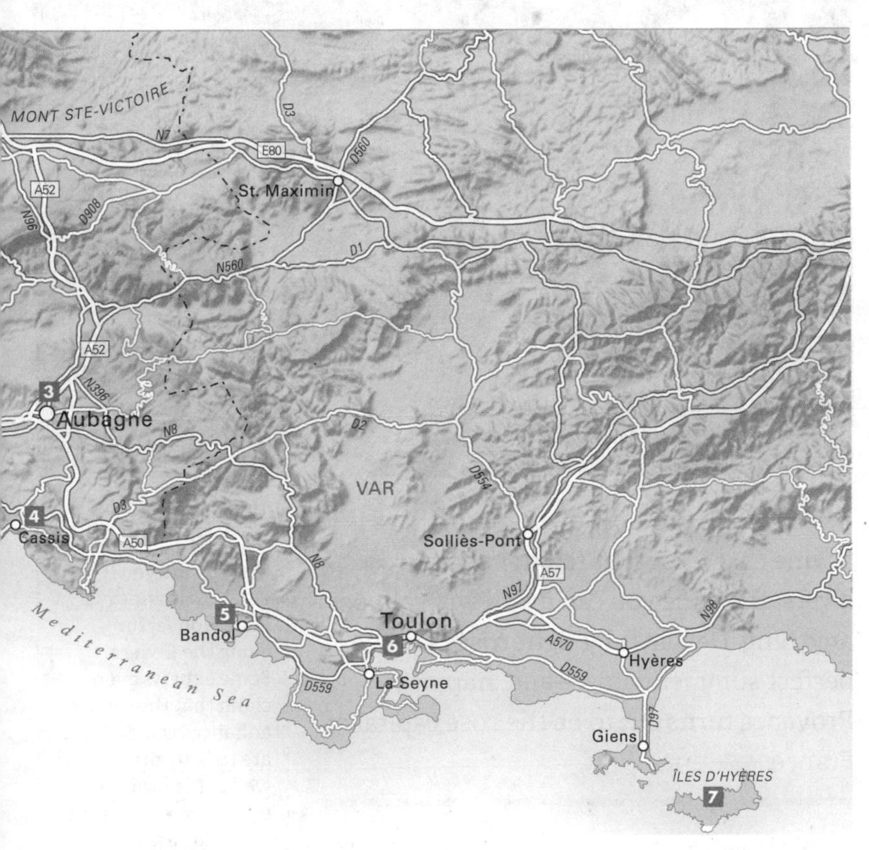
MONT STE-VICTOIRE
N7
E80
D3
D560
A52
St. Maximin
N96
D908
D1
N560
A52
N396
3
Aubagne
N8
D2
VAR
D554
D3
4
Cassis
A50
N8
Solliès-Pont
A57
N97
Mediterranean Sea
5
Bandol
Toulon
6
A570
Hyères
N98
D559
La Seyne
D559
D97
Giens
ÎLES D'HYÈRES
7

PROVENCE'S WINES

As the world has now discovered, there is a wine that is neither red nor white: rosé, a versatile wine you can drink with almost anything. Delightfully, light rosés are the perfect summer wines—and, happily, Provence turns out to be the rosé capital of France.

The Mediterranean embodies a long tradition of making fruity, dry rosés, and Provence has several appellations counting rosé as up to three-quarters of their production. Demand for it has grown greater since people have discovered that rosés are not just for summer. Still, it came as shocking news to learn the French consume more rosé than white wine. How could the most educated drinkers in the world prefer *pink* wine over a buttery white Burgundy? Fingers pointed directly to three main regions that have developed an amazingly sophisticated rosé wine culture: the Côtes du Rhône, Côtes de Provence, and Côteaux d'Aix-en-Provence.

LA VIE EN ROSÉ

One sip and you'll agree: rosé wines taste wonderful along the Riviera. Some experts even claim that the sea air enhances them. Rosés are usually drunk well chilled, whether to quench arid thirsts or to hide a less-than-rounded finish. Although considered less serious wines than their red and white companions, rosés have improved in recent years. Try a top-rated Bandol (perhaps from Domaine Tempier or Domaine de la Bastide Blanch) at least once to see how elegant these wines can be.

The **Côtes de Provence** region runs across the Var toward Marseille to the west and Grasse to the east. The dry whites, fruity rosés, and medium-bodied reds of Château Minuty (☎ *04–94–56–12–09* 🌐 *minuty.com*) are on most area wine lists. Château Sainte-Marguerite (☎ *04–94–00–44–44* 🌐 *www.chateausaintemarguerite.com*) produces full-bodied reds, lively rosés, and tasty whites.

Côteaux d'Aix-en-Provence stretches from the Rhône River to the St-Victoire mountain. Its rosés are often described as "zingy" or "fruity," and its reds and whites range from solid to reasonable. Look for stellar rosés from Château Gassier (☎ *04–42–66–38–74* 🌐 *www.chateau-gassier.fr*) and Château Beaupré (☎ *04–42–57–33–59* 🌐 *www.beaupre.fr*).

Bandol rivals Châteauneuf-du-Pape as the region's reigning red. Domaine Tempier (☎ *04–94–98–70–21* 🌐 *www.domainetempier.com*) produces distinctive reds and stunning rosés.

Top **Côtes du Rhône** choices include La Bastide Saint Dominique (☎ *04–90–70–85–32* 🌐 *www.bastide-st-dominique.com*) and Château de Campuget (☎ *04–66–20–20–15* 🌐 *campuget.com*).

The evocative whites and pale rosés of **Cassis** are prized in France for their delicate floral notes and salt-tinged freshness. La Dona Tigana (☎ *09–65–04–26–54* 🌐 *www.domaineladonatigana.com*) is renowned, as is Cassis Bodin (☎ *04–42–01–00–11* 🌐 *www.vins-cassis-bodin.fr*).

Châteauneuf-du-Pape is the king of reds in Provence, with noted names such as Domaine Chante Cigale (☎ *04–90–83–702–57* 🌐 *www.chantecigale.com*) and Château Rayas (☎ *04–90–83–73–09* 🌐 *chateaurayas.fr*). Fortia, Usseglio (both Raymond and Pierre), Domaine de Vieux Télégraphe, Ogier, and Beaucastel are other great producers.

Beaumes de Venise is an appellation that is world-renowned for its sweet wines from the muscat grape, made here since the 14th century. The pale-gold wines can be zesty or delicate and floral with a high alcohol content (more than 15%) and can pair well with savory dishes like foie gras.

Just above Beaumes de Venise, muscular **Gigondas** reds are gaining ground. For an excellent selection of mostly organic or biodynamic wines, the Caveau du Gigondas (☎ *04–90–12–41–00* 🌐 *www.rhonea.fr*)—where the tastings are free—is a must.

It's no wonder that some of the world's greatest artists were inspired by the landscapes here. The sun-drenched angular red rooftops, the dagger-narrow cypresses, the picture-perfect port towns, and the brooding massifs fire the imagination in a deep, soul-stirring way.

Cézanne colored his canvases in daubs of russet and black-green, the rough-cut structure of bluff and twisted pine inspiring a building-block approach to painting that for others gelled into Cubism. Marcel Pagnol painted pictures with words: the smells of thyme and rosemary, the sounds of thunder behind rain-starved hills, the quiet joy of opening shutters at dawn to a chorus of blackbirds in an olive grove. Cézanne and Pagnol, native sons of this region east of the Rhône, were both inspired to eloquence by the primordial landscape and its echoes of antiquity. And yet, like most who come here, they were equally fascinated with the modern Provençal world and the melding of the ancient with the new.

A visit to this region can encompass the best of urban culture, seaside, and arid backcountry. Aix is a manageable city with a leisurely pace, beautiful old mansions, and a lively arts scene, due in part to its university. Marseille offers the yang to Aix's yin. Its brash style, bold monuments, and spectacular sun-washed waterfront center evoke Naples or modern Athens. Alas, Marseille is often maligned for its crime rate and big-city energy, and, hence, often unfairly neglected by visitors.

Up in the dry inland hills, Pagnol's hometown of Aubagne showcases local life, with a farmers' market in the plane tree–lined town center and makers of *santons* (terra-cotta figurines) at every turn. The lovely port villages of Cassis and Sanary-sur-Mer and the beach town of Bandol allow time to watch the tides come and go, though for the ultimate retreat, take the boat to the almost tropical Îles d'Hyères. Like most of this region, these islands are a true idyll, but even more so for being car-free.

MAJOR REGIONS

Aix-en-Provence. For one day, join all those fashionable folks for whom café-squatting, people-watching, and boutique-hopping are a way of life in Aix-en-Provence, then track the spirit of its most famous native son, Paul Cézanne. Head into the countryside to visit the Jas de Bouffan, his family estate, and Montagne Sainte-Victoire, the main "motif" for this giant of modern art.

Marseille. France's second-largest city is the place to enjoy the colorful sights and smells of a Mediterranean melting pot, where far-flung cultures have mingled ever since the Greeks invaded around 600 BC. Tour its cathedrals and museums, visit its spiffed-up Vieux Port's architectural gems, and then head east to Aubagne to walk its Circuit Pagnol.

The Central Coast. Stretching along the eastern coastline from Marseille are the famously beautiful calanques—rocky fjords that probe deep into the coastline and are punctuated with both pretty seaside towns that conjure up the St-Tropez of the 1940s and the sun-drenched vineyards of picture-perfect Bandol.

Cassis is the jewel of this region, a harbor protected by the formidable 1,300-foot Cap Canaille. Just inland, amid the dry white hills with views of the sparkling ocean below, lies the peaceful market town of Aubagne. Toulon, an enormous naval base and a tough big city, has long, sandy beaches and a charming, up-and-coming Old Town. East of Toulon is Hyères, an elegant Belle Époque–era town, where you catch the ferry to Porquerolles, the best of the wild and beautiful Îles d'Hyères.

Planning

When to Go

High season falls between Easter and October, but if you come in winter, you may be pampered with warm sun and cool breezes. When the mistral attacks (and it can happen in any season), it channels all its forces down the Rhône Valley and blasts into Aix and Marseille like a hurricane. But, happily, the assault may last only one day. (This is not the day, however, to opt for a boat ride from Cassis or Porquerolles; aim instead for the sheltered streets of Aix.)

Planning Your Time

To make the most of your time, divide your days between big-city culture, back-country tours, and waterfront leisure. You can "do" Marseille in an impressive day or weekend trip, but its backstreets and tiny ports reward a more leisurely approach. Aix is as much a way of life as a city charged with must-sees; allow time to hang out in a Cours Mirabeau café and shop the side streets.

Aubagne is most charming on a market day (Tuesday, Thursday, Saturday, or Sunday). Cassis merits at least a day to explore the calanques and enjoy a seaside lunch; Bandol is less appealing unless you're committed to beach time. The complete seaside experience can be found on the island of Porquerolles, one of the Îles d'Hyères.

Take the time to enjoy a late-morning or early-afternoon stroll, a two-hour lunch, and a little siesta—this is, fundamentally, what makes living in Provence so charmingly worthwhile. And even if Aix-en-Provence, Marseille, and Toulon are bustling cities, you'll note that much of general life comes to a halt between midday and 2, and everything is closed on Sunday (except the markets, which are open until about 1 or 1:30). Many shops are also closed on Monday, so plan accordingly.

Keep your sense of humor intact, and learn the Gallic shrug (a typical shoulder movement that can mean anything from "I don't know" to "I really don't care") when you are politely refused service because you are too early or too late. It's a different mentality, one focused on the quality of life for everyone and emphasizing the value of savoring the important things.

To really take advantage of the area, start your trip in a large and vibrant city center like Marseille. From here you can spiral out to Aix, Aubagne, and the coast with ease via train, car, or bus. If you want a stylish and delightful mix of urban chic and country-town beauty, though, Aix-en-Provence can't be beat for a kick-off point.

Getting Here and Around

Public transportation in Marseille, Aix, and the Central Coast is well organized, with most areas accessible by plane, train, bus, or boat.

Flying in is a good option, as Marseille has one of the largest airports in France and regular flights come in from Paris and London. The Toulon-Hyères airport is smaller but also has frequent flights.

If you prefer the more scenic route, note that the high-speed TGV trains go directly to Marseille, Aix-en-Provence, and Toulon from Paris in about the same time as a flight, and a big selection of local and regional trains will take you to the towns along the Central Coast. Another advantage is that train stations tend to be central and more easily accessible than airports.

There is a moderately good network of buses run by a large number of independent bus companies, but check with the local tourism offices for the one you need since the "who's who" in the bus world here is confusing.

If driving, don't count on your rental car having GPS. Get a good map, and familiarize yourself with the towns and cities along your route first, since those are the signs you'll follow.

AIR

The large Aéroport de Marseille Provence in Marignane is about 20 km (12 miles) northwest of the city center. Regular flights come in daily from Paris and London. Delta Airlines flies direct from New York to Nice (about 190 km [118 miles] from Marseille and about 150 km [93 miles] from Toulon). Airport shuttle buses to Marseille center leave every 20 minutes 4:30 am–12:10 am daily (€10); shuttles to Aix leave hourly 8 am–11:10 pm (€10).

AIRPORT INFORMATION Marseille Provence Airport. (*Marignane*) ✉ *Marseille* ☎ *08–20–81–14–14* 🌐 *www.marseille.aeroport.fr.*

BOAT

If you find yourself without a yacht on this lovely coastline, it's easy to jump on a tourist cruiser, whether you putter from calanque to calanque between Marseille and Cassis or commute to the car-free Îles d'Hyères. Many boats have glass bottoms for underwater viewing, and most let you climb onto the top deck and face the wind as the cruiser bucks the waves.

BUS

A good network of private bus services (confusingly called *cars*) strikes out from Marseille's *gare routière* (bus station), adjacent to the Metro Gare St-Charles train station, and carries you to points not served by train. Tickets cost €1.70 and multiple-ticket *carnets* are available.

From Marseille, buses link many destinations, including Aix-en-Provence (€6, 1 hour, leaving every 20 minutes); Nice (€33.50, 3 hours, serviced by Phocéens Cars, five buses daily); Cassis (€6.30, 1½ hours, every 20 minutes); Carpentras (€20, 2 hours, three buses daily); and Cavaillon (€14.70, 1 hour, three buses daily).

As for Aix-en-Provence, it has a dense network of bus excursions from its station. To/from destinations include Marseille (€6, 1 hour, every 20 minutes); Arles (€10, 1½ hours, two to five daily); and Avignon (€18, 1½ hours, two to four daily). Aix-en-Provence has a municipal bus that services the entire town and outlying suburbs (such as Jas de Bouffon). A ticket costs €1.20.

A *navette* (shuttle bus) connects La Rotonde/Cours Mirabeau with the bus and train station, and one heads out to the TGV station (departing from bus station),

One look at the flower-filled fields of the Bouches du Rhône region, and you'll quickly understand why Van Gogh, Gauguin, and Monet loved Provence.

which is some 13 km (8 miles) west of town and the Marseille-Provence airport.

BUS INFORMATION Aix-en-Bus. ✉ *300 av. Guiseppe Verdi* ☎ *09–70–80–90–13* 🌐 *www.aixenbus.fr.* **Aix-en-Provence gare routière.** ✉ *Av. de la Europe* ☎ *08–09–40–04–15.* **Lepilote/Cartreize.** ☎ *08–00–71–31–37* 🌐 *www.lepilote.com.* **Marseille gare routière.** ✉ *3 pl. Victor Hugo, St-Charles* ☎ *04–91–08–16–40.* **Phocéens Cars.** ☎ *04–93–85–62–15* 🌐 *www.phoceens-cars.com.*

CAR

The A6/A7 toll expressway (*péage*) channels all traffic from Paris toward the south. At Orange, A7 splits to the southeast and leads directly to Aix. From there A51 leads to Marseille. Also at Aix, you can take A52 south via Aubagne to Cassis and A50, the coastal autoroute tollway.

The Aix–Marseille–Toulon triangle is well served by a network of autoroutes with a confusing profusion of segmented number-names (A50, A51, A52, A55). Hang on to your map and follow the direction signs. As with any major metropolis, it pays to think twice before driving into Marseille: if you want to visit only the port neighborhoods, it may be easier to make a day trip by train.

However, you'll need to drive to visit the smaller ports and bays outside the center. To approach downtown Marseille, aim for the A51, which dovetails down from Aix. It plops you conveniently near the Vieux Port, while A55 crawls through industrial dockside traffic. The autoroute system collapses inconveniently just at Toulon, forcing you to drive right through jammed downtown traffic. When mapping out your itinerary, remember that all the coastal towns hereabouts line up for easy access between Marseille and Toulon, so you can wind up cruising along A50, which follows the coastline, and take in all the sights.

Although Marseille is one of the biggest cities in France, it's only a matter of minutes before you're lost in deep backcountry on winding, picturesque roads that lead to Cassis or Aubagne and beyond. Beautiful back roads between Aix, Marseille, and Aubagne carry you through Cézanne and Pagnol country; the N96 between Aix and Aubagne is worth skipping the freeway for. The D559 follows the coast, more or less scenically, from Marseille through Cassis to Hyères.

TRAIN

The high-speed Méditerranée line ushered in a new era in TGV (Trains à Grande Vitesse or Trains at Great Speed) travel in France. This route enables you to travel from Paris's Gare de Lyon to Marseille in just three hours. Not only is the idea of Provence as a day trip now possible (though, of course, not advisable), you can even whisk yourself there directly upon arrival at Paris's Charles de Gaulle airport. In addition, with high-speed service now connecting Aix, Nîmes, Avignon, and Marseille, travelers without cars will find a Provence itinerary much easier to pull off.

For full information on the TGV *Méditerranée,* log onto the SNCF website (handily in English). You can purchase tickets on this website or through RailEurope, and you should always buy your TGV tickets well in advance for the most savings. Note that although tickets are cheapest two or more months out, they're sometimes reduced around 11 pm the night before in the off-season.

There's also frequent local-train service to other towns from the region's main TGV stops. From Aix, trains travel to, among other destinations, Marseille (€8.30, 30 minutes, 44 trains daily); Nice (€39, 5½ hours, eight trains daily); and Cannes (€35, 5½ hours, eight trains daily). Marseille has train routes to Aix-en-Provence (€8.30, 30 minutes, 44 trains daily); Avignon (€17, 1 hour, leaves hourly); Nîmes (€30, 1½ hours); Arles (€16, 1 hour); and Orange (€23, 1½ hours). Once in Marseille, you can link up with the coastal train route for connections to all the resort towns eastward to Monaco and Menton. You can also catch trains to Cassis, Bandol, Aubagne, and Toulon.

Marseille has a fine metro system. Most of the two metro lines service the suburbs, but several stops in the city center can help you get around quickly, including the main stop at Gare St-Charles, Colbert, Vieux Port, and Notre-Dame. A ticket costs €1.70, and multiple carnet tickets are available.

TRAIN INFORMATION Aix-en-Provence Gare SNCF. ✉ *Av. Victor Hugo* ☎ *08–92–35–35–35.* **Marseille Gare St-Charles.** ☎ *08–00–11–40–23.* **SNCF.** ☎ *3635* 🌐 *www.sncf.com.*

Hotels

Area accommodations range from luxury villas to modest city-center hotels. This is no longer just converted *mas* (farmhouse) country. Nonetheless, hotels in this region favor Provençal flavor and aim to provide outdoor space at its loveliest, from gardens where breakfast is served to parasol pine–shaded pools. The bigger cities will always have somewhere to stay, but the good and reputable hotels book up quickly at certain times of the year. June, July, and August are considered to be high season, so reserve ahead of time. In the larger cities, particularly Marseille, be careful to note where your hotel is located because, even if the hotel is deluxe, there are unsavory neighborhoods that can make for an unpleasant, if not downright scary, stay (especially at night).

Restaurants

One eats late in Provence: rarely before 1 pm for lunch (and you may find yourself still at the table at 4 pm) and 8 or 9 pm for dinner. Be prepared for somewhat disdainful looks ("Tourists!") and slow responses if you try to come any earlier.

Most restaurants close between lunch and dinner, even in summer, and no matter how much you are willing to spend or how well dressed you are, you will be firmly turned away. If you are craving an afternoon glass of rosé *bien frais* and a light snack, most cafés and brasseries in larger towns and cities have all-day hours.

In smaller villages, some cafés stay open all day, and, near the seaside, head to a small beach or roadside sandwich kiosk or the local *boulangerie* (bakery), which usually has a selection of fresh bread and treats. If you're more intrepid, sample Provençal life in one of the smoky, lottery-playing, coffee-and-pastis-drinking *tabacs* that line every main street in the south. You'll find they also often have basic fare for a reasonable price.

⇨ *Hotel and restaurant reviews have been shortened. For full information, visit Fodors.com. Hotel prices are the lowest cost of a standard double room in high season. Restaurant prices are the average cost of a main course at dinner or, if dinner is not served, at lunch.*

What It Costs in Euros			
$	**$$**	**$$$**	**$$$$**
HOTELS			
under €125	€125–€225	€226–€350	over €350
RESTAURANTS			
under €18	€18–€24	€25–€32	over €32

Visitor Information

The regional tourist offices—the Comité Départemental du Tourisme du Var, the Comité Départemental du Tourisme des Bouches-du-Rhône, and Comité Regional du Tourisme de Provence-Alpes-Côte d'Azur—have extensive documentation on lodging, restaurants, rentals, hikes, and attractions.

CONTACTS Comité Départemental du Tourisme des Bouches-du-Rhône. ✉ *13 rue de Brignoles, Marseille* ☎ *04–91–13–84–13* 🌐 *www.myprovence.fr.* **Comité Départemental du Tourisme du Var.** ✉ *1 bd. de Strasbourg, Toulon* ☎ *04–94–18–59–60* 🌐 *www.visitvar.fr.* **Comité Regional du Tourisme de Provence-Alpes-Côte d'Azur.** ✉ *12 pl. Joliette, Marseille* ☎ *04–91–56–47–00* 🌐 *provence-alpes-cotedazur.com.*

Aix-en-Provence

32 km (20 miles) north of Marseille; 64 km (40 miles) northwest of Toulon.

Longtime rival of edgier, more exotic Marseille, the lovely town of Aix-en-Provence (pronounced "*ex*") is gracious, cultivated, and made all the more cosmopolitan by the presence of some 40,000 university students. In keeping with its aristocratic heritage, Aix quietly exudes well-bred suavity and elegance—indeed, it is now one of the 10 richest townships in France.

The influence and power it once had as the old capital of Provence—fine art, noble architecture, and graceful urban design—remain equally important to the city today. And, although it is true that Aix owns up to a few modern-day eyesores, the overall impression is one of beautifully preserved stone monuments, quietly sophisticated nightlife, leafy plane trees, and gently splashing fountains. With its thriving market, vibrant café life, spectacularly chic shops, and superlative music festival, it's one Provence town that really should not be missed.

Aix's artistic roots go back to the 15th century, when the town became a center of Renaissance arts and letters. A poet himself and patron of the arts, the king encouraged a veritable army of artists to flourish here. At the height of its political, judicial, and ecclesiastical power in the 17th and 18th centuries, Aix profited from a surge of private building, each *grand hôtel particulier* meant to outdo its neighbor. It was into this exalted elegance that artist Paul Cézanne (1839–1906) was born, though he drew much of his inspiration not from the city itself but from the raw countryside around it, often painting scenes of Montagne Sainte-Victoire.

A schoolmate of Cézanne's made equal inroads on modern society: the journalist and novelist Émile Zola (1840–1902) attended the Collège Bourbon with Cézanne and described their friendship as well as Aix itself in several of his works. You can sense something of the vibrancy that nurtured these two geniuses in the streets of modern Aix.

The city's famous Festival d'Aix (International Opera Festival) has imported and created world-class opera productions as well as related concerts and recitals since 1948. Most of the performances take place in elegant, old Aix settings, and during this time the cafés, restaurants, and hotels spill over with the *beau monde* who've come to Aix especially for the July event.

GETTING HERE AND AROUND

Aix lies at a major crossroads of autoroutes: one coming in from Bordeaux and Toulouse, then leading up into the Alps toward Grenoble; the other a direct line from Lyons and Paris, and it's a quick half hour from Marseille. The Aix-en-Provence TGV station is 10 km (6 miles) west of the city and is served by regular shuttle buses. The old Aix train station is on the slow Marseille–Sisteron line, with trains arriving roughly every hour from Marseille St-Charles. The center of Aix is best explored by foot, but there is a municipal bus service that serves the entire town and the outlying suburbs. Most leave from La Rotonde in front of the tourism office.

TOURS

Tourist Office Tours

WALKING TOURS | FAMILY | Two-hour walking tours in English are organized by the Aix tourist office; check the schedule on its website. A tour of Cézanne landmarks leaves from the tourist office daily from mid-June to mid-September; it follows the bronze plaques in the city sidewalks. Reserve ahead with the tourist office. ✉ *Aix-en-Provence* 🎫 *From €10.*

VISITOR INFORMATION

CONTACTS Aix-en-Provence Tourist Office. ✉ *Les Allées, 300 av. Giuseppe Verdi, Aix-en-Provence* ☎ *04–42–16–11–61* 🌐 *www.aixenprovencetourism.com.*

Sights

The famous Cours Mirabeau, a broad, shady avenue that stretches from one grand fountain to another, bisects old Aix into two distinct neighborhoods. Below the cours, the carefully planned Quartier Mazarin is lined with fine 17th- and 18th-century mansions. Above, the Old Town twists and turns from square to fountain square, each turn leading to another row of urban boutiques and another buzzing cluster of café tables.

If you turn a blind eye to these enticing distractions, you can see the sights of Aix in a day's tour—but you'll be missing the point. The music of the fountains, the theater of the café crowds, and the painterly shade of the plane trees are what Aix is all about.

Ancienne Halle aux Grains (*Old Grain Market*)

NOTABLE BUILDING | Built in 1761, this former grain market serves as a post office today—a rather spectacular building for a prosaic service. The frieze, portraying an allegory of the Rhône and Durance rivers, is the work of Aix sculptor Jean Chaste (1726–93); he also created the fountain out in front. That's a real Roman column at the fountain's top. ✉ *Pl. Richelme, Aix-en-Provence.*

Paul Cézanne, Superstar

Picasso called him "the father of us all." He helped catapult Picasso into Cubism. And nearly every artist working today owes a huge debt to the man who erased the traces of traditional art—Paul Cézanne (1839–1906), Aix-en-Provence's most famous native son. His images of Mont Sainte-Victoire and his still life works are the founding icons of 20th-century painting. With them, he invented a new visual language and immortalized his Provençal homeland.

When Cézanne abandoned Aix's art academy for the dramatic landscapes of the surrounding hills, he became smitten with Provence's stark, high-noon light, and he rejected Impressionism's softer hues. Instead of mixing colors to create shadows like Monet, he simply used black. Rather than employing translucent haze to create an effect of distance, he relied on ruler-straight Provençal streets (laid out by ancient Romans) to hurtle the eye from foreground to background.

In the end, Cézanne imposed himself on the landscape, not vice versa. So why not do the same? Aix has a Cézanne Trail through town marked with copper "C" studs. The tourist board also has brochures that guide you through Cézanne Country—the roads leading to Le Tholonet and Mont Sainte-Victoire.

The two most moving locales are just outside the city. Bastide du Jas de Bouffan, Cézanne's cherished family home—and a lifelong source of inspiration for the artist, who moved there at age 20—evidenced the rise of his father to prominence from hatmaker to banker. Four large decorative murals here bear the signature "Ingres"—an ironic reference to a successful and more traditional painter of the time that was the young artist's jab at his father, who preferred a more prosaic career for his son.

Indeed, Cézanne's relationship with his father was complicated. Born out of wedlock, Cézanne himself had a 17-year affair with Hortense Piquet and hid his own son (also born out of wedlock) from his father to inherit the family fortune. Regardless, Cézanne remained at Jas de Bouffan until his mother's death, in 1897, left him too brokenhearted to stay, and the house was sold.

One mile north of Aix's center and amid an overgrown olive grove is Les Lauves, the studio the artist built in 1901. The high point in this area lies a mile along the Chemin de la Marguerite: the belvedere spot from which the artist painted his last views of Mont Sainte-Victoire (indeed, he died shortly after being caught in a storm here).

★ **Atelier Cézanne** (*Cézanne's Studio*)
HISTORIC HOME | Just north of the *vieille ville* (Old Town) loop you'll find Cézanne's studio. After the death of his mother forced the sale of the painter's beloved country retreat, Jas de Bouffan, he had this atelier built and some of his finest works, including *Les Grandes Baigneuses* (*The Large Bathers*), were created in the upstairs workspace. But what is most striking is the collection of simple objects that once featured prominently in his portraits and still lifes—redingote, bowler hat, ginger jar—all displayed as if awaiting his return. The atelier is behind an obscure garden

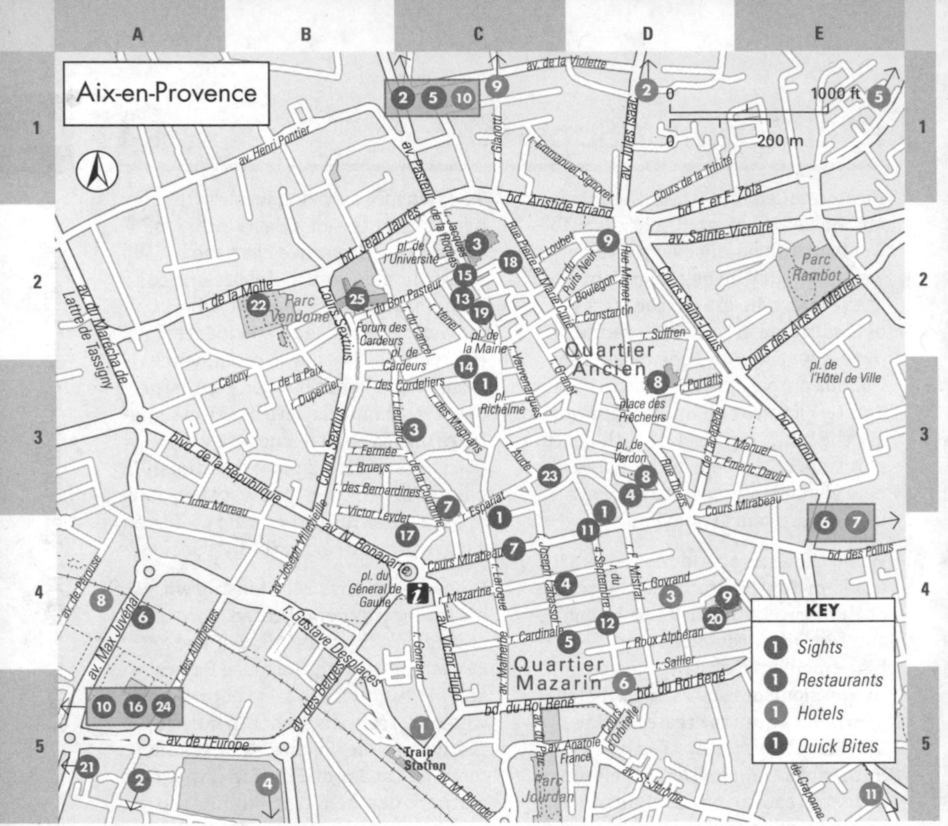

Sights

1 Ancienne Halle aux Grains C3
2 Atelier Cézanne C1
3 Cathédrale St-Sauveur C2
4 Caumont Centre d'Art D4
5 Collège Mignet D4
6 Conservatoire de Musique Darius-Milhaud A4
7 Cours Mirabeau C4
8 Église de la Madeleine D3
9 Église St-Jean-de-Malte D4
10 Fondation Vasarely A5
11 Fontaine d'Eau Chaude D4
12 Fontaine des Quatre Dauphins D4
13 Hôtel de Châteaurenard C2
14 Hôtel de Ville C3
15 Hôtel Maynier d'Oppède C2
16 Jas de Bouffan A5
17 La Rotonde C4
18 Musée des Tapisseries C2
19 Musée Estienne de Saint-Jean C2
20 Musée Granet D4
21 Pasino A5
22 Pavillon de Vendôme B2
23 Place d'Albertas C3
24 Site-Mémorial du Camp des Milles A5
25 Thermes Sextius B2

Restaurants

1 Café Le Grillon D4
2 Gaodina A5
3 Il Était une Fois C3
4 La Fromagerie du Passage D3
5 Le Mas Bottero C1
6 Le Saint Estève E4
7 Les Vieilles Canailles C3
8 Mickaël Féval D3
9 Vintrépide D2

Quick Bites

1 Mana Espresso C4

Hotels

1 Boutique Hôtel Cézanne C5
2 Château de Fonscolombe D1
3 Hôtel Cardinal D4
4 Hôtel Le Pigonnet B5
5 Hôtel Sainte-Victoire Vauvenargues E1
6 La Maison d'Aix D5
7 Les Lodges Sainte-Victoire E4
8 Renaissance Aix en Provence Hotel A4
9 Villa Gallici C1
10 Villa La Coste C1
11 Villa Saint-Ange E5

gate on the left as you climb Avenue Paul-Cézanne. ✉ *9 av. Paul-Cézanne, Aix-en-Provence* ☎ *04–42–21–06–53* 🌐 *www.atelier-cezanne.com* 🎫 *€7* ⏲ *Closed Jan., Sun. and Mon. Feb., and Sun. Dec.*

Cathédrale St-Sauveur

CHURCH | Many eras of architectural history are clearly delineated and preserved here. The cathedral has a double nave—Romanesque and Gothic side by side—and a Merovingian (5th-century) baptistery, its colonnade mostly recovered from Roman temples built to honor pagan deities. The deep bath on the floor is a remnant of the total-immersion baptisms that used to occur here, marking the forsaking of one's old life (going down into the water) for a new life in Christ (rising up from the water). Shutters hide the ornate 16th-century carvings on the portals, opened by a guide on request. The guide can also lead you into the tranquil Romanesque cloister next door, with carved pillars and slender columns.

The extraordinary 15th-century *Triptyque du Buisson Ardent* (*Mary and the Burning Bush*) was painted by Nicolas Froment in the heat of inspiration following his travels in Italy and Flanders, and depicts the generous art patrons King René and Queen Jeanne kneeling on either side of the Virgin, who is poised above a burning bush. To avoid light damage, it's rarely opened for viewing; check with the tourist office beforehand. ✉ *Pl. des Martyrs de la Résistance, Aix-en-Provence* ☎ *04–42–23–45–65* 🌐 *www.cathedrale-aix.net.*

★ Caumont Centre d'Art

ARTS CENTER | Part of the Culturespaces network of museums and monuments, this arts center is a jewel in the organization's impressively laden crown and is one of Aix's top cultural attractions. Given that the center is housed in the glorious Hôtel de Caumont, one of the city's most spectacular 18th-century mansions, it's no wonder that its period rooms are a joy to behold. It hosts two world-class art exhibitions per year in beautifully conceived spaces (the inaugural show was devoted to Venetian master Canaletto), and there are daily screenings of the film *Cézanne in the Aix Region* and a series of jazz and classical performances. The elegant gardens have been painstakingly restored to their original 18th-century layout, and you can enjoy a drink, light lunch, or dessert in the garden restaurant. The indoor Café Caumont is easily Aix's most elegant. ✉ *3 rue Joseph Cabassol, Aix-en-Provence* ☎ *04–42–20–70–01* 🌐 *www.caumont-centredart.com* 🎫 *From €7.*

Collège Mignet

COLLEGE | It's within these walls that Cézanne and his schoolmate Emile Zola discussed their ideas. Cézanne received his *baccalauréat* cum laude here in 1858 and went on to attend a year of law school to please his father. ✉ *Rue Cardinale at Rue Joseph-Cabassol, Aix-en-Provence.*

Conservatoire de Musique Darius-Milhaud

COLLEGE | In a striking modern edifice designed by architect Kengo Kuma in the Forum Culturel (which includes the Pavillon Noir dance center), the Darius Milhaud Music Conservatory celebrates the music of Marseille's native composer, who spent several years of his childhood in Aix and returned here to die. Milhaud (1892–1974), a member of the group of French composers known as Les Six, created fine-boned, transparent works influenced by jazz and Hebrew chant. Aix has yet to make a museum of his memorabilia, but you can visit during its eclectic series of student performances, jazz and classical concerts, and dance recitals. ✉ *380 av. Wolfgang Amadeus Mozart, Aix-en-Provence* ☎ *04–88–71–84–20.*

Cours Mirabeau

STREET | **FAMILY** | Shaded by a double row of tall plane trees, the Cours Mirabeau is one of the most beautiful avenues anywhere, designed so its width and length would be in perfect proportion with the height of the dignified 18th-century hôtels particuliers lining it. You can view this lovely assemblage from one of the dozen or so cafés that spill onto the pavement. ✉ *Aix-en-Provence.*

Église de la Madeleine

CHURCH | Though the facade now bears 19th-century touches, this small 17th-century church still contains the center panel of the fine 15th-century *Annunciation Triptych,* attributed to the father of Jan Van Eyck, the greatest painter of the Early Netherlandish school. Some say the massive painting on the left side of the transept is a Rubens. The church is used regularly for classical concerts. ✉ *Pl. des Prêcheurs, Aix-en-Provence.*

Église St-Jean-de-Malte

CHURCH | This 12th-century church served as a chapel of the Knights of Malta, a medieval order of friars devoted to hospital care. The church was Aix's first attempt at the Gothic style, and it was here that the counts of Provence were buried throughout the 18th century; their tombs (in the upper left) were attacked during the revolution and have been only partially repaired. ✉ *Rue Cardinale and rue d'Italie, Aix-en-Provence.*

★ Fondation Vasarely

ART MUSEUM | After three decades of neglect, the Centre Pompidou's splendid 2019 retrospective of the father of "op-art" placed Victor Vasarely in his rightful place among the great artists of the later 20th century. Whether a fan of the genre or not, a visit to this exhilarating museum, a short drive or bus ride (lines 2 and 20) from Aix center, will delight art fans of all ages. The building itself is an architectural wonder, composed of 16 hexagonal galleries each housing six of the artist's monumental tapestries, mosaics, paintings, or sculptures. Upstairs, a detailed timeline of Vasarely's life and work reveals the versatility and genius of an artist both of and ahead of his time. ✉ *1 av. Marcel Pagnol* ☎ *04–42–20–01–09* 🌐 *www.fondationvasarely.org* 🎫 *€15.*

Fontaine d'Eau Chaude (*Hot Water Fountain*)

FOUNTAIN | FAMILY | Deliciously thick with dripping moss, this 18th-century fountain is fed by Sextius's own thermal source. It seems representative of Aix at its artfully negligent best. In sunny Provence, Aix was famous for its shade and its fountains; apropos, James Pope-Hennessy, in his *Aspects of Provence,* compares living in Aix to being at the bottom of an aquarium, thanks to all the fountains' bubbling waters and the city's shady streets and boulevards. ✉ *Cours Mirabeau, Aix-en-Provence.*

Fontaine des Quatre Dauphins (*Four Dolphins Fountain*)

FOUNTAIN | FAMILY | Within a tiny square at a symmetrical crossroads in the Quartier Mazarin, this lovely 17th-century fountain has four graceful dolphins at the foot of a pine-cone-topped obelisk. Under the shade of a chestnut tree and framed by broad, shuttered mansions, it makes an elegant ensemble worth contemplating from the park bench. ✉ *Pl. des Quatre Dauphins, Aix-en-Provence.*

Hôtel de Châteaurenard

GOVERNMENT BUILDING | Across from a commercial gallery that calls itself the Petit Musée Cézanne (actually more of a tourist trap), this 17th-century mansion once hosted Louis XIV—and now houses government offices. This means that during business hours you can slip in and peek at the fabulous 18th-century stairwell, decorated in flamboyant trompe-l'oeil. Pseudo-stone putti and caryatids pop into three dimensions—as does the false balustrade that mirrors the real one in stone. ✉ *19 rue Gaston de Saporta, Aix-en-Provence.*

Hôtel de Ville (*City Hall*)

GOVERNMENT BUILDING | Built between 1655 and 1678 by Pierre Pavillon, the Hôtel de Ville is fronted by a

Did You Know?

Broad, shady Cours Mirabeau bisects old Aix, dividing it into two neighborhoods: the carefully planned, mansion-filled Quartier Mazarin and the Old Town, where boutiques and cafés line twisty streets.

The museums and churches in Aix-en-Provence are overshadowed by the city itself, with its beautiful fountains, elegant mansions, and charming set pieces like the Place de l'Hôtel-de-Ville.

pebble-encrusted courtyard set off by a wrought-iron gateway. At the back, a double stairway leads to the Salle des Etats de Provences, the old regional assembly room (where taxes were voted on), hung with interesting portraits and pictures of mythological characters. From the window, look for the unmistakable 16th-century clock tower with an open ironwork belfry. The tree-lined square in front—where cafés set up tables right into the center of the space—is a popular gathering place. ✉ *Pl. de L'Hôtel-de-Ville, Aix-en-Provence* ☎ *04–42–91–90–00.*

Hôtel Maynier d'Oppède

COLLEGE | This ornately decorated mansion houses the **Institut d'Études Françaises** (Institute of French Studies), where foreign students take French classes. During the Festival d'Aix in July, the hotel's courtyard is used for a series of classical concerts. ✉ *23 rue Gaston de Saporta, Aix-en-Provence* ☎ *04–42–21–70–92.*

Jas de Bouffan

HISTORIC HOME | Cézanne's father bought this lovely property 1 km (½ mile) west of the center of town in 1859 to celebrate his rise from hatmaker to banker. The budding artist lived at the estate, whose name translates as "the sheepfold," until 1899 and painted his first images of Mont Sainte-Victoire—foundations of 20th-century art—from the grounds. Today the salons are empty, but the estate is full of the artist's spirit, especially the Allée des Marronniers out front. **■ TIP→ The site is closed for renovations until 2025. Check with the central tourist office before visiting, as access has traditionally been via guided tours arranged through the office.** ✉ *80 rte. de Valcros (D64), Aix-en-Provence* ☎ *04–42–16–10–91* 🌐 *www.cezanne-en-provence.com.*

La Rotonde

FOUNTAIN | **FAMILY** | If you've just arrived in Aix's center, this sculpture-fountain is a spectacular introduction to the town's rare mix of elegance and urban bustle. It's a towering mass of 19th-century attitude. That's Agriculture yearning toward Marseille, Art leaning toward Avignon, and Justice looking down on

Cours Mirabeau. But don't study it too intently—you'll likely be sideswiped by a speeding Vespa. ✉ *Pl. de Gaulle, Aix-en-Provence.*

Musée des Tapisseries

ART MUSEUM | In the 17th-century **Palais de l'Archevêché** (Archbishop's Palace), this museum showcases a sumptuous collection of tapestries that once decorated the bishops' quarters. There are 17 magnificent hangings from Beauvais and a series on the life of Don Quixote from Compiègne. Temporary exhibitions highlight contemporary textile art. The main opera productions of the Festival d'Aix take place in the broad courtyard. ✉ *28 pl. des Martyrs de la Resistance, Aix-en-Provence* ☎ *04–42–23–09–91* *€4* *Closed Tues.*

Musée Estienne de Saint-Jean (*Museum of Old Aix*)

HISTORY MUSEUM | You'll find an eclectic assortment of local treasures inside this 17th-century mansion, from faience to santons (terra-cotta figurines) to ornately painted furniture. The building is lovely, too. ✉ *17 rue Gaston de Saporta, Aix-en-Provence* ☎ *04–42–16–11–61* *€4* *Closed Tues.*

★ **Musée Granet**

ART MUSEUM | Once the École de Dessin (Art School) that granted Cézanne a second-place prize in 1856, the former priory of the Église St-Jean-de-Malte now showcases eight of Cézanne's paintings, as well as a nice collection of his watercolors and drawings. Also hanging in the galleries are 300 works by Bonnard, Picasso, Klee, Rubens, David, and Giacometti. ✉ *Pl. St-Jean-de-Malte, Aix-en-Provence* ☎ *04–42–52–88–32* *www.museegranet-aixenprovence.fr* *From €6.50* *Closed Mon.*

★ **Pavillon de Vendôme**

HISTORIC HOME | This extravagant Baroque villa was built in 1665 as a country house for the Duke of Vendôme. Its position just outside the city's inner circle allowed the duke to commute discreetly from his official home on Cours Mirabeau to this retreat, where his mistress, La Belle du Canet, was comfortably installed. The villa was expanded and heightened in the 18th century to draw attention to the classical orders—Ionic, Doric, and Corinthian—on parade in the row of neo-Grecian columns. Inside the cool, broad chambers you can find a collection of Provençal furniture and artwork. Note the two, curious, giant Atlantes that hold up the interior balcony. ✉ *32 rue Celony, Aix-en-Provence* ☎ *04–42–91–88–75* *www.aixenprovence.fr* *€4* *Closed Tues.*

Place d'Albertas

PLAZA/SQUARE | **FAMILY** | Of all the elegant squares in Aix, this one is the most evocative and otherworldly. Set back from the city's fashionable shopping streets, it forms a horseshoe of shuttered mansions, with cobbles radiating from a simple turn-of-the-20th-century fountain. It makes a fine setting for the chamber music concerts that are held here in summer. ✉ *Intersection of Rue Espariat and Rue Aude, Aix-en-Provence.*

Site-Mémorial du Camp des Milles

HISTORIC SIGHT | This museum and memorial is France's only still-intact deportation camp, where 10,000 men, women, and children of 38 nationalities (2,000 of whom were eventually transferred to Auschwitz) were detained over three years, before the structure was repurposed as an armaments factory. Direct contact with internment areas, including sleeping and dining quarters and hiding places, makes for a rare immediacy. Traces of the many artists and intellectuals who were detained here, including Surrealist artists Max Ernst and Hans Bellmer and novelist Lion Feuchtwanger, can be found in the many artworks displayed (all made here), and the graffiti still vibrantly intact on the walls. At the conclusion of the visit, you retrace the deportees' path to a railroad wagon parked near the main building, a sobering reminder of a terrible chapter in French history. ✉ *40 ch. de la Badesse, Aix-en-Provence* ☎ *04–42–39–17–11* 🌐 *www.campdesmilles.org* 🎫 *€9.50.*

Thermes Sextius (*Thermal Baths of Sextius*)
HOT SPRING | Warm natural springs first discovered under the leadership of Sextius, the Thermes now house the glass walls of an ultramodern health spa. The small fountain in the interior marks the warm spring of the original 18th-century establishment. Today, the facility's offerings include a great gym, pressure showers, mud treatments, and underwater massages. ✉ *55 av. des Thermes, Aix-en-Provence* ☎ *04–42–22–81–82* 🌐 *www.thermes-sextius.com.*

Restaurants

Café Le Grillon
$ | **FRENCH** | Dating back 100 years, this is among the Cours Mirabeau's oldest cafés. Its old-fashioned interior and terrace facing the pretty square give it a certain Provençal charm, and you'll find a menu of French brasserie classics along with the usual café fare. **Known for:** historic setting; standard brasserie fare; perfect setting facing Cours Mirabeau. 💲 *Average main: €17* ✉ *49 cours Mirabeau, Aix-en-Provence* ☎ *04–86–22–44–44* 🌐 *cafelegrillon.com.*

Gaodina
$$ | **MODERN FRENCH** | If you have a car and feel like a long, leisurely lunch or dinner in the countryside, this leafy spot 7 km (4 miles) from Aix is a good choice. On nice days, you can sip the local wines under tall plane trees and take in the bucolic views before enjoying fresh local specialties prepared with care and precision. **Known for:** lovely country setting; reliably fresh; sustainable and eco-friendly. 💲 *Average main: €22* ✉ *1075 Chem. du Mont Robert, Aix-en-Provence* ☎ *06–65–67–53–26* 🌐 *www.gaodina.com* ⏲ *No dinner Sun.*

★ Il Était une Fois
$$ | **FRENCH** | At one of Aix's best "bistronomic" (gastronomic bistro) eateries, a stone's throw from the Cours Mirabeau, diners swoon for the small but delicious and beautifully presented selection of upscale French classics—crusted lobster with feta and coriander, squash samosas and homemade goose pâté, or roasted veal giblets with gouda-cauliflower and black truffle. Don't be alarmed by the small à la carte menu; it means you're only served what's market fresh that day. **Known for:** rigorous chef who loves to innovate; delicious dishes featuring both meat (especially organ meats) and fish; great-value set menus. 💲 *Average main: €24* ✉ *4 rue Lieutaud, Aix-en-Provence* ☎ *04–42–58–78–56* 🌐 *www.iletaitunefois-aix.fr* ⏲ *Closed Tues. and Wed. No dinner Sun.*

La Fromagerie du Passage
$$ | **FRENCH** | You can't sample all of France's 600 types of cheese at La Fromagerie du Passage, but there's a decadent selection of 20 or so, all *fait maison* by Laurent and Hervé Mons, who won the prestigious Meilleurs Ouvriers (Best Craftsman of France) award for outstanding cheese maker. The waiters lyrically—and patiently—explain the region or texture of each cheese and suggest a wine with the right composition to bring out the subtle (and not so subtle) flavors. **Known for:** quality handcrafted cheeses; copious cheese and charcuterie plates; delicious sandwiches to stay or go. 💲 *Average main: €20* ✉ *Passage Agard, 55 cours Mirabeau, Aix-en-Provence* ☎ *04–42–22–90–00* 🌐 *www.lafromageriedupassage.com* ⏲ *Closed Mon.*

★ Le Mas Bottero
$$$$ | **FRENCH** | If you're headed from Aix to the Vaucluse or any point north of the city, do what the local gourmands do and get thee to this gastronomic restaurant 23 km (14 miles) northwest of

It's easy to understand why Cézanne painted so many *nature morte* (still life) paintings once you see the delectable delights on sale in many of the town squares.

Aix on France's famous Nationale 7 (D7). A veteran of top kitchens from London to Switzerland, chef Nicolas Bottero struck out on his own in 2017, creating cuisine of utmost refinement but without a trace of fussiness and following the seasons and the local producers. **Known for:** knowledgeable sommelier helps pair wines by the glass or bottle; all-vegetarian menus; bright, modern dining room. *Average main: €41 ✉ 2340 rte. d'Aix RN7, Saint-Cannat, Aix-en-Provence ☎ 04–42–67–19–18 🌐 lemasbottero.com ⏲ Closed Mon. and Tues.*

★ Le Saint Estève

$$$$ | MODERN FRENCH | A short drive from Aix over scenic Route Cézanne, this elegant restaurant on the grounds of Les Lodges hotel has an inspired menu—and who wouldn't be inspired with these breathtaking views of Cézanne's beloved mountain? Michelin-starred chef Julien Le Goff doesn't have far to look for the locally sourced products such as wild *trompette de la mort* mushrooms for a luscious dish of langoustines, mussels, and lemon-infused bouillon or line-caught turbot with French caviar, crispy potatoes, and a Champagne emulsion. **Known for:** stupendous views of Cezanne's Mont Sainte-Victoire; elaborate fixed-price menus; lovely terrace. *Average main: €70 ✉ 2500 rte. Cézanne, Le Tholonet ☎ 04–42–27–10–14 🌐 www.leslodges-saintevictoire.com ⏲ Closed Mon. Jan.–Mar. No dinner Sun.*

★ Les Vieilles Canailles

$$ | WINE BAR | Most recently the chef at Alain Ducasse's Monaco palace, the thirtysomething chef at the helm of this cozy wine bar is passionate about tracking down the best local ingredients, whether it's the juicy tomatoes with your roasted octopus salad or the Camargue rice with your succulent lamb. And he's no less scrupulous about wines, with a penchant for small natural and biodynamic producers from every region of France. **Known for:** chalkboard menu of daily specials; unbeatable prices for fixed menus; small space that fills up quick so reserve in advance. *Average main:*

€20 ✉ 7 rue Isolette, Aix-en-Provence ☎ 04–42–91–41–75 🌐 vieilles-canailles.fr ⏲ Closed Sun. and Mon.

★ Mickaël Féval

$$$ | MODERN FRENCH | This is the kind of place that young cooks dream of working in to learn the ropes, and Féval, quite young himself, has trained many a Michelin-acclaimed chef. After earning his fame in Paris, Féval opened this casual-elegant dining room, tucked away on a typically picturesque Aix side street, with a menu of dishes so masterful and flavorful that the restaurant soon became a local benchmark. **Known for:** gorgeous presentation; market-fresh dishes that change frequently; impeccable service. *$ Average main: €32 ✉ 11 Petite rue St-Jean ☎ 04–42–93–29–60 🌐 www.mickaelfeval.fr ⏲ Closed Sun. and Mon.*

★ Vintrépide

$$ | FRENCH | At this sleek little wine bar, an understated decor belies splendid cuisine that easily stands up to some of Aix's more pricy gastronomic tables, but with much less fuss. In keeping with the wine bar ethos, plates are small (all the better to pair with wines by the glass) but beautifully conceived and sometimes thrilling—think foie gras with apricot confit, sea bream and wild mushrooms, or zucchini flowers stuffed with ricotta and mint. **Known for:** zero snob appeal; delicious desserts; under the tourist radar. *$ Average main: €20 ✉ 48 rue du Puits Neuf, Aix-en-Provence ☎ 04–28–31–16–41 🌐 www.vintrepide.com ⏲ Closed Sun. and Mon.*

Coffee and Quick Bites

Mana Espresso

$ | CAFÉ | FAMILY | If you're hankering for a good cup of coffee (not found in the more standard cafés around Aix), you won't go wrong here. The clientele is mainly students and locals—who know a reliably excellent brew when they taste one—and breakfast pastries and a small menu of snacks accompany the long list of coffee drinks, teas, and other beverages. **Known for:** coffee fit for connoisseurs; homemade snacks; lingering encouraged. *$ Average main: €14 ✉ 14 rue Courteissade, Aix-en-Provence ☎ 04–86–22–44–44 🌐 www.cafesmana.com ⏲ No dinner.*

Hotels

Boutique Hôtel Cézanne

$$ | HOTEL | FAMILY | Three blocks from Cours Mirabeau and the train station, this smart, spiffy, and cozily stylish hotel is a very handy option. **Pros:** spacious rooms; Clarins bath products; location in the heart of things. **Cons:** some rooms get street noise; no pool; breakfast room gets crowded. *$ Rooms from: €175 ✉ 40 av. Victor-Hugo, Aix-en-Provence ☎ 04–42–91–11–11 🌐 boutiquehotelcezanne.com/en ⇨ 55 rooms 🍽 No Meals.*

Château de Fonscolombe

$$$ | HOTEL | This gracious 18th-century country château and wine estate combines a deeply Provençal setting with chic yet comfy rooms and suites in either the historic château or a more modern wing. **Pros:** extensive grounds and wooded walking paths; activities around food and wine; luxurious spa. **Cons:** pool is on the small side; expensive restaurant; not close to the action of Aix-en-Provence. *$ Rooms from: €330 ✉ Rte. de Saint-Canadet, Le Puy-Sainte-Réparde ☎ 04–42–21–13–13 🌐 www.fonscolombe.fr ⇨ 50 rooms 🍽 No Meals.*

Hôtel Cardinal

$ | HOTEL | This eccentric and slightly threadbare inn in an elegant 18th-century house is the antithesis of slick, which, coupled with the location in the Quartier Mazarin, makes it a favorite with writers, artists, and musicians at festival time—and at any time with guests who appreciate the charm of novel furnishings and the music of the bells of St-Jean-de-Malte. **Pros:** excellent rates; rooms are clean and bright; central location. **Cons:** rooms can be noisy and hot in summer; bathroom decor is a throwback to the 1970s; some rooms have only handheld showers. $ *Rooms from: €105* ✉ *24 rue Cardinale, Aix-en-Provence* ☎ *04–42–38–32–30* 🌐 *www.hotel-cardinal-aix.com* 🛏 *35 rooms* 🍴 *No Meals.*

★ Hôtel Le Pigonnet
$$$ | HOTEL | FAMILY | Cézanne painted Sainte-Victoire from what is now the large flower-filled terrace of this enchanting abode, and you can easily imagine former guests Princess Caroline, Iggy Pop, and Clint Eastwood swanning their way through the magnificent, pool-adorned, topiary-accented garden or relaxing in the spacious, light-filled guest rooms. **Pros:** stunning garden setting; beautiful spa; in the center of the city. **Cons:** not all rooms have balconies; some bathrooms on the small side; breakfast not included in room price. $ *Rooms from: €310* ✉ *5 av. du Pigonnet, Aix-en-Provence* ☎ *04–42–59–02–90* 🌐 *en.hotelpigonnet.com* 🛏 *44 rooms* 🍴 *No Meals.*

★ Hôtel Sainte-Victoire Vauvenargues
$$$ | HOTEL | If your heart is set on staying in Aix center, this snazzy hotel 16 km (10 miles) outside of Aix—in a classic Provençal landscape at the foothills of Cezanne's Mont Sainte-Victoire—will make you think again. **Pros:** beautiful walking trails; spacious terraces; great on-site pool and restaurant. **Cons:** outside the city center; no nightlife apart from luxurious dining; on the expensive side. $ *Rooms from: €290* ✉ *33 av. des Maquisards, Aix-en-Provence* ☎ *04–42–54–01–01* 🌐 *www.hotelsaintevictoire.com* 🛏 *17 rooms* 🍴 *No Meals.*

La Maison d'Aix
$$$$ | HOTEL | Ancient and modern blend harmoniously at this elegant boutique hotel set in an 18th-century mansion once inhabited by a French woman named Henriette, to whom four spacious, beautifully decorated rooms pay homage. **Pros:** lovely pool; romantic vibe; terraces with great views. **Cons:** no elevator; pricey; some baths lack privacy. $ *Rooms from: €400* ✉ *25 rue du 4 Septembre, Aix-en-Provence* ☎ *04–42–53–78–95* 🌐 *www.lamaisondaix.com* 🛏 *4 suites* 🍴 *No Meals.*

★ Les Lodges Sainte-Victoire
$$$$ | HOTEL | Although it's just outside Aix and amid 10 acres of woods, olive groves, and vineyards, with Cézanne-immortalized Mont Sainte-Victoire as a backdrop, this hotel eschews the rustic-country-inn aesthetic in favor of a sophisticated, deluxe-contemporary style. **Pros:** has one of the city's best restaurants; four swanky private villas; beautiful grounds and views of Mont Sainte-Victoire from the infinity pool. **Cons:** outside the city center; some first-floor rooms lack views; decor a little dark on cloudy days. $ *Rooms from: €400* ✉ *2250 rte. Cézanne, Le Tholonet* ☎ *04–42–24–80–40* 🌐 *www.leslodges-saintevictoire.com* 🛏 *35 rooms* 🍴 *No Meals.*

★ Renaissance Aix en Provence Hotel
$$$ | HOTEL | FAMILY | After all of Aix's old-world charm, this five-star hotel with all the modern conveniences makes a nice contrast. **Pros:** plentiful buffet breakfasts; excellent location; great restaurant and fitness room. **Cons:** parking not included in the price; breakfast very good but expensive; very contemporary if you're looking for old-world charm. $ *Rooms from: €250* ✉ *320 av. Wolfgang Amadeus Mozart, Aix-en-Provence* ☎ *04–86–91–55–00* 🌐 *www.marriott.com* 🛏 *133 rooms* 🍴 *No Meals.*

★ Villa Gallici
$$$$ | HOTEL | Rooms here are bathed in the lavenders, blues, ochers, and oranges of Aix and feature elegant antiques and gorgeous Souleiado and Rubelli fabrics—a design scheme that truly evokes the swank 19th-century Provence colonized by Parisian barons and dukes. **Pros:** rich fabrics and dashing interiors; beautiful garden spot; 15-minute walk

to town and shops. **Cons:** meals are pricey; no elevator; antique style not for everyone. *Rooms from: €520* *Av. de la Violette, Aix-en-Provence* *04–42–23–29–23* *www.villagallici.com* *Closed Jan.* *22 rooms* *No Meals.*

Villa La Coste

$$$$ | HOTEL | Not only does this vast estate 23 km (14 miles) north of Aix-en-Provence have ultracontemporary, pristine-white guest villas—with touches of wood, concrete, marble, and glass for maximum luminosity—but it also has a luxurious spa and pool, a winery, and a sculpture garden with more than 30 installations by the likes of Richard Serra, Louise Bourgeois, and Andy Goldsworthy. **Pros:** incredible art and grounds open to nonguests (10 am–5 pm) for free; gorgeous setting and views; fantastic restaurants, one headed by a Michelin-starred chef. **Cons:** eye-popping prices; uppity atmosphere not for everyone; more Riviera than Provençal. *Rooms from: €900* *2750 Rte. de la Cride, Le Puy-Sainte-Réparde* *04–42–61–92–92* *www.villalacoste.com* *28 units* *No Meals.*

Villa Saint-Ange

$$$$ | HOTEL | Five 18th-century country cottages house this elegant hotel's unusually spacious guests rooms, where the decor mixes Empire-style wallpapers, Asian carpets, gilt moldings, marble-top desks, and heavy drapery with contemporary velvet chaises longues and modern bathrooms. **Pros:** gorgeous grounds with a heated pool; ground-floor rooms have lovely garden terraces; just a few minutes from the Cours Mirabeau. **Cons:** larger rooms are expensive; still working out service kinks; could use more shelf space in some bathrooms. *Rooms from: €480* *7 traverse St Pierre, Aix-en-Provence* *04–42–95–10–10* *www.villasaintange.com* *34 rooms* *No Meals.*

Nightlife

To find out what's going on in town, pick up a copy of the events calendar *Le Mois à Aix* or the bilingual city guide *Aix la Vivante* at the tourist office.

★ Celeste

COCKTAIL LOUNGES | Very late to the craft cocktail scene, Aix finally has a bar that stands up to its sophisticated cousins in Marseille or even Paris. While there are 10 refreshing and original choices on the cocktail menu, the bartender is happy to customize a drink to your taste, offering helpful tips on rare or unusual spirits (there is no beer or wine served here). The cozy room, complete with comfy chairs and sofas, has a friendly vibe and the outdoor tables are lovely on hot Provence nights. *44 rue Mignet, Aix-en-Provence* *06–89–70–59–62* *www.facebook.com/BarCelesteAix.*

Performing Arts

Festival d'Aix

MUSIC FESTIVALS | In late June and July, opera and music lovers descend on Aix to see world-class opera productions in the courtyard of the Palais de l'Archevêché and other of the city's most beautiful venues. The repertoire at this internationally acclaimed festival is varied and often offbeat, featuring works like Britten's *Curlew River* and Bartók's *Bluebeard's Castle* as well as the usual Mozart, Puccini, and Verdi. Most of the singers, however, are not celebrities, but rather an elite group of students who spend the summer with the Academie Européenne de Musique, training and performing under the tutelage of stars like Robert Tear and Yo-Yo Ma. *Aix-en-Provence* *04–34–08–02–17* *festival-aix.com/fr.*

Grand Théâtre de Provence

CONCERTS | Jessye Norman inaugurated this contemporary 1,350-seat concert hall in 2007 and it has since matured into the city's primary year-round venue for world-class musical performances of all kinds and for all audiences, including classical, opera, recitals, jazz, and world music. It is also a major host of the Festival d'Aix. ✉ *380 av. Max Juvénal, Aix-en-Provence* ☎ *04–42–91–69–70* 🌐 *www.lestheatres.net.*

Le Ballet Preljocaj
BALLET | Angelin Preljocaj has created original productions for the New York City Ballet and the Paris Opera Ballet, and his modern-dance troupe, Ballet Preljocaj, is based at the monolithic Pavillon Noir, designed by architect Rudy Ricciotti. From September through May, the Pavillon hosts contemporary ballet and modern dance performances featuring an international roster. Note that admission to the 6 pm rehearsals is free. ✉ *530 av. Wolfgang Amadeus Mozart, Aix-en-Provence* ☎ *04–42–93–48–00* 🌐 *preljocaj.org.*

Shopping

Unlike the straightforward country-fair atmosphere of markets in nearby Aubagne, those in Aix are filled with rarefied, high-end delicacies that stand shoulder to shoulder with garlic braids. You can find fine olive oils from the Pays d'Aix (Aix region), barrels glistening with olives of every hue and blend, and vats of tapenade (crushed olive, caper, and anchovy paste). Melons, asparagus, and mesclun salad are piled high, and dried sausages bristling with Provençal herbs hang from stands.

A food and produce market takes place every morning on Place Richelme. Just up the street, on Place Verdun, is a good, high-end *brocante* (collectibles) market Tuesday, Thursday, and Saturday mornings.

Be sure to try a *calisson,* an Aixois delicacy made of almond paste and candied fruit. The confection is cut into almond shapes and stacked high in *confiserie* windows.

In addition to its old-style markets and jewel-box candy shops, Aix is a dazzlingly sophisticated modern shopping town—perhaps the best in Provence. The winding streets of the *vieille ville* above Cours Mirabeau—focused around Rues Clémenceau, Marius Reinaud, Espariat, Aude, Fabrot, and Maréchal Foch—have a plethora of goods, including high-end designer clothes.

BOOKS

Book in Bar
BOOKS | This cozy bookshop near Cours Mirabeau is not only a great place to buy and read English-language books, but also to meet other English speakers. ✉ *4 rue Joseph Cabassol, Aix-en-Provence* ☎ *04–42–26–60–07* 🌐 *www.bookinbar.com* ⏲ *Closed Sun.*

CANDY

★ Le Roy René
FOOD | FAMILY | Aix's most famous purveyor of calissons offers an assortment of the delicate almond pastries in gourmet flavors and enticing colors along with the white-frosted classic. The Rue Gaston de Saporta location is the flagship, but its wonderful museum just outside the city center (✉ *5380 Rte. d'Avignon*) delves into the history and making of this sweet and is well worth a visit. The shop also sells fruit syrups, biscuits, cakes, nougats, and a variety of other beautifully packaged candies that are perfect for gifts. ✉ *11 rue Gaston de Saporta, Aix-en-Provence* ☎ *04–42–26–67–86* 🌐 *www.calisson.com.*

Leonard Parli
FOOD | FAMILY | Near the train station, Leonard Parli offers a lovely selection of calissons. ✉ *35 av. Victor Hugo, Aix-en-Provence* 🌐 *www.leonard-parli.com.*

Maison Béchard
FOOD | FAMILY | The most picturesque shop specializing in calissons is the venerable bakery Béchard, founded in 1870. ✉ *12 cours Mirabeau, Aix-en-Provence* ☎ *04–42–26–06–78* 🌐 *maisonbechard.fr.*

Maison Weibel
FOOD | FAMILY | This Aix institution since 1954 is chock-full of sweets that look good enough to immortalize in a still life, let alone eat. Its version of the iconic Provençal calisson is hands down the best around. ✉ *2 rue Chabrier, Aix-en-Provence* ☎ *04–42–23–33–21* 🌐 *www.maisonweibel.com.*

CLOTHING

Blow Up
SECOND-HAND | This vintage store has everything from funky fashions to cool cameras. ✉ *26 rue Boulegon, Aix-en-Provence* ☎ *04–42–58–36–62* 🌐 *blowupvintage.com.*

Catimini
CHILDREN'S CLOTHING | FAMILY | The French chain Catimini offers an imaginative, jazzy stock of kids' sweaters, jackets, and dresses. ✉ *9 rue des Chapeliers, Aix-en-Provence* ☎ *04–42–27–51–14* 🌐 *www.idkids.fr/boutique-catimini.*

Gago
WOMEN'S CLOTHING | Particularly noteworthy on the fashion front is Gago, which sells stylish designer wear for women including Céline, Balanciaga, and Comme des Garçons. ✉ *20–24 rue Fabrot, Aix-en-Provence* ☎ *04–42–27–60–19* 🌐 *gago.fr/en.*

Gérard Darel
WOMEN'S CLOTHING | Contemporary fashions with an emphasis on classic French tailoring, Gérard Darel is known for chic day-to-evening dresses and sleek trench coats. It sells accessories, too. ✉ *13 rue Fabrot, Aix-en-Provence* ☎ *04–42–26–38–45* 🌐 *gerarddarel.com.*

HOUSEHOLD ITEMS/FURNITURE

Santons Fouque
OTHER SPECIALTY STORE | FAMILY | Aix's most celebrated santon (miniature statue) maker was established in 1936. ✉ *65 cours Gambetta, Aix-en-Provence* ☎ *04–42–26–33–38* 🌐 *www.santons-fouque.com.*

Activities

Because it's there, in part, and because it looms in striking isolation above the plain east of Aix, its heights catching the sun long after the valley lies in shadow, Cézanne's beloved Montagne Sainte-Victoire inspires climbers to conquest. The Grande Randonée stretches along its long, rocky crest from the village of Le Tholonet at its western end all the way east to Puyloubier. Along the way you'll traverse Beaurecueil (with splendid views of the mountain), St-Antonin-sur-Bayon's woods and fields, the vineyards of Puyloubier and Pourrières, and the green valley of Vauvenargues.

An alternate route climbs the milder north slope from Les Cabassols. Along the way it peaks at 3,316 feet at Pic des Mouches, from where the view stretches around the compass. Pick up detailed maps at the tourist office or check the Aix-en-Provence tourism website (🌐 *www.aixenprovencetourism.com/en*).

Marseille

32 km (20 miles) south of Aix; 66 km (41 miles) northwest of Toulon.

Popular myths and a fishy reputation have led Marseille to be unfairly maligned as grungy urban sprawl plagued with impoverished neighborhoods and louche politics. It is often given wide berth by travelers in search of a Provençal idyll. A huge mistake. Marseille, even its earliest history, has maintained its contradictions with a kind of fierce and independent pride.

Yes, there are sketchy neighborhoods and some modern eyesores, but there is also tremendous beauty and culture. Cubist jumbles of white stone rise over a picture-book seaport, bathed in light of blinding clarity, crowned by larger-than-life neo-Byzantine churches, and framed by massive fortifications. Neighborhoods teem with immigrant-friendly life, and souklike African markets smell deliciously of spices and coffees. The labyrinthine Old Town radiates pastel shades of saffron, marigold, and robin's-egg blue.

Called Massalia, this was the most important Continental shipping port in antiquity. It flourished for 500 years as a typical Greek city, enjoying the full flush of classical culture, its gods, its democratic political system, its sports and theater, and its naval prowess. Caesar changed all that, besieging the city in 49 BC and seizing most of its colonies. In 1214, Marseille was seized again, this time by Charles d'Anjou, and, in 1481, it was annexed to France by Henri IV. The city's biggest transformation, however, took place under Louis XIV, who pulled down its walls in 1666 and expanded the port to the Rive Neuve (New Riverbank).

Marseille was devastated by plague in 1720, losing more than half its population. By the time of the Revolution, the city was on the rebound again, with flourishing soap-manufacturing and oil-processing industries that encouraged a wave of immigration from Provence and Italy. The 1869 opening of the Suez Canal made Marseille 19th-century Europe's greatest boomtown. With another influx of immigrants, the city quickly acquired the multicultural population it maintains to this day.

GETTING HERE AND AROUND

The main train station is Gare St-Charles on the TGV line, with frequent trains from Paris, the main coast route (Nice/Italy), and Arles. The gare routière is on Place Victor Hugo. Here you can find Cartreize buses into the Bouches du Rhône and Eurolines coaches between Marseille, Avignon, and Nice via Aix-en-Provence.

Marseille has a very good local bus, tram, and métro system (€1.70 for 60 minutes of use), and the free César ferry (immortalized in Pagnol's 1931 film *Marius*) crosses the Vieux Port every few minutes. Itineraries for wherever you want to go in the Bouches-du-Rhone can be found on 🌐 *www.lepilote.com.*

Le Vélo is Marseille's citywide self-service electric bicycle network. Grab a bike, take it to your destination, and then pick up another when you're ready to move on. With a one-month pass (€6), the first 30 minutes and each additional hour cost only €0.50.

CONTACTS RTM. ✉ *6 rue des Fabres, Marseille* ☎ *04–91–91–92–10 for bus and tram timetables* 🌐 *www.rtm.fr/en.*

TOURS

★ Culinary Backstreets Marseille

FOOD AND DRINK TOURS | There's no better way to discover Marseille's vast culinary riches (and Marseille itself) than on foot with bilingual journalist and unabashed food lover Alexis Steinman. Her small, five- to six-hour tours and tailor-made itineraries explore all the hidden culinary corners of a city ripe for discovery—with tasting and sampling all along the way. ✉ *Marseille* 🌐 *culinarybackstreets.com* 🎫 *From €120.*

Icard Maritime

BOAT TOURS | **FAMILY** | Boats make round trips several times a day to the Calanques de Cassis from Marseille's Quai de la Fraternité (Quai des Belges). This company offers 2½-hour to 3½-hour excursions. ✉ *1 quai Marcel Pagnol, Marseille* ☎ *04–91–33–03–29* 🌐 *www.icard-maritime.com* 🎫 *From €30.*

Tourist Office Tours

WALKING TOURS | **FAMILY** | A variety of walking tours are offered several times a week and include the Old Town and port, the Cours Julien and street art, and Marseille by night. Tickets and schedules are available at the tourist office, and you can request tours in English. ✉ *Marseille* 🎫 *From €10.*

VISITOR INFORMATION

CONTACTS Marseille Tourist Office. ✉ *11 la Canebière, La Canebière* ☎ *08–26–50–05–00 (€0.15 per min)* 🌐 *www.marseille-tourisme.com* Ⓜ *Vieux Port.*

Although Marseille is France's second-largest city, it functions more like a conglomerate of neighborhoods—almost distinct little villages. One of these microcosms is the Neapolitan-style maze of picturesque lanes, cafés, artist ateliers, and chic boutiques called Le Panier. Site of the first Greek settlements and the country's oldest neighborhood, it merits intimate exploration. Don't miss the striking museum complex of the Vieille Charité.

The recently transformed Vieux Port is the most scenic walk in town—from its old fish market to the astonishing Musée des Civilisations de l'Europe et de la Méditerranée (MuCEM), the Villa Méditerranée, and the Musée Regards du Provence.

Exploring Le Panier and the Quai du Port introduces you to Marseille's history, but a walk in the Quai de Rive Neuve gives you the big picture. Either from the crow's-nest perspective of Notre-Dame-de-la-Garde or from the vast green Jardin du Pharo, you'll take in spectacular Cinemascope views of this great city. Wear good walking shoes, and bring your wide-angle lens.

Directly east of the Vieux Port, La Canebiére once served as the dividing line between those Marseillais who had money and those who did not. It has, however, lost much of its former glory and is now dominated by shopping malls and fast-food restaurants. Its architecture and 19th-century wedding-cake facades still make for an interesting walk, though, and it's a great place from which to make forays through the North African neighborhood along Rue Longue-des-Capucins to the lively cafés and boutiques of bohemian Cours Julien via Rue d'Aubagne and on to the Palais Longchamp and its fine-arts and natural-history museums.

Along the coast east of Marseille's center, a series of pretty little *anses* (ports) leads to the more famous and far-flung calanques. These miniature inlets are really tiny villages, with pretty, balconied, boxy houses (called *cabanons*) clustered around bright-painted fishing boats. Don't even think about buying a cabanon of your own, however; they are part of the fishing community's heritage and are protected from gentrification.

Abbaye St-Victor

CHURCH | Founded in the 4th century by St-Cassien, who sailed into Marseille full of fresh ideas on monasticism that he acquired in Palestine and Egypt, this church grew to formidable proportions. With a Romanesque design, the structure would be as much at home in the Middle East as its founder was. The crypt, St-Cassien's original, is preserved beneath the medieval church, and in the evocative nooks and crannies you can find the 5th-century sarcophagus that allegedly holds the martyr's remains. Upstairs, a reliquary contains what's left of St-Victor, who was ground to death between millstones, probably by Romans. There's also a passage into tiny catacombs where early Christians worshipped St-Lazarus and Mary Magdalene, said to have washed ashore at Stes-Maries-de-la-Mer, in the Camargue. ✉ *3 rue de l'Abbaye, Rive Neuve* ☎ *04–96–11–22–60* Ⓜ *Vieux Port or Estrangin Préfecture.*

Bar de la Marine

RESTAURANT | Even if you've never read or seen Marcel Pagnol's trilogy of plays and films *Marius, Fanny,* and *César* (think of it as a three-part French *Casablanca*), you can still get a sense of its earthy, Old Marseille feeling at the bar in which it was set. The walls are blanketed with murals, and comfortable café chairs fill the place—all in an effort to faithfully

The heart of Marseille is the Vieux Port (Old Port), with its small boats and portside cafés.

reproduce the bar as it was in the days when the bartender César, his son Marius, and Fanny, the shellfish girl, lived out their salty drama of love, honor, and the call of the sea. ✉ *15 quai de Rive Neuve, Vieux Port* ☎ *04–91–54–95–42* Ⓜ *Vieux Port.*

Cathédrale de la Nouvelle Major

CHURCH | This gargantuan, neo-Byzantine, 19th-century fantasy was built under Napoléon III—but not before he'd ordered the partial destruction of the lovely 11th-century original, once a perfect example of the Provençal Romanesque style. You can view the flashy interior (think marble and rich red porphyry inlay) of the newer of the two churches; the medieval one is being restored. ✉ *Pl. de la Major, Le Panier* Ⓜ *Joliette.*

Château Borély

ART MUSEUM | A gracious 18th-century château houses the collections of the Musée des Arts Décoratifs, de la Faïence, et de la Mode (Museum of Decorative Arts, Faïence, and Fashion). The bright exhibition rooms feature brilliant lacquered ceilings and installations by French artists and designers, all the better to show off the gorgeous tapestries; furniture; Marseille faience pottery dating from the early 17th century; 18th-century hand-painted murals; and fashions from the 15th to 21st century. Touring the museum, taking in the château's large park, and grabbing a bite to eat in the café is the perfect way to spend an afternoon in this lovely part of the city. ✉ *132 av. Clot Bey, Prado* ☎ *04–91–55–33–60* 🌐 *musees.marseille.fr* 🎫 *€6* ⏲ *Closed Mon.* Ⓜ *Rond-Point du Prado, then Bus No. 19, 44, or 83.*

Château d'If

JAIL/PRISON | In the 16th century, François I recognized the strategic advantage of an island fortress to survey the mouth of Marseille's vast harbor, and he built this imposing edifice. Indeed, it was such an effective deterrent that it never saw combat and was eventually converted into a prison. It was here that Alexandre Dumas locked up his most famous character, the Count of Monte Cristo. Though the count

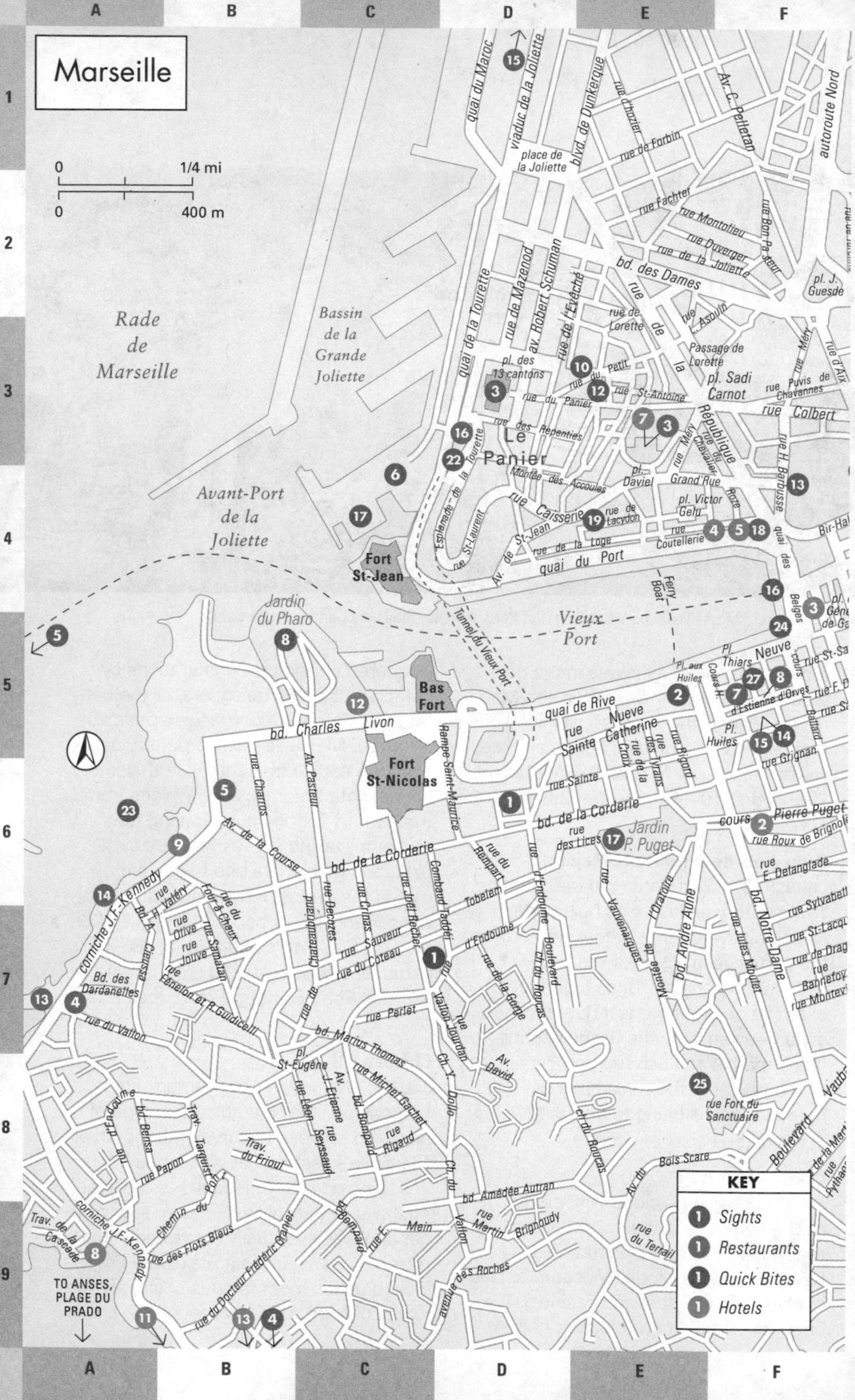

Marseille
0
1/4 mi
0
400 m
Rade de Marseille
Bassin de la Grande Joliette
Avant-Port de la Joliette
Le Panier
Vieux Port
Fort St-Jean
Bas Fort
Fort St-Nicolas
Jardin du Pharo
Jardin P. Puget
Ferry Boat
Tunnel du Vieux Port
quai du Maroc
viaduc de la Joliette
blvd. de Dunkerque
rue d'Horizer
rue de Forbin
Av. C. Pelletan
autoroute Nord
place de la Joliette
rue Fachter
rue Montolieu
rue Duverger
rue de la Joliette
rue Bon Pasteur
bd. des Dames
pl. J. Guesde
quai de la Tourette
rue de Mazenod
av. Robert Schuman
rue de l'Evêché
rue de Lorette
rue de la République
rue L. Asouin
Passage de Lorette
pl. Sadi Carnot
rue Méry
rue d'Aix
rue Puvis de Chavannes
rue Colbert
pl. des 13 cantons
rue du Petit
rue St-Antoine
rue du Panier
rue des Repenties
rue du Chevalier
rue H. Barbusse
Montée des Accoules
pl. Daviel
Grand'Rue
pl. Victor Gelu
rue Roze
quai des Belges
Esplanade de la Tourette
rue St-Laurent
rue Caisserie
rue de Lacydon
Av. de St-Jean
rue de la Loge
rue Coutellerie
quai du Port
Bir-Hakeim
Pl. aux Huiles
Cours H.
Pl. Thiars
rue Neuve
cours
rue St-Saëns
d'Estienne d'Orves
rue F. D
Pl. Huiles
Rattard
rue Grignan
quai de Rive
rue Sainte Catherine
rue des Tyrans
rue de la Croix
rue Rigord
rue Sainte
bd. Charles Livon
Rampe Saint-Maurice
rue Charros
Av. Pasteur
bd. de la Corderie
cours Pierre Puget
rue Roux de Brignoles
rue E. Delanglade
rue des Lices
rue du Rempart
rue d'Endoume
Boulevard
rue Vauvenargues
Montée de l'Oratoire
bd. André Aune
rue Jules Moulet
bd. Notre-Dame
rue Sylvabelle
rue St-Lacq
rue de Drag
rue Bannefoy
rue Montevi
Av. de la Course
corniche J.F.-Kennedy
rue H. Valéry
rue du Four à Chaux
rue Olive
rue Jouve
rue Samatan
Bd. A. Ciccolla
rue Fénelon et R. Guidicelli
rue Chateauneuf
rue Decorzes
rue Crinas
rue Sauveur
rue du Coteau
rue Tobelem
rue Jean Rechers
rue Combaud Tadéi
ch. du Roucas
rue de la Gorge
Bd. des Dardanelles
rue du Vallon
rue Perlet
bd. Marius Thomas
pl. St-Eugène
rue Léon
Av. J. Erienne
bd. Bompard
rue Michel Gachet
rue Seyssaud
rue Rigaud
rue Vallon Jourdan
Ch. Y. Dollo
Av. David
ch. du Roucas
rue Fort du Sanctuaire
Boulevard Vauban
rue de la Mare
rue Pythagore
rue d'Endoume
bd. Bensa
Trav. Targuist
Trav. du Frioul
rue Papon
Chemin du Pont
rue des Flots Bleus
rue du Docteur Frédéric Granier
Ch. du Vallon
bd. Amédée Autran
rue E. Mein
rue Martin Brignoudy
Av. du Bois Scare
rue du Terrail
avenue des Roches
Trav. de la Cascade
corniche J.F.-Kennedy
TO ANSES, PLAGE DU PRADO
KEY
Sights
Restaurants
Quick Bites
Hotels

Sights

1 Abbaye St-Victor D6
2 Bar de la Marine......... E5
3 Cathédrale de la Nouvelle Major....... D3
4 Château Borély B9
5 Château d'If A5
6 Cosquer Méditerranée C4
7 Cours Julien............. H5
8 Jardin du Pharo......... B5
9 La Canebière............ G4
10 La Vieille Charité......... E3
11 Le Centre d'Art MaMo...................... I9
12 Le Panier.................. E3
13 Le Port Antique F4
14 Les Arcenaulx............. F5
15 L'Estaque................ D1
16 Marché aux Poissons... F4
17 MuCEM C4
18 Musée Cantini........... G5
19 Musée des Docks Romains E4
20 Musée d'Histoire de Marseille............ G4
21 Musée Grobet-Labadié I2
22 Musée Regards de Provence............ D3
23 Musée Subaquatique de Marseille............ A6
24 Navette Maritime........ F5
25 Notre-Dame-de-la-Garde E8
26 Palais de Longchamp I2
27 Place Thiars.............. F5
28 Rue Longue-des-Capucins/ Rue d'Aubagne.......... G4
29 Unité d'Habitation Cité Radieuse I9

Restaurants

1 AM by Alexandre Mazzia H9
2 Cantoche G5
3 Chez Etienne E3
4 Chez Fonfon A7
5 Chez Michel............. B6
6 Copains I6
7 Coquille F5
8 Grandes Halles du Vieux Port............. F5
9 La Boîte à Sardine........ I3
10 La Cantinetta H4
11 La Mercerie G4
12 Le Capucin.............. G4
13 L'Epuisette............... A7
14 Le Restaurant Peron ... A6
15 Les Arcenaulx............ F5
16 Regards Café............ D3
17 Sépia & Julis E6
18 Une Table au Sud........ F4

Quick Bites

1 La Tisserie............... C7
2 L'Épicerie Idéale G4
3 Torrefaction Noailles... G4

Hotels

1 Alex Hôtel............... G2
2 C2 Hotel.................. F6
3 Grand Hotel Beauvau Vieux-Port-MGallery F4
4 Hôtel Hermès............. F4
5 Hôtel la Residence du Vieux Port................ F4
6 Hôtel Saint Ferréol...... G5
7 Intercontinental Marseille Hôtel Dieu E3
8 Le Petit Nice Passedat................. A9
9 Les Bords de Mer....... B6
10 Mama Shelter............ I6
11 nhow Marseille A9
12 Sofitel Vieux-Port....... C5
13 Tuba B9

was fictional, the hole through which Dumas had him escape is real enough, on display in the cells. On the other hand, the real-life Man in the Iron Mask, whose cell is also erroneously on display, was not imprisoned here. It's worth taking a trip here if only to ride the Frioul If Express boat (🎫 *€10.80* 🌐 *04–96–11–03–50*) from/to Quai des Belges and to take in the views from the fortress's broad terrace. ✉ *Marseille* ☎ *08–26–50–05–00* 🌐 *www.chateau-if.fr* 🎫 *€11.10.*

Cosquer Méditerranée

HISTORY MUSEUM | FAMILY | Move over Lascaux and Chauvet, France's newest underground odyssey takes you back 33,000 years and 121 feet "undersea." In 1985, diver Henri Cosquer discovered a mostly submerged cave with chambers containing more than 500 evocative images of bison, horses, deer, ibex, aurochs, seals, jellyfish, and human hands. On this simulated visit at Marseille's Villa Mediterranée, groups of six, equipped with headsets, are taken by cable car though a near-perfect replica of the cave to learn the story of these mysterious drawings, the original artists, and their relationship to the animals they depicted. ✉ *Promenade Robert Laffont, Esp. J4, Vieux Port* ☎ *04–91–31–23–12* 🌐 *www.grotte-cosquer.com* 🎫 *€16* Ⓜ *Vieux Port or Joliette.*

Cours Julien

PLAZA/SQUARE | FAMILY | This center of bohemian *flânerie* (hanging out) is a lovely place to relax by the fountain, in the shade of plane trees, or under a café umbrella. Its low-key and painterly tableau is framed by graceful 18th-century buildings, and the warren of streets surrounding it is full of young fashion designers, vintage shops, and hip boutiques. ✉ *La Canebière* Ⓜ *Notre Dame du Mont or Noailles.*

Jardin du Pharo (*Pharo Garden*)

GARDEN | FAMILY | The Pharo, another larger-than-life edifice built to Napoléon III's epic tastes, was a gift to his wife, Eugénie. It's a conference center now, but its green park has become a magnet for city strollers who want to take in panoramic views of the ports and fortifications. ✉ *Above Bd. Charles-Livon, Pharo* 🎫 *Free* Ⓜ *Vieux Port.*

La Canebière

STREET | This wide avenue leading from the port, known affectionately as the "Can o' Beer" by American sailors, once figured in popular songs and operettas and was once crammed with cafés, theaters, bars, and tempting stores full of zoot suits and swell hats. It's noisy but dull today, yet you might still take pleasure in studying its grand 19th-century mansions. ✉ *La Canebière* Ⓜ *Vieux Port, Noailles, or Réformés Canebière.*

La Vieille Charité (*Center of the Old Charity*)

HISTORY MUSEUM | FAMILY | At the top of the Panier district lies this superb ensemble of 17th- and 18th-century architecture, which was originally designed as a hospice for the homeless by Marseillais artist-architects Pierre and Jean Puget and which now houses two museums. While visiting the complex, be sure to walk around the inner court to study the retreating perspective of triple arcades and to admire the Baroque chapel with its novel, egg-peaked dome.

The larger of the two museums is the **Musée d'Archéologie Méditerranéenne** (Museum of Mediterranean Archaeology), with a sizable collection of pottery and statuary from classical Mediterranean civilization; unfortunately, descriptions of these items are rudimentary (e.g., "pot"). There's also an exhibit on the mysterious Celt-like Ligurians who first peopled the coast; alas, displays focus more on the digs than the finds. However, the Egyptian collection—the second-largest in France after the Louvre's—is evocative, with mummies, hieroglyphs, and sarcophagi exhibited in a tomblike setting.

Displays in the upstairs **Musée d'Arts Africains, Océaniens, et Amérindiens** (Museum of African, Oceanic, and American Indian Art) are theatrical: spectacular masks and sculptures are mounted along a black wall, lighted indirectly, and labeled across the aisle. The complex also has changing exhibitions that might focus on fine art, photography, filmmaking, or cultural anthropology, among other things. ✉ *2 rue de la Charité, Le Panier* ☎ *04–91–14–58–80* 🌐 *www.vieille-charite-marseille.com* 🎫 *Exhibitions from €7* Ⓜ *Joliette.*

Le Centre d'Art MaMo

NOTABLE BUILDING | Eighteen stories up, atop Le Corbusier's colossal Cité Radieuse—undertaken in 1947–52 to house the displaced of World War II—this sun-drenched sculpture center, complete with a theater and garden, replaces an ugly gym, added in 1964, that had obscured Le Corbusier's original tiled rooftop terrace. Conceived by notorious Paris designer (and Marseille native) Ito Morabito, aka Ora-Ito, the roof of the famous building has been restored to its original glory, complete with Charlotte Perriand–designed details, and now hosts a rotating schedule of sculpture exhibitions in the summer. The building still houses an apartment complex, shops, a hotel, and a well-regarded restaurant. ✉ *280 bd. Michelet, Prado* ☎ *01–42–46–00–09* 🌐 *www.mamo.fr* 🎫 *Free* ⏲ *Closed Tues.* Ⓜ *Rond-Point du Prado.*

Le Panier

NEIGHBORHOOD | **FAMILY** | The heart of old Marseille is a maze of narrow cobblestone streets lined by shuttered pastel houses and punctuated by *montées* (stone stairways) and tiny squares. Long decayed and neglected, the quarter is now a principal focus of urban renewal. In the past few years, an influx of "bobos" (bourgeois-bohemians) and artists has sparked gentrification, bringing charming B&Bs, chic boutiques, lively cafés, and artists' ateliers. Although wandering this picturesque neighborhood at will is a pleasure, be sure to stroll along Rue du Panier, the Montée des Accoules, Rue du Petit-Puits, and Rue des Muettes. ✉ *Marseille* Ⓜ *Colbert Hôtel de Région.*

Marseille City Pass

If you plan to visit several of Marseille's museums, buy a City Pass (€27 for 24 hours, €37 for 48 hours, €43 for 72 hours) at the tourism office or online. It covers the entry fee for all the city's museums, as well as public transit, a ride on the petit train, and a boat ride to the Frioul islands or the If Castle, with entrance to the monument. The 72-hour pass also includes a guided city tour.

Le Port Antique

GARDEN | **FAMILY** | This garden in front of the Musée d'Histoire de Marseille stands on the location of the city's classical waterfront and includes remains of the Greek fortifications and loading docks. Restored in 2013, the site, with several nearly intact boats (now exhibited in the museum), was discovered in 1967 when roadwork was being done next to the Bourse (Stock Exchange). ✉ *Rue Henri Barbusse, Vieux Port* ☎ *04–91–55–36–00* 🌐 *www.musee-histoire-marseille-voie-historique.fr* 🎫 *Free* ⏲ *Closed Mon.* Ⓜ *Vieux Port.*

Les Arcenaulx (*The Arsenal*)

STORE/MALL | In this broad, elegant stone armory, built for Louis XIV, a complex of upscale shops and restaurants has given the building—and neighborhood—new life. Its bookstore has a collection of art books and publications on Marseille, as well as gifts, perfume, clothing, and local specialties like olive oil, chocolates, and nougat. A book-lined restaurant serves sophisticated cuisine. ✉ *25 cours*

Feisty Marseille flaunts its love of the sea at the famous, harborside Marché aux Poissons (Fish Market).

d'Estienne d'Orves, Vieux Port ☎ *04–91–59–80–30* 🌐 *www.les-arcenaulx.com* Ⓜ *Vieux Port.*

L'Estaque

TOWN | At this famous village north of Marseille, Cézanne led an influx of artists eager to capture its cliff-top views over the harbor. Braque, Derain, and Renoir all put its red rooftops, rugged cliffs, and factory smokestacks on canvas. Pick up the English-language itinerary "L'Estaque and the Painters" from the Marseille tourist office, and hunt down the sites and views they immortalized. The town is a little seedy these days, but there are cafés and a few fish shops that make the most of the nearby Criée (fishermen's auction), which moved here from Marseille's Quai de Rive Neuve. A novel way to see Cézanne's famous scenery is to take a standard SNCF train trip from the Gare St-Charles to Martigues; it follows the L'Estaque waterfront and (apart from a few tunnels) offers magnificent views.

Marché aux Poissons (*Fish Market*)

MARKET | **FAMILY** | Up and going by 8 am every day, this market—immortalized in Marcel Pagnot's *Fanny* (and Joshua Logan's sublime 1961 film adaptation)—puts on a vivid and aromatic show of waving fists, jostling chefs, and heaps of still-twitching fish from the night's catch. Hear the thick soup of the Marseillais accent as blue-clad fishermen and silk-clad matrons bicker over prices, and marvel at the rainbow of Mediterranean creatures swimming in plastic vats before you, each uglier than the last: the spiny-headed *rascasse* (scorpion fish), dog-nosed *grondin* (red gurnet), the monstrous *baudroie* or *lotte* (monkfish), and the eel-like *congre.* "Bouillabaisse" as sold here is a mix of fish too tiny to sell otherwise; the only problem with coming for the early morning show is that you have to wait so long for your bouillabaisse lunch. ✉ *Quai de la Fraternité, Vieux Port* Ⓜ *Vieux Port.*

MuCEM

HISTORY MUSEUM | FAMILY | Made up of three sites designed by Rudy Ricciotti, MuCEM (Museum of European and Mediterranean Civilizations) is all about new perspectives on Mediterranean cultures. Themes like "the invention of gods," "treasures of the spice route," or "at the bazaar of gender" are explored here. At one of the sites, you can access the 12th-century Fort St-Jean, built by Louis XIV with guns pointing *toward* the city to keep the feisty, rebellious Marseillais under his thumb.

If you're not the queasy type, walk across the suspended footbridge over the sea; it provides spectacular photo ops and unique panoramas. On the other side, you can visit a Mediterranean garden and a folk-art collection. A third building—the Center for Conservation and Resources, near the St-Charles train station—holds the museum's permanent collection of paintings, prints, drawings, photographs, and objects. The museum's popular café, bistro, and restaurant (reservations required), overseen by star chef Gérald Passédat, are all great for meals and for taking in the views. ✉ *7 promenade Robert Laffont, Vieux Port* ☎ *04–84–35–13–13* 🌐 *www.mucem.org* 🎫 *From €11* ⏲ *Closed Tues.* Ⓜ *Joliette.*

Musée Cantini

ART MUSEUM | Set in a beautifully restored 17th-century house, this lovely little museum has one of France's foremost collections of Fauve and Surrealist art. It's a must for fans of the genres, with paintings by Signac, Dufy, Léger, Ernst, Arp, and Bacon, as well as Kandinsky and Dubuffet. ✉ *19 rue Grignan, Préfecture* ☎ *04–91–54–77–75* 🌐 *musees.marseille.fr* 🎫 *€6* ⏲ *Closed Mon.* Ⓜ *Estrangin Préfecture.*

Musée des Docks Romains (*Roman Docks Museum*)

HISTORY MUSEUM | FAMILY | In 1943, Germans destroyed the neighborhood along the Quai du Port—some 2,000 houses—displacing 20,000 citizens, but this act of brutal urban renewal, ironically and literally, laid the ground open for new discoveries. When Marseille began to rebuild in 1947, workers dug up the remains of a Roman shipping warehouse full of the terra-cotta jars and amphorae that once lay in the bellies of low-slung ships. The Musée des Docks Romains was created around the finds and demonstrates the scale of Massalia's shipping prowess. ✉ *2 pl. de Vivaux, Vieux Port* ☎ *04–91–91–24–62* 🌐 *musees.marseille.fr* 🎫 *€6* ⏲ *Closed Mon.* Ⓜ *Vieux Port.*

★ **Musée d'Histoire de Marseille** (*Marseille History Museum*)

HISTORY MUSEUM | FAMILY | With the Port Antique in front, this modern, open-space museum illuminates Massalia's history with a treasure trove of archaeological finds and miniature models of the city as it appeared in various stages of history. Best by far is the presentation of Marseille's Classical halcyon days. There's a recovered wreck of a Roman cargo boat, its 3rd-century wood amazingly preserved, and the hull of a Greek boat dating from the 4th century BC. The model of the Greek city should be authentic—it's based on an eyewitness description by Aristotle. ✉ *2 rue Henri Barbrusse, Vieux Port* ☎ *04–91–55–36–00* 🌐 *www.musee-histoire-marseille-voie-historique.fr* 🎫 *Free; €6 (special exhibits)* ⏲ *Closed Mon.* Ⓜ *Vieux-Port or Noailles.*

Musée Grobet-Labadié

HISTORY MUSEUM | This lovely and intimate museum houses the private art collection—ranging from 15th- and 16th-century Italian and Flemish paintings to Fragonard and Millet—of a wealthy 19th-century merchant family. Most of the works are displayed in situ, amid the beautifully appointed rooms of the family's 1873 mansion, so you get a real sense of the era's cultivated tastes in both fine and decorative arts. ✉ *140 bd. Longchamp, La Canebière* ☎ *04–91–62–21–82* 🌐 *musees.marseille.fr* 🎫 *€6* ⏲ *Closed Mon.*

Musée Regards de Provence

ART MUSEUM | This beautifully renovated 1948 architectural gem by Fernand Pouillon was once Marseille's *station sanitaire,* where every immigrant entering France was systematically "disinfected" to guard against epidemic. An absorbing 45-minute film (in English) and the intact machinery tell a fascinating story of Marseille as "gateway to the East." The light-filled second floor has spaces dedicated to the museum's permanent collection of 18th- to 20th-century paintings depicting Provence and the Mediterranean Sea, as well as to temporary exhibitions of works by contemporary painters. There's also a lovely boutique. **■ TIP→ The museum café (open until 7) has some of the best views of the redeveloped new port and is a great place for a gourmet lunch, a light snack on the terrace, or a restorative beverage.** ✉ *Av. Vaudoyer, Rive Neuve* ☎ *04–96–17–40–40* 🌐 *www.museeregardsdeprovence.com* 🎫 *€8.50* ⏲ *Closed Mon.* Ⓜ *Joliette or Vieux Port.*

Musée Subaquatique de Marseille

OTHER MUSEUM | **FAMILY** | Prepare to get wet—preferably equipped with snorkel, flippers, and some goggles—at France's only underwater museum. Exhibits, which are 109 yards off Catalans beach at a depth of 15 feet, consist of 10 submerged sculptures that highlight marine diversity and the human capacity to both destroy or save what remains of this fragile and beautiful ecosystem. ✉ *Plage des Catalans, Marseille* ☎ *06–24–82–27–01* 🌐 *www.musee-subaquatique.com/fr* 🎫 *Free.*

★ Navette Maritime

TRANSPORTATION | **FAMILY** | In keeping with the Vieux Port's substantially spiffed-up image, the Marseille regional transportation service now offers efficient public ferry service, with hourly departures from the eastern side to Pointe Rouge (8 am–7 pm), L'Estaque (8:30 am–7:30 pm), and Les Goudes (8:50 am–7:50 pm). The nominal ticket charge (€5, available only on board) is well worth it for the fun and convenience of crossing the port by boat. ✉ *Pl. des Huiles on Quai de Rive Neuve side and Hôtel de Ville on Quai du Port, Vieux Port* 🌐 *www.rtm.fr* 🎫 *€5 (free with métro pass)* Ⓜ *Vieux Port.*

Notre-Dame-de-la-Garde

CHURCH | Towering above the city and visible for miles around, this overscaled neo-Byzantine monument was erected in 1853 by Napoléon III. The interior is a Technicolor bonanza of red-and-beige stripes and glittering mosaics, and the gargantuan *Madonna and Child* on the steeple (almost 30 feet high) is covered in real gold leaf. While the panoply of ex-votos, mostly thanking the Virgin for deathbed interventions and shipwreck survivals, is a remarkable sight, most impressive are the views of the seaside city at your feet. ✉ *Rue Fort du Sanctuaire, off Bd. André Aune, Garde Hill* ☎ *04–91–13–40–80* 🌐 *notredamedelagarde.fr* Ⓜ *Estrangin Préfecture.*

Palais de Longchamp

ART MUSEUM | **FAMILY** | Inaugurated in 1869, this grandiose hilltop palace was built to commemorate the completion of an 84-km (52-mile) aqueduct bringing the water of the Durance River to the open sea. The massive, classical-style building surrounds—with impressive symmetrical grace—a series of fountains and has a museum in each of its wings. In the **Musée des Beaux-Arts** (Fine Arts Museum) are 16th- and 17th-century paintings, including several by Rubens; French 19th-century paintings by such artists as Courbet, Ingres, and David; and fine marble sculptures and drawings by the Marseille architect Pierre Puget. There are also delightful sculptures by caricaturist Honoré Daumier. In addition to prehistoric and zoological artifacts, the **Muséum d'Histoire Naturelle** (Natural History Museum) has a large aquarium with fish from around the world. ✉ *Eastern end of Bd. Longchamp, La Canebière* ☎ *04–91–14–59–30, 04–91–14–59–50* 🌐 *musees.*

Did You Know?

Marseille's Notre-Dame-de-la-Garde is impressive inside—with a neo-Byzantine interior of Technicolor stripes and mosaics—and out. It's visible for miles around, and the views from it are spectacular.

marseille.fr *Musée des Beaux-Arts: €6. Muséum d'Histoire Naturelle: free.* *Closed Mon.* *Longchamp.*

Place Thiars

PLAZA/SQUARE | An ensemble of 18th-century Italianate buildings frames this popular center of activity, bounded by Quai Neuve, Rue Fortia, Rue de la Paix Marcel-Paul, and Cours d'Estienne d'Orves, where one sidewalk café spills into another, and every kind of bouillabaisse is yours for the asking. At night, the neighborhood is a fashionable hangout for young professionals on their way to and from the theaters and clubs on Quai de Rive Neuve. ✉ *Rive Neuve* *Vieux Port.*

Rue Longue-des-Capucins/Rue d'Aubagne

STREET | **FAMILY** | As you wander along these streets, you may feel you have been transported to a Moroccan souk (market). Shops that serve the needs of Marseille's large and vibrant North African community have open bins of olives, coffee beans, tea, spices, chickpeas, couscous, peppers, and salted sardines. Tiny shoebox cafés sell African sweets, and the daily Marché de Noailles in the surrounding maze of streets is the city's most vibrant and colorful market. ✉ *La Canebière* *Noailles.*

★ Unité d'Habitation Cité Radieuse

NOTABLE BUILDING | Considered at the time a radical experiment in collective living, Le Corbusier's masterpiece "habitat system" was completed in 1952. The mammoth building, set in the middle of a green park with unobstructed views of the sea, contains 337 apartments with 23 different floor plans that were groundbreaking in their simplicity, functionality, and practicality. Each came with views; light; and on-site access to a restaurant, a bar, shops, childcare, a rooftop jogging track, a playground, and a stage. The tourist office's guided tours (reservations can be made online) of the UNESCO World Heritage site take you to a model apartment, the rooftop, and several common areas. The Cité also now houses a restaurant, bar, hotel, and the MaMO arts center—all open to the public. ✉ *280 bd. Michelet, Marseille* *www.marseille-tourisme.com/experience* *€10* *Closed Sun.*

Restaurants

★ AM by Alexandre Mazzia

$$$$ | **FRENCH** | Architect, artist, creator, whatever you call him, one thing's for sure—you won't soon forget the master chef who was awarded a Michelin star within nine months of opening his namesake restaurant. Dishes such as charred satay tuna in tapioca speckled with bright green fish eggs and served with wasabi ice cream showcase his experience working in French, African, and Asian kitchens. **Known for:** exquisite small dishes; unusual pairings in your choice of four set menus; far-flung influences. *Average main: €140* ✉ *9 rue François Rocca, Prado* ☎ *04–91–24–83–63* *www.alexandre-mazzia.com* *Closed Sun.–Tues.*

Cantoche

$$ | **FRENCH** | Run by two sisters who are as committed to using local, sustainable ingredients as they are to coaxing all the goodness from the humble vegetable, this bright, popular lunchtime eatery is set amid boutiques on a pedestrian street minutes from the old port. Seated either in the chic dining room or on the sunny terrace, you can tuck into homemade veggie and goat cheese pizza drizzled with local olive oil or slow-cooked pork with nigella seed croquettes. **Known for:** delicious, imaginative dishes; veggie-centric; lively, fun crowd. *Average main: €18* ✉ *13 rue Haxo, Vieux Port* ☎ *04–91–70–24–99* *www.cantochemarseille.com* *No dinner* *Vieux Port.*

Chez Etienne

$$ | **PIZZA** | A well-known hole-in-the-wall, this small pizzeria is filled daily with politicos, professionals, and other loyal patrons, who provide a soundtrack of laughter and chatter in the rich Marseille patois. Brace yourself for an epic meal, starting with a large anchovy pizza from the wood-burning oven, and then, perhaps, digging into fried squid, eggplant gratin, or a slab of rare grilled beef. **Known for:** stupendous pizza; lots of local flavor; huge portions. *$ Average main: €20 ✉ 43 rue de Lorette, Le Panier ☎ 04–91–90–65–45 ⏲ Closed Sun. Ⓜ Colbert Hôtel de Région.*

Chez Fonfon

$$$$ | SEAFOOD | Tucked into the tiny fishing port of Vallon des Auffes, this local landmark has one of the loveliest settings in greater Marseille. A variety of fresh seafood, impeccably grilled, steamed, or roasted in salt crust, is served in two pretty dining rooms with picture windows overlooking the fishing boats that supply your dinner. **Known for:** some of the city's best bouillabaisse; catch of the day; wonderful setting. *$ Average main: €55 ✉ 140 rue du Vallon des Auffes, Vallon des Auffes ☎ 04–91–52–14–38 🌐 www.chez-fonfon.com.*

Chez Michel

$$$$ | BRASSERIE | This beachside Michelin-starred brasserie near the Jardin du Pharo is considered the last word in bouillabaisse and draws a knowing local clientele willing to shell out a few extra euros (€80) for this authentic classic. Before dining, the fish are paraded by your table and then ceremoniously filleted before being served with the classic accompaniments of a spicy rouille and buttery croutons. **Known for:** cozy atmosphere; small but excellent menu; bouillabaisse that's worth the splurge. *$ Average main: €80 ✉ 6 rue des Catalans, Pharo ☎ 04–91–52–30–63 🌐 www.restaurant-michel-13.fr.*

Copains

$ | MODERN FRENCH | We'd love to keep this friendly restaurant a secret, but the chefs craft dishes of such rare subtlety and sophistication (especially at this price range) and the wine list has such a dazzling array of affordable options by the bottle or the glass, that it seems wrong not to share among *copains*. Though à la carte is possible, opt for the excellent-value prix-fixe menus to try dishes like pan-fried octopus and soppressata ham, hay-smoked Aubrac steak with parsnip purée and anchovy condiment, or foie gras with trout caviar and passion fruit. **Known for:** friendly atmosphere; great price-to-quality ratio; chefs who accommodate special requests. *$ Average main: €17 ✉ 93 rue de Tilsit, Cours Julien ☎ 09–53–60–99–91 🌐 copains-restaurant.fr ⏲ Closed Sun. and Mon. No lunch Tues.–Thurs. Ⓜ Baille or Notre Dame du Mont.*

Coquille

$$ | SEAFOOD | For fresh seafood dishes and delicious pizzas grilled on an open fire, head over to this marine-themed restaurant set on a vast terrace across from Marseille's new Les Grandes Halles du Vieux Port market. The menu features a variety of scintillating pizzas, as well as heaping plates of crustaceans on ice, mussels in a spicy saffron sauce served with hand-cut fries, and whole roasted fish. **Known for:** oven-grilled seafood and pizzas; friendly ambience; generous servings. *$ Average main: €18 ✉ 8 Rue Euthymènes, Vieux Port ☎ 04–91–54–14–13 ⏲ No lunch Mon. and Tues. Ⓜ Vieux Port.*

Grandes Halles du Vieux Port

$ | INTERNATIONAL | FAMILY | To experience all of the city's culinary diversity under one covered-marketplace roof, head to the food stalls at the new Grandes Halles du Vieux Port, which is open 9 am to midnight. Here you can order the freshest catch of the day or vegetarian dishes, as well as gourmet sandwiches, classic pizzas, and authentic tapas to take away or to enjoy on the outdoor terrace. **Known for:** variety of Mediterranean food stalls; great for vegetarians; convivial atmosphere. *$ Average main: €12 ✉ 30 Cr Honoré d'Estienne d'Orves, Vieux Port ☎ 🌐 www.lesgrandeshalles.com Ⓜ Vieux Port.*

★ La Boîte à Sardine

$$ | **SEAFOOD** | Owner Fabien Rugi puts his formidable energy into serving the freshest possible, Mediterranean-inflected seafood dishes, so at this restaurant you—with or without the help of a waiter—choose your fish from the catch of the day on ice. You might start with the grilled shrimp, which is too good to have with anything but a squirt of lemon, perhaps followed by the grilled baby squid or Rugi's version of fish-and-chips—fried hake with crisp chickpea-flour pancakes (a Provence specialty) and house-made aioli. **Known for:** must-try sea-anemone beignets; delicious local wines; convivial atmosphere. *$ Average main: €22 ✉ 2 bd. de la Libération, La Canebière ☎ 04–91–50–95–95 🌐 www.laboiteasardine.com ⏲ Closed Sun. and Mon. No dinner Ⓜ Réformés Canebière.*

★ La Cantinetta

$ | **ITALIAN** | **FAMILY** | Ask any Marseille food enthusiast where they go for great Italian food, and they're sure to mention this legendary spot, which is renowned as much for its food and flowing wine as for its camaraderie. Options include gorgeous plates of charcuterie topped with giant Parmesan shavings, fragrant bowls of steaming risotto, and line-caught fish of the day; just save room for the towering *tiramisu maison.* **Known for:** convivial atmosphere; generous dishes; excellent list of Mediterranean wines. *$ Average main: €17 ✉ 24 cours Julien, Cours Julien ☎ 04–91–48–10–48 🌐 restaurantlacantinetta.fr ⏲ Closed Sun. Ⓜ Noailles.*

★ La Mercerie

$$$ | **FRENCH** | A decor that mixes distressed walls with minimalist industrial-style lighting and sleek designer chairs is your first clue that this neobistro and wine bar in Marseille's emerging Noailles neighborhood is impossibly hip. British chef Harry Cummins, lately of Paris's gastronomic mecca Frenchie, uses local, seasonal ingredients to craft subtle, imaginative dishes that are highly satisfying to all yet also sensitive to the needs of vegetarians and those with food allergies. **Known for:** all the rage among young foodies; healthy dining; secluded outdoor terrace. *$ Average main: €28 ✉ 9 cours St-Louis, Noailles ☎ 04–91–06–18–44 🌐 www.lamerceriemarseille.com ⏲ Closed Tues. No lunch Thurs. Ⓜ Noailles, Vieux-Port-Hôtel de Ville.*

★ Le Capucin

$$ | **FRENCH** | Fresh from the kitchens of Michelin-star chef Lionel Levy, Sylvain Touati has swiftly shown what he can do in this kitchen of his own, where he turns out brasserie-type dishes that are hearty and satisfying as well as innovative and sophisticated. Not one dish on the menu disappoints, nor does the chic dining room—which is airy and bright at lunchtime and lively at night—or the brilliant barman who concocts some of the best craft cocktails in town. **Known for:** fearless innovation in dishes that feel like instant classics; French comfort food; excellent craft cocktails. *$ Average main: €20 ✉ Mercure Hotel, 48 La Canebière, La Canebière ☎ 04–30–22–03–12 🌐 www.brasserielecapucin.com Ⓜ Noailles.*

L'Epuisette

$$$$ | **SEAFOOD** | The views at this fine seafood restaurant are of crashing surf on one side and the port of Vallon des Auffes on the other. Chef Guillaume Sourrieu has acquired a big reputation (and a Michelin star) for a menu of sophisticated, catch-of-the-day dishes—perhaps Atlantic turbot in citrus rind with oxtail ravioli or sea bass slowly baked in a salt-butter crust and walnut oil—and a superb wine list. **Known for:** stupendous seafood; lovely setting; fixed-price menus worth the high price. *$ Average main: €55 ✉ 158 rue du Vallon des Auffes, Pharo ☎ 04–91–52–17–82 🌐 www.l-epuisette.com ⏲ Closed Sun., Mon., and last 2 wks in Aug.*

Le Restaurant Peron

$$$$ | **SEAFOOD** | The stylish, modern darkwood interior and large windows overlooking the sea here are magnets for hip

young professionals. The staff is efficient, and meals are well presented and tasty. **Known for:** to-die-for views; reasonable prix-fixe menus; great spot to watch the sunset. *Average main: €43 56 Corniche J.F. Kennedy, Endoume 04–91–52–15–22 www.restaurant-peron.com Closed Sun. and Mon.*

Les Arcenaulx

$$$ | **FRENCH** | At this red-walled, library-like haven in a stylish book-and-boutique complex of a renovated arsenal, you can have a sophisticated regional lunch and read while you're waiting. If you've had your fill of fish, indulge in the grilled fillet of beef with fried artichokes and sweet onion. **Known for:** very good bouillabaisse; extensive wine list; nice setting in a lively square. *Average main: €26 25 cours d'Estienne d'Orves, Vieux Port 04–91–59–80–30 www.les-arcenaulx.com Closed Sun. Vieux Port.*

Regards Café

$ | **MODERN FRENCH** | Nearby yet removed from the bustle of the Vieux Port and MuCEM's crowded cafés, this luminous, lunch-only dining room in the Musée Regards de Provence has panoramic new port and city views. Chef Thierry Lennon's cooking is worthy of the setting and features dishes like roasted cod with saffron risotto or tender duck breast with honeyed red cabbage. **Known for:** perfect spot for a quick coffee, lunch, or apéro; beautiful views of the boats leaving for Corsica and Sicily; reservations needed (unless you want to enjoy the buffet out on the terrace). *Average main: €16 Allée Regards de Provence, Rive Neuve 04–96–17–40–45 www.museeregardsdeprovence.com Closed Mon. No dinner Joliette or Vieux Port.*

Sépia & Julis

$$ | **MODERN FRENCH** | In a leafy garden perched at the heights of Marseille, the stylish Sépia eatery and lively Julis terrace bar make the perfect stop on your descent from Sainte-Marie Majeure cathedral or after exploring the chic up-and-coming St-Victor neighborhood. Chef Paul Langlère sources local ingredients to create such masterful dishes as rich cuttlefish stew; poached cod with leeks braised in red wine; and, for dessert, the ethereal mille-feuille filled with pastis cream. **Known for:** magical small seafood plates to share (or not); natural and organic wines; spectacular setting with sea and city views. *Average main: €18 2 rue Vauvenargues, St-Charles 09–83–82–67–27 www.restaurant-sepia.fr Closed weekends Vieux Port or Estrangin Préfecture.*

Une Table au Sud

$$$$ | **SEAFOOD** | Chef Ludovic Turac—a candidate on TV's *Top Chef 2011* and one of the youngest Michelin-starred chefs in France—has evolved into a serious, mature, and highly appreciated local celebrity while at the helm of this now tried-and-true favorite. A Mediterranean menu changes every two months depending on what's in season. **Known for:** creamy, fishy Milkshake de Bouille-Abaisse; great views of the Vieux Port; vegetarian-friendly options. *Average main: €38 2 quai du Port, Vieux Port 04–91–90–63–53 www.unetableausud.com Closed Sun. and Mon. Vieux Port.*

Coffee and Quick Bites

La Tisserie

$ | **CAFÉ** | If you're hankering after a great coffee, you can't go wrong at this chic café in the up-and-coming Saint-Lambert village district of the city. **Known for:** coffee roasted on premises; outdoor seating; can buy beans to go. *Average main: €8 142 Rue d'Endoume, St-Victor 04–91–89–22–69 www.tisserie.coffee.*

★ L'Épicerie Idéale

$ | **FRENCH** | For a fresh, seasonal lunch, try this chic little outpost that is part restaurant and part gourmet grocer. Imaginative Mediterranean-inflected salads and light dishes are healthy and delicious, and they pair well with a gourmet soda, Marseille microbrew, or a local rosé. **Known for:** great value meals; perfect for gourmet discoveries and gifts; fresh, seasonal dishes and salads. *Average main: €13 11 rue d'Aubagne, Noailles 09–80–39–99–41 www.epiceriel-ideal.com Closed Mon. Noailles, Vieux-Port-Hôtel de Ville.*

Torrefaction Noailles

$ | **CAFÉ** | **FAMILY** | The scent of roasting coffee emanates from this popular spot on the lively Canébière, Marseille's central spine. The coffee is good, but the hot chocolate is famous (it's so thick you may need a spoon to finish it); enjoy either option and a homemade pastry at the counter, alongside locals sharing the day's gossip. **Known for:** old-world setting; velvety hot chocolate; local flavor. *Average main: €7 56 La Canebière, La Canebière 04–91–55–60–66 www.noailles.com Noailles.*

Hotels

Alex Hôtel

$ | **HOTEL** | This reasonably priced boutique hotel, in a beautiful historic building across from St-Charles train station, has contemporary rooms done in rich neutral tones and equipped with flat-screen TVs and iPhone docking stations. **Pros:** great prices; convenient to the train station and a 15-minute walk to the old port; lovely breakfast. **Cons:** nearby restaurants aren't great; rooms lack character; not in the city center. *Rooms from: €123 13–15 pl. des Marseillaises, St-Charles 04–13–24–13–25 www.hotelalex.fr 21 rooms No Meals Gare St-Charles.*

C2 Hotel

$$$ | **HOTEL** | Previously occupied by a prominent Marseille family, this 19th-century home now holds 20 beautifully designed accommodations. **Pros:** a few minutes from the port; impeccable service; intimate spa with steam room, Jacuzzi, and pool. **Cons:** extra charge for breakfast; some of the lighting in common areas is a bit too neon; rooms vary drastically in size. *Rooms from: €279 48 rue Roux de Brignoles, St-Charles 04–95–05–13–13 www.c2-hotel.com 20 rooms No Meals Estrangin Préfecture.*

Grand Hotel Beauvau Marseille Vieux-Port-MGallery

$$ | **HOTEL** | Chopin spent the night and George Sand kept a suite in this historic hotel overlooking the Vieux Port. **Pros:** in the heart of the city; rooms are quiet; lovely views of the old port. **Cons:** some rooms quite small; service can be distracted when busy; a sea view will cost you. *Rooms from: €220 4 rue Beauvau, Vieux Port 04–91–54–91–00 all.accor.com 73 rooms No Meals Vieux Port.*

Hôtel Hermès

$ | **HOTEL** | Although the rooms are rather snug, this modest city hotel is right around the corner from the Quai du Port and is a good value. **Pros:** location and price add up to excellent value; lovely staff; nice rooftop terrace. **Cons:** rooms are small and the bathrooms even smaller; no bar on rooftop; few frills. *Rooms from: €103 2 rue Bonneterie, Vieux Port 04–96–11–63–63 www.hotelmarseille.com 29 rooms No Meals Vieux Port.*

★ **Hôtel La Résidence du Vieux Port**

$$$ | **HOTEL** | **FAMILY** | The flat, glass-and-concrete facade of this postwar structure grants all the port-facing rooms here broad views of the Vieux Port all the way to Notre-Dame-de-la-Garde. **Pros:** great price for such an ideal location; superb views of the Vieux Port; cheerful decor and service. **Cons:** terrace views are partially obstructed by concrete railings; breakfast not included in price unless chosen when booking; some bathrooms on the small side. *Rooms from: €250 18 quai du Port, Vieux Port*

☎ *04–91–91–91–22* 🌐 *www.hotel-residence-marseille.com* 🛏 *51 rooms* 🍽 *No Meals* Ⓜ *Vieux Port.*

Hôtel Saint Ferréol

$ | **HOTEL** | Set back from the port in the heart of the shopping district, this cozy, charming, little hotel offers a warm reception and a homey breakfast-room-cum-bar. **Pros:** cheerful and helpful service; central location; inexpensive. **Cons:** some rooms are small; street-facing rooms can be noisy; decor a little dated. Ⓢ *Rooms from: €105* ✉ *19 rue Pisançon at Rue St-Ferréol, Vieux Port* ☎ *04–91–33–12–21* 🌐 *www.hotel-stferreol.com* 🛏 *18 rooms* 🍽 *No Meals* Ⓜ *Vieux Port.*

★ Intercontinental Marseille Hôtel Dieu

$$$ | **HOTEL** | Housed in Marseille's majestic 18th-century Hôtel Dieu, a beloved landmark built according to plans by Jacques Hardouin-Mansart, architect to Louis XIV, this place has been transformed into a gleaming palace—even if you don't stay here, it's worth stopping by for a drink on the sprawling terrace, with gorgeous views of the old port. **Pros:** a one-stop luxury spot with excellent pool, spa, and restaurants; splendid views from open-air bar; rates include breakfast. **Cons:** only a fifth of rooms have a terrace; such indulgence does have a price; a bit of a snobby atmosphere. Ⓢ *Rooms from: €315* ✉ *1 pl. Daviel, Vieux Port* ☎ *04–13–42–42–42* 🌐 *marseille.intercontinental.com* 🛏 *194 rooms* 🍽 *Free Breakfast* Ⓜ *Vieux Port.*

Le Petit Nice Passedat

$$$$ | **HOTEL** | On a rocky promontory overlooking the sea, this fantasy villa was bought from a countess in 1917 and converted to a sleek hotel-restaurant, where the Passédat family has been getting it right ever since—especially in the famous restaurant, which is one of only two in Provence with three Michelin stars. **Pros:** has one of the coast's best restaurants; breathtaking views; lovely pool area. **Cons:** leave your impatience at the door when you dine here; restaurant closed Sunday and Monday; hard to reach city center by public transport. Ⓢ *Rooms from: €850* ✉ *17 rue des Braves, Endoume* ☎ *04–91–59–25–92* 🌐 *www.passedat.fr* 🛏 *16 rooms* 🍽 *No Meals.*

★ Les Bords de Mer

$$$ | **HOTEL** | Entering this dazzling little hotel is like walking straight into the surf, perched as it is right over the Marseille waterfront with every one of its (tiny) rooms overlooking the turquoise-blue Mediterranean. **Pros:** eye-popping views of the sea and balconies in every room; beautiful rooftop pool; excellent location. **Cons:** breakfast not included; rooms are minuscule; no bar. Ⓢ *Rooms from: €300* ✉ *52 Corniche Président John Fitzgerald Kennedy, Endoume* ☎ *04–13–94–34–00* 🌐 *www.lesbordsdemer.com/en* 🛏 *19 rooms* 🍽 *No Meals.*

Mama Shelter

$$ | **HOTEL** | Manufacturing hip is this urban chain hotel's claim to fame (not surprising, as it's the brainchild of designer Philippe Starck), and it has the formula down pat—offbeat (preferably artsy) neighborhood, check; plenty of graffiti in the interior design, check; functional, minimalist rooms, check; sexy touches, check. **Pros:** buffet breakfasts can't be beat; great on-site nightlife; cool vibe. **Cons:** not always a bargain; not to everyone's taste; iffy neighborhood. Ⓢ *Rooms from: €140* ✉ *64 rue de la Loubière, Cours Julien* ☎ *04–84–35–20–00* 🌐 *mamashelter.com* 🛏 *127 rooms* 🍽 *No Meals* Ⓜ *Baille or Notre Dame du Mont.*

nhow Marseille

$$$ | **HOTEL** | Sleek, with stunning 360-degree views of the bay and the islands, this white-on-white hotel features designs by Starck, Zanotta, and Emu. Service is prompt and unobtrusive, and the huge windows make for a light-filled reception area. **Pros:** the view out to sea is truly remarkable; rooms are large, most with balconies; saltwater pool. **Cons:** service sorely lacking; too many

rooms for a personalized welcome; minimalist style not for everyone. 💲 *Rooms from: €270* ✉ *200 corniche J. F. Kennedy, Endoume* ☎ *04–91–16–19–00* 🌐 *www.nh-hotels.com/hotel/nhow-marseille* 🛏 *160 rooms* 🍽 *No Meals.*

★ Sofitel Vieux-Port

$$$ | **HOTEL** | **FAMILY** | Its plum location next to the beautiful Palais de Pharo and park and its legendary service make this more than a standard-issue, five-star luxury property, but views from the rooftop terrace put it right up there with the city's top hotels. **Pros:** exemplary service; stupendous views; great spa, restaurant, and bar. **Cons:** pool can be crowded in summer; some rooms on the small side; not an intimate hotel. 💲 *Rooms from: €330* ✉ *36 bd. Charles Livon, Pharo* ☎ *04–91–15–59–00* 🌐 *www.sofitel-marseille-vieuxport.com* 🛏 *134 rooms* 🍽 *No Meals* Ⓜ *Vieux Port.*

Tuba

$$$ | **HOTEL** | A stay at one of this property's intimate cabanons—traditional fisherman's cottages—gets you the full Mediterranean experience of endless sea and sun just outside your door. **Pros:** eye-popping sea views; set within the national park and Marseille; top-notch restaurant. **Cons:** village gets crowded in summer; loud music from the bar; expensive small dishes at restaurant. 💲 *Rooms from: €230* ✉ *2 bd. Alexandre Delabre, Marseille* ☎ *04–91–25–13–16* 🌐 *tuba-club.com* 🛏 *5 rooms* 🍽 *No Meals.*

Nightlife

Thanks to Marseille's vibrant multicultural mix, a type of music has evolved that fuses Arabic music with the rhythms of Provence, Corsica, and southern Italy and weaves in touches of reggae and rap.

BARS AND PUBS

Red Lion

PUBS | This bar is a mecca for English speakers, who pour onto the sidewalk, beer in hand, pub style. There's live music, DJs on the weekend, and a lounge for the die-hard rugby and soccer fans who can't go without watching a game. ✉ *231 av. Pierre Mendès France, Vieux Port* ☎ *04–91–25–17–17* 🌐 *www.pub-redlion.com.*

R2 Le Rooftop Marseille

DANCE CLUBS | Atop the Terrasses shopping center, Le Réctoire and its terrace, Le Rooftop—together called R2—are a popular restaurant by day and a chic cocktail bar and club by night. Dance on the rooftop to live music and DJ beats, or sip a drink on the sprawling terrace while taking in spectacular views of the J4 Pier (home of MuCEM) and Marseille's big-ship port. Both establishments are open until 2 am six days a week (they close at 7 pm on Monday), a rarity in Marseille. ✉ *9 quai du Lazaret, La Joliette* ☎ *04–91–45–61–98* 🌐 *lerooftopdesterrasses.com* Ⓜ *La Joliette.*

MUSIC CLUBS

Au Son des Guitares

CABARET | The music is live, and the crowd is lively at this fashionable cabaret-bar that's a Marseille institution. ✉ *18 rue Corneille, Vieux Port* ☎ *04–91–33–11–47* Ⓜ *Vieux Port.*

Docks des Suds

LIVE MUSIC | At this vast venue, host to the Fiesta des Suds each autumn, you'll find world and Latin music year-round. ✉ *12 rue Urbain V at Bd. de Paris, Vieux Port* ☎ *04–91–99–00–00* 🌐 *www.dock-des-suds.org* Ⓜ *National.*

La Caravelle

LIVE MUSIC | Restaurant by day, club and tapas bar by night, La Caravelle harks back to prewar jazz clubs, but without the smoke. There are great views over the port and live music two nights a week. ✉ *Hotel Belle Vue, 34 quai du Port, Vieux Port* ☎ *04–91–90–36–64* 🌐 *www.lacaravelle-marseille.com* Ⓜ *Vieux Port.*

L'Affranchi

LIVE MUSIC | For rap and techno, try L'Affranchi. ✉ *212 bd. de St-Marcel, La Canebière* ✥ *Via A50 (direction Aubagne)*

☎ 04–91–35–09–19 ⊕ www.l-affranchi.com Ⓜ Dromel, then Bus No. 15; or Timone, then Bus No. 40 (return on night Bus No. 540).

 Performing Arts

ARTS CENTERS

Espace Julien

CONCERTS | Rock, pop, jazz, and reggae concerts, along with the occasional comedy and alternative theater performance, are held here. *✉ 39 cours Julien, Préfecture ☎ 04–91–24–34–10 ⊕ www.espace-julien.com Ⓜ Notre Dame du Mont.*

Le Silo

ARTS CENTERS | This venue in a modern, waterfront building hosts classical and contemporary concerts, as well as theater productions and dance performances. *✉ 35 quai du Lazaret, La Canebière ☎ 04–91–90–00–00 ⊕ www.cepacsilo-marseille.fr Ⓜ Désirée Clary or Joliette.*

OPERA

Opéra Municipal de Marseille

CONCERTS | Operas and orchestral concerts are held at the Opéra Municipal. *✉ 2 rue Molière, Vieux Port ☎ 04–91–55–11–10 ⊕ opera.marseille.fr Ⓜ Vieux Port.*

PUPPET SHOWS

Théâtre Massalia

MUSIC | FAMILY | A young audience thrills to entertainment with puppets, dance, and music—occasionally in English. It's by the Gare St-Charles. *✉ Theatre Massalia, 41 rue Jobin, La Canebière ☎ 04–95–04–95–75 ⊕ www.theatremassalia.com Ⓜ St-Charles.*

THEATER

Badaboum Théâtre

THEATER | FAMILY | At Badaboum, adventurous, accessible productions for children are performed. *✉ 16 quai de Rive Neuve, Vieux Port ☎ 04–91–54–40–71 ⊕ www.badaboum-theatre.com Ⓜ Vieux Port.*

Théâtre National de Marseille La Criée

THEATER | A strong repertoire of classical and contemporary works is performed here. *✉ Quai de Rive Neuve, Vieux Port ☎ 04–91–54–70–54 ⊕ www.theatre-lacriee.com Ⓜ Vieux Port.*

 Shopping

Although you should stock up on *savon* (soap) de Marseille, the city has lots more to offer. Offbeat clothing by local designers, vintage finds, and hip accessories made in Marseille abound around Cours Julien. Nearer the Vieux Port, high-end designer boutiques mingle with chic fashion chains and edgy-elegant concept stores along Rues Grignan, Paradis, and Saint.

You could spend a day (or more!) browsing at Les Docks Village, Les Terrasses du Port, and Les Voûtes de la Major. This trio of quayside complexes has helped to revitalize Marseille's up-and-coming neighborhood of La Joliette.

CLOTHING

★ JoggingJogging

MIXED CLOTHING | In addition to chic men's and women's sportswear and casual attire by a small but choice selection of crème de la crème European designers, this beautifully conceived boutique sells lingerie, shoes, hats, books, linens, ceramics, photographs and graphic art, and Aesop skin care. Everything is handpicked by the charming owner, who is also a well-known French fashion photographer. The shop's cozy courtyard café is the perfect place to recharge your shopping batteries. *✉ 103 rue Paradis, Pharo ☎ 04–91–81–44–94 ⊕ www.joggingjogging.com Ⓜ Estrangin Préfecture.*

Marianne Cat

WOMEN'S CLOTHING | A curated selection of sophisticated, superchic European-designed clothes, shoes, scarves, jewelry, and accessories for women is displayed in a soaring 18th-century space. *✉ 53 rue Grignan, Belsunce ☎ 04–91–55–05–25 ⊕ www.facebook.*

com/boutiquemariannecat Ⓜ *Estrangin Préfecture.*

Sessùn

WOMEN'S CLOTHING | Emma François draws her inspiration from music to create subtle, timeless clothes that are both French and intercontinental. Leave room in your suitcase for at least a Sussùn scarf. ✉ *6 rue Sainte, Vieux Port* ☎ *04–91–52–33–61* 🌐 *en.sessun.com* Ⓜ *Vieux Port.*

Sugar

WOMEN'S CLOTHING | This Marseille-based chain sells reliably chic sportswear in luscious colors. Mix-and-match separates include everything from sexy pencil skirts to jaunty peacoats and those long French scarves. ✉ *16 rue Lulli, Vieux Port* ☎ *04–91–33–47–52* 🌐 *sugarproduct.com.*

FOOD

Four des Navettes

FOOD | **FAMILY** | This famous bakery, up the street from Notre-Dame-de-la-Garde, has made orange-spice, shuttle-shape *navettes* in the same oven since it opened in 1781. These cookies are modeled on the little boat that, it is said, carried Lazarus and the Three Marys (Mary Magdalene, Mary Salome, and Mary Jacobe) to the nearby shore. ✉ *136 rue Sainte, Pharo* ☎ *04–91–33–32–12* 🌐 *www.fourdesnavettes.com* Ⓜ *Vieux Port.*

La Maison du Pastis

WINE/SPIRITS | The selection of pastis, anisettes, and absinthes in this smart little shop is dizzying, but to really savor these unique liqueurs, sign up online for one of the 90-minute tastings. ✉ *108 quai du Port, Vieux Port* ☎ *04–91–90–86–77* Ⓜ *Vieux Port.*

Saladin Épices du Monde

FOOD | A veritable Ali Baba's cave in the heart of the souklike Arab market, this colorful shop brims with eye-popping mounds of dried fruit and nuts, exotic condiments, grains, and every spice under the sun. ✉ *10 rue Longue des Capucins, Noailles* ☎ *04–91–33–22–76* 🌐 *www.saladin-epicesdumonde.fr* Ⓜ *Noailles.*

GIFTS AND CRAFTS

★ Chez Laurette

OTHER SPECIALTY STORE | Ex-fashion designer Laure Traverso (Marc Jacobs, Paul & Joe) escaped the Paris treadmill to open her own wildly creative concept store that spotlights all things French that are also sustainable, ethical, design-conscious, and just plain cool. Discoveries abound: look for chic emerging fashion labels, beautiful leather and straw bags, shoes, belts, avant-garde jewelry, lingerie, handmade home furnishings, and organic cosmetics made in Provence. There's even a grocery corner with local microbrews, chocolates, and teas. ✉ *16 rue Edmond Rostand, Marseille* ☎ *04–88–04–31–70* 🌐 *chez-laurette.com.*

Fragonard

PERFUME | Since 1926, the Riviera-based perfumer has been bottling the sun, sea, and all the luscious scents of Provence in colorful vials. Its popular fragrances—orange flower, rose-lavender, verbena, jasmine, vetiver, the signature Coeur du Soleil, and so many more—come in perfumes, candles, soaps, shower gels, and home fragrances. You'll also find gifts, stylish Mediterranean clothing, and fashion accessories. ✉ *Bd. Jacques Saade, La Joliette* ☎ *04–91–45–35–25* 🌐 *www.fragonard.com.*

★ Herboristerie Père Blaize

OTHER SPECIALTY STORE | This popular shop has been mixing herbal treatments on the same premises since 1805. At the *laboratoire,* trained herbalists use dried local and exotic herbs or plant extracts to customize a concoction for whatever ails you—from sleep issues to digestive troubles. At the contemporary tearoom across the street, you can sip an infusion and purchase packaged herbal teas, loose herbs, spices, coffee, honey, beauty products, books, and traditional candies. ✉ *4–6 rue Meolan et du Père*

Blaize, Noailles ☎ *04–22–67–80–11* 🌐 *www.pereblaize.fr* Ⓜ *Canabière Capucins, Vieux Port.*

★ Maison Empereur

DEPARTMENT STORE | FAMILY | If "made in France" sounds good to you, head to this 190-year-old Marseille institution, which sells all things French. The main store carries everything from housewares and hardware to timeless perfumes, classic toys, and true Savon de Marseille. A second shop across the street (✉ *8 rue des Recolettes*) has irresistible clothing and accessories for women, men, and kids, including wool or sheepskin slippers, rakish straw hats, cashmere capes, chunky wool sweaters, and cotton work shirts. ✉ *4 rue des Récolettes, Marseille* ☎ *04–91–54–02–29* 🌐 *empereur.fr.*

Savonnerie Marseillaise de la Licorne

COSMETICS | One of Marseille's oldest manufacturers sells fragrant soap in blocks, ovals, or fanciful shapes—all of it made using the highest olive oil content possible (72%) and natural essential oils from Provence. Call ahead for a guided tour (in English) of this atmospheric factory to see the whole process done on traditional machines. ✉ *34 cours Julien, Cours Julien* ☎ *04–96–12–00–91* 🌐 *www.savon-de-marseille-licorne.com* Ⓜ *Notre Dame du Mont.*

SHOPPING CENTERS AND MALLS

Les Docks Village

MALL | One of La Joliette's three new quayside shopping centers, Les Docks Village consists of six massive shipping warehouses, each restored by a notable architect, to create stylish, upbeat commercial spaces. The one-of-a-kind shops here sell everything from beauty products, jewelry, clothes, and accessories to housewares, art, and sporting goods—all with a focus on great design. Picturesque cafés and restaurants, several with outdoor terraces, round out the offerings. ✉ *10 pl. de la Joliette, La Joliette* 🌐 *www.lesdocks-marseille.com* Ⓜ *Joliette.*

Les Terrasses du Port

MALL | A modern, three-story, glass-and-steel structure—one of three shopping centers along the restored harbor in La Joliette—houses 160 of the best-loved French clothing chains, such as Petit Bâteau, Comptoir des Cotonniers, and the Marseille-based American Vintage, as well as a branch of Le Printemps department store. Refuel in one of the cafés, or head to the rooftop terrace, where you can have a drink or meal while watching cruise ships sail off to Corsica. ✉ *9 quai du Lazaret, La Joliette* ☎ *04–88–91–46–00* 🌐 *www.lesterrassesduport.com* Ⓜ *Joliette.*

Les Voûtes de la Major

MALL | Under these graceful vaulted arches, built in the 1850s as part of the Sainte Marie de la Major cathedral and now incorporated into one of La Joliette's three new shopping complexes, you'll find lovely cafés and shops, including the design giant Habitat; French perfumer Fragonard; and chocolatier L'Espérantine, specializing in chocolates made with olive oil. The superb Les Halles de la Major gourmet food court has a tempting variety of foods for snacks, meals, or coffee breaks, which you can enjoy indoors or on the wide outdoor terrace with superb views of the J4 Pier and the harbor. Check the website for details on the weekly program of arts events. ✉ *Quai de la Tourette, La Joliette* 🌐 *www.lesvoutesdelamajor.com* Ⓜ *Joliette.*

Activities

Marseille's waterfront position makes it easy to swim and sunbathe within the city sprawl. From the Vieux Port, Bus 83 or 19 takes you to the vast green spread of reclaimed land called the **Parc Balnéaire du Prado.** Its waterfront is divided into beaches, all of them public and well equipped with showers, toilets, and first-aid stations. The beach surface varies between sand and gravel. You can also find your own little beach on the tiny, rocky **Îles de Frioul**; boats leave from the Vieux Port and cost €11.10.

Aubagne

15 km (9 miles) east of Marseille; 10 km (6 miles) north of Cassis.

This easygoing, plane tree–shaded market town (pronounced "oh- *bahn-yuh*") is proud of its native son, the dramatist, filmmaker, and chronicler of all things Provençal, Marcel Pagnol, best known to Anglophones as author of *Jean de Florette, Fanny,* and *Manon des Sources* (*Manon of the Springs*). Here you can spend the morning exploring the animated market or digging through used Pagnol books and collectibles in the Old Town.

Try to visit Aubagne on a market day (Tuesday, Thursday, Saturday, or Sunday), when the sleepy center is transformed into a tableau of Provençal life. The Tuesday market is the biggest, and it's sure to have santon figurines, as Aubagne claims the title of santon capital of Provence.

GETTING HERE AND AROUND

Trains run every 20–30 minutes between Marseille and Aubagne (€4.30, 20 minutes). By bus, Le Pilote's No. 240 runs from Marseille every 20–30 minutes (€2.40, 30 minutes). By car, take the A50 from Marseille to Exit 6 on the A501.

BUS CONTACTS Le Pilote. ☎ *08–00–71–31–37* 🌐 *www.lepilote.com.*

TOURS

To avoid hiking the 12-km (7-mile) or 20-km (12-mile) loop through the *garrigues* (scrubland) above Aubagne, join the bus tour of Marcel Pagnol landmarks that leaves from the tourist office on Wednesday at 3 in July and August. The cost is €12; request an English-speaking guide in advance.

VISITOR INFORMATION

CONTACTS Aubagne Tourist Office. ✉ *8 cours Barthélémy, Aubagne* ☎ *04–42–03–49–98* 🌐 *www.tourisme-paysdaubagne.fr.*

Sights

Circuit Pagnol

TRAIL | FAMILY | Even if you haven't read Pagnol's works or seen his films, you can enjoy the Circuit Pagnol, a series of hikes (some up to 20 km [12 miles] long) in the raw-hewn, arid garrigues behind Marseille and Aubagne. Here Pagnol spent his idyllic summers, described in his *Souvenirs d'un Enfance* (*Memories of a Childhood*), crunching through the rosemary, thyme, and scrub oak at the foot of his beloved Garlaban.

When he became a famous playwright and filmmaker, he shot some of his best work in these hills, casting his wife, Jacqueline, as the first Manon of the Springs. After Pagnol's death, Claude Berri came back to the Garlaban to find a location for his remake of *Manon des Sources,* but found it so altered by brush fires and power cables that he chose to shoot farther east instead, around Cuges-les-Pine and Riboux. (The lovely village and Manon's well were filmed in Mirabeau, in the Luberon.)

Although the trails no longer travel amid pine-shaded olive orchards, they still let you explore primeval Provençal countryside with spectacular views of Marseille and the sea. To access the marked trails by yourself, drive to La Treille northeast of Aubagne, and follow the signs. For maps or an accompanied tour with literary commentary, contact the tourist office. ✉ *Aubagne.*

Farmers' Market

MARKET | FAMILY | Aubagne on a market day is a feast in more ways than one. Depending on the season, for sale are fresh local asparagus, vine-ripened tomatoes and melons, and mesclun scooped by the gnarled fingers of blue-aproned ladies in from the farm (Tuesday, Thursday, and weekends, 8–1:30). The weekend markets make more of regional products; those labeled Pays d'Aubagne must be organically raised. Although they're not as social as markets in Aix, these farmers' markets are more authentic. ✉ *Cours Voltaire, Aubagne.*

Le Petit Monde de Marcel Pagnol (*The Small World of Marcel Pagnol*)
OTHER ATTRACTION | FAMILY | You can study miniature dioramas of scenes from Pagnol stories here. The characters are all santons, including superb portraits of a humpback Gerard Dépardieu and Yves Montand, resplendent in moustache, fedora, and velvet vest, just as they were featured in *Jean de Florette*. For more information, contact the tourist office. ✉ *Esplanade de Gaulle, Aubagne* 🎫 *Free* 🕓 *Closed Sun.*

Musée de la Légion Étrangère (*Museum of the Foreign Legion*)
HISTORY MUSEUM | FAMILY | Another claim to fame for Aubagne: it's the headquarters for the French Foreign Legion. The legion was created in 1831, and accepts recruits from all nations, no questions asked. The discipline and camaraderie instilled among its motley team of adventurers have helped the legion forge a reputation for exceptional valor—a reputation romanticized by songs and films in which sweaty deeds of heroism are performed under the desert sun. The Musée de la Légion Étrangère does its best to polish the image by way of medals, uniforms, weapons, and photographs. ✉ *Caserne Viénot, Aubagne* ✣ *Coming from Marseille, take left off D2 onto D44A just before Aubagne* ☎ *04–42–18–12–41* 🌐 *www.legion-etrangere.com* 🎫 *Free* 🕓 *Closed Mon.*

Hotels

★ La Magdeleine by Mathias Dandine
$$$ | HOTEL | FAMILY | Once the home of a marquis, this splendid Provençal property, tucked away under towering plane trees—with lovely gardens, a swimming pool, picturesque walkways, and a pétanque court—combines a serene natural setting with gracious lodging and outstanding dining thanks to its owners, the Michelin-starred chef Mathias Dandine and his wife. **Pros:** owned by one of Provence's great chefs; romantic yet perfect for families; warm welcome. **Cons:** only 28 rooms; books quickly in summer; outdoor dining can be hot on summer days. $ *Rooms from: €240* ✉ *2 Rond point des Charrons, Aubagne* ☎ *04–42–32–20–16* 🌐 *relais-magdeleine.com* 🛏 *28 rooms* 🍽 *No Meals.*

Cassis

30 km (19 miles) southeast of Marseille; 10 km (6 miles) north of Aubagne.

Surrounded by vineyards, flanked by cliffs, guarded by the ruins of a medieval castle, and nestled around a picture-perfect fishing port, Cassis is one of the prettiest coastal towns in Provence. Known for its delicate white wines and wild calanques, it is a quiet fishing village out of season and inundated with sun worshippers in summer.

Its pastel houses, set at rakish angles and framing the port and harbor, attracted early-20th-century artists including Dufy and Matisse. Even the mild rash of parking-garage architecture in the outer neighborhoods can't spoil the effect of unadulterated charm.

Stylish without being too recherché, Cassis's picture-perfect harbor is in the shadow of the ruddy Cap Canaille, Europe's highest sea cliff, and provides shelter to numerous pleasure boaters. Sailors can restock their galleys at its markets, replenish their Saint James nautical duds in its boutiques, and relax with a bottle of local wine and a platter of sea urchins in one of its waterfront cafés.

GETTING HERE AND AROUND

By car, leave the A50 from Marseille or Toulon and take Exit 8 for Cassis. The D559 from Marseille to Cassis is dramatically beautiful, continuing along the coast

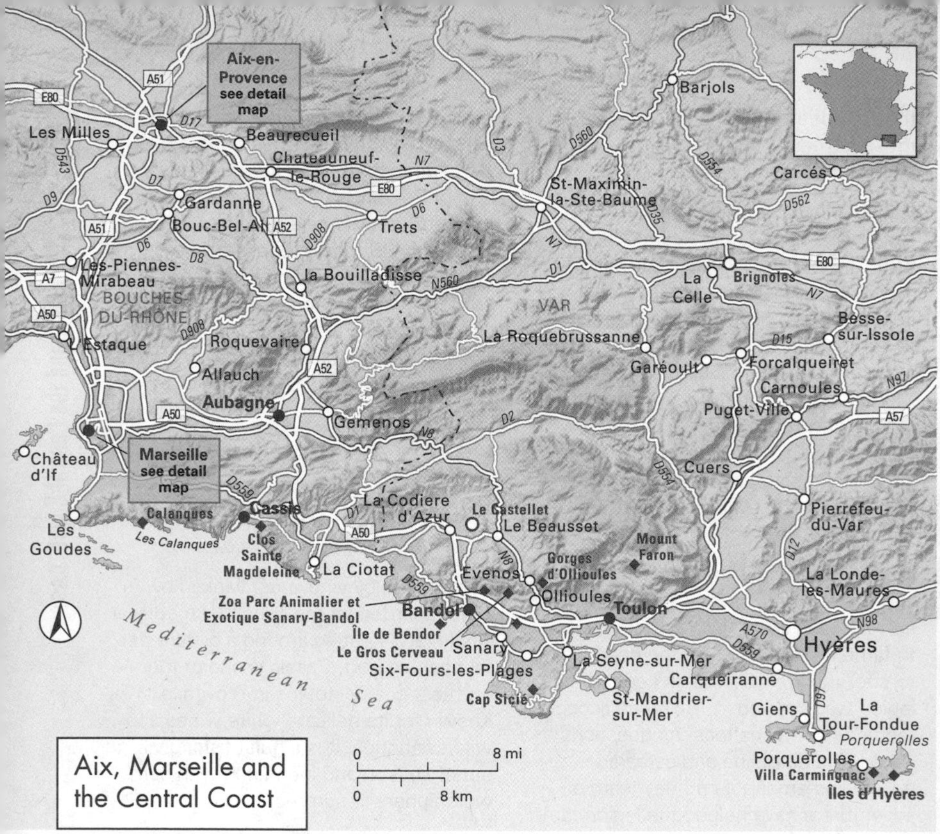

Aix, Marseille and the Central Coast

to Toulon, but it might be too curvy for motion-sickness sufferers.

Hourly trains between Marseille and Toulon stop at Cassis. Although the station is about 3 km (2 miles) from the town center, a shuttle runs into town at least once an hour. There is also the M6 Marseille–Cassis bus, which takes an hour.

TOURS

La Visite des Calanques

BOAT TOURS | FAMILY | This company offers scenic boat tours of the calanques from the wooden kiosk at Quay St-Pierre near the tourist office. A 60-minute, three-calanques tour runs every 60 minutes (10–4, Feb.–Apr. and Oct.–Nov). or every 30 minutes (9:30–6, May–Sept.). Longer explorations last over two hours and cover up to nine inlets. Tickets must be purchased (at the kiosk) at least 30 minutes in advance; larger groups of 15 or more can reserve ahead. ✉ *Quai St-Pierre, Cassis* ☎ *04–42–01–03–31* 🌐 *www.lavisitedescalanques.com* 🎫 *From €17.*

VISITOR INFORMATION

CONTACTS Cassis Tourist Office. ✉ *Quai des Moulins, Cassis* ☎ *04–28–01–01–03* 🌐 *www.ot-cassis.com.*

Sights

Calanques

BODY OF WATER | FAMILY | Touring the calanques, whose fjordlike finger bays probe the rocky coastline, is a must. Either take a sightseeing cruise in a boat that dips into each calanque in turn (tickets, sold at the eastern end of the port, are €19–€33, depending on how many calanques you see) or hike across the cliff tops, clambering down the steep sides to these barely accessible retreats. One boat trip

From Cassis, be sure to take an excursion boat to the calanques, the rocky finger-coves washed by emerald and blue waters.

lets you swim in the turquoise waters under Cap Canaille, but that must be booked at the kiosk in the morning (four to five departures per day, depending on the weather and water temperature).

Although of the calanques closest to Cassis, Port Miou is the least attractive—it was a *pierre de Cassis* (Cassis stone) quarry until 1982 when the calanques became protected sites—it now has an active leisure and fishing port. Calanque Port Pin is prettier, with wind-twisted pines growing at angles from white-rock cliffs. But with its tiny beach and jagged cliffs looming overhead, covered with gnarled pine and scrub and its rock spur known to climbers as the "finger of God," Calanque En Vau, reachable via a challenging two-hour hike both there and back (or your own private boat), is a small piece of paradise.

Château de Cassis
CASTLE/PALACE | This castle has loomed over the harbor since the invasions of the Saracens in the 7th century, evolving over time into a walled enclosure with stout watchtowers. It's private property today and best viewed from a sunny portside terrace. ✉ *Cassis.*

Clos Sainte Magdeleine
WINERY | If you love wine, pick up a "Through the Vineyards" brochure from the tourist office. There are 11 domaines open for tastings and buying, but the most spectacularly sited is the Clos Sainte Magdeleine set on the slopes of towering Cap Canaille. The boutique of this well-established AOC winery, noted for its delicately balanced whites and an elegant rosé, offers tastings Tuesday through Saturday. ✉ *Av. du Revestel, Cassis* ☎ *04–42–01–70–28* 🌐 *www.clossaintemagdeleine.fr.*

Restaurants

★ Brasserie du Corton
$$$ | **MODERN FRENCH** | Though this brasserie is less formal (and less expensive) than its sister restaurant, three-star La Villa Madie, its dishes are no less tasty. Depending on what's in season

and available from local growers and fishermen, the menu in the handsome dining room or on the terrace might include artisanal sausages and braised fennel with squid-ink gnocchi; tandoori monkfish medallions with asparagus, lime crème Chantilly, and Indian spices; or the catch of the day straight from the wood-fired oven. **Known for:** year-round "casual" dining from a Michelin-starred chef; excellent selection of Cassis whites and rosés; panoramic bay views. *Average main: €28* *Anse de Corton, 30 Av. du Revestel, Cassis* *04–96–18–00–00* *lavillamadie.com/la-brasserie-du-corton* *Closed Tues. and Wed. No dinner Mon.*

★ La Villa Madie

$$$$ | FRENCH | Chef Dimitri Droisneau may profess his cuisine to be humble, but it's worth changing out of your beachwear (closed-toe shoes are required) to dine at the three-Michelin-starred restaurant he runs with his wife, Marielle. Standout dishes include the delicately grilled Mediterranean rouget with almonds and fennel that's drizzled with an urchin-and-saffron sauce. **Known for:** a top choice in the region; brilliant seafood dishes; huge wine list. *Average main: €90* *Anse de Corton, Av. de Revestrel-anse de Corton, Cassis* *04–96–18–00–00* *www.lavillamadie.com* *Closed Jan.–mid-Feb., Tues., and Wed. No dinner Mon.*

Hotels

Hotel de la Plage Mahogany

$$$ | HOTEL | FAMILY | Capitalizing on the village's gorgeous bay views is just one of this lively, Art Deco–style boutique hotel's many virtues—it also has light-drenched guest rooms (some with private balconies), a spa with a steam room and solarium, two restaurants (one on the beach), and an irresistible wine bar. **Pros:** one suite has a private pool; on the beach; stylish, beach-chic decor. **Cons:** no rooms for people with reduced mobility; on a very busy road; not all rooms face the bay. *Rooms from: €230* *19 Av. de l'Amiral Ganteaume, Cassis* *04–42–01–05–70* *www.hotelmahogany.com* *28 rooms* *No Meals.*

★ Les Roches Blanches

$$$$ | HOTEL | Featuring views of the port and the Cap Canaille, this cliff-side villa has shed its former Art Deco–style decor for a spiffy contemporary look featuring things like plush velvet chairs and huge modern baths. **Pros:** captivating vistas; beautiful pools and spa; most rooms have balconies. **Cons:** hard to find (use your GPS); breakfast is expensive; in-room dining could be better. *Rooms from: €485* *Rte. des Calanques, Cassis* *04–42–01–09–30* *www.roches-blanches-cassis.com* *Closed Nov.–Mar.* *24 rooms* *No Meals.*

Activities

Cassis Calanques Plongée

DIVING & SNORKELING | The calanques region has some of the best diving in France, and this operator offers daily (weather permitting) cave dives to view fish and brightly colored coral. *06–71–52–60–20* *www.cassis-calanques-plongee.com.*

JCF Boat Services

BOATING | If you don't feel up to a rugged hike to the calanques, you can rent (with or without a license) a semi-rigid boat here for a half- or full-day excursion. *1 Quai des Moulins, Cassis* *06–75–74–25–81* *jcfboat.com.*

Narval Plongée

DIVING & SNORKELING | FAMILY | Fabienne Henry leads divers to the Cassidaigne Lighthouse, Riou Archipelago, and the calanques. Novice divers and children are welcome, and underwater photography courses are also offered. *11 av. de la Viguerie, Cassis* *04–42–01–87–59* *www.narval-plongee.fr.*

Touring the Calanques

To hike the calanques, you need to gauge your skills. The GR98 (marked with red-and-white bands) is the most scenic route, but it requires scrambling down the sheer walls of En Vau; be sure to stay on approved paths. The alternative is to follow the red markers and approach En Vau from behind. If you're ambitious, you can hike the length of the GR98 between Marseille and Cassis, following the coastline, a distance of roughly 30 km (18 miles). Remember, access in the calanques is restricted and can be prohibited at any time due to high winds and fire risk. To check weather conditions, call ☎ *08–11–20–13–13.* Information for the next day is available by 6 pm the evening before.

For calanque boat tours, get to the port around 10 am or 2 pm and look for a vessel that's loading passengers. Two of the best choices are the *Notos II* and the *Moby Dick III*—they have huge windows and full commentary in English. But a slew of alternative boats won't leave you stranded. Round trips should include at least three calanques and average €21.

Bandol

25 km (16 miles) southeast of Cassis; 15 km (9 miles) west of Toulon.

Its name is synonymous with wine to most of the world, but Bandol is also a popular and highly developed coastal resort town. In the 1920s, the Riviera's high-society glamour stretched this far west, and the seaside mansions here rivaled those in Cap d'Antibes and Juan-les-Pins. Although today, the old port is a massive gray parking lot, and the Old Town that fronts the quays is lined with seafood snack shops, generic brasseries, and palm trees, westward, toward the Baie de Renecros, are some of the Belle Époque houses that once made Bandol famous.

In high season the harbor is filled with yachts, and the waterfront promenade is packed with tourist crowds. A portside stroll up the palm-lined Allée Jean Moulin feels downright Côte d'Azur. If you're not a beach lover, pick up an itinerary from the tourist office and visit a few Bandol vineyards just outside of town.

GETTING HERE AND AROUND

Trains run between Marseille and Bandol every half hour (€10, 45 minutes). By car, take the A50 toward Toulon (Exit 12).

VISITOR INFORMATION

CONTACTS Bandol Tourist Office. ✉ *Pavillon du Tourisme, Allée Alfred Vivien, Bandol* ☎ *04–94–29–41–35* 🌐 *www.bandoltourisme.fr.*

Sights

Cap Sicié

SCENIC DRIVE | Head south on the D16 to the D2816 around the cape for a tremendous view across the Bay of Toulon.

Gorge d'Ollioules

SCENIC DRIVE | Head north on D11 to Ollioules; just past the village, follow N8 (toward Le Beausset) through a 5-km (3-mile) route that twists its scenic way beneath the chalky rock faces of the Gorge d'Ollioules. ✉ *Bandol.*

Île de Bendor

ISLAND | **FAMILY** | Boats leave every half hour to make the 2-km (1-mile) trip to Île de Bendor. The island was only a large rock until pastis magnate Paul Ricard bought it in the 1950s and tastefully transformed it into a tourist center with fine beaches, charming cottage shops, an "espace Ricard" highlighting Paul Ricard's lifetime works, and the Museum of Wine and Spirits. Although there is a surprisingly varied selection of island restaurants, a picnic is a nice option, too. ✉ *Bandol* 🌐 *www.lesilespaulricard.com.*

Le Castellet

TOWN | **FAMILY** | On the D559, perched high above the Bandol vineyards, the village of Le Castellet has narrow streets, 17th-century stone houses, and (alas!) touristy shops designed for beach lovers on a rainy day. ✉ *Bandol.*

Le Gros Cerveau

SCENIC DRIVE | On the D20, take a left at Ollioules, and follow the winding road along the crest of Le Gros Cerveau. You'll be rewarded first with inland mountain views and then with an expansive view of the coastline. ✉ *Bandol.*

Notre-Dame de Pépiole

CHURCH | Just east of Bandol on the D559, past the smaller resort of Sanary, as you turn left onto the D63 you'll see signs pointing to the small stone chapel of Notre-Dame de Pépiole. It's hemmed in by pines and cypresses and is one of the oldest Christian buildings in France, dating from the 6th century and modeled on early churches in the Middle East. The simple interior has survived the years in remarkably good shape, although the colorful stained glass that fills the tiny windows is modern—composed mainly of broken bottles. ✉ *Bandol.*

Zoa Parc Animalier et Exotique Sanary-Bandol (*Sanary Bandol's Exotic Garden and Zoo*)

ZOO | **FAMILY** | Three kilometers (2 miles) north of Bandol via the D559 is this zoo and garden, where cacti and exotic tropical plants grow to remarkable sizes. In a small zoo setting, animals such as flamingos, gibbons, and gazelles frolic in shady gardens. ✉ *131 av. Pont d'Aran, Sanary-sur-Mer* ✣ *Exit Bandol from A8, take first right (direction Rte. de Beausset) and follow signs to zoo* ☎ *04–94–29–40–38* 🌐 *www.zoaparc.com* 🎟 *€14.50.*

Restaurants

Restaurant "René 'Sens par Jean-François Bérard"

$$$$ | **MODERN FRENCH** | Chef Jean-François has taken the reins from his illustrious father, René (who consults on the menu), but the Mediterranean-inspired Provençal cuisine that put this restaurant on the map is as scrumptious as ever. The menu emphasizes local seafood, and the dishes—perhaps ravioli stuffed with goat cheese, sorrel, and Parmesan in a lemon chicken broth or red mullet wrapped in seaweed, lightly grilled, and topped with peas and rosemary—often use ingredients from the kitchen's own garden. **Known for:** good-value set menus; Michelin-starred cuisine; lovely setting. Ⓢ *Average main: €65* ✉ *Hostellerie Bérard, 6 rue Gabriel-Péri, La Cadière-d'Azur* ☎ *04–94–90–11–43* 🌐 *hotel-berard.com/en* ⏲ *Closed Mon. and Tues. mid-Sept.–mid-July.*

Hotels

Hostellerie Bérard

$$ | **HOTEL** | Master chef René Bérard is as celebrated for his haute cuisine as he is for his elegant country inn with breathtaking views of the countryside and everything required for a pampered weekend on the hotel premises. **Pros:** very welcoming; elegant gourmet restaurant and a more casual alternative; charming village setting. **Cons:** it's easy to get lost in the sprawling hallways; outdated decor in common spaces; expensive breakfast. Ⓢ *Rooms from: €170* ✉ *7 rue Gabriel-Péri, 6 km (4 miles) north of Bandol, La Cadière-d'Azur* ☎ *04–94–90–11–43* 🌐 *www.hotel-berard.com* ⏲ *Closed Jan.–mid-Feb.* 🛏 *40 rooms* 🍽 *No Meals.*

Hôtel Île Rousse Thalazur
$$$ | **HOTEL** | A view over the infinity pool to the (private) beach and sea greets you at this luxury spa hotel two steps from Bandol's port. **Pros:** excellent restaurant; lovely saltwater pool; nice sea views from the rooms. **Cons:** spa closes early; extras are expensive; decor lacks character. *Rooms from: €340* *25 bd. Louis Lumière, Bandol* *04–94–29–33–00* *www.thalazur.fr/bandol/hotel* *67 rooms* *No Meals.*

Toulon

38 km (24 miles) southeast of Cassis; 67 km (42 miles) east of Marseille.

Best known for a daylong World War II attack during which 75 French ships were deliberately sunk to keep them out of the hands of advancing Germans, Toulon has doggedly kept its place as France's leading naval port. It's also a city of contrasts: crowded with unsightly postwar high-rises yet surprisingly beautiful with its tree-lined littoral; a place with some unappealing nightlife, and yet, by day, charming and colorful with its restaurant scene. What's more, although Toulon looks much like any modern French city, it has splashes of local color.

The port area features a sunny waterfront filled with yachts and pleasure boats, some of which you can hire for trips to the Îles d'Hyères, around the bay, or to Corsica and Sardinia. In the Old Town, you'll also find Les Halles—a produce and local-delicacies market set in a beautifully restored Art Deco building—as well as a maze of streets lined with hip boutiques and renovated medieval and Renaissance houses.

Park your car under Place de la Liberté, follow Boulevard de Strasbourg, and turn right onto Rue Berthelot to reach Old Town's heart of pedestrian-only streets. Wander through Place des Trois Dauphins, with its mossy and fern-lined fountain, or stop in the café-filled Place Puget; Victor Hugo lived in No. 5 when he was researching *Les Misérables*. One block east, the Cours Lafayette becomes a wonderfully animated, authentic Provençal morning market (Tuesday–Sunday), and the Hôtel de Ville has evocative Baroque figures carved by the Marseillais sculptor Pierre Puget.

Visit the Mémorial du Débarquement de Provence via a vertiginous six-minute cable car ride up Mont Faron. In addition to thrilling 360-degree views of the Riviera and Toulon Bay, you'll also get a riveting account of the French and Allied forces attack on August 15, 1944.

GETTING HERE AND AROUND

Toulon is on the main TGV line from Paris (around 3 hours 50 minutes, €35–€126, depending on when you go and the type of ticket) and is served by regional and local trains from Marseille and Nice. By car, take the A50 from Marseille in the west and if you are coming from the east, the A57. The coastal D559 goes between Marseille and Toulon via Bandol.

Toulon has a great network of inner-city buses run by the RMTT. Bus 23 goes to the beaches at Mourillon, Bus 40 to the cable car.

BUS CONTACTS RMTT. *Toulon* *04–94–03–87–03* *www.reseaumistral.com.*

VISITOR INFORMATION

CONTACTS Toulon Tourist Office. *12 pl. Louis Blanc, Toulon* *04–94–18–53–00* *toulontourisme.com.*

Sights

Brignoles
TOWN | Although it's known as the market center for the wines of the Var, Brignoles's largest attraction is still the Abbaye de la Celle, a 12th-century Benedictine abbey that served as a convent until the 17th century and was abandoned until Maria Fournier, owner of the Île de Porquerolles, opened it

as a hotel in 1945. It's now the site of celebrated chef Alain Ducasse's culinary hideaway, Hostellerie de l'Abbaye de La Celle. In general, however, the town has staunchly continued to resist change. In fact, the simple Romanesque chapel housing a 14th-century Christ figure—a widely acclaimed masterpiece by an unknown artist—still serves as the parish church. ✉ *45 km (28 miles) north of Toulon, Brignoles.*

★ Mémorial du Débarquement de Provence
HISTORY MUSEUM | FAMILY | On the site of a crucial fort at the summit of Mont Faron, this museum recounts the planning and execution of World War II's Operation Dragoon, a mission meant to resecure the French ports of Marseille and Toulon and cut off German reinforcements. The story unfolds via firsthand accounts in French and English from men and women who fought for the French Resistance, descriptions of life under the occupation, a detailed timeline, and an 11-minute film showing original footage of the August 15, 1944, invasion—and its vast destruction—which was a decisive turning point in the war. ✉ *8488 Rte. du Faron, Toulon* ☎ *04–94–88–08–09* 🌐 *www.memorialdu-montfaron.fr* 🎫 *€6.*

Mont Faron
MOUNTAIN | FAMILY | Rising 1,900 feet above the town, with panoramas of Toulon, the surrounding countryside, and the sea, Mont Faron can be reached by the circular Route du Faron in either direction or in six minutes by cable car from Boulevard Admiral Jean-Vence. At the top, the World War II memorial commemorates the mountain fort's role in the Provence débarquement of August 1944 and the liberation of Toulon. There is also a zoo that acts as a breeding center for a dozen types of wild cats, including lions, tigers, jaguars, lynxes, and pumas. ✉ *Toulon* ☎ *04–94–92–68–25 for téléphérique* 🌐 *www.telepherique-faron.fr* 🎫 *Téléphérique €8.50 round-trip, zoo €17.50.*

Musée d'Art de Toulon
ART MUSEUM | The collection here includes paintings by Vernet and Fragonard, postwar abstract art, and works by the cartoon-influenced Di Rosa brothers. ✉ *113 bd. Maréchal Leclerc, Toulon* ☎ *04–94–36–81–15* 🎫 *Free* ⏲ *Closed Mon.*

Musée National de la Marine (*Naval Museum*)
HISTORY MUSEUM | FAMILY | Part of a network of marine museums around France, this branch, lodged in the graceful 18th-century section of the Toulon arsenal, is particularly fascinating. The rich maritime history in this part of the Mediterranean comes alive via model ships, paintings, mastheads, and a pictorial account of the city's role in World War II. ✉ *Pl. Monsenergue, Toulon* ☎ *04–22–42–02–01* 🌐 *www.musee-marine.fr/toulon* 🎫 *€7* ⏲ *Closed Tues.*

Restaurants

Beam! Kitchen
$$ | MODERN FRENCH | FAMILY | Under the soaring beams of Le Telegraph, a cultural space in Toulon's old central post office, this trendy new restaurant delivers the food and the fun. After a frothy cocktail apéro, you can tuck into dishes like Toulon bay oysters with tomato cubes and crisp nori seaweed flecked with fennel flowers or a rich tartiflette made with reblochon cheese and pancetta. **Known for:** menu changes daily; imaginative cocktails; vegetarian friendly. $ *Average main: €19* ✉ *2 rue Hippolyte Duprat, Toulon* ☎ *06–27–54–27–06* 🌐 *www.facebook.com/beamkitchentoulon* ⏲ *Closed Sun. and Mon. No dinner Tues. and Wed. No lunch Sat.*

Il Parasole di Marco
$ | ITALIAN | You couldn't have a more perfect setting for chef Marco Casolla's

Continued on page 224

Simple preparations, like grilled vegetables with crusty bread, are best enjoyed with the region's famous rosé wine.

CUISINE OF THE SUN

Don't be surprised if colors and flavors seem more intense in Provence. It could be the hot, dry climate, which concentrates the essence of fruit and vegetables, or the sun beaming down on market tables overflowing with produce. Or maybe you're seeing the world anew through rosé-tinted wine glasses. Whatever the reason, here's how to savor Provence's *incroyable* flavors and culinary favorites.

Provence's rustic cuisine, based on local tomatoes, garlic, olive oil, anchovies, olives, and native wild herbs—including basil, lavender, mint, rosemary, thyme, and sage—has more in common with other Mediterranean cuisines than it does with most regional French fare. Everywhere you'll find sun-ripened fruit dripping with nectar and vegetables so flavor-packed that meat may seem like a mere accessory.

The natural bounty of the region is ample, united by climate—brilliant sunshine and fierce winds—and divided by dramatically changing landscapes. In the Vaucluse, scorched plains give way to lush, orchard-lined hills and gently sloped vineyards. The wild Calanques of Marseille, source of spiky sea urchins, ease into the tranquil waters of St-Tropez, home to gleaming bream and sea bass. Provence's pantry is overflowing with culinary treasures.

PROVENCE'S TOP REGIONAL DISHES

Ratatouille

Fougasse

AÏOLI

The name for a deliciously pungent mayonnaise made with generous helpings of garlic, *aïoli* is a popular accompaniment for fish, meat, and vegetable dishes. The mayonnaise version shares its name with "grand aïoli," a recipe featuring salt cod, potatoes, hard-boiled eggs, and vegetables. Both types of aïoli pop up all over Provence, but they seems most beloved in Marseille. In keeping with Catholic practice, some restaurants serve grand aïoli only on Fridays. And it's a good sign if they ask you to place your order at least a day in advance. A grand aïoli is also a traditional component of the Niçois Christmas feast.

BOUILLABAISSE

Originally a humble fisherman's soup made with the part of the catch that nobody else wanted, bouillabaisse—the famous fish stew—consists of four or five kinds of fish: the villainous-looking *rascasse* (red scorpion fish), *grondin* (sea robin), *baudroie* (monkfish), *congre* (conger eel), and *rouget* (mullet). The fish are simmered in a stock of onions, tomatoes, garlic, olive oil, and saffron, which gives the dish its golden color. When presented properly, the broth is served first, with croutons and rouille, a creamy garlic sauce that you spoon in to suit your taste. The fish comes separately, and the ritual is to place pieces into the soup to enjoy after slurping up some of the broth.

BOURRIDE

This poached fish dish owes its anise kick to pastis and its garlic punch to aïoli. The name comes from the Provençal *bourrido*, which translates less poetically as "boiled." Monkfish—known as *baudroie* in Provence and *lotte* in the rest of France—is a must, but chefs occasionally dress up their bourride with other species and shellfish.

DAUBE DE BOEUF

To distinguish their prized beef stew from *boeuf bourguignon*, Provençal chefs make a point of not marinating the meat, instead cooking it very slowly in tannic red wine that is often flavored with orange zest. In the Camargue, daube is made with the local taureau (bull's meat), while the Avignon variation uses lamb.

Bourride

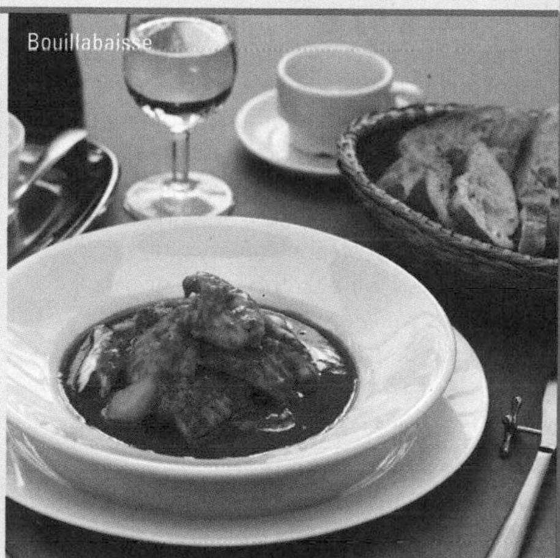

Bouillabaisse

FOUGASSE

The Provençal answer to Italian focaccia, this soft flatbread is distinguished by holes that give it the appearance of a lacy leaf. It can be made savory—flavored with olives, anchovy, bacon, cheese, or anything else the baker has on hand—or sweet, enriched with olive oil and dusted with icing sugar. When in Menton, don't miss the sugary *fougasse mentonnaise*.

LES PETITS FARCIS

The Niçois specialty called *les petits farcis* are prepared with tiny summer vegetables (usually zucchini, tomatoes, peppers, and onions) that are traditionally stuffed with veal or leftover daube (beef stew). Like so many Niçois dishes, they make great picnic food.

RATATOUILLE

At its best, ratatouille is a glorious thing—a riot of eggplant, zucchini, bell peppers, and onions, each sautéed separately in olive oil and then gently combined with sweet summer tomatoes. A well-made ratatouille, to which a pinch of saffron has been added to heighten its flavor, is also delicious served chilled.

SOUPE AU PISTOU

The Provençal answer to pesto, pistou consists of the simplest ingredients—garlic, olive oil, fresh basil, and Parmesan—ideally pounded together by hand in a stone mortar with an olivewood pestle. Most traditionally it delivers a potent kick to *soupe au pistou*, a kind of French minestrone made with green beans, white beans, potatoes, and zucchini.

SOCCA

You'll find socca vendors from Nice to Menton, but this chickpea pancake cooked on a giant iron platter in a wood-fired oven is really a Niçois phenomenon, born of sheer poverty at a time when wheat flour was scarce. After cooking, it is sliced into finger-lickin' portions with an oyster knife. Enjoy it with a glass of chilled rosé.

TIAN DE LÉGUMES

A *tian* is both a beautiful earthenware dish and one of many vegetable gratins that might be cooked in it. This thrifty dish makes a complete meal of seasonal vegetables, eggs, and a little cheese.

delicious pizzas and pasta dishes—inspired by his native Naples and the bounty of the sea—than the white sands of Toulon's Plage du Mourillon. At this beachside terrace restaurant, diners cool off with an apéro spritz in the shade of umbrellas at lunchtime or wrap up a day at the beach over a sunset dinner. **Known for:** thin-crust Neapolitan-style pizzas; well-priced wine by the bottle or glass; endless sea views. *$ Average main: €16 ✉ Plage du Mourillon, Toulon ☎ 07–60–42–94–33 🌐 www.ilparasoledimarco.com ⏲ No dinner Sun.–Tues.*

Le Lido de Toulon
$$ | **SEAFOOD** | At this restaurant on lovely Mourillon Beach, you can sit at tables on the spacious wooden deck or directly on the sand, with pretty views of the bay and the old fort. Toulon's answer to the classic brasserie serves generous seafood platters, an excellent fish soup, and the local catch of the day, as well as heartier French classics such as Charolais beef, truffle risotto, and foie gras. **Known for:** very good seafood, both raw and cooked; open seven days; beachside dining. *$ Average main: €21 ✉ Corniche Frédéric Mistral, Plage du Mourillon ☎ 04–94–03–38–18 🌐 le-lido-de-toulon.fr.*

Hotels

Grand Hôtel des Sablettes-Plage
$$ | **HOTEL** | Set on sandy Les Sablettes Beach, part of the Saint-Mandrier-sur-Mer Peninsula across the harbor from Toulon, this fully restored, Belle Époque–era hotel has bright, casually elegant rooms with a few classic nautical touches and lots of modern amenities. **Pros:** enormous garden terrace is great for breakfast or a drink; two very good restaurants; beach access and an on-site pool. **Cons:** pool is small for a hotel of this size; restaurants book up quickly in high season; rooms vary drastically in size. *$ Rooms from: €170 ✉ 575 av. Charles de Gaulle, Toulon ☎ 04–94–17–00–00 🌐 www.ghsplage.com 79 rooms No Meals.*

★ Hostellerie de l'Abbaye de La Celle
$$$ | **HOTEL** | Chef Alain Ducasse put this beautifully restored property—part of a convent once charged with shaping the future queens of Provence—on the map when he took over both the restaurant (now headed by chef Nicolas Pierantoni) and the inn, where guest rooms mix Louis XVI furnishings with regional accents, and the grounds have private gardens and vineyard views. **Pros:** excellent restaurant; lovely views; true Provençal experience, with all the glamour minus the glitz. **Cons:** restaurant service can be spotty; expensive; no elevator in hotel. *$ Rooms from: €250 ✉ 10 pl. du Général-de-Gaulle, Brignoles ☎ 04–98–05–14–14 🌐 www.abbaye-celle.com ⏲ Restaurant closed Tues. and Wed. mid-Oct.–mid-Apr. and Jan. 10 rooms No Meals.*

★ Lou Calen
$$$$ | **HOTEL** | **FAMILY** | To say this sustainable hotel is unique is an understatement—where else in Provence can you stay in a luxury cave with a bathroom set into the rocks or in a round pigeon tower with sweeping village and countryside views? For the less adventurous, the 200-year-old farmhouse offers a more conventional experience, where each of the large rooms and suites—complete with wood-burning stoves—opens onto a private terrace. **Pros:** an island of repose; in one of France's designated "most beautiful villages"; dining room has a Michelin Green star. **Cons:** quite expensive; some rooms are dark; too much to discover in one night. *$ Rooms from: €560 ✉ 1 cours Gambetta, Cotignac ☎ 04–98–14–15–29 🌐 www.loucalen.com/en/home 14 rooms No Meals.*

Îles d'Hyères

32 km (20 miles) off coast south of Hyères; 29 km (18 miles) southeast of Toulon to ferry departure point.

Strung across the Bay of Hyères and spanning some 32 km (20 miles) is an archipelago whose islands could be locations for a pirate movie. In fact, they have been featured in several, thanks not only to their wild and rocky coastline but also their real pirate history. In the 16th century, the islands were seeded with convicts who were supposed to work the land but instead ran amok, ambushing and sacking passing ships heading for Toulon. Today, the islands consist of three main bodies: Levant, Port-Cros, and Porquerolles.

Part of Levant is military property and is kept strictly guarded with barbed-wire fences. The Domaine Héliopolis (the city of the sun) celebrates harmonious living based on nudism, respect of others and nature. Port-Cros is a magnificent national park with no cars, no smoking, and no dogs. You can hike on pine-scented trails with spectacular views, or follow the underwater path, snorkeling or diving with aquatic life representative of the Mediterranean.

Porquerolles (pronounced "pork-uh-*rohl*") is the largest and most popular escape from the modern world. Its namesake village was originally a retirement colony for Napoleonic officers (the Fort du Petit-Langoustier and the Fort Ste-Agathe, although no longer active, still loom imposingly over the marina), which explains its remarkable resemblance to a military outpost. At the turn of the 20th century, a Belgian engineer named François-Joseph Fournier made a killing in the Panama Canal, then bought Porquerolles at auction as a gift for his new bride. It was only in 1970 that France nationalized the island, leaving Fournier's widow with a quarter of her original inheritance. Her granddaughter now helps run the luxurious Mas du Langoustier.

Off-season, Porquerolles is a castaway idyll of sandy beaches and plunging cliffs along the rocky coastline. Inland, its preserved pine forests, vineyards, and orchards of olives and figs are crisscrossed with dirt roads that you can explore on foot or by bike, which you can rent from one of the numerous outfits in both the port and village. In high season (April–October), day-trippers pour off the ferries, running for the beaches, and T-shirt shops appear out of the woodwork to cater to vacationers' whims.

GETTING HERE AND AROUND

To get to Porquerolles, follow the narrow Giens Peninsula to La Tour–Fondue at its tip. From here, ferries make the 20-minute trip to Porquerolles (every 30 minutes in summer, every 60–90 minutes in winter; €24 round-trip). Ferries for Port-Cros and Levant (€17–€25 round-trip) depart from Port-Saint-Pierre year-round (schedules vary by season). You can also reach the islands by water taxi from these departure points and others along the coast.

VISITOR INFORMATION

CONTACTS Îles d'Hyères Tourist Office. ✉ *Carré du port, Hyères* ☎ *04–94–58–33–76* 🌐 *www.hyeres-tourisme.com.*

Sights

★ Villa Carmingnac

ART MUSEUM | Set amid gardens, vineyards, olive groves, and woods, this stunning outpost of a Paris-based foundation has a world-class art collection that would be right at home in any major city. The foundation is in a renovated farmhouse, whose historic status necessitated creating a separate space to house the art. The result was a 20,000-square-foot, belowground gallery, whose rooms are ingeniously illuminated via a ground-floor pool that doubles as a glass ceiling. You can also see dozens of site-specific works on a stroll through the property. Afterward, sip a glass of local wine at the on-site café. ✉ *Piste de la Courtade, Hyères* ☎ *04–65–65–25–50* 🌐 *www.fondationcarmignac.com.*

Hotels

Le Manoir de Port-Cros

$$$ | RESORT | A mix of southern-coast bourgeois and Provençal touches adds a splash of color to the sunlit, airy rooms of this family-owned hotel, where thoughtful service and absolute calm encourage relaxation. **Pros:** a gentle touch of civilization amid wilderness; lovely setting with enormous old eucalyptus trees; old-world elegance. **Cons:** some south-facing rooms are hot in summer; not open year-round; no Wi-Fi or TV in rooms. *Rooms from: €260* *Île de Port-Cros, Hyères* *04-94-05-90-52* *www.hotel-le-manoirportcros.com* *Closed Oct.–Mar.* *23 rooms* *No Meals.*

Mas du Langoustier

$$$$ | HOTEL | A fabled getaway, the Langoustier has a lobster-orange building, pink bougainvillea, a choice of California modern– or old Provençal–style guest rooms, and a secluded location at the westernmost point of the Île de Porquerolles. **Pros:** rates include breakfast and dinner; one of the prettiest hotels on the island; beach nearby and on-site pool. **Cons:** a hike to get here; no rooms have a sea view; rooms could be brighter. *Rooms from: €500* *Pointe du Langoustier, 3 km (2 miles) from harbor, Ile de Porquerolles* *04-94-58-30-09* *www.langoustier.com* *Closed Oct.–Apr.* *48 rooms* *Free Breakfast.*

Villa Sainte Anne

$$ | HOTEL | This pleasant lodging in the heart of Porquerolles's main village, a five-minute walk from the ferry landing, offers clean, basic rooms with all the amenities. **Pros:** reasonably priced, especially in the off-season; very good on-site restaurants; nice location. **Cons:** there are no sea views; breakfasts are lackluster; rooms lack charm. *Rooms from: €175* *Pl. d'Armes, Hyères* *04-98-04-63-00* *www.sainteanne.com* *Closed Dec.–Mar.* *25 rooms* *No Meals.*

Activities

Centre Immersion Plongée

SCUBA DIVING | Here you can take a diving class, hire a guide, rent diving equipment, and refill scuba tanks. *Port Pothuau, 13 av. des Chalutiers, Hyères* *06-03-49-51-92* *www.immersion-plongee.com.*

Cycle Porquerollais

BIKING | FAMILY | You can rent a mountain bike (*velo tout-terrain*, or VTT) for a day of pedaling the paths and cliff-top trails of Porquerolles. *1 rue de la Ferme, Ile de Porquerolles* *04-94-58-30-32* *velo-porquerolles.fr.*

Locamarine 75

BOATING | This shop rents motorboats to anyone interested, whether or not they have a license. *Port de Porquerolles, Ile de Porquerolles* *06-08-34-74-17* *www.locamarine75.com.*

Chapter 6

THE WESTERN FRENCH RIVIERA

Updated by
Nancy Heslin

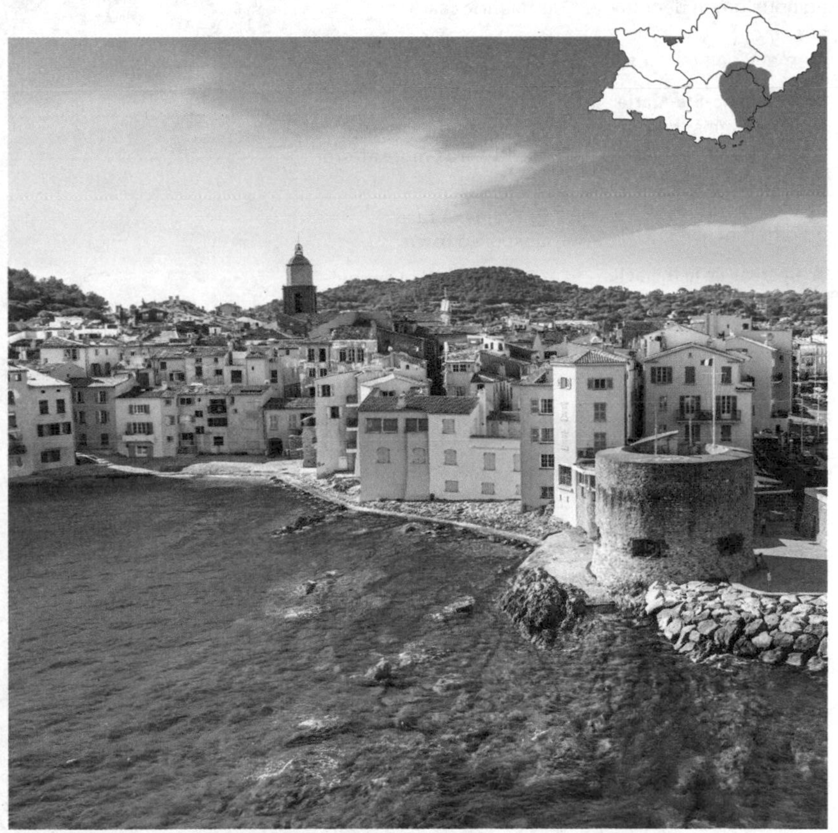

Sights ★★★☆☆ | Restaurants ★★☆☆☆ | Hotels ★★★☆☆ | Shopping ★★☆☆☆ | Nightlife ★★☆☆☆

WELCOME TO THE WESTERN FRENCH RIVIERA

TOP REASONS TO GO

★ **St-Tropez:** Soak up the summer scene in the world's most outlandish fishing port. Just don't forget the fake-tan lotion.

★ **Les Gorges du Verdon:** Peer down into its vertiginous green depths at one of France's most dramatic natural sites.

★ **Moustiers-Ste-Marie:** Houses in this town known for its faience pottery cling to cliffs—often with entrances on different levels.

★ **Château de la Napoule:** In Mandelieu-La-Napoule, discover an extravagant and eccentric château that blends Romanesque, Gothic, and Moroccan styles.

★ **The Estérel Corniche:** The coastline here is a mineral showcase of rock in Technicolor russets, garnets, and flaming oranges.

1 St-Tropez. One of the Riviera's liveliest and glitziest stretches.

2 Ramatuelle. An ancient town with a thriving wine scene.

3 Gassin. A village with gorgeous views over St-Tropez's bay.

4 Grimaud. Home to a romantic castle.

5 Port-Grimaud. A modern version of a Provençal fishing village.

6 Ste-Maxime. One of the Riviera's more affordable towns.

7 Fréjus. A rare unspoiled town.

8 St-Raphaël. A sprawling resort city with a rich port history.

9 Mandelieu-La-Napoule. Dual centers of golf and sailing in the region.

10 Fayence. The most touristy of the Haut Var hill towns.

11 Seillans. An inviting old-fashioned village.

12 La Palud-sur-Verdon. The central town of Gorges du Verdon, France's Grand Canyon.

13 Moustiers-ste-Marie. A striking cliff-side village.

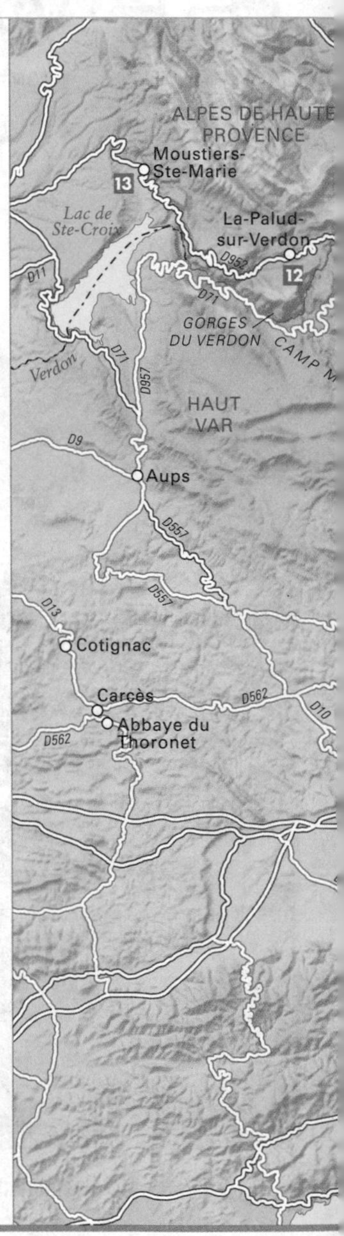

Castellane
D952
N85
Trigance
D71
D21
D563
N85
Mons
ALPES
MARITIMES
N85
D2085
Grasse
LITAIRE DE CANJUERS
D19
11
Seillans
10
Fayence
Bargemon
D2562
D9
D3
D955
D562
Antibes
Mandelieu-
La Napoule
A8
Cannes
Golfe
Juan
9
N98
Draguignan
VAR
La Napoule
Théoule-sur-Mer
D4
N7
D25
N7
MASSIF DE L'ESTÉREL
N7
D7
St-Raphaël
A8
N98
Fréjus
8
7
Corniche de l'Estérel
Golfe
de Fréjus
D25
MAURES
MASSIF DES
N98
Mediterranean Sea
Cap des Sardinaux
6
Ste-Maxime
Port-
Grimaud
Cap de St-Tropez
1
5
Grimaud
4
St-Tropez
Gassin
D93
3
D559
2
Ramatuelle
0
4 mi
0
4 km

The Western Côte d'Azur can supply everything your heart desires—and your purse can withstand. Home to St-Tropez ("St-Trop," or Saint Too Much, as the French call it), the region beckons to both billionaires and backpackers.

Even if the Western Côte d'Azur is considered less glamorous than its counterparts to the east, it's still most often associated with celeb-heavy coastal resorts, where many people don't think twice about spending €1,000 a night for a room. The Var *département* (region) is also, however, a nature-lover's paradise.

Lovely azure waters lap at the foot of the thriving resort towns that include not only the famous St-Tropez, but also Fréjus, St-Raphaël, and Mandelieu-La-Napoule—lower-key places that also beckon sun-starved northerners with stretches of beach and balmy temperatures. Above the coastline, the horizon is dominated by rugged, unspoiled landscapes, from the red-rock heights of the Massif de l'Estérel to the green-black bulk of the Massif des Maures.

Sunburned and, quite possibly, bored beachgoers often head beyond the coastal plateau and into the Haut Var. As the continent climbs gently toward the Alps, the countryside becomes harsh but alluring with raw rock, pine, and scrub oak, as well as glorious vineyard-lined hills that are home to lovely *villages perchés* (perched villages).

Although these historical hill towns make great day trips from the coast, in high season, they're often overrun by busloads of visitors out of Cannes or St-Raphaël. If you have a car and a bit of time, press on to one of France's top natural wonders: the Gorges du Verdon. Roaring with milky-green water and edged by one of Europe's most hair-raising drives, this spectacular chasm draws hard-core hikers who are content with forgoing the local rosé to keep their wits about them as they explore. Backpacks, hiking boots, and picnics are de rigueur until you reach lovely Moustiers-Ste-Marie, an atmospheric center for faience (a type of ceramic). Here, you can treat yourself to a leisurely meal and still more stunning natural views.

MAJOR REGIONS

St-Tropez and the Massif des Maures. Shielded from the mistral by the broad, forested mass of the Massif des Maures, a small expanse of pampered coastline is crowned by the sparkling lights of St-Tropez, itself doubly protected by the hills of the Paillas. A pretty pastel port in winter, in season it becomes glamorous "St-Trop," and *trop* in French means "too much," so you get the idea. For day trips you can escape to the simple life in the hill towns of Ramatuelle, Gassin, and Grimaud. Mere mortals—especially vacationing families on a budget—usually aim for Ste-Maxime across the bay, where the hyperdevelopment typical of the Riviera begins.

Fréjus, St-Raphaël, and the Estérel Corniche. Though the twin resorts of Fréjus and St-Raphaël have become somewhat overwhelmed by waterfront resort culture, Fréjus still harbors a small but charming enclave that evokes both the Roman and medieval periods. East along the coast, the Massif de l'Estérel rears up high above the sparkling water. Its harsh landscape of red volcanic rocks (porphyry), carved by the sea into dreamlike shapes, is softened by patches of lavender, mimosa, scrub pine, and gorse. At the base of the rocks, azure waters churn in and out of castaway coves punctuated by gentle resort bays.

The D559 leads to one of the coast's most spectacular drives, the Corniche de l'Estérel. And if you take DN7, the mountain route to the north, you can lose yourself in the Estérel's desert landscape, far from the sea. Mandelieu and La-Napoule, the resorts that cluster at the foot of the Estérel, are densely populated pleasure ports, with an agreeable combination of cool sea breezes and escapes into the near-desert behind.

Haut Var and the Gorges de Verdon. The hills that back the Côte d'Azur are often called the *arrière-pays,* or backcountry—a catchall term that applies to the hills and plateaus behind Nice as well. Yet this particular wedge of backcountry—north and west of Fréjus—has a character all its own.

If the territory behind Nice has a strong Latin flavor, influenced for centuries by the Grimaldi dynasty and steeped in Italian culture, these westerly hills are deeply, unselfconsciously Provençal. Wild lavender and thyme sprout on dry, rocky hillsides; the earth under scrub oaks is snuffled by rooting boars; and hilltop villages are so isolated and quiet you can hear pebbles drop in their mossy fountains.

The rocky swells behind Cannes and Fréjus are known as the Haut Var, the highlands of the *département* called the Var. The untamed, beautiful, and sometimes harsh landscape beyond these hills lies over the threshold of Haute-Provence, itself loosely defined—more a climate and terrain than a region. Here villages like Fayence and Seillans beckon. You can also explore Moustiers-Ste-Marie, with its faience workshops, and discover the art of this brightly painted tableware. Not far away is La Palud-sur-Verdon, gateway to the spectacular Gorges du Verdon.

Planning

When to Go

Summer days are like the film *Groundhog Day*—every day seems exactly the same as the day before, with the piercing azure blue sky and sticky sunshine heat. July and August are hot, people move slower and, yes, you will sweat. Climate forecasts have become unpredictable, but, as a rule, locals cite August 15 as the beginning of changing weather: clouds tend to roll in frequently, and temperatures drop noticeably in the morning and evening.

March to April and October to November tend to be rainier periods and, of course, the mistral can come at any time, bringing terrible gusts and nippy drafts. To see the Gorges du Verdon in full fall color, aim for early October, though the odds of rain increase as the season advances.

Planning Your Time

Although the off-season sees events like February's Mimosa festival, complete with competing float parades, in La Napoule, most things take place when café life is in full swing, namely from Easter through October. May is mild and often lovely, but the top restaurants and hotels may be booked with spillover from the Cannes Film Festival. Moustiers-Ste-Marie celebrates all things lavender with the LavandEvasion festival the last week of June and first week of July.

Unless you enjoy jacked-up prices, traffic jams, and sardine-style beach crowds, avoid the coast in summer, especially the last week of July and first three weeks of August. Indeed, many of the better restaurants simply shut down to avoid the coconut-oil crowd. Another negative about July and August: it's flash-fire season, and the Estérel is closed to hikers.

Toward the end of the season, there are still things to do. In Bormes-les-Mimosas, you can visit Fort de Brégançon, the president's summer home, open to the public for guided tours during various weeks from July to October. On the first Sunday in September, Fréjus-St-Aygulf cracks open 15,000 eggs as it celebrates the Giant Omelette Festival. In early October, guided walks around hilltop villages near St-Raphaël take place during Var Rambling Week (Semaine Varoise de la Randonnée Pédestre). And even you can afford to shop in St-Tropez during La Grande Braderie—an end-of-season sale held the last weekend of October.

Getting Here and Around

You can visit any spot between St-Tropez and Cannes on an easy day trip, and the hilltop villages and towns on the coastal plateau are just as accessible. Thanks to the efficient A8 highway, you can generally whisk at high speeds to the exit nearest your destination up or down the coast; thus, even if you like leisurely exploration, you can zoom back to your home base at day's end.

Public transportation is not as good here as in other regions of the Riviera and Provence, and some itineraries may require cars. Note, however, that there is no way to avoid the bumper-to-bumper traffic along the Corniche de l'Estérel or from the A8 highway into St-Tropez during the summer season.

Above the autoroute things slow down considerably, and venturing farther north by, say, the 314-km (195-mile) Route Napoléon, is a bigger commitment that should include at least one overnight stop. Driving is the best way to village-hop in the Haut Var and take in the spectacular Gorges du Verdon. Be prepared for some challenging bends along the way, like the Route des Crêtes (D23) from La Palud-sur-Verdon (if white knuckles are not for you, opt for the nearby D952).

If traveling by bus, remember that even if you find a local bus that stops at your village of choice, it won't necessarily drop you in the heart of town. As for waterways, roughly May–September ferries to St-Tropez from Nice (2 hours 30 minutes) and Cannes (1 hour 15 minutes) are scenic, hassle-free transport options.

BOAT

Considering the congestion on the road to St-Tropez, the best way to get there is by taking a train to St-Raphaël and then hopping on Les Bateaux de Saint-Raphaël. These boats, usually two per day April–October (four boats daily during July and August), leave from the Gare Maritime de St-Raphaël in the Vieux Port, take about an hour, and cost €15 one-way.

Bateaux Verts offers a shuttle boat linking St-Tropez and Ste-Maxime mid-February–December. Tickets are €8.40 one-way, and the ride is 20 minutes. Once in St-Tropez, April–September the same company can also take you on a tour around the Calanques de l'Estérel (2–3½ hours, €24.50) or an hour-long tour of the Baie des Canebiers (nicknamed the Bay of Stars) to see some celebrity villas (€14, with an extra €2.80 for a return ticket to Ste-Maxime-St-Tropez).

BOAT INFORMATION Bateaux Verts. ✉ *14 quai Léon Condroyer, Ste-Maxime* ☎ *04–94–49–29–39* 🌐 *www.bateaux-verts.com.* **Bateaux de Saint-Ralphaël.** ✉ *Gare Maritime, Quai Nomy, St-Raphaël* ☎ *04–94–95–17–46* 🌐 *www.bateauxsaintraphael.com.*

BUS

Although high-season traffic en route to St-Tropez can lead to two-plus-hour bus rides, buses along the coast stop at many out-of-the-way places that can't be reached by train. Once operated by separate regional companies (Cartreize, Varlib, Transvaucluse, etc.), there is now one "transport brand" called Zou! for the 06 (Alpes-Maritimes) and 83 (Var) departments. "Express" buses (numbers 1–99) serve major cities with fares based on distance. Flat-fare "Proximity" buses (numbers 100–9999) serve smaller communities.

Timetables are available on the Zou! website and app, as well as at train stations, local bus stations (*gares routières*), and tourist offices, where you can also get information on commercial bus excursions, including day trips out of Fréjus and St-Raphaël into the more popular backcountry towns.

St-Tropez's bus station is on Avenue du Général de Gaulle (at 5 Quai Avancé) and has bus routes run by Zou! This company's 248 routes linking Var municipalities include the popular 876 to/from St-Raphaël (€2.10, 1½ hours, 14 daily), the town with the nearest train station. Some buses stop in Grimaud and Port Grimaud, Ste-Maxime, and Fréjus (€2.10, 1 hour), but check the schedule to be sure. Bus 875 links up with Ramatuelle and Gassin (€2.10, 50 minutes). Bus 878 also connects to Toulon (€2.10, 2 hours).

From St-Raphaël's bus station, located at 100 Rue Victor Hugo next to the train station, all routes are €2.10 except to Nice airport with Bus 90 at Platform 2 at Terminal 2 (€20, 75 minutes). The bus station in Fréjus is on Place Paul-Vernet, and there are several buses from here to St-Tropez.

BUS INFORMATION Zou! ☎ *08–09–40–00–13* 🌐 *services-zou.maregionsud.fr/fr.*

CAR

Driving to Fréjus and Le Muy (exit for St-Tropez) from Cannes is a breeze on the A8 toll highway (€3–€5.70 one-way), but the D25 and D98, which connect you from the A8 to St-Tropez, can move at a snail's pace in July and August. The most scenic route—although again, in the summer it's extremely slow—is the D6098 (La Corniche d'Or) between La Napoule, just east of Cannes, and Fréjus, after which point it turns into the D559. To explore the hill towns and the Gorges du Verdon, small, poky, and pretty roads lead north and west from Fréjus and Cannes, including the famous Route Napoléon.

TRAIN

There are no trains to St-Tropez. The nearest stops are St-Raphaël and Fréjus, the region's major rail hubs from points north and west. Fréjus's main station is on Rue Martin Bidouré, and St-Raphaël's Gare St-Raphaël/Valescure is on Rue Waldeck Rousseau. The latter is also the hub for the coastal TER line between Les Arcs and Nice (it's about 60 minutes from St-Raphaël to Nice, and the fare is €12.80), from where the train begins its scenic crawl along the coast toward Italy, stopping in La Napoule and Cannes.

In St-Raphaël, you can also pick up the direct train from Marseille to Ventimiglia, Italy (there's a stopover in Nice, but you stay on the train) or take the Mandelieu-La-Napoule-Ventimiglia. Either way, count on at least 70–90 minutes.

The train station nearest the Haut Var and the Gorges du Verdon is at Les Arcs, below Draguignan. From there you have to rent a car or get the train to Marseille and take LER Bus 27 to Castellane.

TRAIN INFORMATION SNCF. ☎ *3635* 🌐 *www.sncf-connect.com.* **TGV.** ☎ *3635* 🌐 *www.sncf-connect.com/tgv.*

Beaches

Given their reputation as the world's most glamorous beaches, the reality of *les plages* here often comes as a shock to first-time visitors. Much of the Côte d'Azur is lined with stone and pebble, and the beaches are narrow swaths backed by city streets or roaring highways.

Indeed, on this stretch of the Mediterranean, only St-Tropez has the curving bands of sandy waterfront you've come to expect from all those 1950s photographs—and, even there, the 3-mile Pampelonne Beach has no fewer than 15 restaurants and other businesses and can see as many as 30,000 beachgoers a day.

Note that there's a range of acceptable behaviors on these beaches: some are topless while others are full-on nudist. You'll be able to tell pretty quickly which is which.

Hiking

Check with local tourist office websites for information on hikes in the rugged backcountry of the Massif de l'Estérel. While several *sentiers du littoral* (coastal trails) wind around the St-Tropez Peninsula, *grande randonnées* (national hiking trails) GR51, known as the Balcons de la Méditerranée, and GR49 ascend the Estérel heights. The GR49 intersects with France's most spectacular grande randonnée, the GR4, which threads the Gorges du Verdon.

Hotels

If you've come to this area from other regions in France, you'll notice the sharp hike in hotel prices, and they skyrocket to dizzying heights in summer. St-Tropez's rates vie with those in Monaco. You'll also notice a difference in interior design: the look leans toward "le style Côte d'Azur," a slick, neo–Art Deco pastiche that smacks of Jazz Age glamour.

Up in the hills you can find the charm you'd expect, both in sophisticated inns and in mom-and-pop auberges. Also, the farther north you go, the lower the rates.

If you can't disconnect while on vacation and Wi-Fi is essential, it's best to check with your accommodations beforehand about network access and signal strength.

Restaurants

Restaurants in the coastal resorts are expensive, particularly in St-Tropez, where prices can be higher than even those in Paris . Note, too, that although St-Tropez has one of the country's finest fish markets, just off the port, ordering the catch of the day can be a costly mistake (is one *langouste* really worth 200 euros?). Fortunately, indulging in the *tropézienne*—a rich, local pastry consisting of cream-filled brioche topped with grainy sugar—won't break the bank.

Inland, you'll have a better chance of finding value for your money by tapping into the good home cooking offered at cozy auberges (inns) in hilltop villages. As a rule, the curlier the printing on a menu, the more pretensions a country auberge has; some of the finest post only handwritten chalkboard menus. Your best bet is to order the daily special, which is almost always fresh, and there's no surprise in the price.

Around the Gorges du Verdon, a magnet for hikers and climbers, food becomes less of a priority—expect to find mostly pizzas, salads, and simple hikers' fare.

⇨ *Hotel and restaurant reviews have been shortened. For full information visit Fodors.com. Hotel prices are the lowest cost of a standard double room in high season. Restaurant prices are the average cost of a main course at dinner, or if dinner is not served, at lunch.*

What It Costs in Euros

$	$$	$$$	$$$$
HOTELS			
under €125	€125–€225	€226–€350	over €350
RESTAURANTS			
under €18	€18–€24	€25–€32	over €32

Visitor Information

For information on travel within the Var region—St-Tropez to La Napoule—contact Var Tourism. For Cannes and its surroundings, look to Côte d'Azur Tourisme.

For the Haute-Provence region between Moustiers and Manosque, contact the Agence Développement Touristique des Alpes de Haute-Provence. For the Verdon region, contact Parc Naturel Régional du Verdon.

CONTACTS Alpes de Haute Provence Tourisme. ✉ *Digne-les-Bains* ☎ *04–92–31–57–29* 🌐 *www.tourisme-alpes-haute-provence.com.* **Côte d'Azur Tourisme.** ✉ *Nice* ☎ *04–93–37–78–78* 🌐 *cote-dazurfrance.fr/en.* **Parc Naturel Régional du Verdon.** ✉ *Moustiers-Sainte-Marie* ☎ *04–92–74–68–00* 🌐 *www.parcdu-verdon.fr.* **Tourisme du Var.** ✉ *Toulon* ☎ *04–94–18–59–60* 🌐 *www.visitvar.fr.*

St-Tropez

66 km (41 miles) northeast of Toulon; 84 km (52 miles) southeast of Cannes; 112 km (70 miles) southeast of Nice.

At first glance, St-Tropez isn't all that impressive. It has a pretty port and a photogenic Old Town in sugar-almond hues, but there are many prettier villages in the hills nearby. There are sandy beaches, rare enough on the Riviera, and old-fashioned squares with plane trees and pétanque players, but these are a dime a dozen throughout Provence.

So what made St-Tropez so famous? Two words: Brigitte Bardot. When she showed up here on the arm of Roger Vadim in 1956 to film *And God Created Woman,* the world took notice. Neither the gentle descriptions of writer Guy de Maupassant (1850–93), nor the water-color tones of Impressionist Paul Signac (1863–1935), nor the stream of painters who followed (including Matisse and Bonnard) could focus the world's attention on this seaside hamlet like this one beautiful woman in a scarf, Ray-Bans, and capris.

Anything associated with the distant past seems almost absurd in St-Tropez, but people have been finding reasons to come here since AD 68, when a Roman soldier from Pisa named Torpes was beheaded for professing his Christian faith in front of Emperor Nero, making this a place of pilgrimage. Along medieval streets lined with walled gardens and little squares set with dripping fountains, you can discover historic delights like the Chapelle de la Misericorde, topped by its wrought-iron campanile, and Rue Allard, lined with picturesque houses such as the Maison du Maure.

Despite the big-deal fuss about over-the-top petrodollar parties, megayachts, and paparazzi, this enclave for billionaires is surprisingly small and insulated. The lack of train service, casinos, and chain hotels keeps it that way. Still, in July and August, you must be carefree about the sordid matter of cash. After all, at the most Dionysian nightclub in town, a glass of tap water goes for $28, and, when the party really gets going, billionaires think nothing of "Champagne spraying" the crowds—think World Series celebrations but with $1,000 bottles of Roederer Cristal instead of Gatorade. Complaining about summer crowds, high prices, and poor service has become a tourist sport, and yet these are among the things that contribute to St-Tropez's allure.

GETTING HERE AND AROUND

Getting to St-Tropez can be hellish. There is no direct train service, so your options are car, bus, or boat (from nearby ports like St-Raphaël). Driving can test anyone's mettle, thanks to the crowds, the narrow roads, and the parking situation. If you do decide to rent a car, take the N98 coast road; it's the longest route, but it's also the prettiest, with great picnic stops along the way.

From June through September, you must park at the Parking du Port lot (opposite the bus station on Avenue du Général de Gaulle) and take a shuttle bus into town. At other times, your best options are the Parc des Lices (beneath the Place des Lices) or the Place du XVe Corps in the center of town. Street parking is to be avoided, as exceeding the maximum time limit of three hours and 24 minutes will set you back €30.

A train–bus connection can be made if you're leaving from Nice center: take the train (direction St-Raphaël) from the Gare SNCF Nice Centre-Ville station (€13.90 one-way); from St-Raphaël, there's the daily Bus 876 service with Zou! (€2.10 one-way). Make sure you get to St-Raphaël's bus station early, or you won't get a seat and will be forced to stand for the entire 1½-hour trip.

The other option is to take a 2½-hour boat from the Nice harbor with Trans Côte d'Azur, which has daily trips June–September and costs €74 round-trip (from Cannes, it's only 75 minutes and €60 return).

VISITOR INFORMATION

The Archistoire Saint-Tropez app has two interactive self-guided walks. If you're more of a people person, every Wednesday April–October guided tours (€6) depart in front of the tourist office at 10 am.

CONTACTS St-Tropez Tourist Office. ✉ *Pl. des Lices, 19 Pl. Carnot, St-Tropez* ☎ *04-94-97-45-21* 🌐 *www.sainttropez-tourisme.com/en.*

Sights

Citadelle

MILITARY SIGHT | Head up Rue de la Citadelle to these 16th-century ramparts, which stand in a lovely hilltop park offering a fantastic view of the town and the sea. Amid today's bathing suit–clad sun worshippers it's hard to imagine St-Tropez as a military outpost, but inside the Citadelle's dungeon, the modern Musée de l'Histoire Maritime Tropézienne (St-Tropez Maritime Museum) is a stirring homage to those who served the nation. ✉ *Rue de la Citadelle, St-Tropez* ☎ *04-94-97-59-43* 🎫 *€4, includes museum entry* ⏲ *Closed 2 wks in Nov.*

La Maison des Papillons

OTHER MUSEUM | FAMILY | A block west of Rue Clémenceau, in a pretty house at the end of a typically Tropezien lane, the Butterfly Museum is a delightful place to spend an afternoon. Sweetly aflutter, the 35,000 specimens were a passion of late collector Dany Lartigue, the son of the famous photographer Jacques-Henri. ✉ *17 rue Étienne Berny, St-Tropez* ☎ *04-94-55-90-10* 🎫 *€2* ⏲ *Closed mornings; mid-Nov.–mid-Dec.; and Thurs. and Fri. in Feb.–June, Sept., and Oct.*

Le Sentier du Littoral

TRAIL | To experience St-Tropez's natural beauty up close, consider walking parts of the sentier du littoral, or coastal path, around the peninsula and all the beaches to Cavalaire-sur-Mer. The 12½-km (7-mile) route to Tahiti Beach has longish stretches on sand beach and takes about 3½ hours. Leave from the Tour du Portalet or the Tour Vieille at the edge of the Quartier de la Ponche. Follow the footpath from Plage des Graniers along the beaches and cliffs overlooking the water, often with views toward the Estérel or out to the open sea.

At Tahiti Beach, you can walk the 3 km (2 miles, 50 minutes) back to town or continue another 5 km (3 miles, 90 minutes) along the Plage de Pampelonne to the Bonne Terasse Beach. From here it gets serious, with another 19 km (12 miles, 6 hours) to Cavalaire to complete the entire trail. But you'll need to plan ahead to catch one of the few buses back to St-Tropez. Otherwise, it's 18 km (11 miles) back to town. ✉ *Tour du Portalet, St-Tropez.*

Musée de l'Annonciade

(*Annunciation Museum*)

ART MUSEUM | The legacy of the artists who loved St-Tropez—including Signac, Matisse, Braque, Dufy, Vuillard, and Rouault—has been carefully preserved

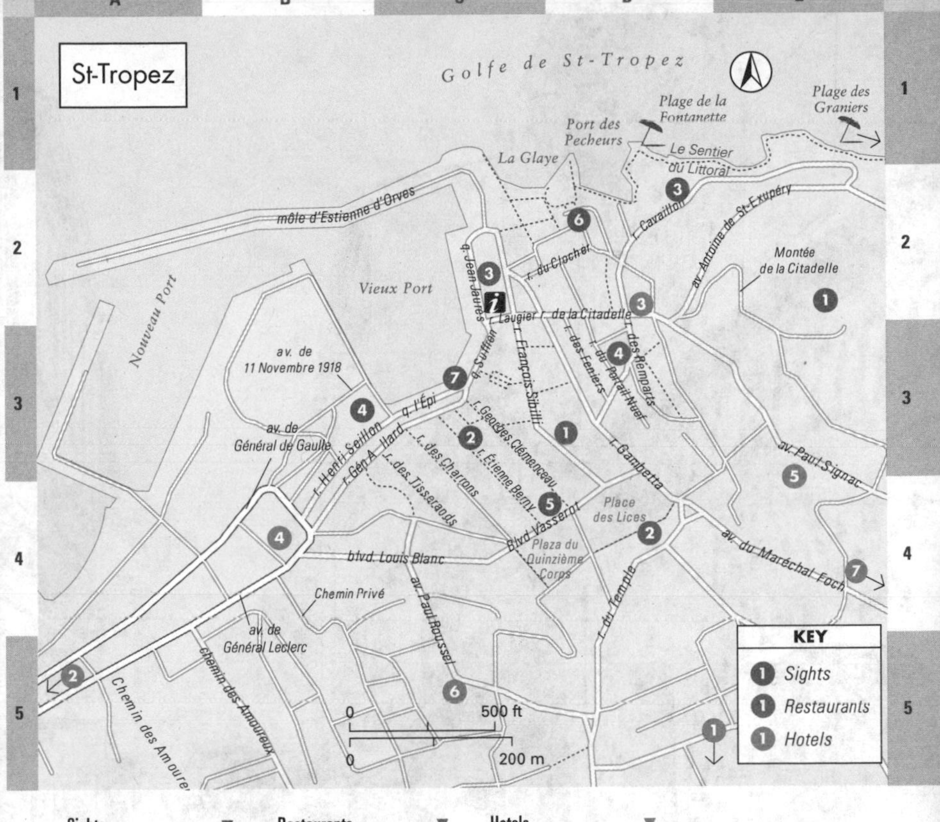

Sights

1 Citadelle E2
2 La Maison des Papillons C3
3 Le Sentier du Littoral ... D2
4 Musée de l'Annonciade B3
5 Place des Lices C4
6 Quartier de la Ponche................... D2
7 Vieux Port................. C3

Restaurants

1 Dior Café des Lices..... D3
2 Le Café................... D4
3 Le Girelier................. C2
4 Restaurant Le G'envie D3

Hotels

1 Château de la Messardière............. E5
2 Cheval Blanc St-Tropez A5
3 Hôtel B. Lodge D2
4 Hôtel de Paris Saint-Tropez............ B4
5 Le Byblos E3
6 Lou Cagnard.............. C5
7 Lou Pinet.................. E4

Did You Know?

Many of St-Tropez's charming, narrow streets were designed to break the impact of the fierce mistral winds.

in this extraordinary museum, housed in a 14th-century chapel just inland from the southwest corner of the Vieux Port. Cutting-edge temporary exhibitions feature local talent and up-and-coming international artists, while works—from Impressionism to Expressionism—by established artists line the walls. ✉ *2 pl. Georges Grammont, St-Tropez* ☎ *04–94–17–84–10* 🎫 *€4* ⏲ *Closed Mon. Oct.–June.*

Place des Lices

PLAZA/SQUARE | **FAMILY** | Enjoy a time-out in the social center of the Old Town, where a symmetrical forest of plane trees shades cafés and restaurants, skateboarders, children, and grandfatherly pétanque players. Also called Place Carnot, the square becomes a very affordable feast for both eyes and palate during the markets held here on Tuesday and Saturday mornings. At night, a café seat is as coveted as a quayside seat during the day.

Heading back to the Vieux Port area, take in the boutiques lining Rues Sibilli, Gambetta, and Clemenceau (where you can taste the most decadent *tarte tropézienne* at Marcel & Cavazza)—you never know when that photographer from *Voici* will be snapping away at the *trendoisie*. If you're here on the first weekend in May, check out Les Chefs de Saint-Tropez's three-day *fêtent les producteurs* (🌐 *www.leschefsasainttropez.com*) event featuring local produce, culinary demonstrations, tastings, and a chef's pétanque competition. ✉ *Av. Foch and Bd. Vasserot, St-Tropez.*

Quartier de la Ponche

NEIGHBORHOOD | **FAMILY** | Walk along Quai Suffern where the statue of the Bailli de Suffren, an 18th-century customs official, stands guard. Continue past the quayside streets lined with famous cafés to the Môle Jean Réveille, the harbor wall, where, if the wind isn't too strong, you can walk out for a good view of Ste-Maxime across the sparkling bay, the hills of Estérel, and, on a clear day, the distant Alps. Retrace your steps along the digue to the 15th-century Tour du Portalet, and head onward to the old fishermen's quarter, the Quartier de la Ponche, just east of Quai Jean Jaurès. Here you can find the Port des Pécheurs (Fishermen's Port), on whose beach Bardot did a star turn in *And God Created Woman*. Complete with gulf-side harbor, St-Tropez's Old Town is a maze of twisting, narrow streets—designed to break the impact of the mistral—that open to tiny squares with fountains. Trellised jasmine and wrought-iron birdcages hang from the shuttered windows, and many of the tiny streets dead-end at the sea. The main drag here, Rue de la Ponche, leads into Place l'Hôtel de Ville, landmarked by a *mairie* (town hall) marked out in typical Tropezienne hues of pink and green. Head up Rue Commandant Guichard to the Baroque Église de St-Tropez to pay your respects to the bust and barqúe of St-Torpes, every day but May 17, when they are carried aloft in the Bravade parade honoring the town's namesake saint. ✉ *St-Tropez.*

Vieux Port

NEIGHBORHOOD | **FAMILY** | Bordered by Quai de l'Épi, Quai Bouchard, Quai Peri, Quai Suffren, and Quai Jean Jaurès, Vieux Port is a place for strolling and looking over the shoulders of artists painting their versions of the view on easels set up along the water's edge. Meanwhile, folding director's chairs at the famous portside cafés, Café de Paris and Sénéquier, are well placed for observing the cast of St-Tropez's living theater play out their colorful roles. While here, be sure to take the time to enjoy a scoop of ice cream at Glacier Barvarac on Rue Général Allard. ✉ *St-Tropez.*

The plages (beaches) around St-Tropez are the most isolated on the Côte d'Azur and are among the region's rare stretches where your back doesn't lean up against the coastal highway. For better or worse, the beaches here remained largely unchanged for decades, until 2019. Thanks to a random French law—the 2006 Décret Plage protecting rare flora—the local town hall was able to extend the leases (from 2019 to 2030) of some 20 environmentally respectful beach clubs.

Note that although the neighboring community of Ramatuelle is a hill town, down along the coast, the line between it and St-Tropez is blurred, so some of the beaches and beach clubs are technically in Ramatuelle.

Nikki Beach

BEACH | Off the Route des Plages is this most notorious of all the beach clubs, famous for A-list debauches and a regular clientele of movie megastars and wannabes. But Nikki Beach isn't actually on the beach; rather it is steps from the shore with a pool and restaurant. If you want to mingle with the famous, rent a seaside Opium bed (€120 for maximum three people, drinks *not* included) or a VIP Bed Ponton by the Sea for up to four people; it's typically €120, but this is St-Tropez, so the price may vary depending on the DJ. Just be sure to avoid renting a bed poolside, where the Champagne showers spare no one. Note that there is a free parking lot here, but attendants might, for a variety of reasons, direct you to another lot where you have to pay for parking. **Amenities:** food and drink; parking (fee and no fee); showers; toilets. **Best for:** partiers. ✉ *Rte. de l'Épi, Ramatuelle* ☎ *04–94–79–82–04* 🌐 *saint-tropez.nikkibeach.com* ⏲ *Closed Oct.–Mar.*

Plage de la Bouillabaisse

BEACH | This sandy public beach at the edge of town has lifeguards (mid-June–mid-September), as well as free showers and toilets. You can rent loungers nearby. **Amenities:** lifeguards; parking (no fee); showers; toilets. **Best for:** swimming. ✉ *Quartier La Bouillabaisse, RD98A, St-Tropez.*

Plage des Graniers

BEACH | **FAMILY** | At the southern base of the Citadelle and past the cemetery, the closest beach to the town of St-Tropez is easily accessible on foot (it's part of the sentier du littoral) and the most family-friendly. At the east end, you can rent loungers (€30 plus extra for an umbrella) from the restaurant. There are no toilets or showers. **Amenities:** parking (no fee). **Best for:** swimming. ✉ *Ch. des Graniers, St-Tropez.*

Plage des Salins

BEACH | Situated between Cap des Salins and Point du Capon, this 600-meter public white sand beach is the gateway to a stretch of Pampelonne Beach, although it's more exposed to the wind and the sea can quickly become rough. It's lined by huge umbrella-pine trees, and you can rent loungers from the beach's private section. To the left, by the coastal path, is a quieter cove. **Amenities:** parking (no fee); showers; toilets. **Best for:** swimming. ✉ *Rte. des Salins, St-Tropez.*

★ Tahiti Beach

BEACH | The oldest and most famous of St-Trop's private beaches (Bardot filmed along this stretch) has fine sand, rentable loungers close to the shoreline, restaurants, and toilets. The crowd is definitely north of 35, but, as they don't act their age, there is a lot to see in terms of hardly there swimwear. **Amenities:** showers; toilets; water sports. **Best for:** swimming; walking. ✉ *Quartier du Pinet, Ramatuelle* ☎ *04–94–97–18–02* 🌐 *www.tahiti-beach.com.*

Despite the outrageous prices, St-Tropez does prove itself to be one of the prettiest places on the French Riviera.

Verde Beach by Yeeels

BEACH | Parisian restaurant group Yeeels is the mastermind behind what is one of Ramutuelle's best new beach clubs. Boho loungers (€50 plus another €10 for an umbrella) on Farniente Beach are available starting at 11 am; there's also a selection of magazines to read while you relax. Headed by Ducasse-trained, Michelin-starred chef Thibault Sombardier, the on-site restaurant offers Mediterranean-style oven-roasted, grilled, and marinated dishes at their most tempting (and pricey—an entire watermelon will set you back €70). The St-Trop party gets started here after 4 pm, when DJs crank up the music. **Amenities:** food and drink; toilets; showers. **Best for:** partiers; sunsets; swimming. ✉ *1149 Chemin de l'Epi, Ramatuelle* ☎ *04–94–79–72–23* 🌐 *verdebeach.com/fr_fr.*

Restaurants

Dior Café des Lices

$$$ | **FRENCH** | What could be more fashionable than tucking into exquisite cuisine—prepared by Michelin-starred guest chefs such as Yannick Alleno and Arnaud Donckele—in an enchanting sheltered garden designed by Peter Wirtz at the House of Dior? Meals are reasonably priced for St-Tropez, and the dessert selection is large (consider trying the much-lauded, tiny, round D'Choux pastries, which come in a variety of flavors). **Known for:** huge dessert menu, including famed caramel D'Choux; comparatively reasonable prices; secret garden vibe. $ *Average main: €32* ✉ *13 rue François Sibilli, St-Tropez* ☎ *04–98–12–67–65* 🌐 *www.dior.com* 🕓 *Closed mid-Oct.–Mar.*

Le Café

$$$$ | **BISTRO** | The busy terrace here often doubles as a stadium for different factions cheering on local pétanque players in Place des Lices. Service can be slow, but the setting, the food (say, black truffle and foie gras macaroni with Parmesan or seven-hour lamb confit with spices), and the piano bar with throwbacks to Piaf and Aznavour make this place memorable. **Known for:** well-priced lunch menu; French music nightly; languid service. *Average main: €36 5 pl. des Lices, St-Tropez 04-94-97-44-69 www.lecafe.fr.*

Le Girelier

$$$$ | **SEAFOOD** | Fish, fish, and more fish—sea bass, salmon, sole, sardines, monkfish, lobster, and crayfish all fill the boats that pull into the Old Port and find their way onto the menu here. Although grilled seafood (with a little thyme and perhaps a whisper of olive oil and garlic) is the order of the day, this is also a stronghold for bouillabaisse. **Known for:** fabulous views of Vieux Port yachts; seafood priced by weight (which gets expensive); reasonably priced wine list and lunch menu. *Average main: €45 Quai Jean-Jaurès, St-Tropez 04-94-97-03-87 www.legirelier.fr Closed Nov.–mid-Mar.*

Restaurant Le G'envie

$$$$ | **FRENCH** | It's always a good sign when people are willing to line up for a seat at a tiny joint like this one. Tucked away on an unassuming street behind the port, with views of Notre Dame church, this restaurant is where you come for classic French food without the St-Tropez prices. **Known for:** no-reservations policy; French duck and traditional veal dishes; tiny shaded spot on a tiny street. *Average main: €39 67 Rue Portail Neuf, St-Tropez 04-94-79-85-09 www.facebook.com/LeGRestaurant Closed Mon.*

 Hotels

★ Château de la Messardière

$$$$ | **HOTEL** | **FAMILY** | For unforgettable luxury—whether you're a couple seeking romance or you want a family retreat—head to this historical château just 10 minutes from St-Tropez but a world away from its bronzed beach crowds. **Pros:** stunning grounds; unprecedented offerings for kids; all the touches that make a stay special. **Cons:** eye-popping prices; not all rooms recently renovated; not near the beach. *Rooms from: €1250 2 rte. de Tahiti, St-Tropez 04-94-56-76-00 airelles.com 99 rooms No Meals.*

Cheval Blanc St-Tropez

$$$$ | **HOTEL** | **FAMILY** | Perhaps the most opulent of St-Tropez's luxe hangouts, La Résidence de La Pinède—with its balustraded white villa built in 1936—has been transformed into Cheval Blanc St-Tropez, an LVMH property. **Pros:** only St-Tropez hotel with a private waterfront; three-Michelin-star restaurant; children welcome. **Cons:** insanely expensive; for the price, some rooms are small; only 30 rooms. *Rooms from: €1550 Plage de la Bouillabaisse, St-Tropez 04-94-55-91-00 www.chevalblanc.com/en/maison/st-tropez Closed Oct.–mid-May 30 rooms Free Breakfast.*

Hôtel B. Lodge

$$$ | **HOTEL** | All of the small, delicately contemporary rooms at this attractively priced, four-story charmer overlook the Citadelle's green park, some from tiny balconies. **Pros:** very good value for location; breakfast and Wi-Fi included; all rooms have air-conditioning. **Cons:** four-night minimum stay high season; two parking spots; €10 cancellation fee. *Rooms from: €250 12 rue de l'Aïoli, St-Tropez 04-94-97-06-57 www.hotel-b-lodge.com Closed 5 wks in Jan. and early Feb. 13 rooms Free Breakfast.*

★ Hôtel de Paris Saint-Tropez
$$$$ | HOTEL | When you walk into the lobby of this sleek five-star hotel, you may be too excited about the open space—a novelty at properties in this tiny fishing port—to notice the rooftop pool suspended 15 meters in the air, with its glass floor peering down at you. **Pros:** only hotel in St-Tropez with rooftop pool; unique rooftop bar with 360-degree views; free beach shuttle. **Cons:** some rooms are snug; not always American-level service; five-night minimum stay in summer. *Rooms from: €790 1 traverse de la Gendarmerie, St-Tropez 04–83–09–60–00 hoteldeparis-sainttropez.com Closed Nov.–Feb. 90 rooms No Meals.*

Le Byblos
$$$$ | HOTEL | Forget five stars—this toy Mediterranean village (grouped around courtyards landscaped with palms, olive trees, and lavender) has a "palace" classification, not to mention access to the exclusive Byblos Beach Ramatuelle. **Pros:** excellent (but exclusive) restaurant and bar; best buffet breakfast includes three-, four-, or five-minute hard-boiled egg; beach access with seaside restaurant. **Cons:** minimum four-night stay in July and August; some rooms can be noisy in summer; can be hard to get beach loungers. *Rooms from: €1095 Av. Paul-Signac, St-Tropez 04–94–56–68–00 www.byblos.com Closed late Oct.–Apr. 87 rooms No Meals.*

Lou Cagnard
$$$ | HOTEL | Ground-floor rooms at this pretty little villa with a pool open onto the flower-filled, manicured garden, where breakfast (€18) is served in the shade of a fig tree. **Pros:** walking distance to everything; free parking; accessible for those with mobility issues. **Cons:** three- and five-night minimum stays June–September; strict cancellation policy; breakfast not included. *Rooms from: €340 18 av. Paul-Roussel, St-Tropez 04–94–97–04–24 www.hotel-loucagnard.com Closed Jan.–Mar. 27 rooms No Meals.*

★ Lou Pinet
$$$$ | HOTEL | At this five-star hotel just steps from Place des Lices, the Pariente family gives you a chance to experience the real St-Tropez, away from the madness of the bling-bling crowds. **Pros:** street-food concept restaurant by Riccardo Giraudi; housekeeping twice a day; enormous pool (biggest in St-Tropez). **Cons:** breakfast eggs are extra; multinight minimum stays in high season; not on the beach. *Rooms from: €1350 70 chemin du Pinet, St-Tropez 04–94–97–04–37 www.loupinet.com Closed Oct.–Apr. 34 rooms No Meals.*

Nightlife

Le Quai Saint-Tropez
CABARET | Philippe Shangti, a model-turned-contemporary-photographer, is the artistic manager of this club in the port. The service is friendly; the cocktails and appetizers are creative; and the cabaret-style performances are live, lively, and sometimes provocative. *Quai Jean Jaurès, St-Tropez 04–94–97–04–07 www.lequaisaint-tropez.com.*

Les Caves du Roy
DANCE CLUBS | Incredibly expensive yet always packed, this kitschy disco in the Byblos Hotel is *the* place to see and be seen. When you hear the theme from *Star Wars,* take comfort while you sip your nearly €30 glass of water that someone other than yourself has just spent €25,000 on a Methuselah of Champagne. There's a horrific door policy during high season—don't worry, it's really not you. It's open every night in July and August and weekends only the rest of the year. *Av. Paul-Signac, St-Tropez 04–94–56–68–00 www.lescavesduroy.com.*

VIP Room

DANCE CLUBS | The VIP Room is notorious for drawing flashy, gilded youths with deep pockets. It opens nightly from mid-June to mid-September. ✉ *Residence du Nouveau Port, St-Tropez* ☎ *06–77–07–77–07.*

Performing Arts

Les Nuits du Château de la Moutte

CONCERTS | Every August, exceptional classical music concerts are given in the formidable gardens of the Château de la Moutte. What could be better? The new gourmet food truck and cocktail bar. You can book tickets online or by phone. ✉ *Château de la Moutte, St-Tropez* ☎ *04–94–96–96–94 for info* 🌐 *lesnuitsduchateaudelamoutte.com.*

Shopping

Where else but St-Tropez could you find Vilebrequin 24-carat-gold-embroidered Golden Turtle swim trunks from €8,000? Shopping here is pricey but, nevertheless, irresistible, and, unlike in Cannes, you'll be welcomed into the stores no matter what you look like or what you're wearing. Rue Sibilli, behind Quai Suffren, is lined with outposts of Dior, Louis Vuitton, and other designers as well as all kinds of trendy boutiques—many selling those all-important sunglasses.

ANTIQUES

La Vieille Mer

ANTIQUES & COLLECTIBLES | Unless you have a very large suitcase, you'll probably do more looking than buying at this intriguing antiques shop that specializes in navigational tools, ship lanterns, and other nautical accoutrements of yesteryear. ✉ *11 pl. de l'Ormeau, St-Tropez* ☎ *06–74–07–91–46* 🌐 *www.lavieillemer.fr.*

CLOTHING AND ACCESSORIES

Caroline Dechamby

JEWELRY & WATCHES | Dutch fashion designer and artist Caroline Dechamby hand-paints the rings and leather purses for sale at the space she shares with Carousel Fine Art. The pop artist also works with Swiss watchmakers for her limited-edition art series—in case you can't squeeze one of the paintings that are also for sale into your suitcase. ✉ *6 rue Jean Aicard, St-Tropez* ☎ *02–74–81–68–08* 🌐 *www.caroline-dechamby.com.*

Le Dépot

SECOND-HAND | This consignment store specializes in gently used clothing and accessories from the likes of Chanel, Prada, Hermès, Vuitton, and Gucci. ✉ *12 bd. Louis-Blanc, St-Tropez* ☎ *04–94–97–80–10* 🌐 *www.ledepot-saint-tropez.com.*

Rondini

SHOES | You wear those strappy sandals back home, but are they the real *sandales Tropeziennes*? Here's your chance to pick up the genuine, handmade article at Rodini, St-Tropez's original cobbler, established in 1927. ✉ *18–18 bis rue Clemenceau, St-Tropez* ☎ *04–94–97–19–55* 🌐 *www.rondini.fr.*

La Grande Braderie

La Grande Braderie (annual end-of-season sale) takes place in St-Tropez over the last weekend in October. Hit the shops Friday through Monday from 9 to 9 to look for bargains on items you couldn't afford *en haute saison*. Be prepared for lots of walking and crowds—but with merchandise at 50% off, who cares?

■ **TIP→ Trans Côte d'Azur even runs a special Nice-St-Tropez ferry just for this weekend.**

MARKETS

Fish Market

MARKET | Every morning, this picturesque little fish market opens for business in Place aux Herbes, just past the tourist office. ✉ *Pl. aux Herbes, St-Tropez.*

Place des Lices

MARKET | The aorta of the village, connecting with Rue Gambetta and Rue Allard, this square overflows with regional produce and foods, as well as clothing and *brocantes* (secondhand items), every Tuesday and Saturday morning. ✉ *St-Tropez.*

Activities

Bicycles are an ideal way to get to the beaches. If you're around at the end of September, be sure to check out Les Voiles de Saint-Tropez, one of the most extraordinary modern sailboat regattas.

Rolling Bikes

BIKING | Here you can rent e-bikes for riding around the city or mountain bikes for longer distances. Prices start at €40 for a full 24 hours. Scooter rentals are also an option. ✉ *50 av. Général-Leclerc, St-Tropez* ☎ *04–94–97–09–39* 🌐 *www.rolling-bikes.com.*

Ramatuelle

12 km (7 miles) southwest of St-Tropez.

A hilltop whorl of red-clay roofs and dense inner streets topped with arches and lined with arcades, this ancient market town was destroyed in the Wars of Religions and rebuilt as a harmonious whole in 1620. Now its souvenir shops and galleries attract day-trippers out of St-Tropez, who enjoy the pretty drive through the vineyards as much as the village itself.

In high season though, traffic jams can be spectacular between where St-Tropez ends and Ramatuelle begins, making what should be a short drive more like a three-hour crawl. From mid-June to mid-September, a daily courtesy bus (*navette*) will take you from the parking lots to the top of the village, where there are coastal panoramas from the Moulin de Paillas, a restored old-style windmill with a mechanism made entirely of wood (tours of it are offered on weekends).

The town cemetery is the final resting place of Gérard Philipe, an aristocratic heartthrob who died in 1959 after making his mark in such films as *Le Diable au Corps*. On Thursday and Sunday mornings, there's a market in Place de l'Ormeau, and the town hosts a jazz festival in mid-August.

GETTING HERE AND AROUND

By car from St-Tropez, take the inland D93, then the D61. Zou! buses also offer service from St-Tropez (€2.10).

Sights

Domaine La Tourraque

WINERY | This 100-acre winery, a highly regarded domaine producing wine since 1805, offers tastings year-round and also runs the Village Cellar in town from June through September. You can reserve a spot for the two-hour guided tour in English every Friday at 4 pm (€15). ✉ *Ch. de la Bastide Blanche, Ramatuelle* ✣ *From Ramatuelle, drive toward La Croix Valmer, then follow l'Escalet until you see signs for Domaine la Tourraque* ☎ *04–94–79–25–95* 🌐 *latourraque.fr* 🎫 *€15 for vineyard tour and wine tasting.*

Hotels

Villa Marie

$$$$ | HOTEL | With its circa-1930s feel, exposed beams, chic acid-toned walls, and jewel-tone upholstery, this Italian-villa-cum-hotel amid a 7-acre pine forest is impressive. **Pros:** gorgeous views; kid-friendly; each room has either terrace or balcony. **Cons:** open bathrooms with

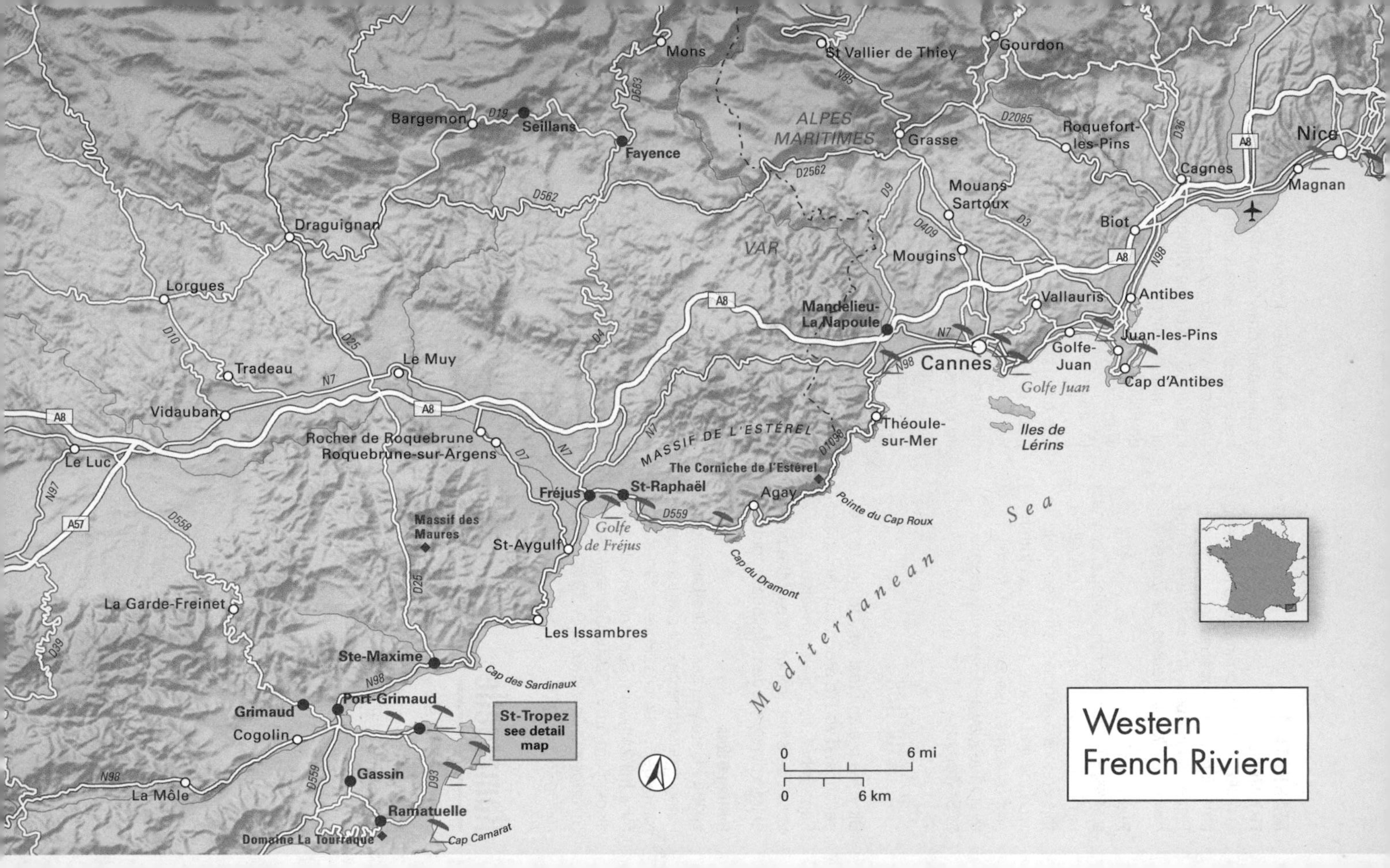
Western
French Riviera
Nice
Magnan
Cagnes
Biot
Antibes
Juan-les-Pins
Cap d'Antibes
Golfe-
Juan
Golfe Juan
Iles de
Lérins
Vallauris
Roquefort-
les-Pins
Gourdon
St Vallier de Thiey
Grasse
Mouans-
Sartoux
Mougins
Cannes
Mandelieu-
La Napoule
Théoule-
sur-Mer
ALPES
MARITIMES
VAR
MASSIF DE L'ESTÉREL
The Corniche de l'Estérel
Pointe du Cap Roux
Agay
Cap du Dramont
St-Raphaël
Fréjus
Golfe
de Fréjus
St-Aygulf
Les Issambres
Mediterranean Sea
Mons
Seillans
Bargemon
Fayence
Draguignan
Lorgues
Le Muy
Tradeau
Vidauban
Le Luc
Rocher de Roquebrune
Roquebrune-sur-Argens
Massif des
Maures
La Garde-Freinet
Ste-Maxime
Cap des Sardinaux
Grimaud
Port-Grimaud
Cogolin
Gassin
Ramatuelle
Domaine La Tourraque
Cap Camarat
La Môle
St-Tropez
see detail
map
0
6 mi
0
6 km
A8
A57
N7
N97
N98
N85
D4
D7
D9
D10
D19
D25
D36
D39
D93
D409
D558
D559
D562
D563
D1098
D2085
D2562
D3

tubs in the middle of room; hard to find; multinight minimum stays required in summer. $ *Rooms from: €900* ✉ *Ch. Val de Rian, Rte. des Plages, Ramatuelle* ☎ *04–94–97–40–22* 🌐 *en.saint-tropez.villamarie.fr* ⏲ *Closed Oct.–mid-May* 🛏 *45 rooms* 🍽 *No Meals.*

Gassin

5 km (3 miles) northwest of Ramatuelle.

Classified as one of Les Plus Beaux Villages en France (Most Beautiful Villages in France), this hilltop town has spectacular panoramas of the Massif des Maures and St-Tropez's bay. In winter, before the summer haze drifts in and after the mistral has given the sky a good scrub, you may be able to make out a brilliant-white chain of Alps on the horizon. There's also less commerce here to distract you; for shops, head to Ramatuelle.

GETTING HERE AND AROUND

From Ramatuelle, follow Chemin des Moulins de Paillas 5 km (3 miles). Otherwise, you can take a Zou! bus (€2.10).

Sights

Massif des Maures

SCENIC DRIVE | Dramatic forest scenery makes taking a drive west and northwest of St-Tropez (take the D98 toward Grimaud) along the D558 worthwhile even if you're not heading up to the A8. This is the Massif des Maures, named for the Moors who retreated here from the Battle of Poitiers in 732 and profited from its strong position over the sea. The largest forest area in the Var reaches an altitude of 2,560 feet. Some 26 villages share the Massif's borders and—amid vineyards and mushroom-shape parasol pines unique to the Mediterranean—crowd the highway (as do cyclists in spring).

The forest is dark with thick cork oaks whose ancient trunks are girdled for cork every 10 years or so, leaving exposed a broad band of sienna brown. Looming even darker and thicker above are chestnut trees, cultivated for their thick, sweet nuts, which you are not allowed to gather from the forest floor, as signs from the growers' cooperative will warn. The best place to sample *châtaignes*—whether in doughnuts, beer, or the famous *marrons glacés* (candied chestnuts)—is at the festival held every October in Collobrières, aka the chestnut capital of the world.

Grimaud

10 km (6 miles) northwest of Gassin.

Once a formidable Grimaldi fiefdom and home to a massive Romanesque château, the hill-village of Grimaud is merely charming today, though the romantic castle ruins that crown its steep streets still command lordly views over the forests and the coast. The labyrinth of cobbled streets is punctuated by pretty fountains, carved doorways, and artisans' gallery-boutiques. Wander along the Gothic arcades of the Rue des Templiers to see the beautifully proportioned Romanesque Église St-Michel, built in the 11th century.

GETTING HERE AND AROUND

From Gassin follow the D61 for about 11 km (7 miles) to the D14 and take the D98 (which also takes you to St-Tropez). Zou! Bus 876 travels here from St-Tropez (€2.10).

Restaurants

Le Magnan

$$$ | **FRENCH** | Just 10 km (6 miles) west of St-Tropez and 4 km (2½ miles) south of Grimaud and the village of La Mole, this bucolic old farmhouse restaurant sits on a hillside over forests dense with cork oak and chestnuts. Whether you eat on the terrace with its views of the Massif des Maures and Gulf of St-Tropez or in the rustic dining room, the food tastes and smells of the surrounding countryside. **Known for:** roast chicken like Maman used to make; large portions; gorgeous views. *Average main: €31* *3085 rte. de Cogolin, RN 98, Le Môle* *04–94–49–57–54* *www.lemagnan.fr* *Closed Mon.–Wed. No lunch Thurs. Closed 10 days early Nov. and 6 wks starting Jan 2.*

Port-Grimaud

6 km (10 miles) east of Grimaud.

Although much of the coast has been targeted with new construction of extraordinary ugliness, this modern architect's version of a Provençal fishing village works. A true operetta set and begun only in 1966, it has grown gracefully over the years, and offers hope for the pink-concrete-scarred coastal landscape.

It's worth parking and wandering along the village's Venice-like canals to admire its Old Mediterranean canal-tile roofs and pastel facades, already patinated with age. Even the church, though resolutely modern, feels Romanesque. There is, however, one modern touch some might appreciate: small electric tour boats (get them at Place du Marché, April through October) that you can rent without a license (€30 for 30 minutes plus €6 per adult) that can carry you and four others from bars to shops to waterfront restaurants throughout the complex of pretty squares and bridges. Market days in the square are Thursday and Sunday.

GETTING HERE AND AROUND

From Gassin, follow the D61 for about 11 km (7 miles) to the D14, and take the D98 (which also takes you to St-Tropez). Zou! Bus 876 (€2.10) runs between Grimaud and the port. From Port Grimaud, a Bateaux Verts ferry (€8.90 one-way; 30 minutes) to St-Tropez runs April to October.

Restaurants

★ La Table du Mareyeur

$$$$ | **SEAFOOD** | Ewan and Caroline Scutcher haven't left Port Grimaud since they married here nearly 36 years ago and set up this waterside gem, now considered one of the Riviera's finest restaurants. In a fun and relaxed atmosphere, they offer the freshest fish and seafood on the coast; certainly the politicians, royalty, and film stars (think Leonardo DiCaprio) who dine portside here among the locals don't complain. **Known for:** meaty oysters perfect for slurping; summertime lunch menu that's quite a deal; celebrity spotting. *Average main: €36* *10–11 pl. des Artisans, Port Grimaud* *04–94–56–06–77* *www.mareyeur.com* *Closed mid-Oct.–late Mar.*

Ste-Maxime

8 km (5 miles) northeast of Port-Grimaud; 33 km (20 miles) northeast of St-Tropez.

You may be put off by its heavily built-up waterfront, bristling with parking garage–style apartments and hotels, and its position directly on the waterfront highway, but compared to overpriced St-Tropez, Ste-Maxime is an affordable family resort with fine, easily accessible, sandy beaches. It even has a sliver of a car-free Old Town (with its only one historic monument, the Tour Carrée) and a stand of majestic plane trees sheltering the central Place Victor-Hugo. Its main beach, north of town, is the wide and sandy La Nartelle.

GETTING HERE AND AROUND

Bateaux Verts ferries connect Ste-Maxime to St-Tropez in 20 minutes (€8.40). By car, if you're coming from the A8, take Exit 36 (Le Muy) and follow the D25. From Fréjus take the RD25. From Grimaud, take the RD558. SNCF trains stop at St-Raphaël where you can connect with a Zou! bus (€2.10).

Restaurants

La Maison Bleue
$$$ | **FRENCH** | Cheerful blue-and-white-checked tablecloths, massive colorful throw cushions, and a polished wood facade give this unpretentious "blue house" on the main pedestrian street a welcoming air. You'll find straightforward fresh pasta like tagliatelle pistou and ravioli and simple grilled meat and fish dishes, accompanied by well-chosen local wines. **Known for:** magical last dinner of any vacation; friendly owner; good value €21 lunch menu. *Average main: €30* *48 rue Paul Bert, Ste-Maxime* *04-94-96-51-92* *www.facebook.com/lamaisonbleuesaintemaxime* *Closed Mon. and Tues. Apr.–June and Sept.–Nov. Closed Dec.–Mar.*

Le Bistrot de Louis
$$$ | **FRENCH** | This place checks all the French-bistro boxes—mouthwatering classic dishes, a chalkboard menu, and a setting on a cobblestone street—with the bonus of friendly service. The three-course €55 menu rounds off the experience, and there is a vegan option. **Known for:** beef Wellington with truffle sauce; accommodating service; location on a quaint pedestrian square. *Average main: €26* *9 pl. Colbert, Ste-Maxime* *04-94-44-88-27* *le-bistrot-de-louis.metro.bar* *Closed Mon. and Jan.–Mar.*

Fréjus

23 km (14 miles) northeast of Ste-Maxime, 37 km (23 miles) northeast of St-Tropez, 65 km (40 miles) southwest of Nice.

Fréjus (pronounced "fray-*zhooss*") has some of the coast's most important historic monuments. Founded in 49 BC by Julius Caesar himself and named Forum Julii, this quiet town was once a thriving Roman shipbuilding port with 40,000 citizens.

In its Roman heyday, Fréjus had a theater, baths, and an enormous aqueduct that brought water all the way from Mons in the mountains, 45 km (28 miles) north of town. Today you can see the remains: a series of detached arches that follow the main Avenue du Quinzième Corps, leading up to the Old Town, with its maze of narrow streets lined with butcher shops, patisseries, and neighborhood stores.

In July and August, the crowds roll in for the sandy beaches by day and the seaside markets by night (8 pm–midnight) as well as for fireworks (Les Nuits de Port-Fréjus) on Friday at 10:30 pm. In September, the town hosts the Giant Omelette festival.

GETTING HERE AND AROUND

By car from St-Tropez and/or Ste-Maxime, you can take the D8. If you're coming from Nice, the direct bus to Fréjus from the Nice–Côte d'Azur airport (No. 3003) takes about an hour and costs €20. By car, you are only 35 minutes from the airport on the A8 highway (Exit 38, Fréjus/St-Raphaël). You can follow the DN7 for a more scenic drive, but it takes a lot more time, particularly with summer traffic. Train travelers will pay €14.50 for the 80-minute journey from the Nice Ville station.

VISITOR INFORMATION

CONTACTS Fréjus Tourist Office. *Le Florus II, 249 rue Jean-Jaurès, Fréjus* *04-94-51-83-83* *frejus.fr.*

Sights

The Fréjus Pass (€6) is valid for seven days and gives you access to four historical landmarks and museums in the city, including those listed here, and can be purchased directly on-site.

Arènes
RUINS | The Arènes (often called the Amphithéâtre) can seat up to 5,000 and is still used for concerts and bullfights. Back down on the coast, a big French

naval base occupies the spot where ancient Roman galleys once set out to defeat Cleopatra and Mark Antony at the Battle of Actium. ✉ *Rue Henri Vadon, Fréjus* ☎ *04–94–51–83–83* 🎫 *€3* ⏲ *Closed Mon. yr-round and Sun. Oct.–Mar.*

Chapelle Cocteau (*La Chapelle Notre-Dame de Jérusalem*)

CHURCH | This eccentric chapel was the last designed by Jean Cocteau as part of an artists' colony that never happened. It's an octagon built around a glass atrium and is embellished with stained glass and frescoes depicting the mythology of the first Crusades. Above the front door, note the tongue-in-cheek painting of the apostles—it features the faces of Coco Chanel, Jean Marais, and poet Max Jacob. ✉ *Av. Nicolaï, La Tour de la Mare, Fréjus* ✣ *5 km (3 miles) north of Fréjus on RN7* ☎ *04–94–53–27–06* 🎫 *€3* ⏲ *Closed Mon. yr-round and Sun. Oct.–Mar.*

Groupe Épiscopal

CHURCH | Fréjus is graced with one of the most impressive religious monuments in Provence. The Groupe Épiscopal is made up of an early Gothic cathedral, a 5th-century Roman-style baptistery, and an early Gothic cloister, its gallery painted in sepia and earth tones with a phantasmagoric assortment of animals and biblical characters. Off the entrance and gift shop is a small museum of finds from Roman Fréjus, including a complete mosaic and a sculpture of a two-headed Hermès. ✉ *48 rue de Fleury, Fréjus* ☎ *04–94–51–26–30* 🌐 *www.cloitre-frejus.fr/en* 🎫 *Cathedral free; cloister, museum, and baptistery €6* ⏲ *Closed. Mon. Oct.–Apr.*

Théâtre Romain

RUINS | Northeast of Old Town and near the Porte de Rome is the Roman theater (circa 1st century). Its remaining rows of arches are mostly intact, and much of its stage, including the orchestra and substructures, are still visible at its center. Today, the site is known as the Théâtre Philippe Léotard (he was born in Fréjus), and it hosts Les Nuits Auréliennes every July. ✉ *Av. du Théâtre Romain, Fréjus* ☎ *04–94–51–83–83* 🎫 *Free* ⏲ *Closed Mon. yr-round and Sun. Oct.–Mar.*

Beaches

The urban beaches—Capitole, République, and Sablettes—draped at the foot of Fréjus are backed by a commercial sprawl of brasseries, beach-gear shops, and realtors (for sun-struck visitors who dream of buying an apartment on the waterfront). The beaches outside the city, however, are public and wide open, with deep sandy stretches toward St-Aygulf. The calanques just south are particularly wild and pretty, with only tiny sand surfaces. During high season, *les plages* are cleaned daily, and lifeguards are on duty.

★ Plage de la République

BEACH | This large, public sand beach, just east of the port and *capitainerie* (harbor master), is close to a restaurant where you can rent a lounger. Arrive early in the summer to claim your spot close to the sea. Note: you'll readily be able to discern the tourists from the locals, who tend to be attired in bottoms-only beach wear. **Amenities:** lifeguards; parking (fee); showers; toilets. **Best for:** sunrise; swimming. ✉ *Bd. Alger, Fréjus.*

Activities

Centre International de Plongée (*International Diving Center*)

SCUBA DIVING | Contact the Centre International de Plongée for diving instruction, equipment rental, and guided outings. ✉ *Port Fréjus, Fréjus* ☎ *04–94–52–34–99* 🌐 *cip-frejus.com.*

St-Raphaël

3 km (2 miles) east of Fréjus; 30 km (19 miles) southwest of Cannes; 68 km (42 miles) southwest of Nice.

This sprawling resort city is right next to Fréjus, with almost no division between the two communities. Along with Fréjus, it serves as a rail crossroads, the two being the closest stops to St-Tropez.

St-Raphaël's busy downtown is anchored by a casino, and although the *vieille ville* might not be the most picturesque, it nevertheless has Palladian and Belle Époque villas circa the 18th and 19th centuries (the tourist office provides a pamphlet). The port has a rich history: Napoléon landed here on his triumphant return from Egypt in 1799; it was also from here that, in 1814, he cast off in disgrace for Elba. And it was here, too, that the Allied forces landed in their August 1944 offensive against the Germans, known as the Champagne Campaign.

Today, St-Raphaël is a major sailing center, has five golf courses nearby, and draws the weary and indulgent to its seawater-based thalassotherapy.

GETTING HERE AND AROUND

There are daily buses to Fréjus (€2.10), or you can take a taxi for about €25. Popular ferries leave from St-Raphaël's Vieux Port for St-Tropez (April–October, €35 round-trip, 1 hour), as well as Îles-de-Léerins and the Calanques de l'Estérel. From St-Raphaël's bus station, next to the train station and on Avenue Victor-Hugo, Zou! Bus 876 links up with St-Tropez (via Grimaud and Ste-Maxime, €2.10, 1½ hours), as well as some towns in the Haut Var and some places along the coastal Corniche de l'Estérel. A taxi from St-Tropez to St-Raphaël will coast at least €115.

If you fly into Nice, take the airport Zou! Express 90 bus from Terminal 2, Quai 7; it's €18 for the 75-minute journey. If you take a taxi, it'll be between €145–€165 (tack on an extra €20–€30 after 6 pm). The TGV Paris–St-Raphaël (from €65 one-way, 5 hours) runs throughout the year, and there are numerous trains arriving from Nice and Cannes. St-Raphaël is the western terminus of the TER line that runs along the Riviera.

Mark Your Calendar

During Les Journées du Patrimoine (🌐 *journeesdupatrimoine.culture.gouv.fr*)—also known as European Heritage Days and usually held the third weekend in September—entrance to participating museums and sites, some of which are usually closed to the public, is free. In addition, the third Sunday in May is La Nuit des Musées (🌐 *nuitdesmusees.culture.gouv.fr*), or European Night of Museums, when museums allow free entry from 8 pm to 1 am.

VISITOR INFORMATION

CONTACTS St-Raphaël Tourist Office. ✉ *99 quai Albert 1er, St-Raphaël* ☎ *04–94–19–52–52* 🌐 *www.saint-raphael.com.*

Sights

Casino Barrière de Saint-Raphaël

CASINO | Looking out over the waterfront, catering to the city's many conventioneers, this casino has 150 slot and 30 video poker machines that operate daily 9 am–3 am (4 am on Saturday). The other games—English roulette, blackjack, and stud poker—however, don't open for play until 9 pm, and you'll need to show your passport. ✉ *Sq. de Grand, St-Raphaël* ☎ *04–98–11–17–77* 🌐 *www.casinosbarriere.com.*

Isn't this why you came to the Riviera? St-Raphaël has one of the finest beach strands along the coast.

★ The Corniche de l'Estérel

SCENIC DRIVE | FAMILY | Stay on the D559 to the D1098, and you'll find yourself careening along a stunning coastal drive, the Corniche de l'Estérel, which whips past tiny calanques and sheer rock faces that plunge down to the sea. At the dramatic Pointe de Cap Roux, an overlook allows you to pull off the narrow two-lane highway (where high-season sightseers can cause bumper-to-bumper traffic) and contemplate the spectacular view up and down the coast.

Train travelers have the good fortune to snake along this cliff side for constant panoramas. It's also a hiker's haven. Some nine trails, ranging from an hour to 4½ hours, strike out from designated parking sites along the way, leading up into the jagged rock peaks for extraordinary sea views. (Don't leave valuables in the car, as the sites are littered with glass from break-ins.) You can download trail maps from the St-Raphaël tourism website or drop by the tourist office across from the train station. There is also a coastal path leaving from St-Raphaël port; you'll see a mix of wild, rocky *criques* (coves and finger bays) and glamorous villas.

Église Notre-Dame-de-la-Victoire

CHURCH | Augmenting the Atlantic City vibe of this modern pleasure port is the gingerbread-and-gilt dome of the neo-Byzantine Église Notre-Dame-de-la-Victoire, which watches over the yachts and cruise boats gliding into the port. ✉ *Bd. Félix-Martin and 19 rue Jean Aicard, St-Raphaël.*

Église San Rafeu

CHURCH | Next to the Museum of Archeology in the vieille ville (Old Town), the 12th-century Église San Rafeu (also known as Église St-Pierre-des-Templiers) is a miniature-scale Romanesque church. It was recently discovered that its foundations lie on top of two other churches dating from the Carolingian era (AD 800–888). Climb up the 129 steps of the 13th-century bell tower, the Tour San Rafeu, for 360-degree panoramic views, and snap away. ✉ *Rue des Templiers, St-Raphaël.*

Musée Archéologique Marin (*Marine Archaeology Museum*)
HISTORY MUSEUM | On the same quiet square as Église San Rafeu, this intimate museum has a fascinating collection of ancient amphorae gleaned from the shoals offshore, where centuries' worth of shipwrecks have accumulated. By studying this chronological progression of jars and the accompanying sketches, you can visualize the coast as it was in its heyday as a Greek and Roman shipping center. Take advantage of the temporary exhibitions held throughout the year (€4). ✉ *Rue des Templiers, St-Raphaël* ☎ *04–94–19–25–75* 🌐 *www.ville-saintraphael.fr* 🎫 *Free* 🕒 *Closed Sun. and Mon. Other hrs vary throughout the year.*

Beaches

St-Raphaël's beaches form a snaking sliver of sand, starting just east of the port and finally petering out against the red cliffs of the Estérel. Collectively, they cover 8 km (5 miles) toward St-Aygulf and include one of the Eastern Var's largest sandy beaches, which is surrounded by a dune. Here you'll find a nudist beach (June–September) and an area where dogs on leashes are permitted. From that point on, you can find tiny calanques and criques for swimming and basking on the rocks.

In high season, beaches are cleaned daily, and lifeguards are on duty at Plage du Veillat, Beau-Rivage, Péguière, Plage du Débarquement, Plage d'Agay, and Plage du Lido. Flags indicate the presence of lifeguards or if the water is too dangerous for swimming.

■ TIP→ To discover the secrets of sites along the shoreline, download the app Piste et Trésor in English and select the game "Saint-Raphaël," a cultural treasure hunt that takes about half a day.

★ Plage Beau-Rivage
BEACH | FAMILY | This is the second public beach in the city center, located between Veillat beach and the port of Santa Lucia. It's divided into two areas, the sandy Handiplage and a large stone pebble beach, and there is a beautiful promenade, shaded by a park with a playground and mini golf. There are showers and toilets, but you can't rent a lounger here. **Amenities:** lifeguards; showers; toilets. **Best for:** sunset; swimming; walking. ✉ *120 bd. Raymond Poincaré, St-Raphaël.*

Plage du Débarquement
BEACH | Named after the Allied landings in August 1944, this is a sand-on-top-of-red-stone beach with great views of the private Île d'Or. From town, head toward Agay until Dramont, where you'll see signs for the pebble beach. **Amenities:** lifeguards; parking (no fee); toilets. **Best for:** swimming. ✉ *1300 bd. de la 36ème Division du Texas, St-Raphaël.*

Plage du Veillat
BEACH | FAMILY | This is the city's main (and its largest) sandy beach, with access for people with disabilities and lifeguard stations during the summer season, when you can also rent a mattress. There are lots of cafés around, and from the Old Port you can take a shuttle to St-Tropez. **Amenities:** lifeguards; parking (fee); showers; toilets. **Best for:** sunset; swimming; walking. ✉ *Corniche Roland Garros and Promenade René Coty, St-Raphaël.*

Restaurants

Récif
$$$$ | FRENCH | This retro restaurant opened when luxe hotel Les Roches Rouges was transformed by French hotelier Valéry Grégo, and it has since picked up one Michelin star. The dinner-only menu is dedicated to gastronomic yet inventive regional dishes, which head chef José Bailly bases on *La Cuisine Provençale de la Tradition*

Populaire, a 1963 cookbook of traditional recipes by René Jouveau. **Known for:** three- and five-course tasting menus only; spectacular seaside setting; hotel guests aren't guaranteed restaurant reservations. *Average main: €128* ✉ *90 bd. de la 36ème-Division-du-Texas, St-Raphaël* ☎ *04–89–81–40–60* 🌐 *www.hotellesrochesrouges.com/en* ⏲ *Closed Mon. and Tues. and Oct.–mid-May.*

Hotels

Excelsior

$$ | **HOTEL** | This urban and friendly hotel combining straightforward comforts and a location on the waterfront in the center of town attracts a regular clientele. **Pros:** minutes from the sea; decent-size rooms; 18 rooms are sea-facing. **Cons:** 30% deposit at time of booking; €14/day public parking; early church bells ring from nearby. *Rooms from: €189* ✉ *Promenade du René Coty, St-Raphaël* ☎ *04–94–95–02–42* 🌐 *www.excelsior-hotel.com* *32 rooms* *No Meals.*

Hôtel Thimothée

$ | **B&B/INN** | This attractive 19th-century villa seems worthy of more than just a two-star rating thanks to well-priced, comfortable rooms and a lovely garden, where grand palms and pines shade a walk leading to the pretty little swimming pool. **Pros:** free parking and free bikes; modern bathrooms; sea-view rooms on top floor worth extra €30. **Cons:** beach and waterfront cafés are a 20-minute walk away; standard rooms are on the small side; reception open only 3:30 pm–8 pm. *Rooms from: €110* ✉ *375 bd. Christian-Lafon, St-Raphaël* ☎ *04–94–40–49–49* 🌐 *www.hotel-thimothee.com* *12 rooms* *No Meals.*

Activities

St-Raphaël is a serious sailing and boating center, with nautical complexes at four different sites along the coast: the Vieux Port, Santa Lucia (by Fréjus-Plage), Le Dramont (at the base of a dramatic little cape below the Estérel), and within Agay's quiet harbor.

To explore the wilds of the Estérel on foot, consider a guided hike led by a qualified staffer from the tourist office.

Club Nautique St-Raphaël

BOATING | For information on boat rentals or sailing lessons, contact this club, founded in 1927. ✉ *26 pl. du Club Nautique, St-Raphaël* ☎ *04–94–95–11–66* 🌐 *www.cnsr.fr.*

France Bike Rentals

BIKING | Canadian Paul Erickson inspired this bike rental company, providing practical info in English to enthusiasts who want to explore the region on two wheels. Rent a bike for your Ironman event or an e-bike by the day or longer (there's a three-day minimum in July) from €55 per day. Rates include saddle bag with tire-repair kit, pump, and helmets, and delivery and pickup can be arranged for an additional fee. ✉ *1387 av. du Gratadis, St-Raphaël* 🌐 *www.francebikerentals.com.*

Golf de Cap Estérel

GOLF | The spectacularly sited 9-hole Golf de Cap Estérel hovers directly over the sea behind Agay. ✉ *RN 98, Agay* ☎ *04–94–82–55–00.*

Mandelieu–La Napoule

32 km (20 miles) northeast of St-Raphaël; 8 km (5 miles) southwest of Cannes; 37 km (23 miles) southwest of Nice.

La Napoule is the small, old-fashioned port village, Mandelieu the big-fish resort town that devoured it. Mandelieu is replete with many sporting facilities and hosts a bevy of sporting events, including sailing regattas, windsurfing contests, and golf championships (there are two major golf courses right in the center of town, by the sea). A yacht-crammed harbor sits under the shadow of some high-rise resort hotels.

La Napoule, on the other hand, offers the requisite quaintness, ideal for a portside stroll, casual meal, beach siesta, or visit to its peculiar castle. Unless you're here for the sun and surf, however, these twinned towns mostly serve as a base for outings to Cannes, Antibes, and the Estérel. In fact, the easternmost beach in Mandelieu dovetails with the first and most democratic beaches of its glamorous neighbor, Cannes.

GETTING HERE AND AROUND

From Terminal 1 or 2 at Nice airport, take the A8 to Exit 40 (about 30 minutes) or from T2 take the 35-minute No. 90 airport bus (direction St-Raphaël, €9). The closest train station is in Cannes, and you can either take a taxi (about €30 to the city center during the day) or catch Bus 22 from Cannes train station, departing frequently throughout the day, for €1.50. It sets you down at "Balcon d'Azur," just past the château.

VISITOR INFORMATION

CONTACTS Mandelieu–La Napoule Tourist Office. ✉ *806 av. de Cannes, Mandelieu-la-Napoule* ☎ *04–93–93–64–64* 🌐 *www.mandelieu-tourisme.com.*

Sights

Château de la Napoule

CASTLE/PALACE | FAMILY | Looming over the sea at Pointe des Pendus (Hanged Man's Point), the Château de la Napoule is a spectacularly bizarre hybrid of Romanesque, Gothic, Moroccan, and Hollywood styles cooked up by the eccentric American sculptor Henry Clews (1876–1937). Working with his architect wife, Clews transformed the 14th-century bastion into something that suited his personal tastes and then filled the place with his own fantastical sculptures. The couple reside in their tombs in the tower crypt, its windows left slightly ajar to permit their souls to escape and allow them to "return at eventide as sprites and dance upon the windowsill." Today the château's foundation hosts visiting writers and artists, who set to work surrounded by Clews's gargoyle-ish sculptures. ✉ *Av. Henry Clews, Mandelieu-la-Napoule* ☎ *04–93–49–95–05* 🌐 *www.lnaf.org* 🎟 *From €7* 🕒 *Closed Mon. and Tues.*

Beaches

There are private beaches nestled in between the seven public beaches, the major difference between public and private being, as it always is, a question of comfort. You can spend the extra euros for a comfortable mattress, access to shade, and the convenience of a nearby restaurant. On the public beach you have to supply your own comforts.

■ TIP→ Beach parking is free in lots when you put a "blue disc" in the windshield. These are available from the tourist office. Also, in July and August, there are two free shuttles, including the Mimoplage, which takes you from the center of town to the beaches.

Plage du Sable d'Or

BEACH | Situated between the casino and Cannes la Bocca, this public sand beach is one of the most beautiful in Mandelieu. There are restaurants and a nautical center nearby, as well as lifeguards on duty. If the views of the Îles de Lérins grow old, head to the neighboring Robinson beach and play some volleyball. **Amenities:** food and drink; lifeguards; showers; toilets. **Best for:** swimming. ✉ *Av. Général-de-Gaulle, Mandelieu-la-Napoule.*

Restaurants

Le Boucanier

$$$ | SEAFOOD | Years ago, former French pro soccer player Wilfrid Gohel teamed up with Eric Chaumier, president of the regional retailers union, and took over this waterfront favorite. They could have just banked on the wraparound views of the marina and château to bring in the dinner crowds, but instead they refined the menu to include grilled bass with smoked salt petals and salmon marinated with pure malt whiskey and sautéed with matcha tea velouté sauce. **Known for:** good value €49 three-course menu; incredible views; vegan, pasta, and kids' options. *Average main: €27 Port de La Napoule, 273 av. Henry Clews, Mandelieu-la-Napoule 04–93–49–80–51 boucanier.fr Closed Mon. Oct.–Mar. No dinner Sun. Oct.–Mar.*

Hotels

Pullman Cannes Mandelieu Royal Casino
$$$ | **HOTEL** | As much a resort as a hotel, this modern waterfront complex with soundproofed rooms has deluxe comforts on a grand scale, with a broad beach terrace, outdoor (unheated) pool, fit lounge, casino, restaurant, and access to the Old Course golf club next door. **Pros:** loungers on the private sand beach; free welcome tray with complimentary half bottles of water replaced daily; beautiful pool. **Cons:** €30 for a taxi to La Croisette in Cannes; not close to any shops; on-site casino open until 4 am, which can mean late-night noise. *Rooms from: €300 605 av. Général-de-Gaulle, Mandelieu-la-Napoule 04–92–97–70–00 www.pullman-mandelieu.com 213 rooms No Meals.*

Activities

Classified as a *station voile* (sailing resort), Mandelieu–La Napoule is a major water-sports center.

Centre Nautique Municipal
BOATING | Small sailboats and windsurfers can be rented from Centre Nautique Municipal, next to the restaurant La Plage. It's open daily year-round. *Av. du Général de Gaulle, Mandelieu-la-Napoule 04–92–97–30–77 www.mandelieu.fr.*

Golf Club de Cannes-Mandelieu
GOLF | Grand Duke Michael of Russia founded the Riviera's first golf course in 1891, known familiarly as the Old Course, and it's been played by all of Europe's royals. Officially it's the International Golf Club Cannes-Mandelieu and has two courses, which are the most visually stunning courses in the south of France. The 18-hole course is shaded by old pine trees and features a ferry across the Slagne River from hole 2 to 3 and again from hole 12 to 13. *Rte. du Golf, Mandelieu-la-Napoule 04–92–97–32–00 www.golfoldcourse.com 18-hole course: €110 (€75 afternoons, hour varies). 9-hole course: €30 18 holes, 6287 yards, par 71; 9 holes, 2316 yards, par 33.*

Fayence

36 km (23 miles) northwest of Mandelieu–La Napoule; 30 km (19 miles) northwest of Cannes; 66 km (41 miles) northwest of Nice.

The most touristy of all the hill towns in the Haut Var backcountry (all of which are called Pays de Fayence), Fayence is easiest to reach from the coast and often filled with busloads of day-trippers. Nonetheless, it has a pretty Old Town at the top, magnificent wraparound views from its 18th-century church down to the Massif des Maures and the Estérel, and a plethora of artisans' galleries and boutiques.

The Four du Mitan museum, where you'll see the original village oven built in 1522, is free to visit and open every day. Fayence is also home to Europe's best gliding club (you can eat at its restaurant) and Pickleball France-Pays-de-Fayence, which has some English-speaking members. Stop by on a Saturday morning near the municipal outdoor sports club, and you can pay a drop-in fee and rent a paddle to get your fix.

GETTING HERE AND AROUND

There are no trains, but Bus 832 travels daily from Cannes (€2.10; 1 hour 20 minutes). It's an hour's drive from Nice airport—take Exit 39 (Fayence/Les Adrets) from the A8. A taxi to/from the airport will cost around €120 (count on more at night).

VISITOR INFORMATION

CONTACTS Fayence Tourist Office. ✉ *Pl. Léon-Roux, Fayence* ☎ *04–94–76–01–02* 🌐 *www.paysdefayence.com.*

Restaurants

Le Temps des Cerises
$$$ | **FRENCH** | You'll find your *bonheur* (happiness) in this popular and centrally located gem of Dutch owner-chef Lodewijk Schröder. From a hearty black Angus steak to a mouthwatering chicken vol-au-vent, the selection is classic French gastronomy (so definitely not vegan or vegetarian-friendly). **Known for:** consistently high-quality meals; homemade ice cream and sorbets; lovely terrace atmosphere on a slightly noisy road. 💲 *Average main: €27* ✉ *2 pl. de la République, Fayence* ☎ *04–94–76–01–19* 🌐 *www.restaurantletempsdescerises.fr* ⏲ *Closed Tues. and Wed.*

Hotels

Moulin de la Camandoule
$$ | **HOTEL** | On 11 acres of streamside greenery, this noble old olive mill has been turned into a lovely country inn—complete with beams, the original millwheel, and a *pressoir* (olive press) in the middle of the bar. **Pros:** gorgeous viney grounds and massive pool; minutes from village; excellent restaurant. **Cons:** arrivals after 6 pm with permission; three-night minimum stay June–September; 25% minimum deposit, full amount paid on arrival. 💲 *Rooms from: €146* ✉ *159 chemin de Notre Dame, Fayence* ☎ *04–94–76–00–84* 🌐 *www.camandoule.com* *11 rooms* *No Meals.*

★ Terre Blanche
$$$$ | **RESORT** | **FAMILY** | Nestled in the countryside, this resort is larger than Monaco and comes with an impressive roster of amenities—four pools, two world-class 18-hole golf courses, a two-story spa, and four restaurants including Michelin-starred Le Feventia. **Pros:** wine cellar with 400 different local Provençal labels; free tea/coffee in suites, sunscreen, and driving range with unlimited balls; kids' club with themes of biodiversity. **Cons:** need car to get here; not all rates include breakfast; visitors tend to stay in the resort and not explore the rest of the countryside. 💲 *Rooms from: €860* ✉ *3100 rte. de Bagnols en Fôret, Tourrettes* ☎ *04–94–39–90–00* 🌐 *en.terre-blanche.com* *115 rooms* *No Meals.*

Seillans

8 km (5 miles) northwest of Fayence; 45 km (28 miles) northwest of Cannes.

Voted one of "France's most beautiful villages" with its ruined château and ramparts, fountains, flowers, and sunny maze of steeply raked cobblestone streets that suddenly break open over valley views, this is an appealing Old Town that still smacks of yesteryear's Côte d'Azur. Its church, a Renaissance remake of an 11th-century structure, is the best spot from which to admire the panorama; it's worth a pause to take in the musty Latin atmosphere.

There are old-style, competitive bakers here, and an active café life on a miniature scale. The French opera composer Gounod and the surrealist Max Ernst were regulars in Seillans—Ernst retired here. Year-round guided tours (from €3; 60 minutes) of the town in English and French start from the tourist office at 10, but you need to reserve a few days in advance (five-person minimum per tour).

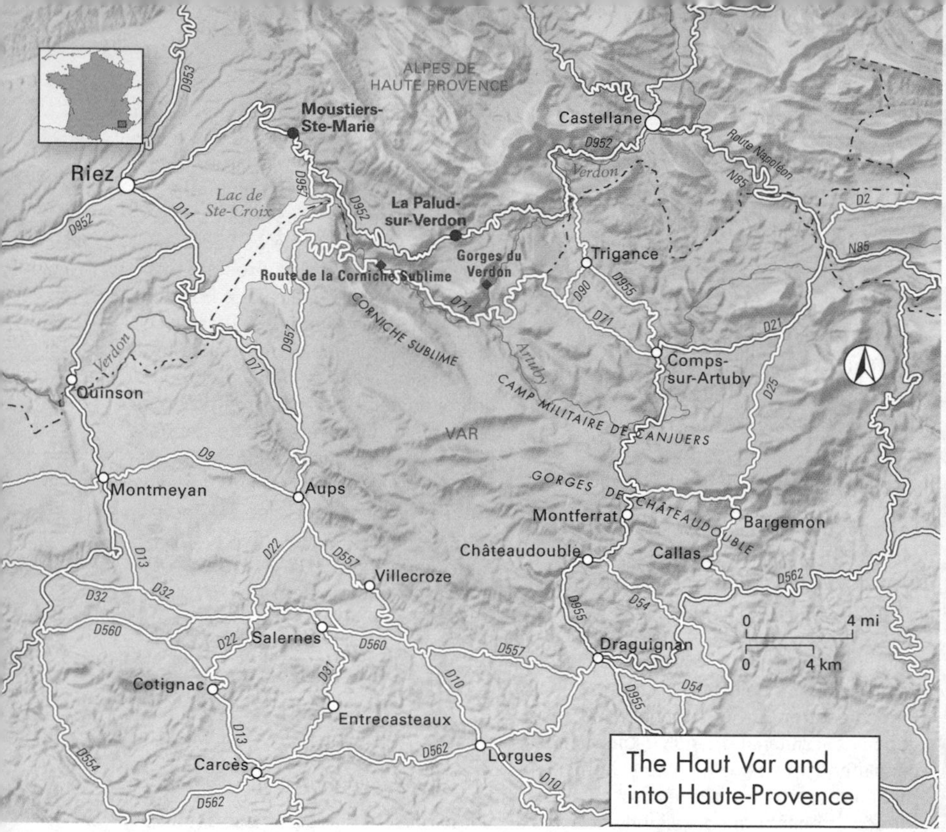

The Haut Var and into Haute-Provence

The Festival Musique Cordiale (🌐 *www.musique-cordiale.com*) takes place over the first two weeks of August at locations such as Chapelle Notre-Dame de l'Ormeau and the 11th-century Église St-Léger, as well as in neighboring villages.

GETTING HERE AND AROUND

From the A8 highway, take Exit 39 (Fayence) and follow the D37/Route du Lac to the D562, then follow the D19 into town. There are a few Zou! buses (€2.10) that can get you here from Cannes and even St-Raphaël.

VISITOR INFORMATION

CONTACTS Seillans Tourist Information Office. ✉ *Waldberg House, Place du Thouron, Seillans* ☎ *04–94–76–01–02* 🌐 *www.paysdefayence.com.*

Sights

Notre-Dame-de-l'Ormeau

CHURCH | Just east of town on the Route de Fayence is the Romanesque chapel Notre-Dame-de-l'Ormeau, which contains a remarkable altarpiece dating from the 16th century. Sculpted portraits of the wise men and shepherds adoring the Christ child, strikingly real in emotion and gesture, contrast sharply with the simple ex-votos that pepper the walls. Guided visits (€5) take place throughout the year on Thursday at 4:30; you need to reserve with the tourist office (five-person minimum). ✉ *Maison Waldberg, Pl. du Thouron, Seillans* ☎ *04–94–76–01–02.*

The 21-km (13-mile) Gorges du Verdon was carved out of solid rock by the fast-flowing Verdon River millennia ago.

Hotels

Hôtel des Deux Rocs

$ | HOTEL | This property exudes Provençal style, with its tiny square with a trickling fountain, venerable plane trees, green valley views, and two massive imposing rocks (and that's just on the outside). **Pros:** old stone house with modern quirky interiors; free Wi-Fi and parking; romantic restaurant. **Cons:** no air-conditioning; damp in wet weather; in need of some renovations. *Rooms from: €90* *Pl. Font d'Amont, Seillans* *04–94–76–87–32* *maisonsmalzac.com* *Closed mid-Nov.–mid-Mar.* *14 rooms* *No Meals.*

La Palud-sur-Verdon

48 km (30 miles) northwest of Seillans.

Though several towns bill themselves as *the* gateway to the Gorges du Verdon, this unassuming village stands in its center, on a plateau just north of the gorge's vertiginous drop (to gain the Gorges's southern flank, enter from the elegant village of Moustiers). It's a hikers' and climbers' town, and—as the Germans and Dutch are more *sportif* than the French—has an international feel. You'll see more beards and Volkswagen vans here than anywhere in France, and you'll probably share a café terrace with backpackers clad in boots and fleece easing off a load of ropes, picks, and cleats.

GETTING HERE AND AROUND

Coming by car (your best option) from the coast, take the A8 highway, get off at the Draguignan exit, then follow the D955 north(ish) past Comps-sur-Artuby to the D952, which you can follow west along a demanding drive—keep your eyes on the road.

VISITOR INFORMATION

CONTACTS Maison des Gorges du Verdon. *Le Château, La Palud-sur-Verdon* *04–92–77–32–02* *www.lapaludsur-verdon.com.* **Maison des Guides du Verdon.** *Rue Principale, La Palud-sur-Verdon* *04–92–77–30–50* *www.escalade-verdon.fr.*

Sights

★ Gorges du Verdon

NATURE SIGHT | FAMILY | You are here for one reason only: to explore the extraordinary Gorges du Verdon, also known as—with only slight exaggeration over another, more famous version—the Grand Canyon. Through the aeons, the jewel-green torrent of the Verdon River has chiseled away the limestone plateau and gouged a spectacular gorge lined with steep white cliffs and sloping rock falls carpeted with green forest. The jagged bluffs, roaring water, and dense wild boxwood create a savage world of genuinely awe-inspiring beauty, whether viewed from dozens of cliff-top overlooks or explored from the wilderness below.

If you're driving from La Palud, follow the dramatic Route des Crêtes circuit (D23), a white-knuckle cliff-hanger not for the faint of heart. When you approach and leave La Palud, you'll do it via D952 between Castellane and Moustiers, with several breathtaking overlooks. The best of these is the Point Sublime, at the east end. Leave your car by the hotel-restaurant and walk to the edge, holding tight to dogs and children—that's a 2,834-foot drop to the bottom. You can also access the famous drive along D71, called the Route de la Corniche Sublime, from Moustiers. Top lookout points here are the Horserider's Cliff, the Balcon de la Mescla, and the Pont de l'Artuby bridge.

Several trails converge in this prime hiking territory. The most spectacular is the branch of the GR4 that follows the bed of the canyon itself, along the Sentier Martel. This dramatic trek, beginning at the Chalet de la Maline and ending at the Point Sublime, was created in the 1930s by the Touring-Club de France and named for one of the gorge's first explorers. Easier circuits leave from the Point Sublime on *sentiers de découverte* (trails with commentary) into the gorge known as Couloir Samson.

Hotels

Hotel des Gorges du Verdon

$$$ | HOTEL | FAMILY | Set at an altitude of 3,000 feet, this four-star Châteaux & Hôtels Collection escape has breathtaking panoramas of La Palud's countryside from the breakfast table, plus plenty of activities for non-hikers. **Pros:** Ping-Pong table, boules, tennis, and heated pool; excellent Cinq Mondes spa; botanical garden. **Cons:** some rooms are small; pricey menu but food is tasty; expensive compared to other local accommodations. *Rooms from: €300* *Rte. de la Maline, La Palud-sur-Verdon* *04–92–77–38–26* *www.hotel-des-gorges-du-verdon.fr* *Closed mid-Oct.–Easter* *30 rooms* *No Meals.*

Le Perroquet Vert

$ | B&B/INN | FAMILY | In a restored 18th-century house on La Palud's only street, this lovely little complex with a B&B, restaurant, and a sports store is run by charming owners. **Pros:** fine bargain prices include free Wi-Fi; free tea and coffee in common area; tasty home-cooked meals. **Cons:** no TV in rooms; free parking is more than 300 feet away in the village; early 10 am checkout, late check-in. *Rooms from: €65* *Rue Grande, La Palud-sur-Verdon* *04–92–77–33–39* *www.leperroquetvert.com* *Closed mid-Nov.–mid-Mar.* *4 rooms* *No Meals.*

Activities

If you're not up to hiking the Sentier Martel, there are other ways to experience the Gorges.

Aboard Rafting

WHITE-WATER RAFTING | FAMILY | Rafting excursions in the Gorges du Verdon run from two to five-plus hours (€50–€80). You can also try canoe-rafting or canyoning, and, for younger members of the family, there's the Adventure Rope Course (€12; 90 minutes). Meeting

The Sentier Martel: Trial by Trail

The Main Show

Threading the Grand Canyon du Verdon is one of France's greatest hiking routes: the Sentier Martel, named in honor of the spelunker-explorer Edouard Martel (1859–1938), who first penetrated the Gorges in 1896 with a canvas canoe, an assistant, and two local trout fishermen. Despite repeated attempts, he didn't manage to negotiate the full canyon's length until 1905.

It was in the 1930s that the Touring Club blasted fire escape–style ladders and catwalks along the precarious rock walls, and drilled two tunnels through solid stone. They added occasional rope railings and steps, buttressed the trail with rock supports, and one of France's most famous hikes was born.

Martel Musts

It's best to depart from the Châlet de la Maline (the Refuge des Malines), striking out on the long descent and then working your way back up gradually to the Couloir du Samson and the Point Sublime (D952). Park your car past the refuge and canteen, 8 km (5 miles) from La Palud-sur-Verdon, and walk 300 yards to the starting point of your descent, just left of the Refuge des Malines. Follow the white and red markings along the way (an X indicates the wrong path; an arrow indicates a change in direction).

You'll encounter all types of terrain—pebbles, stone, muddy soil—and sliding down rocks on your buttocks is a possibility, especially when the alternative is tumbling down, down, and down. Forget about setting a world record, and stop to enjoy lunch along the way so that you can take your eyes off your feet and appreciate the magnificent surroundings. Once you exit the tunnels and cross a small bridge, you'll reach the Parking du Couloir Samson, but even this is not the final destination. Cross the pavement and continue left to finish the ascent to Point Sublime. Markings here are not as visible but paths are solid soil, and you will eventually make it to the top, a rugged terrain where the less daring stop to simply take photos. Have the €3 ready for a nice cold beverage at the only canteen.

Words of Warning

As the Verdon is regulated by two dams, you'll often be confronted with not-so-comforting signs showing a human stick figure running for his life before a tidal wave. This is to warn you to stick to the trail and not linger on the beachlike riverbed when the water is low, as it could rise suddenly at any moment. Bring a flashlight with good batteries; you won't be able to grope your way through the tunnels without it. And be prepared for wet feet—ankle-deep puddles are unavoidable. Dial 112 if you have an emergency.

⚠ In 2022, a lack of water led to a "historic hydrological situation" in the Gorges du Verdon, and rafting and swimming were banned.

Where to Park?

A taxi pickup at Point Sublime must be arranged the previous night for the roughly 14-km (9-mile) return ride. Alternatively, leave a car at the final destination, and ask a taxi (in advance) to transport you to your takeoff point. The best companies are **Taxi Verdun** (☎ *06–81–95–26–98*) and **Taxi de l'Étoile** (☎ *06–07–37–33–78*).

points vary, but many excursions start from Adventure Forest near Castellane. ✉ *Rte. de Moustiers D 952, Castellane* ☎ *04–92–83–76–11* 🌐 *www.rafting-verdon.com.*

La Maison du Canyoning et de l'Escalade
MOUNTAIN CLIMBING | FAMILY | Want to try canyoneering or climbing? Contact La Maison du Canyoning et de l'Escalade May–September for guided outings, varying from 90 minutes (€45) to full-day 5½ hour excursions (€85). The minimum age for participation is six for an introduction to climbing outing; you may be asked to bring lunch. ✉ *1 Pl. de l'Église, Castellane* ☎ *07–85–55–15–30* 🌐 *www.maisondu-canyoning.fr.*

Provisto
BUS TOURS | FAMILY | Leave the hassle of driving these hair-raising roads to someone else. Provisto gives a four-hour minibus tour of the region for up to eight people. ☎ *06–82–93–88–72* 🌐 *provisito.fr.*

Moustiers-Ste-Marie

10 km (7 miles) northwest of La Palud-sur-Verdon.

At the edge of epic wilderness, it's a bit of a shock to find this picture-perfect village of 700 residents tucked into a spectacular cleft in vertical cliffs, its bluffs laced with bridges, draped with medieval stone houses, and crowned with church steeples. The Verdon River gushes out of the rock at the village's heart, and between the two massive rocks that tower over the ensemble, a star swings suspended from a chain.

To most, the name "Moustiers" means faience, the fine, glazed earthenware that has been produced here since the 17th century, when a monk brought in the secret of enamel glazes from Faenza in Umbria. Its brilliant white finish caught the world's fancy, especially when the fashionable grotesques of Jean Berain, decorator to Louis XIV, were imitated and produced in exquisite detail. A colony of ceramists—from large commercial producers to independent artisans—still creates Moustiers faience.

More than 20,000 olive trees grow on the dry stone of Claux hill, so be sure to look for Moustiers olive oil at the Friday morning market, where you'll also find local delicacies like tapenade, handmade cookies, and lavender honey. The town is quite keen to promote French lavender, which is actually a hybrid called lavendin created for the perfume industry a century ago. The community's LavandEvasion event, which includes tours on bike, foot, and hot-air balloon, lets you experience lavender in bloom on the Valensole Plateau, about 30 minutes away. You can also visit the local lavender farm overlooking Sainte-Croix Lake.

If you're in town on Tuesday in spring or fall, 90-minute tours in English (€10–€15) start at 10:30 am, but you need to reserve in advance at the tourist office.

GETTING HERE AND AROUND

There is no shuttle up to the village, so a car is your best bet. From the Côte d'Azur take the A8 highway, exit direction "Draguignan," then "Aups, Les Salles" to Moustiers, found just off D952 (a 90-minute drive from Fréjus). Zou! Bus 51 runs from Nice to Castellane and connects with Zou! Bus 450 to Moustiers (€2.10; 90 minutes).

VISITOR INFORMATION

CONTACTS Moustiers Tourist Office. ✉ *Maison de Lucie, Pl. de l'Église, Moustiers-Sainte-Marie* ☎ *04–92–74–67–84* 🌐 *www.moustiers.fr/en.*

For centuries, the town of Moustiers-Ste-Marie has been known for its fine faience ceramics.

Sights

Chapelle Notre-Dame-de-Beauvoir

CHURCH | Moustiers was founded as a monastery in the 5th century, but it was in the Middle Ages that the Chapelle Notre-Dame-de-Beauvoir (first known as d'Entreroches, or "between rocks") became an important pilgrimage site. You can still climb the steep cobbled switchbacks along with pilgrims, passing modern stations-of-the-cross panels in Moustiers faience. From the porch of the 12th-century church, remodeled in the 16th century, you can look over the roofs of the village to the green valley, a patchwork of olive groves and red-tiled farmhouse roofs. The forerunner of the star that swings in the wind over the village was first hung, it is said, by a crusader grateful for his release from Saracen prison. It takes about 20 minutes to climb the 262 steps, but remember, what goes up must come down—these worn stone steps yield little traction, so be careful. ✉ *Moustiers-Sainte-Marie.*

Musée de la Faïence

OTHER MUSEUM | The small but excellent Musée de la Faïence has concise audiovisual explanations of the craft and displays a chronology of fine pieces. It is housed in a pretty 18th-century *hôtel particulier* (private mansion) with a lovely *salle de mariage* (wedding hall) lined in painted canvas. ✉ *Pl. du Tricentenaire, Rue du Seigneur de la Clue, Moustiers-Sainte-Marie* ☎ *04–92–74–61–64* 🌐 *musee-moustiers.fr* 🎫 *€5* 🕓 *Closed Tues. Closed Jan.–Mar. and weekdays Nov.*

Route de la Corniche Sublime

SCENIC DRIVE | Despite its civilized airs, Moustiers is another gateway to the Gorges du Verdon, providing the best access to the southern bank and the famous drive along D71 called the Route de la Corniche Sublime. (There's also the scenic 23-km [14-mile] route along the northern ridge, Route des Crêtes along the D23, which starts at Castellane and has no fewer than 14 viewpoints that cut through the ridges of the canyon.)

Breathtaking views over withering drop-offs punctuate this vertiginous road just wide enough for two cars if you all hold your breath. The best of the vistas is called the Balcons de la Mescla, with viewpoints built into the cliff face overlooking the torrential whirlpool where the Verdon and Artuby combine. ✉ *Moustiers-Sainte-Marie.*

Hotels

Hôtel les Restanques

$ | HOTEL | Only a 10-minute walk from the village, this motel-style property offers excellent value and has tidy, spacious rooms, some of which open onto a terrace and garden. **Pros:** spacious rooms; lovely view from the pool; free parking and Wi-Fi. **Cons:** rooms facing the pool can get noisy; any cancellation forfeits deposit; no minibar in room. *$ Rooms from: €120* ✉ *Rte. des Gorges du Verdon, D952, Moustiers-Sainte-Marie* ☎ *04–92–74–93–93* 🌐 *www.hotel-les-restanques.com* ⏲ *Closed Nov. 15–Mar. 15* *20 rooms* *No Meals.*

★ La Bastide de Moustiers

$$$ | HOTEL | Gourmands from around the world flock to this lovely 17th-century bastide, transformed by Alain Ducasse, who had 21 Michelin stars to his name in 2023, into a luxury country retreat surrounded by olive and chestnut trees, lavender, and trellises filled with the blooms of rose bushes. **Pros:** outstanding restaurant; peace and quiet with exceptional natural lighting; gorgeous, nature-heavy decor. **Cons:** not really walking distance of village; rooms can feel a tad cramped; set menus at restaurant start at €95. *$ Rooms from: €350* ✉ *Chemin de Quinson, Moustiers-Sainte-Marie* ☎ *04–92–70–47–47* 🌐 *www.bastide-moustiers.com* ⏲ *Closed Nov.–Mar.* *13 rooms* *No Meals.*

Shopping

L'Atelier Soleil

CERAMICS | At this shop next to the Bastide de Moustiers, second-generation potter Franck Scherer custom-makes plates for Alain Ducasse's auberges. You can visit the workshop and buy pieces with tiny flaws at a reduced price. ✉ *Chemin de Quinson, Moustiers-Sainte-Marie* ☎ *04–92–74–61–62* 🌐 *www.soleil-deux.com.*

Le Souquet

FOOD | Stock up here on local olive oils, local food specialties, and cork crafts. ✉ *Rue Marcel Provence, Moustiers-Sainte-Marie* ☎ *06–82–68–84–55.*

Chapter 7

NICE AND THE EASTERN FRENCH RIVIERA

Updated by
Nancy Heslin

Sights	Restaurants	Hotels	Shopping	Nightlife
★★★★☆	★★★★☆	★★★★☆	★★★★☆	★★★☆☆

WELCOME TO NICE AND THE EASTERN FRENCH RIVIERA

TOP REASONS TO GO

★ **Picasso and company:** As artists have long loved the Côte d'Azur, it is blessed with superb art museums, including the Fondation Maeght in St-Paul and the Musée Picasso in Antibes.

★ **Èze:** The most perfectly situated of the coast's *villages perchés,* Èze has some of the most breath-taking views this side of a NASA space capsule.

★ **Nice:** With its bonbon-color palaces, blue Baie des Anges, time-stained Old Town, and Musée Matisse, this is one of France's most colorful cities.

★ **Cap d'Antibes:** Bordering well-hidden mansions and zillion-dollar hotels, the Sentier Tirepoil is a spectacular foot-path along the sea.

1 **Cannes.**

2 **Îles de Lérins.**

3 **Mougins.**

4 **Grasse.**

5 **Valbonne.**

6 **Vallauris.**

7 **Antibes.**

8 **Cap d'Antibes.**

9 **Juan-les-Pins.**

10 **Biot.**

11 **Villeneuve-Loubet.**

12 **Haut-de-Cagnes.**

13 **St-Paul-de-Vence.**

14 **Vence.**

15 **Nice.**

16 **Villefranche-sur-Mer.**

17 **Beaulieu-sur-Mer.**

18 **St-Jean-Cap-Ferrat.**

19 **Èze.**

20 **Roquebrune-Cap-Martin.**

21 **Menton.**

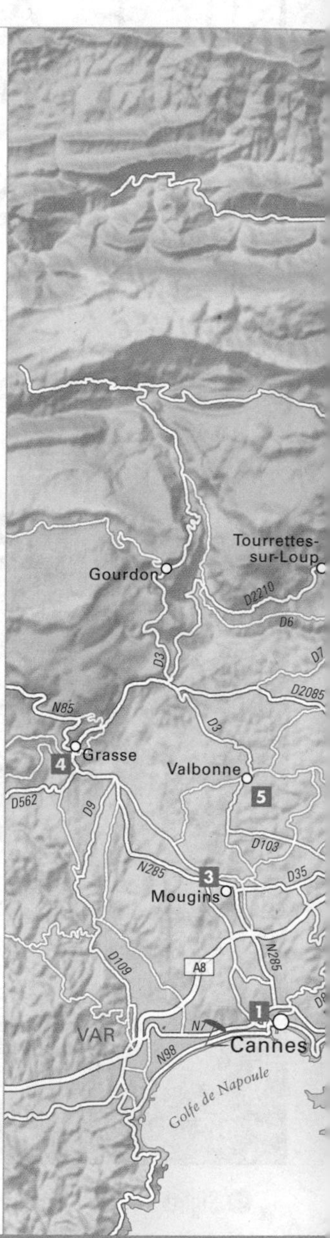

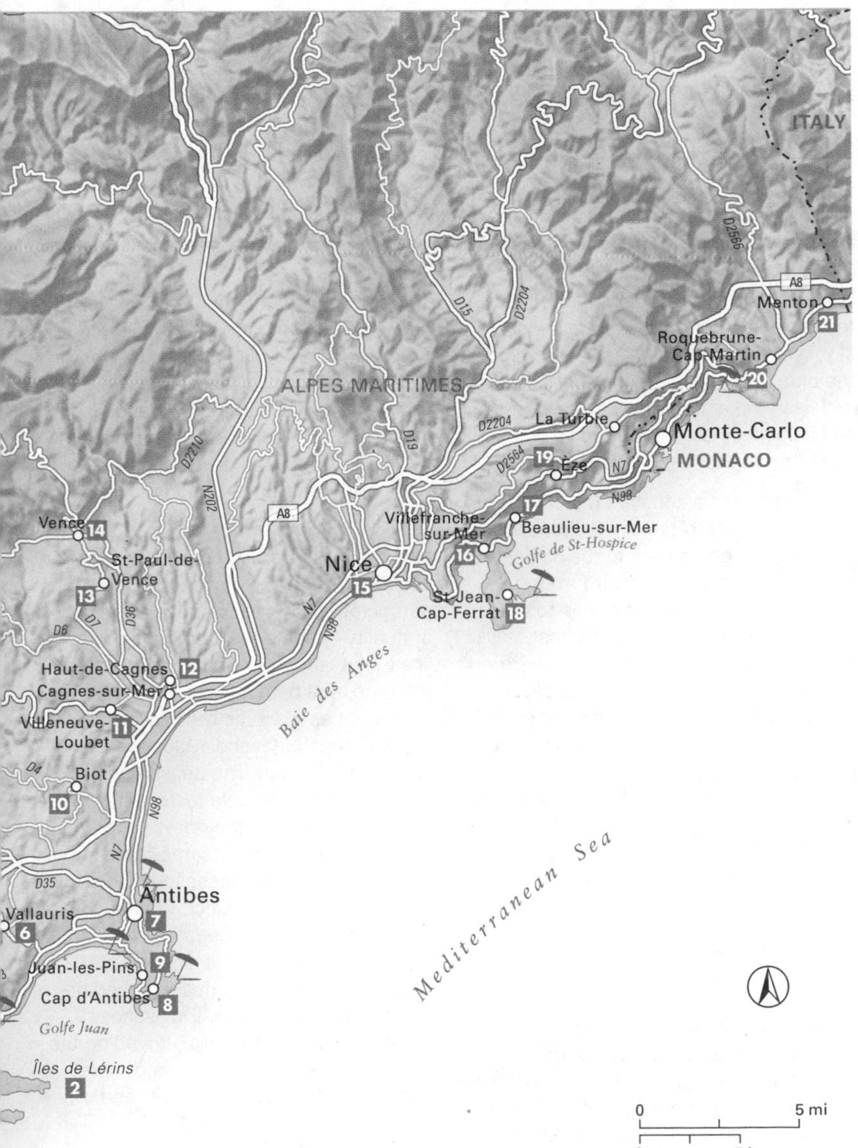
ITALY
D2566
A8
Menton
21
Roquebrune-Cap-Martin
20
D15
D2204
ALPES MARITIMES
D2204
La Turbie
Monte-Carlo
MONACO
D19
D2564
19
Èze
N7
N98
17
D2210
N202
A8
Villefranche-sur-Mer
Beaulieu-sur-Mer
16
Golfe de St-Hospice
Vence
14
St-Paul-de-Vence
Nice
15
13
St-Jean-Cap-Ferrat
18
N7
N98
D7
D36
D6
Baie des Anges
Haut-de-Cagnes
12
Cagnes-sur-Mer
Villeneuve-Loubet
11
D4
Biot
10
N98
N7
D35
Antibes
Vallauris
6
7
9
Juan-les-Pins
Cap d'Antibes
8
Mediterranean Sea
Golfe Juan
Îles de Lérins
2
0
5 mi
0
5 km

With the Alps and pre-Alps playing bodyguard against inland winds and the sultry Mediterranean warming the sea breezes, the eastern slice of the Côte d'Azur is pampered by a nearly tropical climate that sets it apart from the rest of France's southern coast.

This is where the real glamour begins: the dreamland of azure waters and indigo sky; white villas with balustrades edging the blue horizon; evening air perfumed with jasmine and mimosa; palm trees and parasol pines silhouetted against sunsets of apricot and gold.

There has been a constant march to this renowned stretch of Mediterranean coastline, going back to the ancient Greeks, who sailed eastward from Marseille to market their goods to the indigenes. But most of the earliest inhabitants of this region were fishermen and peasants who grew wheat, olives, and grapes for wine. This was not one of those lush regions of France where the living was easy. There were no palaces or gracious châteaux, only small villages, with fortifications here and there for use when Celts, Vandals, Ostrogoths, Saracens, and pirates from Algeria's Barbary Coast were on the rampage.

It was only in the middle of the 19th century that a troupe of kings and queens (including Victoria and dozens of her relatives), Russian grand dukes seeking to escape St. Petersburg's harsh climate, princelings from obscure Balkan countries, English milords, and a rabble of nouveau-riche camp followers began making prolonged visits here. They had mansions and gardens built; luxury hotels sprang up in imitation of their palaces back home. Many have left their architectural mark: Moroccan palaces in Menton, a neo-Greek villa in Beaulieu, and a Russian Cathedral in Nice, as appealing to the eye as the works masterminded by Picasso, Matisse, and Chagall, who were attracted to the region thanks to its intoxicating light.

The rich invaders withdrew to the cooler north for the summer months. No person of quality—and above all no lady of quality—would risk getting tanned like those laboring field hands, and, at the time, sea bathing was shunned by all, except as a drastic medical remedy. Then, in the 1920s and 1930s, people began to like it hot. The peasantry of the West was now pale factory and office workers, and their new badge of leisure and pleasure became the tan that their aristocratic predecessors had so assiduously avoided. Coco Chanel, the famous couturier, made *le bronzage* the chicest of fashion "accessories" in 1923 when she accidentally got scorched on a Mediterranean cruise. Toplessness, and even bottomlessness, arrived on the beaches. Meanwhile, more and more hotels, restaurants, nightclubs, and casinos were built.

The Côte remains a demi-paradise. Day-trippers seeking contrast head inland to *villages perchés* (perched villages) and historic towns—from Mougins, where Picasso spent his last years, to Grasse, with its factories that make perfume from the region's abundant flowers, to the galleries, souvenir shops, and snack stands that crowd the cobblestones of St-Paul-de-Vence. Or you could drive from Cannes to the Italian border in two hours, seeing much of the region courtesy of the swift A8 autoroute and the three parallel corniches that allow you to explore without retracing your steps too often. But like the artists and nobles who paved the way before you, you will likely be seduced to linger.

MAJOR REGIONS

Cannes. Conspicuous consumption, glamorous fanfare, and a host of wannabes characterize the celluloid city of Cannes when its May film fest turns it into a global frat party. But the Louis Vuitton set enjoy this city year-round.

The Pays Grassois. Just behind Cannes, the hills that block the mountain winds rise, sun bleached and jungle green. From the well-groomed Provençal village-slash-bedroom community of Mougins to the hill-city of Grasse, tiled with the greenhouses that feed the region's perfume factories, you'll find charming small towns inviting peace and relaxation. Grasse itself supports modern industry and tourist industry with aplomb, offering a dense Italian-style Old Town as well. Beyond, you can head for the hills of the *arrière-pays* on the Route Napoléon to cities like Valbonne.

Antibes and nearby. The coastline spanning the short distance from Cannes to Antibes and Nice has a personality all its own, combining some of the most accessible waterfront resorts (Juan-les-Pins, Villeneuve, and Cagnes-sur-mer) with one of the most elite (Cap d'Antibes). This is vacationland, with a culture of commercial entertainment that smacks of the worst of Florida in the 1960s. The hot, poky N98, which goes from Antibes to Cagnes, crawls past a jungle of amusement parks, a massive beach disco and casino, and even a horse-race track. The hill towns of Vallauris and Biot cater to souvenir hunters and lunch sorties. But everyone visiting this little piece of the Côte d'Azur, whether staying in a villa or a concrete cube, is after the same experience: to sit on a balcony, to listen to the waves washing over the sand, and to watch the sun setting over the oil-painted backdrop of the Maritime Alps.

The hill towns: St-Paul-de-Vence and Vence. The hills that back the Côte d'Azur are often called the arrière-pays, or backcountry. This particular wedge of backcountry—behind the coast between Cannes and Antibes—has a character all its own: deeply, unselfconsciously Provençal, with undulating fields of lavender watched over by villages perched on golden stone. Many of these villages look as if they do not belong to the last century—but they do, since they played the muse to some of modern art's most famous exemplars, notably Pablo Picasso and Henri Matisse. High in the hills these villages loom, parallel to the sea, smelling fragrantly of wild herbs and medieval history—and soap shops.

So hungry have the hordes that flock to the Riviera become for a taste of Picasso that many of the hill towns have been only too happy to oblige. St-Paul-de-Vence, which once hunkered down against the onslaught of Moors, now opens its pale-blue shutters wide to surges of day-trippers. Galleries and boutiques offer everything from neo–Van Gogh sofa art to assembly-line lavender sachets, and everywhere you'll hear the gentle *breet-breet* of mechanical souvenir *cigales* (cicadas). So if you're allergic to souvenir shops, artsy-craftsy boutiques, and middle-brow art galleries, aim to visit off-season or after hours. Top sights include the famous Colombe d'Or inn and Matisse's sublime Chapelle du Rosaire.

Nice. Walking along the seaside Promenade des Anglais is one of the most iconic Riviera experiences. Add in top-notch museums, a charming old quarter open till all hours, scads of diverse restaurants, and an agenda of first-class festivals all year long, and Nice merits a visit.

The Corniches resorts. Purists and hardcore regional historians insist that this final sunny sliver of coast—from Cap Ferrat to the Italian border—is the one and only, true Côte d'Azur. It is certainly the most dramatically endowed, backed by forested mountains and crystalline Alps, with Mediterranean breezes relieving the summer heat and radiant light soothing midwinter days. And yet it was from these cliffs that for 2,500 years castles and towers held watch over the waters, braced against the influx of new peoples—first the Greeks, then the Romans, the Saracens, trade ships from Genoa, battleships under Napoléon, Edwardian cruise ships on the Grand Tour, and the Allies in World War II.

The influx continues today, of course, in the great waves of vacationers who storm the coast from spring to early fall. The sun shines most brightly on the fabled glamour ports of Villefranche-sur-Mer, Beaulieu, and St-Jean-Cap-Ferrat. Also here are Èze and Roquebrune–Cap-Martin. Then there's Menton, an enchanting Italianate resort where winters can be so mild that lemon trees bloom in January.

Planning

When to Go

The sun always seems to shine in the magical, southeast corner of France. It's no secret that the coast is in its prime July and August, when rain is almost unheard of, but if you're anxious to enjoy the beaches, aim for less-packed June or September. Cannes books early for the film festival in May, so unless you're determined to hover outside the Farfalla with an autograph book, plan to visit in another month. Also, many hotels and restaurants close November–Easter, and those that do thrive year-round tend to shut down in August, at the height of the tourist season, for the traditional *fermeture annuelle*.

The region's short periods of intense rainfall, lasting half a day to a week, most likely happen October–November and March–April, but late spring can also be surprisingly wet (locals swear that it always rains on the first day of the Cannes Film Festival). If you're intent on strolling in shirtsleeves under the palms on a winter day, head for Menton, famous for having one of the mildest climates in France, and, like the rest of the eastern Côte d'Azur, protected by the Estérel from the mistral that razors through Fréjus to the west, and from northern winds by the Alps.

Planning Your Time

How you tackle this stretch of the Côte d'Azur will largely depend on the form of transportation you have chosen. With a car, you can base yourself outside a major resort and combine day trips to Nice, Cannes, and Monaco with a taste of more leisurely Provençal life. If you're dependent on public transportation, you might stay in a larger center such as Nice, where trains will easily take you along the coast and whisk you to such towns as Èze and Antibes and buses hit about every village in the backcountry, including St-Paul-de-Vence.

Should sunbathing be a priority, you might prefer the sandy beaches of Cannes to the pebbles of Nice; in the height of summer, aim for the less populated beaches of St-Jean-Cap-Ferrat, Èze, and Cap d'Ail (where you can now visit the Belle Époque Villa Les Camélias), or grab an early-morning ferry to the Îles de Lérins.

Art is a super-major draw in this area, with must-see museums, such as the Matisse museum in Nice, the Fondation Maeght in St-Paul-de-Vence, the Fernand Léger museum in Biot, and the Picasso museum in Antibes.

There is plenty for music fans, too: Nice and Juan-les-Pins hold major jazz festivals in the summer, and Monaco's springtime Printemps des Arts celebrates music, dance, cinema, and theater. Vence's Nuit du Sud, a world music event that started in 1997, has become so popular that festivalgoers on a flight from Paris once asked the pilot to call organizers to say they were late as they didn't want to miss the show.

Stroll through a kaleidoscopic food market—perhaps the Marché Forville in Cannes, Cours Saleya in Nice, or Menton's Marché des Halles—to see how seriously this area takes fresh produce. Then visit a good local bistro to taste specialties such as *pissaladière* (caramelized onion tart), *soupe de poissons* (fish soup), and, of course, *salade niçoise* (which in Nice contains neither green beans nor potato).

With so much to see, it's tempting to pack too much into a visit to this area, so be sure to set aside some time for relaxing on café terraces—something that the locals have mastered.

Getting Here and Around

As home to France's second-busiest airport, Nice is a natural starting point for seeing the area. The airport is conveniently located 15 minutes from the town center, and you don't have to spend money on a taxi to get there. A tram line stops at both terminals and goes to the port (€1.70), and the relocated Nice–St-Augustin train station is a 15-minute walk from Terminal 1.

French Riviera Pass

The French Riviera Pass (🌐 *en.frenchrivierapass.com*) is your ticket to the region's sights and transportation. Included are things like guided tours, wine tastings, and discounts at museum shops, as well free or reduced entry at attractions in Nice and nearby Côte d'Azur towns like Monaco (oceanography museum), Èze (exotic gardens), and Saint-Jean-Cap-Ferrat (Ephrussi de Rothschild villa and garden). The passes are available for 24 hours (€28), 48 hours (€40), or 72 hours (€59), and an unlimited public-transport add-on costs €4/day.

East and west of Nice, a train route connects all the main coastal towns—a magic carpet ride of convenience for travelers. Buses also spider out, but they can take a good two hours between Nice and Cannes (as opposed to 35 minutes on the train). It's a well-kept secret that the Biot train station is a five-minute walk from Marineland, a major attraction near Antibes. Trains also head up into the hills around Grasse.

Surely the biggest bargain in the South of France is the Zou! bus ticket (€2.10), between Nice and Cannes or Menton. The most scenic route is that taken by Bus 600, which runs every 20 minutes from Nice to Menton along the Moyenne Corniche; note, though, that it can be unpleasantly crowded in high season. (⚠ **Until March 2024, the 600 is replaced with the 607 Nice-Monaco and the 608 Monaco-Menton.**) Buses also connect Nice to Èze village (30 minutes) and St-Paul-de-Vence and Vence (at least an hour); be sure to check the schedule because these buses are not frequent.

■ TIP→ An excellent website to help you calculate your route—bus, tram, train, and boat—across the Riviera is the interactive map on ***services-zou.maregionsud.fr/en.***

AIR

The Nice–Côte d'Azur Airport, often hovering in the top five of PrivateFly's world's most scenic airport landings, has frequent flights between Paris and Nice on Air France and the low-cost airline EasyJet, as well as direct flights on Delta Airlines from New York and from Newark with La Compagnie.

In the off-season, or if you book well in advance, you can find a one-way trip from Paris to Nice for less than €40, which can be cheaper than the train (though baggage fees and airport transfers offset this). The flight time between Paris and Nice is about 1½ hours.

A taxi from the airport into Nice center—say, the Place Masséna—is a flat-rate fare of €32, but a cheaper option is to take the Line 2 tram from either terminal, which from T2 runs daily at 5:24 am to 11:55 pm weekdays (before boarding, you must purchase a €1.70 ticket from the machines at the tram stop).

Regular Nice Airport Xpress buses also serve Cannes, Antibes, Monte Carlo, Roquebrune Cap Martin, and Menton. Note that until March 2024, the 80 Airport-Monaco-Menton (formerly 110) leaves from T2, and, due to roadworks takes a detour after Monaco, bypassing Roquebrune. Take the three-minute tram for free between Terminal 1 and Terminal 2 to get onboard.

⚠ Uber with care: the French government has banned this taxi app because they consider it unfair competition. As a result, there have been disputes at the airport between cabbies and Uber drivers. It's usually best to take the tram or bus.

AIRPORT INFORMATION Aéroport Nice–Côte d'Azur. *✉ Nice ☎ 08–20–42–33–33 (€0.12 per min) 🌐 www.nice.aeroport.fr/en.*

BOAT

The Côte d'Azur is one of the world's most beautiful coastlines, and several companies enable you to take it all in via boat and ferry service. Riviera Lines offers routes between Golfe Juan to Cannes, Monaco, and St-Tropez. Trans Côte d'Azur, with Nice and Cannes departures, has routes including the Corniche de l'Estérel, Monaco, Porquerolles, and St-Tropez, plus specialty excursions that feature nighttime dining and glass-bottom boats. Note that some routes and destinations are available June–October only.

BOAT CONTACTS Riviera Lines. *☎ 04–92–98–71–31 🌐 www.riviera-lines.com.* **Trans Côte d'Azur.** *✉ 20 quai St-Pierre, Cannes ☎ 04–92–98–71–30 🌐 www.trans-cote-azur.com.*

BUS AND TRAM

Along the coast, the train line is the quickest way to get around, but to reach many backcountry spots, you'll have to take a bus out of Cannes (Palm Bus, €1.60 valid up to 59 minutes); Grasse (Sillages, €1.50 valid up to 2½ hours); Antibes (Envibus, €1 valid up to 1 hour); or Menton (Zest bus, €2 valid up to 1 hour). Many bus companies have or are in the process of switching their onboard payment systems; in some cases, it might be slightly cheaper to pay with your credit card or scanning a QR code once on the bus instead of buying a ticket with cash from the driver.

Drivers do give change and hand you a ticket, which you must get stamped (*composté*) in the ticket validator and keep as proof of payment (inspectors often board buses to check). If you plan to use the bus more than once, look into a multiride or weekly pass to save money. Schedules can be found on the bus company's app or website; you can also check tourist office websites. And remember, you must hail a bus to stop; don't presume the driver sees you.

Ligne d'Azur is Nice's main bus network, but regional buses are operated by Zou! Its Bus 600 (which, until March 2024, is renumbered 607), departs every 15 minutes (5:35 am–8:30 pm) from Nice–Port Lympia Fodéré and stops at all the villages between Nice and Monaco along the Corniche Inférieure. At night there is the less frequent service on Bus 601.

For Villefranche, Èze, and Cap d'Ail on the Moyenne Corniche, take Bus 112, which departs Nice Vauban (take the Line 1 tram to get here) six times a day (no Sunday service) and ends at the casino in Monte Carlo. You can also take Bus 82, which goes as far as Èze via Villefranche and runs daily. Bus 655 goes to St-Paul-de-Vence and Vence, stopping first in St-Paul-de-Vence (about 1 hour) while Bus 650 takes you to Grasse (1 hour, 20 minutes); both these buses depart near the airport from Parc Phoenix, a stop on the Line 2 tramway.

In Nice, bus stations are spread across the city and include Vaubun (north and regional buses to Marseille and Aix), Gare SNCF, Station J. Bermond (the main hub), Cathédrale Vieille Ville, Alberti/Gioffredo, and Albert 1er. Lignes d'Azur also operates two modern tram lines, a fast and efficient way to get from the train station to the Old Town and the port. Tickets (which are interchangeable with bus tickets) cost €1.70 one-way and must be purchased before boarding from machines at each stop.

In Cannes, Zou! runs routes from in front of the train station, including Bus 620 to Nice (1½ hours) and Buses 661 and 662 to Grasse (45 minutes). Within Cannes, use Palm Bus, which also serves Mandelieu and Mougins (and runs night buses in summer).

The Antibes bus station is at 1 Place Guynemer, and Bus 620 connects with Cannes to the west and, to the east, both Nice (€1.70, every 15–20 minutes) and Cagnes-sur-Mer, a coastal town also served by train. From there it's an easy connection with adjacent St-Paul-de-Vence and Vence using Zou! Bus 665, which departs every 30–45 minutes from Cagnes Ville's bus station at Square Bourdet. The 620 Nice–Cannes bus stops at the square, too.

Transdev operates Nice Airport Xpress buses to Vallauris/Antibes (No. 82), Cannes (No. 81), Monaco-Roquebrune-Cap-Martin-Menton (No. 80). As of 2023, the express bus serves only Terminal 2 but that could change. From Terminal 1, you can take a three-minute tram ride for free to to Terminal 2. In addition, the Nice-St-Augustin train station is a direct and easy 10- to 15-minute walk. Monaco's buses—Compagnie des Autobus de Monaco—help stitch together the principality's widely dispersed neighborhoods.

BUS INFORMATION Envibus. ✉ *Antibes* ☎ *04–89–87–72–00* 🌐 *www.envibus.fr.* **Lignes d'Azur.** ✉ *3 pl. Masséna, Nice* ☎ *08–10–06–10–06 €0.06/min* 🌐 *www.lignesdazur.com.* **Zou!** ☎ *08–09–40–00–13* 🌐 *services-zou.maregionsud.fr/fr.* **Palm Bus.** ✉ *Cannes* ☎ *08–25–82–55–99* 🌐 *www.palmbus.fr/en.* **Sillages.** ☎ *04–93–36–37–37* 🌐 *sillages.paysdegrasse.fr.* **Transdev/Nice Airport Express Buses.** ✉ *Nice* ☎ *08–09–40–00–13* 🌐 *www.niceairportxpress.com.* **Zest.** ✉ *Menton* ☎ *04–93–35–93–60* 🌐 *www.zestbus.fr.*

CAR

Driving is the best way to traverse the region and reach its backcountry sights. A car also gives you the freedom not only to zip along the A8 between the coastal resorts but also to enjoy the tremendous views from the three corniches that trace the coast from Nice to the Italian border. A car is, of course, a liability in city centers, with parking garages expensive and curbside spots virtually nonexistent.

From Paris, the main southbound artery is A6/A7, known as the Autoroute du Soleil (Highway of the Sun). It passes through Provence and joins the eastbound A8 at Aix-en-Provence. The A8 flows briskly from Cannes to Antibes to Nice and on to Monaco/Menton.

A couple of points worth noting: keep your car doors locked at all times, and keep all bags hidden from view. Also, this is one of the most dangerous driving regions in Europe, and the speeds and aggressive Grand Prix–style maneuvering of some drivers make it impossible to let your guard down. On the A8 toward Italy, tight curves, hills, tunnels, and construction keep things especially interesting. For traffic reports, tune to 107.7 FM or, in English, Riviera Radio 106.5.

TRAIN

Nice is the major rail crossroads for trains arriving from Paris and other northern cities and from Italy, too. To get from Paris to Nice (with stops in Cannes and other resorts along the coast), you can take the TGV, though it only maintains high speeds to Valence before returning to conventional rails and rates. Night trains arrive at Nice in the morning from Paris, Metz, and Strasbourg.

You can easily move along the coastal towns between Cannes, Nice, and Ventimiglia (in Italy) by train on the slick double-decker Côte d'Azur line, a highly pleasant branch of SNCF lines, with more than 40 trains a day. Don't be shocked, though, to see a graffitied clunker pull in. The good news is that all information like departures and arrivals, and train station details, can now be easily searched by city via a one-stop website (🌐 *www.gares-sncf.com*) or Assistant SNCF. Similarly, there is only one central telephone number now (☎ *3635*) for train stations.

The Marseille–Vintimille (Ventimiglia) line heads east to Italy, and Vintimille–Marseille travels west. From Nice, some main stops on this line are: Antibes (€5.20, 25 minutes); Cannes (€7.90, 40 minutes); Menton (€5.90, 40 minutes); and Monaco (€5.90, 25 minutes). Stops on the Mandelieu–Ventimille line include Villefranche-sur-Mer, Beaulieu, Èze-sur-Mer, and Cap d'Ail. No trains run to the hill villages, including St-Paul-de-Vence and Vence.

A word of caution: don't be alarmed by police presence at main stations from Menton to Nice to Cannes. Security has been beefed up, especially with the rise in migrants trying to cross the border from Italy. Also, hold on to your purse, wallet, and belongings when traveling by rail. There are frequent onboard recordings reminding passengers to be careful of pickpockets; it's smart to be especially vigilant while riding the train and bus.

TRAIN INFORMATION Gare Cannes Ville. ✉ *1 rue Jean-Jaurès, Cannes* ☎ *3635* 🌐 *www.garesetconnexions.sncf/fr/gares-services/cannes*. **Gare Nice Ville.** ✉ *Av. Thiers, Nice* ☎ *3635* 🌐 *www.gares-sncf.com*. **SNCF.** ☎ *3635* 🌐 *en.oui.sncf/en*. **TGV.** ☎ *3635* 🌐 *en.oui.sncf/en/tgv*.

Beaches

From intimate pebbly stretches to long swaths of golden sand packed with sun worshippers, from nudist beaches to family-friendly ones, the Côte d'Azur is famed for its magnificent beaches. Cagnes-sur-Mer across to Menton, however, is reviled for its notorious *galets*, round white stones that can make you feel like a fakir lying on a rounded bed of nails instead of nestling into sand. A thin foam mattress, available from the souvenir shops in close beach proximity, can make all the difference—as can a pair of €10 slip-on rubber shoes for navigating the stones. Or consider springing for a sun lounger.

Many beaches are privately operated, renting parasols and mattresses to anyone who pays; if you're a guest at one of the local hotels, you'll get a discount. These beaches also allow you in for free if you are drinking or eating from their menus. The good news is that public beaches (with free toilets during summer and open showers) usually alternate with private *plages,* where you'll pay on average €25 for a mattress, which often includes a parasol. Happily, the sun is free.

■ TIP→ If lodging inland, leave early for the beach: traffic on N98, which lines the coast, often grinds to a halt. Or head down over lunchtime when public beaches are less crowded. And take your own water for drinking and post-swim rinsing. With the region in a severe drought the past several summers, showers have had their taps shut off.

Hotels

Along this golden stretch you'll see the prices rise, even beyond those of the Estérel. The atmosphere changes, too. In the coastal resorts the majority of visitors seem to value proximity to the sea over cachet, and you'll often find yourself far from the land of Provençal cottons and cozy country inns. The interior design here is a peculiar hybrid—vaguely Jazz Age, a little Hollywood—that falls into a loose category known as "Côte d'Azur style."

In Cannes, the grand hotels are big on prestige (waterfront position, awe-inspiring lobbies, high-price sea views) and weak on swimming pools, which are usually just big enough to dip in. In addition, their private beaches are on the other side of the busy street, and you'll have to pay for access, just as nonguests do. The glitziest properties are in Cannes, Monaco, and the Cap d'Antibes. Nice provides a broader range of prices, and you'll find charming family-run hotels around St-Paul-de-Vence and Vence.

Remember that July and August are the busiest months, and hotel prices skyrocket in May during the Monaco Grand Prix and the Cannes Film Festival. It used to be you could plan ahead anytime between April and October to find deals, but, in a post-Covid world, this is not the case. Rates are inflated across April to October. In the off-season, however, you can still find deals if you have flexibility in your travel dates. In addition, renting a rural *gîte* (🌐 *www.gites-de-france.com/en*) allows you to avoid overpriced breakfasts and make the most of the abundance at the markets.

Most hotel rates now include Wi-Fi, but much to the dismay of many travelers, signals can be weak even in the bigger towns or in upscale hotels due to aging infrastructures. Also keep in mind that five-star service is not the same in France as it is stateside. Finally, do your homework if you're sensitive to noise: check that your idyllic seaside accommodation isn't close to the train tracks or the quaint village auberge doesn't face the main square, where things can be loud into the early hours. Chiming church bells lose their charm at 11 pm … and 4 am!

■ TIP→ Don't be surprised at checkout when you see the taxe de séjour (usually around €1–€1.50 per guest per day). This city tax is never included in the price when you book online from travel websites.

Restaurants

Riviera restaurants range from takeout spots to Michelin-star establishments. Throughout the region, however, the "Made in France" and "Nissart cuisine" movements are on the rise in an attempt to protect all that is near and dear to French stomachs against the invasion of Starbucks and Burger King in cities like Nice.

The best way to appreciate a meal in the region is to eat like a local. First, remember that meals here are for lingering conversation, and many restaurants have only one seating a night—so if you're in a rush, don't bother. Order the daily special when possible: it will be fresh and the price clearly labeled. Note that many French restaurants don't appreciate or can't readily accommodate special requests for dishes without something, say, or with something on the side. Also, be cautious when ordering fish priced by the 100g—the bill might cause you to choke on your crème brûlée.

When dining with young children, the staff in some establishments might give you a less than enthusiastic welcome, and fellow diners might cast a side-eye in your direction. It's not that the French are averse to babies, but an evening out is for civilized adults. Finally, waving your platinum card around won't make your waiter smile or serve you any faster, especially in the busier seasons.

⇨ *Hotel and restaurant reviews have been shortened. For full information, visit Fodors.com. Hotel prices are the lowest cost of a standard double room in high season. Restaurant prices are the average cost of a main course at dinner or, if dinner is not served, at lunch.*

What It Costs in Euros

$	$$	$$$	$$$$
HOTELS			
under €125	€125–€225	€226–€350	over €350
RESTAURANTS			
under €18	€18–€24	€25–€32	over €32

Cannes

6 km (4 miles) east of Mandelieu-La Napoule; 73 km (45 miles) northeast of St-Tropez; 33 km (20 miles) southwest of Nice.

Cannes is pampered with the luxurious year-round climate that has made it one of the most popular resorts in Europe. Settled first by the Ligurians and then dubbed Cannoïs by the Romans (after the cane that waved in its marshes), Cannes was an important sentinel site for the monks who established themselves on Île St-Honorat in the Middle Ages.

Its bay served as nothing more than a fishing port until, in 1834, an English aristocrat, Lord Brougham, fell in love with the site during an emergency stopover with a sick daughter. He had a home built here and returned every winter for a sun cure—a ritual quickly picked up by his peers. Between the popularity of Le Train Blue transporting wealthy passengers from Calais and the introduction in 1936 of France's first paid holidays, Cannes became *the* tasteful and expensive stomping ground of the upper crust.

Cannes has been further glamorized by the ongoing success of its annual film festival, as famous as—and, in the trade, more respected than—Hollywood's Academy Awards. About the closest many of us will get to feeling like a film star is a stroll here along La Croisette, the iconic promenade that gracefully curves the sandy, wave-washed coastline, peppered with chic restaurants and prestigious private beaches. This is precisely the sort of place for which the French invented the verb *flâner* (to dawdle, saunter): strewn with palm trees and poseurs, its fancy boutiques and status-symbol hotels—including the recently restored Carlton, the legendary backdrop to Grace Kelly in *To Catch a Thief*—all vying for the custom of the Louis Vuitton set.

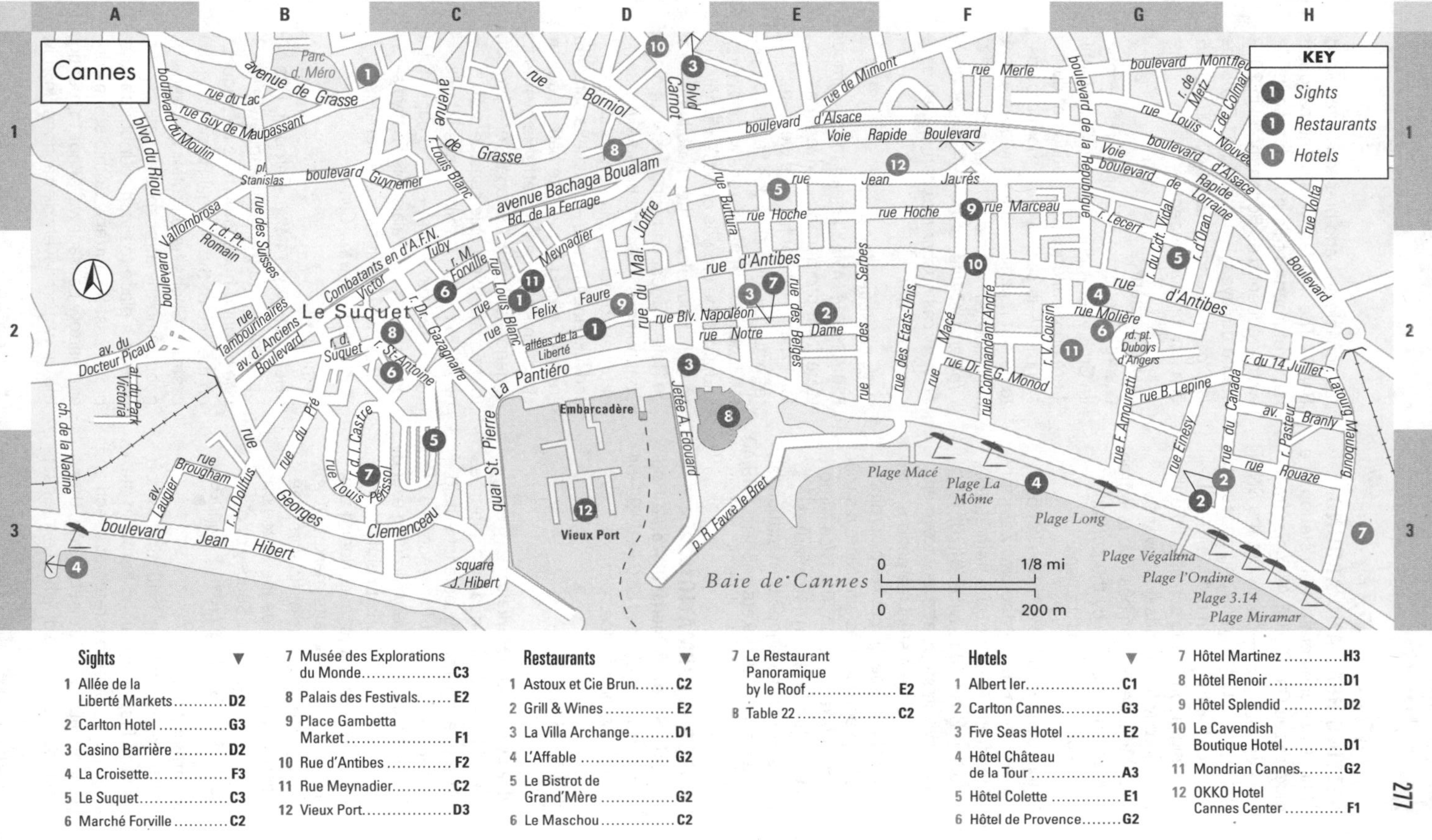

Sights

1 Allée de la Liberté Markets D2
2 Carlton Hotel G3
3 Casino Barrière D2
4 La Croisette F3
5 Le Suquet C3
6 Marché Forville C2
7 Musée des Explorations du Monde C3
8 Palais des Festivals E2
9 Place Gambetta Market F1
10 Rue d'Antibes F2
11 Rue Meynadier C2
12 Vieux Port D3

Restaurants

1 Astoux et Cie Brun C2
2 Grill & Wines E2
3 La Villa Archange D1
4 L'Affable G2
5 Le Bistrot de Grand'Mère G2
6 Le Maschou C2
7 Le Restaurant Panoramique by le Roof E2
8 Table 22 .... C2

Hotels

1 Albert Ier C1
2 Carlton Cannes G3
3 Five Seas Hotel E2
4 Hôtel Château de la Tour A3
5 Hôtel Colette E1
6 Hôtel de Provence G2
7 Hôtel Martinez H3
8 Hôtel Renoir D1
9 Hôtel Splendid D2
10 Le Cavendish Boutique Hotel D1
11 Mondrian Cannes G2
12 OKKO Hotel Cannes Center F1

GETTING HERE AND AROUND

Cannes has one central train station, the modernized Gare SNCF. All major trains pass through here—check out the SNCF app or website for times and prices—but many of the trains run the Mandelieu–Ventimiglia route. You can also take the TGV directly from Paris (just over five hours). Cannes's main bus hub is in front of the l'Hôtel-de-Ville by the port and serves all coastal destinations.

Within Cannes, use Palm Bus (€1.50). For excursions out of the city, Zou! runs routes from in front of the train station, including Bus 600 to Nice (€1.70, 1½ hours), which stops at every town en route. Fares are a steal (be patient, you may not get a seat), but keep in mind that between Cannes and Nice, it's much faster to take the train. The Nice Airport Xpress Shuttle No. 81 (45 minutes), leaves from the Cannes train station, and you can purchase tickets onboard (€19.40 one-way).

VISITOR INFORMATION

CONTACTS Cannes Tourist Office. ✉ *1 bd. de la Croisette, Cannes* ☎ *04–92–99–84–22* 🌐 *en.cannes-france.com.*

Sights

Allée de la Liberté Markets

MARKET | **FAMILY** | Shaded by plane trees and sheltering a sandy pétanque field, this is a little piece of Provence in a big, glitzy resort town. Every morning except Monday, a flower market paints the square in vivid colors, and, during the weekend arts-and-crafts market (10–6), you can find paintings of flowers. The antiques market shares the space on Saturday and the first Sunday of every month. ✉ *Allée de la Liberté, Cannes.*

★ Carlton Hotel

HOTEL | Inaugurated in 1913, the Carlton was the first of the grand hotels to stake a claim on a superb stretch of beach and greenery along La Croisette, and, thus, is the best positioned, which explains its fashionable see-and-be-seen terrace and Bar 58. The film festival's grand banquets have returned to this iconic hot spot, which reopened as Regent hotel in 2023 after a multiyear restoration. ✉ *58 bd. de la Croisette, Cannes* ☎ *04–93–06–40–06* 🌐 *www.ihg.com/regent.*

Casino Barrière

CASINO | The famous Casino Barrière on La Croisette—open 10 am to 3 am (until 4 am on weekends and until 5 am during summer)—is said to draw more crowds to its slot machines than any other casino in France. ✉ *Palais des Festivals, 1 La Croisette, Cannes* ☎ *04–92–98–78–00* 🌐 *www.casinosbarriere.com/fr/cannes-le-croisette.html.*

★ La Croisette

PROMENADE | **FAMILY** | Head to this famous waterfront promenade—which runs for 1½ km (1 mile) from its western terminus by the Palais des Festivals—and stroll beside the palm trees and flowers and amid the crowds of poseurs (fur coats in tropical weather, mobile phones on Rollerblades, and sunglasses at night). Continue east past the broad expanse of private beaches, glamorous shops, and luxurious hotels—but make sure you are not walking in the bike path or a construction site. "La Croisette Reinvents its Legend" is the city's slogan for a project to renovate this iconic seaside strip by 2025. The €160 million face-lift will include red pavement—an homage to the red carpet of the Palais des Festivals—as well as new facilities and amenities. ✉ *Bd. de Croisette, Cannes.*

Le Suquet

NEIGHBORHOOD | **FAMILY** | Climb up Rue St-Antoine into the picturesque *vieille ville* neighborhood known as Le Suquet, on the site of the original Roman castrum. Shops here proffer Provençal goods, and the atmospheric cafés provide a place to catch your breath. The pretty pastel shutters, Gothic stonework, and narrow passageways (not to mention the views) are lovely distractions. In July,

Did You Know?

Europe's upper crust flocked to Cannes's La Croisette beach because they believed that lying on its white sands (instead of the beach pebbles at Nice) was enough to cure most ailments.

The Three Corniches

The lay of the land east of Nice is nearly vertical, as the coastline is one great cliff terraced by three parallel national roads—the **Corniche Inférieure** (sometimes called the Basse Corniche and N98), the **Moyenne Corniche** (N7), and the **Grande Corniche** (D2564)—that snake along its graduated crests. The lowest (*inférieure*) is the slowest, following the coast and crawling through the main streets of resorts, including Monte Carlo. Villefranche, Cap Ferrat, and Beaulieu are some of the towns along this 20-mile-long *route nationale*.

The highest (*grande*) is the fastest, but its panoramic views are blocked by villas, and there are few safe overlooks (this is the road Grace Kelly roared along in *To Catch a Thief*, and, some 27 years later, crashed and died on). The middle (*moyenne*) offers views down over the shoreline and villages and passes through a few picturesque cliff-top towns, including Èze.

you can hear young musicians perform free open-air concerts in the Place de la Castre during the Jeunes Talents festival. ✉ *Rue St-Antoine, Cannes.*

Marché Forville (*Forville Market*)

MARKET | FAMILY | Opened in 1934, this market still draws the chefs, connoisseurs, and voyeurs of Cannes every morning (except Monday, when there's a flea market). You'll see showy displays of still-flipping fish from some 25 local boats alongside glossy local vegetables piled high; cheeses carried down from the mountains; and sausages, olives, charcuterie, oysters, and flower stands. The whole scene gets hosed down by 1 pm, so don't linger too long over breakfast. The nearby Café de l'Horlage (✉ *7 rue du Marché Forville*) is a good spot to relax after browsing. ✉ *Rue du Marché Forville, Cannes* ⏲ *Closed Mon.*

Musée des Explorations du Monde

HISTORY MUSEUM | FAMILY | Housed in an 11th-century château atop a hill, this museum has a wonderful collection of weaponry, artifacts, art, and antiques. There are temporary exhibitions here, as well, and, over the next few years, the museum will be modernized for the first time in its 40-year history. The imposing four-sided Tour du Suquet (Suquet Tower) and its 109 steps were built in 1385 as a lookout against Saracen-led invasions. ✉ *Pl. de la Castre, Le Suquet* ☎ *04–89–82–26–26* 🌐 *www.cannes.com/fr/culture/musees-et-expositions.html* 🎫 *€6* ⏲ *Closed Mon. Oct.–Mar.*

Palais des Festivals

PERFORMANCE VENUE | Pick up a map at the tourist office in the Palais des Festivals, the building that sets the scene for the famous Cannes Film Festival. As you leave the information center, head to your right to see the 24 red-carpeted stairs that A-listers ascend every year. Set into the surrounding pavement, the Chemin des Étoiles (Stars' Walk) enshrines some 150 autographed hand imprints—including those of Depardieu, Streep, and Stallone (the clay imprints are sent to a potter in Vallauris, before being cast in metal in Rhône). From October to April, the Palais hosts music, theater, dance, and comedy performances for surprisingly reasonable prices. And hey, If you forget to snap your own red-carpet moment, the Palais has a special Instagram filter (🌐 *www.instagram.com/ar/555964202082615*) to "awaken your inner star." ✉ *Bd. de la Croisette, Cannes* ☎ *04–92–98–62–77 ticket office* 🌐 *www.palaisdesfestivals.com.*

Place Gambetta Market

MARKET | FAMILY | Just a couple of blocks east of the train station along Rue Jean Jaurès, you can pick up fresh fruit and vegetables, as well as clothes, shoes, belts, and bags at the city's second covered market that's a little less upscale than the Marché Forville. While in the neighborhood, visit the nearby Asian and kosher shops, or stop in for one of the creamiest cappuccinos this side of Italy at Volupté (✉ *32 rue Hoche* ⏲ *Closed Sun.*). ✉ *Pl. Gambetta, Cannes.*

Rue d'Antibes

STREET | FAMILY | Two blocks behind La Croisette lies this attractive high-end shopping street. At its western end is Rue Meynadier, packed with trendy clothing boutiques and fine-food shops. Not far away is the covered Marché Forville, the scene of the animated morning food market. Rue Houche, behind Rue d'Antibes and down from Galleries Lafayette, has lots of boutiques and cafés. ✉ *Cannes.*

Rue Meynadier

STREET | FAMILY | It's hard to imagine 16th-century horse-drawn carriages being pulled down this main street of Cannes that's now home to inexpensive and trendy clothes boutiques, rare food stores, cheese and wine shops, and some of the best butchers in town. At one end of Rue Meynadier is Rue d'Antibes, Cannes's primary high-end shopping street. ✉ *Rue Meynadier, Cannes.*

Vieux Port (*Old Port*)

MARINA/PIER | FAMILY | At the foot of Le Suquet, this narrow, well-protected port harbors luxury yachts and slick little *bateaux de plaisance* (pleasure boats) that creak and bob beside weathered-blue fishing barques. From the east corner, off La Pantiéro at Quai Laubeuf (where a renovated sea wall has a panoramic promenade and heliport), you can catch a 20-minute ferry to the Îles de Lérins. The port and Quai St-Pierre, which runs alongside and has a plethora of restaurants, have emerged from their tattered and tired midlife crisis to become smartly dressed, more energized versions of their former selves. ✉ *Cannes.*

Beaches

Both Cannes and St-Tropez are known for their glorious beaches, and, for decades, little about them changed. Five years ago, however, the season brought electrifying transformation to both St-Tropez's iconic beaches and to the 5-mile stretch of coastline in Cannes. As part a four-year, €50 million project, the largest redevelopment since 1960, 80,000 cubic meters of sand was added to expand beaches from 80 to 130 feet deep on La Croisette.

There are now 25 private and public beaches, including La Môme, Long, Végaluna, L'ondine, 3.14 Plage, and Miramar. Note that the two municipal beaches (*regie municipal*)—Macé, near the Palais des Féstivals, and Zamenhoff, at the Port Canto east end—are cheaper for renting loungers. In addition, every season a big-name chef ends up at one of the private beach restaurants, as at Majestic's La Plage Barrière with BFire by Mauro Colagreco (his Mirazur restaurant in Menton was number one in the world in 2019).

Most beaches along La Croisette are owned by hotels or restaurants, though this doesn't necessarily mean the hotels or restaurants front the beach. It does mean that they own a patch of beachfront bearing their name and from which they rent chaises, mats, and umbrellas (from €25 to €80 per day) to the public and to hotel guests.

Crowds mark the public beaches, which are set amid the private strands and their color-coordinated umbrellas and which offer simple open showers, basic toilets, and loungers that rent for just €6.70 a day. To be slightly removed from traffic and crowds, head west of town, where the open stretches of sand run uninterrupted toward Mandelieu.

Special anti-jellyfish nets are set up July through August along Gazagnaire, Macé, and Plages du Midi beaches, so you can swim in semi-peace. There are a couple of no-smoking beaches in each sea town across the Riviera. In Cannes, these include Bijou Plage (also home to Handiplage) and Plage des Rochers de la Bocca, where anyone caught lighting up is fined €38. Daily in July and August, there is a beach library (Pages à la plage) on La Croisette (check at either Zamenhof or Macé beach), where, for a €10 deposit, you can sign out books for up to two days; English publications are available.

■ TIP→ From June to September, Cannes uses the Tétéoù system for child and beach safety. Look for special poles along the seafront topped with toys (say, a yellow banana or a train), and ask a lifeguard for a bracelet on which to write your child's name and mobile number. Explain to your children that they should go to the nearest pole if lost. If you're not a fan of kids at the beach, lay your towel as far away from these poles as possible.

 Restaurants

Astoux et Cie Brun

$$$ | **SEAFOOD** | A beacon to all fish lovers since 1953, Astoux et Cie Brun deserves its reputation for impeccably fresh *fruits de mer.* Well-trained staffers negotiate cramped quarters to lay down heaping seafood platters, shrimp casseroles, and piles of oysters shucked to order. Open 365 days a year with nonstop service, it is noisy, cheerful, and always busy (so don't expect rapid service). **Known for:** legendary address open 365 days a year; noisy, cheerful atmosphere; arrive early or be prepared for long lines. *$ Average main: €31 ✉ 27 rue Félix Faure, La Croisette ☎ 04–93–39–21–87 🌐 www.chezastoux.com.*

Grill & Wines

$$$ | **FRENCH** | Could it be that Cannes finally has an eatery where good food and friendly service come together? Come for *une verre* on the terrace or a meal in one of two interior rooms, one modern and the other traditional, where the steak-house menu offers more than just grilled Argentine black Angus, Australian Wagyu, and Kobe beef—there are also fish and seasonal vegetarian dishes, as well as plenty of French and world wines. **Known for:** pricey but amazing food; friendly staff who speak English; selection of rums from a producer in Nice. *$ Average main: €32 ✉ 5 rue Notre-Dame, Cannes ☎ 04–93–38–37–10 🌐 grillandwines.com.*

L'Affable

$$$$ | **FRENCH** | When chef Jean-Paul Battaglia decided to set up shop in Cannes, gastronomes were delighted, and he does not disappoint—so much so that it's not uncommon for tourists to eat here more than once during their stay. The roast beef is succulent, and the spicy lobster has just the right kick. **Known for:** signature Grand Marnier soufflé; open kitchen setup and prix-fixe menus; packed (and noisy) atmosphere. *$ Average main: €44 ✉ 5 rue Lafontaine, La Croisette ☎ 04–93–68–02–09 🌐 www.restaurant-laffable.fr ⏲ Closed Mon. and Sun.*

★ La Villa Archange

$$$$ | **FRENCH** | You wouldn't expect to find a restaurant with two Michelin stars set in a residential area, 10 minutes by car from La Croisette, but Bruno Oger promises you an unforgettable evening in this très cozy spot surrounded by centennial trees and gardens. Yes, it's pricey (à la carte from €130 and the two set menus are €230 and €350 without drinks), but you'll have bragging rights that you and Robert De Niro have shared the same chef. **Known for:** impeccable service; wonderful pairings by sommelier; perfectly executed nine-course Inspiration Menu

(€570 with wine). *Average main: €130 ✉ 15 bis rue Notre-Dame des Anges, Le Cannet ☎ 04–92–18–18–28 🌐 bruno-oger.com ⏲ Closed Sun. and Mon. No lunch Tues.–Thurs.*

Le Bistrot de Grand'Mère

$$$$ | FRENCH | La Brouette de Grand'Mère built a following as a charming hole-in-the-wall with a true-blue bistro menu, and although the restaurant has changed its name and location, it has kept its €55 three-course menu that includes wine, fizzy water, a shot of vodka, as well as surprisingly tasty food. It feels especially right in winter. **Known for:** classic bistro menu; wine and bottled water included; generous portions. *Average main: €55 ✉ 1 rue du pré, Cannes ☎ 04–93–38–90–50 🌐 lebistrotdegrand-mere.com ⏲ Closed Sun.*

Le Maschou

$$$$ | FRENCH | If you're tired of choosing from complicated menus, visit this long-popular restaurant in Le Suquet, where you only have to decide what kind of meat you want. Every dinner starts with a gigantic basket of whole raw vegetables—to be cut up and dipped in a selection of sauces—and grilled bread, and then come the generous servings of charcoal-grilled beef, lamb, or chicken (there's also a meat-free menu). **Known for:** beef, lamb, or chicken straight off the grill; quaint and intimate in Le Suquet; signature Tomahawk for two with baked potatoes. *Average main: €55 ✉ 15 rue St-Antoine, Cannes ☎ 04–93–39–62–21 🌐 www.lemaschou.com ⏲ Closed Nov.–Jan. No lunch.*

Le Restaurant Panoramique by Le Roof

$$$$ | FRENCH | When *Hell's Kitchen* presenter and chef Arnaud Tabarec left to open Beam! in Toulon, Lori Moreau stepped in at this trendy restaurant occupying the fifth floor of a former post office with fabulous views over Le Suquet. She shortened the menu, but there is still a good selection of fish and vegetarian dishes, as well as beef and chicken options. **Known for:** magical rooftop; all you can eat Sunday brunch; boisterous ambience. *Average main: €40 ✉ 1 rue Notre-Dame, Cannes ☎ 04–63–36–05–05 🌐 www.fiveseashotel.com/en/panoramic-restaurant.html.*

Table 22

$$$$ | FRENCH | In a city where style often wins out over substance, food lovers treasure this Suquet eatery, run by Noël Mantel, who, among other top-notch jobs, worked with Ducasse at Louis XV in Monaco. The contemporary setting harmonizes with the exquisitely detailed Mediterranean cuisine on the seasonal prix-fixe menus (€39, €49, or €60). **Known for:** one of city's finest restaurants; excellent and varied wine selection; gluten-free, lactose-intolerant, nut-allergy, and vegan options. *Average main: €40 ✉ 22 rue St-Antoine, Cannes ☎ 04–93–39–13–10 🌐 www.restaurantmantel.com ⏲ Closed Sun. and Mon. No lunch.*

Hotels

Albert Ier

$ | HOTEL | In a quiet residential area above the Forville market—a 15-minute walk uphill from La Croisette and beaches—this renovated neo–Art Deco mansion has tastefully decorated earth-tone rooms that are both minimal and tidy. **Pros:** ideal location for price; low nonrefundable rates; delicious coffee and breakfast. **Cons:** need to be in reasonable shape for the walk up the hill; needs some TLC; small rooms. *Rooms from: €95 ✉ 68 av. de Grasse, Cannes ☎ 04–93–39–24–04 🌐 www.albert1er.com 12 rooms No Meals.*

★ Carlton Cannes

$$$$ | HOTEL | To much fanfare, the rebranded Carlton Cannes, the grande dame of La Croisette since 1913, reopened in March 2023 after a multiyear, €350 million renovation, and the work of 750 specialized craftsmen led by restoration specialist Richard Lavelle was evident in the skillful preservation of every detail—from the faience and Carrara marble scales on the lobby floor to the Paolo Venini Art Deco chandeliers. **Pros:** historic spot with high-tech fitness club; largest infinity pool in Cannes; Room 623, the Alfred Hitchcock Suite, where Grace Kelly kissed Cary Grant in *To Catch a Thief*. **Cons:** €30 cocktails; deposit for entire stay is due at time of booking; no business center. *Rooms from: €800 ✉ 58 bd. de la Croisette, Cannes ☎ 04–93–06–40–06 🌐 www.ihg.com/regent 332 rooms 🍽 No Meals.*

Five Seas Hotel

$$$$ | **HOTEL** | Housed in the town's old post office, steps from the Palais des Festivals, Five Seas has plentiful amenities—a rooftop pool, personal shoppers, jogging routes, yacht charters, and dog sitters are all at hand—and a stylish interior that evokes voyages to the Far East. **Pros:** free minibar for nonalcoholic drinks; year-round heated pool; fantastic rates off-season. **Cons:** who needs a bathroom scale when vacationing in France?; can be tricky to find when driving; luxury comes with a hefty high-season price tag. *Rooms from: €450 ✉ 1 rue Notre-Dame, Cannes ☎ 04–63–36–05–05 🌐 www.fiveseashotel.com/en 45 rooms 🍽 No Meals.*

Hôtel Château de la Tour

$$ | **HOTEL** | Nestled in a 5,000-square-meter park a 10-minute drive from Cannes and near a beach, this boutique hotel on a 19th-century property feels like a mini-retreat. **Pros:** hotel is feng shui designed; excellent breakfast of homemade crêpes, eggs, and bacon; parking included in price. **Cons:** 100% of reservation charged with cancellation two days beforehand; uphill location, so mobility issues can arise; Wi-Fi can be spotty. *Rooms from: €219 ✉ 10 av. Font de Veyre, Le Cannet ☎ 04–93–90–52–52 🌐 www.hotelchateaudelatour.com ⏲ Closed Nov.–Mar. 33 rooms 🍽 No Meals.*

Hôtel Colette

$$ | **HOTEL** | Considering its proximity to the beach and Palais des Festivals, this boutique hotel facing the train station is extraordinarily affordable, particularly if you book ahead for stays in the off-season (mid-October through June). **Pros:** stylish contemporary rooms; L'Occitane toiletries; Wii Nintendo free on demand. **Cons:** €25/day parking at nearby car park; Wi-Fi reception isn't great; rooms are on the small side. *Rooms from: €140 ✉ 5 pl. de la Gare, Cannes ☎ 04–93–39–01–17 🌐 www.hotelcolette.com 45 rooms 🍽 Free Breakfast.*

★ Hôtel de Provence

$$ | **HOTEL** | This affordable choice has a fabulous location, and its very gracious owners go the extra distance to ensure guests have the service and experience of a much-higher-caliber modern hotel. **Pros:** close to Cannes city center; all-day continental breakfast for €10.80; free cancellation. **Cons:** only 10 parking places (€19 per night); smallish rooms; no spa or pool, but partners with Institut Aurélie beauty center. *Rooms from: €162 ✉ 9 rue Molière, Cannes ☎ 04–93–38–44–35 🌐 www.hotel-de-provence.com ⏲ Closed Nov.–Mar. 30 rooms 🍽 No Meals.*

Hôtel Martinez

$$$$ | **HOTEL** | A face-lift gave this hotel, part of the Hyatt Group for over a decade, a sleek, 1930s Hollywood–style glamour, and, during a stay here, you'll definitely feel like a celebrity, whether you're lounging on the private beach, La Plage, designed by architect Pierre-Yves Rocher, or enjoying modern Mediterranean cuisine by two-Michelin-star chef Christian Sinicropi in the burl-wood-and-ebony-adorned Palme d'Or restaurant. **Pros:** prestigious setting, impeccable service; decadent and endless breakfast buffet; spacious bathrooms with Fragonard products. **Cons:** smaller rooms have limited closet space; parking is €48/day; some rooms and reception could use a sprucing. *Rooms from: €650 ✉ 73 bd.*

Celebrity-Spotting in Cannes

Remember that, during the Cannes Film Festival, screenings are *not* open to the public, and the stars themselves no longer grace cafés, beaches, or the morning market; they hide in the privacy of the Hôtel du Cap-Eden Roc on the Cap d'Antibes. Your best bets for spotting celebs are at the red carpet events at the Palais des Festivals every evening at 7:30 pm and 10:30 pm or the backstreet exits of big hotels—like the Rue Saint Honoré behind the Majestic—where A-listers dash into their car en route to the Palais about an hour before events. Cannes Cinéphiles (*moncompte.festival-cannes.com*) allows 4,000 members (including foreigners) a chance to view Official Selections, including Competition films and Special Screenings. You can apply online in February.

de la Croisette, Cannes 04–93–90–12–34 www.hyatt.com 410 rooms Free Breakfast.

Hôtel Renoir

$$ | HOTEL | This boutique hotel is in a graceful mansion on a residential backstreet behind the city center and within reasonable walking distance of La Croisette. **Pros:** super-friendly and helpful staff; 15-minute walk to La Croisette; gluten-free bread and almond or soy milk on request at buffet breakfast (€20). **Cons:** affiliated beach is pricey; shower separated by glass screen; small elevator and steep steps at the entrance. *Rooms from: €180 7 rue Edith Cavell, Cannes 04–92–99–62–62 www.hotel-renoir.fr Closed 3 wks in Jan. 31 rooms No Meals.*

Hôtel Splendid

$$ | HOTEL | This hotel in a traditional 1873 palace overlooking La Pantiéro and the Old Port offers contemporary creature comforts, up-to-date bathrooms, and freshly decorated rooms—small doubles facing the sea are a good choice if you covet a waterfront position but can't afford the grand hotels on La Croisette. **Pros:** family-run with flawless service; excellent value; great public beach around the port in La Bocca. **Cons:** hand-held showers in bathtub; breakfast €22; no on-site parking. *Rooms from: €189 Allées de la Liberté, 4–6 rue Félix-Faure, Cannes 04–97–06–22–22 www.splendid-hotel-cannes.fr 62 rooms No Meals.*

Le Cavendish Boutique Hotel

$$ | HOTEL | Lovingly restored by friendly owners Christine and Guy Welter, the giddily opulent former residence of Lord Cavendish and a listed Belle Époque building is a true delight, blending a contemporary palette of "wintergarden" greens and "incensed" reds with 19th-century elegance. **Pros:** few steps from Palais des Festival and beaches; complimentary drinks daily 6:30–8:30 pm; only Cannes hotel that serves breakfast until the last guest has eaten. **Cons:** located on noisy street; one charging point for electric car (€25); €25/day secure car park. *Rooms from: €180 11 bd. Carnot, Cannes 04–97–06–26–00 cavendish-cannes.com/fr 34 rooms No Meals.*

★ Mondrian Cannes

$$$$ | HOTEL | While being transformed into the Mondrian Cannes—the first of the Accor brand's sleek lifestyle hotels to open in France—the former Grand Hotel underwent a massive modernization that not only refreshed the rooms but also added the unique Mr. Nakamoto restaurant and the new Hyde Beach, which is only about 300 feet from the hotel's front door and has its own pier. **Pros:** free bottled water in room; American-style 1950s grill restaurant with a Japanese twist; noon checkout. **Cons:** €42 breakfast; extras can add up (€25 parking); room decor doesn't dazzle. *Rooms from: €420* *45 bd. de la Croisette, Cannes* *04–93–38–15–45* *book.ennismore.com/hotels/mondrian/cannes* *Closed Dec. and Jan.* *75 rooms* *No Meals.*

OKKO Hotel Cannes Center

$$ | ALL-INCLUSIVE | At reception upon checking into this four-star hotel, where the rooms are compact but very functional and chic, you'll be reminded that snacks, hot and cold drinks, and a nightly aperitivo at the 24/7 rooftop bar are included in your rate, as are Nespresso coffee, unlimited national calls (with a €10 credit for international calls), and access to the gym and kitchen facility with fridges and a large communal table. **Pros:** all-inclusive rates, a rarity in Cannes; 10-minute walk to beach and five minutes to main shopping street; early check-in and late checkout possible with direct bookings. **Cons:** if you like your air-conditioning on the frosty side you will be disappointed; louvered bathroom walls not great for nonsolo travelers; parking not included. *Rooms from: €167* *6 bis pl. de la Gare, Cannes* *04–92–98–30–30* *www.okkohotels.com* *125 rooms* *All-Inclusive.*

Nightlife

For most of the year, Cannes is a festival town, and its nightlife reflects pop-up party spots where you need an invitation.

Le Bâoli

DANCE CLUBS | The biggest player on the Cannes nightlife scene, Le Bâoli attracts the likes of the Kardashians, Channing Tatum, Jude Law, and oh, some 3,000 other revelers who pass the door-selection process. It's usually packed until dawn even outside of festival time. If staying up past 10 doesn't interest you, head to Cloud Nine, the 360-degree-panorama rooftop bar that's open June–September for sunset cocktails. *Port Canto, Bd. de la Croisette, La Croisette* *04–93–43–03–43* *www.baolicannes.com/en.*

Zoa Bistrot

COCKTAIL LOUNGES | Open seven days a week until 1 am, Zoa is a sushi eatery that also happens to be *the* place to drink chic cocktails. Be sure to book a table in advance. *2 pl. Charles de Gaulle, Cannes* *04–93–30–00–30* *www.zoasushibar.com.*

Shopping

Whether you're window-shopping or splurging on that little Maria Grazia Chiuri number in the Dior window, you'll find some of the best shopping outside Paris on the streets off La Croisette. For stores carrying designer names, try Rond-point Duboys-d'Angers off Rue Amouretti, Rue des Serbes, and Rue des Belges, all perpendicular to the waterfront.

Rue d'Antibes is the town's main shopping drag, home base to every kind of clothing and shoe shop, as well as mouthwatering candy, fabric, and home-design stores. Rue Meynadier mixes trendy young clothes with high-end food specialties.

Activities

Cannes Stand-up Paddle Evasion

STAND UP PADDLEBOARDING | Near Palm Beach, this is one of the first shops on the Riviera to jump (or stand) on the SUP trend. It's a unique way to take in coastal views, so see Jean-Marc about renting a board, starting at €15 hour for Initiation or Discovery lessons. *5 pl. Franklin Roosevelt, Cannes* *07–69–91–57–01, 06–87–95–45–18* *www.stand-up-paddle-kayak-cannes.com.*

Club Nautique de la Croisette
WATER SPORTS | At its private windsurfing base off Île Ste-Marguerite, this company organizes diving sorties and rents kayaks, windsurfers, and catamarans for 30 minutes or an hour, June–October. ✉ *Bijou Plage, Cannes* ☎ *04–93–45–09–40* 🌐 *www.club-nautique-croisette.fr.*

Elite Rent a Bike
BIKING | This outfitter rents electric, mountain, and racing bikes starting at €32 per day (along with a hefty up to €1,200 safety deposit). If you're more intrepid, consider renting a moped for €75 per day (plus €800 deposit); no special driver's license is required. ✉ *19 av. du Maréchal Juin, Cannes* ☎ *04–93–94–30–34* 🌐 *www.elite-rentabike.com.*

Rivage Croisière Catamaran
SAILING | FAMILY | From May to September, climb aboard a 25-meter, three-crew catamaran for destination paradise: Lérins Islands. Swim and snorkel (kit provided) as the boat moors between the two islands, or go ashore. The full-day trip (€122) departs at 10:15 am every day except Monday and returns at 5:15 pm; it includes lunch onboard. The half-day trip (€65; three hours, no meal) departs at 2 pm. Fireworks cruises are also on the catamaran menu. ✉ *20 quai St-Pierre, Cannes* ☎ *04–92–98–71–31* 🌐 *www.rivage-croisiere.com.*

Îles de Lérins

15–20 minutes by ferry off the coast of Cannes.

When you're glutted on glamour and tired of dodging limos and the leavings of dyed-to-match poodles, catch a boat from Cannes's Vieux Port to one of two Îles de Lérins. On one of these two lovely island getaways you can find car-free peace and lose yourself in a tropical landscape of palms, pines, and tidal pools. Ste-Marguerite Island has more in the way of attractions: a ruined prison-fortress, a museum, and a handful of restaurants. Smaller and wilder, St-Honorat Island is dominated by its active monastery and its 10th-century ruins. Allow at least a half day to enjoy either island; you can see both if you get an early start. Although Ste-Marguerite has some restaurants and snack shops, you would be wise to bring along a picnic and drinks to enjoy the designated areas, which you won't find at St-Honorat.

■ TIP→ A mind-boggling way to experience the islands without the crowds (and earn some serious bragging rights) is the ÖTILLÖ Swinrun Cannes that happens every October. The 24-mile race starts just after sunrise from Ste-Marguerite and includes a 1 mile swim back to Cap de la Croissette on the mainland, before a run along the famous boulevard and by the red carpet at the Palais des Festivals.

GETTING HERE AND AROUND

Buy your tickets to Île Ste-Marguerite from one of the ferry companies at the booths on Cannes's Vieux Port; look for the Horizon Company, which operates year-round. It's a 15-minute ride to Îles de Lérins from Cannes (€17 round-trip; daily approximately every hour on the hour 9–4 in high season, last boat back at 5 pm). Book online for reduced rates.

Boats to Île St-Honorat are run by the monks who inhabit the island, and tickets must be purchased from their own company, Planaria. Île St-Honorat can be reached in 20 minutes (€16.50 round-trip) from the Vieux Port; the schedule varies depending on the month, but from April to mid-October, ferries run every hour 9–5 (8 am on Sundays and holidays) and return 9:30–5:30. For an extra €5.50, you can get a 15-minute tour of the vineyard and sample its wines as part of the Vineyard Wines Excursion.

CONTACTS Horizon Company. ✉ *Quai Laubeuf, Cannes* ☎ *04–92–98–71–36*

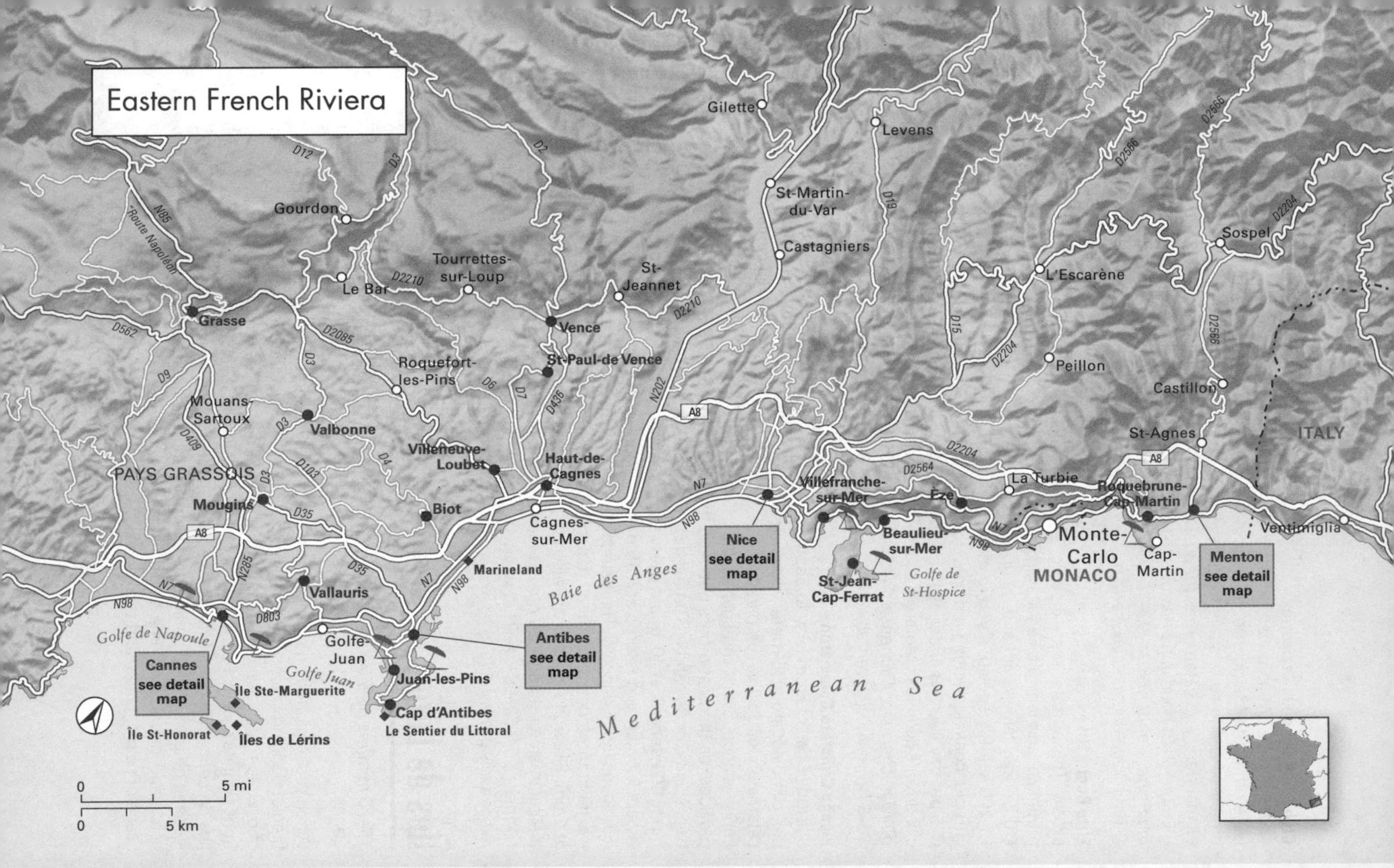

Eastern French Riviera
Gilette
Levens
St-Martin-du-Var
Castagniers
Gourdon
Tourrettes-sur-Loup
Le Bar
St-Jeannet
Sospel
L'Escarène
Grasse
Vence
St-Paul-de-Vence
Roquefort-les-Pins
Peillon
Castillon
Mouans-Sartoux
Valbonne
Villeneuve-Loubet
Haut-de-Cagnes
PAYS GRASSOIS
Mougins
Biot
Cagnes-sur-Mer
St-Agnes
ITALY
La Turbie
Villefranche-sur-Mer
Èze
Roquebrune-Cap-Martin
Beaulieu-sur-Mer
Monte-Carlo
MONACO
Cap-Martin
Ventimiglia
Marineland
Vallauris
Golfe de Napoule
Golfe-Juan
Golfe Juan
Juan-les-Pins
Cap d'Antibes
Le Sentier du Littoral
Île Ste-Marguerite
Île St-Honorat
Îles de Lérins
Baie des Anges
St-Jean-Cap-Ferrat
Golfe de St-Hospice
Mediterranean Sea
Cannes see detail map
Antibes see detail map
Nice see detail map
Menton see detail map
"Route Napoléon"
N85
D12
D3
D2
D2210
D562
D2085
D9
D6
D7
D436
D409
D103
D4
D35
N202
A8
N7
N98
N285
D803
D19
D15
D2204
D2564
D2566
0
5 mi
5 km

www.horizon-lerins.com. **Planaria.** ✉ *Vieux Port, end of parking Laubeuf, Cannes* ☎ *04–92–98–71–38* 🌐 *www.cannes-ilesdelerins.com.*

Sights

Île St-Honorat

ISLAND | Smaller and wilder than Ste-Marguerite, Île St-Honorat is home to an active monastery and the ruins of its 11th-century predecessor. The monks are more famous in the region for their nonreligious activity: manufacturing and selling a rather strong liqueur called Lérina. Retreats at the abbey's *hôtellerie* require a two-night minimum stay, and you must bring your own sheets and towels and obey the rule of silence (even during mealtime). There is no cost, but a donation of €45–€55 per night per person is welcome. There is Wi-Fi but only in a restricted area. **■ TIP→ There are no garbage cans on Île St-Honorat, so be prepared to take any trash you generate back with you to Cannes.** ✉ *Ile St-Honorat* 🌐 *abbayedelerins.com/site/fr.*

★ Île Ste-Marguerite

ISLAND | From the drop-off point on Île Ste-Marguerite, walk left for 10 minutes to see the Fort Royal. Built by Richelieu and improved by Vauban, the fort offers views over the ramparts to the rocky island coast and the open sea. On the southern side of the island, you'll have to get wet to see the underwater eco-museum: its six statues are submerged 92 to 144 yards from the shore at a depth of 10 to 16 feet. The island's two restaurants—L'Escale and La Guérite—are both closed from mid-October to spring. They're also rather pricey, and the service is not as good as the fish; you are paying for food with a view. Public toilets are accessible. ✉ *Ile-Ste-Marguerite.*

Musée de la Mer (*Marine Museum*)

HISTORY MUSEUM | **FAMILY** | This complex is famous for reputedly being the prison of the Man in the Iron Mask. Inside, you can see his cell and hear his story. The truth of his captivity is not certain; however, it is true that many Huguenots were confined here during Louis XIV's religious scourges. You'll also find a Roman boat dating from the 1st century BC and a collection of amphorae and pottery recovered from ancient shipwrecks. ✉ *Fort de l'Île Ste-Marguerite, Ile-Ste-Marguerite* ☎ *04–93–89–26–26* 🎟 *€6.50* ⏲ *Closed Mon. Oct.–May.*

Restaurants

Restaurant La Tonnelle

$$$$ | **FRENCH** | It's hard to believe that this tranquil island is only 20 minutes from Cannes by boat, and that it's the location of a scenic, 19th-century restaurant run by monks from the Île St-Honorat monastery alongside chef Mathias Metge. You're here for the views; although the menu focuses on very fresh grilled fish, prices seem aimed at the stars (literally), and service reflects a "we're the only restaurant on the island" attitude. **Known for:** breezy luxurious atmosphere; wines and liqueurs produced by island monks; snack bar open mid-May–mid-Sept. $ *Average main: €35* ✉ *Abbaye Notre-Dame de Lérins, Ile St-Honorat* ☎ *04–92–99–54–08* 🌐 *tonnelle-abbayedelerins.fr* ⏲ *Closed Nov.–mid-Apr.* ✍ *Reservations required. No dinner.*

Mougins

8 km (5 miles) north of Cannes; 11 km (7 miles) northwest of Antibes; 32 km (20 miles) southwest of Nice.

Passing through Mougins, a popular residential expat community near Cannes, Nice, and the big Sophia-Antipolis business park, you may perceive little more than sleek, upscale, suburban sprawl. But, in 1961, Picasso found more to admire and settled into a *mas* (traditional farm) that became a mecca for artists and art lovers; he died there in 1973.

Over the decades, others of note also colonized the town, including Cocteau, Man Ray, Léger, and Christian Dior.

Despite overbuilding, Mougins claims extraordinary (yet distant) views over the coast and has a charming, gentrified Old Town (which is a *zone piétonne,* or pedestrian zone) on a hilltop above the fray. In addition to a few off-duty celebrities, you'll encounter wealthy Parisians who have chosen to buy a Riviera pied-à-terre here. Where they go, noted chefs follow, and Mougins is now a byword in gourmet circles, with restaurants as well as expensive cafés with pleasant terraces. The town also has plenty of galleries.

GETTING HERE AND AROUND

Getting to Mougins by public transportation is time-consuming. Bus 660 from Cannes or Grasse stops in Mougins; from there it's a 15-minute walk up the hill to the Vieux Village. Alternatively, you could get off at the Val de Mougins stop and call the on-demand 206 Palm Bus to take you up to the Vieux Village (any day except Sunday) or the 208 from the train station in Mouans-Sartoux (from Cannes a 20-minute train ride; €3.50).

From Nice, the 40-minute train to Cannes costs €7.90 one-way. If you don't have time to burn, opt for a taxi (around €50 from Cannes).

FESTIVALS

Les Étoiles de Mougins

CULTURAL FESTIVALS | Since it first started in 2006, hundreds of the world's best chefs have converged in Mougins Village to share their passion with demonstrations, workshops, and tastings in this open-air theater of gastronomy. Free shuttles transport you from the parking lot up to the village where you can roam freely, but you'll need to purchase tickets online for any demonstrations or events. The festival plans to increase its presence abroad, in countries like Italy and Japan, by taking a road tour every other year. ✉ *Vieux Village, Mougins* ☎ *04–92–92–14–00* 🌐 *festival.lesetoiles-demougins.com.*

VISITOR INFORMATION

CONTACTS Mougins Tourist Office. ✉ *39 pl. des Patriotes, Mougins* ☎ *04–92–92–14–00* 🌐 *mouginstourisme.com.*

Sights

Centre de la Photographie de Mougins

ART MUSEUM | This municipal museum officially opened July 2023 in a former presbytery in the heart of the village. The €1.9 million project replaces the former photography museum and looks "to support artistic creation through exhibitions, publications, and artist residencies." François Cheval, the curator and co-founder of the Lianzhou Museum of Photography in China, was named artistic director. There's a bookshop on the main floor and two stories for temporary exhibitions. ✉ *Porte Sarrazine, 43 rue d'Église, Mougins* ☎ *04–22–21–52–12* 🌐 *centrephotographiemougins.com* 🎫 *€6* ⏲ *Closed Tues. Closed Mon. Oct.–Mar.*

★ **Musée d'Art Classique de Mougins**

ART MUSEUM | This hidden gem "highlights the dialogue between the old and the new" with Roman, Greek, and Egyptian art rubbing shoulders with pieces by Picasso, Matisse, Cézanne, Warhol, and Dalí. Expect to come across a sarcophagus alongside a Cocteau or a Hirst sculpture next to an ancient bust. Spread over four floors, the museum also houses antique jewelry and the world's largest private armory collection. ✉ *32 rue Commandeur, Mougins* ☎ *04–93–75–18–22* 🌐 *www.mouginsmusee.com* 🎫 *€14.*

Notre-Dame-de-Vie

CHURCH | To find Picasso's final home, where he lived for 12 years until 1973, follow the D35 south of Mougins 2 km (1 mile) to the ancient ecclesiastical site of Notre-Dame-de-Vie. From his room, Picasso could see the 13th-century bell tower and arcaded chapel, a pretty ensemble once immortalized in a painting by Winston Churchill. The chapel, listed as a historical monument since 1927, is said to date from 1655. Approached through an allée of ancient cypresses, the former priory house Picasso shared with his wife, Jacqueline, overlooks the broad bowl of the countryside (now blighted with modern construction). Unfortunately, his residence was bought by a private investor and is now closed to the public. ✉ *Ch. de la Chapelle, Mougins* *Free* ⏲ *Closed weekdays in May, June, and Sept., and Mon.–Sat. Oct.–Apr.*

Hotels

Le Manoir de l'Etang
$$ | **B&B/INN** | Owner Camilla Richards spent 20 years in London before converting this 19th-century Provençal manor house—in the Bois de Fond Merle, perched over a lotus pond with a spectacular pool and near the Cannes–Mougins golf course—into an upscale inn. **Pros:** friendly welcome from English-speaking owner; exceptional setting with air-conditioning; well-priced restaurant. **Cons:** stone steps difficult for those with mobility issues; Cannes beaches 7-km (4½-mile) drive away; some bathrooms need TLC. *Rooms from: €200* ✉ *66 allée du Manoir, Mougins* ☎ *04–92–28–36–00* ⊕ *www.manoir-de-letang.com* ⏲ *Closed Nov.* *22 rooms* *Free Breakfast.*

Royal Mougins Golf Resort Hotel
$$$ | **RESORT** | What it lacks in Provençal character, this plush hotel on the green makes up for in modern comforts—each suite, decorated in soothing tones of beige and gray, is an independent apartment that has a separate living room as well as a kitchenette. **Pros:** tranquil atmosphere; golf course, outdoor pool, and free parking; kitchenettes have a dishwasher. **Cons:** Wi-Fi can be weak; you need a car to get here; decor a bit lacking. *Rooms from: €300* ✉ *424 av. du Roi, Mougins* ☎ *04–92–92–49–69* ⊕ *www.royalmougins.fr* ⏲ *Closed Jan. and Feb.* *29 suites* *Free Breakfast.*

Activities

Golf Club de Cannes-Mougins
GOLF | Founded in 1923 by members such as Aga Khan and Prince Pierre of Monaco, this course is a stunner. The club has hosted the European Open of Cannes, while the PGA Senior Tour also played here. Nonmembers are welcome (if they have a maximum handicap of 28), and there's a dress code (no long-sleeve shirts or denim). ✉ *1175 av. du Golf, Mougins* ☎ *04–93–75–79–13* ⊕ *www.golfcannesmougins.com* *From €100* *18 holes, 6780 yards, par 72.*

Grasse

10 km (6 miles) northwest of Mougins; 17 km (11 miles) northwest of Cannes; 22 km (14 miles) northwest of Antibes; 42 km (26 miles) southwest of Nice.

Coco Chanel may have first set up shop in Cannes, but when she wanted to create her classic No. 5 fragrance she headed to Grasse. The mild microclimate in what is the perfume capital of the world nurtures nearly year-round shows of tropically hued flowers: orange blossoms, pittosporum, roses, lavender, jasmine, and mimosa. In the past, Grasse's legendary perfume-makers laid blossoms face-down in a lard-smeared tray, then soaked the essence away in alcohol. Today, the scents are condensed in vast copper stills. Only the essential oils are kept, and the water thrown away—except rose water and orange water, which find their way into delicately perfumed pastries.

In Paris and on the outskirts of Grasse, the scents are blended by a professional *nez,* or "nose," who must be able to distinguish some 500 distinct fragrances and may be able to identify up to 3,000. The products carry the names of couturiers like Chanel and Dior as well as such perfume houses as Guerlain. The laboratories where these great blends are produced are off-limits to visitors, but, to accommodate the crowds of inquisitive scent-seekers, Molinard, Fragonard, and Galimard each has a factory that creates simple blends and demonstrates some production techniques. Factory tours are free, and you pass through a boutique of house perfumes on the way out.

If you're looking for a more "scent-sational" experience, create your own perfume at Galimard (you can even order refills online once back home) and be treated to VIP perks, like a glass of Champagne at the end of a workshop. The annual Jasmine Festival takes place over three days at the end of July or early August with traditional floats and puppet shows.

GETTING HERE AND AROUND

The train from Nice takes just over an hour (€11.40), but it's under 30 minutes from Cannes (€4.90). Alternatively, Bus 659 from Nice has daily service to Grasse, and Bus 660 comes from Cannes; both cost €2.10.

Once here, you can get around aboard Le Petit Train de Grasse for a 35-minute circuit of the town, including Place aux Aires, Vieille Ville, and the cathedral. It departs every day (€6.50) but Sunday, April–October, 11–6 from the Cours Honoré Cresp; in summer it operates seven days a week.

VISITOR INFORMATION

CONTACTS Grasse Tourist Office. ✉ *Pl. de la Buanderie, Grasse* ☎ *04–93–36–66–66* 🌐 *www.paysdegrassetourisme.fr/en.*

Sights

Cathédrale Notre-Dame-du-Puy

CHURCH | On a cliff top overlook at the Old Town's edge, this Romanesque cathedral contains no fewer than three paintings by Rubens, a triptych by the famed 15th-century Provençal painter Louis Bréa, and *Lavement des Pieds* (*The Washing of the Feet*) by the young Fragonard. ✉ *Pl. du Petit Puy, Grasse* 🎫 *Free.*

Fragonard

FACTORY | Built in 1782, this perfume factory is open to the public daily for free guided tours, and it has the best boutique: look for the Ma Fougassette (My Sweet Fougasse)—your home will have the wonderful scent of a Provence sweet, soft *fougasse* bread. Sign up for a do-it-yourself-perfume (DIYP) workshop for a more specialized memento of your visit. ✉ *20 bd. Fragonard, Grasse* ☎ *04–93–36–44–65* 🌐 *www.fragonard.com* 🎫 *Free.*

Galimard

FACTORY | Tracing its pedigree back to 1747, Galimard is one of the world's oldest perfume houses. Today, its factory is open to visitors 365 days a year, where for €58 you can create and name your own perfume in a two-hour workshop. They're held daily at 10, 2, and 4 in Galimard's Studio des Fragrances, around the corner at 5 route de Pegomas; for those with more time, try the Haute-Parfumerie workshops with your very own nez to accompany your creations and a decadent Champagne break. ✉ *73 rte. de Cannes, Grasse* ☎ *04–93–09–20–00* 🌐 *www.galimard.com* 🎫 *Free.*

Molinard

FACTORY | Established in 1849, Molinard offers an extensive tour that includes visits to the Soap Factory, the Distillery (witness "the nose" at work concocting new fragrances), and the Cream Room, where the packaging team hand-labels each bottle or pump. For €30—and without a reservation—you can create your perfume in a few basic steps (20 minutes). ✉ *60 bd. Victor Hugo, Grasse* ☎ *04–93–36–01–62* 🌐 *www.molinard.com* 🎫 *Free.*

Did You Know?

The factory of perfume-maker Fragonard is among the places where you can learn how Grasse—whose micro-climate nurtures orange blossoms, roses, lavender, jasmine, and mimosa, among other blooms—became the world's fragrance capital.

Musée d'Art et d'Histoire de Provence (*Museum of the Art and History of Provence*)
ART MUSEUM | Just up from the Fragonard perfumery, the Musée d'Art et d'Histoire de Provence is open daily and has a large collection of faïence from the region, including works from the famous pottery towns of Moustiers, Biot, and Vallauris. ✉ *2 rue Mirabeau, Grasse* ☎ *04–93–36–80–20* 🌐 *www.museesdegrasse.com* 🎫 *€2.*

Musée International de la Parfumerie (*International Museum of Perfume*)
OTHER MUSEUM | With its soaring structure of steel, glass, and teak, the MIP has long been one of the more sleekly spectacular museums along the coast. The contemporary design relies on color-coding to easily trace the 3,000-year history of perfume making (highlights include a fascinating collection of 4,000 antique perfume bottles). Artist contributions, like the "Eye Nose You" project that lets you discover details of the scented body through a photographic lens, add a living dimension to the museum. ✉ *2 bd. du Jeu de Ballon, Grasse* ☎ *04–97–05–58–00* 🌐 *www.museesdegrasse.com* 🎫 *€6.*

Place aux Aires
PLAZA/SQUARE | Below the central cluster of museums and perfumeries, the picturesque Place aux Aires is lined with 17th- and 18th-century houses and their arcades. Every Saturday morning there's a small market selling produce and spices (the bigger market happens Wednesday 8–1, at Place du Cours Honoré Cresp). ✉ *Grasse.*

Vieille Ville (*Old Town*)
NEIGHBORHOOD | Go down the steps to Rue Mirabeau and lose yourself in the dense labyrinth of the Vieille Ville, where steep, narrow streets, austere facades, discreet gardens, and random flights of stairs are thrown into shadow by shuttered houses five and six stories tall. ✉ *Grasse.*

Villa Musée Fragonard
ART MUSEUM | This museum headlines the work of Grasse's own Jean-Honoré Fragonard (1732–1806), who was one of the great French "chocolate-box" artists—so called because they were known for their maudlin artwork of a type that was found on boxes of chocolate at the time. The lovely villa contains a collection of Fragonard's drawings, engravings, and paintings; also on display are works by his son, Alexandre-Evariste, and his grandson, Théophile. ✉ *23 bd. Fragonard, Grasse* ☎ *04–93–36–52–98* 🌐 *www.museesdegrasse.com* 🎫 *Free. €2 includes entry to Museum of the Art and History of Provence* ⏲ *Closed last 3 wks of Nov.*

 Restaurants

Les Delicatesses de Grasse
$$ | **SANDWICHES** | All that perfume sniffing can build an appetite and this is just the place to refuel on cheeses, olives, charcuteries, tapenades, and chuntneys. It's open daily, and you could spend hours lingering over a half bottle of wine and sampling the delicious regional selections that are part of a shared platter (three to four people) for only €30. **Known for:** quaint Provençal deli; great wine pairings; small space so gets crowded quickly. 💲 *Average main: €18* ✉ *7 rue Marcel Journet* ☎ *06–16–02–44–26* 🌐 *les-delicatessesdeg.wixsite.com/monsite.*

 Hotels

La Bastide Saint-Antoine
$$$ | **HOTEL** | This ocher mansion, once the home of an industrialist who hosted the Kennedys and the Rolling Stones, is now the Relais & Chateaux domain of celebrated chef Jacques Chibois, who welcomes you with old stone walls, shaded walkways, an enormous pool, and guest rooms that glossily mix Louis XVI, Provençal, and high-tech delights. **Pros:** choice of Provençal or modern room

Route Napoléon

One of France's most famous and panoramic roads is the Route Napoléon (🌐 *www.route-napoleon.com*), taken by Napoléon Bonaparte in 1815 after his escape from imprisonment on the Mediterranean island of Elba. He landed at Golfe-Juan, near Cannes, on March 1 and forged northwest to Grasse, then through dramatic, hilly countryside to Castellane, Digne, and Sisteron. Commemorative plaques bearing the imperial eagle stud the route, inspired by Napoléon's remark, "The eagle will fly from steeple to steeple until it reaches the towers of Notre-Dame."

Although there are a few lavender-honey stands and souvenir shacks along the way, it's the panoramic views as the curvy but well-maintained road winds up into the Alps that make this a route worth taking. The whole 314-km (195-mile) route from Golfe-Juan to Grenoble takes about five days, but you can just do part of it and still take in lovely scenery. You can also follow the Route Napoléon to Trigance and then on to the spectacular Gorges du Verdon (aka the Grand Canyon du Verdon). From there, you can continue on to the heart of the Var and, in a mere 30 minutes, be amid the beautiful Gorges Country.

decor; coffee machine and organic tea in each room; 1,000 wine references and over 25,000 bottles. **Cons:** restaurant is very expensive; books up far in advance; deposit of 50% of the total stay is charged at time of booking. 💲 *Rooms from: €336* ✉ *48 av. Henri-Dunant, Grasse* ☎ *04–93–70–94–94* 🌐 *www.jacques-chibois.com* 🕓 *Closed 3 wks in Nov.* *16 rooms* 🍴 *No Meals.*

Valbonne

18 km (11 miles) north of Cannes; 14 km (9 miles) northwest of Antibes.

This Provençal hill town has been adopted by the British and a smorgasbord of other nationalities, who work either at the nearby tech park Sophia-Antipolis (France's Silicon Valley) or commute to, say, London or Geneva during the workweek, thanks to low-cost travel from easyJet.

Valbonne exudes a peculiar kind of mixed-country charm, with a plethora of tasteful restorations and restaurants (including Moroccan, Indian, and sushi). Its principal draw is its Old Town, laid out in a grid system in the 16th century by the monks of Lérins. A checkerboard of ruler-straight *ruelles* (little streets) lies within a sturdy rampart of wraparound houses. At the center, a grand *place* is framed by Renaissance arcades and shady elms, perfect for people-watching at one of the cafés, and at the bottom of the village is the 13th-century Abbaye de Valbonne.

You'll find upgraded versions of typical gifts to take home at the Friday Provençal market, one of the region's best, and the first Sunday of the month features an antiques fair. The Maison de la Presse Libris newsstand, beside the pharmacy, has an outstanding selection of international publications. Memoire de Famille (✉ *18 rue Alexis Julien*) sells fabulous and affordable housewares and, just steps away, is Niche Books (✉ *7 rue Grande*), which is owned by two British bookworms.

A few kilometers west of Valbonne you'll find La Pitchoune, Julia Child's former Provençal home in Plascassier. For more than 20 years, it was run by

American Kathie Alex as Cooking with Friends in France, using Julia's kitchen very much as it was in her heyday. Today, Julia's legacy lives on as Le Peetch, an unconventional cooking school offering a recipe-free, all-inclusive, five-night experience.

GETTING HERE AND AROUND

There are two ways to get to Valbonne: by car (all the parking is free!) or by bus. In Cannes, in front of the train station, the daily Bus 663 takes about 40 minutes (€2.10). And from the bus station in Antibes, Bus 10 accesses Valbonne via Biot (35 minutes, €1.50 onboard) and runs seven days a week.

Restaurants

★ Restaurant De Sa Vie

$$$$ | FRENCH | Judging by the crowd of regulars flocking to his restaurant, Daniel Desavie has built quite a reputation for his classic Provençal dishes—hardly surprising given that he was trained for 23 years by the late Roger Vergé at the famous Moulins de Mougins. Try the half lobster with cranberry beans and wild mushrooms salad in herb vinaigrette before tucking into thinly sliced beef with truffle coulis. **Known for:** knowledgeable sommelier; set-price menus at gastronomic restaurant and more relaxed Le Bistrot; free parking. *Average main: €37* ✉ *1360 rte. d'Antibes, Valbonne* ✣ *From Valbonne, follow Rte. de Cannes then take left at Forum roundabout along D103* ☎ *04–93–12–29–68* 🌐 *restaurant-danieldesavie.fr* ⏲ *Closed Sun. and Mon.*

Vallauris

6 km (4 miles) northeast of Cannes; 6 km (4 miles) west of Antibes.

Dominated by a blocky Renaissance château, this ancient village in the low hills above the coast owes its four-square street plan to a form of medieval urban renewal. Ravaged and eventually wiped out by waves of the plague in the 14th century, the village was rebuilt by 70 Genovese families imported by the Abbaye de Lérins in the 16th century to repopulate the abandoned site. They brought with them a taste for Roman planning—hence the grid format in the Old Town—but more importantly, a knack for pottery making. Their skills and the fine clay of Vallauris were a perfect marriage, and the village thrived as a pottery center for hundreds of years.

In the late 1940s Picasso found inspiration in the malleable soil and settled here, giving the flagging industry new life. And it was here that Hollywood goddess Rita Hayworth married Ali Khan on May 27, 1949. Sadly, the town has developed a more shady reputation (so keep your hands on your purse) despite Saudi's King Salman owning a 1930s villa where Churchill and Hollywood celebs stayed, running along 1 km (½ mile) of Vallauris's beachfront.

GETTING HERE AND AROUND

The SNCF Golfe–Juan–Vallauris train station is in Place Pierre Sémard in the center of Vallauris. Tickets cost €6.40 one-way from Nice (30 minutes) and €2.10 from Cannes (only 4 minutes). Bus 8, part of the Envibus network, runs between the Golfe–Juan train station and Vallauris about every 15 minutes (45–55 minutes on Sunday). From Place Guynemer in Antibes, Envibus 5 goes to Vallauris with less frequent departures. Bus 200, connecting Nice and Cannes (€1.50), stops in Golfe–Juan and runs about every 15 minutes.

Sights

Musée National Picasso

ART MUSEUM | In the late 1940s, Picasso settled here in a simple stone house, "le château de Vallauris"—the former priory of the Abbaye de Lérins and one of the rare Renaissance buildings in the region—creating pottery art from the malleable local clay with a single-minded passion. But he returned to painting in 1952 to create one of his masterworks in the château's Romanesque chapel: the vast multipanel oil-on-wood composition called *La Guerre et la Paix* (*War and Peace*). Today the chapel is part of the Musée National Picasso, where several of Picasso's ceramic pieces are displayed. ✉ *Pl. de la Libération, Vallauris* ☎ *04–93–64–71–83* 🌐 *musees-nationaux-alpesmaritimes.fr/picasso* 🎫 *€6* 🕓 *Closed Tues.*

Antibes

15 km (9 miles) southeast of Nice.

Named Antipolis—meaning across from (*anti*) the city (*polis*)—by the Greeks, who founded it in the 4th century BC, Antibes flourished under aristocratic rule of the Romans, who gave it an amphitheater, aqueducts, and baths. The early Christians established their bishopric here, the site of the region's cathedral until the 13th century. It was in the Middle Ages that the kings of France began fortifying this key port town, an effort that culminated in the recognizable star-shape ramparts designed by Vauban.

The young general Napoléon once headed this stronghold, living with his family in a humble house in the Old Town; his mother washed their clothes in a stream. There's still a *lavoir* (public laundry fountain) in the Old Town where locals, not unlike Signora Bonaparte, rinse their clothes and hang them like garlands over the narrow streets.

With its broad stone ramparts scalloping in and out over the waves and backed by blunt medieval towers, it's easy to understand why Antibes (pronounced "Awn-*teeb*") inspired Picasso to paint on a panoramic scale. Stroll Promenade Amiral-de-Grasse along the crest of Vauban's sea walls, and watch the sleek yachts purring out to sea.

Even more intoxicating, just off the waterfront, is the souklike maze of old streets, its market filled with fresh fish and goat cheese, wild herbs, and exotic spices. This is Vieil Antibes, with a nearly Italianate feel, perhaps no great surprise considering that Antibes's great fort marked the border between Italy and France right up to the 19th century.

Monet fell in love with the town, and his most famous paintings show the fortified Vieil Antibes against the sea. He arrived in January 1888 and expected to stay only a few days; three months later, he had shipped off 39 canvases to be exhibited in Paris at the gallery of Vincent van Gogh's brother. To see Antibes as Monet—and Picasso, Cross, Boudin, and Harpignies—once did, head to the tourist office for an English-language pamphlet, complete with a map, on the Painters' Trail, or sign up for a guided walk of it.

GETTING HERE AND AROUND

Antibes has one central train station, the Gare SNCF, which is at the far end of town but still within walking distance of the vieille ville and only a block or so from the beach. Local trains are frequent, coming from Nice (20 minutes, €5.20), Juan-les-Pins, Biot, Cannes (10 minutes, €3.30), and almost all other coastal towns. High-speed TGVs (Trains à Grand Vitesse) also stop in Antibes, but they cost a little more, and you won't be able to board without a ticket.

Bus service, available at Antibes's Gare Routière (✉ *1 pl. Guynemer*) is supplied by Envibus. For local routes or to get to Cannes, Nice, Cagnes-sur-Mer, Juan-les-Pins, take the Zou! 620 (ex-200), which runs every 15 minutes and costs €2.10. A new bus-tram Line A serves 18 stops from Antibes via Biot to Sophia Antipolis, the tech park located near Valbonne (there are plans to extend the route to

Grasse); tickets are cheaper when you buy them on your phone.

TOURS

Antibes Tourist Office Tours

WALKING TOURS | Throughout the year, the tourist office offers guided tours that range from the Painters' Trail and Artists and the Mediterranean to Discovering Old Antibes. June through September, the Gourmet Tour lets you sample local flavor on stops at three local eateries. Tours in English must be reserved in advance with the tourist office. ✉ *Pl. Guynemer, Antibes* ☎ *04–22–10–60–10* 🌐 *www.antibesjuanlespins.com* 🎫 *From €7.*

VISITOR INFORMATION

CONTACTS Antibes Tourist Office. ✉ *Pl. Guynemer, Antibes* ☎ *04–22–10–60–10* 🌐 *www.antibesjuanlespins.com.*

Sights

★ Commune Libre du Safranier (*Free Commune of Safranier*)

NEIGHBORHOOD | **FAMILY** | A few blocks south of the Château Grimaldi, aka the Picasso Museum, is the Commune Libre du Safranier, a magical little neighborhood with a character (and mayor) all its own since 1966 (it's not technically a part of Antibes). The commune even holds its own festivals throughout the year, celebrating a variety of things like chestnuts, grape harvests, and the Christmas Yule log. Not far off the seaside promenade, Rue de la Touraque is the main street to get here, and you can amble around Place du Safranier, where tiny houses hang heavy with flowers and vines, and neighbors carry on conversations from window to window across the stone-stepped Rue du Bas-Castelet. ✉ *Rue du Safranier, Rue du Bas-Castelet, Antibes* 🌐 *www.lacommunelibredusafranier.fr.*

Cours Masséna

MARKET | **FAMILY** | To visit old Antibes, stroll the Cours Masséna, where every day from 6 am to 1 pm (except Monday September–May) a sheltered Provençal market tempts you with lemons, olives, and hand-stuffed sausages. Here both vendors and shoppers take breaks in the shoebox cafés flanking one side. Painters, sculptors, and other artists take over at 3 pm every day (except Monday mid-June–September and Friday, Saturday, and Sunday October–mid-June). From Port Vauban, you'll find the cours by passing through an arched gateway beneath the ramparts and following Rue Aubernon to the old Portail de l'Orme, built of quarried Roman stone and enlarged in the Middle Ages. ✉ *Antibes.*

Eglise de l'Immaculée-Conception (*Cathédrale Notre-Dame*)

CHURCH | This sanctuary served as the region's cathedral until the bishopric was transferred to Grasse in 1244. The church's 18th-century facade, a marvelous Latin mix of classical symmetry and fantasy, has been restored in stunning shades of ocher and cream. Its stout medieval watchtower was built in the 11th century with stones "mined" from Roman structures. Inside is a Baroque altarpiece painted by the Niçois artist Louis Bréa in 1515. ✉ *Rue du St-Esprit, Antibes.*

Musée Archéologie (*Archaeology Museum*)

HISTORY MUSEUM | Promenade Amiral-de-Grasse—a marvelous spot for pondering the mountains and tides—leads directly to the Bastion St-André, a squat Vauban fortress that now houses the Musée Archéologie. In its glory days, this 17th-century stronghold sheltered a garrison; the bread oven is still visible in the vaulted central hall. The museum collection focuses on Antibes's classical history, displaying amphorae and sculptures found in local digs as well as in shipwrecks from the harbor. ✉ *Bastion St-André, Av. Général-Maizières, Antibes* ☎ *04–92–95–85–98* 🎫 *€3* ⏲ *Closed Mon. and Sun. Nov.–Jan.*

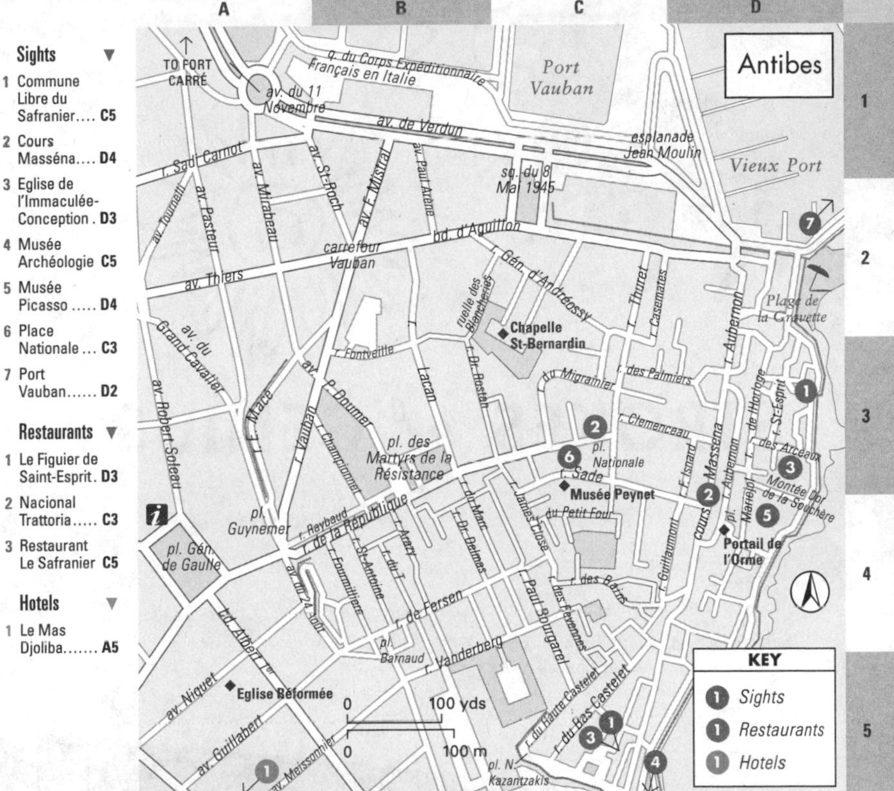

★ Musée Picasso

ART MUSEUM | Rising high over the water, this museum is set in the stunning medieval Château Grimaldi. As rulers of Monaco, the Grimaldi family lived here until the revolution; this fine old castle, however, was little more than a monument until its curator offered use of its chambers to Picasso in 1946, when that extraordinary genius was enjoying a period of intense creative energy. The result was a bounty of exhilarating paintings, ceramics, and lithographs inspired by the sea and by Greek mythology—all very Mediterranean. The château, which became the museum in 1966, houses some 245 works by the artist (but not all are on display), as well as pieces by Miró, Calder, and Léger. The first floor displays more than 100 paintings by Russian-born artist Nicolas de Staël. Download the Picasso Antibes app before your visit. ✉ *Château Grimaldi, Pl. Mariejol, Antibes* ☎ *04–92–90–54–20* 🎫 *€8* 🕒 *Closed Mon.*

Place Nationale

PLAZA/SQUARE | FAMILY | Not far from the Commune quarter, the Old Town invites you to explore its streets lined by a mix of shops, galleries, restaurants, and bakeries. Aim to wind up on Place Nationale, the site of the Roman forum. It's a pleasant place for a drink under the hackberry trees, which allow for the right amount of shade in summer and sunshine in winter. ✉ *Antibes.*

Port Vauban

MARINA/PIER | Whether you approach the waterfront from the train station or park along the Avenue de Verdun, you'll

Continued on page 306

STROKES *of* GENIUS

Le Cantique des Cantiques (oil on canvas)
by Marc Chagall, Musée Chagall

Fleurs et Fruits (gouache cutout) by Henri Matisse, Musée Matisse

A kind of artistic Garden of Eden exists in the minds of many painters, a magical place painted in the vivid colors of imagination—a promised land where they can bask in warm sunshine nearly every day of the year, swim in a placid sea of incredible blue, daub flowers so colorful they would challenge even the most riotous palette, and live life as sensually as they sketch it.

This is the dream would-be Adams sought in the late 19th century when, inspired by Impressionist *plein-air* (open-air) painting, artists abandoned the airless studios of Paris for the sun-kissed towns of the South of France. By the 1920s, a virtual migration of painters and sculptors heeded the siren call of the Mediterranean muse and began to colonize the Côte d'Azur. Signac made St-Tropez the Riviera's first "Greenwich Village"; Cannes attracted Picasso and Van Dongen; Haut-de-Cagnes and St-Paul-de-Vence lured Renoir, Soutine, and Modigliani; and Matisse and Dufy settled in Nice. A veritable "museum without walls," these locales went on to nurture some of the biggest movements in 20th-century art. Creativity was unleashed, cares forgotten, and *le bonheur de vie*—the happiness of life—became a forceful leitmotiv.

The result was an outpouring of art whose exuberance and energy led to the paradise that exists here today: a tightly packed 100-mile stretch of coastline crammed with the houses, gardens, and towns that inspired these artists. Be content to leave their masterpieces to museums scattered around the world, and get ready to savor instead a host of virtual Matisses, 3-D Renoirs, and pop-up Picassos. This rainbow curve of a coast will prove to be an unforgettable road trip through the history of modern art.

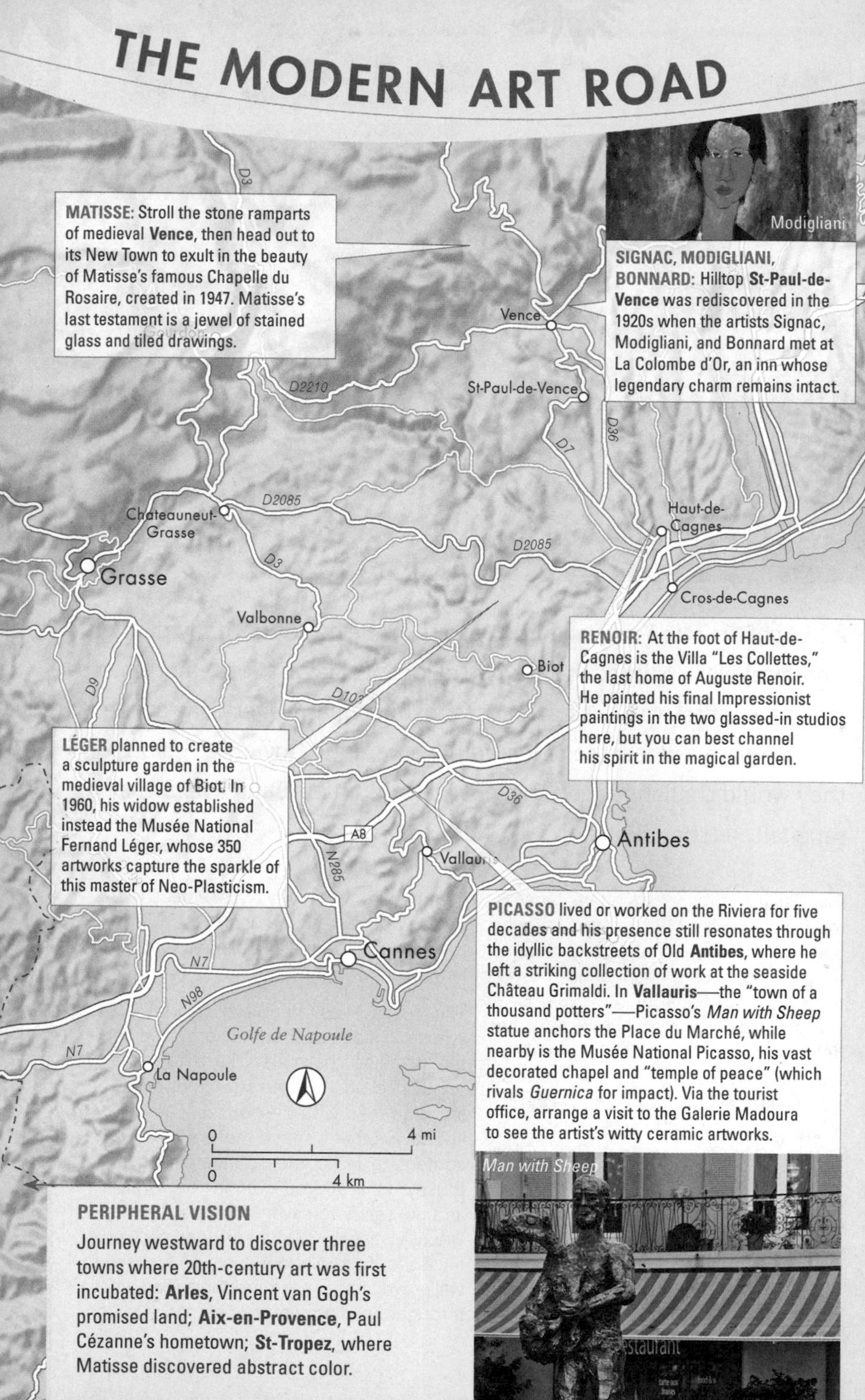
THE MODERN ART ROAD
MATISSE: Stroll the stone ramparts of medieval Vence, then head out to its New Town to exult in the beauty of Matisse's famous Chapelle du Rosaire, created in 1947. Matisse's last testament is a jewel of stained glass and tiled drawings.
Modigliani
SIGNAC, MODIGLIANI, BONNARD: Hilltop St-Paul-de-Vence was rediscovered in the 1920s when the artists Signac, Modigliani, and Bonnard met at La Colombe d'Or, an inn whose legendary charm remains intact.
RENOIR: At the foot of Haut-de-Cagnes is the Villa "Les Collettes," the last home of Auguste Renoir. He painted his final Impressionist paintings in the two glassed-in studios here, but you can best channel his spirit in the magical garden.
LÉGER planned to create a sculpture garden in the medieval village of Biot. In 1960, his widow established instead the Musée National Fernand Léger, whose 350 artworks capture the sparkle of this master of Neo-Plasticism.
PICASSO lived or worked on the Riviera for five decades and his presence still resonates through the idyllic backstreets of Old Antibes, where he left a striking collection of work at the seaside Château Grimaldi. In Vallauris—the "town of a thousand potters"—Picasso's Man with Sheep statue anchors the Place du Marché, while nearby is the Musée National Picasso, his vast decorated chapel and "temple of peace" (which rivals Guernica for impact). Via the tourist office, arrange a visit to the Galerie Madoura to see the artist's witty ceramic artworks.
Man with Sheep
PERIPHERAL VISION
Journey westward to discover three towns where 20th-century art was first incubated: Arles, Vincent van Gogh's promised land; Aix-en-Provence, Paul Cézanne's hometown; St-Tropez, where Matisse discovered abstract color.
D3
Vence
St-Paul-de-Vence
D2210
D36
D7
A8
Châteauneuf-Grasse
D2085
Grasse
Haut-de-Cagnes
Cros-de-Cagnes
Valbonne
Biot
D9
D103
D36
A8
N285
Vallauris
Antibes
Cannes
N7
N98
Golfe de Napoule
N7
La Napoule
0
4 mi
0
4 km

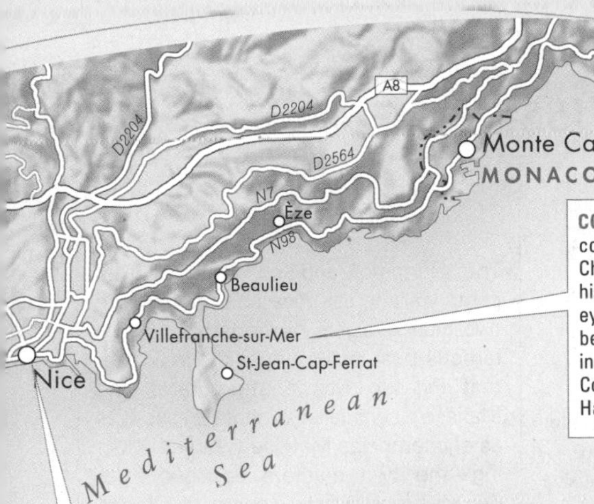

COCTEAU: "The Prince of Poets" covered **Villefranche-sur-Mer's** Chapelle Saint-Pierre in 1957 with his fanciful curlicues, angels, and eyes, while more of his work can be found up the coast in Menton in the seaside Musée Jean Cocteau and the pretty Marriage Hall of the town Hôtel de Ville.

CHAGALL AND MATISSE: A banquet of museums entices the art lover to **Nice**, including the Musée Matisse, the Musée National Marc Chagall, and the Musée d'Art Moderne, but don't forget to stroll to Matisse's favorite spots—the elegant Promenade des Anglais, Jardin Albert 1er, and enchanting Cours Saleya marketplace.

Marc Chagall Museum

"The days follow each other here with a beauty which I would describe as insolent."

—Nietzsche,
writing from Èze, near Beaulieu, 1883

St-Paul-de-Vence

Chapelle du Rosaire, Vence

PICASSO & MATISSE: THE ODD COUPLE

Born: October 25, 1881, in Málaga, Spain.

Died: April 8, 1973, in Mougins, Côte d'Azur.

Personality Profile: Genius, philosopher-sage, egoist.

Claim to Fame: A one-man history of 20th-century art, Picasso changed styles as often as he did mistresses, but he is best known as the founder of Cubism.

Picasso Peeking: Cane fencing has been erected around Picasso's last retreat of Notre-Dame-de-Vie in Mougins by his heirs, and you are obliged to view his majestic Château de Vauvenargues (where he lies buried) through binoculars.

Picasso Peaking: The Musée Picasso in Antibes and his War and Peace Chapel in Vallauris are top spots to view his masterworks.

Best-Known Works: *Les Demoiselles d'Avignon, Guernica, Au Lapin Agile, Minotauomachy.*

Quote: "You see, I have to paint for the both of us now" (on hearing of Matisse's death).

Ceramic Plate by Picasso, Galerie Madoura

PABLO PICASSO

The "North Pole and South Pole" of 20th-century art (to use Picasso's phrase), the two heavyweights of modernism had a famous push-pull friendship. No matter that Picasso was a structuralist and Matisse a sensualist, or that Picasso was as egocentric as Matisse was self-effacing—the two masters engaged in a decades-long artistic "game of chess," often played out as neighbors on the Côte d'Azur. It was Matisse's mesmerizingly beautiful paintings created in Nice in the 1930s that probably inspired Picasso's move to the South of France in 1946. He wound up painting in Antibes, sculpting in Vallauris, wooing in Golfe-Juan, and seducing in Mougins. But their ventriloquous dialogue began in 1906 when they first met in the Parisian salon of Gertrude Stein (who lost little time in baiting the artists against each other).

Matisse had already created a revolution in color; Picasso, 12 years younger, was about to create one in form with *Les Demoiselles d'Avignon*, the "first" 20th-century painting, whose cubistic structure was inspired by African sculpture—as it turns out, Matisse's African sculpture, since Picasso had studied his collection of Senegalese totems. When Picasso moved to the Midi in 1946, Matisse presented him with a dove, which inspired Picasso to create his famous poster in homage to France's newly won peace.

The same year, Picasso was given the keys to Antibes' Château Grimaldi, where he painted 30 canvases depicting mermaids and minotaurs, all prancing about in direct homage to Matisse's famously joyous paintings, *Le Bonheur de Vivre* and *La Danse*.

HENRI MATISSE

What Tahiti was to Gauguin, Nice was to Matisse. Its flower marketplaces, palaces painted in bonbon pastels, and magnificent palm trees soothed and, together with the constantly changing show of light—so different from the relentless glare of St-Tropez (where, in 1904, he first committed chromatic mayhem with his Fauve "wild beast" masterpiece, *Luxe, Calme, et Volupté*)—inspired him.

By 1919, ailing with bronchitis, he had moved to Nice, where he started to paint images of unrivaled voluptuousness: semi-nude odalisques skimpily clad in harem pantaloons and swathed in Moroccan fabrics. Their popular success allowed Matisse to relocate, in 1921, to a rooftop apartment at 1 Place Charles Félix, which magnificently overlooked Nice's Cours Saleya flower market. To view his art, head for the city's Musée Matisse; to see his grave, visit the Monastère de Cimiez cemetery.

But to sense his true spirit, venture to nearby Vence, where he moved in 1943 when Nice was threatened by World War II. Here he created the sublime Chapelle du Rosaire, his masterpiece ("in spite of all its imperfections") of black-on-white tile drawings and exalted stained-glass windows of emerald, blue, and yellow. The intensely competitive Picasso also saw it, of course, as a challenge. So, in 1952–53 he transformed an empty Romanesque chapel in nearby Vallauris into a "temple of peace" with scenes of La Guerre (war) and La Paix (peace). Unlike Matisse, however, he designed no liturgical gear, chasubles, or altar, since Picasso remained an avowed atheist.

Born: December 31, 1869, in Le Cateau, Northern France.

Died: November 3, 1954, in Nice, Côte d'Azur.

Personality Profile: Buddha, bon vivant, hedonist.

Claim to Fame: As father of the Fauves—the phrase "wild beast" described their expressive use of shade and hue—his works simplified design and exalted color.

Meeting Matisse: Musée Matisse in Nice, Rosary Chapel in Vence.

Matisse's muse: A decade before Sister Jacques-Marie inspired Matisse's Chapelle du Rosaire, she had been a nurse and model to him.

Best-Known Works: *Luxe, Calme, et Volupté; La Danse; Jazz; L'Atelier Rouge; Nu Rose.*

Quote: "Picasso sees everything."

La Danse

first encounter an awesome expanse of luxury yachts in Port Vauban. It has an underground parking lot and an attractive esplanade from which you can admire one of Europe's oldest and largest ports home to 1,642 berths—including 18 for superyachts of up to 525 feet. It's no wonder the antiques fair and sailing show chose this spot for their events every spring. With the tableau of snowy Alps looming in the background and the formidable medieval block towers of the Fort Carré (Square Fort) guarding entry to the port, it's difficult to find a more dramatic spot to anchor.

The superbly symmetrical island fortress was completed in 1565 and restored in 1967, but can only be admired from afar. Across the Quai Rambaud, which juts into the harbor, a tiny crescent of sand called La Gravette beach offers swimmers one of the last soft spots on the coast before the famous Riviera pebble beaches begin on strands farther east. ✉ *Antibes.*

 Beaches

Antibes and Juan-les-Pins together claim 25 km (15½ miles) of coastline and 48 beaches (including Cap d'Antibes). In Antibes you can choose between small sandy inlets, such as La Gravette, below the port; the central Plage du Ponteil; Plage de la Salis toward the Cap; rocky escarpments around the Old Town; or the vast stretch of sand above the Fort Carré.

The Plage de la Salis may be one of the prettiest beach sites on the coast, with the dark pines of the cape on one side and the old stones of Antibes on the other, all against a backdrop of Alpine white. Juan-les-Pins is one big city beach, lined by a boulevard and promenade peppered with cafés and restaurants. If you want to follow in Picasso's footsteps, head to the Plage de la Garoupe, halfway down the Cap d'Antibes peninsula and set near the cape's fabulous Sentier Tirepoil footpath: this pretty white-sand crescent is the place locals have always headed to sunbathe and celeb-spot.

 Restaurants

★ Le Figuier de Saint-Esprit

$$$$ | FRENCH | Christian Morisset's Michelin-starred restaurant is named after the 50-year-old fig tree that, along with a canopy of vines, shades the private courtyard. This is one of the region's best restaurants, and the haute-cuisine chef bases his scrumptious set menus on what's available at the daily market. **Known for:** the main culinary attraction of Antibes; charming courtyard; local and organic (and some very fancy) wines. *Ⓢ Average main: €70 ✉ 14 rue Saint-Esprit, Antibes ☎ 04–26–85–67–93 ⊕ www.restaurant-figuier-saint-esprit.fr ⊗ Closed Tues. Closed Wed. Oct.–June, Mon. and Wed. lunch July–Sept., one wk in Feb., last wk in June, and Dec.*

Nacional Trattoria

$$$ | FRENCH | When you've had enough of the "catch of the day" and need a good old dose of red meat—in various cuts, from rump steak to rib to sirloin XXL—this Italian restaurant in old Antibes is the place to go. The selection includes black Angus American, Australian, or Irish beef as well as veal, chicken, and foie gras, and it's all overseen by Nicolas Rondell, head chef at the Michelin-starred Pecheurs in the Cap. **Known for:** steaks priced by the gram; swanky summer terrace; convivial service. *Ⓢ Average main: €25 ✉ 61 pl. Nationale, Antibes ☎ 04–93–61–77–30 ▭ No credit cards ⊗ Closed Mon.*

★ Restaurant Le Safranier

$$ | FRENCH | Part of a tiny Old Town enclave determined to resist the press of tourism, this casual tavern has tables scattered across a sunny terrace on Place Safranier. Chef Gaïatto Olivier is in charge of a refined menu that reflects his five years in the kitchen at the celebrated

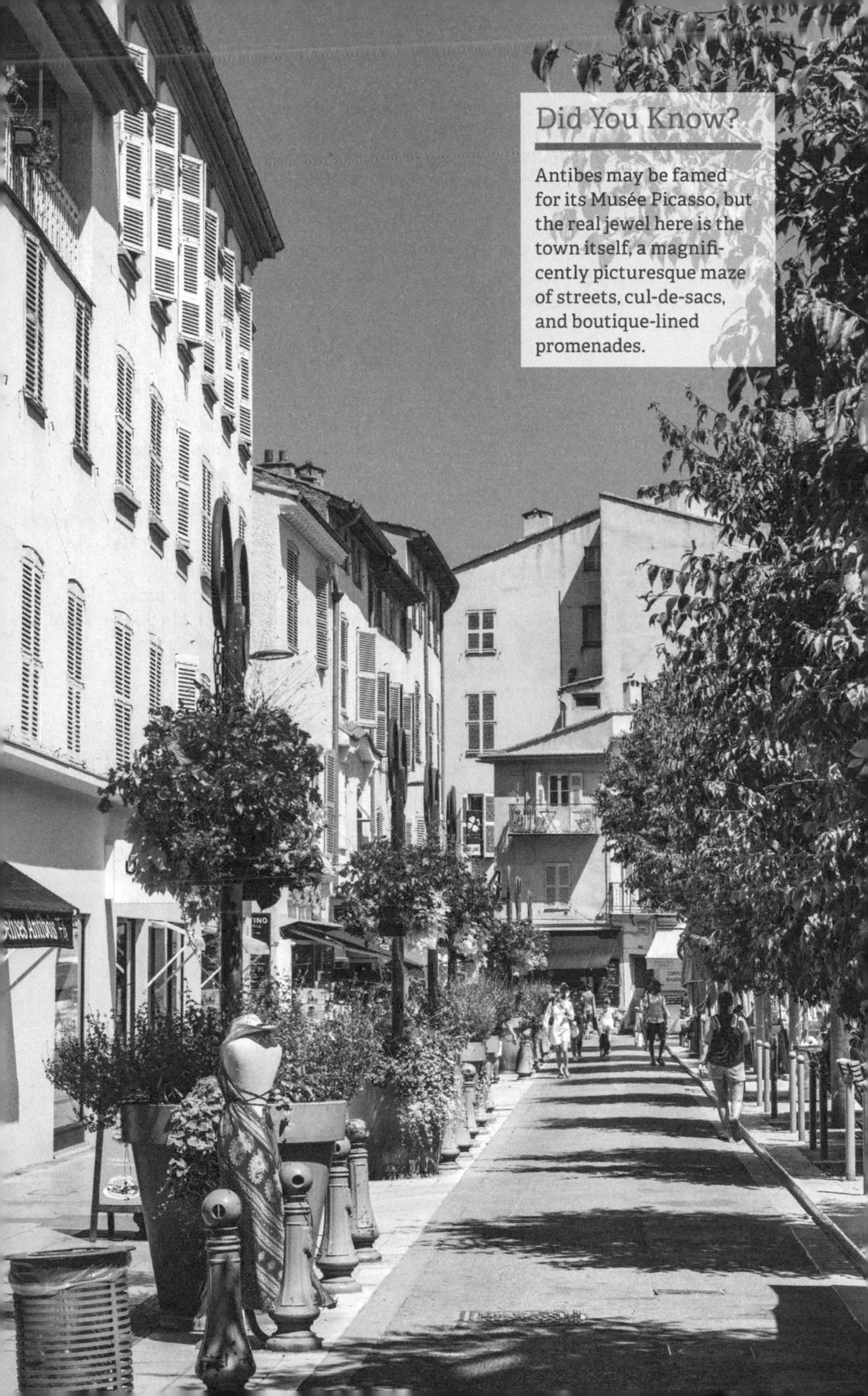

Did You Know?

Antibes may be famed for its Musée Picasso, but the real jewel here is the town itself, a magnificently picturesque maze of streets, cul-de-sacs, and boutique-lined promenades.

Eden Roc—think roasted catch of the day with chickpea stew, chorizo, mussels fennel, and coriander—but at a fraction of the price. **Known for:** pretty terrace tucked away from main streets; affordable menu from celebrated chef; laid-back vibe. *Average main: €22 1 pl. Safranier, Antibes 04–93–34–80–50 www.facebook.com/restaurantlesafranier Closed Mon.*

Hotels

Le Mas Djoliba

$$ | HOTEL | FAMILY | Tucked into a residential neighborhood—on the crest between Antibes and Juan-les-Pins and surrounded by greenery and well protected from traffic noise—this cool, cozy inn feels like the 1920s private home it once was. **Pros:** quiet neighborhood only a seven-minute walk to sandy beach; lovely swimming pool; top-floor family suite with terrace and views of Cap d'Antibes. **Cons:** breakfast €15; parking free but not accessible 24/7; allergy alert: hotel cats. *Rooms from: €225 29 av. de Provence, Antibes 04–93–34–02–48 www.hotel-djoliba.com Closed mid-Nov.–mid-Mar. 15 rooms No Meals.*

Nightlife

Absinthe Bar Antibes

BARS | Take a trip back to the days of Hemingway, and taste some absinthe to find out what that talk of hallucinating is all about; you might just get a hat to commemorate the occasion. This underground establishment is open Tuesday to Sunday and has a piano bar on Friday and Saturday nights. *25 cours Masséna, Antibes 04–93–34–93–00 www.facebook.com/AbsintheAntibes.*

Le Blue Lady Pub

PUBS | Frequented by both French locals and foreigners (and their kids and dogs), this pub is a great place to collect your thoughts over a drink or to hear some live music. The Blue Lady has daytime appeal, too. Beginning at 7:30 am, you can grab a latte, a smoothie, or even an English breakfast (there are newspapers on hand, too). The kitchen is open till 3 pm, so you can stick around for a lunch of burgers, potpies, or fresh salads. *La Galerie du Port, Rue Lacan, Antibes 04–93–34–41–00 www.blueladypub.com.*

Shopping

You can find plenty of eclectic boutiques and galleries in the Old Town, especially along Rue Sade, Rue de la République, and Rue James Close. In addition, Antibes has a trio of antiques and flea markets that occur in different places and days. On Thursday and Saturday there's one in Place Nationale (6–4:30 or 5:30 April to September) and another in Place de Gaulle (same hours). On Sunday from May to September, there's also one in Jardins de la Pinède (8–4:30).

Although you can pick up iconic Savon de Marseille products in the Provençal Cours Masséna market, consider stopping by Le Comptoir des Savonniers on Rue Thuret, where translucent wedges of multicolor soap are cut to size using a special machine and sold by weight. The shop's presentation is so "modern art" you can almost overlook the fact that the soap is imported from Belgium. And if the yacht vibe of Antibes is calling, Criste Marine on Rue Aubernon sells all clothes *marinières*.

Activities

Diamond Diving

DIVING & SNORKELING | Brit Alex Diamond owns this Golfe–Juan dive center, where he offers Discover Scuba courses and equipment rentals. Alex is French government–certified, so he also trains diving instructors. *Rue des Pêcheurs, Vallauris 06–15–30–52–23 www.diamonddiving.net.*

Cap d'Antibes

2 km (1 mile) south of Antibes.

This fabled, 4-mile-long peninsula has been carved up into luxurious estates perched high above the water and shaded by thick, tall pines. Since the 19th century its wild greenery and isolation have drawn a glittering assortment of aristocrats, artists, literati, and the merely fabulously wealthy. Among those claiming a prestigious Cap d'Antibes address over the years are: Guy de Maupassant; Anatole France; Claude Monet; the Duke and Duchess of Windsor; Greek shipping tycoon Stavros Niarchos; and the cream of the Lost Generation, including Ernest Hemingway, Dorothy Parker, Gertrude Stein, and F. Scott Fitzgerald.

Today, the focal point is the Hôtel du Cap Eden Roc, which is packed with stars during the Cannes Film Festival (not surprisingly, as movie studios always pick up the tab for their favorite celebs). Reserve a table for lunch here during the festival and be literally surrounded by celebrities to-ing and fro-ing. Play it cool, though: keep your sunglasses on at all times, and resist the urge to take photos.

GETTING HERE AND AROUND

Envibus 2 (€1.50) connects Cap d'Antibes to downtown Antibes.

Sights

Jardin Thuret (*Thuret Garden*)
GARDEN | To fully experience the Riviera's heady hothouse exoticism, visit this glorious garden, established by botanist Gustave Thuret in 1856 as a testing ground for subtropical plants and trees. Thuret was responsible for introducing the palm tree, which forever changed the look of the French Riviera. On his death, the property was left to the Ministry of Agriculture, which continues to dabble in the introduction of exotic species. Tours from 90 minutes up to three hours can be reserved in advance. ✉ *90 chemin Raymond, Antibes* ✣ *From Port Gallice, head up Chemin du Croûton, turn right on Bd. du Cap, then right again on Chemin Raymond* ☎ *04–92–38–64–70* 🌐 *www6.sophia.inra.fr/jardin_thuret* 🎫 *Free* 🕒 *Closed weekends.*

★ **Le Sentier du Littoral** (*Sentier Tire-poil*)
TRAIL | Bordering over-the-top hotels and estates, this spectacular footpath is nicknamed the Sentier Tire-poil, as the wind along it "ruffles the hair." It stretches about 5 km (3 miles) along the outermost tip of the peninsula, coming full circle around the gardens at Villa Eilenroc over to l'Anse de l'Argent Faux.

Book a guided nature walk through the tourist office, or tackle the route on your own via Plage de la Garoupe, where Cole Porter and Gerald Murphy once hung out and a where paved promenade affords dazzling views over the Baie de la Garoupe and the distant Alps. At the far end of the cape, however, the pavement gives way to a boulder-studded path along 50-foot cliffs, dizzying switchbacks, and thundering breakers. Continue along the path's newer portion to the cove l'Anse de l'Argent Faux, where you can catch your breath before heading up to the entrance of Villa Eilenroc. Then follow Avenue Beaumont to the cape's main road, RD2559.

The walk takes about two hours, and they might be two of the most memorable of your trip, particularly if you tackle it at sunset. Except for fellow walkers on sunny days and, perhaps, a yacht out on the water, civilization disappears along most stretches. Note that signs reading *Attention Mort* (Beware: Death) are reminders that this path can be very dangerous, especially in stormy weather. Indeed, when storm warnings are issued, locked gates might block the route.
■ TIP→ From the station in town take Bus 2 to the Fontaine stop. To return, follow Plage de la Garoupe to Boulevard de la Garoupe,

A gigantic unframed painting come to life, Antibes has been immortalized by countless artists, including Monet, Renoir, and Picasso.

and make a left to reconnect with the bus. ✉ *Antibes.*

Phare de la Garoupe (*Garoupe Lighthouse*)

LIGHTHOUSE | You can sample a little of what draws famous people to this part of the world by walking up Chemin de Calvaire from the Plage de la Salis in Antibes—a distance of about 1 km (½ mile) via a challenging pathway—and taking in the extraordinary views from the hill surmounted by this old *phare* (lighthouse). You can also climb all 114 steps to the top. Next to the lighthouse, the 16th-century double chapel of Notre-Dame-de-la-Garoupe contains ex-votos and statues of the Virgin, all in memory of and for the protection of sailors. **■ TIP→ Reward your trek with a drink or a meal at the Bistrot du Curé next door.** ✉ *Chemin de Calvaire, Antibes* ☎ *04–22–10–60–10.*

★ Villa Eilenroc

HISTORIC HOME | Le Sentier du Littoral passes along the beach at the Villa Eilenroc (designed by Charles Garnier, who created the Paris Opéra), which commands the tip of the peninsula from a grand garden. The site has a café and an eco-museum, as well as a scented garden at the entrance to La Rosaerie (Rose Garden). You can also catch glimpses of the distant Château de la Cröe, another legendary villa. On Wednesdays, September through June, you can wander through the villa's reception salons. Highlights include the Winter Salon's *1,001 Nights* ceiling mural painted by famed Art Deco designer Jean Dunand, display cases filled with memorabilia donated by Caroline Groult-Flaubert (Antibes resident and goddaughter of the great author), and a boudoir with *boiseries* (decorative wooden features) from the Marquis de Sévigné's Paris mansion. Note that the villa is sometimes closed for private events; check the Antibes tourist office's website before you visit. ✉ *460 av. L.D. Beaumont, at peninsula's tip, about 4 km (2½ miles) from Garoupe Bay, Antibes* ☎ *04–93–67–74–33* 🌐 *www.antibesjuanlespins.com* 🎫 *€2.*

Beaches

Plage de la Garoupe

BEACH | FAMILY | Thanks to its perfect oval bay, the finest, softest sand on the Riviera, magnificent views that stretch out to Antibes, and relatively calm waters, this northeast-facing beach is a real jewel—and the first in the country to impose a "No Selfie" zone. Getting the Gucci-clad spillover from the Hotel du Cap-Eden Roc, the high-end private beach clubs here open onto the sand. Quieter folk stick to the public section at the other end, where you can rent loungers online through the tourist office website for only €10 a day. There are also two snack bars. **Amenities:** food and drink; parking (no fee); showers; toilets. **Best for:** swimming. ✉ *Chemin de la Garoupe, Antibes.*

Restaurants

Les Pêcheurs

$$$$ | FRENCH | In 1954, French resistance hero Camille Rayon built a restaurant between two stone fishing huts from the early 20th century, and today it's part of the Relais & Chateau Cap d'Antibes Beach Hotel. Although beef is available, chef Nicolas Rondelli's menu emphasizes fish, and all dishes are complemented by produce from the nearby hills and wines from a formidable list that includes a 2018 Pierre-Yves Colin-Morey Meursault at €2,400 a bottle. **Known for:** Michelin-starred seafood; stunning "Epilogue" desserts; sunset views over the Îles de Lérins and the Estérel. $ *Average main: €65* ✉ *10 bd. Maréchal Juin, Antibes* ☎ *04–92–93–13–30* 🌐 *www.ca-beachhotel.com* ⏲ *Closed Mon. and Tues. Closed mid-Oct.–Mar. No lunch.*

Hotels

★ Hôtel du Cap–Eden Roc

$$$$ | HOTEL | Open since 1870, this extravagantly expensive hotel reminiscent of *The Great Gatsby* era is still the mainstay for A-Listers and those with deep pockets for good reason—with 22 acres of immaculate gardens bordered by rocky shore, it embodies the fantasy of a subtropical French Riviera idyll. **Pros:** hands down one of the world's best hotels, booked well in advance; buffet breakfast included; fascinating glimpse into 20th-century history. **Cons:** if you're not a celebrity, tip big to keep the staff interested; insanely expensive everything; formal dress required for dinner in restaurant and bars. $ *Rooms from: €1400* ✉ *Bd. J.F. Kennedy, Antibes* ☎ *04–93–61–39–01* 🌐 *www.hotel-du-cap-eden-roc.com* ⏲ *Closed mid-Oct.–mid-Apr.* *111 rooms* 🍽 *Free Breakfast.*

★ Hôtel La Jabotte

$$ | HOTEL | At this adorable boutique hotel just steps from a sandy beach, tastefully decorated and colorful rooms surround a central courtyard, where guests relax over a gorgeous breakfast (€10–€15) of fresh-baked pastries and homemade jams. **Pros:** very warm welcome is a pleasant contrast to some of the better-known hotels; free beach umbrellas and mats, SUPs to rent; switch off your mobile phone and save. **Cons:** breakfast not free; often booked up; checkout 10 am. $ *Rooms from: €214* ✉ *13 av. Max Maurey, Antibes* ☎ *04–93–61–45–89* 🌐 *www.jabotte.com* *No credit cards* *9 rooms* 🍽 *No Meals.*

Activities

Supdreams

STAND-UP PADDLEBOARDING | French stand-up paddleboard champion Céline Guesdon runs a school for beginners and experienced paddleboarders on Cap d'Antibes. She also offers Pilates classes to work off those buttery croissants. ✉ *Bd. du Maréchal Juin* ☎ *06–41–96–70–22* 🌐 *www.supdreamschool.com.*

Juan-les-Pins

5 km (3 miles) southwest of Antibes.

From Old Antibes, you can jump on a bus over the hill to Juan-les-Pins, the jazzy younger-sister resort town that, along with Antibes, bracelets the wrist of the Cap d'Antibes. It's a stretch of beach that was "discovered" by the Jazz Age jet set, including F. Scott and Zelda Fitzgerald.

Here, in the 1920s, visitors experimented with the newfangled fad of waterskiing, which is still practiced from the docks of the Belle Rives. Ladies with bobbed hair and beach pajamas exposed lily-white skin to the sun, browning themselves like peasants and flaunting bare, tanned arms. American industrialists had swimming pools introduced to the seaside, and the last of the leisure class, weary of stateside bathtub gin, wallowed in Europe's alcoholic delights.

Although the town of today isn't as glamorous as its history, the scene along its waterfront is still something to behold. Here, thousands of international sunseekers stream up and down the promenade or lie flank to flank on its endless stretch of sand.

GETTING HERE AND AROUND

Regional rail service connects Juan-les-Pins to Nice (25 minutes, €6.40), Cannes (€2.20), and other coastal towns; from the train station, Envibus 15 (€1.50) loops through town, stopping at the public beach. Juan-les-Pins can also be reached from either Nice or Cannes via Zou! Bus 620 (€2.10, 75 minutes).

Sights

Casino Juan-Les-Pins
(*Casino Partouche Juan-les-Pins*)
CASINO | This glassed-in complex houses 75 slot machines, English roulette, and blackjack, which are played every night: the casino is open until 3 am (4 am on Saturday). There's also a panoramic beach restaurant. ✉ *3 av. Guy de Maupassant, Juan-les-Pins* ☎ *04–92–93–71–71* 🌐 *casino-juanlespins.partouche.com.*

Beaches

Antibes and Juan-les-Pins together claim 25 km (15½ miles) of coastline and 48 beaches (including Cap d'Antibes). Juan-les-Pins has eight private beaches and a couple of public beaches, where you can rent loungers for €10–€11 a day. The boulevard and promenade running parallel to the sea are peppered with cafés and restaurants.

Plage d'Antibes les Pins
BEACH | This sandy public beach west of Juan-les-Pins is popular thanks to its size and is thus known as La Grande Plage. You can rent a beach chair from the nearby private beaches that dominate the strip. **Amenities:** showers; toilets. **Best for:** swimming. ✉ *Bd. du Littoral, Juan-les-Pins.*

★ Port de Crouton Plage
BEACH | FAMILY | Covered with fine white sand, this small public beach next to Cap d'Antibes Beach Hotel boasts shallows that slope very gently, making it ideal for kids. It's a protected bay, so there are no waves, just plenty of shallow water that's bathwater-warm in high summer. There are few English tourists, so it offers a real *plage à la Française* experience. **Amenities:** parking (fee); showers; toilets. **Best for:** snorkeling; solitude. ✉ *Bd. Marechal Juin, Juan-les-Pins.*

Hotels

Hotel des Mimosas
$$$ | **HOTEL** | In an enclosed hilltop garden studded with tall palms, mimosas, and greenery, this is the sort of place where only the quiet buzzing of cicadas interrupts silent nights. **Pros:** incredible park with pool; easy 10-minute walk to train station; free parking. **Cons:** two-night

Just add water, and even an overbuilt town like Juan-les-Pins becomes a place worth scrambling for a postage-stamp portion of sun and fun.

minimum some months; free Wi-Fi but signal can be weak; not open year-round. *Rooms from: €250* *Rue Pauline, Juan-les-Pins* *04–93–61–04–16* *www.hotelmimosas.com* *Closed Oct.–Apr.* *34 rooms* *No Meals.*

★ Les Belles Rives
$$$$ | HOTEL | Lovingly restored to 1930s glamour, this fabled landmark proves that what's old is new again, as France's stylish young set make this endearingly *neoclassique* place with lovely Art Deco accommodations one of their latest favorites. **Pros:** views are quite spectacular, but ask for a room with a frontal (not lateral) sea view; lots of water sports; Michelin-starred restaurant with vegetarian set menu. **Cons:** everything at beach costs extra (loungers, towels, umbrella); careful when ordering fish by the gram (it's pricey); thin walls. *Rooms from: €750* *33 bd. Édouard Baudoin, Juan-les-Pins* *04–93–61–02–79* *www.bellesrives.com* *Closed Jan.–early Mar.* *43 rooms* *No Meals.*

Biot

6 km (4 miles) northeast of Antibes; 15 km (9 miles) northeast of Cannes; 18 km (11 miles) southwest of Nice.

Above a stretch of commercial-industrial quarters along the coast from Antibes, the *village perché* of Biot (pronounced "Bee-*otte*") sits neatly on a hilltop, and, as some claim, near an ex-volcano. Threaded with cute alleyways and dotted with pretty *placettes* (small squares), the Old Town is so picturesque that it almost demands you pick up a brush and palette—photographs don't do it justice, especially as it's not on the receiving end of much light.

For centuries home to a pottery industry, known for its fine yellow clay that stretched into massive, solid oil jars, Biot has, in recent generations, made a name for itself as a glass-art town. Despite the new commercialism, however, traces of old Provence remain, especially in the evening after the busloads of shoppers leave and the deep-shaded squares under the plane trees fall quiet. Then you can meander around the edges of the Old Town to find the stone arch gates known as the Porte des Tines and the Porte des Migraniers: they're the last of the 16th-century fortifications that once enclosed Biot. Step into the 15th-century église, which contains an early-16th-century altarpiece that's attributed to Louis Bréa and depicts the Virgin Mary shielding humanity under her cloak; the surrounding portraits are as warmly detailed as the faces and hands in the central panel.

Truly photo-worthy is centuries-old Place des Arcades, the ancient heart of the Old Town, which was first colonized by the Knights Templar and then the Hospitallers of St. John of Jerusalem. Set between the tourist office and the church, just behind Rue Barri, it has an otherworldly grace, with its Gothic arcades and tall palm trees. The picturesquely curved and shop-lined Rue Saint Sébastien is the heart of town.

GETTING HERE AND AROUND

The Biot train station on the coast is 4 km (2½ miles) away, but you can jump on Envibus 10 (€1.50) from outside the station and arrive in the village in less than 15 minutes. Alternatively, you can call IciLa d'Envibus (☎ *04–92–19–76–30*) and organize an individual pickup by minibus—still costing only €1.50. It's available 6:30 am–7 pm on weekdays and 9–noon and 2–5:30 on Saturday within specified zones, which include Cap d'Antibes, Biot, St-Paul-de-Vence, and Valbonne. By car, coming up from the D6007, take the CD4 past Marineland and you'll find signposting straight to Biot.

VISITOR INFORMATION

CONTACTS Biot Tourist Office. ✉ *4 chemin Neuf, Biot* ☎ *04–93–65–78–00* 🌐 *www.biot-tourisme.com.*

Sights

La Verrerie de Biot (*Biot Glassworks*)
FACTORY | FAMILY | On the edge of town, follow the pink signs to La Verrerie de Biot, which has developed into something of a cult industry since its founding in the 1950s. Here you can observe the glassblowers at work; visit the extensive galleries of museum-quality glass art (which is of much better quality than the kitsch you find in the village shop windows); and start a collection of bubbled-glass goblets, cruets, or pitchers, just as Jackie Kennedy did when the rage first caught hold (she liked cobalt blue). Despite the extreme commercialism—there is a souvenir shop, an eco-museum, a boutique of home items, audio tours of the glassworks, a bar, and a restaurant—it's a one-of-a-kind artisanal industry, and the product is made before your eyes. ✉ *5 chemin des Combes, Biot* ☎ *04–93–65–03–00* 🌐 *www.verreriebiot.com* 🎫 *€3, guided visit €6.*

Villeneuve-Loubet

10 km (6 miles) north of Antibes.

You'll spot Villeneuve-Loubet before you land at Nice Airport. The four white curved residential buildings at the end of a lengthy stretch of beaches seem to reach the sky. Then there is the tiny village, its medieval château heavily restored in the 19th century.

Although the area is best known for its sprawl of overbuilt beachfront, heavily charged with concrete high-rises and with all the architectural charm of a parking ramp, if you're a foodie, you may want to make the pilgrimage to the eccentric Musée de l'Art Culinaire.

Sights

Musée de l'Art Culinaire (*Museum of Culinary Arts*)
OTHER MUSEUM | The only museum of culinary art in France is a shrine to the great chef Auguste Escoffier (1846–1935). The epitome of 19th-century culinary extravagance and revered by the French as much as Joan of Arc and De Gaulle, Escoffier was the founding father of the school of haute cuisine Calvin Trillin calls "stuff-stuff-with-heavy," where ingredients are stripped, simmered, stuffed, sauced, and generally intervened with, sometimes beyond recognition. His was the school of food as sculpture—the famous *pièces montées,* wedding-cake spires of spun sugar—and menus of staggering length and complexity. He wowed 'em at the Ritz in Paris and the Savoy and Carlton in London and is a point of reference for every modern chef—if only as a foil for rebellion. In his birthplace, you'll view illustrations of his creations and a collection of fantastical menus, including one featuring the meat of zoo animals killed in the war of 1870. There are paid guided tours, as well as English-language audio guides (€3). ✉ *3 rue Escoffier, Villeneuve-Loubet* ☎ *04–93–20–80–51* 🌐 *en.musee-escoffier.com* 🎫 *€6* ⏲ *Closed early Dec.–mid-Jan.*

Haut-de-Cagnes

14 km (9 miles) southwest of Nice; 10 km (6 miles) north of Antibes.

Could this be the most beautiful village in southern France? Part-time residents Renoir, Soutine, Modigliani, and Simone de Beauvoir are a few who thought so. Bypass the seaside area of town—with its congested freeway overpasses, tourist-oriented shops, and beachfront pizzerias—and instead head inland from the N7, following the brown "Bourg Médiéval" signs and up the steep road to one of the Riviera's most heavenly perched villages.

Even Alice, of Wonderland fame, would adore this steeply cobbled Old Town, honeycombed as it is with tiny piazzas, return-to-your-starting-point-twice alleys, and winding streets that abruptly change to stairways. Many of the pretty residences are dollhouse-like (especially those on Rue Passebon), and most date from the 14th and 15th centuries.

GETTING HERE AND AROUND

Frequent daily trains from Nice or Cannes stop at Cagnes-sur-Mer (get off at Cros-de-Cagnes if you're heading to the beach) from where you take the free year-round daily navette No. 44 to Haut-de-Cagnes. Zou! Bus 620 (€2.10) also stops in Cagnes-sur Mer (which has several beachfront cafés, like Cigalon Plage, open year-round). In July and August, the free shuttle No. 45 takes you to the beach, with a stop (Le Tiercé/Kennedy) near the hippodrome, which hosts special evening events in summer.

By car from Paris or Provence on the A8 take Exit 47 (Villeneuve–Loubet/Cagnes-sur-Mer); if coming from the east (Monaco, Nice), look for Exit 48 (Cagnes-sur-Mer). Polygone Riviera in Cagnes-sur-Mer is France's first outdoor shopping and leisure center. It's open seven days a week and is a big draw—with nearly 110 brands, 25 restaurants, and nine cinemas—so roads in the area can get congested.

VISITOR INFORMATION

CONTACTS Cagnes-sur-Mer Tourist Office. ✉ *6 bd. Maréchal Juin, Cagnes-sur-Mer* ☎ *04–93–20–61–64* 🌐 *www.cagnes-tourisme.com.*

Chapelle Notre-Dame-de-la-Protection
CHURCH | Nearly hidden in the hillside and entered by an obscure side door, the grand Chapelle Notre-Dame-de-la-Protection, with its Italianate bell tower, was first built in the 14th century after the fortress had been destroyed; as a

A top pick for France's most beautiful *village perché*, Haut-de-Cagnes is an enchanting place filled with tiny piazzas, winding alleys, and staircase streets.

hedge against further invasion, they placed this plea for Mary's protection at the village edge. In 1936, the *curé* (priest) discovered traces of fresco under the bubbling plaster; a full stripping revealed that every inch of the apse had been decorated with scenes of the life of the Virgin and Jesus, roughly executed late in the 16th century. From the chapel's porch are sweeping sea views. Even if it's closed when you stop by, be sure to note the trompe-l'oeil "shadows" delightfully painted on the bell tower portal. ✉ *Rue Hippolyte Guis, Cagnes-sur-Mer* ⏲ *Closed Oct.–Mar. and Mon.–Sat.*

Château-Museé Grimaldi

CASTLE/PALACE | **FAMILY** | Crowning Haut-de-Cagnes is the squat, crenellated Château-Museé—an imposing fortress with banners flying from its square watchtower—that was built in 1310 by the Grimaldis (Prince Albert of Monaco's family) and reinforced over the centuries. You are welcomed inside by a grand balustraded stairway and triangular Renaissance courtyard with a triple row of classical arcades infinitely more graceful than the exterior. Beyond lie vaulted medieval chambers, a vast Renaissance fireplace, and a splendid 17th-century trompe-l'oeil fresco of the fall of Phaëthon from his sun chariot.

The château also contains three highly specialized museums: the Musée de l'Olivier (Olive Tree Museum), which highlights the history and cultivation of this Provençal mainstay; the obscure and eccentric Collection Suzy-Solidor, a group of portraits of the cabaret chanteuse painted by her artist friends, including Cocteau and Dufy; and the Musée d'Art Moderne Méditerranéen (Mediterranean Museum of Modern Art), which contains paintings by some of the 20th-century devotees of the Côte d'Azur, including Chagall, Cocteau, and Dufy. If you've climbed this far, continue to the tower and look over the coastline, just as the guards once did while on the lookout for Saracens. ✉ *Pl. du Château, Haut-de-Cagnes* ☎ *04–92–02–47–35* 🎫 *From €4* ⏲ *Closed Tues.*

Musée Renoir

ART MUSEUM | After staying in various places up and down the coast, Auguste Renoir (1841–1919) settled into a house in Les Collettes, just east of the Vieille Ville, which is now the Musée Renoir. He passed the last 12 years of his life here, painting the landscape around him; working in bronze; and rolling his wheelchair through the luxuriant garden tiered with roses, citrus groves, and spectacular olive trees. Today, you can view this sweet and melancholic villa, preserved by Renoir's children, and admire 15 of his last paintings and 30 sculptures. Although up a steep hill, Les Collettes is just a 10-minute walk from Place du Général-du-Gaulle in central Cagnes-Ville. Alternatively, you can take the free No. 45 shuttle in July and August. Speaking of summer, there are guided tours in English (€3) Wednesday through Sunday. ✉ *Chemin des Collettes, Cagnes-sur-Mer* ☎ *04–93–20–61–07* *€6* *Closed Tues.*

Hotels

★ Château Le Cagnard

$$$ | HOTEL | There is no better way to experience old Haut-de-Cagnes's grand castle views than to stay in this acclaimed 13th-century manor, perched on the ramparts of the Grimaldi fortress. **Pros:** free shuttle bus to Cagnes-sur-Mer; gorgeous setting ideal for romance; lots of steps to work off decadent meals. **Cons:** half the rooms are outside the hotel in the village; breakfast €25; no on-site parking. $ *Rooms from: €255* ✉ *54 rue Sous Barri, Cagnes-sur-Mer* ☎ *04–93–20–73–22* *www.lecagnard.com* *30 rooms* *No Meals.*

Le Grimaldi

$$ | HOTEL | This little hotel is smack in the middle of the Haut-de-Cagnes's liveliest square, complete with picture-perfect pétanque games. **Pros:** attentive owners speak four languages, including English; awe-inspiring room views; value prix-fixe lunch under €20. **Cons:** no elevator and steep stairs; parking is difficult; some slanted ceilings can challenge taller guests. $ *Rooms from: €155* ✉ *6 pl. du Château, Cagnes-sur-Mer* ☎ *04-93-20-60–24* *www.hotelgrimaldi.com* *5 rooms* *No Meals.*

St-Paul-de-Vence

18 km (11 miles) northwest of Nice.

This medieval village can be seen from afar, standing out like its companion, Vence, against the skyline. In the Middle Ages, St-Paul-de-Vence was basically a city-state, and it controlled its own political destiny for centuries. By the late 19th century, however, it had faded to oblivion—overshadowed by the growth of Vence and Cagnes—only to be rediscovered in the 1920s, when a few penniless artists began paying for drinks at the local auberge with their paintings. Paul Signac, Amedeo Modigliani, and Pierre Bonnard met at the Auberge de la Colombe d'Or, now a sumptuous inn with walls that are still covered with their sketches and daubs.

Today, the most commercially developed of Provence's hilltop villages, St-Paul-de-Vence is a magical place. Artists are still drawn to its light, its pure air, its wraparound views, and its honey-color stone walls, soothingly cool on a hot Provençal afternoon. Arrive early in the day to get a jump on the cars and tour buses, which can clog the main D36 highway by noon, or plan on a stay-over.

It won't take you long to "do" St-Paul-de-Vence; a pedestrian circuit leads you inevitably through its Rue-Grande to the donjon (fortress tower) and austere Gothic church. The trick is to break away and slip onto mosaic-cobbled backstreets—little more than narrow alleys that often lead to impossibly pretty cul-de-sacs and are lined by shuttered stone houses, where windows and niches spill over with potted flowers and orange trees.

You can also hike from St-Paul-de-Vence to Vence along a scenic path that starts beside the Chapelle Ste-Claire. The walk takes roughly 90 minutes.

GETTING HERE AND AROUND

St-Paul-de-Vence is only 15 minutes from the coast by car: take the Cagnes-sur-Mer highway to Exit 47 or 48 (depending on the direction you're coming from), and look for signs on the RD 436 to La Collle sur Loup/Vence. St-Paul-de-Vence is between the two.

There's no train station, but you can get off at Cagnes-sur-Mer and take Bus 655 (€2.10; 25 minutes), which departs from Nice and Cannes.

VISITOR INFORMATION

CONTACTS St-Paul-de-Vence Tourist Office. ✉ *2 rue Grande, St-Paul-de-Vence* ☎ *04–93–32–86–95* 🌐 *www.saint-pauldevence.com.*

Sights

Café de la Place

RESTAURANT | FAMILY | On your way from the overpriced parking garages, you'll pass a Provençal scene played out with cinematic flair yet still authentic: the perpetual game of pétanque outside the Café de la Place. A sun-weathered pack of men (and it is overwhelmingly men) in caps, cardigans, and workers' blues—occasionally joined by a passing professional with tie and rolled-up sleeves—gathers under the massive plane trees and stands serene, silent, and intent to toss metal balls across the dusty square. Until his death, Yves Montand made regular appearances here, participating in this ultimate southern scenario. Note that although the café is the perfect place to people-watch, don't expect much in terms of food and service. ■ **TIP→ Want to give *pétanque* a go? The tourist office rents balls for €5 per person, and you can play for as long as you want. Pay €8.50 extra, and you'll get your own private English-speaking instructor.** ✉ *Pl. de Gaulle, St-Paul-de-Vence* ☎ *04–93–32–80–03.*

Chapelle des Pénitents Blanc

CHURCH | Jean-Michel Folon had a deep affection for the town of St-Paul-de-Vence, where he befriended artists such as César, so it seems fitting that the decoration of its 17th-century Chapelle des Pénitents Blanc was one of the Belgian artist's last projects before his death in 2005. The overwhelming sensations as you enter the chapel are of peace and clarity: eight oil paintings in pastel colors by Folon collaborator Michel Lefebvre line the walls on either side and four stained-glass windows reinforce the themes of generosity and freedom. Sculptures take the place of the traditional altar and font, and the back wall is covered with a mosaic of the town made up of more than 1 million pieces. The chapel demonstrates the versatility of this artist and reflects the town's ability to celebrate its past while keeping an eye on the future. The tourist office can arrange for a 50-minute *visite* of the chapel in English (€8.50) from Tuesday to Friday, but you'll need to reserve in advance. ✉ *Pl. de l'Eglise, St-Paul-de-Vence* ☎ *04–93–32–86–95 for tourist office* 🎫 *€3* ⏲ *Closed second half of Nov.*

★ Fondation Maeght

ART MUSEUM | Many people come to St-Paul-de-Vence just to visit France's most important private art foundation, founded in 1964 by art dealer Aimé Maeght. High above the medieval town, the small modern art museum attracts 200,000 visitors a year. It's an extraordinary marriage of the arc-and-plane architecture of Josep Sert; the looming sculptures of Miró, Moore, and Giacometti; the mural mosaics of Chagall; and the humbling hilltop setting, complete with pines, vines, and flowing planes of water.

On display is an intriguing and ever-varying parade of important works by modern masters, including Chagall's wise and funny late-life masterpiece *La Vie* (*Life*).

With masterworks by Mirò, Picasso, Giacometti, and Vasarely, the Fondation Maeght in St-Paul-de-Vence is a modern-art treasure trove.

Two extensions in 2023 built toward the forest, due to be completed to mark the 60th anniversary of the Foundation's inauguration in 2024, provide additional exhibition, performance, and conference space, as well as panoramic windows opening to the extensive grounds. The impressive vistas help to beguile even those who aren't into modern art. Café F, should you need time to reflect, is open year-round. Contact the tourist office for a private guided visit in English (€9 plus discounted admission rate of €11). ✉ *623 ch. des Gardettes, St-Paul-de-Vence* ☎ *04–93–32–81–63* 🌐 *www.fondation-maeght.com* 🎫 *€16.*

Restaurants

★ La Colombe d'Or

$$$$ | FRENCH | The food might be a bit overpriced, but where else in the world could you eat in a dining room under a Picasso, on a terrace beside a ceramic Léger mural, or next to a pool amid an idyllic garden with a Calder sculpture? The quirky but unpretentious Provençal menu has hardly changed over 50 years—the hors d'oeuvres de la Colombe (basket of crudité and hunks of charcuterie), salmon quenelles, and Grand Marnier soufflé flambé are as acclaimed as ever. **Known for:** dining amid priceless art; lunch spot for celebs during Cannes Film Fesival; menu that hasn't missed a tasty beat in years. $ *Average main: €40* ✉ *Pl. Général-de-Gaulle, St-Paul-de-Vence* ☎ *04–93–32–80–02* 🌐 *www.la-colombe-dor.com* 🕓 *Closed Nov.–Christmas.*

La Fontaine

$$$ | BISTRO | The new owners of this St-Paul-de-Vence institution in the center of the old village have magically created a contemporary bistro, where a few seats on a second-story terrace (book in advance) overlook the street below. Choose the plat du jour, or order from an à la carte menu with everything from an organic egg to a chicken burger to a Jerusalem artichoke and shimeji-mushroom confit with smoked duck breast. **Known for:** charming village views;

friendly service; head to the tearoom if the restaurant is packed. *Average main: €28 ✉ 10 montée de la Castre, St-Paul-de-Vence ☎ 06–26–20–23–24 ⊕ www.restaurant-la-fontaine-saint-paul-de-vence.fr ⊙ Closed mid-Nov.–Feb.*

Le Tilleul

$$$ | **BISTRO** | Before you plunge into the dense tangle of streets in old St-Paul-de-Vence, stop on the ramparts under the century-old lime tree for a meal or snack at this atmospheric café, where the breezy terrace looks onto the valley and the Alps. The kitchen makes more of an effort than you might expect, turning out colorful salads (crispy goat cheese salad with figs) and pastas at lunch and more serious fare in the evening. **Known for:** fairly priced traditional French dishes with lighter fare; daily tea menu 3–6; charming shaded terrace. *Average main: €30 ✉ Pl. du Tilleul, St-Paul-de-Vence ☎ 04–93–32–80–36 ⊕ www.restaurant-letilleul.com No credit cards.*

Le Vieux Moulin

$$$ | **FRENCH** | From just outside the walled village, you can see this restaurant that was once a 17th-century oil mill. Owner Frédéric Rossi hired the young chef Olivier Depardieu, who did his apprenticeship at the Colombe d'Or and worked at Château Saint Martin, to create regional dishes like risotto with artichokes and langoustines or sea bass with pole-fried vegetables. **Known for:** affordable Provençal dishes; hearty dinners; lots of character and lovely views. *Average main: €25 ✉ Lieu-dit-Ste-Claire, Rte. de Vence, St-Paul-de-Vence ☎ 04–93–58–36–76 ⊕ levieuxmoulin-restaurant.business.site ⊙ Closed mid-Nov.–Feb.*

Hotels

★ La Colombe d'Or

$$$ | **B&B/INN** | Often called the most beautiful inn in France, "the golden dove" occupies a rose-stone Renaissance mansion just outside the walls of St-Paul-de-Vence and is so perfect overall that some contend you haven't really been to the French Riviera until you've stayed or dined here. **Pros:** original art, including works by Picasso and Rodin; gem of a hotel oozing charm and class in a laid-back vibe; famous guests, past and present. **Cons:** some annex rooms have blocked views; menu selection often outshone by the art; hard to get a reservation. *Rooms from: €350 ✉ Pl. Général-de-Gaulle, St-Paul-de-Vence ☎ 04–93–32–80–02 ⊕ www.la-colombe-dor.com ⊙ Closed Nov.–Christmas 25 rooms No Meals.*

Le Hameau

$$ | **B&B/INN** | Less than a mile below tourist-packed St-Paul-de-Vence, with views of the valley and the village, this lovely little inn is a jumble of terraces, trellises, archways, orange trees, olives, and honeysuckle vines. **Pros:** relaxing setting with old-fashioned charm and a pool; walking distance to Maeght Foundation; ask for the independent Nid d'Amour room with cathedral ceiling and skylight. **Cons:** short but uphill walk to St-Paul-de-Vence with no sidewalk; narrow staircase leading to rooms that share building with hotel office; some bookings require two-night minimum. *Rooms from: €225 ✉ 528 rte. de la Colle, St-Paul-de-Vence ☎ 04–83–39–95–94 ⊕ le-hameau.com ⊙ Closed mid-Nov.–mid-Feb. 13 rooms No Meals.*

Vence

4 km (2½ miles) north of St-Paul-de-Vence; 22 km (14 miles) north of Nice.

Plaques guide you through historic squares and *portes* (gates) in Vence, which is slightly more conscious of its past than the more-commercialized St-Paul-de-Vence. The down-to-earth feeling starts in a square just outside the Cité Historique (Historical City), where

Inside La Colombe d'Or

In 1920, the café Chez Robinson was a local hot spot for weekend dancing, which led to owner Paul Roux, a Provençal farmer with an eye for art, to open a small inn called La Colombe d'Or. It could accommodate only three guests, but, soon enough, artists were exchanging paintings for a meal or night's stay with the freethinking owner.

Over the next 20 years, Paul and his wife, Baptiste (known as "Tintine"), developed close relationships with other "thinkers and artists" who had moved to the south of France. Art was fashionable, and thanks to guests such as Picasso, Matisse, and Chagall, the inn was able to expand while maintaining a secluded yet unpretentious atmosphere.

During the course of its history, the inn has welcomed other big names, too, from Charlie Chaplin and Winston Churchill to Elton John and Hugh Grant. There have been setbacks along the way, however. One morning in 1959, Tintine came downstairs to find the walls bare—all the paintings had been stolen (and had never been appraised). The only masterpiece left was a Chagall, as it was apparently too large to fit through the window. This produced the famous line from Chagall "I'm a big-time artist! Why are you not stealing my paintings, too?"

The art collection at the inn and restaurant—both presided over by third-generation manager François Roux and his wife, Danièle—continues to grow, most recently with the acquisition of a large poolside ceramic piece by Irish artist Sean Scully. Indeed, the family's extraordinary sense of style would have delighted Pablo, Georges, and Henri. By the fireplace in the bar hangs a Braque. A table on the dining terrace is shaded by fig trees and lorded over by a ceramic Léger mural of a dove. The pool is amid an idyllic garden bower that's complete with a Calder stabile (one of many works here by Calder, who was apparently in love with François's mother).

Although the Provençal menu hasn't changed much in decades, and its prices are as fabulous as the art collection, having a drink or a meal here is an authentic experience—one that you can enjoy without being a hotel guest. If, however, you have opted to splurge for a night's stay, head upstairs to your room to be bewitched by Louis XIII armoires, medieval four-posters, wooden beams, Provençal borders, and murals. In addition to the main house, the property has two annexes, but regardless of where you stay, your room will be flawless and tasteful.

you'll find cafés and a small morning food market that attracts local producers (look for Tony and his exceptional *socca*, a pancake made with chickpea flour).

Inside the old city's stone walls, the Place du Peyra invites you to linger at restaurant terraces, browse in shops selling tablecloths or pottery, and quench your thirst at a pretty drinking fountain whose water comes directly from the Peyra source. Wander past Place du Peyra and Place Clémenceau, with its ocher-color Hôtel-de-Ville (Town Hall), to Place du Frêne, with an ash tree planted in the 16th century. Be sure to wander Rue du Marché, lined by old-fashioned food shops, including a butcher, a baker, and a fishmonger.

GETTING HERE AND AROUND

As with St-Paul-de-Vence, take the Cagnes-sur-Mer highway to Exit 47 or 48 (depending on the direction you're coming from) and look for signs on the RD 436 to La Colle sur Loup/Vence. St-Paul-de-Vence is between the two.

There's no train station, but you can get off at Cagnes-sur-Mer and take Bus 400 bus (€1.50; 30 minutes), which departs directly from Nice or Cannes. You can rent an electric bike (€0.15 a minute) via the app Bik'Air, which geolocates the nearest available bicycle. Unlike other such operations, Bik'Air has no stations; you simple leave the bike at your destination.

VISITOR INFORMATION

CONTACTS Vence Tourist Office. ✉ *Villa Alexandrine, Pl. du Grand Jardin, Vence* ☎ *04–93–58–06–38* 🌐 *vence-tourisme.com.*

Sights

Cathédrale de la Nativité de la Vierge (*Cathedral of the Birth of the Virgin*)
CHURCH | In the center of the Old Town, the Cathédrale de la Nativité de la Vierge was built in the 11th and 12th centuries on the site of a Roman military drilling field and is a hybrid of Romanesque and Baroque styles. The smallest cathedral in France, it has been expanded and altered many times over the centuries. Note the rostrum added in 1499—its choir stalls are carved with particularly vibrant and amusing scenes of daily life in the Middle Ages. In the baptistery is a ceramic mosaic of Moses in the bulrushes by Chagall. ✉ *Pl. Godeau, Vence* 🎫 *Free.*

★ **Chapelle du Rosaire** (*Chapel of the Rosary*)
CHURCH | On the outskirts of "new" Vence, toward St-Jeannet, is the Chapelle du Rosaire, better known as the Matisse Chapel. The artist decorated it with beguiling simplicity and clarity between 1947 and 1951 as his gift to nuns who had nursed him through illness. It reflects the reductive art style of the era: walls, floor, and ceiling are gleaming white, and the small stained-glass windows are cool greens and blues. "Despite its imperfections I think it is my masterpiece … the result of a lifetime devoted to the search for truth," wrote Matisse, who designed and dedicated the chapel when he was in his 80s and nearly blind. ✉ *466 av. Henri-Matisse, Vence* ☎ *04–93–58–03–26* 🌐 *www.chapellematisse.com* 🎫 *€7* ⏲ *Closed Sun., Mon., and 2 wks in Dec.*

Château du Domaine St. Martin
$$$$ | **HOTEL** | Occupying the site of an ancient Knights Templar fortress and set amid 34 acres of private greenery designed by Jean Mus, this hilltop domain has 180-degree panoramic views and is complete with a helicopter pad. **Pros:** flawless views and service; biodiversity refuge that supports a bird-protection charity and provides nesting boxes; superb Michelin-starred restaurant. **Cons:** buffet breakfast €40; nothing really within walking distance; minimum stay required during some periods. Ⓢ *Rooms from: €950* ✉ *2490 av. des Templiers, Vence* ☎ *04–93–58–02–02* 🌐 *www.chateau-st-martin.com* ⏲ *Closed mid-Oct.–Apr.* *46 rooms* *No Meals.*

L'Auberge des Seigneurs et du Lion d'Or
$ | **B&B/INN** | **FAMILY** | Dating from the 17th century and the only hotel set within Vence's old walls, this former stagecoach inn has been owned by the same family since 1919, and they still go out of their way to make your stay memorable. **Pros:** lovely family atmosphere; excellent food; seasonal fruits and fresh flowers to welcome you. **Cons:** front rooms can be noisy in summer, quieter back rooms lack views; no air-conditioning; strict cancellation policy. Ⓢ *Rooms from: €90* ✉ *Pl. du Frêne, Vence* ☎ *04–93–58–04–24* 🌐 *auberge-seigneurs.fr* *6 rooms* *No Meals.*

Photographs can't do justice to the beauty of St-Paul-de-Vence—one would need to pick up brush and canvas to fully capture its bewitching ambience.

Villa Roseraie

$$ | **B&B/INN** | A quick walk up from Old Vence, this 100-year-old house has charming regional details—mix-and-match old furniture, fine local tiles and fabrics, homemade bath salts and jams—plus there's a giant magnolia outside that spreads its venerable branches over the terrace. **Pros:** spacious rooms with air-conditioning; accommodating owners; ground-floor rooms with private terraces. **Cons:** nearby street noise but at such a great rate, wear earplugs; paid parking (€8/day); coast is a 15-minute drive. *$ Rooms from: €180 ✉ 128 av. Henri-Giraud, Vence ☎ 04–93–58–02–20 🌐 www.villaroseraie.com 🛏 10 rooms 🍽 Free Breakfast.*

Performing Arts

★ Nuits du Sud

FESTIVALS | Since 1997, world-music lovers have taken over Place du Grand Jardin in mid-July for four weeks, with up to 9,000 revelers a night gyrating to various beats. Even if you don't want to buy concert tickets, come for the atmosphere and share a picnic—the music will find you no matter where you are. *✉ 39 rue de 8 Mai 1945, Vence ☎ 04–93–58–40–17 🌐 www.nuitsdusud.com.*

Nice

176 km (110 miles) east of Aix-en-Provence; 33 km (20 miles) northeast of Cannes; 20 km (12½ miles) southwest of Monaco.

United with France only since 1860, Nice has a unique culture that stems from a very distinct history. It was on Colline du Château (now château-less) and at the Plage des Ponchettes, in front of the Old Town, that, in 350 BC, the Greeks established the market port of Nikaia, which became Marseille's chief coastal rival. The Romans established themselves a little later on the hills of Cimiez (Cemenelum), previously occupied by Ligurians and Celts.

After falling to Saracen invasions, Nice regained power and became an important port in the early Middle Ages. So cocksure did it become that, in 1388, the city and the hill towns behind it effectively seceded from the county of Provence, under Louis d'Anjou, and allied with Savoie as the Comté de Nice (Nice County). Thus began Nice's liaison with the House of Savoy, and, through it, with Piedmont and Sardinia. It was a relationship that lasted some 500 years, tinting the culture, architecture, and dialect in rich Italian hues.

By the 19th century, the port of Nice rivaled the neighboring port of Genoa. Tourism became another source of income, as the English and Russian nobility were enamored of the extraordinary climate and superb waterfront position. The stone mansions and hotels developed to accommodate them created a nearly solid wall of masonry, separated from the beach by what was originally called the Camin deis Anglés (the English Way) and is now known as the Promenade des Anglais.

Many of Nice's most delightful attractions—the Cours Saleya market, the Old Town streets, the Hotel Negresco, and the Palais Masséna—are on or close to the famous 10-km (6-mile) promenade, which was listed as a UNESCO World Heritage site in 2021. Although this waterfront crescent is still a big draw, the redevelopment of Nice's port, around the other side of the Colline du Château, has made it easier to take in the Genoese architecture or peruse the antiques at the Puces de Nice, along Quai Papacino.

In addition, Nice has been given the "Family Plus" label—meaning that it has things like free strollers, play areas, and restaurants with child-friendly activities. It also is one of France's most LGBTQ+-friendly cities, known for its In&Out and Zefestival film festivals and its Pink Parade and Lou Queernaval street parties. Some establishments even display the *Nice irisée naturellement* logo, indicating that they have taken part in training provided by Nice's Convention and Visitors Bureau, a member of the International Gay and Lesbian Travel Association.

GETTING HERE AND AROUND

As the main point of entry into the French Riviera region, Nice has France's second-largest airport, which sits on a peninsula between Antibes and Nice, 6 km (4 miles) southwest of the city. You can also reach Nice by Zou! Bus 600 (the Nice–Monaco–Menton, which, until spring 2024, is redirected as Bus 607 Nice–Monaco and Bus 608 Monaco–Menton), Bus 620 (Nice Antibes–Cannes), and Bus 665 (St-Paul-de-Vence and Vence).

The fastest way to get around the city is by tram. Lignes d'Azur operates three efficient lines, which run daily from early in the morning until late at night: L1 travels to Old Nice, Place Masséna, and the train station; the west–east L2 serves both airport terminals and ends at the port; and the newest L3 runs from Terminal 2 to Nice-Saint Isidore. Tickets cost €1.70 one-way, and you must buy them before boarding from automated machines at each tram stop.

Tram tickets can be used to transfer to city buses, also run by Lignes d'Azur and costing €1.70. At stops, remember to wave your hand, as if hailing a cab, to indicate to the bus driver that you want to get on.

There are designated bike paths in the city and along the promenade as far as Antibes, and Vélobleu (☎ *04–93–72–06–06* 🌐 *www.velobleu.org/en*) bikes are available at 161 stations across town. It costs €3 per day or €7 per week for a regular bike and €4 a day for an e-bike, with no added fees under half an hour. Sign up with any cell phone (international numbers included) or look for the few stations that accept credit cards directly.

During Nice's annual Carnaval, gargantuan floats, often ridden by the famous *grosses têtes*—literally, "fat heads"—fill the streets of old Nice with fantasy.

FESTIVALS

★ Nice Carnaval

FESTIVALS | FAMILY | Nice hosted its first edition of Carnaval in 1294, and today it's the third-largest celebration of its type in the world, drawing nearly a million spectators to free and paid events for all ages along the Promenade du Paillon off Place Masséna. One of the highlights of this massive themed event, which lasts for 15 days and culminates on Mardi Gras, is the Flower Battle—a parade of 18 floats, each decorated with 3,000 fresh flowers, during which people toss 5,000 tonnes of locally grown mimosa blossoms in a tradition started by the British (who originally threw eggs, flour, and confetti plaster). ✉ *Office du Tourisme, 5 promenade des Anglais, Nice* ☎ *04–97–13–36–66* 🌐 *www.nicecarnaval.com/en.*

VISITOR INFORMATION

CONTACTS Nice Tourist Office. ✉ *5 promenade des Anglais, Nice* ☎ *04–92–14–46–14* 🌐 *www.explorenicecotedazur.com/en.*

Sights

Framed by the "château"—really a rocky promontory—and Cours Saleya, Old Town is the best place to experience Nice's historic feeling. Its grid of narrow streets, with houses five and six stories high and jewel-box Baroque churches on every other corner, creates a magic that seems utterly removed from the Côte d'Azur fast lane.

Nice takes on a completely different character west of Cours Saleya thanks to broad city blocks; vast neoclassical hotels and apartment houses; and a series of inviting parks dense with palm trees, greenery, and fountains. From the Jardin Albert Ier, once the delta of the Paillon River, the famous Promenade des Anglais stretches the length of the city's waterfront.

The original promenade was the brainchild of Lewis Way, an English minister in the growing community of British who were drawn to Nice's climate. They needed a proper walkway on which to

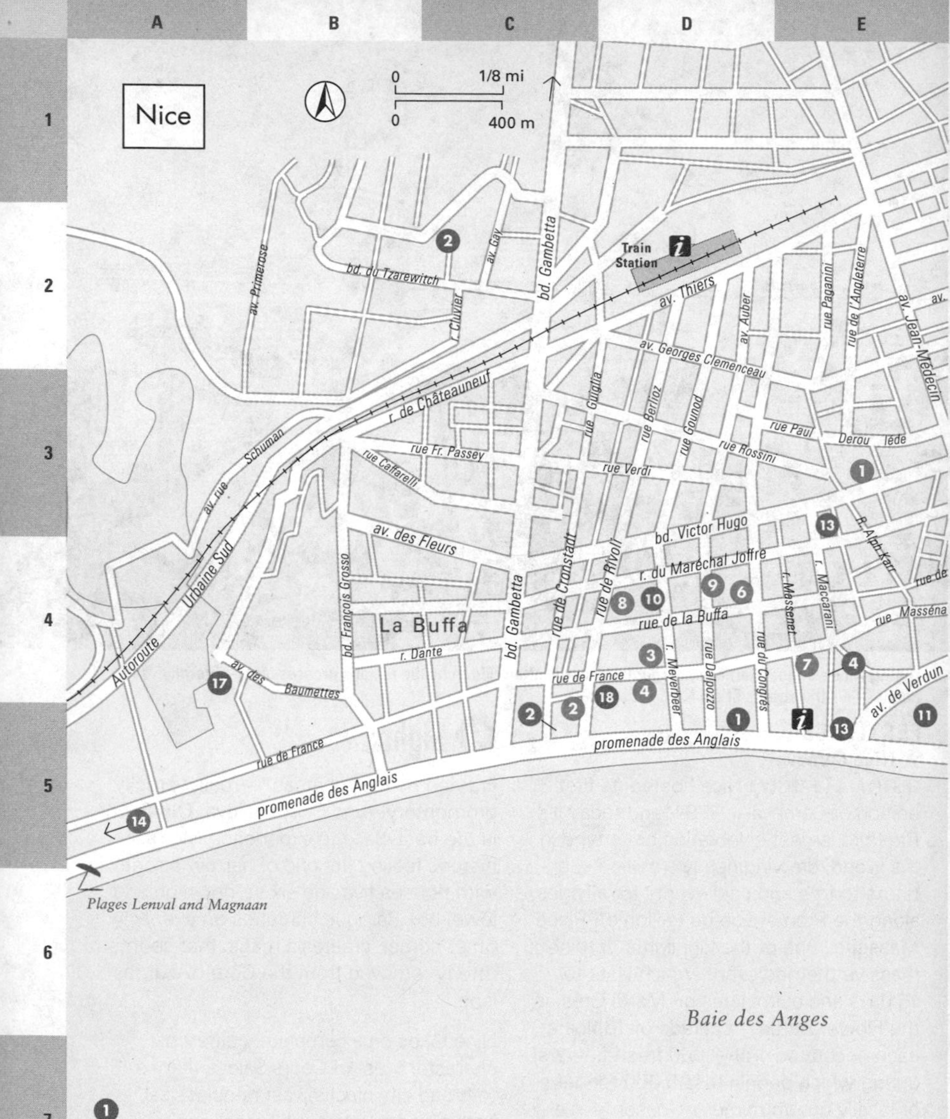

Sights

1 Casino du Palais de la Méditerranée........ **D5**
2 Cathédrale Orthodoxe Russe St-Nicolas...... **C2**
3 Cathédrale Ste-Réparate........... **G4**
4 Chapelle de la Miséricorde............ **G5**
5 Chapelle Sainte-Rita.. **G5**
6 Cimetière du Château.................. **H4**
7 Colline du Château..... **I4**
8 Cours Saleya........... **G5**
9 Eglise du Gésù......... **G4**
10 Église St-Martin........ **H4**
11 Jardin Albert Ier....... **E5**
12 La Crypte Archéologique de Nice.................. **H3**
13 Le Ruhl Casino Barrière Nice........... **E5**
14 Monastère de Cimiez..................... **I1**
15 Musée Archéologique.......... **I1**
16 Musée de Préhistoire Terra Amata............ **J4**
17 Musée des Beaux-Arts............. **A4**
18 Musée Masséna....... **D4**
19 Musée Matisse......... **I1**
20 Musée National Marc Chagall............ **F1**
21 Palais Lascaris......... **G4**
22 Place Garibaldi.......... **H3**
23 Place Masséna......... **F4**
24 Port de Nice............ **I5**
25 Promenade de Paillon.................... **F4**

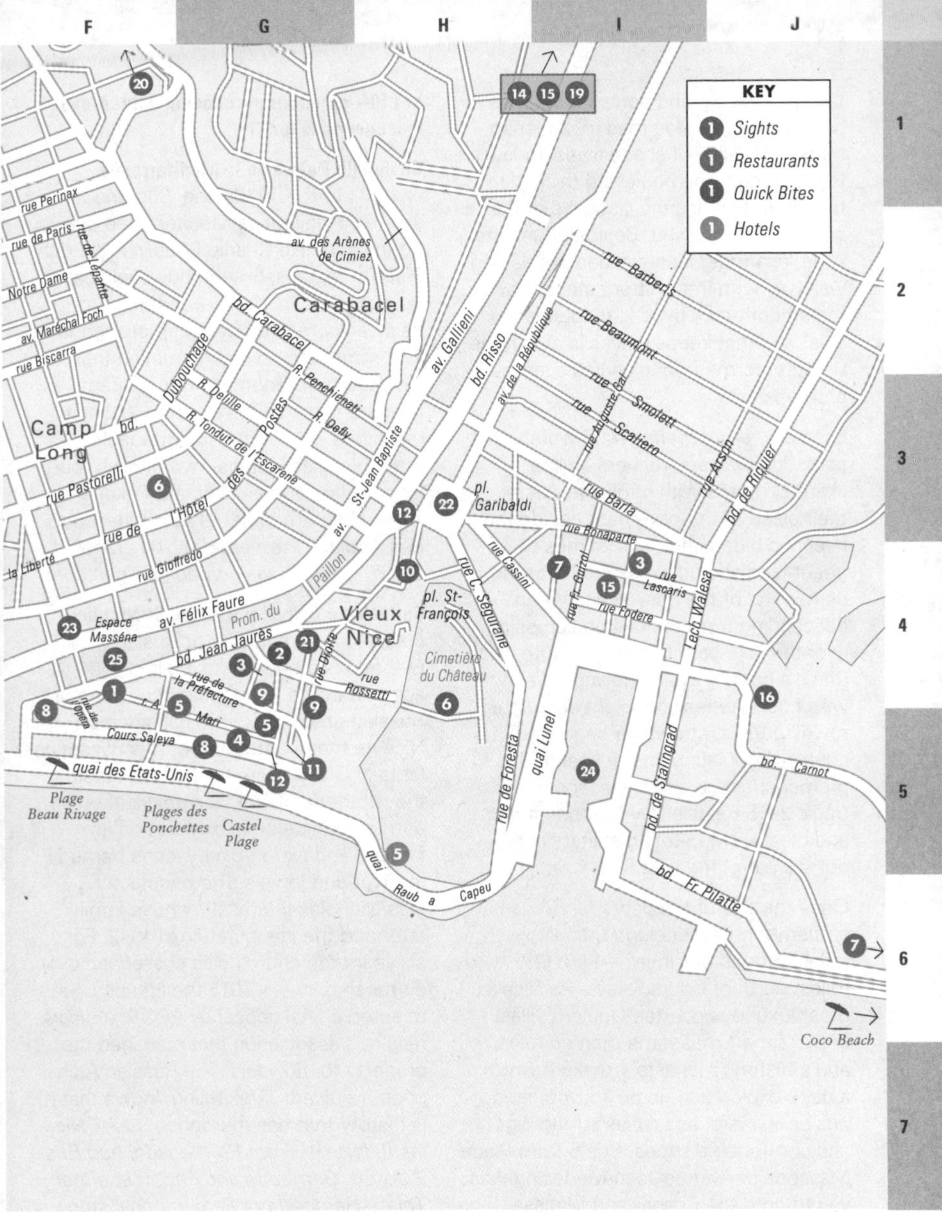

Restaurants

1 Attimi F4
2 Chantecler C5
3 Chez Pipo Socca I4
4 La Femme du Boulanger E4
5 La Merenda G4
6 La Part des Anges F3
7 La Réserve de Nice ... J6
8 Le Bistro Gourmand F5
9 Le Bistrot d'Antoine ... G4
10 Le Canon D4
11 Le Panier G5
12 Le Safari G5
13 Le Séjour Café E3
14 Lycée Hotellier Paul Augier A5
15 Restaurant Jan I4

Quick Bites

1 Café des Chineurs A7
2 Glacier Fenocchio G4

Hotels

1 Hotel Boscolo Nice E3
2 Hôtel Negresco C5
3 Hôtel Suisse D4
4 La Fontaine D4
5 La Perouse H5
6 Nice Garden Hotel D4
7 Solara E4
8 Villa Rivoli D4
9 Windsor D4

take the sea air, and pooled resources to build a 6½-foot-wide road meandering through an alley of shade trees. Today, this is a multilane boulevard thick with traffic—in fact, it's the last gasp of the coastal highway N98. Beside it runs the wide, charming, sun-washed pedestrian walkway with intermittent steps down to the smooth-rock beach; its foundation is a seawall that keeps waves in all but the wildest storms from sloshing over the promenade.

Each day, *promeneurs*—sun worshippers, dog walkers, runners, in-line skaters, moms with strollers—vie for their piece of the pavement beside the hypnotic blue water. Sometimes they get entangled and exchange barbs, so be mindful of the busy scene when descending from the bus and crossing over the bike path to the sea. Note, too, that it's best to avoid strolling here in the wee hours, when you might encounter rowdy drunks, strewn garbage, and couples copulating on the beach. The promenade was also the scene of the tragic 2016 Bastille Day terrorist attack, and machine-gun-toting military personnel still patrol the area.

Once the site of the powerful Roman settlement, Cemenelum, the hilltop neighborhood of Cimiez—4 km (2½ miles) north of Cours Saleya—is Nice's most luxurious quarter. Opulent villas, important art museums, Roman ruins, and a historic monastery make it worth a day's exploration. To do so, you need bus or taxi fare, as well as strong legs and comfortable shoes. Bus 5 from Place Masséna or Avenue Jean-Médecin takes you to both the Chagall and Matisse museums (Stop: Musée Matisse); from the latter you can visit the ruins and monastery. If you opt to drive, arm yourself with a map and a navigator.

■ TIP→ For many years, all of Nice's municipal museums were free, and they still are for residents. Although admission for visitors is reasonable—generally €5 or €10—consider purchasing a three-day museum pass for €15.

Casino du Palais de la Méditerranée

CASINO | In the 1920s and '30s, the swanky Palais de la Méditerranée drew performers like Charlie Chaplin and Edith Piaf. The establishment, however, lost its glory and, in 1990, everything but its swanky facades was demolished to accommodate new construction that included hotel rooms and restaurants as well the casino. Choose from 170 slot machines, 38 electric roulette tables, three blackjack tables, two English roulette tables, and an Ultimate Poker and Texas Hold'em table. ✉ *15 promenade des Anglais, Promenade* ☎ *04–92–14–68–00* 🌐 *www.casinomediterranee.com.*

Cathédrale Orthodoxe Russe St-Nicolas

CHURCH | This magnificent Russian Orthodox cathedral was built in 1896 to accommodate the sizable population of Russian aristocrats who had adopted Nice as their winter home. This Byzantine fantasy is the largest of its kind outside the motherland, with six gold-leaf onion domes, rich ceramic mosaics on its facade, and extraordinary icons framed in silver and jewels. The benefactor was Nicholas II himself, whose family attended the inauguration in 1912. For six years the church was challenged over ownership, but in 2013 the French courts rejected a final appeal by ACOR, a *niçois* religious association that managed the property for 80 years. The Russian Archpriest rejoiced: "This ruling shows that it is history that has triumphed." ✉ *Av. Nicolas II, Nice* ✥ *From Promenade, hop Bus 7 up Bd. Gambetta and get off at either Thiers-Gambetta or Parc Imperial stop, or walk 15 mins west from train station* ☎ *09–81–09–53–45* 🌐 *www.sobor.fr.*

Cathédrale Ste-Réparate

CHURCH | An ensemble of columns, cupolas, and symmetrical ornaments dominates the Vieille Ville, flanked by an 18th-century bell tower and glossy ceramic-tile dome. The cathedral's interior, completely restored to a bright palette of ocher, golds, and rusts, has elaborate plasterwork and decorative frescoes on every surface. ✉ *3 pl. Rossetti, Old Town* 🌐 *cathedrale-nice.fr.*

Chapelle de la Miséricorde

CHURCH | A superbly balanced *pièce-montée* (wedding cake) of half-domes and cupolas, this chapel is decorated within an inch of its life with frescoes, faux marble, gilt, and crystal chandeliers. A magnificent altarpiece by Renaissance painter Ludivico Brea crowns the ensemble. Visits are limited to 2:30 to 5:30 pm on Tuesday. ✉ *7 cours Saleya, Old Town* ⏲ *Closed Wed.–Mon. and July, and Aug.*

Chapelle Sainte-Rita (*Église de l'Annonciation*)

CHURCH | Officially known as the Église de l'Annonciation, this 17th-century Carmelite chapel is a classic example of pure Niçoise Baroque, from its sculpted door to its extravagant marble work and the florid symmetry of its arches and cupolas. ✉ *1 rue de la Poissonerie, Old Town* 🌐 *www.sainte-rita.net.*

Cimetière du Château (*Cemetery*)

CEMETERY | This solemn cluster of white tombs looms prominently over the city below, providing a serene or macabre detail of daily life, depending on your mood. Under Nice's blue skies, the gleaming white marble and Italian mix of melodrama and exuberance in the decorations, dedications, photo portraits, and sculptures are somehow oddly life-affirming. Founded in 1783, there are 2,800 graves here—with prominent names like Jellinek-Mercedes and Leroux—in three sections, to this day segregating Catholics, Protestants, and Jews. ✉ *Allée François-Aragon, Nice.*

Colline du Château (*Château Hill*)

CITY PARK | **FAMILY** | Although nothing remains of the once-massive medieval stronghold but a few ruins left after its 1706 dismantling, the name *château* still applies to this high plateau-like park, from which you can take in extraordinary views of the Baie des Anges, the length of Promenade des Anglais, and the red-ocher roofs of the Old Town. Children can blow off energy at the playground, while you enjoy a picnic with panoramic views and a bit of shade. You can also partake in the Communist party's annual Fête du Chateau in June or try yoga from May to October every Tuesday (€10, meet-up at the snackbar "La Citadelle"). It's 213 steps to the top or you can use the free elevator next to the Hotel Suisse; alternatively, ascend the hill slower from the port side, near Place Garibaldi, which is a more gentle climb. ✉ *Promenade des Anglais, east end, Nice* 🎟 *Free.*

★ Cours Saleya

NEIGHBORHOOD | **FAMILY** | This long pedestrian thoroughfare—half street, half square—is the nerve center of Old Nice, the heart of the Vieille Ville, and the stage for the city's marketplace and café life. Shoppers come to smell the roses (and mimosas and orange blossoms) before browsing at stalls selling local produce, spices, olives, and little gift soaps in the single row set-up, the overflow of which sprawls into leafy Place Pierre Gautier. Market days are Tuesday through Saturday, 6 am to 5:30 pm and Sunday 6 am to 1:30 pm. Arrive early, especially in summer, to avoid being at the mercy of the crowd (and a target for the rampant pickpockets).

On Monday morning, antiques and *brocantes* (collectibles) draw avid vintage hounds, and, from June to September, there's also an artisanal craft market selling jewelry, pottery, purses, and paintings. At Place Charles Félix on the east end of Cours Saleya is the imposing yellow stone building where Matisse lived on the third and then fourth floor from 1921 to 1938. Today, there's no plaque that bears his name, only a broken shutter of his workshop to serve as a commemoration. Its future remains uncertain, but for many Niçois,

No wonder Matisse lived in a building overlooking the Cours Saleya, a thoroughfare whose marketplace is one of the most colorful in France.

this building is a part of Nice's heritage. ⊠ *Cours Saleya, Old Town.*

Eglise du Gésù

CHURCH | If Nice's other chapels are jewel boxes, this is a barn. Broad, open, and ringing hollow after the intense concentration of sheer matter in the Miséricorde and Ste-Rita, it seems austere by comparison. That's only because the decoration is spread over a more expansive surface. If it's possible, this 17th-century Baroque chapel is even more theatrical and over-the-top than its peers. Angels throng in plaster and fresco, pillars spill over with extravagantly sculpted capitals, and from the pulpit (to the right, at the front) the crucifix is supported by a disembodied arm. ⊠ *Corner of Rue Droite and Rue du Jésus, Nice.*

Église St-Martin (*Église St-Augustin*)

CHURCH | This serene Baroque structure at the foot of the château anchors the oldest church-parish in Nice. Built in 1405, it was here that Martin Luther preached in 1510 and Garibaldi was baptized in 1807. ⊠ *Rue Sincaire, Nice.*

Jardin Albert Ier (*Albert I Garden*)

GARDEN | Along Promenade des Anglais, this luxurious garden stands over the delta of the River Paillon, underground since 1882. Every kind of flower and palm tree grows here, thrown into exotic relief by night illumination. Home base for many city festivals with its Théâtre de Verdure and also Ciné Prom in the summer, the garden is the starting point for Nice's Promenade du Paillon. ⊠ *2–16 av. de Verdun, New Town* *Free.*

La Crypte Archéologique de Nice

RUINS | Via steel walkways, explore (by tour only) this half-acre archaeological crypt beneath Place Garibaldi. It contains the remains of a 14th-century tower and aqueduct that were razed by Louis XIV and only uncovered during excavations for Nice's tram system at the beginning of this century. The Centre du Patrimoine (Heritage Center) offers one-hour guided tours for up to 15 people, but you must reserve with them directly at 14 rue Jules-Gilly. The meeting point—Place Jacques Toja—is just off Place Garibaldi.

■ **TIP→ Wear "sensible shoes," as heels can't be worn in the crypt.** ✉ *Pl. Jacques Toja, Old Town* ☎ *3906* 🎫 *€7.*

Le Ruhl Casino Barrière Nice

CASINO | Renovated to the tune of €5 million, Le Ruhl is the biggest "machine park" on the Côte d'Azur luring in the summer vacationers and the winter convention crowd with vivid colors and fiber-optic lighting. Some flock into the hushed gaming room for poker and blackjack; others try their luck at one of the 282 slot and 36 electronic English roulette machines. ✉ *1 promenade des Anglais, New Town* ☎ *04–97–03–12–22* 🌐 *www.casinosbarriere.com/en/nice.html.*

Monastère de Cimiez

RELIGIOUS BUILDING | This fully functioning monastery is worth the pilgrimage. You can find a lovely garden, replanted along the lines of the original 16th-century layout; the **Musée Franciscain,** a didactic museum tracing the history of the Franciscan order; and a 15th-century church containing three works of remarkable power and elegance by Bréa. ✉ *Pl. du Monastère, Cimiez* ☎ *04–93–81–00–04* 🌐 *stemariedesanges.free.fr* 🎫 *Free* ⏲ *Museum closed Sun.*

Musée Archéologique (*Archaeology Museum*)

HISTORY MUSEUM | **FAMILY** | Next to the Musée Matisse, this museum has a large collection of objects extracted from digs around the Roman city of Cemenelum, which flourished from the 1st to the 5th centuries. Among the fascinating ruins are an amphitheater, frigidarium, gymnasium, baths, and sewage trenches, some dating from the 3rd century. ■ **TIP→ It's best to avoid midday visits on warm days.** ✉ *160 av. des Arènes-de-Cimiez, Cimiez* ☎ *04–93–81–59–57* 🌐 *www.musee-archeologie-nice.org* 🎫 *€5* ⏲ *Closed Tues.*

Musée de Préhistoire Terra Amata

HISTORY MUSEUM | **FAMILY** | During the digging for the foundation of a building in 1966, the shovels uncovered the remains of a temporary settlement once used by elephant hunters thousands of years ago. Now the site is a museum with models and other displays—including one with an actual human footprint, calcified in the sand—that reconstruct the ancient beach-camp known as Terra Amata (Beloved Land). Films explain the lifestyle of what are among the oldest known inhabitants of Europe. Recorded commentaries and the museum's app are available in English. ✉ *25 bd. Carnot, Nice* ☎ *04–93–55–59–93* 🌐 *www.musee-terra-amata.org* 🎫 *€10* ⏲ *Closed Tues.*

Musée des Beaux-Arts (*Jules-Chéret Fine Arts Museum*)

ART MUSEUM | Originally built for a member of Nice's Old Russian community, the Princess Kotschoubey, this Italianate mansion is a Belle Époque wedding cake, replete with one of the grandest staircases on the coast. After the *richissime* American James Thompson took over and the last glittering ball was held here, the villa was bought by the municipality as a museum in the 1920s. Unfortunately, many of the period features were sold, but in their place are paintings by Degas, Boudin, Monet, Sisley, Dufy, and Jules Chéret, whose posters of winking *damselles* distill all the *joie* of the Belle Époque. From the Hôtel Negresco area, the museum is about a 15-minute walk up a gentle hill; guided tours in English can be arranged. ✉ *33 av. des Baumettes, New Town* ☎ *04–92–15–28–28* 🌐 *www.musee-beaux-arts-nice.org* 🎫 *€10* ⏲ *Closed Mon.*

Musée Masséna (*Masséna Palace*)

CASTLE/PALACE | This spectacular Belle Époque villa houses the Musée d'Art et d'Histoire (Museum of Art and History), where familiar paintings from French, Italian, and Dutch masters line the walls. Be sure to see the palace gardens, set with towering palm trees, a marble bust of the handsome General Masséna, and the Jardin de la Légion d'Honneur (a memorial to victims of the July 14 tragedy), all backdropped by the ornate trim of the Hôtel Negresco; this is one of Nice's most imposing oases. ✉ *65 rue de France, New Town* ☎ *04–93–91–19–10* 🎫 *€10* ⏲ *Closed Tues.*

★ Musée Matisse

ART MUSEUM | In the 1960s, the city of Nice bought this lovely, light-bathed, 17th-century villa, surrounded by the ruins of Roman civilization, and restored it to house a large collection of Henri Matisse's works. The Fauvist artist settled along Nice's waterfront in 1917, seeking a sun cure after a bout with pneumonia, and remained here until his death in 1954. During his years on the French Riviera, Matisse maintained intense friendships and artistic liaisons with Renoir, who lived in Cagnes, and with Picasso, who lived in Mougins and Antibes. He eventually moved up to the rarefied isolation of Cimiez and took an apartment in the Hôtel Regina (now an apartment building, just across from the museum), where he lived out the rest of his life. He walked often in the parklands around the Roman remains and was buried in an olive grove outside the Cimiez cemetery.

The museum's collection includes several pieces the artist donated to the city before his death; the rest were donated by his family. In every medium and context—paintings, gouache cutouts, engravings, and book illustrations—the collection represents the evolution of his art, from Cézanne-like still lifes to exuberant dancing paper dolls. Even the furniture and accessories speak of Matisse, from the Chinese vases to the bold-printed fabrics with which he surrounded himself. A series of telling black-and-white photographs captures the artist at work. **■ TIP→ You can't enter the museum with a backpack or travel bag, so have a €1 coin handy for a locker.** ✉ *164 av. des Arènes-de-Cimiez, Cimiez* ☎ *04–93–81–08–08* 🌐 *www.musee-matisse-nice.org* 🎫 *€10* ⏲ *Closed Tues.*

Musée National Marc Chagall (*Marc Chagall Museum of Biblical Themes*)

ART MUSEUM | Inaugurated in 1973, this museum has one of the finest permanent collections of Chagall's (1887–1985) late works. Superbly displayed, 17 vast canvases depict biblical themes, each in emphatic, joyous colors. Chamber music and classical concert series also take place here, though extra admission fees may apply. Bus stops outside. ✉ *Av. du Dr-Ménard, Cimiez* ☎ *04–93–53–87–20* 🌐 *musees-nationaux-alpesmaritimes.fr/chagall* 🎫 *€8 or €10, depending on exhibition* ⏲ *Closed Tues.*

Palais Lascaris

CASTLE/PALACE | A listed heritage building, this palace was built in 1648 for Jean-Baptiste Lascaris-Vintimille, *marechal* to the Duke of Savoy. The magnificent vaulted staircase, with its massive stone balustrade and niches filled with classical gods, is surpassed in grandeur only by the Flemish tapestries (after Rubens) and the extraordinary trompe-l'oeil fresco depicting the fall of Phaëthon. With a little luck, you'll be in time for one of the many classical concerts performed here. Note, however, that the building has no elevator. ✉ *15 rue Droite, Old Town* ☎ *04–93–62–72–40* 🎫 *€10* ⏲ *Closed Tues.*

Place Garibaldi

PLAZA/SQUARE | FAMILY | Surrounded by grand vaulted arcades stuccoed in rich yellow, this square could have been airlifted out of Turin. In the center, the shrinelike fountain sculpture of Garibaldi seems to be surveying you as you stroll under the very attractive arcades and lounge in the surrounding cafés. Les Artisanales, the market for local crafts (jewelry, ceramics, leather goods, clothes, accessories) sets up the first Sunday of the month (9–7), and an antiques market takes place on the third Saturday of every month (7–5). **■ TIP→ Behind**

Far from the city center, the Musée Matisse draws thousands of art lovers every month to take the long bus ride up the hill to the Cimiez suburb.

Place Garibaldi is the so-called Antique Quarter, with important antiques stores and emporiums like the Puces de Nice along the streets Antoine-Gautier, Emmanuel-Philibert, Catherine-Ségurane, Martin-Seytour, and Foresta. ✉ *Old Town.*

Place Masséna

PLAZA/SQUARE | FAMILY | As Cours Saleya is the heart of the Vieille Ville, so this impressive and broad square is the heart of the entire city. It's framed by early-17th-century, Italian-style arcaded buildings, their facades stuccoed in rich red ocher. The lively and boisterous space hosts an event—from Carnaval to the Christmas market—at least once a month, and Promenade du Paillon runs through it. Nespresso has a boutique here if you need a free coffee to perk you up. ✉ *Pl. Masséna, Nice.*

Port de Nice

MARINA/PIER | FAMILY | In 1750, the Duke of Savoy ordered a port to be dug to shelter the approach of the city's maritime traffic. It's still a safe harbor for freighters, fishing boats, and yachts, and its redevelopment has made it easier to take in the area's Genoese architecture or peruse the antiques at the Puces de Nice emporium and other shops along Rue Robilant, near the large Port Lympia parking lot.

From June to mid-October (daily 10–7), the free shuttle *Lou Passagin* ferries you across the port from the Quai Lunel to Quai d'Entrecasteaux. In June, keep an eye out for the Fête du Port—a gastronomical explosion (and one of the rare occasions when you'll witness the French walk and eat simultaneously) outmatched only by fire-eaters and fireworks. From the port, you can take Bus 33 to visit the 16th-century Fort du Mont-Alban, which has exceptional views of Bordighera and Saint-Jean-Cap-Ferrat all the way over to Baie des Anges (those curvy white buildings) and Antibes. ✉ *Old Town.*

Promenade de Paillon

CITY PARK | FAMILY | Running behind Old Town, this 30-acre park is known as the Coulée Verte (Green Belt). It serves as a playground for kids, a refuge for adults (who take advantage of the free Wi-Fi), and a venue for many of the city's annual and one-off events, like April Fool's Day (in French, Poisson d'Avril, or Fish Day). No matter when you visit, there's plenty to photograph here. ✉ *Promenade de Paillon, Nice.*

Beaches

Nice's beaches extend all along the Baie des Anges, backed full-length by the Promenade des Anglais and a thriving and sophisticated downtown—hence, don't be surprised if you see power-suited executives stripping down to some Lycra, tanning over their lunch hour, and then suiting back up for the afternoon's work a block or two away. The absence of sand (there's nothing but those famous Riviera pebbles, *les galets*) helps maintain that dress-for-success look.

The downside of the location: the otherwise stylish streets downtown tend to fill with underdressed, sunburned tourists caked with salt during beach season. Enterprising vendors cruise the public beach waterfront, hawking ice cream, slabs of watermelon, coffee, ice-cold sodas, and beer.

Posh private beaches, some of which share names with public beaches, have full-service restaurants and bars, color-coordinated mattresses and beach umbrellas, and ranks of tanners with phones glued to their ears. Several of these beaches lure clients with water-skiing, parasailing, windsurfing, and Jet-Skiing; if you're looking for a particular sport, check the signs posted at the entrance with the restaurant menus. Fees for private beaches average €20–€45 for a mattress (you'll pay more for the row closest to the sea) and €5 for a parasol with access to a dressing room and bathroom/shower.

Private beaches alternate with open stretches of public frontage that have free toilets and open "showers" (a cold elevated faucet for rinsing off salt), which will be turned off if there are drought conditions, so consider bringing your tap water for a DIY rinse. Note, too, that Centenaire and Lenval beaches are smoke-free, and Centenaire and Carras are "handiplages," accessible with a wheelchair.

From mid-June to mid-September, all private and public beaches have lifeguards (9–6:30). Check the flags to see if it's safe to swim: yellow means the water quality is poor (blue is good), orange means danger (from waves or jellyfish), and red means no swimming. Jellyfish have an unpredictable presence, so keep an ear open for the word "*méduse*," look for it on the signboards in front of private beach areas, or check the website 🌐 *meduse.acri.fr/carte/carte.php.*

Castel Plage

BEACH | At the east end of the promenade, near Hotel Suisse, there is both a large public beach and a private one, where the water is calm and clear (you can rent a lounger at the latter for about €25, with umbrella). The public beach is composed of large stones, which are more comfortable to walk on than pebbles. Jellyfish are also less of a problem in this corner due to the currents. **Amenities:** lifeguards (private beach, seasonal); showers. **Best for:** snorkeling; sunrise; sunset; swimming. ✉ *8 quai des États-Unis, Nice* 🌐 *www.castelplage.com/en.*

Coco Beach

BEACH | East of the Promenade, past the port and La Réserve restaurant and a few steps below street level, is one of Nice's quieter strands, with very clear water, few tourists (locals tend to spread their towels here), and hardly any jellyfish. The catch? The beach is more slabs of rock than sand, and the coastline here is exposed to wind. Many fish move about below, making this an excellent place for snorkeling. **Amenities:** food and drink;

Like the Rio of France, Nice is lined with a gigantic crescent beach whose prime spot, the Promenade des Anglais, is home to many palace-hotels.

lifeguards (seasonal); parking (street); showers. **Best for:** snorkeling; solitude; swimming. ✉ *Av. Jean Lorrain, Nice.*

Plage Beau Rivage

BEACH | Across from Cours Saleya, the Riviera's largest private beach is one of Nice's nicest; you can gain access by renting a pricey lounger for the day via phone. The beach itself is stony, so wear water shoes. If there are jellyfish sightings, you'll see a written warning of "méduse" on a beach board; ditto for strong winds. Steps from Beau Rivage on the Prom is Nice's own Statue of Liberty (look carefully, as she's only 4½-feet tall). **Amenities:** food and drink; lifeguards; showers; toilets. **Best for:** sunset; swimming. ✉ *107 quai des États-Unis, Nice* ☎ *04–92–00–46–80* 🌐 *plagenicebeaurivage.com.*

Plages des Ponchettes

BEACH | **FAMILY** | Almost at the end of the promenade and in front of Old Town, this basic stony stretch is a popular spot, with a melange of tourists and locals of all ages all day. In summer it has sandy volleyball courts. Keep an eye out for jellyfish. **Amenities:** lifeguards (seasonal); toilets. **Best for:** snorkeling; sunrise; sunset; swimming. ✉ *Quai des États-Unis, Nice.*

Plages Lenval and Magnan

BEACH | Locals come early—with umbrellas, chairs, and coolers in tow—to these two sizable public beaches around the halfway point of the promenade. As both are stone beaches with occasional jellyfish, water shoes are best for getting in and out of the sea. Lenval is a no-smoking beach with pay-to-use underground hot showers, toilets, and lockers, as well as portable toilets in the summer; it has no lifeguards or first aid station. These are, however, provided at neighboring Magnan, which is wider and lower than street level. This area is less touristy, so expect to see topless torsos. **Amenities:** lifeguards (Magnan, seasonal); showers; toilets. **Best for:** sunrise; swimming. **■ TIP→ When the winds pick up, this area can be dangerous, so watch for the warning**

flags, and avoid swimming for 24 hours after a storm. ✉ *Promenade des Anglais, Nice.*

Restaurants

Attimi

$$ | **ITALIAN** | Specializing in salads, pizzas, and pastas—prepared on the spot from local produce—this place offers a refreshing, light alternative to all those heavy French dishes. But Attimi is as hot as the lasagna Bolognese it serves, so you'll need to reserve or eat early. **Known for:** thin-crust pizza; terrace seating with great people-watching; long lines that are worth waiting in. *Average main: €20* ✉ *10 pl. Masséna, Nice* ☎ *04–93–91–05–26* 🌐 *www.attimi.fr.*

Chantecler

$$$$ | **MEDITERRANEAN** | Long a showplace for Riviera luxury, the Negresco is replete with Régence-fashion salons decked out with 18th-century wood boiserie and Aubusson carpets. Its main dining room, the Michelin-starred Chantecler has been playing musical chefs for the past few years and currently features a new-generation culinary artist, Virginie Basselot, and her selections of impressive haute cuisine. **Known for:** a leader in French haute cuisine; formal dress code; giant wine cellar. *Average main: €80* ✉ *Hôtel Negresco, 37 promenade des Anglais, Promenade* ☎ *04–93–16–64–00* 🌐 *www.hotel-negresco-nice.com* *Closed Mon. and Tues. No lunch.* *Jacket required.*

★ **Chez Pipo Socca**

$ | **FRENCH** | There are plenty of places where you can sample socca in Old Town, but if you want to understand why so much fuss is made in Nice over the chickpea pancake, this out-of-the-way café behind the port is the place to go. As per usual, a batter of chickpea flour, water, olive oil, and salt is baked in giant copper tins in a wood-fired oven, but here, the cook expertly scrapes the surface of the nearly-cooked dough with a metal spatula so that it comes out extra-crispy. **Known for:** authentic Niçois food; arrive at 5:30 opening to avoid long wait; cash-only policy. *Average main: €7* ✉ *13 rue Bavastro, Port Nice* ☎ *04–93–55–88–82* 🌐 *www.chezpipo.fr* *No credit cards* *Closed Mon. and Tues. July and Aug.*

★ **La Femme du Boulanger**

$$ | **FRENCH** | Although lunch and dinner are delicious, this the place to come for a breakfast of freshly sliced country breads, mouthwatering Ö Jardin Sucré jams (say, raspberry and violet or apple-pear with hazelnut), and organic yogurts—all made in France. Sure, you can still have your flaky croissant, but here the friendly owners deliver a toaster to your table to grill the bread exactly to your liking. **Known for:** the best breakfast (and brunch) in Nice; outstanding dinner; French countryside vibes. *Average main: €22* ✉ *3 rue Commandant Raffali, New Town* ☎ *04–89–03–43–03* 🌐 *www.facebook.com/femmeduboulanger* *No credit cards.*

★ **La Merenda**

$$$ | **FRENCH** | The back-to-bistro boom climaxed here when Dominique Le Stanc retired his crown at the Negresco to take over this tiny, unpretentious landmark of Provençal cuisine. For decades he has worked in a miniature open kitchen creating ultimate versions of stuffed sardines, tagliatelle with pistou, slow-simmered *daubes* (beef stews), and the quintessential stockfish (the local lutefisk)—but don't worry, pizza is an option, too. **Known for:** real deal when it comes to French bistro; amazing food for the price; cash-only policy and reservations only in person or via social media. *Average main: €32* ✉ *4 rue Raoul Bosio, Old Town* ☎ 🌐 *www.lamerenda.net* *No credit cards* *Closed weekends and 1st 2 wks in Aug.*

La Part des Anges

$$ | **FRENCH** | This wine shop with some 300 labels and a few tables and chairs at the back is really about *vins*

naturels—unfiltered, unsulfured wines made by small producers from hand-harvested grapes—but the often-simple food served here also happens to be excellent. Whether you choose a charcuterie or cheese plate or one of the handful of hot dishes (like spaghetti with razor clams or octopus cooked in red wine), you can expect it to be generous and fresh. **Known for:** natural and organic wines; informative staff; lunch in the heart of the cellar. *Average main: €18 ✉ 17 rue Gubernatis, New Town ☎ 04–93–62–69–80 🌐 lapartdesanges-nice.com ⏲ Closed Sun.*

La Réserve de Nice

$$$$ | FRENCH | Chef Jêrome Cotta knows what it takes to earn restaurant acclaim, and his originality and attention to detail are reflected in creations like mille-feuille of foie gras caramelized with maple syrup; fig marmalade flavored with port wine, cranberry, and red-currant jelly; and cod fillet cooked in frothy butter, shallots, and cocoa beans stewed with bacon in a fine truffle bouillon. It's easy to run up a bill of €200 per couple with drinks here, but the panoramic views, especially upstairs, from the Art Deco building jutting over the sea cannot be faulted. **Known for:** seaside location with excellent views; trendy sea bar; set menu €95 and €120. *Average main: €54 ✉ 60 bd. Frank Pilatte, Mont Boron ☎ 04–97–08–14–80 🌐 www.lareservedenice.com ⏲ Closed Sun. and Mon.*

Le Bistro Gourmand

$$$$ | BISTRO | This restaurant, steps from the Hotel Beau Rivage and with an outdoor terrace, focuses on the preservation of French cuisine. The sommelier amazingly seems to know your order before you do; a decent bottle of red will set you back around €50. **Known for:** five-course Legend Menu for only €118; famous soufflé; impressive wine list. *Average main: €35 ✉ 3 rue Desboutin, Old Town ☎ 04–92–14–55–55 🌐 www.bistrotgourmand.net.*

★ Le Bistrot d'Antoine

$$ | BISTRO | You won't find any "concept" cooking here, just pure French bistro fare at its finest—beef salad with anchovy dressing, butter risotto with truffles, sliced leg of lamb, and traditional pork casserole. Save room for the day's dessert, such as the wonderfully warm peach-and-frangipane tart. **Known for:** excellent prices; jaw-droppingly tasty food; reservations necessary. *Average main: €24 ✉ 27 rue de la Préfecture, Old Town ☎ 04–93–85–29–57 ⏲ Closed Sun. and Mon.*

★ Le Canon

$$$ | FRENCH | With a handwritten menu board, wine bottles as far as the eye can see, and a low-key assemblage of chairs and tables that look like they came out of a 1970s-era attic, this is the kind of authentic French bistro people travel to Provence for. Owner Sébastien Perinetti and chef Elmahdi Mobarik source the freshest hyperlocal produce to bring you a parade of taste sensations, all seductively priced. **Known for:** organic food and natural wine; changing menu influenced by local suppliers; long leisurely meals. *Average main: €27 ✉ 23 rue Meyerbeer, New Town ☎ 04–96–79–09–24 🌐 www.lecanon.fr ⏲ Closed weekends. No dinner Wed.*

Le Panier

$$$$ | FRENCH | In an intimate space on a tiny street, just behind Cours Saleya, this restaurant has a chalkboard menu of dishes that showcase the natural skill of chef Aurélien Martin. The choice of market-fresh seasonal cuisine is easy, as there's one four-course menu for lunch and either a four- or a five-course menu for dinner. **Known for:** uncomplicated French cooking; regularly changing prix-fixe menus; reservations necessary for charming outside seating. *Average main: €65 ✉ 5 rue Barillerie, Nice ☎ 04–89–97–14–37 🌐 www.restaurantlepanier.com ⏲ Closed Tues. and Wed. No lunch Thurs.*

Le Safari

$$$ | **FRENCH** | The Cours Saleya's desirable terrace tables provide an excuse for many of the restaurants along this strip to get away with culinary murder, but that's not the case at Le Safari, which pays more attention than most to ingredients and presentation. Choose from traditional Niçois dishes—the fish soup served with croutons, spicy mayonnaise, and cheese is particularly good—and Italian-inspired fare such as creamy risotto. **Known for:** Niçois dishes appreciated by locals; lively outdoor eating; colorful dining room. *Average main: €30* *1 cours Saleya, Port Nice* *04–93–80–18–44* *www.restaurantsafari.fr.*

★ Le Séjour Café

$$$ | **FRENCH** | Owners Renaud and Marilène Geille, who used to run Les Viviers back in the day, pack this popular eatery by offering exceptional surroundings, fabulous food, and flawless service. The fish dishes are supreme, lightly accentuated by seasonal vegetables, and the *magret carnard* seems reinvented. **Known for:** small space so reservations a must; charming service; excellent sweet-and-salty desserts. *Average main: €30* *11 rue Grimaldi, New Town* *04–97–20–55–35* *www.sejourcafe.com* *Closed Sun. and Mon.*

Lycée Hotellier Paul Augier

$ | **FRENCH** | Popular with both locals and expats, the three restaurants at the Paul Augier Hospitality and Tourism School, attended by 1,200 pupils and apprentices, serve lunch weekdays and dinner some evenings—and everything is prepared by aspiring young chefs. The fifth-floor La Rotonde is the most sophisticated and expensive of the three restaurants, but, still, the set lunch menu is just €28 without drinks, and set dinner menus start at €35. **Known for:** three-course meals at a steal, from €28 at lunch; unique way to experience local Nice; chefs who could very well become the world's best. *Average main: €15* *163 bd. René Cassin, Nice* *04–93–72–77–77* *www.lycee-paul-augier.com* *No credit cards* *Closed weekends.*

Restaurant Jan

$$$$ | **FRENCH** | Chef Jan Hendrik van der Westhuizen is the first South African to be awarded a Michelin star, which he earned within two years of opening this self-titled restaurant in the port. Because of this, it can be tough to get reservations to sample a menu that might feature such innovative dishes as veal cheeks, potatoes *dauphinoise,* potato puree, trumpet mushrooms, foie gras, and lavender mayonnaise. **Known for:** set menus with pairing options; homemade bread and ice cream; reservations require deposit. *Average main: €165* *12 rue Lascaris, Port Nice* *04–97–19–32–23* *janonline.com/restaurantjan* *Closed Sun., Mon., and 2 wks in late Nov. No lunch.*

Coffee and Quick Bites

Café des Chineurs

$$ | **CAFÉ** | The best place to grab a bite in Place Garibaldi, this café has an eclectic feel that's as appealing as the food and friendliness—and it's a fabulous location for people-watching. **Known for:** great people-watching; convenient location; romantic. *Average main: €18* *1 rue Cassini, Old Town* *04–93–89–09–62.*

★ Glacier Fenocchio

$ | **CAFÉ** | **FAMILY** | For fresh, homemade, gelato-style ice cream offered in a rainbow of flavors and colors, stop at Glacier Fenocchio any day of the week from 9 am to midnight, March to November. There's also a choice of sorbets made with locally grown citrus, including orange, mandarin, and lemon. **Known for:** 90-plus flavors; open day and night; beer-flavored sorbet. *Average main: €8* *2 pl. Rossetti, Old Town* *04–93–62–88–80* *www.fenocchio.fr* *Closed mid-Nov.–Carnival.*

A magnificent wedding-cake extravaganza, the Hotel Negresco—once the haunt of the Beatles and the Burtons—is the icon of Nice.

Hotels

Hotel Boscolo Nice

$$$$ | **HOTEL** | A top-notch restoration completed in 2023 has transformed this Belle Époque extravaganza into a supermodel of a hotel, where the lobby feels otherworldly (think the white-on-white, Rococo-ed rooms at the end of Kubrick's *2001: A Space Odyssey*), and the white-and-cream guest rooms have things like cascading, diamondlike ceiling lights, sculpted rose door handles, and the very latest in push-button luxury. **Pros:** near shops and restaurants; striking spa; five blocks from the beach, but who cares when you have the rooftop Bclub?. **Cons:** service can be hit and miss; skip the hotel's €65 airport taxi and book direct for €32 flat rate; €39 breakfast (but lots of cafés close by). *Rooms from: €495 ✉ 12 bd. Victor Hugo, New Town ☎ 04–97–03–89–83 🌐 boscolocollection.com/nice/en 112 rooms No Meals.*

Hôtel Negresco

$$$$ | **HOTEL** | This white-stucco slice of classic Riviera extravagance accommodates well-heeled guests in elegant, uniquely decorated rooms replete with swagged drapes, fine antiques, and a few quirky touches (like plastic-glitter bathtubs). **Pros:** with 6,000 works of art it's like staying in a museum; best bar on the Riviera; spa and private beach. **Cons:** €35 breakfast; check whether room has bathtub or shower; strict cancellation policy. *Rooms from: €650 ✉ 37 promenade des Anglais, Promenade ☎ 04–93–16–64–00 🌐 www.hotel-negresco-nice.com 128 rooms No Meals.*

Hôtel Suisse

$$$$ | **HOTEL** | Charging modest prices for a spectacular view from the top end of the seafront, where the promenade winds around to the port, the acclaimed Hôtel Suisse far outclasses most other hotels in this price range, although be prepared for a small reception area and a *très petit* elevator. **Pros:** balconies with quintessential sea views; clean, modern rooms; accessible prices in low season. **Cons:** pricey breakfast (but you can walk to Cours Saleya market); parking nearby (€30/day); busy website with pop-up notices. *Rooms from: €380* *15 quai Raubà Capéù, Port Nice* *04–92–17–39–00* *www.hotel-nice-suisse.com* *38 rooms* *No Meals.*

La Fontaine

$$ | **HOTEL** | Fifty meters from the waterfront and the Negresco, this immaculate, modern hotel on a bustling shopping street offers a friendly welcome from its house-proud owners—for a great price. **Pros:** central location; leafy courtyard; anti-allergy flooring and pillows. **Cons:** rooms overlooking the street can be noisy; expensive breakfast; Wi-Fi can be dodgy. *Rooms from: €151* *49 rue de France, New Town* *04–93–88–30–38* *www.hotel-fontaine.com* *29 rooms* *No Meals.*

La Perouse

$$$$ | **HOTEL** | Just past Old Town, at the foot of the town's château, this secret treasure cuts into the cliff (an elevator takes you up to reception), and the best rooms—including Raoul Dufy's favorite—not only have views of the azure sea, they also look down into an intimate garden dotted with lemon trees. **Pros:** complete renovation in 2023; heated cliff-side pool April–September; big savings with prepaid bookings. **Cons:** some windows face a stone wall; not good for those with mobility issues; €18 breakfast. *Rooms from: €520* *11 quai Rauba Capeu, Le Château* *04–93–62–34–63* *www.hotel-la-perouse.com* *56 rooms* *No Meals.*

Nice Garden Hotel

$ | **HOTEL** | It's hard to believe that this little gem of a hotel, with its own courtyard garden, is smack in the middle of Nice, next to the pedestrian shopping streets and a five-minute walk from the Old Town. **Pros:** delicious garden breakfast (€12) with homemade jam; extremely helpful owner; short walking distance to everything. **Cons:** parking is down the street at public garage; two-night stay minimum during certain times; rooms are smallish. *Rooms from: €85* *11 rue du Congrès, New Town* *04–93–87–35–62* *www.nicegardenhotel.com* *9 rooms* *No Meals.*

Solara

$ | **HOTEL** | One block from the beach and two from Place Masséna, this tiny budget hotel has small but bright rooms worthy of a more upscale establishment. **Pros:** ideal base near the beach; top-floor terraces overlooking pedestrian street; soundproof windows. **Cons:** rooms on the small side; tricky to find by car; at these rates, rooms book up in advance. *Rooms from: €119* *7 rue de France, New Town* *04–93–88–09–96* *www.hotelsolara.com* *12 rooms* *No Meals.*

Villa Rivoli

$$ | **HOTEL** | Not only is this Belle Époque hotel (circa 1890) in the chic Quartier des Musiciens and just a couple of blocks up from the beach, but it has very reasonable rates. **Pros:** friendly and helpful service; period-authentic French feel; location and value. **Cons:** hotel parking €18 per day and neighborhood parking is difficult; lower-ground-floor category rooms can be musty; no elevator. *Rooms from: €144* *10 rue de Rivoli, New Town* *04–93–88–80–25* *www.villa-rivoli.com* *24 rooms* *No Meals.*

Windsor

$$ | **HOTEL** | Most of the rooms at this memorably eccentric hotel have either frescoes with mythological themes or works that feature an artist's whimsy, but the real draws are the excellent service, the location three blocks from the beach, and the garden—a city-center oasis of lemon, magnolia, and palm trees. **Pros:** private pool and garden in heart of city; good dining options on-site and nearby; online promos include a free night's stay. **Cons:** artist-inspired interior design isn't for everyone (look online before

booking!); street-facing rooms can be noisy; ultraviolet elevator is cool the first time but annoying by the end of the week. $ *Rooms from: €190* ✉ *11 rue Dalpozzo, New Town* ☎ *04–93–88–59–35* 🌐 *www.hotelwindsornice.com* *57 rooms* *No Meals.*

Nightlife

For the most part, nightlife here consists of having a late dinner. Although there are a few clubs in the Old Town–Port district and a few bars in the pedestrian area, Nice is not a city for singles—and it's certainly not a city for roaming around late at night.

BARS

The Aston Club

BARS | Don't forget your camera when heading up to this panoramic bar on the seventh floor of the Aston La Scala Hotel. The views of old Nice and the Promenade du Paillon across to the airport are spectacular, and drink prices are more than reasonable. There's live music Thursday, Friday, and Saturday evenings, and, in the summer, the action moves to the rooftop Moon Bar, where there's a pool (for guests) and a 360-degree view. Note that there are 23 steps from the hotel lobby to the bar's elevator. ✉ *12 av. Felix Faure, Centre Ville* ☎ *04–93–17–53–00* 🌐 *hotel-aston.com.*

★ Bar Le Relais

BARS | If you're all dressed up and have just won big, invest in a drink in the intimate walnut-and-velour Bar Le Relais in the iconic Hôtel Negresco. It's worth the price (€17 for a glass of local red wine, or €6 for Perrier) just to get a peek at the washrooms. There is live music every evening, and in the summer an outdoor bar hosts a nightly DJ. ✉ *37 promenade des Anglais, Promenade* ☎ *04–93–16–64–12* 🌐 *www.hotel-negresco-nice.com.*

DANCE CLUBS

Le Glam

DANCE CLUBS | The city's most colorful LGBTQ+ club has DJs who compel you to dance to the best mixes around. It welcomes all clubbers in the know, with only one requirement: be you. It's open from 11 pm to 4 am Friday to Sunday, with a happy hour (11 pm–midnight) that includes two free drinks with the €12 entry. ✉ *6 rue Eugène Emmanuel, Nice* ☎ *06–60–55–26–61* 🌐 *www.leglamnice.com.*

Performing Arts

CONCERTS

Acropolis

ARTS CENTERS | Classical music, ballet performances, traditional French pop concerts, and even dog shows take place at Nice's convention center, the Acropolis. ✉ *Palais des Congrès, Esplanade John F. Kennedy, Nice* ☎ *04–93–92–83–00* 🌐 *www.nice-acropolis.com.*

Conservatoire National

ARTS CENTERS | The regional conservatory in Cimiez has a mixed calendar of events, from classical concerts to dance. ✉ *127 av. de Brancolar, Cimiez* ⊕ *Take Bus No. 15 to Cdt. Gérôme stop* ☎ *04–97–13–50–00* 🌐 *www.conservatoire-nice.org.*

Opéra de Nice

OPERA | A half-block west of Cours Saleya stands a flamboyant Italian-style theater designed by Charles Garnier, architect of the Paris Opéra. Today it's home to the Opéra de Nice, with a permanent chorus, orchestra, and ballet corps. The season runs September through June, and tickets start at €6. If you are under 30, head to the box office an hour before showtime for €5 tickets. ✉ *4 rue St-François-de-Paule, Old Town* ☎ *04–92–17–40–79* 🌐 *www.opera-nice.org/en.*

Théâtre de Verdure

MUSIC | Built in 1945, the Théâtre de Verdure can seat 1,850 people or provide standing room for 3,200. It's a great spot for concerts and theater. Keep an eye out for the summer calendar for the Ciné Prom, when you can watch big-screen movies here. ✉ *Jardin Albert Ier, Espace Jacques Cotta, Nice* 🌐 *www.tdv-nice.org.*

FILM AND THEATER

Cinéma Rialto

FILM | What you will find here is the city's biggest selection of foreign- and English-language films, with some Cannes Film Festival screenings, too. What you won't find are concessions stands and popcorn. ✉ *4 rue de Rivoli, Cimiez* 🌐 *cinemarialto.fr.*

Théâtre National de Nice

THEATER | Headed by Muriel Mayette-Holt, the Théâtre National de Nice hosts 40 productions from all over Europe as part of an initiative to become a center for innovative European theater. Tickets range from €5 to €35, and on the "*Entre spectateurs*" section of the website, you can find people selling or exchanging their tickets for a cheaper price. ✉ *Promenade des Arts, Centre Ville* ☎ *04–93–13–90–90* 🌐 *www.tnn.fr.*

Shopping

Nice's main shopping street, Avenue Jean-Médecin, runs inland from Place Masséna; all needs and most tastes are catered to in its big department stores (Galeries Lafayette, Monoprix, and the split-level Étoile mall). Line 1 of the tramway has made this mini Champs-Elysées all the more accessible, so expect crowds on Saturday and note that most shops are closed on Sunday.

Luxury boutiques, such as Emporio Armani and Chanel, line Rue du Paradis (Louis Vuitton is at the end of the street on Avenue de Suède), while Tiffany and Cartier can be found along Avenue de Verdun. Rue de France and Old Town have more affordable offerings from independent shops.

Alziari

FOOD | This tiny shop sells olive oil by the gallon (and other quantities), packaged in containers featuring its famous, old-fashioned, blue-and-yellow labels. ✉ *14 rue St-François-de-Paule, Old Town* 🌐 *www.alziari.com.fr.*

Confiserie Florian du Vieux Nice

FOOD | Open every day except Christmas, this shop is a good source for candied fruit (a Nice specialty). It's on the west side of the port, near the Marché aux Puces. ✉ *14 quai Papacino, Old Town* 🌐 *www.confiserieflorian.com.*

La Promenade des 100 Antiquaires

ANTIQUES & COLLECTIBLES | France's third-largest *regroupment* of antiques collectors forms a triangle from Place Garibaldi to the port (Quai Papacino) and along Rue Catherine Ségruane at the bottom of the château. Shops along Rue Antoine Gautier and Rue Emmanuel Philibert are worth exploring, as is Marché aux Puces de Nice, an emporium with 30 stalls under one roof in Quai Lunel. In addition, Place Garibaldi hosts a morning antiques market on the third Saturday of the month. ✉ *Old Town.*

Mademoiselle

SECOND-HAND | You have to hand it to the French: they even do secondhand fashion right. Steps away from the Hôtel Negresco, Mademoiselle is a must-stop shop in Nice. Chanel, Dior, Louis Vuitton, Hermès—you name it, the gang's all here, at least in vintage terms. In addition to luxury-brand clothes, there are shoes, bags, and belts—all of it excellently priced and gorgeously displayed by owner Sephora Louis. ✉ *41 rue de France, New Town.*

Maison Auer

CHOCOLATE | The venerable house of Henri Auer has been selling chocolate and candied fruit since 1820. ✉ *7 rue St-François de Paule, Old Town* 🌐 *www.maison-auer.com.*

Oliviera
FOOD | Come here for the best selection of Provençal olive oils in town. Oliviera is run by the passionate Nadim Beyrouti, who also serves Mediterranean dishes made with the finest local ingredients. ✉ *8 bis rue du Collet, Old Town* ☎ *04–93–13–06–45* 🌐 *oliviera.com.*

Star Dog Boutique
PET STORES | For the jet-set pet, Star Dog Boutique has iPawds (a plush toy with FaceBark, DogTube, and Bark Street Journal apps), Doggle sunglasses, and Oh My Dog! cologne to get Fido's tail wagging. ✉ *40 rue de France, New Town* ☎ *04–97–03–27–40.*

 Activities

Nice is one giant outdoor arena, and the Promenade is the racetrack. From the Ironman Nice triathlon to the Nice-Cannes Marathon 41.195-km (26.21-mile), and from the five-day, nonstop No Finish Line to the 10-km (6-mile) Prom'Swim (not to mention the cycling, kayaking, sailing ... and even skiing), there are plenty of options to work off that breakfast croissant while taking in some spectacular scenery. Check out Swimrun Côte d'Azur (🌐 *swimruncotedazur.com*) if you want find area events that will let you experience more of the region and meet other sporty folk.

Glisse Evasion
PARASAILING | **FAMILY** | If the idea of parasailing (€50 for 10 minutes) seems a bit terrifying, note that you'll see nothing but elated smiles from satisfied customers. Stand-up paddleboards and kayaks are also for rent from €10. You'll find this outfitter across from the Negresco Hotel. ✉ *29 promenade des Anglais, Promenade* ☎ *07–61–83–41–02* 🌐 *www.glisse-evasion.com.*

Villefranche-sur-Mer

10 km (6 miles) east of Nice.

Nestled discreetly along the deep scoop of harbor between Nice and Cap Ferrat, this pretty watercolor of a fishing port seems surreal, flanked as it is by the big city of Nice and the assertive wealth of Monaco. The town is a stage set of brightly colored houses—the sort of place where Pagnol's *Fanny* could have been filmed. Fishermen skim up to the docks here in weathered-blue *barques,* and the streets of the Vieille Ville flow directly to the waterfront, much as they did in the 13th century.

Some of the prettiest spots in town are around Place de la Paix, Rue du Poilu, and Place du Conseil, which looks out over the water. The deep harbor, in the caldera of a volcano, was once preferred by the likes of Onassis and Niarchos and the royals on their yachts. But the character of the place was subtly shaped by the artists and authors who gathered at the Hôtel Welcome—Diaghilev and Stravinsky, taking a break from the Ballet Russe in Monaco; Somerset Maugham and Evelyn Waugh; and, above all, Jean Cocteau, who came here to recover from the excesses of Paris life.

Nowadays, the population consists mainly of wealthy retired people, though families do head here to enjoy its sandy (well, gravelly) beach and jellyfish-free zones. The only fly in the ointment is Villefranche's popularity: between the endless stream of cruise ships sending their passengers ashore in very, very large numbers and Netflix fans following in the footsteps of *Emily in Paris* (not to mention a flood of new construction so villas now virtually elbow each other out of the way up the hillsides), the town's physical beauty has become more challenging to appreciate peacefully.

Still and all, quaint alleyways and the heavenly panoramas of the town from

Did You Know?

The colorful harbor of Villefranche-sur-Mer surrounds one of the deepest and most beautiful bays on the Riviera.

on high nicely remind you why everyone headed here in the first place, and the natural light will always captivate. A piece of advice: wear sensible shoes as cobblestone is no friend to thinly soled footwear (and there are lots of steps).

GETTING HERE AND AROUND

Villefranche is a major stop on the Marseille–Ventimiglia coastal train route, with more than 40 arrivals every day from Nice (€2.10; 6 minutes). Buses connect with Nice and Monaco via Zou! Bus 600 (€2.10), which until March 2024 is replaced by Bus 607, and Ligne d'Azur Buses 15 and 80 (€1.70). Public parking is tricky to find, and most of it is paid (from €1.80 per hour) between 9 am and 7 pm.

VISITOR INFORMATION

CONTACTS Villefranche-sur-Mer Tourist Office. ✉ *Jardin François Binon, Villefranche-sur-Mer* ☎ *04–93–01–73–68* 🌐 *www.tourisme-villefranche-sur-mer.com.*

Sights

Chapelle St-Pierre

CHURCH | So enamored was Jean Cocteau of this painterly fishing port that he decorated the 14th-century Chapelle St-Pierre with images from the life of St. Peter and dedicated it to the village's fishermen. ✉ *Quai de l'Amiral Courbet, Villefranche-sur-Mer* ☎ *04–93–76–90–70* 🎫 *€3* ⏲ *Closed Mon., Tues., and mid-Nov.–mid-Dec.*

Citadelle St-Elme

MILITARY SIGHT | Restored to perfect condition, the stalwart 16th-century Citadelle St-Elme anchors the harbor with its broad, sloping stone walls. Beyond its drawbridge lie the city's administrative offices and a group of minor gallery-museums, with a scattering of works by Picasso and Miró. Whether or not you stop into these private collections (all free of charge), you're welcome to stroll around the inner grounds and circle the imposing exterior. ✉ *Harbor, Villefranche-sur-Mer* 🎫 *Free.*

Église St-Michel

CHURCH | This modest Baroque church, above Rue Obscure, contains a movingly realistic sculpture of Christ carved in fig wood by an anonymous 17th-century convict. ✉ *Pl. Poullan, Villefranche-sur-Mer.*

Rue Obscure

STREET | Running parallel to the waterfront, the extraordinary 14th-century Rue Obscure (Dark Street) is entirely covered by vaulted arcades; it sheltered the people of Villefranche when the Germans fired their parting shots—an artillery bombardment—near the end of World War II. **■ TIP→ If playing tourist is building up your appetite, Focacceria Mei on Rue du Poilu (the next street up) has the best takeaway in town.** ✉ *Villefranche-sur-Mer.*

Beaches

★ Plage des Marinières

BEACH | To the east of the port is the biggest beach you'll find in Villefranche, but it's only about 1 km (½ mile) long. Popular because the shoreline is protected from winds, this beach has coarse sand and lifeguards in the summer. Note that the SNCF train line runs parallel, so the noise factor is a consideration. There are no loungers, but there are jellyfish nets (though they aren't 100% foolproof). **Amenities:** lifeguards; showers; toilets. **Best for:** snorkeling; sunrise; swimming. ✉ *Promenade des Marinières, Villefranche-sur-Mer.*

Restaurants

Cosmo Bar

$$$ | **MEDITERRANEAN** | Facing the Cocteau chapel with an enviable view of the sea from its terrace, this modern brasserie could easily get away with being merely mediocre. Instead, it serves fresh, colorful Mediterranean dishes ranging from an addictive *anchoïade*—crudités with anchovy dip—to omelets. **Known for:** fantastic views; casual yet memorable French Riviera dining; terrace seating (reserve to nab a spot). $ *Average main: €25* ✉ *11 pl. Amélie Pollonnais, Villefranche-sur-Mer* ☎ *04–93–01–84–05* 🌐 *www.restaurant-lecosmo.fr.*

Hotels

Hôtel de la Darse

$ | **HOTEL** | The most desirable rooms at this simple yet welcoming 1950s hotel have balconies with sweeping panoramas—so who needs luxury fittings and fabrics when you can have a view of the old harbor for a reasonable rate? Even the kid's breakfast (€5) is half the regular price. **Pros:** splurge for terrace; away from the crowds of town; good deal for Villefranche. **Cons:** no elevator; a walk to the center of town; early-morning-delivery noise. $ *Rooms from: €100* ✉ *32 av. Général de Gaulle, Villefranche-sur-Mer* ☎ *04–93–01–72–54* 🌐 *www.hoteldeladarse.com* ⏲ *Closed mid-Dec.–early Jan.* *21 rooms* *No Meals.*

Hôtel Provençal

$$ | **HOTEL** | Within walking distance of the port, this inexpensive, family-run hotel might not look like much from the outside, but it is friendly and accommodating. **Pros:** balconies with sea view (ask for this when booking); high-quality breakfast served on the terrace; super beverage prices at bar. **Cons:** modest decor; village-facing rooms may have street noise; bit of a hike up to hotel from beach. $ *Rooms from: €161* ✉ *4 av. Maréchal Joffre, Villefranche-sur-Mer* ☎ *04–93–76–53–53* 🌐 *www.hotelleprovencal.fr* ⏲ *Closed mid Oct.–Apr.* *43 rooms* *No Meals.*

★ Hôtel Welcome

$$$ | **HOTEL** | Somerset Maugham holed up in one of the tiny crow's-nest rooms at the top, Jean Cocteau lived here while writing *Orphée,* and Elizabeth Taylor and Richard Burton used to tie one on in the bar—and this waterfront landmark remains a formidable and flawless retreat. **Pros:** excellent English-speaking service; artistic heritage makes for a nostalgic trip into the Roaring '20s; paddleboard and kayak rentals. **Cons:** some rooms are oddly shaped—narrow and long—so they feel small; expensive parking in summer; style may feel overly nautical to some. $ *Rooms from: €249* ✉ *3 quai Amiral Courbet, Villefranche-sur-Mer* ☎ *04–93–76–27–62* 🌐 *www.welcomehotel.com* ⏲ *Closed mid-Nov.–Christmas* *35 rooms* *No Meals.*

Beaulieu-sur-Mer

4 km (2½ miles) east of Villefranche; 14 km (9 miles) east of Nice.

With its back pressed hard against the cliffs of the corniche and sheltered between the peninsulas of Cap Ferrat and Cap Roux, this once-grand resort basks in a tropical microclimate that earned its central neighborhood the name "Petite Afrique." The town was favored by members of 19th-century society that included the Empress Eugénie, the Prince of Wales, and Russian nobles.

GETTING HERE AND AROUND

With frequent arrivals and departures, Beaulieu is a main stop on the Marseille–Ventimiglia coastal train line. From Beaulieu's train station the hourly Bus 81 (€1.70) connects with neighboring St-Jean-Cap-Ferrat. Bus 600 (until 2024, it's Bus 607) takes you to/from Nice/Monaco, while Bus 84 goes to Nice via Villefranche.

VISITOR INFORMATION

CONTACTS Beaulieu Tourist Office. ✉ *Pl. Georges Clemenceau, Beaulieu-sur-Mer* ☎ *04–93–01–02–21* 🌐 *www.otbeaulieusurmer.com.*

Sights

Promenade Maurice-Rouvier

PROMENADE | FAMILY | Today Beaulieu is usually spoken of in the past tense and has taken on a rather stuffy character. Its small beach, however, attracts families with children, and on the Promenade Maurice-Rouvier, a paved pedestrian path that begins not far from the Villa Kerylos, you can stroll the waterfront, past grand villas and their tropical gardens, all the way to St-Jean-Cap-Ferrat. The 30-minute walk winds along the Baie des Fourmis (Bay of Ants)—whose name alludes to the black rocks that appear to be "crawling" up from the sea—and has great views of the sparkling Mediterranean and surrounding mountains. ✉ *Beaulieu-sur-Mer.*

★ Villa Kerylos

HISTORIC HOME | One manifestation of Beaulieu's Belle Époque excess is the eye-popping Villa Kerylos, a 1902 mansion built in the style of classical Greece (to be exact, of the villas that existed on the island of Delos in the 2nd century BC). It was the dream house of amateur archaeologist Théodore Reinach, who hailed from a wealthy German family, helped the French in their excavations at Delphi, and became an authority on ancient Greek music. He commissioned an Italian architect from Nice, Emmanuel Pontremoli, to surround him with Grecian delights: cool Carrara marble, rare fruitwoods, and a dining salon where guests reclined to eat *à la grecque.* It's one of the most unusual houses in the south of France. ✉ *Impasse Gustave-Eiffel, Beaulieu-sur-Mer* ☎ *04–93–01–01–44* 🌐 *www.villakerylos.fr/en* 🎫 *€11.50.*

Restaurants

La Reserve

$$$$ | MEDITERRANEAN | This Michelin-starred hotel restaurant—a marvel of light and color—has been a crown jewel of the Mediterranean since it opened in 1880. Chef Julien Roucheteau uses fresh Mediterranean ingredients in original takes on classic dishes like langoustine tails roasted in hazelnut butter, and the four- (€165) and six-course (€195) set menus are a better value than ordering à la carte. **Known for:** perfect wine pairings; seaside location with gorgeous views; fabulous desserts. $ *Average main: €85* ✉ *5 bd. General Leclerc, Beaulieu-sur-Mer* ☎ *04–93–01–00–01* 🌐 *www.reservebeaulieu.com* ⏲ *Closed Nov.–mid-Dec. No lunch May–Oct.*

St-Jean-Cap-Ferrat

2 km (1 mile) south of Beaulieu on D25.

One of the most exclusive addresses in the world, the peninsula of Cap Ferrat is moored by the luxuriously sited pleasure port of St-Jean. From its portside walkways and crescent of beach you can look over the sparkling blue harbor to the graceful green bulk of the corniches.

Yachts purr in and out of port, and their passengers scuttle into cafés for takeout drinks to enjoy on their private decks. On shore, the billionaires come and go, and trade gossip (like who purchased the world's most expensive house, the 14-bedroom Villa Les Cedres) while residents of Cap Ferrat fiercely protect it from curious tourists. The town's grand old villas are hidden, for the most part, in the depths of tropical gardens. You can nonetheless try to catch glimpses of them from the Coastline Promenade.

GETTING HERE AND AROUND

Bus 81 accesses the cape from Nice. The humor is not lost that a bus fare of €1.70 brings you to one of the most exclusive pieces of land on the planet.

VISITOR INFORMATION

CONTACTS St-Jean-Cap-Ferrat Tourist Office. ✉ *5 and 59 av. Denis Semeria, St-Jean-Cap-Ferrat* ☎ *04–93–76–08–90* 🌐 *www.saintjeancapferrat-tourisme.fr.*

Baroness Ephrussi de Rothschild spared no expense—a garden full of roses, a house full of Renaissance treasures—in creating her estate above the sea in St-Jean-Cap-Ferrat.

Sights

Coastline Promenade

PROMENADE | FAMILY | While Cap Ferrat's villas are sequestered for the most part in the depths of tropical gardens, you can nonetheless walk its entire coastline promenade if you strike out from the port. From the restaurant Capitaine Cook, cut right up Avenue des Fossés, turn right on Avenue Vignon, and follow Chemin de la Carrière. The 11-km (7-mile) walk passes through lush flora and, on the west side, follows white cliffs buffeted by waves.

When you've traced the full outline of the peninsula, veer up Chemin du Roy past the fabulous gardens of the Villa des Cèdres, owned by King Leopold II of Belgium at the turn of the last century. Indeed, the king owned several opulent estates along the French Riviera, undoubtedly paid for by his enslavement of the Belgian Congo. Past the gardens, you can reach the Plage de Passable, from which you cut back across the peninsula's wrist.

A shorter loop takes you from town out to the Pointe de St-Hospice, much of the walk shaded by wind-twisted pines. From the port, climb Avenue Jean Mermoz to Place Paloma and follow the path closest to the waterfront. At the point are an 18th-century prison tower, a 19th-century chapel, and unobstructed views of Cap Martin. Two other footpath maps start at the tourist office (✉ *59 avenue Denis-Séméria*); the shorter one takes you from town out to the Pointe de St-Hospice, and much of it is shaded by wind-twisted pines. From the port, climb Avenue Jean Mermoz to Place Paloma and follow the path closest to the waterfront or the Promenade Maurice Rouvier, which runs along the eastern edge of the peninsula.

You'll stumble on reasonably priced cafés, pizzerias, and ice-cream parlors on the promenade of the Plage de St-Jean. The best swimming in the region is a bit farther south, past the port, at Plage

Paloma. Keep trekking around the wooded area, where a beautiful path (*sentier pédestre*) leads along the outermost edge of Cap Ferrat. Other than the occasional yacht, all traces of civilization disappear, and the water is a dizzying blue. ✉ *St-Jean-Cap-Ferrat.*

★ Villa Ephrussi de Rothschild

HISTORIC HOME | Between the port and the mainland, the floridly beautiful Villa Ephrussi de Rothschild bears witness to the wealth and worldly flair of the baroness who had it built. Constructed in 1905 in neo-Venetian style (its flamingo-pink facade was thought not to be in the best of taste by the local gentry), the house was baptized "Île-de-France" in homage to the Baroness Béatrice de Rothschild's favorite ocean liner. In keeping with that theme, her staff wore sailing costumes, and her ship travel kit is on display in her bedroom. Precious artworks, tapestries, and furniture adorn the salons—in typical Rothschildian fashion, each is given over to a different 18th-century "époque." Upstairs are the private apartments of Madame la Baronne, which can only be seen on a guided tour offered around noon.

The grounds are landscaped with no fewer than seven gardens and topped off with a Temple of Diana. Be sure to allow yourself time to wander here, as this is one of the few places on the coast where you'll be allowed to experience the lavish pleasures characteristic of the Belle Époque Côte d'Azur. Tea and light lunches, served in a glassed-in porch overlooking the grounds and spectacular coastline, encourage you to linger. ✉ *Av. Ephrussi, St-Jean-Cap-Ferrat* ☎ *04–93–01–33–09* 🌐 *www.villa-ephrussi.com* 🎫 *€16.*

Beaches

★ Plage de Paloma

BEACH | This lovely, shade-dappled stretch of sand is at the bottom of a steep hill only five minutes away on foot from the glamorous village of Saint-Jean. It's also at the heart of a battle for survival as the French government begins to enforce a new law that all beach structures must be dismountable. In 1973, Saint-Jean, with its shallow bay, soft sand, and some of the Riviera's clearest waters, was given a special "natural and remarkable site" status, including the construction of its jetty, which currently can't be dismounted. If the mayor tears it down, nothing can be rebuilt in its place. The public beach remains open, and for now so is the private Paloma Beach (€50/day for a lounger plus another €8 for an umbrella). **Amenities:** lifeguards; showers; toilets; water sports. **Best for:** snorkeling; sunrise; swimming. ✉ *Av. Jean Mermoz, St-Jean-Cap-Ferrat.*

Restaurants

Le Pacha du Sloop

$$$ | **SEAFOOD** | Catering to the yachting crowd, this established portside restaurant has outdoor tables surrounding a tiny "garden" of potted palms. The focus is on fish, of course—*soupe de poisson* (fish soup), St-Pierre (John Dory) steamed with asparagus, and roasted whole sea bass. **Known for:** long-running portside eatery; terrace views of yachts; good value for Cap Ferrat. 💲 *Average main: €25* ✉ *Port de St-Jean-Cap-Ferrat, St-Jean-Cap-Ferrat* ☎ *04–93–01–48–63* 🌐 *www.facebook.com/lepachadusloop* ⏲ *Closed Wed.*

Hotels

Brise Marine

$$$ | **HOTEL** | With a Provençal-yellow facade, blue shutters, balustraded sea terrace, and pretty pastel guest rooms, Brise Marine embodies a picturesque Cap Ferrat hotel. **Pros:** views, views, views; excellent value for location; very close to Paloma Beach. **Cons:** some rooms are small; parking €18 a day;

no restaurant on-site. $ *Rooms from: €235* ✉ *58 av. Jean Mermoz, St-Jean-Cap-Ferrat* ☎ *04–93–76–04–36* 🌐 *www.hotel-brisemarine.com* ⏲ *Closed Nov.–Feb.* 🛏 *16 rooms* 🍽 *No Meals.*

★ Grand-Hôtel du Cap-Ferrat, a Four Seasons Hotel
$$$$ | **HOTEL** | **FAMILY** | Now managed by the Four Seasons, this extravagantly expensive hotel at the end of the peninsula has long been the exclusive playground for Hollywood's elite, and it continues to set *the* standard for discreet Cap-Ferrat luxury, with amenities like Michelin dining and two new private villas (Beauchamp and Clair-Soleil). **Pros:** every detail is well thought out and every need promptly attended to; elegant, state-of-the-art spa; picnic experience in chef's garden. **Cons:** forget it if you're on a budget (breakfast alone is €60); this level of luxury can be overwhelming; can feel snooty. $ *Rooms from: €1040* ✉ *71 bd. du Charles du Gaulle, St-Jean-Cap-Ferrat* ☎ *04–93–76–50–50* 🌐 *www.fourseasons.com/capferrat* ⏲ *Closed Dec.–Feb.* 🛏 *74 rooms* 🍽 *No Meals.*

Royal Riviera
$$$$ | **HOTEL** | Parisian design guru Grace Leo Andrieu revamped this former *residence hôtelière* for British aristocrats, and it now invites guests on an intimate voyage into neo-Hellenic style with an admiring wink at the nearby Villa Kerylos; elegant 1950s-retro furnishings; and wallpaper and fabrics that provide splashes of turquoise, lemon, aniseed, and red currant. **Pros:** excellent service and concierge; gorgeous property with gym and spa; heated outdoor pool and private beach. **Cons:** some small rooms facing railroad; €38 breakfast; pricey rates. $ *Rooms from: €395* ✉ *3 av. Jean Monnet, St-Jean-Cap-Ferrat* ☎ *04–93–76–31–00* 🌐 *www.royal-riviera.com/en* ⏲ *Closed mid-Nov.–mid-Jan.* 🛏 *96 rooms* 🍽 *No Meals.*

Èze

2 km (1 mile) east of Beaulieu; 12 km (7 miles) east of Nice; 7 km (4½ miles) west of Monte Carlo.

Medieval and magnificent, towering like an eagle's nest above the coast and crowned with ramparts and the ruins of a château, Èze (pronounced "*ehz*") is, unfortunately, the most accessible of all the perched villages. So even during off-season, its streets flood with tourists, some not-so-fresh from the beach; indeed, it was one of the first towns to post pictorial warnings that say, in effect, "No Shoes, No Shirt, No Service." It does, however, get very quiet at night, and it is spectacularly sited, with streets that are steep—in places, suitable only for the flamboyantly fit—and time-stained stone houses that huddle together in storybook fashion. No wonder U2 frontman Bono and guitarist The Edge have beachside villas here.

Colonized millennia ago by the Romans, who may have built a temple here to the Egyptian goddess, Isis (hence the town name), this mountain aerie was much coveted by locals seeking to avoid raiding Saracens. By the 19th century, only peasants were left, but when the Riviera became fashionable, Èze's splendid views up and down the coast were alluring to fabled visitors that included lots of crowned heads; Georges Sand; Friedrich Nietzsche; and Consuelo Vanderbilt, who, when she tired of being Duchess of Marlborough, traded in Blenheim Palace for a custom-built house here.

GETTING HERE AND AROUND

By car, you should arrive using the Moyenne Corniche, which deposits you near the gateway to Èze Village. Buses 112 and 82 from Nice also use this road, but Bus 600 (until March 2024, take the 607 Nice-Monaco bus for €2.10 each) goes by the sea, and Bus 116 heads up the Grande Corniche from Nice (€1.70).

The "eagle's nest" village of the Riviera, Èze perches 1,300 feet above the sea; travelers never fail to marvel at the dramatic setting.

By train, you'll arrive at the station in Èze-sur-Mer, where a daily electric shuttle bus (*navette*) takes you up to hilltop Èze, a trip that, with its 1,001 steep switchbacks, takes a full 15 minutes (keep this in mind if you're hiring a taxi to "rush" you down to the train station). You could instead walk from the train station up the Nietzsche Path to the village (90 minutes at least). High heels are not allowed, and the trek isn't advised in the dark.

VISITOR INFORMATION

CONTACTS Èze Tourist Office. ✉ *Pl. du Général de Gaulle, Èze* ☎ *04–93–41–26–00* 🌐 *www.eze-tourisme.com.*

Sights

★ Jardin Exotique
GARDEN | Set 1,310 feet above sea level, this is one of the Riviera's most visited sites. Full of rare succulents and Jean-Philippe Richard sculptures, the botanical garden is also blessed with superlative views: from this crest-top locale you can pan all the way from Italy to St-Tropez—on a clear day, you can even see Corsica. Just a few feet from the entrance, take a timeout lunch at the Nid d'Aigle, an inexpensive eatery that features focaccias and salads and is quaintly set on stone levels rising up around a tall tree. ✉ *20 rue du Château, Èze* ☎ *04–93–41–10–30* 🌐 *www.jardinexotique-eze.fr* 🎫 *€7.*

Restaurants

Cap Estel–La Table de Patrick Raingeard
$$$$ | **FRENCH** | For more than 50 years, celebs have holidayed and dined at Cap Estel along Èze's *bord de mer,* enjoying its private 5-acre peninsula with all-encompassing views of the Mediterranean. Chef Patrick Raingeard's Michelin-star set menus are worthy of the location and may start with six oysters "Pearls Monte-Carlo," followed by Charolais beef fillet with chard cannelloni, and then finish with "the all-chocolate tube." There is a four-course vegetarian menu (€145), and the produce often comes directly from the hotel's garden. **Known for:** great

brunch; paradisical views; produce from the hotel's garden. *Average main: €175* *1312 av. Raymond-Poincaré* *04–93–76–29–29* *www.capestel.com* *Closed Jan.–Mar.*

Hotels

★ Château de la Chèvre d'Or

$$$$ | **HOTEL** | Bordered by gardens that hang from the mountainside in nearly Babylonian style, this hotel encompasses an entire stretch of the village, streets and all, and, in addition to divine accommodations, it delivers breathtaking Mediterranean views—at a price. **Pros:** insane views; fabulous heated infinity pool; Michelin-starred restaurant plus three other dining choices. **Cons:** no elevator; cobbled walk to reach hotel; some rooms have bathtub shower. *Rooms from: €675* *Rue du Barri, Èze* *04–92–10–66–66* *www.chevredor.com* *Closed Nov.–Mar.* *45 rooms* *No Meals.*

Roquebrune–Cap-Martin

5 km (3 miles) east of Monaco.

Amid the frenzy of overbuilding that defines this last gasp of the coast before Italy, two twinned havens have survived, each in its own way: the perched Vieille Ville of Roquebrune, which gives its name to the greater area, and Cap-Martin—luxurious, isolated, exclusive, and the once-favored retreat of the Empress Eugénie and Winston Churchill. With its lovely tumble of raked tile roofs and twisting streets, fountains, archways, and squares, Roquebrune village has managed to avoid commercialization and remain charming.

Rue Moncollet is lined with arcaded passageways and medieval houses, and Somerset Maugham—who once memorably described these environs as a "sunny place for shady people"—resided in the town's famous Villa Mauresque (still private) for many years. Irish poet W.B. Yeats died at the Hôtel Idéal Séjour in Roquebrune-Cap-Martin in 1939. He was buried at the nearby St. Pancras graveyard, as he had instructed his wife, "If I die, bury me up there and then in a year's time when the newspapers have forgotten me, dig me up and plant me in Sligo." The war prevented his body's repatriation, and it was subsequently discovered that the poet had been disinterred in 1946, and his bones had been mixed with others in the ossuary. His "remains" were finally transferred and reburied in County Sligo, Ireland in 1947.

At sea level, you can discover the "Cap" by walking the 4-km (2½-mile) *sentier*, a pine-shaded foot path from the Cap-Martin-Roquebrune train station along the sea to the beach on the Menton side. Along the way, visit Eileen Gray's Villa E-1027 and Le Corbusier's cabanon, a UNESCO World Heritage site. Zest Bus18 (€2.10) will bring you back to your starting point.

GETTING HERE AND AROUND

Despite its small size, there are two train stations here: Cap-Martin-Roquebrune, which allows access to the isolated beach and the Monte-Carlo Country Club during the Rolex Masters tennis tournament, and Carnolès, a stop closer to Menton and steps from several beaches along the promenade. Regional trains run direct between Nice or Cannes (€5.20, 30 minutes; €11.50, 70 minutes, respectively), but not all stop at Cap Martin.

From the Carnolès Roquebrune train station, the Zest Bus 21 (€2.10) makes eight trips a day into town or the Roquebrune–Cap-Martin train station; otherwise, it's a one-hour hike up, though there are lots of stairs and benches for resting. The Nice–Menton Bus 600 (Bus 608 until March 2024), which runs from the bus station in Nice every 15 minutes (€2.10), also stops in the lower part of Roquebrune.

■ TIP→ From Carnolès train station, you can access the scenic Corbusier foot trail (an easy-to-follow stone path with lots of steps both up and down) that traces the tip of Cap Martin and back to the Roquebrune–Cap-Martin train station before continuing on to Monaco. For more on Roquebrune's four circuit trails, see the tourism website.

VISITOR INFORMATION

CONTACTS Roquebrune-Cap-Martin Tourist Office. ✉ *218 av. Aristide Briand, Roquebrune-Cap-Martin* ☎ *04–93–35–62–87* 🌐 *roquebrune-cap-martin.fr/informations.*

Beaches

★ Plage de la Buse

BEACH | FAMILY | The entirely public Plage de la Buse, also known as Cabbé Beach, is a wonderfully small, fine-pebble strand, with zero star-chasers and strutting high heels. It's protected from the elements by the curved south-facing wall of a huge villa (whose gardens add a lovely tropical feel), making it ideal for novice swimmers. Access is down 50 steps from the Cap-Martin train station (where there are a few parking places) or Le Corbusier trail, but it's completely BYO: towel, umbrella, and water/drinks. There's no bathroom, but the tiny and wonderful Le Cabanon restaurant serves lunch and dinner. **Amenities:** showers. **Best for:** solitude; swimming. ✉ *Sentier du Corbusier, Roquebrune-Cap-Martin.*

Menton

1 km (½ mile) east of Roquebrune; 9 km (5½ miles) east of Monaco.

The least pretentious and most overlooked of the Côte d'Azur resort towns, Menton rubs shoulders with the Italian border and owes some of its balmy climate to the protective curve of the Ligurian shore. Its Cubist skew of terra-cotta roofs, yellow-ocher houses, and churches featuring Baroque arabesques and ceramic-tile steeples all evoke the villages of the Italian coast. There's also a touch of Spain—in the fantastical villas, exotic gardens, and whimsical patches of ceramic color—and a soupçon of Morocco, Corsica, and Greece. Menton is, in fact, the best of all Mediterranean worlds.

At first glance, the beaches here don't seem very glamorous, but Les Sablettes is an unexpected jewel that faces the multicolored Old Town and has knee-deep water for easy wading. Next to it, Plage Rondelli caters to those who cannot do without a lounger. The two strands are connected by the Esplanade des Sablettes, a decklike walkway running from Place Fontana to Square Victoria and featuring four drinking fountains, 12 lighted pergolas, misters, and free Wi-Fi.

Menton's near-tropical climate and 316 days of sunshine a year nurture orange and lemon trees that hang heavy with fruit in winter. There's another Florida parallel: the warmth attracts senior citizens intent on escaping northern fog and ice to bask on waterfront benches after their morning dips and to browse in downtown shops later in the day. That said, Menton is less expensive than Nice, so it attracts younger generations, too. The farther east you head, the more intriguing and colorful the city becomes.

GETTING HERE AND AROUND

Trains run all day from Nice and Monaco, and there are a couple of bus options. Zou! Bus 600 (€2.10) travels from Menton to Nice (until March 2024, this route is via the Menton–Monaco Bus 608). The Nice airport express Bus 80, which stops at Monte-Carlo Casino, takes about an hour and costs €19 one-way. To get to Monaco via Roquebrune from the village, take Zest Bus 21 or 22, or, if passing through Beausoleil, take Bus 18 or 24 (also €2.10), which goes along the seaside to the border.

FESTIVALS

Festival de Musique (*Chamber Music Festival*)

MUSIC FESTIVALS | During the first two weeks of August, this festival's classical concerts take place at four locations around town, including the stone-paved plaza outside the church of St-Michel. Last-minute tickets can be purchased for €15 at the venue just before the show, and, for €5, a shuttle will pick you up from town hall. ✉ *Menton* ☎ *04–83–93–70–20* 🌐 *www.festival-musique-menton.fr.*

Fête du Citron (*Lemon Festival*)

CULTURAL FESTIVALS | FAMILY | This full-blown lemon love-in runs from mid-February through the first week of March. Floats decorated with real fruit glide through town, and musicians are on hand with entertainment. Think of it as France's answer to the Rose Bowl Parade, minus the football and add the NFT. That's right, in 2023 the festival launched a token collection. ✉ *Menton* ☎ *04–92–41–76–50* 🌐 *www.fete-du-citron.com.*

TOURS

Heritage Tours

WALKING TOURS | FAMILY | Menton acquaints you with its rich architectural heritage by offering regular *visites due patrimoine* (heritage tours) to its gardens, cemetery, museums, and villas. Details about each tour (including points and time of departure) can be found at the Menton tourist office or the **Maison du Patrimonie.** ✉ *Le Palais de l'Europe, 8 av. Boyer, Menton* ☎ *04–92–41–76–76* 🌐 *www.menton.fr* 🎫 *From €6.*

VISITOR INFORMATION

CONTACTS Menton Tourist Office. ✉ *Le Palais de l'Europe, 8 av. Boyer, Menton* ☎ *04–83–93–70–20* 🌐 *www.menton-riviera-merveilles.fr.*

Sights

The Côte d'Azur was famed for its panoply of grand villas and even grander gardens built by Victorian dukes, Spanish exiles, Belgian royals, and American blue bloods. Although its hothouse crescent blooms everywhere with palm and lemon trees and jungle flowers, nowhere else does it bloom so extravagantly as in Menton, famous for its temperate climes and 24-karat sun.

Basilique St-Michel

CHURCH | This majestic basilica dominates the skyline of Menton. Beyond the beautifully proportioned facade—a 19th-century addition—the richly frescoed nave and chapels contain several works by Genovese artists plus a splendid 17th-century organ. Volunteers man the doors here, so you may have to wait for the church to open (usually from 3 pm to 5 pm) before visiting. The parvis is the site of concerts during the August Menton music festival. ✉ *Parvis St-Michel, 22 rue St-Michel, Menton* ⏲ *Closed Tues., Thurs., and weekends.*

Casino Barrière

CASINO | At this modern downtown recreation complex, the sea views through huge bay windows may distract you from the slot machines. The casino is open daily from 11 am to 2 am (4 am Friday and Saturday). ✉ *2 av. Félix-Faure, Menton* ☎ *04–93–10–16–16* 🌐 *www.casinosbarriere.com/fr/menton.html.*

Chapelle de l'Immaculée-Conception

CHURCH | Just above the main church, the smaller Chapelle de l'Immaculée-Conception (aka Pénitents Blancs) answers St-Michel's grand gesture with its own pure Baroque beauty. The sanctuary, dating from 1687, is typically closed to the public; however, on Wednesdays between 2:30 pm and 3:15 pm, you can try and slip in to see the graceful trompe l'oeil over the altar and the ornate gilt lanterns early penitents carried in processions. ✉ *Pl. de la Conception, Menton.*

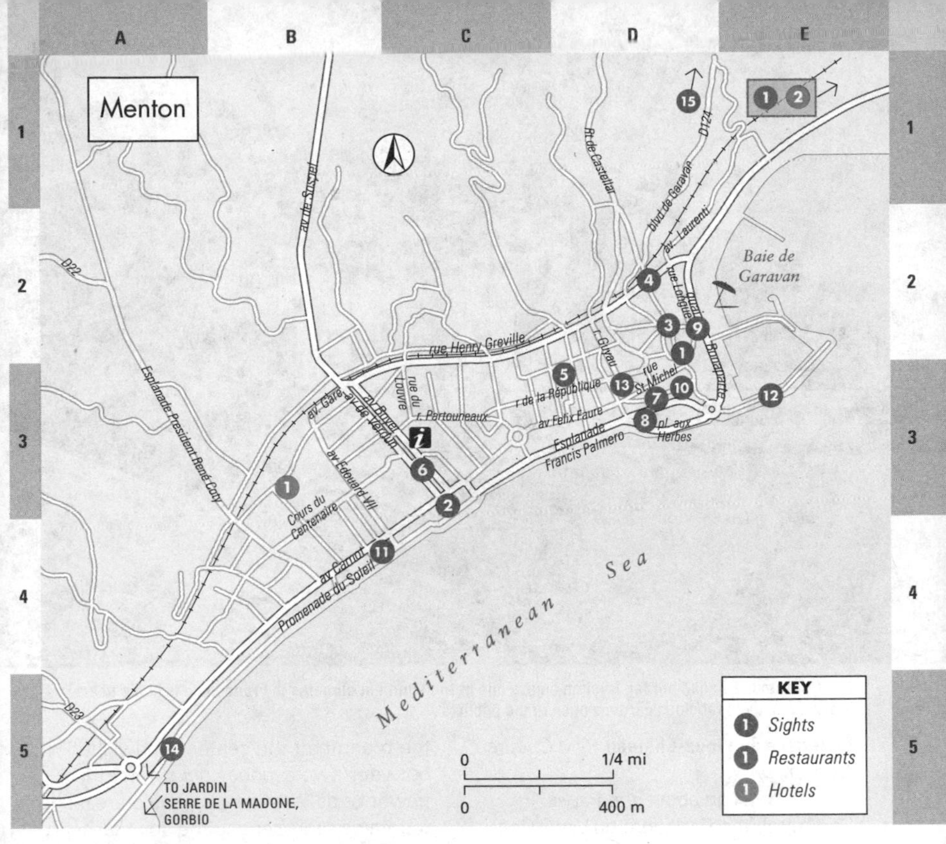

Sights

1 Basilique St-Michel D2
2 Casino Barrière C3
3 Chapelle de l'Immaculée-Conception D2
4 Cimetière du Vieux-Château D2
5 Hôtel de Ville D3
6 Jardins Biovès C3
7 Marché Couvert (Les Halles) D3
8 Musée Jean Cocteau D3
9 Parvis St-Michel D2
10 Place aux Herbes D3
11 Promenade du Soleil ... B4
12 Quai Napoléon III E3
13 Rue St-Michel D3
14 Serre de la Madone A5
15 Val Rahmeh Botanical Garden D1

Restaurants

1 Mirazur E1

Hotels

1 Hôtel Lemon B3
2 Napoléon E1

Not far from the Italian border, Menton enjoys one of the sunniest climates in France and is home to an amazing array of fabulous gardens open to the public.

Cimetière du Vieux-Château (*Old Château Cemetery*)

CEMETERY | High above the Parvis St-Michel, the Cimetière du Vieux-Château lies on the terraced plateau where once stood a medieval castle. The Victorian graves here are arranged by nationality, with an entire section dedicated to Russian royalty. The birth and death dates often attest to the ugly truth: even Menton's balmy climate couldn't reverse the ravages of tuberculosis. ✉ *Ch. du Trabuquet, Menton.*

Hôtel de Ville

GOVERNMENT BUILDING | The 19th-century Italianate Hôtel de Ville conceals a treasure by painter Jean Cocteau: he decorated the Salle des Mariages (Marriage Room) with vibrant allegorical scenes. Today it is used for civil marriages. ✉ *17 av. de la République, Menton* 🎫 *€2* ⏲ *Closed weekends.*

Jardins Biovès (*Biovès Gardens*)

GARDEN | FAMILY | Directly in front of the tourist office, the broad tropical Jardins Biovès stretches 2,600 feet across the breadth of the center, sandwiched between two avenues. Its symmetrical flower beds, exotic trees, sculptures, and fountains representing the spiritual heart of town are free to visit, except during the Fête du Citron, when they display giant sculptures constructed out of 15 tons of citrus fruit, and also at Christmas, when it has a more festive feel. ✉ *8 av. Boyer, Menton.*

Marché Couvert (Les Halles) (*Covered Market*)

MARKET | FAMILY | Between the lively pedestrian Rue St-Michel and the waterfront, the marvelous Marché Couvert (Les Halles) is considered one of the best (but pricey) food markets in France. Its Belle Époque facade is decorated in jewel-tone ceramics, and it's equally colorful and appealing inside, where, each day, some 30 merchants sell homemade bread (one gluten-free) and mountains of cheese, oils, fruit, and Italian delicacies daily (be sure to try the local dish, *barbbajuans,* a fritter stuffed with Swiss chard and ricotta). On Saturday, there is a clothing market outside at Place Fornari. Across from the market, the Italian Café Sini sells to-die-for apricot croissants and mouthwatering pizzas. ✉ *Quai de Monléon, Menton.*

★ Musée Jean Cocteau

ART MUSEUM | On the waterfront opposite the market, a squat medieval bastion crowned with four tiny watchtowers houses this extraordinary museum, France's memorial to the eponymous artist-poet-filmmaker (1889–1963). Cocteau spotted the fortress, built in 1636 to defend the port, as the perfect site for a group of his works. The museum has nearly 1,800 *oeuvres graphiques,* and about 990 are original Cocteaus, a donation from the late California businessman and Holocaust survivor Severin Wunderman's personal collection. This is a must-see. ✉ *2 quai Monléon, Menton* ☎ *04–92–10–97–10* 🌐 *museecocteau-menton.fr* 🎫 *€5* 🕓 *Closed Tues.*

Parvis St-Michel

PLAZA/SQUARE | **FAMILY** | Up a set of grand tiered stairs that lead from the Quai Bonaparte, the Parvis St-Michel is a broad plaza paved in some 250,000 round white and gray stones patterned in the coat of arms of the Grimaldi family. The plaza was created in the 17th century by Prince Honoré II; the letter H is incorporated into the design as a kind of signature at the base of his great gift to the city. ✉ *Menton.*

Place aux Herbes

PLAZA/SQUARE | **FAMILY** | Right by the market, the pretty little Place aux Herbes is a picturesque spot for a pause on a park bench, a drink, or a restaurant meal in the deep shade of the plane trees. ✉ *Menton.*

Promenade du Soleil

PROMENADE | **FAMILY** | Stroll the length of Menton's famous beachfront along the Promenade du Soleil: broad, white, and studded with palm trees, from Plage du Fossan in front of the covered market Marché des Halles westward to Plage de la Piscine, next to the indoor municipal swimming pool Les Bains du Cap (€7.50 entry). A little farther along the seaside walkway, Le Paradis de la Glace ice cream parlor is a reward any time of year. ✉ *Menton.*

Quai Napoléon III

MARINA/PIER | To get a feel for the territory, start your exploration at the far east end of the Vieille Ville and walk out to the end of the Quai Napoléon III, which juts far out into the water. Above the masts of pleasure boats, all of Menton spreads over the hills, and the mountains of Italy loom behind. This is the place to be at sunrise. ✉ *Menton.*

Rue St-Michel

STREET | **FAMILY** | Serving as the main commercial artery of the Vieille Ville, Rue St-Michel is lined with shops, cafés, and orange trees. ✉ *Menton.*

Serre de la Madone

GARDEN | **FAMILY** | With a temperate microclimate created by its southeastern and sunny exposure, Menton attracted a great share of wealthy horticultural hobbyists, including Major Lawrence Johnston, a gentleman gardener best known for his Cotswolds wonderland, Hidcote Manor. He wound up buying a choice estate in Gorbio—one of the loveliest of all perched seaside villages, 10 km (6 miles) west of Menton—and spent the 1920s and '30s making the Serre de la Madone a masterpiece.

Johnston brought back exotica from his many trips to South Africa, Mexico, and China, and planted them in a series of terraces, accented by little pools, vistas, and stone steps. Although most of his creeping plumbago, pink belladonna, and night-flowering cacti are now gone, his garden has been reopened by the municipality. If you don't have a car, you can reach it from Menton via Zest Bus 7 (€2.10). ✉ *74 rte. de Gorbio, Menton* ☎ *04–93–57–73–90* 🎫 *€10* 🕓 *Closed Mon. and Nov. and Dec.*

Val Rahmeh Botanical Garden

GARDEN | FAMILY | This garden is particularly delightful in the fall, when the hibiscus and brugmansias are in bloom. Planted by Maybud Campbell in the 1910s and cherished by connoisseurs, it bursts with rare ornamentals and subtropical plants and is adorned with water-lily pools and fountains. The tourist office can also give you directions to other gorgeous gardens around Menton, including the Fontana Rosa, the Villa Maria Serena, and the Villa Les Colombières. ✉ *Av. St-Jacques, Menton* ☎ *04–92–10–97–10* 🌐 *www.jardinbotaniquevalrahmehmenton.fr/fr* 🎫 *€7* ⏲ *Closed Tues.*

Restaurants

★ Mirazur

$$$$ | MODERN FRENCH | Chef Mauro Colagreco—who learned his craft in Latin America before working with the likes of Bernard Loiseau in Burgundy and both Alain Passard and Alain Ducasse in Paris—now helms this innovative establishment, which has garnered three Michelin stars and is frequently cited as the world's best restaurant. Colagreco is one of the young chefs whose style has been dubbed *la jeune cuisine*—for him, the plate is a palette, and each of the ingredients, which are often gathered from the on-site vegetable garden, has its precise place and significance. **Known for:** inventive gastronomic cuisine by Argentinean-Italian chef; sensational views of the coast cannot match the flavor; requires reservations at least six months in advance. [$] *Average main: €450* ✉ *30 av. Aristide Briand, Menton* ☎ *04–92–41–86–86* 🌐 *www.mirazur.fr* ⏲ *Closed Mon. and Tues., early Jan., and 2 wks mid-Nov. No lunch Wed.*

Hotels

Hôtel Lemon

$ | HOTEL | Subtropical gardens and 19th-century architecture are two of Menton's main attractions, and this hotel a few minutes' walk from the train station gives you a taste of both and at prices rarely seen along the Riviera. **Pros:** plenty of charm at rock-bottom prices; five minutes to the sea; rooms are basic but tasteful. **Cons:** parking can be difficult; some street noise; no air-conditioning. [$] *Rooms from: €123* ✉ *10 rue Albert 1er, Menton* ☎ *04–93–28–63–63* 🌐 *www.hotel-lemon.com* *16 rooms* 🍽 *No Meals.*

Napoléon

$$$ | HOTEL | This elegantly modern hotel in Garavan, east of the town center next to Italy, is hard to beat when it comes to value, given that attentive service, a fitness room overlooking a solar-heated swimming pool, and contemporary furnishings all make it feel like a luxury hotel even though it's not. **Pros:** fantastically warm service; sea and mountain views from.upper floors; very accessible with grab bars, shower stools, and elevator. **Cons:** bit of a walk from the town center; parking can be difficult (€12/day); no restaurant on-site. [$] *Rooms from: €272* ✉ *29 porte de France, Menton* ☎ *04–93–35–89–50* 🌐 *www.napoleon-menton.com* *46 rooms* 🍽 *No Meals.*

Chapter 8

MONACO

8

Updated by
Nancy Heslin

Sights ★★★☆☆ | Restaurants ★★★☆☆ | Hotels ★★★☆☆ | Shopping ★★★★☆ | Nightlife ★★★☆☆

WELCOME TO MONACO

TOP REASONS TO GO

★ **Monte Carlo:** Even if you aren't a gambler, the gold leaf and over-the-top rococo in the casino are definitely worth a long look.

★ **Grace Kelly:** Follow in Grace Kelly's footsteps with a visit to the Palais Princier, the official residence of the "royal" family, including the actress's grandson, heir apparent Prince Jacques.

★ **Parks:** Yes, Virginia, you can afford to visit Monte Carlo—that is, if you stroll through the free Japanese or rose gardens. Or for a few euros, head to the vertiginous Jardin Exotique de Monaco, which offers magnificent views of the country.

★ **Museums:** One of the world's best oceanography museums, the Musée Océanographique is an architectural masterpiece in its own right.

★ **Beaches:** Monaco's gorgeously renovated waterfront is well known for its private clubs and people-watching.

Monaco covers just 473 acres and would fit comfortably inside New York's Central Park. (That said, it also reaches a height of 528 feet, so bring some walking shoes.) Despite its compact nature, everybody drives here, whether from the Palais Princier perched on the Rock in Old Town down to the superyacht-lined port in La Condamine or up to Casino Gardens in the heart of Monte Carlo.

1 Monaco. **The principality's sensational position on a broad peninsula that bulges into the Mediterranean seduces billionaires and A-Listers, as well as those who just want to see how the 1% live. One out of every three people is a multimillionaire here, with the microstate boasting the world's most expensive property to buy ($1 million per 14.6 square meters, according to the Knight Frank Wealth Report 2022) and to rent (up to $220,000 a month).**

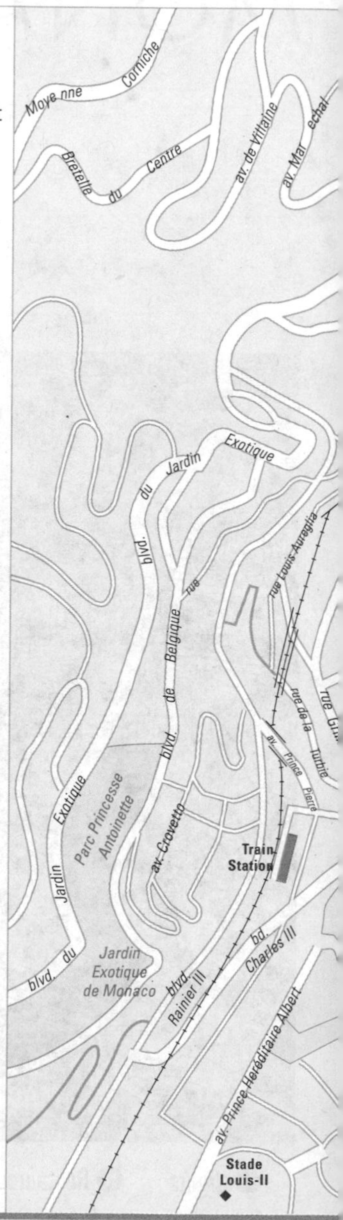

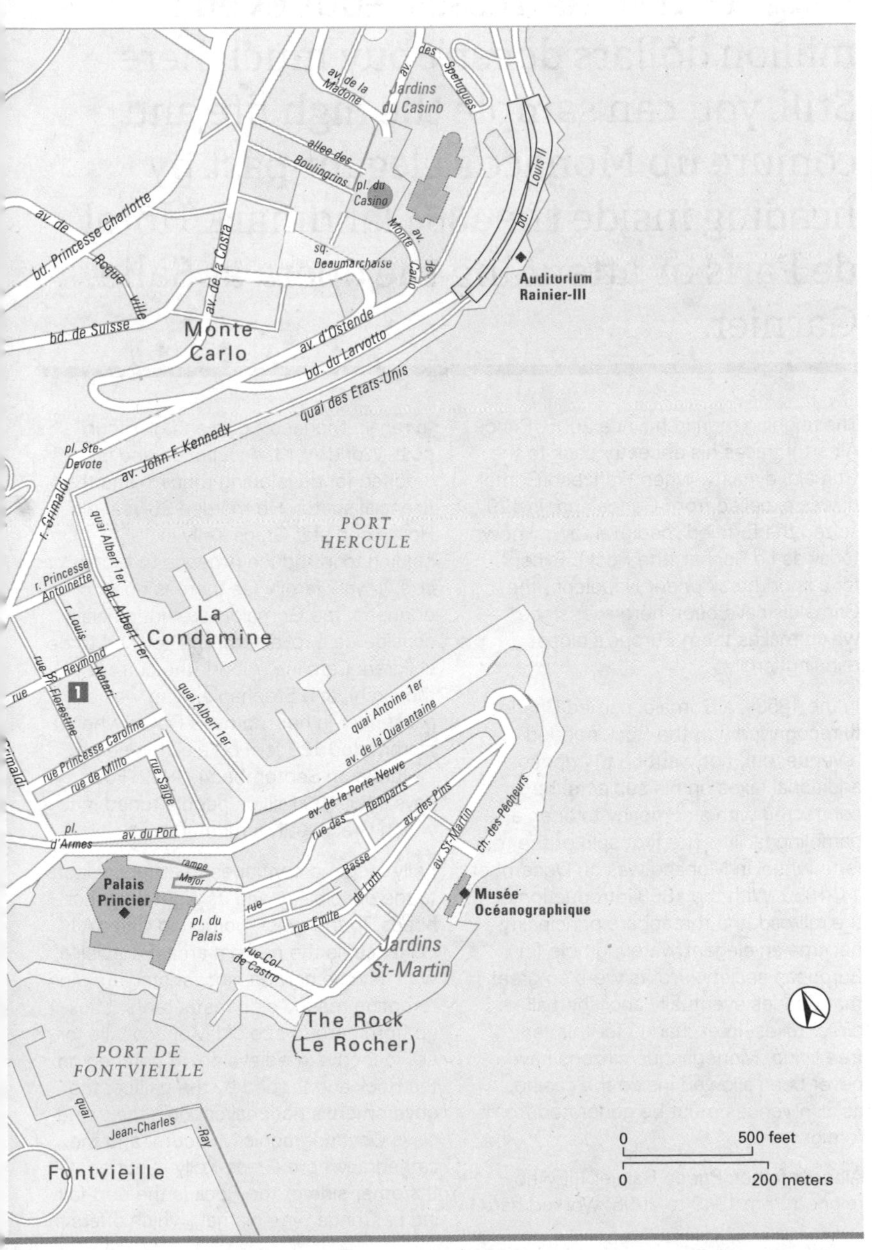
av. de la Madone
av. des Spelugues
Jardins du Casino
allee des Boulingrins
pl. du Casino
bd. Louis II
av. Princesse Charlotte
bd. Princesse Charlotte
av. de la Costa
sq. Beaumarchaise
av. de Monte Carlo
Auditorium Rainier-III
av. de Roque ville
bd. de Suisse
Monte Carlo
av. d'Ostende
bd. du Larvotto
quai des Etats-Unis
pl. Ste-Devote
av. John F. Kennedy
r. Grimaldi
quai Albert 1er
PORT HERCULE
r. Princesse Antoinette
bd. Albert 1er
r. Louis Notari
La Condamine
rue S. Reymond
rue Pr. Florestine
1
quai Albert 1er
quai Antoine 1er
av. de la Quarantaine
rue Princesse Caroline
rue de Millo
rue Saige
Grimaldi
av. de la Porte Neuve
rue des Remparts
av. des Pins
ch. des Pecheurs
av. St-Martin
pl. d'Armes
av. du Port
rampe Major
Palais Princier
rue Basse
rue de Loth
Musée Océanographique
pl. du Palais
rue Emile
Jardins St-Martin
rue Col. de Castro
The Rock (Le Rocher)
PORT DE FONTVIEILLE
quai Jean-Charles -Ray
Fontvieille
0 500 feet
0 200 meters

This compact, fairy-tale, Mediterranean destination is one of the world's most sought-after addresses—but even a million dollars doesn't buy much here. Still, you can sample the high life and conjure up Monaco's elegant past by heading inside the 1864 landmark Hôtel de Paris or attending the opera at Salle Garnier.

The reigning monarch since 2005, Prince Albert II traces his ancestry back to the Grimaldi dynasty, when Franceso Grimaldi was expelled from Genoa and, in 1297, seized the fortified medieval town known today as Le Rocher (the Rock). Except for a short break under Napoléon, the Grimaldis have been here ever since, which makes them Europe's oldest reigning family.

In the 1850s, a Grimaldi named Charles III recognized that the Rock needed revenue, but, not wanting to impose additional taxes on his subjects, he contracted with a company to open a gambling facility. The first spin of the roulette wheel in Monaco was on December 14, 1856. With the 1868 introduction of the railroad, the threadbare principality became an elegant watering hole for European society. Profits were so great that Charles eventually abolished all direct taxes. In exchange for this tax-free living, Monégasque citizens have never been allowed inside the casino, as all revenues must be generated from foreigners.

Albert's father, Prince Rainier III, who reigned from 1949 to 2005, worked hard to regain Monaco's glitz and glamour post–World War II occupation and is credited for developing tourism and the financial sector. He married 26-year-old Hollywood star Grace Kelly in 1956, helping to introduce America to Monaco's "royal" family (as there is no king or queen, the Grimaldis are not officially considered a royal family). They had three children: Caroline, Albert (the current monarch), and Stephanie, who was a passenger in her mother's Rover when it plummeted 120 feet off a cliff in nearby La Turbie on September 4, 1982. Four days later, 100 million people tuned in to watch Grace Kelly's funeral on TV.

Kelly's legend continues to attract visitors to the principality and its eight neighborhoods. To the west, bordering Cap d'Ail in France, is the newest area, Fontvieille, with its rose garden, soccer stadium, and tempting marina-side restaurants. Look up from here to see old Monaco-Ville (or Le Rocher), a medieval town perched on the Rock and topped by the palace, the government's national council, the world-class Oceanographic Museum, and the cathedral where Grace Kelly is buried. On the other side of the Rock is the port-facing La Condamine district, which offers a smorgasbord of eateries and pedestrian shopping streets and connects to Casino Square, the Metropole shopping center (Monaco's very high-end version of a mall), and the illustrious Hôtel de Paris.

To the east, the Larvotto beachfront and a two-level walkway with restaurants and bars—including places where you can spend €28 for a glass of water—is next to Monaco's €2 billion land reclamation called Portier Cove. The 15-acre eco-neighborhood will feature residences, a garden, and even a marina when it opens by 2026. The Exotic Garden district, way up behind Fontvielle, includes the magical *jardins,* Villa Paloma art museum, the Museum of Prehistoric Anthropology, and Princess Antoinette Park, where you can play badminton or miniature golf. The mostly residential La Rousse and Les Moneghetti round off Monaco's neighborhoods.

Planning

When to Go

The beaches are at their best in June or September (even Monégasques escape the swelter of July and August), but to avoid the shiploads of high-season travelers, visit in the fall or winter. The temperatures won't be as high, but you'll still get color from reflecting diamonds. Don't even think about coming during the Grand Prix at the end of May or during the Monaco Yacht Show, which is held over four days in September.

Getting Here and Around

Monaco may be less than 2 square kilometers but it is famous for its traffic jams. (Don't even get the locals started about the noise and construction!) So forget driving in town. If you're flying into the Nice airport, a taxi to Monaco costs a flat fee of €95 (there's no Uber in Monaco).

A more affordable option is the Nice AirportXpress, the 80 bus (formerly No. 110) to Menton, which has several stops in Monaco including at the tourist office in front of the Casino (45 minutes, €19 one-way). The last bus leaves from Terminal 2 at 8:30 pm; this service does not currently stop at Terminal 1. However, from T1 you have the option of walking 10–15 minutes to the new Nice Saint-Augustin train station and taking a 35-minute ride for €5.40. Rest assured the walkway is well lit in the evening.

From Nice, Monaco is serviced by regular trains along the Cannes–Ventimiglia line; from Nice Ville, the main station, the journey costs €4.40 one way and takes 21 minutes. By bus, Lignes d'Azur Bus No. 607 departs from the Port in Nice, but can be very crowded in high season. You can pay the €2.50 fare onboard. Note this line used to be the 100 Nice-Menton direct but until April 2024, the journey is divided into two bus lines: 607 and 608 Monaco-Menton.

Monaco is a relatively easy place to navigate on foot, especially if you take advantage of its 78 public elevators, 35 escalators, and 8 travelators. But if you're looking for an insider's view, native Jean-Marc Ferrié at Monaco Rando (🌐 *www.monaco-rando.com*) gives guided walking tours in English on a variety of topics, from the secrets of the Rock and the Grand Prix Circuit to the four-hour Via Alpina with stunning overviews of the principality. Prices run €15–€50 per person.

BUS

Compagnie des Autobus de Monaco operates a bus service that threads the avenues of the principality, and all six lines stop at the tourist office, at the top of the Casino gardens. Purchase your ticket on board from the driver for €2 cash, or tap your credit card and save

€0.50. You can also save by buying in advance online. A 24-hour pass (€5.50) can by bought online or from an agent.

The company also operates both the bateau-bus, a solar electric boat from Quai des États-Unis to the casino side of the port (it runs daily 8 am–8 pm and costs €2) and MonaBike, which has 300 electric bikes that you can rent (from €1) using a valid credit card. The Monapass app is a one-stop payment platform for all these transport services. It also helps with street parking.

■ TIP→ From the tourist office you can take the 18 or 24 Zest bus (€2 from driver; €1.80 with credit card on bus) to/from Menton.

Across the street, heading west, the Nice airport bus stops at Casino Monte Carlo.

BUS INFORMATION Compagnie des Autobus de Monaco. ☎ *377/97–70–22–22* 🌐 *www.cam.mc.*

Hotels

Even off-season, hotels cost more here than in nearby Nice or Menton. Reserve as far ahead as possible during events (like Monaco Grand Prix) and festivals (like Printemps des Arts) and brace yourself for skyrocketing rates. For the cost-conscious, Monaco is the ultimate day trip by train.

Restaurants

With numerous Michelin-starred restaurants, there is no shortage of decadent dining in the principality, but with 140 nationalities calling Monaco home, the food scene is quite diverse, too. From the lunch hot spot A Cantina run by a 40-year-old Monégasque chef to Sexy Tacos, where chef Pepe Olivares, who hails from Mexico City, has won the loyalty of locals, Monaco has never been more appetizing.

⇨ *Restaurant and hotel reviews have been shortened. For full information, visit Fodors.com. Restaurant prices are the average cost of a main course at dinner, or if dinner is not served, at lunch. Hotel prices are the lowest cost of a standard double room in high season.*

What It Costs in Euros

$	$$	$$$	$$$$
HOTELS			
under €125	€125–€225	€226–€350	over €350
RESTAURANTS			
under €18	€18–€24	€25–€32	over €32

Visitor Information

CONTACTS Monaco Tourist Office. ✉ *2a bd. des Moulins, Monte Carlo* ☎ *377/92–16–61–66* 🌐 *www.visitmonaco.com.*

Sights

Casino de Monte-Carlo

CASINO | Place du Casino is the center of Monte Carlo and a must-see, even if gambling is not your thing. The hopeful descend from tour buses and enter the gold-leaf splendor of the 1863 casino to tempt fate beneath the gilt-edge rococo ceiling. Some spend much more than planned here, as did the French actress Sarah Bernhardt, who once lost 100,000 francs.

The main gambling hall is the Salle Europe, where you can play roulette and Texas Hold'em, while the slot machines stand apart in the Salle des Amériques. Bring your passport, as you have to be at least 18 to enter. There's a €17 admission to the period gaming rooms (open from 2 pm), where a dress code applies (no runners, shorts, or jeans with holes). To see what the fuss is all about without tempting fate, you could just book lunch

Monaco's Belle Époque opulence is epitomized by its famed Casino de Monte-Carlo, which is particularly stunning at night.

in the casino's Salon Rose. ✉ *Pl. du Casino, Monte Carlo* ☎ *377/98–06–21–21* 🌐 *www.montecarlosbm.com.*

Collection des Voitures Anciennes
(*Collection of Vintage Cars*)
OTHER MUSEUM | FAMILY | Prepare to be wowed by the Prince of Monaco's car collection, which is now in a huge, state-of-the-art facility at the port. The assemblage of 100 or so vintage cars features everything from a 1903 De Dion-Bouton to a Lamborghini Countach. Most were owned by Prince Albert's father, Rainier; exceptions include the Lexus from Albert's wedding to Charlene Wittstock in 2011 and Charles Leclerc's Ferrari SF90, which the F1 driver—the only Monégasque to race for the Prancing Horse—donated in 2021. ✉ *54 rte. de la Piscine* ☎ *377/92–05–28–56* 🌐 *www.mtcc.mc/en* 🎟 *From €8.*

Jardin Exotique de Monaco
(*Tropical Garden*)
GARDEN | A half-hour walk (uphill!) west from the palace brings you to this garden, where the views of the coastline are spectacular and an amazing variety of cacti and succulents clings to the sheer rock face. Indeed, the garden, which opened in 1933, traces its roots back to when Monaco's near-tropical climate nurtured plants that visitors from the northlands would have found exotic.

Also on the grounds—or actually under them and down 300 steps—are the Grottes de l'Observatoire, amazing grottoes and caves filled with stalagmites and spotlit with fairy lights. In addition, the on-site Musée d'Anthropologie has exhibits on general prehistory and regional Paleolithic discoveries. Note that the garden has been undergoing a multiyear restoration that's slated to be complete in early 2024; before visiting, check to be sure that it has reopened and to confirm hours and admission fees. **■ TIP→ You can hop on the No. 2 Jardin Exotique Bus (€2 onboard) in front of the casino tourism office or one of Monaco's 79 elevators (perhaps at Bd. de Belgique, Av. Pasteur, or Av. Hector Otto) to take you up, up, and away.**

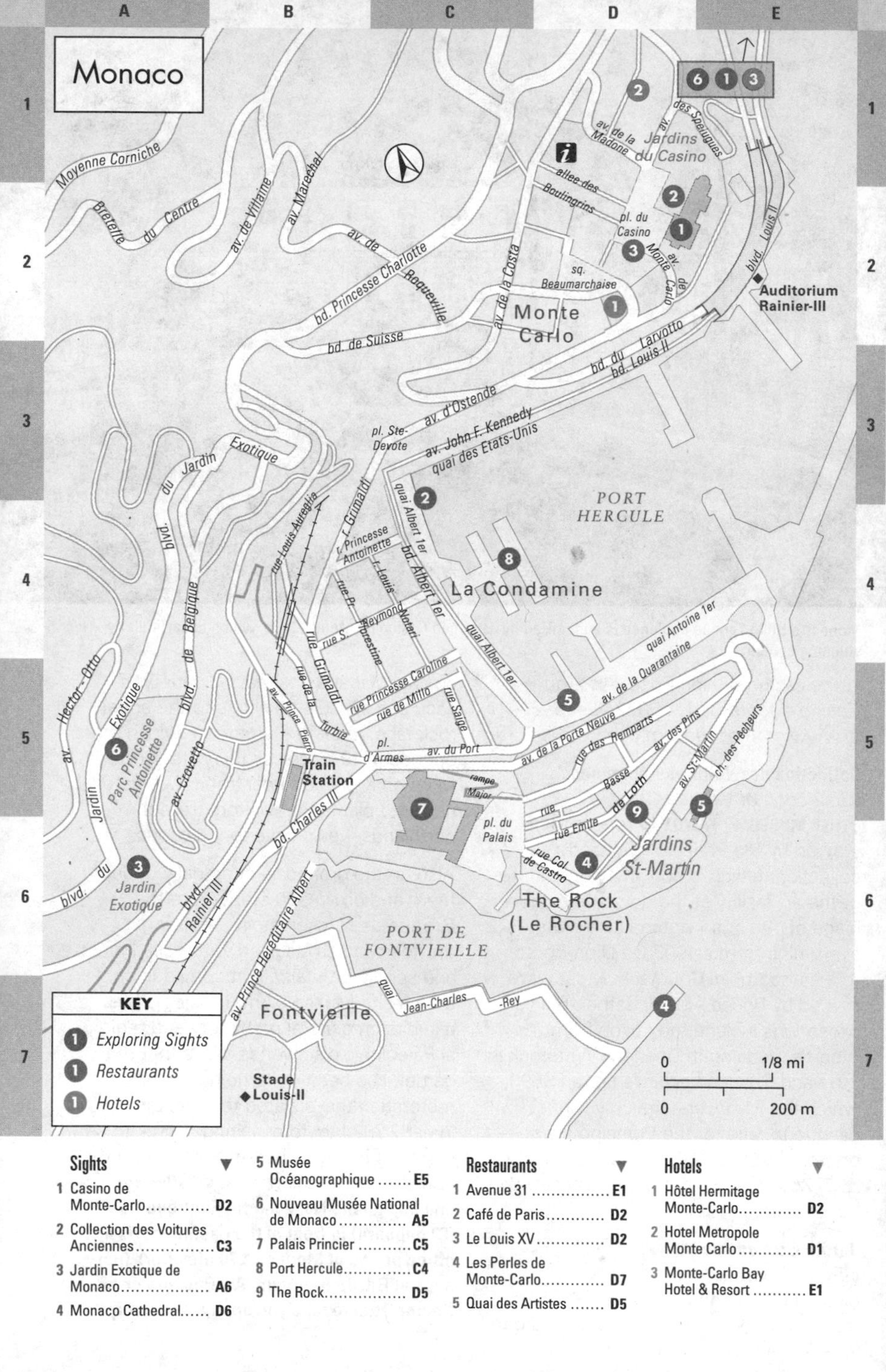

Sights

1 Casino de Monte-Carlo **D2**
2 Collection des Voitures Anciennes **C3**
3 Jardin Exotique de Monaco.................. **A6**
4 Monaco Cathedral...... **D6**
5 Musée Océanographique **E5**
6 Nouveau Musée National de Monaco **A5**
7 Palais Princier **C5**
8 Port Hercule.............. **C4**
9 The Rock................ **D5**

Restaurants

1 Avenue 31 .... **E1**
2 Café de Paris............ **D2**
3 Le Louis XV **D2**
4 Les Perles de Monte-Carlo............. **D7**
5 Quai des Artistes **D5**

Hotels

1 Hôtel Hermitage Monte-Carlo............. **D2**
2 Hotel Metropole Monte Carlo **D1**
3 Monte-Carlo Bay Hotel & Resort **E1**

Monaco on a Budget

As you might expect, dining is expensive in Monaco, and even the most modest hotels cost more than in nearby Nice or Menton. If you're frugal, however, you can find ways to avoid breaking the bank. For instance, because Monaco is very accessible by train, you can make it a day trip. After all, some 55,000 employees commute each day from elsewhere to Fontvieille, the closest thing Monaco has to a business district.

While here, you can stroll the Princess Grace Rose Garden and the Monte-Carlo Japanese Garden for free. Or film Instagram Live from aboard the solar electric Bateau Bus (€2), which crosses Port Hercule from Quai des Etats-Unis to Quai Antoine 1er (no one has to know you are not on a yacht!). If you love art, visit the luminous and free-of-charge Opera Gallery next to the Hermitage. Note, too, that the two branches of the Nouveau Musée National de Monaco (Villa Sauber and Villa Paloma) are free on Sunday. To really see the stars, catch one of the nightly (from June to September) films at the Open Air Cinema in the Parking du Chemin des Pêcheurs. Finally, Monaco's public toilets are free (although it's good to tip the attendant a euro).

There are ways to save money on food, too. Pick up fresh edibles at the daily Place d'Armes market in La Condamine or a buttery croissant for €1.50 at the iconic Pâtisserie Riviera. Alternatively, eat portside at the very affordable Société Nautique, Monaco's rowing club, where you don't have to be a member to dine and the water views are impressive. If you want panoramic vistas instead, head up the Rock for lunch at Club Bouliste du Rocher, Monaco's pétanque club, where nonmembers can order a three-course €20 lunch. Or you could just join Monaco's working class (yes, really), and grab a slice at Guidi's in Fontvieille.

✉ 62 bd. du Jardin Exotique 🌐 www.jardin-exotique.mc 🎫 €7.40.

Monaco Cathedral

CHURCH | Follow the crowds down the last remaining streets of medieval Monaco to the 19th-century Cathédrale de l'Immaculée-Conception, which contains the tomb of Princess Grace and Prince Rainier III, as well as a magnificent altarpiece painted in 1500 by Louis Bréa. From September to June, Monaco's Boys Choir (Les Petits Chanteurs) provides the music for Sunday mass at 10:30 am. *✉ 4 rue Colonel Bellando de Castro, Monte Carlo ☎ 377/99–99–14–00 🌐 diocese.mc.*

★ Musée Océanographique
(*Oceanography Museum*)

SCIENCE MUSEUM | **FAMILY** | This museum, in a splendid Edwardian structure perched dramatically atop a cliff, was built under Prince Albert I to house specimens collected on amateur explorations, including those led by Jacques Cousteau from 1957 to 1988. The main floor Whale Room has skeletons and taxidermy of enormous sea creatures, as well as early submarines, diving gear dating from the Middle Ages, and a few interactive science displays. The main draw, however, is the aquarium, a blockbuster complex of backlighted tanks containing more than 600 species of marine life. Be sure to try one of the two escape games—the

30-minute Discovery Escape or the 60-minute Escape Experience—that you can play in teams. Round off your visit with a meal in the museum's La Terrasse restaurant, set at 85 meters above the sea. ✉ *Av. St-Martin* ☎ *377/93–15–36–00* 🌐 *musee.oceano.org* 🎫 *€19; €25 combined with Prince's Palace or with Prince's Car Collection.*

Nouveau Musée National de Monaco

OTHER MUSEUM | Monaco's national museum actually occupies two buildings at opposite ends of town. One of the surviving structures from the Belle Époque, Villa Sauber, with its welcoming rose garden, is in the Larvotto Beach area (take the elevator down from Place des Moulins). Next door to the Jardin Exotique is Villa Paloma, with its fabulous stained-glass windows. The museums are open to the public only during exhibitions, so check the website for more information. ✉ *Villa Sauber, 17 av. Princesse Grace* ☎ *377/98–98–91–26* 🌐 *www.nmnm.mc* 🎫 *€6.*

Palais Princier

CASTLE/PALACE | The famous Rock, crowned by the palace where the princely family resides, stands west of Monte Carlo. On May 6, 1955, it's where Grace Kelly first met her future husband, Prince Rainier. An audio guide leading you through this sumptuous historical structure, built in the 13th century and expanded and enhanced over the centuries, reveals an extravagance of 16th- and 17th-century frescoes, as well as tapestries, gilt furniture, and paintings. The renovated private apartments, the "Grands Appartements," are open to the public from early April through October, but there is no wheelchair access.

The Relève de la Garde (Changing of the Guard) takes place outside the front entrance of the palace every day promptly at 11:55 am. In addition, beginning in mid-July, a summer concert series is held at 9:30 pm in the palace courtyard; you can buy tickets through the Orchestre Philharmonique de Monte-Carlo (🌐 *www.opmc.com*). ✉ *Pl. du Palais* ☎ *377/93–25–18–31* 🌐 *www.palais.mc* 🎫 *From €10* ⏲ *Closed mid-Oct.–Mar.*

Port Hercule

MARINA/PIER | **FAMILY** | It's a blissful downhill hike from Monte Carlo to the port along Boulevard Albert 1er, where pleasure boats of every length flash white and blue. Pop-up grandstands line the street for Grand Prix, and the far corner of the port is where the Institut Océanographique launches research boats to study aquatic life in the Mediterranean, as its late director Jacques Cousteau did for some 30 years. From here, you can also access the seawall—aka the renovated digue—and use the ladder to take a dip in the Mediterranean (just beware of the jellyfish).

From La Condamine, you can catch a glimpse of the yachting club, one of the world's most prestigious and a staple on the local social circuit, where musicians such as Elton John and Duran Duran have performed. Steps from the club, at La Poissonnerie on Quai l'Hirondelle, you can witness the catch of the day from Monaco's fourth-generation (and only!) fisherman, Eric Rinaldi. He supplies many of Monaco's private chefs, including those who work on yachts. Surely you can afford €8 to try one of the freshest ever Mediterranean prawns. Burger alert: There are several tasty burger joints in La Condamine, from Gruber's on Rue Princess Caroline to Steak 'n Shake near the train station.

★ The Rock

HISTORIC DISTRICT | **FAMILY** | Most of Monaco's sights are concentrated—with tidy, self-conscious charm—on the broad plateau known as Le Rocher, or the Rock. Here, in the medieval heart of Monaco, you'll find the cathedral, palace, Musée Océanographique, and the delightful St- Martin Gardens, the country's first public garden (open since 1816). Only vehicles with Monaco license plates can drive through the gate, but the No. 1 or 2 buses will get you to the top. If you're feeling energetic, climb the 42 steps of the Rampe Majeur from Place d'Armes, behind the right corner of the port. You can also approach the Rock by elevator from the seafront at the port's farthest end, though this, too, requires some walking.

Although area businesses are predominately souvenir stores that cater to cruise visitors, there are a few unique establishments, including Chocolaterie de Monaco, which has been open since 1920; the award-winning La Montgolfière restaurant; and Les 5 Saveurs (✉ *6 bis rue Basse*), a shop that sells Panier des Sens natural, made-in-Marseilles cosmetics and soaps that are favored by Monaco residents.

 Beaches

La Note Bleue

BEACH | **FAMILY** | Probably the best known of the private beaches, La Note Bleue is one of several strands at the newly revamped Larvotto Beach. It has live music every Wednesday year-round, a restaurant serving breakfast and Mediterranean-Asian food from noon to night, and—most essential—loungers to rent (€30 per day) from mid-April to mid-October. It's also a jellyfish-free zone, with nets that keep their tentacles at bay. **Amenities:** food and drink; showers; toilets. **Best for:** sunrise; swimming. ✉ *Plage du Larvotto, Av. Princesse Grace* ☎ *377/93–50–05–02* 🌐 *www.lanotebleue.mc.*

Plage du Larvotto

BEACH | **FAMILY** | Just off Avenue Princess Grace, one of the world's most costly streets on which to own property, is the only free public beach in Monaco. After two years of extensive renovations, it now has a pristine beachfront (protected by jellyfish nets) along with a promenade, bike lanes, and shops. Restaurants vary from Italian (Giacomo) to Mexican (Sexy Tacos), and across the street, you'll find mind-blowing Japanese at the Niwaki, which is owned by the Sass Café family. Although the beach's €50 million face-lift is impressive, some complain it's too contemporary, and you'll have to put up with construction noise next door where the €2 billion, land-extension Portier Cove project is underway. **Amenities:** food and drink; lifeguards; showers; toilets; water sports. **Best for:** sunrise; sunset. ✉ *Av. Princesse Grace.*

Plage Mala

BEACH | This stretch of sandy, shaded land is easily one of the most idyllic and stylish of the Riviera beaches—one where impressive cliffs tower above coves that are fantastic places to snorkel. Nearby are private beach restaurants where you can rent loungers; note, though, that in high season they can cost a whopping €100 per day. The 3½-km (2-mile) Mala footpath runs to Plage Marquet in Fontvieille in Monaco—a 20- or 30-minute walk where the only challenging leg is the 100-plus-step access to Mala beach itself. **Amenities:** food and drink; lifeguard; showers. **Best for:** snorkeling; swimming; walking. ✉ *Av. Raymond Gramaglia, Cap-d'Ail.*

Restaurants

Avenue 31

$$$$ | **ITALIAN** | You could easily walk past this unassuming restaurant—near Larvotto Beach along one of the world's most expensive streets—and not have a clue that its four eating areas are packed with locals loyal to chef Andréa Lanzillotta. Locally sourced ingredients go into its simple salads, pizzas, pastas, and fish or grilled beef dishes, all of which are reasonably priced (for Monaco) and won't leave you feeling heavy like dishes at some Michelin-starred restaurants. **Known for:** tucked-away local hot spot; known for its pizzalike "skizza"; organic kale salad for vegans. $ *Average main:*

€40 ✉ 31 av. Princesse Grace, Monaco ☎ 377/97–70–31–31 🌐 www.avenue31.mc.

Café de Paris

$$$$ | BRASSERIE | The landmark Belle Époque Brasserie 1900—better known as Café de Paris—reopened in summer 2023 after an ambitious renovation. Supercilious and super-professional waiters still fawn gracefully over titled preeners, jet-setters, and tourists enjoying classic fare (shellfish, steak tartare, matchstick frites), but now there is an additional floor. **Known for:** ultimate spot for people-watching; cool new Amazonico rooftop restaurant overlooking casino; nonstop food service. *$ Average main: €45 ✉ Pl. du Casino ☎ 377/98–06–76–23 🌐 www.montecarlosbm.com.*

★ Le Louis XV

$$$$ | FRENCH | Only in Monaco can opulence be served on a plate, and only at Alain Ducasse's flagship, three-Michelin-star restaurant in the Hôtel de Paris, can you taste it. At Louis XV, Ducasse embraces the Riviera's *art de vivre* and simplicity, with dishes like grilled local fish and oysters from Maison Giol with salicornia (seaweed) and pistachio praline. **Known for:** meal of a lifetime from a celebrity chef; 350,000 bottles of wine with 3,700 references; restaurant manager Claire Sonnet picked up Michelin's 2023 Service Award. *$ Average main: €140 ✉ Hôtel de Paris, Pl. du Casino ☎ 377/98–06–88–64 🌐 www.ducasse-paris.com ⊗ Closed Tues. and Wed. No lunch weekdays ⛃ Jacket required.*

★ Les Perles de Monte-Carlo

$$$ | SEAFOOD | Tucked away at the far end of the Fontvieille Port, with spectacular views of the cathedral and the oceanography museum suspended on the Rock above, this restaurant with a few unpretentious wooden tables and chairs is where celebrities like Clooney and Pitt were rumored to come for a *dégustation* (tasting). Whether they were dining next to a prince, a model, or an everyday local, it wouldn't matter to the owners—two marine biologists from Brittany—as to them, everyone is made to eat the freshest of shellfish, crustaceans, and fish. **Known for:** hands down best seafood (and most affordable meal) in Monaco; unique location akin to eating on a yacht; small space so reservations necessary. *$ Average main: €25 ✉ 47 Quai Jean Charles Rey ☎ 377/97–77–84–31 🌐 www.perlesdemontecarlo.com ⊗ Closed Sun. No dinner Sat.–Wed.*

Quai des Artistes

$$$$ | FRENCH | This warehouse-scale, neo–Art Deco bistro on the port packs in Monaco residents. The people-watching is optimal no matter where you sit while tucking into rich brasserie classics (think lamb shank on the bone with potato puree, rosemary, and spicy gravy) or the restaurant's renowned oysters and seafood platters. **Known for:** boisterous ambience and great people-watching; big terrace; French brasserie classics with a twist. *$ Average main: €39 ✉ 4 quai Antoine Ier ☎ 377/97–97–97–77 🌐 quaidesartistes.com.*

Hotels

Hôtel Hermitage Monte-Carlo

$$$$ | HOTEL | FAMILY | The epitome of elegance and discretion, this hotel is where the gold-plated crowd comes *not* to be seen; even if you don't stay here, visit the lobby to admire Gustav Eiffel's glass-dome Art Nouveau vestibule. **Pros:** unrivaled meals and views in Michelin-starred restaurant; best lobby bar in Monaco; free guest access to Thermes Marins wellness center. **Cons:** very expensive; can be noisy; you have to leave at some point. *$ Rooms from: €850 ✉ Sq. Beaumarchais ☎ 377/98–06–86–83 🌐 www.montecarlosbm.com 🛏 278 rooms 🍽 No Meals.*

★ Hotel Metropole Monte Carlo

$$$$ | **HOTEL** | This Belle Époque hotel, set on land that once belonged to Pope Leo XIII, has pulled out all the stops in its decor—famed Paris designer Jacques Garcia has given the rooms his signature hyper-aristocratic look while the late Karl Lagerfield was the architect behind the Odyssey pool and lounge; it's also home to Yoshi, the only Japanese restaurant on the French Rivera to have been awarded a Michelin star. **Pros:** flawless and attentive service; next to the luxury Metropole Shopping Center; one of the best spas in Europe. **Cons:** expensive; parking extra; check-in from 3 pm only. [$] *Rooms from: €720* ✉ *4 av. de la Madone* ☎ *377/93–15–15–35* 🌐 *metropole.com* *125 rooms* *No Meals.*

Monte-Carlo Bay Hotel & Resort

$$$$ | **HOTEL** | Perched on a 10-acre peninsula, with 75% of its rooms offering sea views, this highly acclaimed luxury resort—which immodestly bills itself as "a natural Eden reinvented"—seeks to evoke the Côte d'Azur's 1920s heyday with its neoclassical columns and arches, exotic gardens, lagoon swimming pool, casino, and concert hall. **Pros:** one of two proper beach resorts in Monaco; close to nightlife, restaurants, and Larvotto Beach; free access to Monte Carlo Casino. **Cons:** breakfast extra; free Wi-Fi only for maximum of two devices; might seem a little too over-the-top, even for Monaco. [$] *Rooms from: €640* ✉ *40 av. Princesse Grace* ☎ *377/98–06–20–00* 🌐 *www.montecarlosbm.com* *334 rooms* *No Meals.*

Nightlife

Jimmyz

DANCE CLUBS | This legendary disco at Sporting Monte-Carlo is not for lightweights: the partying is as serious as the need to be seen, so if surgically enhanced faces and body parts or paying €28 for a water upset you, then stay at your hotel. Note that the club doesn't even open until 11:30 pm. ✉ *Sporting Monte-Carlo, Av. Princesse Grace* ☎ *377/98–06–70–68* 🌐 *www.montecarlosbm.com.*

Performing Arts

OPERA

Opéra de Monte-Carlo

OPERA | Charles Garnier, the designer of the Salle Garnier Opera House, with its 18-ton gilt-bronze chandelier and extravagant frescoes, also built the Paris Opéra, but it was American-born Princess Alice, married to Prince Albert I, who made it a cultural destination. It hosts not only the coast's most significant performances of opera but also of dance and orchestral music. ✉ *Pl. du Casino* ☎ *377/98–06–28–00* 🌐 *www.opera.mc.*

Shopping

Shopping is pricey here, but it can also be a lot of fun. The Promenade Princess Charlene, behind Casino Square in the One Monte-Carlo complex (where people pay up to €250,000 a month in rent!), is the heart of the most high-end shopping street in all the Riviera. Four of the biggest fashion houses are here side by side—Cartier, Louis Vuitton (spread over three floors), Chanel, and Fendi—amid newer labels that include Ralph & Russo and Harry Winston.

The 60 street-level luxury shops along Avenue des Beaux-Arts include Prada Femmes, Bulgari, Alexander McQueen, and Piaget. You can find the same haute couture and luxury labels at the very casual secondhand shop the Queen Bee at Place de la Crémaillère, run by stylist Katie Holmes (no, not of Tom Cruise fame).

Princess Stephanie's daughter, Pauline Ducruet, has launched a gender-neutral clothing line called Alter Designs, but you can only shop online. The sole couture made in Monaco is by fashion designer Isabell Kristensen, who was Princess Charlene's maid of honor and also designed her bridal gown. Isabell's ultrafeminine gowns and cocktail dresses can be seen in her boutique on the Rock (✉ *18 rue Princesse Marie de Lorraine*). You can also pick up a bottle of her Monaco perfume (€65), a celestial scent made for Albert and Charlene's wedding.

One of the few independent perfume shops in Monaco is Parfumerie Edith Harlay in the shopping center in Fontvieille. Run by a Monégasque local, it has hundreds of scents to choose from including niche perfumes like Serge Lutens.

Another made-in-Monaco product can be found at the atelier l'Orangerie (✉ *9 rue de la Turbie*). The delicious orange liqueur—a perfect cocktail when mixed with prosecco—was created by Irish-Italian Philip Culazzo, who discovered a way to use the bitter oranges produced by Monaco's 600 trees. He also launched a liqueur as a nod to Monaco's national tree—carob—and a citrus gin.

■ TIP→ Get the Carlo app, which automatically gives you 5% cash back on all purchases with Carlo-affiliated merchants. These include Les Perles de Monte-Carlo restaurant and Larry King, the customer-friendly hair salon at the Hotel de Paris, open seven days a week.

Activities

AUTO RACING

Grand Prix de Monaco

AUTO RACING | The Grand Prix de Monaco typically takes place the last Sunday of the Cannes Film Festival in May, but Formula One's new owners, Liberty Media, would like that date to be more flexible. Even with all the new worldwide F1 races to chose from, diehard fans still flock to Monaco and drop €10,000 per person to stand on a balcony overlooking the course. If that's too rich for your budget, pick up tickets for the Thursday practice and qualifying rounds (€30 for Place du Casino seats), or drive the course for free when it opens that same night at 7:30 pm. Tickets for the Historic Grand Prix of Monaco, which takes place two weeks earlier on the same track every other year, run from €25. On alternate years, you can see the Formula E, the electric-car racing series. 🌐 *www.formula1.com*.

SPAS

Les Thermes Marins de Monte-Carlo
(*Sea Baths of Monte-Carlo*)

SPAS | Opened in the 1990s, this thalassotherapy (seawater-therapy) facility stretches along the port's upper side between the landmark Hôtel de Paris and its sister, the Hermitage, and can be accessed directly from either hotel. Within the sleek, 6,600-square-meter, multilevel complex, you can pursue every creature comfort, from underwater massage and seaweed body wraps to a 45-minute La Prairie Caviar Instant Lifting Treatment for €190. To get over jet lag, spend a couple of minutes in two cold chambers at -60°C and then -110°C as part of a cryotherapy treatment, which also helps sleep disorders and has anti-aging benefits. ✉ *2 av. de Monte-Carlo, Monaco* ☎ *377/98–06–69–00* 🌐 *www.montecarlosbm.com*.

Index

A

B

C

M

N

O

P

Q

R

S

T

U

V

W

Z

Photo Credits

Front Cover: Robert Harding / Alamy Stock Photo [Description: Beach parasols, Nice, Alpes Maritimes, Provence, Cote d'Azur, French Riviera, France, Europe]. **Back cover, from left to right:** Luboslav Tiles/Shutterstock. LiliGraphie/Shutterstock. Martin M303/Shutterstock. **Spine:** StevanZZ/Shutterstock. **Interior, from left to right:** Nedjat Nuhi/Shutterstock (1). Bbsferrari/iStockphoto (2-3). Boris Stroujko/Shutterstock (5). **Chapter 1: Experience Provence and the French Riviera:** IR Stone/Shutterstock (6-7). Gkuna/iStockphoto (8-9). Ville de Nice (9). Fabio Michele Capelli/Shutterstock (9). Alain Hocquel (10). Elementals/Shutterstock (10). Sergey Dzyuba/Shutterstock (10). Féria d'Arles_Lionel-Roux (11). Photo Roland Michaud / Archives Fondation Maeght (11). Featureflash Photo Agency/Shutterstock (12). Courtesy_Parfums Galimard (12). Seray.T/Crtpaca (12). Alain Hocquel (12). Tomas Marek/Dreamstime (13). Hocquel_A (13). Beachrex.com (13). Pierre Behar, Balloïde Photo - Christophe Bauthe (13). Garsya/Shutterstock (14). Johan Thelander/Shutterstock (14). Biset V (14). Yoan Navarro (15). HLphoto/shutterstock (20). Barmalini/Shutterstock (20). T. Duval (20). Jerome Kelagopian (21). Chez Pipo/SteeveBernardo (21). Ralf Liebhold/Shutterstock (22). Esterel Côte d'Azur (23). RobsonAbbott/iStockphoto (24). @OT CASSIS (24). Trabantos/iStockphoto (24). Courtesy_Saint-Rémy de Provence (24). Eric Valenne geostory/Shutterstock (24). Mihai-Bogdan Lazar/Shutterstock (25). Leonid Andronov/ Shutterstock (25). Alain Hocquel (25). Delort_V (25). Carlos Sanchez Pereyra/Dreamstime (25). Trabantos/Shutterstock (26). Voyageur8/Shutterstock (27). Anaïs Fournié (28). Cagnes-sur-Mer (28). Roland Michaud/Archives Fondation Maeght (28). Nice Code01/F. Follet (29). Metriognome/Shutterstock.com (29). **Chapter 3: Nîmes and the Alpilles:** Katja Wickert/Shutterstock (51). Guillaume Piolle/wikipedia.org (54). Anjci/Flickr (55). Andy Hawkins/Flickr (55). Lamax/Shutterstock (64). Mike Tumchewics, Fodors.com member (67). Ermess/Shutterstock (73). Ventdusud/Shutterstock (77). Keith Hider/Shutterstock (81). Judal/Shutterstock (89). Scott Brenner/Flickr (93). EQRoy/Shutterstock (97). **Chapter 4: Avignon and the Vaucluse:** Ecstk22/Shutterstock (101). Pablo Debat/Shutterstock (111). Eleni Mavrandoni/Shutterstock (114). Minerva Bloom, Fodors.com member (116). Tomas Marek/Shutterstock (118). Travel-Fr/Shutterstock (127). StevanZZ/Shutterstock (143). Nikolay Dimitrov - ecobo/Shutterstock (143). Wirestock Creators/Shutterstock (144). Trabantos/ Shutterstock (145). RossHelen/Shutterstock (145). Boris Stroujko/Shutterstock (146). Brilliance stock/Shutterstock (146). Brilliance stock/Shutterstock (147). Marina VN/Shutterstock (148). David Hughes/Shutterstock (149). Photocreo Michal Bednarek/Shutterstock (149). Serge Goujon/Shutterstock (149). Massimo Santi/Shutterstock (157). **Chapter 5: Aix, Marseille, and the Central Coast:** RossHelen/Shutterstock (165). Nadia & Massimo/Flickr (168). Nadia & Massimo/Flickr (169). Mon Oeil 59/Shutterstock (169). Emily Marie Wilson/Shutterstock (173). Christian Mueller/Shutterstock (181). Travelview/Shutterstock (182). Philip Lange/Shutterstock (185). Sergii Figurnyi/Shutterstock (193). Owen Franken/VieuxPortFranken (198). Francesco Bonino/Shutterstock (201). Marako85/Shutterstock (215). Rawpixel.com/Shutterstock (221). Tanya_F/iStockphoto (222). Anastasiia Soshenkova/Shutterstock (222). MychkoAlezander (223). Bonchan/Shutterstock (223). **Chapter 6: The Western French Riviera:** Proslgn/Shutterstock (227). Marco Rubino/Shutterstock (238). Try Media/iStockphoto (241). Steve Allen/Shutterstock (252). Gunold/Dreamstime (259). JoelMielle/iStockphoto (263). **Chapter 7: Nice and the Eastern French Riviera:** Mkinct/The French Riviera (265). Oleg P/Shutterstock (279). ArtMediaFactory/Shutterstock (293). Chris Hellier / Alamy Stock Photo (300). Mageplotter Travel / Alamy Stock Photo (301). Kunstbilder-Galerie.de/Amadeo Modigliani/Wikimedia Commons (302). M-Louis/Flickr (302). Bibiana Castagna/Shutterstock (303). Stocknshares/iStockphoto (303). United Archives GmbH / Alamy Stock Photo (304). Galerie Madoura (304). Wikimedia Commons/Library of Congress, Prints and Photographs Division, Van Vechten Collection, reproduction number LC-USZ62-103699 DLC (305). Henri Matisse/Wikimedia Commons (305). ArtMediaFactory/Shutterstock (307). Proslgn/Shutterstock (310). Alexandre Rotenberg/Shutterstock (313). Renaud d'Avout d'Auerstaedt/Wikipedia.org (316). Adrian Scottow/Flickr (319). Idealink Photography/Alamy (323). Michelle Silke/Shutterstock (325). Rostislav Glinsky/Shutterstock (330). Margarita Hintukainen/ Shutterstock (333). Proslgn/Shutterstock (335). The Leading Hotels of the World (339). Sabine Klein/Shutterstock (344). Dimitrisurkov/Dreamstime (348). Giancarlo Liguori/Shutterstock (351). Xbrchx/Shutterstock (357). **Chapter 8: Monaco:** Ostill/Shutterstock (359). Monte Carlo Société des Bains de Mer (365). **About Our Writers:** All photos are courtesy of the writers except for the following: Nancy Heslin, courtesy of LDWimages.

**Every effort has been made to trace the copyright holders, and we apologize in advance for any accidental errors. We would be happy to apply the corrections in the following edition of this publication.*

Notes

Notes

Notes

Fodor's PROVENCE AND THE FRENCH RIVIERA

Publisher: Stephen Horowitz, *General Manager*

Editorial: Douglas Stallings, *Editorial Director;* Jill Fergus, Amanda Sadlowski, *Senior Editors;* Brian Eschrich, Alexis Kelly, *Editors;* Angelique Kennedy-Chavannes, *Assistant Editor;* Yoojin Shin, *Associate Editor*

Design: Tina Malaney, *Director of Design and Production;* Jessica Gonzalez, *Senior Designer;* Jaimee Shaye, *Graphic Design Associate*

Production: Jennifer DePrima, *Editorial Production Manager;* Elyse Rozelle, *Senior Production Editor;* Monica White, *Production Editor*

Maps: Rebecca Baer, *Senior Map Editor,* David Lindroth, Mark Stroud (Moon Street Cartography), *Cartographers*

Photography: Viviane Teles, *Senior Photo Editor;* Namrata Aggarwal, Neha Gupta, Payal Gupta, Ashok Kumar, *Photo Editors;* Jade Rodgers, *Photo Production Intern*

Business and Operations: Chuck Hoover, *Chief Marketing Officer;* Robert Ames, *Group General Manager*

Public Relations and Marketing: Joe Ewaskiw, *Senior Director of Communications and Public Relations*

Fodors.com: Jeremy Tarr, *Editorial Director;* Rachael Levitt, *Managing Editor*

Technology: Jon Atkinson, *Executive Director of Technology;* Rudresh Teotia, *Associate Director of Technology;* Alison Lieu, *Project Manager*

Writers: Nancy Heslin, Jennifer Ladonne

Editor: Laura M. Kidder

Production Editor: Monica White

13th Edition

ISBN 9-781-64097-642-9

ISSN 1944-2912

SPECIAL SALES

This book is available at special discounts for bulk purchases for sales promotions or premiums. For more information, e-mail SpecialMarkets@fodors.com.

PRINTED IN CANADA

10 9 8 7 6 5 4 3 2 1

About Our Writers

Since swapping Canada for the Côte d'Azur in 2001, writer **Nancy Heslin** has distinguished herself as the region's go-to media personality, a role that has resulted in her taking the TGV with Tom Cruise to Marseille, lunching with Prince Albert in Monaco, and sipping Champagne with Paris Hilton in St-Tropez. A French citizen since 2010, the former editor-in-chief of *Forbes Monaco* and *ÖTILLÖ Swimrun* magazine founded Good News Monaco and hosts a successful podcast, *Nancy & PJ Finally Get Together.* For this edition, Nancy updated the Travel Smart, Western French Riviera, Nice and the Eastern French Riviera, and Monaco chapters.

Jennifer Ladonne has been investigating the far corners of France for Fodor's and other travel publications since 2004, when she left her longtime home of Manhattan for the less frenzied pleasures of Paris. Now a regular features writer for the magazine *France Today,* she also co-authored Fodor's *Around Paris with Kids,* writes frequent articles for Fodor's blog, and has contributed to the *Fodor's Paris* dining, hotels, and shopping sections for many years. Beguiled by the south of France since a revelatory trip long ago, Jennifer spends as much time as possible south of the Monts de Vaucluse and has been nurturing a passionate long-distance love affair with Marseille. For this edition, she channeled her ardor into updating the following chapters: Experience; Nîmes and the Alpilles; Avignon and the Vaucluse; and Aix, Marseille, and the Central Coast.